A COMPANION TO SCRIPTURE STUDIES

Volume I. General Introduction to the Bible

BY THE RIGHT REVEREND
JOHN E. STEINMUELLER, S.T.D., S.Scr.L.,V.F.

Consultor of the Pontifical Biblical Commission
Former Professor of Sacred Scripture and Hebrew
at the Seminary of the Immaculate Conception, Huntington, N. Y.
Pastor of St. Barbara's Parish, Brooklyn, N. Y.

REVISED AND ENLARGED EDITION

NEW YORK CITY

Published by

JOSEPH F. WAGNER, INC.
for
THE LUMEN CHRISTI PRESS

Nihil Obstat
Michael J. Cantley, S.T.L.
Censor Deputatus

Imprimatur
Bryan Josephus McEntegart, D.D., LL.D.
Episcopus Bruklyniensis

Bruklyni
Die v februarii, 1962

The *Nihil Obstat* and *Imprimatur* are official declarations that a book or pamphlet is free of doctrinal and moral error. No implication is contained therein that those who have granted the *Nihil Obstat* and *Imprimatur* agree with the contents, opinions or statements expressed.

Revised and Enlarged Edition

FOREWORD

A careful survey of the contents, scope and purpose of this volume will suggest immediately at least two good reaons for its publication.

Its sacred and sublime subject-matter is the Bible and more particularly the Old Testament.

Now, the character of the Bible has been authoritatively defined for us by the Council of Trent and the Council of the Vatican in the words: "The Bible embraces the Books which are written under the inspiration of the Holy Ghost, and, therefore, have God for their Author. It is clear, consequently, that the Bible does not only contain the Word of God but is the Word of God."

Surely then a book which treats of the revelation of the Mind and Will of God, is devoted to a holy and exalted theme which not only richly merits but also commands our serious interest and concern.

St. Paul, in his letter to his beloved disciple, St. Timothy, refers to the supereminent dignity and incomparable excellence of Scripture when he says: "All Scripture is inspired by God" (2 Tim. 3, 16 f). And the Fathers of the Church uniformly declare that the Bible is a "Letter written by your Heavenly Father and transmitted by the sacred writers to the human race in its pilgrimage so far from its heavenly Country" (Encyclical "Providentissimus Deus").

The inestimable value and precious usefulness of Scripture are impressively described by the Apostle to the Gentiles when he declares in the passage above referred to: "All Scripture . . . is useful for teaching, for reproving, for correcting, for instructing in justice that the man of God may be perfect, equipped for every good work."

The volume herewith presented, as already noted, deals particularly with the Old Testament, and its obvious and practical purpose generally is to provide the recognized requisites for a systematic study, clear understanding and correct interpretation of the Bible. The student or reader therefore is favored with a clear and concise consideration of such outstanding questions as inspiration, interpretation, textual rendition, historical backgrounds, and geographical setting of these divinely inspired writings.

iii

The author presents these subjects with scholarly ability, in logical relationship and systematic grouping. I might observe as deserving of special approval that there is no undue tendency to emphasize highly speculative theories but rather a readily discernible and commendable disposition to favor a fruitful exegetic development of the divinely inspired meanings and lessons latent in the text beneath. He is apparently mindful of the truth: "The letter indeed killeth, but the spirit quickeneth" (2 Cor. 3, 6).

Very interesting and instructive comments are offered in regard to prominent and important persons, places, ceremonials, and customs described in the biblical narrative.

It is, of course, true that the Old Testament is more easily intelligible, engrossingly interesting, and significantly impressive today than ever before. And this fact is due, after giving proper acknowledgment to scholarly scriptural study in itself, to the enlightening and helpful influence provided by the most recently accumulated and related data of archæology, philology, anthropology, ethnology, and history.

The useful and practical results of these scientific studies and findings have been happily apparent in increased accuracy of understanding the chronological sequence of biblical events, a considerable reinforcement of reliable norms of biblical interpretation, a more refined appreciation of biblical literary excellence, a truer insight into the moral and spiritual aspirations of the people of Israel, a more comforting and salutary realization of God's interest in and care of His chosen people on earth, and a more definite and comprehensive outline of the imperial background of Assyria, Babylon, Persia, Arabia, Greece, and Rome, in the foreground of which, and throughout the various epochs of its own existence, Israel fulfilled its most significant historical destiny.

All these matters are interesting and useful, it is true; but we must always realize that they are only of relative worth and of secondary importance in comparison with the primary religious purpose and essential spiritual value of the Word of God itself.

May, then, this new scriptural treatise be favored with the fullest degree of success and blessing in rendering the Word of God more widely known, more sincerely appreciated, and more faithfully followed in the minds, hearts and lives of its fortunate readers!

✠ THOMAS E. MOLLOY,
Bishop of Brooklyn.

Feast of the Nativity B.V.M., 1941.

PREFACE

When this first volume of *A Companion to Scripture Studies* (General Introduction to the Bible) appeared twenty-one years ago, it was graciously greeted by Catholic and non-Catholic Scripturists, in various critical reviews both here and abroad, as a valuable contribution to Biblical scholarship in the English language. Since that time it has been reprinted frequently, gratifying proof that it has become a successful textbook, particularly for seminarians, as well as secure general guide.

Much has transpired over the intervening years in the world of Scripture, and my own desire to make the present volume — later its two associates — wholly current has been implemented by the urgings of seminary professors of Scripture as well as of former students.

During the period of Pope Pius XII (1939-1958) there appeared some important documents giving the greatest encouragement to Biblical research, especially to the study of literary forms. Worthy of mention are the encyclicals *Divino afflante Spiritu* (1943) and *Humani generis* (1950) as well as the Letter of the Pontifical Biblical Commission to Cardinal Emmanuel Suhard (1948). To these have been added the recent *Monitum* of the Holy Office (1961). During this entire period much new archæological material from the Near East has been discovered, deciphered, evaluated; all this now throws a great new light upon Bible interpretation. Then, too, within the past fifteen years the Dead Sea, or Qumran, Scrolls were added to Biblical research material.

Much of this new material has been analyzed, synthesized and incorporated in this revised volume. In addition, a new section, entitled "Archæology" — taken from our *Catholic Biblical Encyclopedia: Old Testament* — has been included to bring this subject abreast of the latest discoveries. All bibliographies throughout this volume have been completely revised, with special stress, wherever possible, on English references.

Our determination to face modern Biblical problems squarely and to offer solutions according to the traditional mind of the Church will, it is hoped, make this volume — General Introduction to the Bible — a treasury of useful information for all who use it.

THE AUTHOR

St. Barbara's Parish,
Brooklyn, New York

To His Excellency
THE MOST REV. BRYAN J. McENTEGART, D.D., LL.D.
BISHOP OF BROOKLYN

TABLE OF CONTENTS

I. LIST OF ABBREVIATIONS

A.J.S.L.L.	*The American Journal of Semitic Languages and Literature*
A.N.E.T.	*Ancient Near Eastern Texts*
A.T.A.	*Alttestamentliche Abhandlungen*
B.A.	*The Biblical Archaeologist*
B.A.S.O.R.	*Bulletin of the American Schools of Oriental Research*
B.S.	*Biblische Studien*
B.Z.	*Biblische Zeitschrift*
B.Z.F.	*Biblische Zeitfragen*
C.B.E.N.T.	*Catholic Biblical Encyclopedia: New Testament*
C.B.E.O.T.	*Catholic Biblical Encyclopedia: Old Testament*
C.B.Q.	*Catholic Biblical Quarterly*
C.E.	*Catholic Encyclopedia*
C.R.	*Clergy Review*
D.B.	*Denziger-Bannwart (13th ed.)*
D.D.L.B.	*Dictionnaire de la Bible (Vigouroux)*
D.D.L.B. Suppl.	*Dictionnaire de la Bible Supplement (Pirot)*
E.B.	*Enchiridion Biblicum*
E.R.	*Ecclesiastical Review*
H.D.B.	*Hasting's Dictionary of the Bible*
H.P.R.	*Homiletic and Pastoral Review*
I.B.	*Institutiones Biblicae (6th ed.)*
J.A.O.S.	*Journal of the American Oriental Society*
J.B.L.	*Journal of Biblical Literature*
J.E.	*Jewish Encyclopedia*
J.O.N.E.S.	*Journal of Near Eastern Studies*
K.B.R.L.	*Kalt, Biblisches Reallexikon (1st ed)*
LXX.	*Septuagint*
M.G.	*Migne Greek*
M.L.	*Migne Latin*
M.T.	*Massoretic Text*
Orntl.	*Orientalia*
R.B.	*Revue Biblique*
Theol. St.	*Theological Studies*
V.D.	*Verbum Domini*
Vulg.	*Vulgate*
Z.K.Th.	*Zeitschrift für Katholische Theologie*
*	*Non-Catholic writers*

II. ABBREVIATED TITLES OF BOOKS OF THE BIBLE

Abd.	Abdias	Lam.	Lamentations
Agg.	Aggeus	Lev.	Leviticus
Apoc.	Apocalypse	Mach.	Machabees
Bar.	Baruch	Mal.	Malachias
Cant.	Canticle of Canticles	Matt.	Matthew
Col.	Colossians	Mich.	Micheas
Cor.	Corinthians	Nah.	Nahum
Dan.	Daniel	Num.	Numbers
Deut.	Deuteronomy	Os.	Osee
Eccles.	Ecclesiastes	Par.	Paralipomenon
Eph.	Ephesians	Pet.	Peter
Esd.	Esdras	Phil.	Philippians
Est.	Esther	Philem.	Philemon
Ex.	Exodus	Prov.	Proverbs
Ez.	Ezechiel	Ps.	Psalm
Gal.	Galatians	Pss.	Psalms
Gen.	Genesis	Rom.	Romans
Hab.	Habacuc	Sam.	Samuel (1, 2 Kings)
Heb.	Hebrews	Sir.	Sirach (Ecclesiasticus)
Isa.	Isaias	Soph.	Sophonias
Jas.	James	Thess.	Thessalonians
Jer.	Jeremias	Tim.	Timothy
Jon.	Jonas	Tit.	Titus
Jos.	Josue	Tob.	Tobias
Jdgs.	Judges	Wis.	Wisdom
Jud.	Judith	Zach.	Zacharias
Kgs.	Kings (3, 4 Kings)		

GENERAL INTRODUCTION TO THE BIBLE

Bibliography: Moriarty, F. L., "Bulletin of the Old Testament," in *Theol. St.*, XVI (1955), 397-413; Collins, J. J., "New Testament Abstracts" (Weston, Mass. 1956-); Bibliographie Biblique (Montreal, 1958); *Religious and Theological Abstracts (Youngstown, Ohio, 1958-); see also periodicals *Biblica*, B.Z., C.B.Q., R.B., V.D., etc.

GENERAL INTRODUCTION: Grannan, C. P., "A General Introduction to the Bible" (4 vols., St. Louis, 1921); "Institutiones Biblicae" (6th ed., Rome, 1951); *Willoughby, H. R., "The Study of the Bible: Today and Tomorrow" (Chicago, 1947); Perella, G. M., "Introduzione generale alla Sacra Bibbia" (Turin, 1948; Sp. ed. by J. Prado, Madrid, 1950); Schildenberger, J. "Vom Geheimnis des Gotteswortes. Einführung in das Verständnis der Hl. Schrift (Heidelberg, 1950); Charlier, C. "La lecture chretienne de la Bible" (4th ed., Maredsous, 1951; English ed., London, 1957); Höpfl, H.-Leloir, L., "Introductio Generalis in Sacram Scripturam" (6th ed., Rome, 1958).

GENERAL AND SPECIAL INTRODUCTIONS TO THE OLD AND NEW TESTAMENTS: Cornely, R., "Historicae et Criticae Introductionis in U. T. Libros Sacros Compendium" (10th ed. by A. Merk, Paris, 1930); Höpfl, H., "Introductionis in Sacros Utriusque Testamenti Libros Compendium," vol. II (5th ed. by Miller, A. and Metzinger, A., Rome, 1946); vol. III (5th ed. by Gut B., and Metzinger, A., Rome, 1949); Lusseau-Collomb, "Manuel d'Etudes Bibliques" (7 vols., Paris, 1930-35); Pope, H., "The Catholic Student's Aids to the Bible" (5 vols., 2nd ed., London, 1926-1938); Prado, J., "Praelectionum Biblicarum Compendium" (3 vols., 5th ed., Turin, 1950-52); Renié, P. J., "Manual d'Ecriture Sainte" (5 vols., 4th ed., Lyons-Paris, 1948 ff); Robert, A., and Tricot, A., "Initiation biblique" (3rd ed., Paris, 1954; Engl. ed. by P. Arbez and M. McGuire, vol. I, 1951; vol. II, 1955); Robert, A., and Feuillet, A., "Introduction à la Bible," vol. I, 2nd ed. (Tournai-Paris, 1959), vol. II (Tournai-Paris, 1959); Schumacher, H., "Handbook of Scripture Study" (3 vols., St. Louis, 1922-25); Steinmueller, J. E., and Sullivan, K., "Catholic Biblical Encyclopedia: Old and New Testament" (2 vols., 3rd printing, New York, 1959).

The word *Bible* is derived from the Greek word βιβλίον, which means "a book." The Greek Church used the plural of the word (βιβλία) to designate the entire collection of sacred writings. This quasi-technical term passed over to the Latin Rite with this difference: the Greek neuter plural became a Latin feminine singular, and hence we have the expression *Biblia Sacra*. For this reason the singular number is found in all modern languages of the Western Church. This techni-

1

cal term, *"The Bible,"* therefore represents the book of books, or "The Book" *par excellence.*

The Greek Fathers often applied various collective names to the Bible—for example, the Sacred Scriptures, the Holy Letters, the Scriptures, or simply the Scripture. These expressions are also found in the New Testament to designate the Old Testament. Besides these names, the Jews also use the term "Torah" (though this is more often restricted to the Pentateuch) and "The Twenty-Four Books."

The Latin Fathers, however, popularized the expression, the "Old and New Testaments." A testament (Hebr., *berith*) signifies primarily a pact or covenant made between God and man. The Old Testament, therefore, is a covenant made between God and the Hebrew nation, and concluded through their representative Moses on Mount Sinai. The New Testament is a covenant made between the Heavenly Father and mankind, and concluded through man's representative, Jesus Christ, the God-Man, who sealed this contract on Golgotha with His blood.

The Bible can be defined as a collection of sacred books which were composed under the positive influence of the Holy Spirit, were written at various times and in various places by men whom God had chosen for this purpose, and were received by the Church as inspired.

The Bible, as we know it from the Vulgate, contains seventy-two books, divided into chapters and verses;[1] it consists of two parts, the Old and the New Testaments. The Jews, whom Protestants generally follow, only recognize thirty-eight books of the Old Testament. By means of a peculiar division the Old Testament was at one time reduced to twenty-two books to correspond with the number of the letters of the Hebrew alphabet. The general division followed by the Jews is: the Torah or the Law, the Prophets, and the Holy

---

[1] The division of the Bible into chapters generally used today is attributed to Stephen Langton (1214); our modern verse division in the Old Testament is attributed to Sanctes Pagninus (1528) and in the New Testament to Robert Stephanus (1555).

Writings. In accordance with the Decree "Sacrosancta" of the Council of Trent, however, Catholic scholars recognize forty-five books of the Old Testament; some scholars still speak of forty-six or even forty-seven books.[2] The general division of the Old Testament into historical, didactic, and prophetical books also includes the seven deutero-canonical books. The New Testament contains twenty-seven books, of which seven are deutero-canonical, and the general division is the same as that of the Old Testament: historical, didactic, and prophetical.

This collection of sacred books, forming the Bible, enjoys a greater dignity and excellence than any other written book. First of all, the contents of the Bible is most sacred, for it centers round the mystery of the redemption of man or, as many of our modern scholars are wont to call this contents, *Heilsgeschichte*, that is, salvation history. The Old Testament remotely and proximately prepared the way for the Messias, whereas the New Testament presents us with His advent and explains to us His nature and mission. Hence, the often repeated saying: "Novum Testamentum in Vetere latet, Vetus Testamentum in Novo patet." St. Jerome therefore rightly remarks: "Ignoratio Scripturarum ignoratio Christi est," that is, to be ignorant of the Scriptures means to be ignorant of Christ. Secondly, the Bible is essentially incomparable with any other written book, because it is the word of God; that is, it has God as its principal Author and the hagiographer or sacred writer as the instrumental cause.

[2] See page 74.

PART I

BIBLICAL INSPIRATION

Bibliography: Bea, A., "De Scripturae Sacrae Inspiratione Quaestiones Historicae et Dogmaticae" (2nd ed., Rome, 1935); Benoit, P., "L'inspiration," in "Initiation Biblique" of Robert and Tricot (3rd ed., Paris, 1954, pp. 5-45); *idem*, "Note complémentaire sur l'inspiration," in R.B., 63 (1956), 416-422; Billot, L., "De inspiratione S. S." (4th ed., 1929); Brinkmann, B., "Inspiration und Kanonizität des Hl.Schrift in ihrem Verhältnis zur Kirche," in "Scholastik," 33 (1958), 208-233; Costello, C. J., "St. Augustine's Doctrine on the Inspiration and Canonicity of Scripture" (Washington, D. C., 1930); Dorsch, A., "De Inspiratione S. Scripturae" (2nd ed., Innsbruck, 1927); Durand, A., in C.E., s.v. *Inspiration;* Florit, E., "Ispirazione Biblica" (2nd ed., Rome, 1951); Fonck, L., "Der Kampf um die Wahrheit der Hl.Schrift seit 25 Jahren" (Innsbruck, 1905); Goettsberger, J., "Autour de la question biblique," in B.Z., 3 (1905), 225-250; Jones, A., "Biblical Inspiration: A Christian Rendezvous?" in "Scripture," 10 (1958), 97-109. Lagrange, M. J., "Inspiration des livres saints," in R.B., 5 (1896), 199-220; *idem,* "L'inspiration et les exigences de la critique," in R.B., 5 (1896), 496-518; Mangenot, E., "Inspiration," in V.D.B.; Pesch, C., "De Inspiratione S.S." (Freiburg i.B., 1925), and "Supplementum" (ibid., 1926); Rahner, K., "Über die Schriftinspiration" (Freiburg i.B., 1959); Steinmueller, J. E., "Some Problems of the O.T." (New York, 1936); Tromp, S., "De S.Scripturae inspiratione" (5th ed., Rome, 1953); Vosté, J. M., "De Scripturarum Veritate" (Rome, 1924); *idem,* "De natura et extensione inspirationis biblicae" (Rome, 1924); *idem,* "De divina inspiratione et veritate Sacrae Scripturae" (2nd ed., Rome, 1932); Courtade, G., art. "Inspiration," in "Supplement au Dictionnaire de la Bible," 4 (1949), 482-559; cf. also MacKenzie, R. A. F., "Some Problems in the Field of Inspiration," in C.B.Q., 20 (1958), 1-8; Stanley, D. M., "The Concept of Biblical Inspiration," in "Proceedings," Cath. Theol. Soc. of Am. (1958), 65-95; Smyth, K., "The Inspiration of the Scriptures" in "Scripture," 6 (1954), 67-75.

General Remarks

The word *inspiration* is derived from the Latin *inspirare*, which means to breathe into. In the secular sense, it may signify inhalation, influence (whether mental or creative), and an expression of opinion.

4

As a religious and technical term, it means a *divine act,*
and is derived from the expression *divinitus inspirata* found
in the Vulgate. This expression is the literal translation of
the Greek word θεόπνευστος (2 Tim. 3, 16), which is generally
understood by Greek grammarians and the Fathers in the
passive sense, that is, inspired by God.[1]

In the Bible and in tradition the word has a variety of
meanings. It is applied to the divine act by which God gives
and conserves physical life (cf. Gen. 2, 7; Wisd. 15, 11; Acts
17, 24 f). It refers to the spiritual life (cf. Sir. 4, 12); for
this reason theologians hold that actual grace effects an illumination of the intellect and an inspiration of the will.
Canonists at times also call a canonical election a divine inspiration. Finally, inspiration is a kind of supernatural motion by which men are impelled to teach others what God
wants them to teach; when this is performed orally, there is a
question of prophetical inspiration, and when accomplished in
writing, there is a question of biblical inspiration. It is with
this latter inspiration that we are chiefly concerned.

In regard to the inspiration of the Sacred Scriptures three
factors must be distinguished. First, there is the primary
efficient cause, which is the Holy Spirit, who supernaturally
acts upon man. The Bible is attributed to the Holy Spirit
by appropriation, because every action of God *ad extra* is
common to the three Persons of the Blessed Trinity. Secondly, there is the subject of inspiration, which is man, the
instrument of the Holy Spirit. Finally, there is the end or
terminus of inspiration, which is the book or the word of God.

The canonical books contained in the Bible can be called
sacred or holy for various reasons: either in view of the
writers or hagiographers (who were holy men), or in virtue of
the contents of the books (which contain the history of man's
salvation and redemption) or in virtue of the purpose of the

---

[1] Similar words are θεοδίδακτος (taught by God: 1 Thess. 4, 9);
θεόδοτος (given by God); θεόπεμπτος (sent by God); θεόκλητος (called
by God); θεόγνωστος (known by God); θεόκτιστος (created, made by
God); etc.

books (which is to teach men religious truths, strengthen them in the practice of virtue), but chiefly because of the origin of the books (which were written under the special divine influence that is called inspiration).

The fact of inspiration is a dogma that must be believed by divine faith (i.e., on the authority of God revealing). That the Sacred Scriptures are inspired (i.e., written under a special divine influence), is known from the two sources of revelation, the Bible and sacred tradition (i.e., the witness of the Fathers, theologians, and the Decrees of the Church).

CHAPTER I

THE EXISTENCE OF INSPIRATION

In proving the inspiration of the Sacred Scriptures from the two sources of revelation, the Bible and tradition, we must bear in mind that these two authorities are not here quoted formally as dogmatic sources of revelation, but as reliable historical sources possessing the highest degree of human authority. Thus, in establishing the existence of inspiration a vicious circle is avoided.

Art. 1. The Proofs of Inspiration from Sacred Scripture Itself [1]

(a) INSPIRATION OF THE OLD TESTAMENT

There are two passages in the New Testament which explicitly refer to the Old Testament as inspired, namely, 2 Tim. 3, 16 and 2 Pet. 1, 20 f.

In the former passage St. Paul alludes to the *fact of inspiration* of the Old Testament books, after he had advised his disciple, St. Timothy, to persevere in the faith that he had from his infancy learned from others and from the Sacred Scriptures: "All Scripture is inspired by God πᾶσα γραφὴ θεόπνευστος and useful for teaching, for reproving, for correcting, for instructing in justice; that the man of God may be perfect, equipped for every good work. The entire sentence suggests a particular supernatural influence of God in regard to the origin of the Old Testament. In the second passage the Prince of the Apostles, St. Peter, refers to the *nature of inspiration* and specifically to the prophecies of the Old Testament: "This, then, you must understand first of all, that no prophecy

---

[1] Cf. Steinmueller, J. E., "The Bible: Its Meaning, Inspiration, Authors, Canon," in H.P.R., 37 (1937) 1316 f.

7

of Scripture is made by private interpretation. For not by will of man was prophecy brought at any time; but holy men of God spoke (ελάλησαν) as they were moved (φερόμενοι) by the Holy Spirit." Hence, the words of the prophets are not the products of their own imagination, nor may these prophecies be explained by a mere human interpretation, but their utterances are from God (i.e., they are of divine origin). In other words, their discourses must be attributed to the Holy Spirit as the principal cause.

These two texts complement each other. The first speaks more clearly of the fact of inspiration, while the latter explains more fully the nature of inspiration, though it does not necessarily allude to all the Sacred Books of the Old Testament.

Although the Old Testament does not give any explicit proofs of its own inspiration, there are indirect arguments which are strengthened by their cumulative force. First of all, the sacred writers were prophets in the widest sense of the word, for they spoke in the name of God and were His interpreters (cf. Ex. 4, 15 f; 7, 1 f). In some of them there was a divine impulse or motion to speak, and they could not resist this impulse (cf. Jer. 20, 7 f). Other prophets also spoke of future events, and their predictions were verified in time (cf. Isaias, Jeremias, Daniel, etc.). Secondly, these prophets were often commanded by God to write down their utterances (Ex. 17, 14; 34, 27; Deut. 31, 19; Bar. 2, 28; Isa. 8, 1; 30, 8; Apoc. 1, 11; 2, 1. 8. 12; etc.). Finally, the literary accomplishments of these prophets were designated by significant titles, as "the Book of the Law of Yahweh" (Jos. 24, 26; 2 Esd. 8, 8), or "the Book of Yahweh" (Isa. 34, 16), or "the Law of Yahweh" (1 Par. 16, 40), or "the Sacred Books" (1 Mach. 12, 9; cf. Prologue of Sir.; Dan. 9, 2; 2 Mach. 2, 13).

Similarly, implicit references to the inspiration of the Old Testament books may be found from the manner in which Jesus and His followers quoted from and used these books.

The books, or collection of books (whether they were legal

or historical, prophetic or didactic), which we call the Old
Testament, were commonly accepted by Jesus Christ and the
members of the primitive Church as "the Scripture" (John 2,
22; 10, 35; Gal. 3, 8.22; 1 Tim. 5, 18; 1 Pet. 2, 6; 2 Pet. 1, 20),
"the Scriptures" (Matt. 21, 42; 22, 29; John 5, 39; Acts 17, 2.11;
18, 24; Rom. 15, 4; 16, 26), "the Holy Scriptures" (Rom. 1, 2),
"the Sacred Writings" (2 Tim. 3, 15), "the Word of God" (Mark
7, 13), or "the Oracles of God" (Rom. 3, 2) because of their
divine origin.

Just as the Jews of their time, they in their teaching regarded
the Old Testament scrolls with greatest esteem, profound reverence by ascribing to them (1) *absolute*, unimpeachable, infallible *authority* and (2) a *special influence of the Holy Spirit*
in their composition.

(1) Authoritative Usage of Old Testament Books. — Christ
quoted the Old Testament as a strong, infallible authority
against His enemies to support His position and to strengthen
His arguments (e.g., against the devil in Matt. 4, 4.7.10; cf. also
John 5, 39. 45-47), declared that the Scriptures cannot be broken
(John 10, 35), and that their prophetic utterances must be fulfilled to the last jot or tittle (Matt. 5, 17f; cf. 26, 24. 31. 54;
Luke 16, 17; 18, 31; 24, 44; John 13, 18). Similarly the collection of Old Testament books was regarded by the Apostles to
be clothed with firm, unassailable, spiritual authority, to be a
source of firm faith as well as a trustworthy guide for daily
living, and to possess permanent, apologetic, kerygmatic value.
As such it was used by Peter (Acts 2, 16-21; 3, 18; 1 Pet. 2, 6-8),
James (Acts 15, 15-18), and very frequently by Paul (Rom. 1,
17; 4, 3. 17; 15, 9-12; 1 Cor. 1, 19; Gal. 3, 10f). The Four
Evangelists also call to the close, critical, serious attention of
all Christians the absolutely necessary fulfillment of the
prophetic Scriptures even in the slightest details. St. Matthew,
in particular, alludes most frequently to the amazing necessity
of God's plans and promises being fulfilled (Matt. 1, 22f; 2, 15.
17f. 23; 4, 14-16; 8, 17; 12, 17-21; 13, 35; 21, 4f; 27, 9f; cf. also
John 19, 24. 28. 36; Acts 1, 16). This unwavering faith, wonderful confidence and absolute trust expecting the fulfillment of

prophetic utterances were based upon the firm, deep, unshaken conviction shared by all pious Israelites throughout their entire history that these scrolls and the messages contained therein were of divine origin and that Yahweh would live up to His promise made to Israel and to mankind, and that consequently the Holy Scriptures could be used and quoted with the greatest authority.

(2) Special Influence of the Holy Spirit. — The reason why the Old Testament books were considered so authoritative was precisely because they were regarded to be of divine origin and to have been written under some special influence of the Holy Spirit (Matt. 22, 43ff and Mark 12, 36 quoting Ps. 109 [110], 1; cf. Matt. 22, 31ff quoting Ex. 3, 6; Matt. 15, 4 quoting Ex.20, 12; etc.) It was this same Holy Spirit (promised by Jesus during His earthly ministry and conferred first upon His intimate followers on the first Christian Pentecost) who spoke in the Scriptures: thus, according to the *kerygma* of Peter through (the mouth of) David (Acts 1, 16. 20 introducing quotations from Ps. 68 [69], 26 and 108 [109], 8), through the prophets (1 Pet. 1, 10-12); according to the preaching of Paul through Isaias, the prophet (Acts 28, 25-27) quoting Isa. 6, 9ff), through unnamed sacred writers (Heb. 3, 7-11 quoting from Ps. 94 [95], 7-11; Heb. 9, 8-10 referring to Mosaic ordinances; Heb. 10, 15-17 quoting from Jer. 31, 33); according to the members of the *Urkirche*, or primitive Apostolic Church, through the mouth of their father, or ancestor, David (Acts 4, 25 ff quoting from Ps. 2, 1). It is also noteworthy that in place of this same Holy Spirit some passages speak of God Himself (e.g., Zachary, the father of John the Baptist in his *Benedictus*: "as he promised through the mouth of his holy ones the prophets from of old" (Luke 2, 70): this *Benedictus* is based upon various prophetical and messianic passages of the Old Testament. In Heb. 4, 4 it is God Himself who spoke on the seventh day, and then a quotation from Gen. 2, 2 is given. Occasionally the word "Law" is used in place of the word "God" (e.g., the Law says) in introducing a Biblical citation (1 Cor. 14, 21; cf. Gal. 3, 18).

Thus the respectful, reverential, and deferential attitude of Jesus and the members of His established Church toward the commonly recognized collection of Old Testament scrolls was based upon the belief in the divine authority, origin and influence of these books; in a few words, upon their divine inspiration.

(b) INSPIRATION OF THE NEW TESTAMENT

While the New Testament has no explicit proofs of its own inspiration, there are two passages which can be cited as indirect arguments for it. In his Second Epistle, composed about A.D. 66-67 when the first three Gospels and nearly all of the Pauline Epistles (excepting 2 Timothy) were in circulation, St. Peter wrote: "Therefore, beloved, while you look for these things, endeavor to be found by him without spot and blameless, in peace. And regard the long-suffering of our Lord as salvation. Just as our most dear brother Paul also, according to the wisdom given him, has written to you, as indeed he did in all his epistles, speaking in them of these things. In these epistles there are certain things difficult to understand, which the unlearned and the unstable distort, just as they do the rest of the Scriptures also, to their own destruction" (2 Pet. 3, 14-16). By the phrase "according to the wisdom given him," St. Peter seems to be alluding to the charism of inspiration given to St. Paul, and there is also a comparison made between the Pauline Epistles and "the rest of the Scriptures." In the second passage St. Paul is probably quoting from the Gospel of his disciple, St. Luke: "For the Scripture says, 'Thou shalt not muzzle the ox that treads out the grain,' and 'The laborer is worthy of his wages'" (1 Tim. 5, 18). Both citations, Deuteronomy 25, 4 and Luke 10, 7, seem to be included in the same phrase: "For the Scripture says."

Art. 2. The Proofs of Inspiration from Tradition

The Church throughout her entire history teaches the

inspiration of the Sacred Scriptures, and by the term inspiration supposes not only the dignity and excellence of the sacred
books, but also the action of the Holy Spirit in their composition.

(*a*) *The Doctrine of the Fathers*.[2]—From the very beginning of the Church the Fathers distinguished between the
books of the Bible and secular literature, acknowledged these
books to be of incontestable authority, and made use of them
in the liturgy of the Church. These Fathers ascribe various
qualities to these sacred books.

These books are spoken of as containing *indisputable truth*,
either because their authority was derived from the Holy
Spirit who had spoken in them or had revealed what the
prophets wrote, or because these writings are divine. Thus, St.
Clement R., St. Justin M., St. Irenæus, St. Hippolytus, St.
John Chrysostom, St. Hilary.

The Fathers call these books *inspired by God* (θεόπνευστος,
inspiratus). Thus, St. Ignatius A., St. Justin M., Theophilus
A., St. Irenæus, Origen, Tertullian, St. Cyril A., St. Gregory of
Nyssa.

They maintain that God is the *author of the Bible* (thus, St.
Cyril J., St. Gregory the Great, St. Isidore S.); that He *dic-
tated* the Bible and *spoke* to us through it (thus, St. Irenæus,
St. John Chrysostom, St. Jerome, St. Augustine).

The Fathers also assert that the sacred writers were the
instruments of God (thus, St. Justin M., Athenagorus, Theophilus A., St. Jerome, St. Gregory the Great).

(*b*) *The Doctrine of the Scholastics*.[3]—St. Bonaventure
may be cited as one of the outstanding Franciscans who wrote
on the Bible; he taught that God is the author of the Bible,
and by imparting revelations to the prophets and to others He
furnished it with authoritative certitude; the Bible is therefore
infallible. Among the Dominicans, St. Thomas Aquinas in the

---

[2] Cf. Bea, A., *op. cit.*, 3-6.

[3] Cf. Bea, A., *op. cit.*, 7-10; Merk, A., in I.B., 26-31; Pesch, C., *op. cit.*,
140-201.

Summa (2. 2., qq. 171-174) treats of *prophecy,* and of inspiration as a kind or species of prophecy; his exposition of the subject (the essence, the cause, the manner, and the division of prophecy) is so complete that very little of importance has been added to the nature of inspiration since his day. Worthy of mention is also Henry of Ghent, who laid particular stress on the doctrine of instrumental causality and called God the principal Author and the human writers the secondary authors of Sacred Scripture.

Art. 3. The Ecclesiastical Magisterium

It is very significant that in the second century the authority of the Old Testament was opposed by Marcion, a Gnostic, and in his book entitled *Antitheses* he denied the divine origin of the books of the Old Testament. In the fourth century the Manicheans also set aside the writings of the Old Testament. Against this heresy the Fathers strenuously defended the divine origin of the Old and New Testaments, as well as the equal authority of both (e.g., St. Irenæus, Tertullian, etc.). Afterwards this doctrine of the Fathers was formally proposed by the Church. In the *ancient rule of faith* (fifth century) we have: "Si quis dixerit vel crediderit, alterum Deum esse priscæ legis, alterum evangeliorum, anathema sit" (E.B., 28); and according to the *ancient statutes of the Church* (fifth-sixth centuries) the bishop was to ask of the candidate to be ordained: "Si novi et veteris testamenti, id est, legis et prophetarum, et apostolorum unum eundemque credat auctorem et Deum" (E.B., 30).

This same doctrine of the Old and New Testaments having the one and the same author, God, was often reasserted. It is found in the symbol proposed in 1053 by St. Leo IX to Peter, Bishop of Antioch (E.B., 38), in the profession of faith required by Innocent III in 1208 of the Waldensians (E.B., 39), in the profession of faith made by Michael Palæologus at the Second Council of Lyons in 1274 (E.B., 40), in the Decree for the Jacobites by Eugenius IV at the time of the Council of Florence in 1441,[4] in the Decree "Sacrosancta" of the Council of Trent issued on April 8, 1546 (E.B., 57), in the Dogmatic Constitution "Dei Filius" of the Vatican Council on April 24, 1870 (E.B., 77), in the Encyclical "Providentissimus Deus" of Leo XIII in 1893 (E.B., 81. 124 f), in the Encyclical "Spiritus Paraclitus" of Benedict XV in 1920 (E.B., 448).

The word "author" in these documents is not to be restricted to merely the *economy* of the Old and New Testaments, but must be made to include the *writings* of both Testaments. This is evident from the early documents opposing the Manicheans.

Appendix

(a) *The Doctrine of Protestants on Inspiration.*[5]—The *early Protestants* acknowledged the inspiration of the Bible, but did not properly understand its nature. The Bible was taken to be the *sole rule of faith,* to possess supreme authority and to enjoy unrivalled pre-eminence, and inspiration and revelation were held to be one and the same thing. External proofs or criteria for the existence of inspired books of the Bible were rejected and only internal criteria based upon one's personal experiences, religious feelings or sociological spiritual effects were substituted (*Luther, *Zwingli, *Calvin, *Beza; cf. also chapter V). Since the Bible became regarded as having been dictated by the Holy Spirit, its human element became gradually neglected, and finally totally denied. Hence, such strictly orthodox authorities as *John Buxtorf, Sr. and Jr. (sixteenth century), and the *Helvetian Formula of Consent (1675) went to such extremes as asserting that even the vowel points and accents of the Hebrew text had been revealed to the sacred writers. This

---

[4] "Unum atque eumdem Deum Veteris et Novi Testamenti, hoc est Legis et Prophetarum atque Evangelii, profitetur auctorem, quoniam eodem Spiritu Sancto inspirante utriusque Testamenti sancti locuti sunt" (E.B., 47).

[5] Dodd, C. H., "The Authority of the Bible" (New York, 1929); Reid, J. K. S., "The Authority of Scripture" (London, 1957).

automaton, mechanical recording or total passivity of the sacred writers was the common view held by the early Protestant theologians.

This rigorous theology espousing the total passivity of the sacred writers was denied by the *Pietists*[6] or Spiritualists in the seventeenth and eighteenth centuries; for example, *Spencer (d.1705), *Franck (1628), and *Breithaupt. The formal profession of *deism*,[7] according to the articles laid down by *Lord Herbert of Cherbury in England (d.1698), admitted a purely natural religion, which consisted in the knowledge of religious truths attained by reason alone. This doctrine of the deists was introduced into Germany and developed into pure *rationalism*.[8] Rationalists such as *Semler (d.1791), *Kant, *G. Paulus, *D. F. Strauss, etc., asserted that the only divine element in the Bible is that which has a permanent value in ethics, whereas everything else represents the human element which must be appraised according to grammatical and historical rules.

Semirationalism was founded by *Schleiermacher (d. 1834) and developed by *Rothe. According to these critics inspiration was nothing more than the spirit of Christ, received by the disciples of Christ and transmitted to the Church. Hence, for the Holy Spirit inspiring they substitute the spirit of the Christian community. This communal spirit, they say, was also to be found in the apocryphal books. As the Old Testament arose from another spirit, it did not enjoy the same inspiration as the New Testament.

Among modern Protestant theologians very few acknowledge the true inspiration of the Bible. Those who do not follow the principles of rationalism emphasize the divine revelation in the Bible, that is, the divine message to man. The more conservative of these scholars assert that the sacred books are the result of the same Divine Providence which has ruled and shaped

---

6 Cf. Lauchert, F., in C.E., s.v., *Pietism*.
7 Cf. Aveling, F., in C.E., s.v. *Deism*.
8 Cf. Aveling, F., in C.E., s.v. *Rationalism*.

history.[9] Others hold that the Scriptures are divine, because they awaken in the heart of the hearer or reader a religious faith, a sense of piety or edification (e.g., *K. Barth, E. Brunner, etc.). Still others maintain that the books of the Bible were written by men who experienced a religious enthusiasm similar to the poets.

The theories of rationalism developed into *modernism*, which was condemned by Pope Pius X in the Decree "Lamentabili" on July 3, 1907 (propositions 9 f, 12; cf. E.B., 200 f, 203), and the Encyclical "Pascendi" on September 8, 1907 (cf. E.B., 278-281). In accordance with this modernistic view, *Loisy, commenting upon the Decree, stated that God is the author of the Bible in the same way that He is the architect of the Basilica of St. Peter at Rome.

(b) *The Doctrine of the Jews on Inspiration.*—The Jews have always regarded the Old Testament as divine. *Philo held inspiration was a sort of ecstasy and had various degrees, the greatest of which was given to Moses. *Josephus also maintained that the Bible was of divine origin. The early rabbinical schools admitted the divine origin of the Bible, but attributed revelation solely to the Torah or Pentateuch. According to some of these rabbis, God orally taught Moses everything that he was to write; according to others, God gave Moses the complete written Torah or dictated it to him in its entirety. According to these same rabbis the Nebiim (Prophets) and Kethubim (Holy Writings) were inspired through God's presence (shekinah), or were written by the sacred writers in accordance with traditions handed down to them from the period of Moses (to whom God had originally revealed the contents of these books), or were revealed to the preëxisting souls of these sacred writers on Mount Sinai. During the Middle Ages, *Maimonides defended the various degrees of inspiration for the sacred writers; plenary inspiration was attributed to Moses, while the rest of the sacred

[9] Cf. * Stewart, A., in H.D.B., s.v. *Bible;* * Sanday, W., "Inspiration" (Bampton Lectures, 3rd ed., London, 1896).

writers enjoyed lesser degrees of inspiration. Modern Jewish theologians have abandoned literal dictation or mechanical inspiration, but maintain that "the Spirit of God" was in the sacred writers and that biblical inspiration differs from purely human inspiration.[10]

[10] Cf. * Kaufman, K., in J.E., s.c. *Inspiration*. Cf. also * St. B., IV.1, 415-451.

Chapter II

THE NATURE OF INSPIRATION

"The books of the Old and New Testament, whole and entire, with all their parts, as enumerated in the Decree of the same Council [Trent] and in the ancient Latin Vulgate, are to be received as sacred and canonical. And the Church holds them as sacred and canonical, not because, having been composed by human industry, they were afterwards approved by her authority, nor only because they contain revelation without errors, but because, having been written under the inspiration of the Holy Spirit, they have God for their Author. Hence, because the Holy Spirit employed men as His instruments, we cannot, therefore, say that it was these inspired instruments who, perchance, have fallen into error, and not the primary author. For, by supernatural power, He so moved and impelled them to write—He was so present to them—that the things which He ordered, and those only, they first rightly understood, then willed faithfully to write down, and finally expressed in apt words and with infallible truth. Otherwise, it could not be said that He was the Author of the entire Scripture" ("Providentissimus Deus," in E.B., 125).

Inspiration may therefore be defined as a supernatural influence of the Holy Spirit on the sacred writers, moving and impelling them to write in such a manner that they first rightly understood, then willed faithfully to write down, and finally expressed in apt words and with infallible truth all the things, and those only, which He ordered.

The analysis of this definition shows that there are three factors in inspiration: first, God as the Inspirer (active inspiration); second, the hagiographer as the inspired one or the receiver of the inspiration (passive inspiration); third, the book as the terminus of the inspiration (terminative inspiration).

Art. 1. Active Inspiration

("For, by supernatural power, He . . .," "Providentissimus Deus.")

Inspiration is one of those actions which theologians call *ad extra*, and which are common to the three Divine Persons of the Blessed Trinity. It is, however, attributed to the Holy Spirit by appropriation, because the Holy Spirit proceeds from the Father and the Son through spiration, and because inspiration is a grace. This influence of God is something positive, physical, and supernatural.

This influence belongs to the charismatic gifts of God, because it is given primarily for the good of others. Then, too, inspiration has this in common with every actual grace that it is a transitory participation of the divine power. Yet, it differs from actual grace, a divine aid, which man uses when and how he wishes. In the charismatic gifts it is not man who makes use of the supernatural forces, but it is God who uses the natural forces of man to attain His end, namely, the common good of the Church. As a charismatic gift, inspiration differs from the gift of tongues or of miracles.

Art. 2.   Passive Inspiration

("They first rightly understood, then willed faithfully to write down, and finally expressed in apt words and with infallible truth," "Providentissimus Deus.")

From these words we may see that through inspiration God influences man's noblest faculties, namely, his intellect, will, memory, and imagination.

In developing the concept of inspiration, Catholic theologians follow two principal and different thought patterns. (a) Since various ecclesiastical documents state that God is the Author of the Bible, some Catholic scholars (e.g., J. Franzelin) examine the requirements necessary for anyone to be called an author of a book, and then propose the essential elements required for divine inspiration. This school of thought begins with the idea of author or authorship, and by asking itself for the strict requirements of the authorship of a (divine) book, it makes a clear distinction between the *formal* and *material* elements in the mind of the hagiographers and contained in the Bible. Accordingly, the formal elements, which are the ideas or thoughts contained in the Bible, must come *directly* from the Holy Spirit. The material elements, which contain the words, modes of expression or literary forms, come *indirectly* under the influence of the Holy Spirit, but this negative, effective assistance is guaranteed by His positive presence ever ready to prevent error or falsehood.

(b) The Thomistic school (e.g., M.-J. Lagrange) begins with the concept expressed by the verb "inspire," or the philosophical principle of instrumental causality, and from this concludes that God is the Author of the Bible. At the same time they explain in what sense God can be called the literary Author of Holy Writ. This reasoning is based upon St. Thomas' formula of dual authorship, divine and human, that is, principal and instrumental ("Auctor principalis sanctae Scripturae est Spiritus Sanctus . . . homo autem fuit auctor instrumentalis" (Quodlibet, VII, a. 14 ad 5) and his application of God's action upon secondary or instrumental causes according to their proper nature.

It would seem that these two methods should be combined to give us a better insight into the nature of inspiration. From tradition we know that God is the Author of the Bible. Hence, He must perform those acts which a man performs when he writes a book. God must conceive a book in His divine mind and must will it to be written. But God in the fulfillment of His plan uses men as His instruments. Hence, in the sacred writer there must also arise some acts, if the book is to be written. At the same time man must remain free, and yet be subordinate to the divine acts.[1]

THE TWO EXTREMES

Aside from these methods of explaining the nature of inspiration, there are some unsatisfactory ones. Some scholars go to the extreme of asserting that *God is the only Author* of the Bible and the human writers employed by Him act as passive instruments or mere machines. Both *Philo and *Josephus proposed this concept of inspiration. The early Protestants

[1] Cf. Bea, A. *op. cit.*, 43; *idem,* "Die Instrumentalitätsidee in der Inspirationslehre," in "Studia Anselmiana" (Rome, 1951), 47-65. Cf. Stanley, D. M., "The Concept of Biblical Inspiration," in "Proceedings," The Catholic Theological Society of America (1958), 65-89.

hardly differed from this view, when they asserted that God selected every word and actually dictated it to the sacred writer, who merely functioned as a passive instrument. But this explanation of the nature of inspiration cannot be reconciled with the fact that the ideas, mode of expression, and method of proposing various ideas differ so exceedingly in the Bible. Then, too, the sacred writers themselves tell us that they collected their material after much time, pain, and effort (cf. 2 Mach. 2, 24. 27; Luke 1, 1 ff). We know also that they at times employed various sources or documents for the composition of their books (e.g., Books of Kings).

There are other scholars who go to the other extreme. They assert that the *sacred writers are the only authors* in the proper sense of the word, and that God exercised either no influence or only a moral influence upon them.   (a) Lessius, Bonfrerius, Haneberg, etc., held that God is the Author of the Bible through *consequent approbation;* that is, the books were composed solely by the individual efforts of the sacred writers, but afterwards God, either directly or through His Church, declared the books to be free from error. But, needless to say, this view was declared erroneous by the Vatican Council. (b) Others limited inspiration to a mere *negative influence,* that is, a mere external assistance whereby God is prepared to prevent any errors from creeping into the Scriptures. This assistance, enjoyed by the infallible magisterium of the Church in definitions of faith and morals, does not of itself and by itself suffice for inspiration. The essence of inspiration requires a positive influence of God upon the mental faculties of the sacred writers. God is the Author by a physical causality, and by a supernatural power He elevates and applies the spiritual and material faculties of the sacred writer in the complete composition of the book.[2]

2 Cf. Grannan, C. P., *op. cit.,* III, 112-140.

(a) THE INTELLECT [3]

The intellect of man, or his mind, is the cognitive faculty which seeks for, thinks or reasons about and knows the truth. We ordinarily say man's intellect, or mind, is illumined or enlightened.

St. Thomas (2, 2, q. 173, art 2; *De Ver.* q. 12, art. 7) distinguishes between the acceptance of things (*acceptatio rerum*) and the judgment of the things accepted (*judicium de rebus acceptis*) that may go on in the mind of the sacred writer.

(1) The Acceptance of Things.—St. Thomas teaches that the reception of truths does not necessarily pertain to biblical inspiration, and modern scholars agree that the communication of truths by newly impressed species is not one of the formal elements of inspiration, because the sacred writers often could, by their own natural powers, come to the knowledge of truth. Nevertheless, for the purpose of selecting things naturally known to them, they needed the *assistance of a supernatural light.* The sacred writers themselves tell us that they gathered their material after expending much time and effort (cf. Luke 1, 1 ff; 2 Mach. 2, 19 ff), that they made use of various sources (cf. Prov. 30, 1; 31, 1; 1 Par. enumerates seventeen sources), that they are narrating events personally experienced (cf. Matthew, John, Acts in the "we" sections).

The Use of Sources by the Sacred Writers.—The fact that the sacred writers made use of sources and documents in the composition of their books, does not make these sources inspired. Inspiration refers only to the judgment passed upon the material taken and used. Hence, it would not be repugnant to inspiration if a sacred writer borrowed from non-Hebrew or pagan sources. But his dependence upon such sources should be judged according to other criteria (e.g., age, language, style, etc.).

The Distinction and Nexus between Revelation and Inspira-

[3] Cf. Bea, A., "De Scripturae Sacrae Inspiratione, etc.," 46-58; Desroches, A., "Jugement pratique et Jugement speculatif chez l'Ecrivain inspiré" (Ottawa 1958).

tion.—The word "revelation" has a variety of meanings. In the *strict sense* of the word, it means the divine manifestation of occult or strictly supernatural truths through the infusion of new species (*acceptatio rerum*). In this sense revelation does not belong to the essence of inspiration. The hagiographer does not always need this kind of revelation for his book. In the *broader sense* of the word, revelation is understood of any divine communication or God's message to man. In this sense the Bible is considered as revealed and the object of divine faith; that is, the Bible must be believed on the authority of God speaking. But the extent of these communicated truths must not be restricted to these divine writings, because tradition is also an independent source of divine revelation.

(*2*) *The Influence of God upon the Intellect to Judge the Accepted Things.*—According to St. Thomas (2. 2, q. 174, art. 2), the principal element in prophetic knowledge is *judgment;* that is, the intellect of the sacred writer is elevated and applied with the assistance of a supernatural light, so that it may infallibly judge the truths to be written.

There are various judgments that must be elicited by the sacred writer. He must judge about the truth and certitude of the material, and unite these separate judgments with one another (theoretical judgments). He must judge what he is going to write, what documents he is going to use in his book (practical judgments). He must judge how he is to express himself—for example, the kind of literature (narrative, poetic, didactic), mode of expression, apt words, figures of speech, etc. (literary judgments).

Theoretical Judgment.—In order that the sacred writer may elicit those judgments which God conceived in His mind and wishes to communicate to humanity by means of the Sacred Scriptures, and in order that the hagiographer may be certain about these judgments, God must move his intellect in such a manner that he elicits these judgments as true and certain. From the time of Origen this divine movement of the intellect of the sacred writer is called *illumination*. A supernatural light elevates the intellectual faculties to understand things that are divine, and strengthens these faculties to judge according to divine truth.

Practical Judgment.—That the entire production of a book may proceed principally from God, and not from man, it is necessary that man's practical intellect be determined by some previous divine motion to such an extent that the practical judgment (i.e., only those judgments determined to be used in the composition of the book) will infallibly follow. God moves the intellect to elicit infallibly this judgment, and this motion is something internal. Mere external incentives or occasions are insufficient, even though they are present (e.g., the requests made to St. Mark by the Roman community for the gospel of St. Peter).

Literary Judgment.—The external form of expression is an activity commanded by the will, but is formally elicited by the practical intellect. Since this intellectual activity belongs to the composition of the book, God must also move the intellect of the sacred writer in this regard, because the sacred writer is the instrument of God, not only in regard to its internal mental conception, but also in regard to the book itself, which cannot exist without some determined external form.

Importance and Power of This Supernatural Influence upon the Intellect.—Because of this supernatural influence described above, the Bible has certain specific characteristics which distinguish it from all other books. First, it is *immune from error*. Though the sacred writers may privately share the ideas of their contemporaries, yet when a judgment between truth and falsehood must be made, they are influenced by God to such an extent that whatever is formally asserted is affirmed without error. Secondly, the Bible has an *excellence all its own*. Even if this excellence is not sufficient to prove the inspiration of the Bible, yet it confirms the supernatural origin of the Bible. This excellence is evident from the contents proposed and the origin of the Bible. It contains a simple, yet sober, description of historical truths confirmed by modern discoveries; it contains doctrines, both righteous and sublime, accommodated to the intelligence of all. The Sacred Scriptures originated among a people less cultured than many of its neighbors (e.g., the Egyptians, the Babylonians, the Phœnicians, etc.); the authors often had very little education (e.g., Amos). Whenever these books were written, there is a marvellously correct judgment given in difficult matters being discussed by even contemporaneous philosophy or religious systems (e.g., the doctrine of the Logos by St. John).

Though many of the sacred writers were *conscious of their inspiration,* yet, the necessity of one's consciousness of inspiration does not belong to the essence of inspiration. In fact, some of them were not aware of their own inspiration (cf. Luke 1, 1-4; 2 Mach. 2, 20-31), and some sacred books were not recognized to be of divine origin by the contemporaries of the hagiographers, as is evident from the history of the Canon.

(b) THE WILL [4]

We commonly say that the will is moved, urged, impelled, determined, induced, or persuaded to give its consent to any proposal and to what God wills absolutely.[5]

(1) The Necessity of the Motion of the Will.—This necessity is expressed in the Encyclicals "Providentissimus Deus" (E.B., **125**) and "Spiritus Paraclitus" (E.B., **448**), and follows from the concept of a "book." A book represents not merely ideas and their coördination in the mind, but also their outward expression in writing. If God wishes to be the Author of an inspired book, He must move the will of man to perform those acts necessary for its outward expression. If the actual writing of these ideas proceeds from man only, without any divine motion or assistance, God could not be called the

---

[4] Cf. Bea, *op. cit.,* 68-70.
[5] Cf. Grannan, *op. cit.,* III, 47.

Author of the book in the proper sense of the word, but only the Author of the thoughts contained in the Bible.

(*2*) *The Nature of This Motion.*—This is defined by its purpose and scope. (i) In order that God may be called the principal Author of a book, the act of man's will must be dependent upon the act of the divine will, which states that this book must be written and must be written in a definite manner. This impulse or influence upon the will of the hagiographer must be *infallibly efficacious* and must *proceed from the absolute will of God.* (ii) This divine impulse upon the will of the sacred writer must be *physical* and *immediate.* Were this impulse merely moral and mediate, man, but not God, would be the principal cause. (iii) This impulse must be such that the sacred writer, even though he infallibly follows the divine motion, remains *free.*

(c) The Executive Faculties

Inspiration must also extend its influence to the executive mental faculties, the memory and the imagination. Whether this influence should be considered as a mere negative assistance or as a positive direction, is disputed among theologians.

CHAPTER III

THE EXTENT OF INSPIRATION

We are not here concerned with the question: "What books are inspired?" This question will be answered in the discussion on the history of the Canon. Here we are concerned only with the question: "How far does inspiration extend among the books?" To what extent do we find it in the Bible? Must inspiration be predicated of all the assertions in the Bible, or may it be restricted only to certain categories of truth?

The Council of Trent (April 8, 1546) stated that "those entire books with all their parts as have been accustomed to be read in the Catholic Church" must be considered as sacred and canonical (E.B., 60). Afterwards, Holden (d. 1662) restricted inspiration to those things pertaining to doctrine or having some relation with doctrine. The Vatican Council (1870) repeated the words of the Council of Trent (E.B., 79). Afterwards, however, Professor Rohling of Germany (1872), who later retracted his opinion, and the French layman Francis Lenormant (1880-1884), whose book was put on the Index on December 19, 1887, held that inspiration must be restricted to faith and morals, and those things intimately connected with them. Cardinal Newman,[1] whose opinion was neither retracted nor condemned officially, asserted that *res obiter dictae* (i.e., things of minor importance, as e.g., Tobias' dog wagging its tail [Tob. 11, 9]; Paul's cloak left behind at Troas [2 Tim. 4, 13], etc.) were not inspired (1884). In Italy, Salvatore di Bartolo (1888), whose book was placed on the Index, exempted secular matters from the province of inspiration.

This question about the general extension of inspiration has been settled by the Encyclical "Providentissimus Deus" of

---

[1] Cf. Duggan, J., "Num sententia Cardinalis Newman de inerrantia S.S. defendi possit?" in V.D., 18 (1938), 219-234.

28   A COMPANION TO SCRIPTURE STUDIES

November 18, 1893, which repeated the words of the Council of Trent and of the Vatican: ". . . the entire books with all their parts" (E.B., 124). These same words are also contained in the Encyclical "Divino afflante Spiritu" of September 30, 1943 (E.B., 538).

Art. 1. The Theological Proofs for This General Extension

(a) *Councils and Decrees of the Church.*—(1) The Tridentine and Vatican Councils issued formal dogmatical decrees. The encyclicals "Providentissimus Deus" of Leo XIII and "Divino afflante Spiritu" of Pius XII, even though they were not "ex cathedra" pronouncements, nevertheless are of supreme value and oblige in conscience.

The doubt, however, still remains as to what is meant precisely by the expression "all their parts." Some scholars (e.g., Billot, Schiffini, etc.) interpret these words in the *physical* sense to mean every particular part, even the smallest parts (i.e., everything without exception). Others (e.g., Pesch, De San, etc.) hold that the word "part" must be taken in a broader sense, that is, according to a *moral* evaluation. This latter interpretation seems more in conformity with the mind of the Councils, which wished to safeguard particular pericopes or individual passages in the Vulgate and to state that the books of our Latin Vulgate Bible must be recognized in their integral form. Since therefore these Councils speak of this word "part" with a connotation other than that which we now have in mind, their Decrees cannot be directly or immediately applied to settle the question of the general extension of inspiration.

(2) The "Providentissimus Deus" has given the authentic interpretation of the Church, and refers directly to the question of the extension of inspiration that had been so often discussed in the years prior to this pronouncement. The Encyclical urges the faithful in a question of the truth or falsehood of a passage to consider primarily "what God has said,"

rather than "the reason and purpose which He had in mind in saying it." And so the Roman Pontiff, Leo XIII, denies the distinction between things inspired because of their religious content and those which are *obiter dicta*. He positively teaches that "all the books which the Church receives as sacred and canonical are written wholly and entirely, with all their parts, at the dictation of the Holy Spirit" (E.B., 124). Hence, inspiration by its very nature embraces wholly and entirely everything written by the hagiographer.

(3) This same doctrine was confirmed by the Decree of Pius X in his "Lamentabili," which condemns the proposition: "Divine inspiration is not to be extended to all Scripture in such a way as to preserve each and all its parts from error" (E.B., 202). This doctrine is repeated by Benedict XV in the "Spiritus Paraclitus": "He (i.e., Leo XIII) also teaches that divine inspiration extends to every part of the Bible without the slightest exception, and that no error can occur in the inspired text" (E.B., 455). This same Encyclical, speaking with regard to the inerrancy of the Bible, rejects the distinction of those who try "to distinguish between what they style the primary or religious and the secondary or profane element in the Bible" (E.B., 454). The same Holy Father approved a decision of the Pontifical Biblical Commission on June 18, 1915, in which it was stated that everything which the hagiographer asserts, enunciates, suggests must be held as having been asserted, enunciated, suggested by the Holy Spirit (E.B., 420).

(b) *The Fathers.*—The Fathers both explicitly teach and practically apply the doctrine of the universal extension of inspiration. Every text, even though it does not formally treat of a religious topic, is quoted as the word of God. They deny that there can be any contradiction in the Bible. Never do they even suggest the possibility of falsehood or error in purely historical parts.

(c) *Theological Proofs.*—(1) The general extension of inspiration to every part of the Bible follows directly from the

nature of inspiration. The sacred writer is an instrument in regard to everything that he writes in his book. Hence, undoubtedly all his judgments expressed in sentences are embraced by the divine act of inspiration. Everything, therefore, without exception comes under the influence of God, the principal cause. Leo XIII aptly expressed this in the words: "They wrote those things, and only those things, which the Holy Spirit ordered them to write."

(2) An indirect proof is also derived from the fact, as will be shown later, that everything contained in the Bible is immune from error. This infallibility or immunity from error is the result of inspiration and includes everything in the Bible.

Art. 2. The Particular Extension of Inspiration

The question still remains whether in the expression *parts* individual words are to be included. In other words, should verbal inspiration be admitted?

The proponents of verbal inspiration either in the broad or in the strict sense do not understand by it mechanical dictation, which means that God dictated every word through sensible sounds or the infusion of words (i.e., by internal suggestion or by stirring the phantasy in such a manner that the sacred writer reads these words as from a book). This view was defended by *Philo and *Josephus, by most Protestants in the seventeenth century, and by the Catholics, Estius, Gregory of Valencia, Bañez, Billuart, etc. We must note here that the word *dictation*, employed by Cardinal Billot and the Encyclical "Providentissimus Deus," does not imply mechanical transcription, but rather composing, teaching, inspiring.

This rigorous theory of verbal inspiration cannot be defended. It asserts that the sacred writers were mere passive instruments. It cannot explain the diversity of style, language, words, phrases, etc. It cannot explain the literary imperfections in the Bible nor the peculiar differences prevailing between sacred writers treating the same theme.

In the first place, we must remember that to give a light to determine an individual word does not mean the same thing as to give or to infuse or to supply or to dictate a determined word to the hagiographer. All Catholic scholars are agreed that the divine influence in inspiration positively extends to the judgments or thoughts of the sacred writer, but differ as to whether this influence extends positively or negatively to the hagiographer's very words.

The proponents of *verbal inspiration in the broad sense* (e.g., Hurter, Franzelin, Pesch, Cornely, Vigouroux, Merk, Lattey, etc.) proceed from the notion of author and distinguish between the formal and material elements in the Bible. They agree that words of supreme importance (e.g., Logos, the words of the institution of the Blessed Eucharist, the various mysteries of the Trinity, Incarnation, etc.) are directly inspired, but in regard to other words God assists merely negatively. The formal element consists in the communication of the contents or ideas, while the material element consists in the form or the wording, its literary character, external form, phraseology, vocabulary, etc. Just as a human writer, so too may God be called an author, if He is solely responsible for the ideas and leaves the selection of the words to the hagiographer. Thus, God is the principal Author even though the concrete form of these thoughts through language is determined by the instrument alone, provided this form reproduces faithfully His ideas. Yet, these very words are not entirely subtracted from the divine influence. God influences them negatively; that is, He must impede inept or unsuitable words from creeping into the text of the sacred writer. This is commonly called negative assistance.

In this theory inspiration influences the words of the hagiographer, not through a positive divine influence, but through the *positive divine presence and negative assistance,* by reason of which God is prepared to impede any words that would not suitably express His thoughts. This effect is positive and not negative, because it would be impossible for improper or inept words to be used or applied. It is just like a mother, who is teaching her infant how to walk. She takes it by the hand and then leaves it walk alone. But she is always on hand and ready to assist, lest the child fall. Thus, positive assistance is required only when the author is about to use some misleading expression.

The proponents of *verbal inspiration in the strict sense* (e.g., Scheeben, Lagrange, Grannan, Billot, Poels, Tanquerey, Höpfl, Ruffini, Bea, etc.) hold that the influence of inspiration on the sacred writer is also positive in regard to the external form or writing, and we are inclined to endorse this theory.

The divine action, by which the intellectual faculties of the sacred writer are elevated and also applied in the composition of a book, must also reach the very effect (i.e., the wording of the book). Whatever the human author does in composing the book, he does under divine influence, since the true notion of a principal and instrumental cause requires that the entire effect must be attributed to both. But merely negative assistance in the selection of words does not suffice, because then the material part of the book would be subtracted from the positive divine influence (i.e., true inspiration).

There are two principal arguments employed by all who defend strict verbal inspiration: (1) the philosophical argument from the notion of causality; (2) the psychological argument.

(1) *The Philosophical Argument from the Notion of Causality.*—The same effect must be ascribed to the principal cause and to the instrumental cause, but not in such a manner that one part of the book comes from God solely and another from man solely. But all comes from each, but from each in a different manner. The total effect is ascribed to the principal cause and the same total effect also to the instrument. "Thus, the Bible is the joint production of God and man. It is all from God, its source and principal author, and it is all through man, its channel, and all by man, its secondary, subordinate, instrumental author. The conclusion is: The Bible is never to be regarded as merely human nor as merely divine, nor as

partly human and partly divine, but as all human and all divine. All human, because written by man, and all divine, because inspired by God. These two factors are everywhere present and should be everywhere recognized, if we are to understand the Bible in its true light" (Grannan, *op. cit.*, III, 52).

(2) *The Psychological Argument.*—There is an intimate connection between our words and our thoughts, and if these are separated vivisection results, according to Cardinal Billot.

In the psychological order there is such a connection between the external word (whether oral or written) and the internal word or thought of the mind, that they cannot be separated, except through divine intervention or through a miracle; for no thought is possible, unless it makes some trace upon the sensible faculty or phantasy. Every word expressed terminatively represents an idea that was in our mind, and when an idea is in our mind, there immediately arises some sensible sign to express that idea.

Corollary 1. Divine inspiration does not take away the manner of thinking or writing proper to the individual writers; this divine action elevates and applies their faculties, but does not destroy them. Hence, biblical inspiration does not take away the sacred writer's freedom, because even though under the divine impulse he says infallibly what God wishes him to say, yet he retains freedom in the selection of phrases or words.

Corollary 2. Divine inspiration does not exclude linguistic peculiarities or irregularities in syntax. "In inspiration God adapts Himself to the instrument used; He accommodates Himself to the complex nature of the man He has chosen to be His living, intelligent, willing, active, plastic instrument. Thus, God speaks, acts, and writes by him, and with him, and through him in the production of the book. Making all due allowance for the many and very considerable differences between an intelligent, living instrument and an inert, lifeless instrument, we need not hesitate to say that God uses man as his instrument very much as a man uses a pen or other instrument to write with" (Grannan, *op. cit.*, III, 54). In so far as God does not change the nature of the intelligent instrument, but uses it in accordance with its nature and elevates it, the variety of style and diction is thus easily explained: *Quidquid recipitur ad modum recipientis recipitur.* Thus, a Paderewski or a Kreisler necessarily had to accommodate himself to the tonal possibilities of his instrument, the piano or violin.

Corollary 3. This divine inspiration does not require that the very words spoken by Christ and reported in the four Gospels must be revealed to the Evangelists just like modern tape recordings. These words or discourses of Jesus recorded by Apostolic witnesses (Matthew, John) and their assistants (Mark, Luke) faithfully and accurately render the substance, the gist of the main ideas, thoughts or meaning of Our Lord's teaching in their own free stylistic way without having re-courses to invented speeches clothing any of His messages. For this faithful and accurate reporting it sufficed if the Evangelists, aided by this supernatural light, wrote down the thoughts and words as these Apostolic witnesses remembered them or as they were transmitted by the Apostles and other witnesses. Thus, the Evangelists could record the words and also the deeds of Jesus in different ways (just as modern reporters for various newspapers do by giving a full or modern account, or by summarizing the same speeches or deeds of a person) without being contradictory. Hence, those views are manifestly *untenable* which suppose: a) that the discourses of Jesus in the Gospels, especially "in his (John's) Gospel are theological meditations devoid of historical truth concerning the mystery of salvation" ("Lamentabili," n. 16 [E.B., 207]); b) or that His words are the definite formulations of His spiritual message by the *Urgemeinde* or primitive Church (a position maintained by some scholars of various historical and literary schools); c) or that prior to Pentecost there could not be a faith in the divinity of Christ (for the contrary, cf. "Lamentabili," n. 27 [E.B. 218]) or an incipient faith in the Trinity, so that some Gospel phrases, words or expressions, which were by Catholic tradition up to now commonly accepted as those of Jesus, must be ascribed to this primitive Church as a liturgical addition or interpretation of His words.[2]

Corollary 4. This divine inspiration does not exclude personal labor exercised by the hagiographers in the composition of their books. If the Holy Spirit had suggested every word to them, then this fact-finding or word-finding process would not have been necessary.

Corollary 5. If the human hagiographer employed a secretary or scribe who gave the book its external literary form (as St. Paul for his Epistle to the Hebrews), then charismatic inspiration must also be conceded to this secretary or scribe. The same may be said if a book is composed successively by many authors or revisers. Inspiration is primarily destined for man, and not primarily for the book.

Corollary 6. This divine inspiration must be carefully distinguished from literary authenticity which is not necessarily an object of faith. The divine origin of an entire canonical book is guaranteed, even though the human author is unknown or several unknown collaborators participated, and even though we know nothing of the period in which the book was composed.[3]

Corollary 7. Various versions of the Bible are said to be equivalently inspired, that is, in so far as they express exactly the words of the original text and are equivalent to the words of the original text. Hence, it follows that the original text always possesses a greater dignity than the versions or translations.

---

[2] D. M. Stanley maintains that Matt. 28, 18 ff with the precise Trinitarian formula is a liturgical addition: "To assume that our Lord would have made such a precise allusion to the Trinity antecedent to the Pentecostal revelation is to shut one's eyes to the historical process by which Christian dogma was gradually imparted to the apostolic Church" (cf. "Liturgical Influences on the Formation of the Four Gospels," in C.B.Q., 21 (1959), 29.

[3] Cf. Robert and Tricot, "Guide to the Bible," 18 ff.

CHAPTER IV

THE EFFECT OF INSPIRATION: INERRANCY

Bibliography: Vosté, J.-M., "De scripturarum veritate iuxta recentiora Ecclesiae documenta" (Rome, 1924); De Courte, G. "Inspiration et inerrance," in *Supplément au Dictionnaire de la Bible,* 4 (1949), 482-559; Florit, E., "La verità della S. Scrittura" (Rome, 1951); Weisengoff, J. P., "Inerrancy of the Old Testament in Religious Matters," in C.B.Q., 17 (1955), 128-137; Coppens, J., "L'inspiration et l'inerrance biblique," in "Ephemerides theologicae Lovanienses," 33 (1957), 36-57; Forestell, J. T., "The Limitation of Inerrancy," in C.B.Q., 20 (1958), 9-18.

From the very fact that the sacred writers were divinely inspired it necessarily follows that the Sacred Scriptures are both *de facto* and *de jure* free from all error. The Catholic Church has always taught this. "For all the books which the Church receives as sacred and canonical are written wholly and entirely, with all their parts, at the dictation of the Holy Spirit; and so far is it from being possible that any error can coëxist with inspiration, that inspiration not only is essentially incompatible with error, but excludes and rejects it as absolutely and necessarily as it is impossible that God Himself, the supreme Truth, can utter that which is not true. . . . And so emphatically were all the Fathers and Doctors agreed that the divine writings, as left by the hagiographers, are free from all error that they labored earnestly, with no less skill than reverence, to reconcile with each other those numerous passages which seem at variance" ("Providentissimus Deus," cf. E.B., 124, 127). This Catholic dogma of Biblical inerrancy was also stressed in modern times by Benedict XV in his Encyclical "Spiritus Paraclitus" (E.B., 450) and by Pius XII in his Encyclical "Divino afflante Spiritu" (E.B., 538-540).

This Biblical inerrancy, though absolute and universal, requires some explanation, since not everything in the Bible presents the Word of God in the same way, tone or stress, nor does everything therein enjoy the same degree of truth. Hence, certain restrictions or clarifications must be made for this inerrancy to be properly understood; namely, it must be applied only to the autographs and must be predicated solely of those truths which the sacred writer as such affirms and precisely according to the meaning by which he affirms these truths.

This absolute inerrancy must be directly attributed to the original texts of the sacred writers. This inerrancy applies to transcriptions (as the Massoretic Text and Greek New Testament text) and translations (as the Septuagint, Vulgate, etc.) in the measure in which they represent faithfully the original autographic manuscripts; and, although inspiration does not *per se* exclude error from the literary transmission of the text, yet, *de facto*, divine providence has faithfully preserved the Sacred Scriptures in regard to their substance. "It is true, no doubt, that copyists have made mistakes in the text of the Bible; this question, when it arises, should be carefully considered on its merits, and the fact not too easily admitted, but only in those passages where the proof is clear" ("Providentissimus Deus," cf. E.B., 124). These copyists' mistakes do not alter the substantial faithfulness of the text.

The object of this inerrancy must be restricted to those statements which the sacred writer as such *affirms* and, secondly, according to the sense by which he is affirming these truths.

1. These infallibly true affirmations or statements include not only those explicitly ascribed by the hagiographers to God (1 Cor. 7, 10), but also everything that "he asserts, enunciates, suggests" (E.B., 420). Hence, whatever the sacred writer affirms, he also teaches this, and this is also taught by God.

a) In the Bible there are many *inspired statements by the sacred writers themselves.*[1] Thus, for example, in the epistles of St. Paul there are to be found inspired references that are historical, doctrinal or even personal, as facts about his life, feelings, intentions, solemn protests, prayers, etc. This same Apostle expresses his doubts about situations (1 Cor. 1, 16;

---

[1] Cf. Merk-Bea, "Institutiones Biblicae," 75-78; Höpfl-Leloir, "Introductio Generalis, etc." 86-91.

2 Cor. 12, 2ff), and it is God who does not wish to remove
this doubt from His instrumental cause, but moves him to
confess his doubt or ignorance about matters. Similarly, harsh
imprecations, as in the cursing Psalms described in highly
colored poetry and very expressive Oriental imagery as well
as the bitter feelings truly expressed in the thoughts of some
sacred writers, were not immoral judgments, but are indications of a very strong sense of justice calling upon God to
repair injury or damage inflicted, to punish sinners who are
the enemies of God, His people and His religion, to vindicate
their national, religious or personal rights, and to restore their
prestige as God's elected people; this heavenly cry for justice
is not so perfect as the spirit of charity advocated by Jesus
Christ and His followers.[2] Finally, the advice, opinion or com-
mandment which an inspired author gives (1 Cor. 7, 6), even
though he may distinguish it from that revealed by the
Lord (1 Cor. 7, 12.25.40; cf. also 7, 10), is true and good.

b) We frequently find inserted in the Bible the *sayings,
conversations, letters, documents, etc., of others.* The question
arises: What is the attitude or intention of the sacred writer
toward this material? He may acknowledge the fact that he
is quoting, make mention of his sources, give at least substantially the words of others. This is called *explicit, or formal,
citation.* This external material may contain historical truth,
that is, *veritas citationis,* wherein the quotation agrees with
the sources from which it is derived. It is the Word of God
by reason only of God's attestation that these things were
written or said. *Per se* the sacred writer neither approves nor
disapproves, but suspends his judgment, unless this is indicated.
Neither is the material intrinsically divine and infallible.
Thus, the historical books relate various conversations; for
instance, those of Joseph and his brethren, Samuel and Saul,
Jonathan and David, Christ and the Jews, Paul and Festus.
Then, too, the poetical books of the Old Testament, as the

[2] Cf. Steinmueller, J. E., "Some Problems, etc.," 218-220.

Canticle of Canticles and Job, give long conversations between persons.

This material may also contain objective truth, that is, *veritas rei citatae*, where there is an agreement between the contents of a citation and the facts in the case. It is the Word of God by reason of its contents and hence intrinsically divine and infallible. We can determine in many cases from the persons speaking or from circumstances whether the sacred writer makes this material his own and approves of it. Thus, intrinsically and objectively true are the sayings uttered by God and the prophets in the Old Testament, and by Christ, the angel Gabriel, the Blessed Virgin Mary, the Apostles as special organs of revelation, by those filled with the Holy Spirit in the New Testament.

Some documents, decrees and letters from non-inspired sources have been incorporated at times by the inspired hagiographers in their books. None of their material *per se* enjoys any greater authority than it had before, and it becomes objective truth only when it is approved by God (Job 42, 8) or by an inspired writer (Acts 17, 28; Tit. 1, 12ff.). It is the task of the Biblical scholar to determine when the sacred author approves of his sources.

2. This inerrancy must be limited to the meaning which the sacred writer and God through him wish to express. This meaning must not be extended to any meaning that can be reconciled with the biblical text. This literal sense, which the hagiographer expressed, is to be determined by the principles of exegesis with special attention being given to the literary forms, the study of which has been encouraged by Pius XII in his Encyclical "Divino afflante Spiritu." He writes: "Let the interpreter . . . endeavor to determine the peculiar character and circumstances of the sacred writer, the age in which he lived, the sources, written or oral, to which he had recourse and the forms of expression he employed . . . the supreme rule of interpretation is to discover and define what the writer intended to express" (E.B., 557). And again: "By this knowl-

edge and exact appreciation of the modes of speaking and writing in use among the ancients can be solved many difficulties raised against the veracity and historical value of the Divine Scriptures and . . . this study contributes to a fuller and more luminous understanding of the mind of the Sacred Writer" (E.B., 560).

All Catholic scholars admit the fact of biblical inerrancy, but the method of explaining and applying this inerrancy to the natural sciences and historical parts of the Bible varied since the latter part of the last century and particularly since the end of World War I when our knowledge of the history, culture and religion of the Fertile Crescent countries (e.g., Sumerians, Babylonians, Assyrians, Hittites, Egyptians, Canaanites, etc.) was considerably increased. This has been called the "Biblical Problem" for Catholic exegetes.

Art. 1. Sacred Scripture and Science

Bibliography: Peters, N., "Bibel und Naturwissenschaft nach den Grundsätzen der kath. Theologie" (Paderborn, 1906); Steinmueller, J. E., "Some Problems, etc," 1-23; Schwegler, T., "Der Beitrag der Naturwissenschaft zur Schrifterklärung," in "Studia Anselmiana" (Rome, 1951), 424-442.

The natural sciences, as such, are not professedly or directly taught in the Bible, but only by reason of their nexus with religious truths. The Bible as a religious book was intended primarily by God to teach men infallibly about faith and morals, to inculcate theoretical truths and practical duties necessary for salvation. For this purpose the natural sciences have the least nexus with religion and are only casually mentioned in the Bible. "The Holy Spirit did not intend to teach men those things which were in no way useful to salvation" (St. Augustine, *Gen. ad. lit.*, II. 9).

The difficulties arising from astronomy, cosmology, geology, psychology, botany, and zoology do not constitute contradictions to the teachings of the Bible and the natural sciences.

Confronted with these same difficulties from the natural sciences, St. Augustine everywhere in his works declared that no possible contradiction can exist between the Bible and the natural sciences. He insisted (a) that the Sacred Scriptures were free from any error, that this must be believed even if we cannot solve all the difficulties and problems (Ep. 28 and 82; *Contra Faustum Man.*); (b) that between the Bible and the secular sciences no possible contradiction can exist, and for this reason neither the theologian nor the physicist should make rash assertions or assert what is not known as known (*Gen. ad lit.*, I, 18, 37, I, 19, 39, and I, 21, 41 cited by the "Providentissimus Deus"); and (c) that the Bible does not speak of the natural phenomena scientifically or exactly, but accommodated itself to the popular way of thinking (*De actibus cum Felice; Gen. ad lit.*, II, 9, 20, cited by the "Providentissimus Deus").

These principles of St. Augustine were reaffirmed by Pope Leo XIII in his Encyclical "Providentissimus Deus," and were made more explicit and more emphatic. The Encyclical laid down three principles for the correct interpretation of biblical references to the natural sciences (E.B., 121). (a) The sacred writers "did not seek to penetrate the secrets of nature." Hence, many of their assertions and phrases must be understood according to the external appearance of natural objects and not according to their essential or intrinsic nature. (b) The sacred writers "described and dealt with things in more or less figurative language," that is, they made use of pictures and similitudes taken from nature to illustrate spiritual doctrines. (c) The sacred writers made use of "terms which were commonly used at the time, and which in many instances are daily used at this day," that is, they deliver a popular account and accommodate themselves to the intelligence of their audience.

These three principles of Pope Leo XIII are sufficient to explain all the apparent contradictions between the Bible and the natural sciences. Hence, the sacred writers remained children of their own times, and did not by reason of inspiration receive any special revelation or more profound knowledge of the natural sciences than their contemporaries. Their language in describing the natural phenomena was therefore relatively true.

Art. 2. Sacred Scripture and History

Bibliography: Bea, A., *op. cit.*, 97-101; Bonaccorsi, G., "Questioni Bibliche" (Bologna, 1904); Delattre, A., "Autour de 'a Question Biblique" (Liège, 1904); Durand, A., "Dictionnaire Apologétique," II (4th ed., Paris, 1915); Fonck, L., "Der Kampf, etc."; Idem, "Die Irrtumslosigkeit der Bibel vor dem Forum der Wissenschaft" (Einsiedeln, 1919); Goettsberger, J., "Autour, etc."; Grannan, C., "A General Introduction, etc.," III (St. Louis, 1921), 85-102; von Hummelauer, F., "Exegetisches zur Inspirationsfrage," in B.S., IX, iv (1904); Lagrange, M. J., "A Propos de L'Encyclique Providentissimus," in R.B., IV (1895), 48-64; Idem, "L'inspiration et les exigences, etc.," in R.B., V (1896), 199 f; Idem, "La méthode historique" (Paris, 1904; English edition, London, 1905); Idem, "Eclaircissement sur la méthode historique" (Paris, 1905); Idem, "Addenda et Notanda," in R.B., XVI (1919), 593-600; Prat, F., "La Bible et l'Histoire" (Paris, 1904), 40 ff.; Steinmueller, J. E., "Some Problems, etc.," 29-35; * Noth, D. M., "History and the Word of God in the Old Testament," in "Bulletin of the John Rylands Library," 32 (Manchester, 1950), 194-206; McKenzie, J. L., "The Two-Edged Sword" (Milwaukee, 1956).

A more difficult problem than that of the application of inerrancy to the natural or physical sciences appears when we treat of some historical passages (e.g., the story of Susanna in the Book of Daniel) or even of some entire books, especially of the Old Testament (e.g., Esther, Judith, Tobias). Do all the facts narrated in the pericopes or books of the Bible (especially where mere secular facts are narrated without any bearing on faith or morals) enjoy real, objective historicity? Are all the events described facts that really happened in real life? Any event, even though it happened in ordinary life or secular history without any apparent religious connotation, merits objective reality and truth, if the hagiographer formally affirms that this even really took place. The Biblical problem, however, is this: Does the sacred writer extend this prerogative of objective truth to everything that he speaks of, whether the matters are religious or purely secular (cf. Luke in regard to the mission of John the Baptist or to the time of Christ's birth)?

In the past some Catholic scholars, who were aware of

some serious historical difficulties in the Bible, approached this problem in a threefold way: (a) the Bible in some passages or even some books, just like the natural, physical sciences, could be considered as having the exterior appearance of truth; (b) the Bible has various literary forms, the truth of which is not always absolute, but may be relative; (c) the Bible indulges in implicit citations in which the sacred writer merely incorporates or inserts material into his book, but does not wish to become a responsible witness to its truth. See below.

However, the opponents of these methods followed a stricter, traditional method. These scholars (e.g., Brucker, Delattre, Fonck, Hugo, Billot, etc.) were partly aided by some decisions of the ecclesiastical magisterium which agreed to some extent to their principles, the application of which, however, was restricted.

From the serious discussions which had taken place between these two schools of thought and diverse methods of approaching the Biblical problem, there was gradually evolved a general harmony of principles. This harmony was attained by eliminating from the more liberal school those ideas which conflicted with Catholic principles of inerrancy and by restricting within just limits some ideas espoused by the strict traditionalists. This harmony has been stressed by Pius XII in his "Divino afflante Spiritu," which encourages scholars to study and apply "the literary forms," or "genres," of the Bible. "Catholic commentators . . . in demonstrating and proving its (i.e., the Bible's) immunity from error, should also make a prudent use of this means, that is, to what extent the manner of expression or the literary mode adopted by the sacred writer may lead to a correct and genuine interpretation; . . . this part of his office cannot be neglected without serious detriment to Catholic exegesis" (E.B., 560).

(a) BIBLE HISTORY ACCORDING TO APPEARANCE

The three principles laid down by Pope Leo XIII in the

interpretation of the natural sciences were made to apply also to historical facts by some Catholic scholars. They maintained that the sacred writers did not always present us with strict historical truth, because they followed at times popular opinions and traditions, even though these might be false. Assuming that the "Providentissimus Deus" had given a more liberal interpretation of inspiration, Lagrange applied this criterion of apparent, non-objective history to the Old and New Testaments,[1] while von Hummelauer used this principle to invent various literary forms for the Old Testament, and Prat developed a system of implicit citations. Goettsberger denied that this interpretation could be placed upon the Encyclical, and insisted that the Bible considered in itself demanded non-objective history.

Neither the Encyclical nor the subject considered in itself justify the negation of real, objective history in the Bible.

The sentence which led Lagrange and others to form a false conclusion was: "The principles here laid down will apply to cognate sciences, and especially to history" (E.B., 123). But these words in their context do not refer to the method permitted in interpreting the natural sciences according to apparent truth (E.B., 121), but rather urge us to apply a like line of argument against false natural science as well as against false profane history (E.B., 122). Pope Benedict XV clarified the issue when he gave an authentic interpretation to these words: "And if Leo XIII does say that we can apply to history and cognate subjects the same principles which hold good for science, he yet does not lay this down as a universal law, but simply says that we can apply a like line of argument when refuting the fallacies of adversaries and defending the historical truth of Scripture from their assaults" ("Spiritus Paraclitus," in E. B., 458).

The Church through her Pontifical Biblical Commission amplified the words of both Leo XIII and Benedict XV, when in a Decree it stated that those books which are regarded as his-

---

[1] Cf. "Historical Criticism, etc.," *loc. cit.,* 44, 180-213. 234 f.

torical, either wholly or in part, are to be properly regarded as really history and objectively true. The question had been asked: "Whether we may admit as a principle of sound exegesis the opinion which holds that those books of Holy Scripture which are regarded as historical, either wholly or in part, sometimes narrate what is not really history properly so-called and objectively true, but only have the appearance of history and are intended to convey a meaning different from the strictly literal or historical sense of the words." The answer was as follows: "In the negative; excepting always the case—not to be easily or rashly admitted, and then only on the supposition that it is not opposed to the teaching of the Church and subject to her decision—that it can be proved by solid arguments that the sacred writer did not intend to give a true and strict history, but proposed rather to set forth, under the guise and form of history, a parable or an allegory or some meaning distinct from the literal or historical signification of the words" (June 23, 1905; E. B., 161).

When we consider the subject in itself, we must admit that the critical methods employed by modern historians in writing history are not always verified in the ancient documents. The Bible in recording ancient history may omit some facts, neglect the chronological order, give a mere summary of discourses, etc., yet in spite of these limitations the ancient history of the Bible is not false, nor has the Bible led men into error.[2] Be-

---

[2] The genuine historicity of Israel has been upheld by the Protestant scholar * D. M. Noth (*op. cit.*, 204) ; "If it is correct that the proper sphere of divination in the Old Testament is the history of Israel, that is tantamount to saying that the field of the operation of the word of God is the historically conditioned event, even in its minutest details. Thereby, and precisely on that account, is the genuine historicity of Israel strongly emphasized in the Old Testament." This position, however, has been seriously challenged by the Jesuit scholar, J. L. McKenzie (*op. cit.*, 60-71), who alleges as his fundamental thesis that there is only one kind of history, that is, the modern idea of history which goes back to the period of the Greeks. Everything else before that time in the ancient Semitic world consisted mainly of stories, folklore, etc., but no history, because no one was capable of writing any kind of history. ". . . the Old Testament gives us stories of the remembered past of the Hebrews . . . The men whom He (i.e., God) used could tell a story, but they could not write history; . . if God wishes to write a history, He would have to choose other instruments and, in this instance, other times and countries" (63).

tween history and the natural sciences a threefold distinction exists. (a) Their *subject-matter* is different. The events recorded in ancient history are no longer subject to our immediate perception, but on the contrary physical phenomena are being constantly repeated and are subject to the perception of our senses. (b) Their *effects* are different. Ancient human experiences cannot be repeated, nor are they regulated by specific forms of action. Were the sacred writer, as an historian, to judge merely according to external appearances and not according to objective truth, he would lead people necessarily into error. On the contrary, since physical phenomena are being constantly repeated, they can be checked by the reader of the Bible when the sacred writer makes a judgment according to external appearances. (c) Their *ends* are different. History is to be found everywhere in the Bible. The Old Testament treats of creation, the development of the human race, the election of the Hebrews as God's chosen people and their preparation under the special divine guidance for the coming of the Messias. The New Testament is presented as the fulfillment of the Old Testament, and treats of the life of Jesus Christ and the development of the Church established by Him. On the contrary, the natural sciences are rarely and then only casually mentioned in the Bible. In general, they have little or no relation with eternal salvation.

(b) New Literary Forms in the Bible

Bibliography: von Hummelauer, F., "Exegetisches zur Inspirationsfrage," in B.S., 9, iv (1904); Steinmueller, J. E., "Some Problems, etc.," 36–45; Steinmueller, J. E.—Sullivan, K., art. "Literary Forms" in C.B.E.O.T., I, 637–639.

A literary form of a book or pericope is a certain, general, external pattern of writing regulated by custom in a certain epoch or region and expresses the meaning intended by the author. The literary forms, like styles in architecture, are expressions of a certain culture and period.

The Bible contains various kinds of literature, and to interpret correctly various texts or books we must carefully distinguish between the various literary forms employed and then apply to them the rules of hermeneutics and exegesis. The subject-matter, the literary style, and the constant ecclesiastical interpretation will help to differentiate the varieties of literature.

It is obvious to every reader of the Bible that various literary forms are found in its pages. The general categories of poetic, didactic, and narrative literature also admit various subdivisions. Inspiration is compatible with every kind of literature, provided the literary form does not include anything immoral or erroneous, or does not lead us into error.

Every literary form contains some truth according to its specific genre. Thus, the truth expressed by the sacred writer in the matters of the natural sciences, poetry or history may vary and not be the same. The truth which the hagiographer intends to convey to his readers will depend upon the literary form which he chooses to clothe his thoughts, ideas or message. "The Catholic commentator, in order to comply with the present needs of biblical studies, in explaining the Sacred Scripture and in demonstrating and proving its immunity from all error, should also make prudent use of this means, determine, that is, to what extent the manner of expression or the literary mode adopted by the sacred writer may lead to a correct and genuine interpretation" ("Divino afflante Spiritu," E.B., 560). Again from the same Encyclical: "For of the modes of expression which, among ancient peoples, and especially those of the East, human language used to express its thought, none is excluded from the Sacred Books, provided the way of speaking adopted in no wise contradicts the holiness and truth of God" (ibid., E.B., 559).

Hence, those literary forms must be excluded from the Bible which would convey or imply false doctrine or immoral teaching, or in which the sacred writer would lead or attempt to make his (first) readers accept fiction for fact or truth. Such literary forms would be unworthy of the Holy Spirit.

Of the various scholars (e.g., Lagrange, Prat, etc.) who advocated various literary forms for the historical genre, von

Hummelauer brought these into a clever, but defective, system. He distinguished, besides history properly so called, between nine kinds of literary forms in the narrative literature or historical books of the Old Testament: (a) fable; (b) parable; (c) historical epic; (d) religious history; (e) ancient history; (f) popular tradition or folklore; (g) liberal narrative; (h) midrash; (i) prophetical and apocalyptical narrative. These nine categories (of which d, e, f, g are the more important ones) share this in common, that they have only the form of history or use history as a literary robe, whereas in reality they contain, either wholly or partially, non-historical, legendary or fabulous material. Each and every one of these categories has its own degree of truth according to its own literary form intended by the sacred writer, but none of them represent full historical truth.

(a-b) The fable and parable are proposed under a narrative form, but are fictitious and lack any historical basis. (c) The historical epic is some historical fact treated poetically. In this category von Hummelauer places the Psalms dealing with the creation of the world and the description of the ten Egyptian plagues narrated in the Book of Wisdom (chs. 16-19). (d) Religious history has for its purpose the religious edification of its readers. From the abundance of the material at his disposal, the sacred writer chooses that which is apt to stimulate spiritually his audience and presents it in such a way as to render this religious edification more effective. The sacred writer does not vouch for the accuracy of all the historical facts that he uses. (e) Ancient history is such as one reads among the Greeks and Romans. It was compiled without a complete and accurate investigation of documents and sources, as is the case today among critical historians. According to von Hummelauer, this category embraces the biblical narratives from Josue to Paralipomenon. Truth is had only when there is a general agreement between the narrative and objective history, but due allowances must be made for freedom of expression as in the historical epic. (f) Popular tradition (e.g., the origins of races and families) has an historical nucleus, but also includes many legendary or fabulous additions. In this category von Hummelauer would place the Book of Genesis, especially the ten Toledoth (i.e., Generations). (g) A liberal or free narrative is an historical romance, a sort of historical epic. An historical event is taken, and then fictitious persons, events, and conversations are added for moral instruction. In this category von Hummelauer places Ruth, Tobias, Judith, and Esther. (h) Midrash Haggada, a form of literature peculiar to the Hebrews, is a biblical narrative interpreted in a rather free manner to inculcate some ethical truths. In this category von Hummelauer places the Book of Job. (i) The prophetical and apocalyptical narratives are only mentioned briefly by him.

The underlying weakness of von Hummelauer's theory was that it was based more upon his keen and intuitive imagination to solve real and apparent historical difficulties than upon the accurate research into the ancient literature of the Near East and Egypt, little of which was known when he wrote his famous article for the *Biblische Studien*.

As we have seen above, Pope Pius XII in his Encyclical "Divino afflante Spiritu" has strongly encouraged the scientific study of thought patterns, the literary forms of the ancient Semites, if we wish to obtain the correct and genuine meaning intended by the sacred writer and to safeguard the inerrancy, truth, authority and trustworthiness of the Bible. As special aids to obtain this meaning at times, research must be carried out in allied sciences (e.g., history, archæology, ethnology, etc.) and in the entire domain of the ancient literature of the East (cf. *ibid.*, E. B., 558).

In the diligent pursuit of these literary forms some abuses and dangers are to be avoided: of making false, forced, exaggerated claims for similarities with or dependence upon profane sources; of misunderstanding the unique, supernatural character of the Isrælite religion and the firmness of the Hebrew traditions; of applying preconceived, Hegelian, evolutionary principles in rigidly fixed, stereotyped, assembly-line fashion to the history and religion of Israel.

Perhaps with these and other dangers in mind Pope Pius XII wrote in his Encyclical "Humani Generis" (Aug. 12, 1950): "In a particular way must be deplored a certain too free interpretation of the historical books of the Old Testament. Those who favor this system, in order to defend their cause, wrongly refer to the Letter which was sent not long ago to the Archbishop of Paris by the Pontifical Commission of Biblical Studies . . . If, however, the ancient writers have taken anything from popular narrations (and this may be conceded), it must never be forgotten that they did so with the help of divine inspiration, through which they were rendered immune from any error in selecting and evaluating those documents.

"Therefore, whatever of the popular narrations have been inserted into the Sacred Scriptures must in no way be considered on a par with myths or other such things, which are more the product of an extravagant imagination than that of striving for truth and simplicity which in the Sacred Books, also of the Old Testament, is so apparent that our ancient writers must be admitted to be clearly superior to the ancient profane writers" (E.B., 618).

Hence, more extensive, legitimate, Semitic literary forms or types are now being established for the entire Bible, including history. What particular labels or designations are pinned upon them because of their fundamental thought patterns will be found in Biblical interpretation: see Part IV: HERMENEUTICS.

(c) IMPLICIT CITATIONS

Bibliography: Prat, F., in *Etudes,* 86 (1901), 474 ff, 93 (1902), 614 ff; *idem,* "La Bible et l'Histoire" (Paris, 1904), 40 ff; Steinmueller, J. E., *op. cit.,* 206-213.

At the beginning of this chapter the attitude of the sacred writer toward explicit citations was discussed. But what is his attitude toward implicit quotations? When he makes use of a document or source without acknowledging the fact or without making mention of his source material, he is said to indulge in implicit citation.

In their composition the sacred writers often made use of historical sources without mentioning the sources by name or the manner in which they made use of them. For example, the hagiographer may propose various genealogies, and since he could not have a personal knowledge of successive generations, he must have derived these genealogies from various sources. Again, he may cite only one source, as for the Books of Samuel (cf. 2 Sam. 1, 18) which cover a period of more than 130 years. Again, the author of the Books of Paralipomenon, written after the exile, states that "the ark has been there to this day" (2 Par. 5, 9), although at that time there was no ark in the temple. Hence, the question arises: "Do the sacred writers, in taking their material from various documents, make this material their own and assume responsibility for its objective truth, or do they simply borrow this material and leave the responsibility to the author of the source?"

Father Prat states that there are many implicit citations in the Bible, and that the general principle to follow is that the sacred writers make these their own only when these citations are either explicitly or equivalently approved by them. It is the task of the readers to determine according to the norms of historical criticism what citations the sacred writers did not make their own, and what is true and what is false. According to Fr. Prat, we cannot say that the sacred writers approved of the errors or led the readers into error, because the first readers for whom the books were destined knew that the hagiographers drew their citations from various sources; but we of today must determine by the laws of literary criticism and the mode of expression to what extent the sacred writers should win our faith in the things that they related.

It is obvious that such an approach to the historical books of the Bible would lead to pure subjectivism and would soon leave the mind uncertain about many things related in the Bible. The general norm to be followed is that, when the sacred writer implicitly cites any source, he wishes to accept the responsibility for it and wishes also to approve of the same, unless the context tells us otherwise. This is also the practice of modern historians. Were they to mix indiscriminately sources which meet their approval with sources upon which they pass no judgment or which they even doubt, surely the average reader would soon be led into error.

The Pontifical Biblical Commission on February 13, 1905, laid down the principles to guide scholars in answering difficulties arising by reason of implicit citations. The question had been asked: "Is it allowable for a Catholic commentator to solve difficulties occurring in certain texts of Holy Scripture, which apparently make historical statements, by asserting that we have in such texts tacit or implied quotations from documents written by a non-inspired author, and that the inspired author by no means intends to approve of these statements or make them his own, and that these statements cannot, in consequence, be regarded as free from error." To this the Commission replied: "In the negative; except in the case when, subject to the mind and decision of the Church, it can be proved by solid arguments, first, that the sacred writer really does cite another's sayings or writings, and secondly, that he does not intend, in so doing, to approve them or make them his own" (E.B., 160).

CHAPTER V

THE CRITERIA OF INSPIRATION

Bibliography: Ruwet, J., "De criterio inspirationis N.T.," in V.D., XXI (1941), 89-98; Smyth, K., "The Criterion of New Testament Inspiration," in C.B.Q., II (1940), 229-244; *Dodd, C. H., "The Authority of the Bible" (New York, 1929); *Reid, J. K, S., "The Authority of Scripture" (London, 1957); Crehan, J. H., "Who Guarantees the Bible?" in *Scripture,* 4 (1950), 231-236.

A criterion is a test or some recognized principle by which we can determine the correctness of a conclusion or judgment. Accordingly, the criterion of inspiration is the test or principle by which we distinguish inspired books from non-inspired books. Such a biblical criterion should have various requisites: (a) it should by its *very nature* be apt to bear witness to the fact of inspiration; (b) it should be *universally applicable* to only and all the inspired books without exception; (c) it should be *universally adapted* to the capacity of all men, since there is a question of something that must be believed; (d) it should be *infallibly true.* Such a criterion is necessary, because the inspiration of the Bible is a dogma of the Church, and on the basis of such a criterion we must make an act of *divine faith.*

With the advent of Protestantism and its simultaneous rejection of the teaching authority of the Church, various internal insufficient criteria were set up to decide the inspiration of a book. These were based upon the book itself, the reader of the book, the writer of the book, and the Author of the book. But for most modern Protestants[1] this question is not of great importance, since they explain inspiration as a sort of *religious enthusiasm,* and the inspired books are not considered any longer as "the rule of faith," but simply as a witness of the religious conscience of primitive Christianity; hence, there is

[1] Cf. Reid, J. K. S., *op. cit.,* 11-28.

no essential difference between the Bible and other religious books of that period.

The *Bible books,* whether in their matter or their form, are insufficient to serve as a criterion for their own inspiration. This has been commonly termed as the Anglican criterion. The matter contained in a sacred book may be historical or doctrinal, and everyone acknowledges the sublimity, holiness, and harmony of the doctrines of the Bible. But the decisive question is not what the book contains, but rather under what conditions it was written, because the matter of a book does not enter into the strict and proper concept of inspiration. Furthermore, there are books of the Old Testament with dry genealogies and statistical details, narratives of human misdoing which are not apt to serve as material for spiritual reading. The literary form (i.e., the elegance of language) is not sufficient to prove the inspiration of a book. Some of the books of both the Old and New Testaments are recognized to be inferior in style. The criteria of style and literary quality are subjective, and depend to a large extent upon the psychological disposition of the reader.

The fruits produced in the mind of the *reader* by a book are also an insufficient criterion for the inspiration of that book. These fruits are claimed to be deep religious sentiments of faith, hope, and charity for God and man, etc. Luther[2] declared he could tell inspired from non-inspired books *ex gustu et sapore,* just as he could tell good from bad food. Undoubtedly deep religious emotions are sometimes aroused by reading and meditating upon the Scriptures, and all admit that the Bible has exercised a salutary influence upon mankind. Yet, such a criterion is purely subjective. Impressions from reading the Bible vary from person to person, and even with the same person at different periods. Some books of the Old Testament, though recognized as inspired, never excite any religious emotions in man. Yet, the *Imitation of Christ,* a non-inspired book, arouses the deepest religious emotions. Such a criterion,

---

[2] Cf. Reid, J. K. S., *op. cit.,* 56-102.

therefore, being neither objective nor universal, but purely arbitrary, does not suffice to prove a book inspired.

Neither the *prophetic* or *apostolic* origin of a book nor the *writer's own witness* to the inspiration of his book is a sufficient criterion. The prophetic and apostolic offices are not the same as the charism of inspiration. The inspiration to speak is not the same as the inspiration to write. Such prophets as Elias and Eliseus, such Apostles as Philip, Bartholomew and Simon, did not write inspired books. It cannot be proved that the Apostles could write only under the influence of inspiration, and that everything that they wrote had to be inspired. Besides, there are New Testament writings which were not written by Apostles (Mark, Luke, Acts), and it is probable that St. Paul wrote an Epistle between our First and Second Epistles to the Corinthians, and the inspiration of this lost Epistle is still disputed. On the other hand, the Epistle of St. Barnabas, though ascribed by many to the Apostle, was never recognized as inspired. Nor is the witness of the sacred writer about his own inspiration a sufficient criterion. It is possible, though not necessary, that the sacred writer might learn of his own inspiration by divine revelation; but should he in this case wish to communicate that knowledge to others, his witness could produce only human, not divine, faith. If the sacred writer confirmed the witness of his inspiration by a miracle, this would be a sufficient criterion for his bystanders, but not for the universal Church or for future generations; there would be required in addition a morally certain transmission of this witness through the ages by some infallible authority, and this amounts to saying that the teaching authority of the Church is the immediate criterion of inspiration. Exception must be made for an Apostle, whose witness to the inspiration of his writing or the writing of others would suffice, because the Apostles by virtue of their office enjoyed the prerogative of personal infallibility.

The pietistic or Calvinistic[3] criterion, by which *God the Au-*

---

[3] Cf. Reid, J. K. S., *op. cit.*, 29-55.

thor reveals to the individual Bible reader which books are inspired and their interpretation, is insufficient. This inner witness of the Holy Spirit by private revelation might be present in special and rare cases, but since most frequently this witness can be reduced to illusions and hallucinations, certainty based upon this criterion is impossible. The bitter controversies among the early Reformers about the extension of the Canon and the inspired content of some books are sufficient refutation of this theory.

Ecclesiastical Magisterium[4]

The only objective, infallible, and universal criterion of inspiration is Catholic tradition. *The Catholic position is that the formal witness of God to the inspiration of the Sacred Scriptures was revealed to the Apostles and handed down by them to the whole Church; that it has been preserved from error by divine ecclesiastical tradition, and is being legitimately proposed by the teaching office of the Church.* Briefly, we know what books are inspired and what books are not inspired by the witness of the Catholic Church, which is the same as the testimony of God Himself. That this criterion is sufficient, is proved by its very nature, the doctrine of the Fathers, and the practice of the Church.

Inspiration is a divine supernatural action. If this action is considered actively as it is in God, it is totally beyond our finite comprehension. If this action is considered passively as it is in the sacred writer, then, as we saw above, his witness alone does not suffice for us to believe by divine faith that his book was inspired. If this action is considered terminatively as it is manifested in the sacred books, these books either in their matter or their form are insufficient to serve as a criterion of inspiration. Hence, there must be another manner by which the divine supernatural action is made known to us, and this is by the witness of God Himself through revelation. Since

[4] Cf. Bea, A., *op. cit.*, 129-138.

this revelation must be believed by all men at all times, it could not have been accomplished in any other way than through Christ and the Apostles, and it cannot be conserved and interpreted in any other way than through the divine tradition of the Church and her teaching office.

The doctrine of the Fathers both in the East and West clearly shows that they recognized divine ecclesiastical tradition as the criterion for inspired books. Their witness may be aptly summarized in the words of St. Augustine: "I would not believe the gospel, unless the authority of the Catholic Church affected me" (*Contra Manich.*, 5, 6; M.L., XLII, 176).

The Catholic Church, as in other revealed truths, did not immediately give a dogmatical definition about what books are inspired. Yet, from her very beginning she vindicated for herself the right to declare what books were inspired. This right she exercised by determining what books were to be read in her religious assemblies, and what books were to be excluded as apocryphal. Gradually then various catalogues of inspired books were gathered by ecclesiastical authority in the various local churches for public reading.

PART II

BIBLICAL CANON

Bibliography: Aicher, G., "Das A.T. in der Mischna," in B.S., 11, iv (1906); Batiffol, P., 'L'Eglise Naissante—Le Canon du Nouveau Testament," in R.B., 12 (1903), 10-26, 226-233; Dausch, P., "Der Kanon des Neuen Testamentes," in B.Z.F., 1, v (4th ed., 1921), 177-219; Dennefeld, L., "Histoire des Livres de l'Ancien Testament" (Paris, 1919); Fell, W., "Der Bibelkanon des Flavius Josephus," in B.Z., 7 (1909), 1-16, 113-122, 235-244; Jacquier, E., "Histoire des Livres du Nouveau Testament" (2 vols., 2nd ed., Paris, 1903-1905); *von Harnack, A., "'Die Entstehung des Neuen Testaments und die wichtigsten Folgen der neuen Schöpfung" (Leipzig, 1914); Lagrange, M. J., "Histoire ancienne du Canon du Nouveau Testament" (Paris, 1933); *idem,* in R.B., 44 (1935), 212-219; Reilly, W. S., "Le Canon du Nouveau Testament et le Critère de la Canonicité," in R.B., 30 (1921), 195-205; Zarb, S. M., "De historia canonis utriusque testamenti" (Rome, 1934); Brinktrine, J., "Nach welchen Gesichtspunkten wurden die einzelnen Gruppen des neutestamentlichen Kanons geordnet?" in B.Z., 24 (1938), 125-135; Reid G. J., in C.E. s.v. *Canon;* *Strack-Billerbeck, "Kommentar zum Neuen Testament aus Talmud und Midrasch," Exkurs 16 (Munich, 1928), 415-451; *Zeitlin, S., "An Historical Study of the Canonization of the Hebrew Scriptures" (Philadelphia, 1933); Goettsberger, J., "Einleitung in das A.T." (Freiburg i. B., 1927); Costello, C. J., "St. Augustine's Doctrine on the Inspiration and Canonicity of Scripture" (Washington, D. C., 1930); Höpfl, H., "Authenticité. Canonicité," in *Suppl. de la Bible* (Paris, 1928), 666-676, 1022-1045; *Zahn, T., "Forschungen zur Geschichte d. neutest. Kanons u. d. altschristl. Literatur" (Leipzig, 1929); Dewailly, L.-M., 'Canon du Nouveau Testament et histoire des dogmes" in *Vivre et Penser,* 1 (1941), 78-93; Cotter, A. C., "Lost Books of the Bible," in *Theol. St.,* 6 (1945), 206-228.

General Remarks

Inspiration teaches us that God is the principal Author and the sacred writer the instrumental cause of the Bible, and that all its books were written under the divine influence.

From this it logically follows that the Bible must be considered as God's book. But many religious books have been written during the period of the Old and New Covenants. The question therefore arises: *what particular books* enjoy the prerogative of divine origin and authority? At present the individual books of the Bible are gathered together and placed in some logical sequence; thus, in the Old Testament the historical books are followed by the didactical books, and the prophetical books are put in the last place; the only exceptions to this sequence are the First and Second Books of Machabees, which are placed at the very end. In the New Testament, which has the same general division, the five historical books are followed by twenty-one didactical books, and finally there is the one prophetical book, the Apocalypse.

But this present arrangement did not always prevail. There was a time when certain books were not formally accepted as canonical by the Church. The treatise called *Biblical Canon*, therefore, seeks to explain the history of this collection of religious books, and tries to show why this collection is recognized as inspired. Specifically then, the Church does not add anything to the inspiration of a book; she merely tells us that these individual books which we have in our Bible are inspired.

(1) The Etymology and Meaning of the Word "Canon."— The word *canon* and its derivatives *canonical* or *canonicity* come to us from the Greek word κανών, which was taken from the old forms κάνη, κάννα. The word also appears in the Semitic languages, for example, in the Hebrew form *qaneh* and the Assyro-Babylonian *qanū*.

The primary sense of the word is a cane, a reed, a rod, a rule, which was used to draw straight lines or to measure distances; in this sense the Hebrew word *qaneh* is often applied in the Old Testament. From this primitive material meaning it came to be taken in the metaphorical sense of a *rule* or *norm of conduct* in ethics, or the *canon* or *rule* or *model* of elegant style and language in literature.

The word *canon* can have either an active or a passive meaning. Hence, the word *canonical* can mean either something which regulates or measures, or something which is regulated or measured.

(2) The Use of the Word "Canon" in the New Testament.— In the New Testament the word is applied in the passive sense,

as a definitely fixed space within the limits of which one's commission or one's sphere of activity is confined (cf. 2 Cor. 10, 13. 15 f); it is also used in the metaphorical or active moral religious sense, as a rule or standard, principle or law, of living and acting (cf. Gal. 6, 16; Phil. 3, 16). The Apostolic Fathers and ecclesiastical writers, therefore, apply the word *canon* to the rule of faith and Christian morals. Later, however, this word began to be applied to the Sacred Scriptures.

(*3*) *The Application of the Word "Canon" to the Sacred Scriptures.*—Some scholars (e.g., Cornely, Lagrange, etc.) believe that the word *canon* was first applied by Origen to mean the collection of the Sacred Scriptures. The original Greek work of Origen in which this word occurs has not been preserved, but the term occurs in the Latin translation of St. Jerome and Rufinus. Thus, it remains doubtful whether the corresponding word in Greek was κανών or ἐνδιάθετος as found in Origen's extant writings. It is also to be noted that this latter word found in Eusebius is translated by Rufinus as canonical. Again, others (e.g., Lagrange) believe that the *Monarchian Prologues* to the Gospels, in which the word *canon* appears, belong to the third century, but Dom Morin has shown that these *Prologues* are the work of Instantius, who lived in the latter part of the fourth century.

The first person known with certainty to apply the terms *canon, canonized,* to the Sacred Scriptures was the Greek Father, St. Athanasius, about A.D. 350. After this time the term *canon* and its derivatives often occur among the Greeks (e.g., *Synopsis Sacræ Scripturæ,* the Council of Laodicea, Amphilochius, etc.), as well as amongst the Latins (e.g., Rufinus, St. Jerome, St. Augustine, etc.).

It seems probable that the noun *canon* was first used, and that from this the adjectival form *canonical* and the verbal form *canonize* were derived. It also seems very likely that the passive sense of the word *canon* was at first employed; that is, the term was used to denote the collection of books which the Church recognized as sacred and which she declared to be inspired. Later the active sense was applied to the word, whereby these books were recognized to be the rule of faith and morals because of their divine origin.[1]

These two senses, the passive and active, can be combined in the definition of the Canon, which is *the catalogue of books which the Catholic Church has declared to be divinely inspired, and which she regards as a partial and remote rule of faith and morals.*

The older Jewish literature has no such designation as the word Canon for the books of the Bible, but it indirectly refers to the Canon of the Bible, when it speaks of books which "render the hands unclean."

(4) The Kinds of Canonical Books.—There was a time when the inspiration of some books was acknowledged by all, and that of other books was denied or doubted by some. The books placed in the Canon from the very beginning and the inspiration of which was never doubted were called ὁμολογούμενοι, that is, accepted books. The books which were the subject of discussion and doubt at any time or anywhere were called ἀντιλεγόμενοι or ἀμφιβαλλόμενοι, that is, contested or contradicted books. Since the sixteenth century, however, the terms proto-canonical and deutero-canonical books, introduced by Sixtus of Sienna to express the same things, are commonly used.

There are seven deutero-canonical books of the Old Testament: Tobias, Judith, Wisdom, Sirach, Baruch, First and Second Books of Machabees; besides these, there are some fragments of two other books—Esther 10, 4-16, 24 (Vulg.) and Daniel 3, 24-90; 13; 14. There are seven deutero-canonical books of the New Testament: the Epistle to the Hebrews, the Epistle of St. James, the Second Epistle of St. Peter, the Second and Third Epistles of St. John, the Epistle of St. Jude, and the Apocalypse; besides these there are some individual deutero-canonical passages (such as Mark 16, 9-20; Luke 22, 43 f; John 5, 4; 8, 1-11).

Catholic scholars claim inspiration for both classes of ca-

[1] Cf. Zarb, S. M., *op. cit.*, xvi ff; Höpfl, H., *op. cit.*, I, 27-30.

nonical books, carefully distinguishing them from the apocryphal books. Protestants, however, in their classification of the books of the Old Testament, call our deutero-canonical books the apocryphal books, and our apocryphal books the pseudepigraphal books.

(5) *Inspiration and Canonization.*[2]—Inspiration differs from canonization in a threefold manner: in time, thought, and causality.

(a) Inspiration is simultaneous with the composition of the book, and accompanies the sacred writer until the book is completed. Canonization, however, is something subsequent to inspiration, and may follow centuries after the book has been written, as is evident from the history of the deutero-canonical books. Inspiration, therefore, is independent of canonization, but canonization is not independent of inspiration. The Church is limited in her jurisdiction, for she can only canonize an inspired book. Hence, all canonical books are necessarily inspired, but not all inspired books are necessarily canonized.

(b) In the order of thought inspiration is *in itself* absolute and dependent upon God alone; whereas canonization is *quoad nos,* i.e., relative to us, incomplete and dependent upon inspiration and the Church. Canonization does not affect the book, but merely changes our attitude towards the book and makes us certain by faith that this book is of divine origin.

(c) Inspiration has God for its causality. It is God who inspires and gives the sacred writer the divine impulse to write. On the other hand, canonization depends upon the Church, as in the Old Law it depended upon the synagogue. Briefly then, God inspires the book; the Church canonizes the book. God is the Author of the book; the Church is the publisher of the book.

[2] Cf. Grannan, C., *op. cit.,* III, 156-159.

Chapter I

THE HISTORY OF THE OLD TESTAMENT CANON

There is no Jewish document of the pre-Christian period which gives us a complete list or catalogue of the inspired books of the Old Testament. Yet, there is much evidence that authentic collections of the sacred inspired books were in existence. The Hebrew Bible with its threefold classification of the Law, the Prophets, and the Sacred Writings was given its definite form during the Christian period, and some of these books, parts or fragments of them, go back to the pre-Christian or early Christian Period, as we know from the Dead Sea Scrolls.

Jews and Protestants recognize or acknowledge only the proto-canonical books of the Old Testament, whereas Catholics and the Oriental Churches accept not only the proto-canonical books, but also the deutero-canonical books and fragments of the Old Testament.

Art. 1. The Old Testament Canon of the Jews

(a) The Various Documents about the Canonical Books of the Jews

Before considering these documents in detail, it may be useful to state in general the origin and the development of the Canon. *The origin of the Canon is rightly traced back to Moses.* On several occasions Moses was ordered by God to write down his experiences and the laws (cf. Ex. 17, 14; 24, 4. 7; 34, 27; Num. 33, 2; Deut. 31, 9. 24). Many *references* to *Moses and his Law* are contained in the prophetical as well as the historical books of the Old Testament. To this Law of Moses even *Josue added his writing* (Jos. 24, 26). Samuel wrote the law of the kingdom in a book and laid this beside the ark of the covenant (I Sam. 10, 25). King Ezechias (727-699 B.C.) ordered the Levites to make use of the Psalms of

David and Asaph in the temple liturgy (2 Par. 29, 30), and he likewise commanded the Proverbs of Solomon to be collected (Prov. 25, 1). King Josias (640-609 B.C.) renewed the covenant with the Lord *on the basis of the Mosaic Law* which was found in the temple (4 Kgs. 23, 1-3; 2 Par. 34, 29-32). Then, too, many of the prophets wrote down their utterances (cf. Isa. 34, 16; Jer. 36, 4). Thus, then, we can readily admit the *gradual development and accumulation of scrolls* which comprised the sacred literature of the Hebrews.

(*1*) *The Samaritan Pentateuch.*—The Samaritan Pentateuch, written in Phœnician script, contains merely the five Books of Moses and these alone were recognized by the Samaritans. This is one of the oldest documents proving the existence and canonicity of the first collection of the sacred books of the Bible.

During the rule of Zorobabel (c. 536-516 B.C.) the Samaritans wished to show their religious solidarity with the Jews by offering to help rebuild the temple, but their offer was refused (1 Esd. 4, 1 ff). It was, however, only during the time of Nehemias (c. 430 B.C.) that certain abuses were corrected and there were expelled from the Jewish community some individuals (2 Esd. 13, 28) who, according to Josephus (*Antiq.*, XI, 7 f), played an important rôle (c. 330 B.C.) in the erection of the schismatic temple on Mount Garizim. Thus, according to these two sources the definite division between the Jews and the Samaritans took place between 430 and 330 B.C. Later on these Samaritans (as during the period of Antiochus IV Epiphanes, 175-164 B.C.) denied that they were religiously affiliated with the Jews (cf. Josephus, *Antiq.*, XII, 5, 5; also John 4, 9).

From this we may conclude that amongst the Jews as well as among the Samaritans of the fifth or fourth century B.C. there was a firm conviction that the five books of Moses were considered as canonical or authoritative, and were to be used as reliable, trustworthy guides of their conduct with God and their neighbors.

(*2*) *Esdras.*—Jewish tradition has preserved many records

which are both real and legendary about the activity of Esdras
—for example, his collecting the books of the Bible, his dictating them from memory, his transcribing them into the Aramaic script, his closing the Canon, etc.

In the Bible we read that in the seventh year of Artaxerxes
I Longimanus (458 B.C) Esdras the priest and scribe returned
from Babylon to Jerusalem with many of the Jewish exiles
(1 Esd. 7). He read and explained the Law of Moses to the
people, who then obliged themselves under oath to its observance (444 B.C.: cf. 2 Esd. 8-9). It is very probable that this
Law, as read and explained by Esdras, contained the entire
Pentateuch.

The Bible, however, makes no mention of the Jewish claims
that he either collected or preserved the books of Sacred Scripture, but his zeal for the Mosaic Law as well as his deep spir-
ituality would incline us to believe that this was so (cf.
apocryphal 4 Esd. 14, 18-47). Nevertheless, nowhere do we
read that he closed the Canon of the Bible, but rather the
contrary is true, since the genealogical lists, given in the two
books bearing his name, include names of men who lived at
least one hundred and fifty years after his death.[1]

(3) *Nehemias.*—In the twentieth year of Artaxerxes (445
B.C), Nehemias returned from Babylon to Jerusalem. The
Second Book of Machabees, written about the middle of the
second century B.C., cites a letter that the Palestinian Jews
wrote to their coreligionists in Egypt. Amongst other things
they mention the literary activity of Nehemias. "And these
same things were set down in the memoirs and commentaries
of Nehemias: how, having made a library he gathered together
out of the countries the books of the kings and of the prophets
and of David, and the epistles of kings concerning the holy
gifts" (2 Mach. 2, 13).

There is no mention of the Pentateuch or Torah in this letter
because its wide circulation made its collection unnecessary.
"The books of the kings and of the prophets" may mean either

---

[1] Cf. Grannan, C., *op. cit.*, III, 173.

one collection of the canonical Books of Kings and Prophets
or two distinct collections: the one containing the Books of the
Kings (i.e., Josue, Judges, Samuel, and Kings),[2] while the other
collection embraced the Prophets in general (i.e., without any
definite extension) [3] or the later Prophets (as Isaias, Jeremias,
Ezechiel, and the Minor Prophets).[4] "The books of David,"
strictly speaking, signify the Psalms of David, but they could
also allude to the entire Psalter. "The epistles of kings concerning the holy gifts" refers undoubtedly to the original letters
of grants made by the foreign kings, (especially the Persian
rulers), and not necessarily to the Books of Esdras or to 1
Esdras 6, 2-12; 7, 11-26; 2 Esdras 2, 7 ff.

From this letter cited in the Second Book of Machabees we
cannot conclude that Nehemias, who collected various books,
collected only canonical books. Nor can it be inferred that he
closed the Canon of the Old Testament. It is, however, noteworthy that, according to the Bible, Nehemias and not Esdras
is identified with the collection of the Scriptures. This activity
of Nehemias is almost entirely ignored by later Jewish tradition.

(4) The Greek Septuagint Translation (250-100 B.C.).[5]—
From the period of Esdras and Nehemias to the time of Jesus
ben Sirach (i.e., from the fifth to the second century B.C.), there
is no document which refers to the collection of the sacred
books, except the Septuagint.

The Letter of Aristeas, written about the end of the third
century B.C., narrates the origin of this Greek version. Although this letter is commonly regarded as apocryphal, it is
recognized to be very old. Many things that it relates are
legendary; yet, it is now commonly admitted that the Pentateuch translation of which it speaks was made during the time
of Ptolemy II Philadelphus (285-246 B.C.), because Demetrius,
a Jewish writer living at the time of Ptolemy IV Philopator

[2] Cf. Goettsberger, J., *op. cit.,* 355; Schmidt, N., in J.E., s.v. *Bible Canon,* 145[b].
[3] Cf. Goettsberger, J., *op. cit.,* 355.
[4] Cf. Schmidt, N., in J.E., s.v. *Bible Canon,* 145[b].
[5] Cf. Zarb, S., *op. cit.,* 16-20.

(222-205 B.C.), made use of this Greek version. It is also generally conceded that the Greek version of the Prophets and some Hagiographa had been completed by the middle of the second century B.C., and the reason for this assertion is based upon the Prologue of ben Sirach, which written in the year 130 B.C. presupposes the existence of a Greek version of "the Law, the Prophets, and other books." At the time of Our Lord all our books of the Old Testament were already extant in the Greek version.

The Letter of Aristeas states that the Pentateuch was translated from the Hebrew into the Greek with the permission of the high priest at Jerusalem, who had sent the manuscript from Jerusalem from which this translation was made. This seems to have been also the case with the other books of the Old Testament. Thus, it can be legitimately inferred that only those books were translated and recognized as sacred writings, which had been previously accepted by the principal community at Jerusalem.

It is of great importance to note that the Greek Alexandrian version contains not only the proto-canonical books found in the Hebrew Bible, but also the seven deutero-canonical books and passages from the Books of Esther and Daniel.

These deutero-canonical books and fragments were excluded from the Canon by the Jews and are not found in the Hebrew Bible. This doctrine of the Jews unconsciously influenced some ecclesiastical writers, who either called these books into doubt or rejected them. The Protestants, following the footsteps of the Jews, excluded these books from the Bible and called them apocryphal books.

(5) *The Book of Sirach or Ecclesiasticus.*—This book, which is of greatest importance for the history of the Canon, was originally written in Hebrew c.200-180 B.C. Jesus ben Sirach, the author, in his Hymn of Praise for the Fathers (chs. 44-49) mentions in passing some of the books of the Old Testament. All of the proto-canonical books, with the exception of Esther and Daniel, are mentioned. None of the deutero-canonical books, with the possible exception of Baruch, is alluded to.

(6) *The Prologue of Sirach or Ecclesiasticus.*—The book itself was according to the prologue translated into Greek about the year 130 B.C. by the grandchild of Jesus ben Sirach. In this prologue the grandchild three times makes mention of the Sacred Scriptures as "the Law, and the Prophets, and the other books." From this prologue it is evident that the Bible was then divided into two collections, which were definitely closed and called "the Law and the Prophets," whereas the indefinite term "the other books" seems to indicate that a third collection was in the process of formation and had not as yet reached its final state.

(7) *Judas Machabee.*—In a second letter from the Palestinian Jews to their coreligionists in Egypt, the Second Book of Machabees, having made mention that Nehemias of old had once collected the sacred books, passes on to say that Judas now did the same. "And in like manner Judas also gathered together all such things as were lost by the war we had, and they are in our possession. Wherefore if you want these things, send some who may fetch them to you" (2 Mach. 2, 14 f).

After purifying the temple, Judas Machabee (166-161 B.C.) placed there copies of the Sacred Scriptures to replace those which Antiochus IV Epiphanes had burnt with fire (1 Mach. 1, 59 f). This document from the Second Book of Machabees does not say anything about the number or the names of the books. Undoubtedly they were the same as those collected by Nehemias, together with those written after his time. It is certain that at this time all the books collected by Nehemias had been in the Greek collection of the Alexandrian Jews, and that these Jews of the dispersion were in the habit of receiving the sacred books from the principal community at Jerusalem.

These documents dating from the pre-Christian period are of great value in tracing the history of the formation of the Canon of the Old Testament. The Jewish documents written during the early Christian period are more numerous, and many of them are specifically more definite.

At the time of Our Lord the Jews in the Roman Empire were divided into two principal classes: the Hellenistic and the

Palestinian Jews. In the former class were the Alexandrian Jews with their principal scholar, Philo. In the latter class were the Essenes, the Sadducees, and the Pharisees.

(8) The Hellenistic Jew, Philo.—It is certain that the Jews of the dispersion, as long as they followed the Alexandrian version, recognized both the proto-canonical and deutero-canonical books of the Old Testament. It is also certain that they, when they began in the second century to make use of the Greek version of Aquila, determined to follow exclusively the Palestinian Canon, which contained only the proto-canonical books.

Philo,[5a] the Jewish philosopher of Alexandria, died after A.D. 38. Nowhere does he *ex professo* treat of the Canon of the Old Testament. Besides the Pentateuch, to which he attributed a greater degree of inspiration, he acknowledged other books as sacred. Since, however, he fails to refer to eight or nine proto-canonical books and omits any mention of the deutero-canonical books, it is difficult to determine precisely what books were recognized by him as sacred and what books were rejected by him. It is, however, possible that already at his time the deutero-canonical books, rejected by the Palestinian Pharisees, began to be rejected in the dispersion.[6]

(9) The Essenes and the Sadducees.—Both the Essenes,[6a] (cf. Josephus, *Bella Jud.,* II, 8, 8) and the Sadducees (cf. Josephus, *Antiq.,* XIII, 10, 6, XXVI. 1, 4; Origen, St. Jerome, etc.) acknowledged the authority of the Pentateuch. Besides these five books of Moses, the Essenes recognized the books of the Prophets (cf. Josephus, *Bella Jud., ibid.*) ; the contents of this collection is not specified, but possibly it could be identified with the second collection of the Pharisees.

This scant information helps little, however, in determining

[5a] Cf. Bentwich, N.,"Philo-Judaeus of Alexandria" (Philadelphia,1940).
[6] Cf. Zarb, S., *op. cit.,* 26-28.
[6a] In the Essenian Qumran library consisting of hundreds of Biblical and non-Biblical manuscripts and dating between the Hasmonean Period (135-37 B.C.) and the destruction of the settlement (A.D. 68), there are canonical, apocryphal and hitherto unknown books, but no list of commonly recognized canonical books. Cf. Steinmueller, J. E.-Sullivan. K., art. "Scroll," in C.B.E.O.T.

the Canon of the Old Testament. The principal Jewish sources for the early Christian period are of Pharisaical origin or influence.

(10) The Fourth Book of Esdras.—This apocryphal apocalypse, written after the destruction of the temple by Titus (about the end of the first century of our era) either in Hebrew or Aramaic by a Palestinian Jew, reduces the number of sacred books to *twenty-four.*

The book contains a legendary description of Esdras' worries over the destruction of the Law by Nabuchodonosor. Shortly before his death he is filled with the prophetical spirit "that I might write all that has happened in the world since the beginning, even the things which were written in thy law, in order that men may be able to find the path, and that they who live at last may live" (v. 22). This prophetical spirit enabled Esdras, according to the apocryphal book, to dictate to five scribes for forty consecutive days ninety-four books, of which twenty-four were to be read by the worthy and the unworthy, and the other seventy (the nature of which is still undetermined by scholars) were to be delivered only to the learned. The number twenty-four corresponds with the numbers of books in the Palestinian Canon: namely, the five books of Moses, eight Prophets, and eleven Hagiographa.

(11) Josephus Flavius.[7]—Josephus was born between September 13, A.D. 37, and March 15, 38, and died shortly after September 13, 93. His writings, therefore, are almost contemporaneous with the preceding documents. In his book against Apion (I. 7 f) he asserts that the Jews do not have myriads of discordant and conflicting books, but only *twenty-two,* which contain the history of all past time and which are justly regarded as divine. Of these, five are the books of Moses, thirteen are the prophetical books, which were written from the death of Moses to the reign of Artaxerxes I (465-424 B.C.), and the remaining four books contain hymns to God and precepts of men.

[7] Cf. Zarb, S., *op. cit.,* 29-35; * Bentwich, N., "Josephus" (Philadelphia, 1940).

"Then from the time of Artaxerxes to our own time, our history has been written down very particularly, but these books have not been considered worthy of the same credit as the books of earlier date, because there has not been an exact succession of prophets. But what credence we have given to all those books of our own nation is evident from our conduct; for though so long a time has passed, no one has ever been so bold as to add anything to them whatever. But all Jews are instinctively led, from the moment of their birth, to believe that these books contain divine oracles and to abide by them, and if need be, gladly die for them."

Although Josephus makes mention of only *twenty-two books* of the Bible, yet this number according to most modern scholars agrees with the twenty-four given in the Fourth Book of Esdras and the Talmud. The number twenty-two is symbolical for Josephus and represents the number of letters of the alphabet; it is obtained, not by deducting two books mentioned in the other documents, but by uniting the Book of Ruth with Judges and the Book of Lamentations with Jeremias.

Josephus does not strictly follow the division of the Palestinian Canon into three collections of the Law, the Prophets, and the Hagiographa. The first collection of books in both Canons agree—the books of Moses, or the Law. The extent of the second and third collections of books differ. In the Palestinian Canon eight books are listed in the second collection, whereas Josephus gives the number as thirteen, which most likely were the Books of Josue, Judges, Samuel, Kings, Jeremias, Ezechiel, Isaias, the Twelve Prophets (i.e., those of the Palestinian Canon), and the Books of Esdras, Paralipomenon, Esther, Job, and Daniel. In the Palestinian Canon eleven books are listed as the third collection of the Hagiographa, whereas Josephus gives the number as four books, which most likely were the Psalter and the three books of Solomon (i.e., the Books of Proverbs, Canticles, and Ecclesiastes).

Josephus distinguishes between two classes of books. The

first class (i.e., the books of the Bible) enjoy the greatest authority; the other class of books, though holy, are inferior in authority. The reasons given by him for this distinction are doctrinal and chronological: doctrinal, because the second class of books were written when there was no succession of prophets, and chronological, because the second class of books were written after the time of Artaxerxes I. Josephus, therefore, closes the Canon with Esdras, and hence those books written prior to the period of Esdras belong to the Sacred Scriptures, the others written after the scribe's time, among which were some deutero-canonical books, were of lesser authority, because there was no succession of prophets.

(12) *The Mishna.*[8]—In this collection of the Jewish Tannaites nearly all of the books of the Palestinian Canon are cited with the exception of Nehemias (which was considered as one book with Esdras, which, however, is cited), Abdias, Nahum, Habacuc, Sophonias, and Aggeus (which, however, belonged to the Book of Minor Prophets), and finally Daniel (which is cited in the Tosephta and Mechilta, other Jewish sources). The Mishna also cites some of the deutero-canonical books, mention of which will be made later.

(13) *The Older Versions Based Immediately upon the Hebrew Text.*—Among the older versions worthy of mention is the *Syriac Peshitto.* When this version was made from the Hebrew text, either shortly before the Christian era (or in the first or second century of our era, according to other authorities) by Jews (or Jewish Christians) of Syria, it only contained the proto-canonical books, with the exception, however, of the Books of Paralipomenon, Esdras-Nehemias, and Esther. These, together with the deutero-canonical books, were added

[8] The Talmud signifies literally "teaching, inference, or doctrine," and is commonly applied to a collection of works embodying the oral tradition in contradistinction to the written Law (i.e., the Torah). This collection consists of two parts: the Mishna and the Gemara. The *Mishna* (i.e., repetition) is the name applied to the collection of traditions of various Jewish teachers concerning the Mosaic Law. This collection was made at the end of the second century after Christ at Tiberias by Rabbi Juda han-Nasi, and about one hundred and fifty teachers are mentioned.

in the third or fourth century. All of these books are now contained in the Canons of the Nestorians and the Jacobites.

Having rejected the Alexandrian version, the Jews began in the second century to produce their own Greek versions. Three are worthy of mention. The versions of *Aquila and Symmachus* contained only the proto-canonical books, whereas the version of *Theodotion* contained not only the proto-canonical books but also the deutero-canonical parts of the Book of Daniel.

(14) The Babylonian Talmud.—The last document in rabbinical literature to reach us is contained in a *Baraita* [9] of the Babylonian Talmud, tractate *Baba Bathra* (Last Gate). The text was written after the second century, but its content represents a tradition of the preceding period; it enumerates the books of the Jewish Canon in their order and gives their authors.

"The rabbis taught: The order of the Prophets is as follows: Joshua, Judges, Samuel, Kings, Jeremiah, Ezekiel, Isaiah, and the Twelve (Minor Prophets). . . . The order of the Hagiographa is as follows: Ruth, Psalms, Job, Proverbs, Ecclesiastes, Song of Songs, Lamentations, Daniel, Esther, Ezra, and Chronicles. . . . And who wrote these? Moses wrote his book, and the section of Balaam (Num. 23 f), and Job. Joshua wrote his book and the last eight verses of Deuteronomy (narrating the death of Moses). Samuel wrote his book, Judges, and Ruth. David wrote the Psalms with the collaboration of ten Elders, viz., Adam, Melchizedek, Abraham, Moses, Heman, Jeduthun, Asaph, and the three sons of Korah. Jeremiah wrote his book, Kings, and Lamentations. Hezekiah

---

They are commonly called the Tannaites (from Tannaim, i.e., teachers). Their title was *rabbi* (i.e., my master or teacher); very seldom, however, was the title *rabban* (i.e., our teacher or master) applied to them. The second part, the *Gemara*, represents the completion of the Talmud by subsequent authors, called Amoraim, who, as teachers after Rabbi Juda han-Nasi, expounded the Mishna (from 219 to 359 in Palestine and from 219 to 500 in Babylonia). The former is called the Palestinian revision and the latter the Babylonian revision of the Talmud.

[9] Baraita (i.e., that which is external), material handed down but not incorporated in the Mishna.

and his associates wrote Isaiah, Proverbs, Song of Songs, and Ecclesiastes. The men of the Great Assembly wrote Ezechiel, the Twelve, Daniel, and Esther. Ezra wrote his book and the genealogy of Chronicles down to himself, and Nehemiah completed it" (Baba Bathra, ff. 14ᵇ and 15ᵃ).[10]

This document expresses a rather novel opinion about the origin of some sacred books. The order of books for the second and third collection differs to some extent from that given in the Massoretic Text or Hebrew Bible. Although the number of books is not explicitly stated, yet, when these individual books are added together, they make a total of *twenty-four,* which is equivalent to thirty-eight proto-canonical books according to our computation.

In this catalogue there is no mention of the seven deutero-canonical books; namely: (1) Tobias; (2) Judith; (3) Wisdom; (4) Sirach; (5) Baruch; (6-7) the First and Second Books of Machabees. Thus, if Jeremias and Lamentations are taken as one book, the total is *forty-five.* But some Catholic scholars consider Jeremias and Lamentations as two separate books, and speak of forty-six books. Still others consider Baruch 6 (the epistle of Jeremias) as a separate book, and speak of forty-seven books.

Talmudic Canon	*Order of Books*	*Our Computation*
I. (5) Torah	5	5
II. Nebiim		
(1) Josue	6	6
(2) Judges	7	7
(3) Samuel	8	8-9
(4) Kings	9	10-11
(5) Jeremias	10	12
(6) Ezechiel	11	13
(7) Isaias	12	14
(8) Twelve Prophets	13	15-26

[10] Cf. *Strack-Billerbeck, *op. cit.,* 424 f; *Cohen, A., "Everyman's Talmud" (London, 1934), 149 ff.

III. Hagiographa

(1) Ruth	14	27
(2) Psalms	15	28
(3) Job	16	29
(4) Proverbs	17	30
(5) Ecclesiastes	18	31
(6) Canticles	19	32
(7) Lamentations	20	— (with
(8) Daniel	21	33 Jeremias)
(9) Esther	22	34
(10) Esdras	23	35-36
(11) Chronicles	24	37-38

Further documentary evidence beyond the second century of our era is unimportant, since even the modern Hebrew Bibles, with the exception of some small changes in the order of books, agree with the Talmud both in regard to the number of books and the division into three collections. This Jewish tradition about the extent of the Canon is further confirmed by the Canon of Melito, the Bishop of Sardis [11] (died before 195), and the Canon of Origen [12] (185/186-254/255).

(15) Documents about Individual Proto-Canonical Books. —The proto-canonical books are acknowledged by all, and are contained both in the Hebrew Bibles as well as the Alexandrian version, which however does not follow the Jewish division into three collections.

The *Law* or *Torah* was the foundation of the Jewish religion, and both Jews and Christians acknowledge that it substantially emanated from Moses. Thus, the beginning of the Canon goes back to Moses.

[11] Cf. Eusebius, *Eccl. Hist.*, IV, 26. It is uncertain, however, from the context whether Melito wished to declare the Jewish or the Christian Canon.

[12] Cf. Eusebius, *Eccl. Hist.*, VI, 25. Either Origen is merely citing the books which were at his time considered as contained in the Hebrew Canon, or he is merely giving his private opinion and preference, knowing that the public policy of the Church was to include the deuterocanonical books, which he also included in his *Hexapla*.

Amongst the *earlier Prophets* are listed Josue, Judges, Samuel, and Kings. These four historical books form a continuous history from the time of Josue (c. 1400 B.C.) to the Babylonian exile (586 B.C.), and received their definite literary form either in Palestine or Babylon immediately after the deportation of the Jews into the exile. These books, therefore, were accepted as canonical during the period of the exile.

The *later Prophets* according to the Talmud are Jeremias, Ezechiel, Isaias, and the Twelve Prophets. These books do not follow the strict chronological order and arrangement of the earlier Prophets, except perhaps the Book of the Twelve Prophets, which was probably-arranged in chronological order after the death of the last prophet Malachias and thus received its definite arrangement as a minor collection after the exile. However, it should be noted that the books written before the exile had already been acknowledged as sacred before their final arrangement in the Palestinian Canon.

This second collection consisting of eight books was acknowledged by all at the beginning of the second century B.C. This is evident from the Prologue of the Book of Sirach and the Hymn of Praise of the Fathers in the same book. Nevertheless, the Book of Ezechiel [13] was almost placed among the apocryphal books shortly before the destruction of the temple (A.D. 70), when the school of Shammai thought that it was at variance with the Pentateuch, and that its reading (chs. 1 and 10) might bring dangers to the Jewish faith. But due to the influence of Rabbi Chananyah ben Hezekiah, who harmonized the difficulties between the Books of Moses and Ezechiel, the book was retained as canonical.

The *Hagiographa* included books about which there were serious discussions.[14] Of the three books of Solomon the least objection was found against Proverbs, and the greatest against Ecclesiastes and the Canticle of Canticles. Then too doubts were raised against the Books of Esther and Ruth. Some of

---

[13] Cf. *Strack-Billerbeck, *op. cit.,* 426.
[14] Cf. *Strack-Billerbeck, *op. cit.,* 426-433.

these disputes lasted almost until the end of the second century of our era.

Since some of these proto-canonical books which are contested had been recognized as canonical at the time of Sirach (e.g., Proverbs, Ezechiel), and since various definite canonical catalogues were in circulation (e.g., Josephus and the Talmud), we can conclude that these disputes and discussions concern books already canonized and that they are not indications of the incipient formation of a Canon.

(16) *Documents about Individual Deutero-Canonical Books and Passages.*—The use of the deutero-canonical books in the dispersion and especially in Egypt is certain. This is evident from the presence of these books in the Alexandrian version, which was used not only in Egypt but also throughout the entire dispersion until the second century after Christ. These books, however, were also familiar to and recognized by the Jews of Palestine. Let us, therefore, consider these deutero-canonical books and passages individually and their usage particularly among the Palestinian Jews.

The Book of Baruch (chs. 1-5) and the Epistle of Jeremias (Bar. 6).—At the time of Daniel, the Book of Baruch seems to have been united with that of Jeremias, because Daniel explicitly states that he read in Jeremias the number of the years of the captivity (Dan. 9, 2; Jer. 25, 11 f; 29, 10), and then in the same context he literally depends upon Baruch (compare Dan. 9, 5 with Bar. 1, 17; Dan. 9, 7 with Bar. 1, 15 f; Dan. 9, 15 with Bar. 2, 11 f). Modern scholars also point out that one and the same translator translated Jeremias, Baruch, and the Epistle of Jeremias from the Hebrew into the Greek, and thus these three books had been considered as one, a fact that is also confirmed by early church documents. The author of the Second Book of Machabees (2, 2) seems to allude to the Epistle of Jeremias, and a short time afterwards the eleventh apocryphal Psalm of Solomon cites Baruch 5, 4 ff as an authoritative writing. Origen also made use of a Hebrew text of the Book of Baruch, and his diacritical marks to this book are still preserved in some codices. Finally, the Apostolic Constitutions (5, 20) of the fourth century tell us that Baruch was being read in the synagogues. The Epistle of Jeremias was known to the Qumran people, and reference to it may be found in the Dead Sea Scrolls.

The Book of Judith.—All modern scholars agree that the original language of this book was Semitic. St. Jerome made use of an Aramaic text for his Vulgate translation, and Hebrew texts of the book are also extant. Besides, the exegesis to this book appears in various rabbinical Midrashim, and the author of the apocryphal Psalms of Solomon seems to allude to it. These facts show that both the Palestinian and the Babylonian Jews made use of the book.

The Book of Tobias.—This book was current in many languages, Hebrew, Aramaic, Syriac, Greek, and Latin. St. Jerome made use of an Aramaic text for his Vulgate translation, and an exegesis to the book exists in a seventh-century Aramaic Midrash. These facts prove that the Palestinian and Babylonian Jews thought highly of the book. This book was utilized by the Qumran community as we know from the Dead Sea Scrolls.

The Book of Ecclesiasticus or Sirach.—Most modern scholars concede that the original language of this book was Hebrew. The strongest argument for its canonicity is found in its Prologue; it supposes this book to have been received as canonical by the Palestinian coreligionists of the translator. In fact, this book was held in such great esteem by the Palestinian Jews that it was quoted by the author of the apocryphal Psalms of Solomon and by the rabbis like the rest of the Sacred Scriptures. The Qumran people were acquainted with Ben Sira as we know from the Dead Sea Scrolls.

The Book of Wisdom.—This book was originally written in Greek. St. Epiphanius in the fourth century declared that this book, as well as the Book of Sirach, was being contested by the Jews. About the same time Eustathius quotes Wisdom 18, 14 ff, as if this text had been in the Jewish Canon.[15]

---

[15] Cf. Goettsberger, J., *op. cit.*, 366.

The First and Second Books of Machabees.—The First Book of Machabees was written in Hebrew, whereas the Second Book was written in Greek. Both books were diligently used by the Jews. The author of the apocryphal Psalms of Solomon and Josephus (*Antiq.*, XII, 6, 1 ff) made use of the First Book, whereas the author of the apocryphal Psalms of Solomon, Philo, and St. Paul (Hebr. 11, 35) allude to the Second Book. The celebration of the Feast of Hanuka or the Dedication of the Temple is based upon the use of either of these two books. Finally, the Second Book of Machabees was employed by the author of the apocryphal work called the Fourth Book of Machabees.

The Deutero-Canonical Parts of Daniel.—All of these parts were contained in the version of Theodotion, and it is probable that the version of Symmachus had the history of Susanna (Dan. 13).

The Deutero-Canonical Parts of Esther (10, 4-16, 24 Vulg.). —This arrangement in the Vulgate, though not chronological, is due to St. Jerome. In their Greek sequence these chapters form part of a consecutive history. The original text of these deutero-canonical parts was Semitic, and Josephus (*Antiq.*, XI, 6) quotes these chapters in the same manner as the rest of the book.

The usage of the deutero-canonical books and passages by the Jews shows that these were everywhere highly esteemed. Although they were rejected by the Palestinian Jews in the first century of our era, yet they were never declared by them to be erroneous or false, and despite their rejection from the Palestinian Canon, Josephus made use of them as genuine sources for his history of the Jewish people.

The force of these arguments for the canonical value of these books and passages is increased, when we consider the relationship which existed between the various Jewish communities. After the Babylonian exile all Jews, whether they lived in Babylon or in Egypt or elsewhere, recognized the primacy and jurisdiction of the Jerusalem community in matters religious. For this reason the Alexandrian community obtained permission from the high priest to translate the sacred books into the Greek,[16] and also received directly from the Jerusalem community the Book of Esther (11, 1 Vulg.) and other books (2 Mach. 2, 14 f). The Jews in Babylonia (Zach. 7) and in Egypt [17] acted in the same manner. Pilgrimages were made to Jerusalem by the Hellenistic Jews (Acts 2, 5-11), who also paid an annual tax for the maintenance of the temple and the daily sacrifices. If, therefore, sacred books were used and acknowledged as sacred and canonical in the dispersion, the natural inference would be that these same books had been at one time acknowledged as sacred and canonical by the principal community of Jerusalem.

(17) *The Palestinian and Alexandrian Canons.*—The relationship between these two Canons is explained in various ways by modern scholars. Goettsberger maintains that Judaism, whether in Palestine or in Alexandria, never explicitly recognized more than the twenty-four books mentioned in the Palestinian Canon. Cornely, * Schuerer, Mangenot, Höpfl, etc., believe that there were two independent Canons, one in Palestine (containing only the proto-canonical books), the other in the dispersion (including also the deutero-canonical books).

The opinion defended by Kaulen-Hoberg, Zarb, etc., seems the more probable. It defends the original unity of the two Canons with the proto-canonical and deutero-canonical books because of the intimate relationship which existed between the various Jewish communities, explains satisfactorily the gradual process whereby the deutero-canonical books and passages were eliminated until in the first century of our era they were totally rejected from the Palestinian Canon, which was then followed by the Jewish dispersion.

The deutero-canonical books and passages were rejected because of four criteria, which the Pharisees invented when they were subjecting all the books of the Bible to a reëxamination. (a) The first criterion was the conformity of a book with the

---

[16] Cf. Letter of Aristeas.
[17] Cf. Elephantine Papyri.

Pentateuch. Thus, the Book of Ezechiel had been questioned because of its apparent difficulties with the Torah or the Law. (b) The second criterion was the age of the book. No book was considered canonical which was written after the time of Esdras. (c) The third criterion was that the book had to be written in Hebrew. Thus, books written either in Aramaic or Greek were rejected. (d) The fourth criterion was that the book had to be written in Palestine. For this reason the Books of Daniel and Esther were assigned to the men of the Great Assembly by the Babylonian Talmud.

These four Pharisaical criteria, placing a limitation upon inspiration and prophecy, are theologically indefensible, and yet they are of great importance in explaining the history of the formation of the Palestinian Canon. These artificial norms having been invented, only the proto-canonical books were recognized in the process of reëxamining the Canon of the Old Testament. Since the deutero-canonical books and passages of the Alexandrian version did not meet the requirements of these four criteria, they were rejected. The Book of Baruch and the Epistle of Jeremias lacked Palestinian origin; the Book of Sirach and the First Book of Machabees were written after the time of Esdras; the Book of Tobias and the fragments of Daniel and of Esther were composed originally in Aramaic and probably also outside of Palestine; the Book of Judith was probably written in Aramaic; and the Book of Wisdom and the Second Book of Machabees were written in Greek.

According to the Pharisaical criteria, the Palestinian Canon was definitely closed about the end of the first century, perhaps at the Synod of Jamnia. Having determined the canonical books, the rabbis also determined the text itself and "made a fence around it."

(b) The History of the Formation of the Canon of the Old Testament [18]

Now that we have seen what books are contained in the

[18] Cf. Zarb, S., *op. cit.*, 78-112.

Palestinian and Alexandrian Canons, the question remains: how were these various books, written at different times, places, languages, collected to form the Canon of the Old Testament?

(1) Two Ancient Opinions in Regard to the Formation of the Canon.—One Jewish tradition based upon the apocryphal Fourth Book of Esdras attributes the formation of the Canon to Esdras alone. Some of the Fathers and ecclesiastical writers (e.g., St. Irenæus, Clement of Alex., Tertullian, Origen, Eusebius, St. Basil, St. John Chrysostom, St. Jerome, etc.) believed that Esdras was responsible for the formation of the Canon, but did not exclude the deutero-canonical books. The second Jewish tradition attributes the formation of the Canon to the men of the Great Assembly (Hebr., *kenéseth haggedolah*) associated with Esdras. This latter opinion is more commonly held by Jewry, and was explained at length by * Elias Levita (d. 1549) and by its principal exponent among Protestants, * John Buxtorf, Sr.

The common tendency today is to reject both these opinions, in particular the one maintaining that Esdras was the author of the Canon. The arguments upon which these opinions are based are either false or insufficient, and many other arguments, which are historically true or very probable, have been totally neglected. All scholars now admit that the Fourth Book of Esdras is apocryphal. Besides, the Great Assembly consisting of a body of 120 men, founded at Jerusalem by Esdras in the fifth century B.C. and existing till the time of Simon the Just (c. 300 B.C.), has been declared a rabbinical fiction by * Schuerer, Goettsberger, Felten, Zarb, and others.

(2) The Threefold Division of Books in the Palestinian Canon.—The threefold division of the Old Testament into the Pentateuch, the Prophets, and the Sacred Writings is not based upon three different degrees of inspiration, nor upon a distinction between the prophetical office and prophetical gifts, nor upon three stages in the religious development of the people (monotheism, prophetism, and Judaism), but upon three different aspects in the evolution of the synagogal liturgy.

The threefold division of books must be explained independently of the question of the canonicity of the books. These books were considered inspired and canonical long before they were placed in any of the three collections. The first and second collections were important for the liturgical services of the Jews. The third collection alone seems to have had some nexus with the definite formation of the Palestinian Canon.

In the first collection of books was the Torah or Pentateuch, which possessed a certain priority. The explanation of the Mosaic Law or its liturgical usage is evident from the history of the Jews both in the pre-exilic as well as in the post-exilic period. To facilitate the reading of the Pentateuch, it was divided into various sections to be read at determined intervals. Thus, it was completely read in some localities in the course of seven years, in others in the course of three and a half years, three years, or one year. This liturgical usage of consecutive reading presupposed its canonical authority. The sole usage of the Pentateuch for the liturgy in the very beginning by no means excluded the admission and recognition of other sacred and canonical books, as yet ungrouped in special collections. The sole usage of the Pentateuch in the very beginning also explains the reason why this original collection of five books was translated first into Greek at Alexandria.

After the Pentateuch had been selected for the liturgy, a second collection of books was formed. Those books which were more suitable to illustrate the Mosaic Law were selected for this. From this collection there was no consecutive reading before the middle of the seventh century of our era, yet the custom of reading from the Prophets prevailed at the time of Christ (cf. Luke 4, 17; Acts 13, 15). It is unknown whether this custom was introduced at the time of the Machabees or by the Pharisees in opposition to the Sadducees who disregarded the prophetical books.

The third collection, lacking the intrinsic unity prevailing in the other two collections, is made up of smaller sub-collections, some of which were used in the liturgy. Thus, the Psalter, used in the liturgical services, was combined with the

Books of Job and Proverbs because of their special system of rhythm. The Psalter, being used from ancient times in the liturgy, can be considered sacred and canonical long before it was placed as the second book among the Hagiographa. Another small sub-collection consists of the five Megilloth (Hebr. for scrolls): Ruth, Canticles, Ecclesiastes, Lamentations, and Esther. Of these books Esther was used in pre-Christian times in the liturgy to be read on the Feast of Purim; the Lamentations were introduced about the second or third century of our era to be read on the anniversary of the destruction of Jerusalem; the other three were added at a still later period [19]—Ruth to be read on the second day of the Feast of Pentecost, Canticles on the octave of the Passover, and Ecclesiastes on the Feast of Tabernacles. The other books of this collection (e.g., Daniel, Esdras, Nehemias, Paralipomenon) seem never to have been used in the liturgy.

This third collection was formed in the first century of our era, according to the above-mentioned criteria of the Pharisees, who definitely closed the Palestinian Canon. All the remaining writings, which were equally holy and canonical (i.e., the deutero-canonical books and passages), were excluded from their Canon. Hence, the division into three collections cannot explain the history of the formation of the Canon of the Old Testament.

(3) *The Probable Opinion about the Formation of the Canon.*—In the Old Testament the faithful had the greatest respect for the prophets sent to them by God. Their utterances, whether oral or written, were considered as sacred or canonical.

Moses was the first prophet to write down the utterances of the Lord (cf. Ex. 17, 14; 24. 4. 7; 34, 27; Num. 33, 2; Deut. 31, 9. 24), and thus laid the foundation of the Canon. His Pentateuch was not only recognized as divine and canonical in the passive sense, but also in the active sense of a rule of faith to be observed by all (i.e., as the Torah, the Law). The inspira-

[19] Cf. * Blau, L., in J.E., s.v. *The Five Megilloth.*

tion of the Pentateuch is assumed by the other books of the Old Testament, when they refer to it as the Book of the Law of God (Jos. 24, 26 in MT; 2 Esd. 8, 8) or the Book of the Law of the Lord (2 Par. 17, 9; 34, 14), or the Law of the Lord (1 Par. 16, 40; 2 Par. 31, 4; Luke 2, 23). After the exile Esdras read the Pentateuch publicly to the people, who bound themselves by oath to its fulfillment (2 Esd. 8, 8 ff); but he was not the first to promulgate the Law, and hence he was not the first to have laid the foundation of the Canon.

The second collection consists of many more books, some of which were written long after the time of Moses (e.g., the books of the post-exilic prophets). This collection is divided into two parts: the earlier Prophets (Josue, Judges, Samuel, and Kings) and the later Prophets (Jeremias, Ezechiel, Isaias, the Minor Prophets). These books written by prophets, sometimes by divine command (cf. Isa. 34, 16; Jer. 30, 2; 36, 2-8), were almost immediately recognized as sacred and canonical (cf. Jos. 24, 25 f; 1 Sam. 10, 25) independently of their position in this or that collection of scrolls. The second collection could only have been formed after the exile, or more precisely in the second century B.C. This collection had not yet been organized when the Alexandrian Jews were translating the sacred books into Greek, because one and the same translator was responsible for the Books of Jeremias (placed by the Palestinian Jews in the second collection), of Lamentations (placed by them in the third collection), and of Baruch (declared by them to be apocryphal). That the inspired value of a book is independent of the formation of a canonical collection may also be seen in the citations of Daniel from the Books of Jeremias and Baruch. Daniel quotes from the Book of Jeremias before there is any thought of a second collection.

The books of the third collection enjoyed inspired authority long before they were assembled into one collection. There is evidence of the existence of a collection of Psalms (2 Par. 29, 30) and a Book of Proverbs (Prov. 25, 1) prior to the exile, and the author of the Book of Sirach at the beginning of the second century B.C. quotes nearly all the proto-canonical books of the third collection. The reason why the books of this third collection (recognized as sacred and canonical even before the formation of a second collection) were relegated to the last position, was their general non-usage in synagogal readings or services. Of this collection only the five Megilloth are now used on appointed days. The first formal and explicit mention of this third collection is made in the Babylonian Talmud, but this collection must have already existed in the second half of the first century of our era, since the mention of twenty-four books by the Fourth Book of Esdras presupposes it. Josephus makes no mention of this threefold collection, because he is enumerating the books independently of their liturgical usage. The Alexandrian version, much older than the enumeration of Josephus, does not follow the arrangement of the three collections of the Palestinian Canon, but, while having the proto-canonical and deutero-canonical books, arranges them according to a systematic and chronological order. These books and their arrangement as found in the Alexandrian version were accepted by the Church. The deutero-canonical books, lacking not inspiration but only the Pharisaical criteria, were thus included in the Christian Canon.

Art. 2.   The Old Testament Canon of the Christians

Had the Church accepted the Palestinian Canon, this also would have been binding upon all Christians, but only because of the value placed upon it by her. The Church, however, did not receive this Canon, but rather the Alexandrian, which included the deutero-canonical books and passages, and she thereby showed that she is the only legitimate and final authority determining the extent of the Canon.

The Canon of the Church prevailed within a short time. The New Testament literature, going back to the period when Christianity was striving to a large extent to make converts from Judaism, makes no explicit or formal mention of the deutero-canonical books or passages, but nevertheless alludes to some of them. As time went on, the number of writers explicitly favoring the Alexandrian Canon increased, and in the African councils of the fourth century the last doubts about the extent of the Old Testament Canon were removed.[20]

(a) THE NEW TESTAMENT AND THE OLD TESTAMENT CANON

Our Lord calls the Old Testament "the Scriptures" (John 5, 39), "Moses and the Prophets" (Luke 24, 27), "the Law of Moses, the Prophets, and all the Psalms" (Luke 24, 44). The citation of Christ found in St. Matthew's Gospel, "from the blood of Abel the just unto the blood of Zacharias the son of Barachias" (23, 25), may refer to Genesis 4, 8 and the Second Book of Paralipomenon 24, 21 f (i.e., the last book of the third Jewish collection), but it does not necessarily exclude the deutero-canonical books.[21] Of the books of the Old Testament Our Lord mentions directly or indirectly by name "Moses" (i.e., the Pentateuch, John 5, 46 etc.), Isaias (Luke 4, 17 ff), Osee (Matt. 9, 13), Jonas (Matt. 12, 40), Zacharias (Matt. 26, 31), Malachias (Matt. 11, 10), and the Psalms (Matt. 21, 16). Similarly, the Apostles themselves were acquainted with a collection of the Old Testament books (Acts 17, 2), and also refer to "the books of the Prophets" (Acts 7, 42) and "the book of Psalms" (Acts 1, 20), etc.

In the entire New Testament there are from 270 to 350 citations from the Old Testament, and of these less than fifty disagree with the Septuagint version. Citations, however, are missing for the following proto-canonical books: Ruth, First and Second Esdras, Esther, Abdias, Nahum, Ecclesiastes, and Canticles. No scholar would deny the canonicity of these proto-canonical books in the primitive Christian Church simply because of the omission of references to them in the New Testament; their content did not serve the purpose of the sacred writers.

There are no explicit, formal citations from the deutero-canonical books in the New Testament. But there is a series

[20] Cf. Goettsberger, J., op. cit., 370 f.
[21] Cf. Zarb, S., op. cit., 118 f.

of passages which show traces of these Old Testament writings. It suffices to give the following examples:

Hebrews 1, 3 . . . . Wisdom 7, 26
Hebrews 11, 35 . . . . 2 Machabees 6, 18--7, 42
Matthew 27, 39-42 . . . . . . Wisdom 2, 17 f
Ephesians 6, 13-17 . . . . . . Wisdom 5, 18-20
Romans 1, 20-32 . . . . Wisdom 13—14
Romans 9, 21 . . . . Wisdom 15, 7
James 1, 19 . . . . Sirach 5, 13
Matthew 6, 14 . . . . Sirach 28, 2

At the time of Our Lord and the Apostles, the Septuagint version was used by all the Jews of the dispersion, and the sacred writers of the New Testament made diligent use of a Greek version which contained the deutero-canonical books and passages. Had these not been considered inspired, surely the Apostles and their disciples would have warned the early Christian readers and determined exactly the authentic catalogue of sacred books.

The only passage in the New Testament which may contain a possible allusion to an apocryphal book is Jude 14 f. Hence, nowhere in the New Testament is there an explicit citation, in which an apocryphal book is assumed as canonical.[22]

(b) THE OLD TESTAMENT CANON DURING THE PATRISTIC PERIOD

The Greek Septuagint [23] was the only Bible text of the Old Testament that was universally read in the primitive Church both in the East and in the West, until the Old Latin (trans-

---

[22] Cf. Goettsberger, J., *op. cit.*, 372-374; Steinmueller, J. E.—Sullivan K., art. "Old Testament Quotations," in C.B.E.N.T., 466-471.

[23] Among the Greek Papyri part of the Book of Sirach is contained in Papyrus 964 or Chester Beatty Papyrus XI, probably of the fourth century of our era, and some deutero-canonical passages of the Books of Daniel and Esther are contained in Papyri 967 and 968 or Chester Beatty Papyri IX and X, probably of the first half of the third century (cf. Kenyon, F. G., "The Text of the Greek Bible," London, 1937, 44-46). Among the great codices or principal uncials *Codex Sinaiticus* of the fourth century, though incomplete, contains the deutero-canonical Books of Tobias, Judith, 1 and 2 Machabees, Wisdom, and Sirach, and also the apocryphal books, 3 and 4 Machabees; *Codex Alexandrinus* of

lated from the Septuagint) and the Old Syriac versions were made. However, not only the proto-canonical but also the deutero-canonical books are found both in the Latin and Syriac versions.

Early Christian art in the catacombs indicates a keen appreciation for the writings of the Old Testament. Representations were made from all of the deutero-canonical books, excepting the Books of Wisdom and Sirach, the contents of which are hardly adaptable for reproduction. Thus, we find representations from the Books of Daniel (3, 24 ff; 13; 14), Tobias, Judith, Baruch, and Machabees.[24] It is to be particularly noted that the apocryphal books are totally ignored.

The Apostolic Fathers and earliest ecclesiastical writers either allude to the deutero-canonical books or quote them as Sacred Scripture. The following schematical form represents this early period. The sign "x" expresses an allusion to a book, and the asterisk (*) a citation from it.

	Tob.	Jud.	Bar.	Wisd.	Sir.	1 Mach.	2 Mach.	Esth.	Dan.
Didache [25]				*	x				
St. Clement R. [26]	x	*		*	x			*	x
Ep. Barnabas [27]				*					
St. Ignatius [28]		x							
St. Polycarp [29]	*								
Shepherd of Hermas [30]	x			x	*		*		
Martyrdom of St. Polycarp [31]		*							
St. Irenæus [32]			*	*					*
Clement A. [33]	*	*	*	*	*	*	*	*	*
St. Hippolytus [34]	*		*	*	*	*	*		*
Tertullian [35]		*	*	*	*	*	*		*
Origen [36]	*	*	*	*	*	*	*	*	*
St. Cyprian [37]	*		*	*	*	*	*		*

the fifth century contains all the proto-canonical and deutero-canonical books, and also the apocryphal books, 3 Esdras, 3 and 4 Machabees, Psalm 151, and the Psalms of Solomon; *Codex Vaticanus* of the fourth century contains all the proto-canonical and deutero-canonical books with the exception of the 1 and 2 Machabees, and also has the apocryphal book, 3 Esdras. The apocryphal books in these codices were not considered by many as canonical or sacred books (cf. Zarb, S., *op. cit.*, 125-128).

(c) The Old Testament Canon in the Ecclesiastical Decisions

St. Augustine (d. 430) gave a complete Canon without the addition of any apocryphal works (cf. *De doctr. christ.*, II, 8; M.L., XXXIV, 41). In his domain and under his influence the first ecclesiastical decisions were given about the extent of the Old Testament Canon. These, however, were of local authority. The Council of Hippo (A.D. 393), the decisions of which were confirmed by the two Councils of Carthage (397 and 419), determined the Canon exactly as it is today (E.B., 16-20).

---

[24] For the representations from these books see D.D.L.B., II, 155 f.

[25] *Didache* (90-100), V, 2 = Wisd. 12, 7; X, 3 = Wisd. 1, 14; IV, 5 = Sir. 4, 36; X, 3 = Sir. 18, 1.

[26] St. Clement of Rome (96/98), LXI, 2 = Tob. 13, 6. 10; LV, 4 f = Jud. 8 ff; III, 4 = Wisd. 2, 24; VII, 5 = Wisd. 12, 10; XXVII, 5 = Wisd. 11, 22 and 12, 12; LIX, 3 = Sir. 2, 11; LV, 6 = Esth. 15, 5; XLV, 7 = Dan. 3, 19 ff.

[27] Epistle of Barnabas (c. 100), VI, 7 = Wisd. 2, 12.

[28] St. Ignatius Martyr of Antioch (d. 109) in *Ep. ad Eph.*, XV, 1 = Jud. 16, 14.

[29] St. Polycarp (c. 115) in *Ep. ad Philip.*, X, 2 = Tob. 4, 10 and 12, 9.

[30] The Shepherd of Hermas (c. 140), in Mand. V, ii, 3 = Tob. 4, 19; Mand. I, 1 = Wisd. 1, 14; Vis. III, vii, 3 = Sir. 18, 30; Mand., I = 2 Mach. 7, 28.

[31] The Martyrdom of St. Polycarp (155/156), XIV, 1 = Jud. 9, 12. 14.

[32] St. Irenæus (135/140—202/203) in *Adv. Hær.*, V, 35, quotes Baruch as Jeremias; a number of passages from the Book of Wisdom are given in *Adv. Hær.*, IV, 38, 3; the history of Susanna and that of Bel and the dragon are mentioned in *Adv. Hær.*, IV, 26, 1, and V, 54, 2.

[33] Clement of Alexandria (150—211/216) recognized all the deutero-canonical books and passages as sacred and canonical (cf. Zarb, S., *op. cit.*, 136 f). Cf. Ruwet, J., "Clement d'Alexandrie: Canon des Ecritures et Apocryphes," in *Biblica*, 29 (1948), 71-99.

[34] St. Hippolytus (170/175—236) is certain to have cited all the deutero-canonical books and passages, with the exception of Judith and Esther (cf. Zarb, S., *op. cit.*, 174 f).

[35] Tertullian (160—240/250) quotes all the deutero-canonical books, with the exception of Tobias and the deutero-canonical parts of Esther (cf. Zarb, S., *op. cit.*, 181).

[36] Origen (185/186—254/255) does not follow in practice the Palestinian Canon given above, but in his general writings he makes use of all the deutero-canonical books and passages (cf. Zarb, S., *op. cit.*, 137-142; Goettsberger, J., *op. cit.*, 379). Cf. Ruwet, J., "Duo textus Origenis de canone A.T.," in *Biblica*, 2 (1921), 57-60; Merk, A., "Origines und der Kanon des A.T.," in *Biblica*, 6 (1925), 200-205.

[37] St. Cyprian (210-258) quotes all the deutero-canonical books and passages, with the exception of Judith and the deutero-canonical parts of Esther (cf. Zarb, S., *op. cit.*, 181).

Though these Councils were locally restricted in their jurisdiction, yet their Canon was more than a local ordinance. It expressed the view of the universal Church, for we read: "Ita ut de confirmando isto canone transmarina Ecclesia consulatur" (i.e., the proposed Canon with the deutero-canonical books and passages was sent to Rome for confirmation).

This same Canon was proposed on February 20, 405, by Pope St. Innocent I in his letter to Bishop Exsuperius of Toulouse (E.B., 21).

The so-called Decree of Gelasius (492-496) likewise has this same complete Canon (E.B., 26).

These individual decisions of local churches were reflections of the universal Church, and remained the criterion until the fifteen century. In 1441 the Council of Florence in its Decree for the Jacobites published anew the same Canon, with proto-canonical and deutero-canonical books (E.B., 47).

The Council of Trent in its Decree "Sacrosancta" of April 8, 1546, formally and definitely canonized all the books of the Old Testament, including the deutero-canonical books and passages for the first time (E.B., 57, 60). Since the time of this Decree it is an article of faith to believe that the deutero-canonical books and passages of both Testaments are also inspired.[37a]

Although the Vatican Council (1869-1870) did not repeat the Canon of sacred books determined by the Council of Trent, yet, it confirmed the Decree "Sacrosancta."

(d) The Effects of the Palestinian Canon upon Christian Writers [38]

In the history of the Church various isolated attempts were

[37a]Cf. Maickle, A., "Der Kanon der biblischen Bücher u.das Konzil von Trient" (Freiburg i.Br., 1929); Dunker, P. G., "De singulis S.Scripturae libris controversis in Concilio Tridentino," in "Studia Anselmiana" (Rome, 1951), 66-93; idem, "The Canon of the Old Testament at the Council of Trent," in C.B.Q., 15 (1953), 277-299.

[38]Cf. Goettsberger, J., op. cit., 378-384; Gigot, F., op. cit., 50 ff. Ruwet, J., "Le Canon Alexandrin des Ecritures. Saint Athanase," in Biblica, 33 (1952), 1-29; Synave, P., "Le canon Scriptuaire de Sainte Thomas d' Aquin," in R.B., 33 (1924), 522-533.

made to determine the Old Testament Canon in such a manner as to depreciate or even to exclude the deutero-canonical books and passages.   These attempts were unsuccessful and were due to peculiar influences.

The Canons of Bishop Melito of Sardis and of Origen have been discussed above. St. Athanasius (295-373) in the thirty-ninth of his festal epistles acknowledges twenty-two books of the Bible (i.e., the proto-canonical books, including Baruch and the Epistle of Jeremias), and relegates the deutero-canonical books to the pious but not canonical works. But in his writings he also makes use of the deutero-canonical books, to which he theoretically denied canonical value. St. Cyril of Jerusalem (315-386) enumerates twenty-two books (i.e., the proto-canonical books, including Baruch and the Epistle of Jeremias), and says of the "doubtful or controverted" books (i.e., the deutero-canonical books) that they are put aside in the second rank. But his practice also is more liberal than his theory, since he cites these books as Sacred Scripture. This disagreement between theory and practice is also found in St. Epiphanius (315-403) and St. Gregory of Nazianzus (329-390). Although the authenticity of the sixtieth Decree of the Council of Laodicea (c. 360: cf. E.B., 12), with its catalogue of twenty-two books (inclusive of Baruch and the Epistle of Jeremias), is disputed, yet the Decree shows evidence of the belief prevailing in Asia Minor about this period.

The West to a large extent received its theological training from the East. Hence, traces of the limited Canon can also be found in the Latin Church. St. Hilary of Poitiers (d. 367) reproduces the catalogue of Origen (i.e., his list of twenty-two books, inclusive of the Epistle of Jeremias), and then says: "some have added Tobias and Judith, making twenty-four, after the letters of the Greek alphabet." Rufinus (d. 410) of Aquileia distinguishes between twenty-two canonical books which are authoritative in matters of faith, and ecclesiastical books which should not be used for that purpose, but are read in the churches: namely, Wisdom, Sirach, Tobias, Judith, and Machabees. Yet, despite their theories, both he and St. Hilary made use of the deutero-canonical books as divinely inspired Scriptures. Although St. Jerome (d. 420) often rejects the deutero-canonical books as apocryphal, he espouses this theory as his private opinion, knowing full well that these books were being read by the Church and were being advocated by his contemporaries. His practice at times contradicts his theory, for he cites the deutero-canonical books as divinely inspired Scriptures.

There can be little doubt that the Alexandrian Canon from the earliest times had come into the hands of the early Christian communities at Alexandria, Antioch, Africa, and Rome. When some of the Fathers from Origen to St. Jerome fix the number of books at twenty-two or twenty-four, they do not follow the earlier tradition of the Church, but rather their private estimate based upon the Jewish Palestinian tradition.[39] St. Augustine, a contemporary of St. Jerome, teaches this earlier tradition. The testimonies of later writers, who doubted the inspiration of some or all of the deutero-canonical books, were so small in number that they were unable to shake the universal belief in the complete Canon of the Old Testament. Among these may be mentioned: Theodore of Mopsuestia (350-428), Junilius Africanus (c. 551), Leontius of Byzantium (d. 543), St. Gregory the Great (540-604), St. John of Damascus (d. 754), Nicephorus of Constantinople (d. 829), Walafrid Strabo (d. 849), Notker of St. Gall (d. 912), Hugh of St. Victor (d. 1141), Peter of Clugny (d. 1156), John of Salisbury (d. 1180), Peter Comestor (d. 1179), Rupert of Deutz (1070-1135), Hugh of St. Cher (d. 1263), Nicholas of Lyra (d. 1340), Alphonse Tostatus (d. 1455), Antoninus of Florence (d. 1459), Cajetan (d. 1534).

These isolated testimonies and opinions never demanded a formal decision on the part of the universal Church. However, to settle once and for always the question of the extent of the Canon against the Protestant Reformers of the sixteenth century, the Council of Trent for the first time formally and defi-

[39] Cf. * Swete, H. B., "An Introduction to the O.T. in Greek" (2nd ed., Cambridge, 1914), 224.

nitely canonized both the proto-canonical books and the
deutero-canonical books and passages.

(e) THE CANON OF THE OLD TESTAMENT IN THE OTHER CHRISTIAN CHURCHES [40]

(1) The Greek Church.—In the beginning the same uncer-
tainty prevailed in the Greek as in the Latin Church. However, in 692 at the Council of Trullo the Canon of the Roman
Church was completely accepted. Even after the Greek
Schism in the ninth century under Photius, the same Canon
was retained. When the Patriarch Cyril Lukaris (d. 1638),
who was favorable to Protestantism, tried to reintroduce the
Canon of the Council of Laodicea, the Synods of Constantinople (1638), Jassy (1642), Jerusalem (1672) proclaimed their
acceptance also of the deutero-canonical books. Since the
eighteenth century the deutero-canonical books began to be
rejected by the Greek Church, due to the influence of Russian
writers and theologians. From this time on the influence of
Protestantism was felt, so that the deutero-canonical books
were rejected by some theologians and excluded from their
catechisms. However, no official decision has been given on
the matter.

(2) The Syrian Church.—It is difficult to determine the
Syrian Canon in the earliest period. The Syriac Peshitto of
the Old Testament originated in Jewish or Judeo-Christian
circles (first century B.C. to second century of our era), and
originally lacked also some of the proto-canonical books, such
as Paralipomenon, Esdras-Nehemias, and Esther. The Syrian
writer Aphraates (middle of the fourth century) made use of
Judith, Baruch, fragments of Daniel, perhaps also of Wisdom.
St. Ephraem (d. 373) has no commentaries on the deutero-
canonical books, but cites these as well as the proto-canonical
books. A catalogue of the Old Testament, dating from 350 to
400, omits the proto-canonical Books of Canticles and Ecclesiastes, as well as the deutero-canonical Books of Tobias and

[40] Cf. Goettsberger, J., *op cit.*, 384-388; Zarb. S., *op. cit.*, 192-248.

Baruch. Hence, it is incorrect to maintain that the old Syrian Church did not recognize the deutero-canonical books.

In the subsequent period the Syrian Church recognized also the deutero-canonical books. The *Codex Ambrosianus* of the Syriac Peshitto (sixth century) contained Judith, Wisdom, Sirach, Baruch, Apocalypse of Baruch, Epistle of Jeremias, Fourth Esdras, First to Fifth Machabees, but Tobias is missing. The Syrohexapla of Paul of Tella (618) includes all the deutero-canonical books. Amongst the *Jacobites* there exists a "Book of Women," which included Ruth, Esther, Judith, and Susanna. Jacob of Edessa (d. 708) refers to the words of Baruch, Wisdom, Esther, Judith, and Sirach. Barhebræus, the most prolific writer of the Jacobites (d. 1286), comments upon Sirach, Wisdom, Daniel (3, 24 ff, and 13 f), cites Machabees, mentions Baruch, does not seem to consider Paralipomenon as inspired, and omits in his writings Esdras and Nehemias. The *Nestorians* separated Paralipomenon, Esdras-Nehemias, and Esther from the other proto-canonical books. Jesudad, Bishop of Hadad (c. 852), recognized a Canon of twenty-two books. The Nestorian rival of Barhebræus, Ebedjesu (d. 1318), includes in his Canon Sirach, Wisdom, Judith, Esther, Daniel Minor (Dan. 13, 1-64), Letter of Baruch, the Jewish Mishna, Josephus with First to Fourth Machabees, Apocalypse of Asiatha, and Tobias. The Canon of Ibn Chaldum (d. 1406) mentions five books of Moses, Josue, Judges, Ruth, Judith, First to Fourth Kings, Paralipomenon, First to Third Machabees, Esdras, Esther, Psalms, five books of Solomon, minor and major Prophets, Sirach.

Hence, from the earliest times witness can be given for most of the deutero-canonical books.

(*3*) *The Ethiopian Church.*—The Ethiopians were converted to Christianity by the Syrians. Their Old Testament Canon includes the deutero-canonical Books of Tobias, Judith, Wisdom, Sirach, and Baruch; First and Second Machabees are added as an appendix. They also recognize a great number of apocryphal writings.

(*4*) *The Armenian Church.*—Moses of Chorene (c. 1000),

the historian, speaks of twenty-two books of the Old Testament. This undoubtedly is the Jewish Canon. However, the outstanding writers of the fifth century (e.g., John Manderkuni, Eznik, Lazarus of Pharp, and Elische) also mention the deutero-canonical books.

(5) *The Coptic Church.*—The Canon of the Copts follows essentially that of the Catholic Church, and is free from apocryphal books.

(6) *The Protestants.*—Carlstadt (1520) excluded the deutero-canonical books from the Canon as apocryphal; six of them were considered as sacred books (apocryphi, tamen agiographi), but Baruch together with the deutero-canonical passages from Daniel and Esther were recognized as completely apocryphal. The Zürich Bible of 1529 placed them in the appendix. Luther's first German translation (1534) has them in the appendix with the title "Apocrypha." The Gallican Confession,[41] the Anglican Confession, and the Swiss Confession II (1546) were very tolerant towards the deutero-canonical books, but from the time of the Synod of Dordrecht (1618) the Reformers bitterly attacked these books and emphasized their human origin (cf. the Synod of Westminster 1643-53). Thenceforth they were no longer regarded as belonging to the Sacred Scriptures, and were to be removed from the Bibles. This was followed out strictly by the Puritans in Scotland, who demanded that the deutero-canonical books be no longer printed in the Bible (cf. Apocryphal-Struggle of 1825-1827, 1850-1853). For this reason the British Bible Societies omitted them from their Bibles, but on the other hand the Lutherans printed the Bible along with these so-called apocryphal books. Most of the modern theologians, however, wish a Canon only for historical appearances, but do not wish to be bound to it.

[41] In the Confession of 1559 we read: "utiles, non sunt tamen ejusmodi, ut ex iis constitui possit articulus fidei."

CHAPTER II

THE HISTORY OF THE NEW TESTAMENT CANON

It is easier to trace the history of the New Testament Canon. From the earliest period of Christianity there is evidence from the Apostolic Fathers, apologists, and ecclesiastical writers, as well as from Biblical manuscripts, to show in what great esteem these inspired books of the New Testament were held. This esteem for the Sacred Scriptures of the New Testament was no less great than the reverence of the Church for the books of the Old Testament contained in the Septuagint version, which was so frequently quoted by the sacred writers of the New. Both Testaments were held to be inspired and to have God as their Author.

After Our Lord ascended into heaven, the Apostles, in accordance with the mandate given them, began to preach His gospel and establish His spiritual kingdom, the Church, throughout the world. During this period of missionary activity they were the inspired authors of the sacred books of the New Covenant. These consisted partly of books dealing with the life of Our Lord and His Apostles (the four Gospels and the Acts), partly of letters addressed either to individual churches or to the Church in general, and partly of prophecies concerning the Church (e.g., the Apocalypse). This collection of religious books, however, was limited in time and authorship. Unlike the books of the Old Testament, the inspiration of which extended over a period of more than a thousand years, the sacred books of the New Testament were confined to the brief period between Our Lord's death and the death of the last Apostle. The origin of the books of the New Testament can be roughly placed between A.D. 40 and 100. With the death of the last Apostle, St. John, public revelation ceased and no inspired, canonical book appeared after that time.

The Apostles were filled with the gifts of the Holy Spirit on Pentecost, and were endowed with personal infallibility in regard to faith and morals. Unlike the Prophets of the Old Testament, who without any previous special instruction were divinely chosen for their sublime mission from the great multitude of the Jewish nation and were impelled to prophesy and at times to write, the Apostles were personally instructed by Our Lord and prepared for their particular kerygmatic mission. This entire new religious literature of the New Testament, with the exception of two books, was written by eyewitnesss. But these two books, the Gospels of St. Mark and St. Luke, were written according to the teachings of St. Peter and St. Paul respectively. These books by the Apostles and by two of their disciples were held from the very beginning in equal esteem with the books of the Old Testament. The Apostolic Fathers and the subsequent ecclesiastical writers quote freely from both Testaments as from sacred, inspired books.

The Formation of the Canon of the New Testament.— This formation was a *slow process,* and *various difficulties* had to be encountered. The first dificulty was that of *communication.* Modern methods of personal contact (printing, postal service, telegram, telephone, radio, television, etc.) were lacking. Books had to be transcribed or copied by hand and sent by special messengers to churches situated in various parts of the Roman Empire. Another difficulty encountered was the *geographical extent of the Church.* Many of the Apostolic Epistles were sent to particular churches, some of whose cities or towns played no important role in the Roman Empire. Considerable time elapsed before these Epistles were copied on papyrus rolls or codices and then forwarded to adjacent or far-distant Christian communities. If the original Epistle, no matter how important it may seem to us now, happened to be addressed to a small community off the main Roman highways, considerable time would have to elapse before other Christian communities could become aware of this particular Apostolic letter. A third and likewise serious difficulty encountered was the *propagation of religious books by heretics,* who proposed false doctrines and represented their books as sacred and inspired. Hence arose the necessity of definitely establishing what books or epistles were really of divine origin. The inspired books had to be separated from the apocryphal books, even though some of these apocryphal books were orthodox in spirit or doctrine and had been accepted by individual local communities.

The Canon of the New Testament consists of twenty-seven books. In the first three centuries seven books were generally, but not universally, accepted. These *seven deutero-canonical books* are: *the Epistle to the Hebrews, the Epistle of St. James, the Second Epistle of St. Peter, the Second and Third Epistles of St. John, the Epistle of St. Jude, and the Apocalypse.* There was, however, a serious discussion about only three of these seven books, namely, the Epistle to the Hebrews, the Second Epistle of St. Peter, and the Apocalypse. Yet, there was no general doubt even about these three, but only a temporary hesistance or passing indecision.[1]

Agreement in Tradition about the New Testament Canon.— Toward the end of the fourth century almost absolute harmony existed in the universal Church about the extent of the Canon of the New Testament, and this harmony prevailed in ecclesiastical tradition until the Council of Trent found it necessary formally and definitely to canonize the twenty-seven books of the New Testament.

Art. 1.   The Formation of the Canon of the New Testament to A.D. 150 [2]

(a) *The Writings Containing the Gospel of Jesus Christ.*— Our Lord came to establish a new spiritual order, to advocate new principles of holiness and daily living more perfect than those preached by the Pharisees. The Messianic prophecies

[1] Cf. Grannan, C. P., *op. cit.,* III, 202.
[2] Cf. Lagrange, M. J., "Histoire ancienne, etc.," 8 ff.

in the Old Testament had been fulfilled in Him. He did not come to destroy, i.e., to make people regard as worthless or ridiculous, the Law of Moses and the Prophets, but to perfect them, i.e., to bring them to their logical and divinely intentioned conclusions (Matt. 5, 17), and to establish a new Covenant between God and mankind.

The fulfillment of the Law and the Prophets is contained in the gospel which was preached by Our Lord and His disciples and which was later put into writing by the Apostles. These writings comprise the books of the New Testament.

These writings containing the kerygmatic teachings of the inspired writers, of the Apostles and the two disciples, St. Mark and St. Luke, were considered authoritative. St. Peter places the Pauline Epistles on a par with the rest of the Sacred Scriptures (2 Pet. 3, 15-17), and St. Paul probably refers to the Gospel of his disciple as Scripture (1 Tim. 5, 18; Luke 10, 7). St. Clement of Rome, in a passage important for the history of the Canon, vindicated the right of the ministry to continue the work of the Apostles, and, writing in the name of the Roman Church, he explicitly asserts that St. Paul's Epistle to the Corinthians was written under the inspiration of the Holy Spirit (XLVII, 1 ff).

(b) *The Writings of the New Testament Considered as Sacred Scripture.*—These sacred writings contain the gospel of Jesus Christ, and therefore bestow an incontestable authority upon the shepherds of the Church so that they could demand obedience from the faithful (cf. St. Ignatius of Antioch in *Ep. ad Phila.*, VIII, 2). The written Gospel of Jesus Christ, contained in the four Gospels and Apostolic writings, is something very vital, and possesses the same authority as the sacred books of the Old Testament (cf. *Ep. Barnabas*, IV, 14; St. Ignatius of Antioch in *Ep. ad Phila.*, V, 1 f, also *Ep. ad Smyrn.*, V, 1, VII, 2; St. Polycarp in *Ep. ad Philip.*, II, 1, III, 2, XII, 1; Pseudo or Second Clement, II, 4, XIII, 4, XIV, 2). The New Testament literature, therefore, was not intended merely as a consulting library, but was to be a library of momentous importance for Catholic living and action.

(c) *The New Testament Literature as Liturgical Reading.*— The early Christians read in their churches not only the sacred books of the Old Testament but also the writings of the Apostles. The first traces of public reading go back to St. Paul (cf. Col. 4, 16; 1 Thess. 5, 27; also 2 Pet. 3, 15 f). But the first writer to speak of the *liturgical* usage of the New Testament literature in Christian assemblies is St. Justin the Martyr (c. 100/110—163/167), who says: "And on the day called Sunday, all who live in cities or in the country gather together to one place, and the memoirs of the Apostles or the writings of the Prophets are read as long as time permits" (*I Apol.*, LXVII, 3 f). These *memoirs of the Apostles* are, according to the other writings of St. Justin, the Gospels. It seems, however, very likely that the Pauline Epistles were also used for liturgical reading. At the end of the second century most books of the New Testament were being read during divine services, because the Muratorian Fragment, having mentioned the Canon of the New Testament books, says of the Apocalypses of John and Peter: "which latter some of us do not wish to be read in the church" (E.B., 6).

(d) *The Menace of the Apocryphal Literature.*—The members who made up the primitive Church were drawn from Judaism and paganism, and from both these two sources there arose dangers to the authoritative teaching of the successors of the Apostles. Some of the converts from Judaism tried to impose the obligations of the Mosaic Law upon the members of the Church. Other converts from paganism tried to adulterate the Apostolic doctrine with false philosophical ideas. From this twofold tendency the principal heresies, especially Gnosticism, arose within the primitive Church.

Both of these groups had their own writings opposed to the pure faith of the Apostles and their successors, so that confusion at times arose. Since the Apostles enjoyed irrefragable authority, their names were at times assumed for heretical apocryphal writings, which were edited in the form of Gospels (e.g., the Gospels of Thomas, of Matthias, of Philip, of Judas Iscariot, etc.). But it is noteworthy that amongst the Apostolic Fathers there is no citation from these apocryphal books as sacred, inspired writings of the New Testament.

At the time of the Apostles, if we prescind from the Judaizers mentioned in the Pauline Epistles, there is little evidence of struggles within the Church between the Christians and their heretical adversaries. The writings of the Apostles refer more to the inner spiritual life of the Church than to an external struggle against heretics. At most, there were present germs of future heresies, which became apparent during the period of the Apostolic Fathers and ecclesiastical writers. These heretics made use of the New Testament literature to propagate their false doctrines, thus indirectly bearing witness to the canonical value of some New Testament books.

The Jewish Christian tendency had as its principal exponent Cerinthus, a late contemporary of St. John the Apostle in Asia Minor. He and his followers made use of the Gospel of St. Matthew, but rejected the authority of St. Paul. Even though Cerinthus was hostile to the Apostles, and in particular to St. John, he acknowledged that St. John was the author of the Apocalypse and other writings.[3] After the death of Cerinthus many other heresies arose from the same Jewish legalistic tendency. The Naaseni or Ophites acknowledged the four Gospels, seven Pauline Epistles (Romans, First and Second Corinthians, Ephesians, Galatians, Philippians, and probably that to the Hebrews), and the Apocalypse. Later this sect made use of the apocryphal Gospels according to the Egyptians and of Thomas. The Peratæ made use of the Gospel of St. John and two Epistles (First Corinthians and Colossians). The Sethites acknowledged the Gospels of St. Matthew

---

[3] Cf. Zarb, S., *op. cit.*, 300.

and St. John, and three Epistles (First and Second Corinthians and Philippians). The Ebionites and Nazarenes received the Gospel of St. Matthew, but refused to accept the authority of St. Paul, whom they declared to be an apostate from the Mosaic Law.

The pagan Christian tendency had as its first proponent Simon Magus, who was acquainted with the Gospels of St. Matthew and probably of St. John, and alluded to 1 Corinthians and 1 Peter. His followers also spread some of their private writings under the name of Christ and His disciples, and they maintained schools in Syria, Egypt, and Rome until the third century. Menander, the successor and pupil of Simon Magus, is mentioned by St. Irenæus (cf. *Adv. Haer.*, I, xxiii, 5). Basilides, a pupil of Menander, propagated his Gnostic doctrines at Alexandria, Egypt (A.D. 120-140), and acknowledged many writings of the New Testament (the Gospels of St. Luke and St. John, the Epistle to the Romans, 1 and 2 Corinthians, Ephesians, and perhaps 1 Timothy); he seems also to have been acquainted with the Gospels of St. Matthew and St. Mark, and 1 Peter. Carpocrates, a contemporary of Basilides at Alexandria, acknowledged the canonical Gospels and some of the Pauline Epistles. Valentinus, one of the most important proponents of Gnosticism, was born in Egypt and lived in Rome from 140 to 160. Besides acknowledging the books of the Old and New Testaments, he claimed to have received his manner of interpreting the Sacred Scriptures from a certain Theodas, a disciple of St. Paul. His principal pupils in the West were Heracleon and Ptolemæus, and in the East Marcus.

(e) *The Earliest Evidence for the Deutero-Canonical Books of the New Testament.*—Since these writings are the most contraverted of the canonical books, a survey will point out their usage by the Apostolic Fathers. The sign "x" expresses an allusion to a book, and an asterisk (*) a citation from it.

	Hebr.	2 Pet.	2 John	3 John	James	Jude	Apoc.
Didache [4]	x						x
St. Clement R. [5]	*	x			x		x
Ep. Barnabas [6]		x					
St. Ignatius [7]					x		
St. Polycarp [8]	x		x		*		
Papias [9]							x
Ps. Clement [10]	*				*		*
Shepherd of Hermas [11]	*	x			*		*
Martyrdom of St. Polycarp [12]							*
St. Justin Martyr [13]	x				x		*

[4] The *Didache* also quotes from the Gospels of St. Matthew and St. Luke, and from the following Epistles: Romans, 1 Corinthians, and 1 Peter; it alludes to the Gospels of St. Mark and St. John, and to the following Epistles: Ephesians, 1 and 2 Thessalonians, 1 Timothy, and Titus. Cf. X, 3 = Hebr. 3, 4; X, 3 = Apoc. 4, 11; XVI, 4 = Apoc. 13, 2.13.

[5] St. Clement of Rome in his First Epistle to the Corinthians also quotes from the Gospels of St. Matthew and St. Luke, and from the following Epistles: Titus and Hebrews. He alludes to the Gospel of St. Mark, the Acts, and to the following Epistles: Romans, 1 and 2 Corinthians, 1 Timothy, and 1 Peter. Cf. XXXVI, 2 = Hebr. 1, 3 f; XI, 1 = 2 Peter 2, 6 f; XII, 1 = James 2, 25; XXX, 2 = James 4, 6; XXXIV, 3 = Apoc. 22, 12.

[6] The Epistle of Barnabas also quotes from the Gospels of St. Matthew and St. Mark, and from the following Epistles: Romans, 2 Timothy, Titus, and 1 Peter. It alludes to the Gospel of St. Luke, and to the Epistle to the Galatians. Cf. XV, 4 = 2 Pet. 3, 8.

[7] St. Ignatius Martyr of Antioch also quotes from the Gospels of St. Matthew, St. Luke, and St. John, the Acts, and from the following Epistles: Romans, 1 and 2 Corinthians, Ephesians, Colossians, and 1 Thessalonians. He alludes to 2 Thessalonians, 2 Timothy, and 1 Peter. Cf. *Ep. ad Eph.*, V, 3 = James 4, 6.

[8] St. Polycarp also quotes from the four canonical Gospels, the Acts, and the following Epistles: Romans, 1 and 2 Corinthians, Galatians, Ephesians, Philippians, Colossians, 2 Thessalonians, 1 and 2 Timothy, 1 Peter and 1 John. Cf. *Ep. ad Philip.*, VI, 3 = Hebr. 12, 28; XII, 2 = Hebr. 6, 20 and 7, 3; VII, 1 = 2 John 7; XII, 3 = James 1, 4.

Art. 2. The Crisis of Marcionism and Montanism, A.D. 150-210.[14]

Up to the time of St. Justin the Christians had learned directly from the Apostles the teaching of Our Lord. The writings of the Apostles were considered rules of faith and conduct. Tertullian, writing about 200, aptly sums up this doctrine with the words: "The Roman Church unites the Law and the Prophets in one volume with the writings of the Evangelists and Apostles, from which she drinks in her faith" (*De præscr.*, XXXVI).

Marcion (135/140—170), the heretic, is the most important second-century witness for the history of the Canon. He extended the pagan Christian tendency to its extreme limits. In his work called *Antitheses* he rejected the entire Old Testament, and of the New Testament writings he acknowledged only an abbreviated form of St. Luke's Gospel and the first ten Pauline Epistles. Consequently, he repudiated the Pastoral Epistles, the Epistle to the Hebrews, and other Apostolic writ-

[9] Papias, Bishop of Hierapolis in Phrygia (c. 130), definitely refers to the Gospels of St. Matthew and St. Mark, and alludes to the Gospel of St. John, 1 Peter, and 1 John. Andrew of Cæsarea maintains that Papias taught that the Apocalypse was inspired.

[10] Pseudo-Clement (A.D. 140) also quotes from the four Gospels, Acts, all of the Pauline Epistles (with the exception of Philemon), 1 Peter, and 1 John. Cf. XI, 6 = Hebr. 10, 23; XV, 1 = James 5, 19 f; XVII, 7 = Apoc. 11, 13.

[11] The "Shepherd of Hermas" also quotes from the four Gospels, the Acts, and from the following Epistles: Romans, 2 Corinthians, Ephesians, Philippians, 1 Thessalonians, and 1 Peter. It alludes to 1 Corinthians, 2 Thessalonians, 1 and 2 Timothy, and 1 John. Cf. Vis. II, ii, 7 = Hebr. 11, 33; Vis. II, iii, 2 = Hebr. 3, 12; Vis. III, vii, 2 = Hebr. 3, 12; Vis. IV, iii, 4 = 2 Pet. 2, 20; Sim. VIII, vi, 4 = James 2, 7; Mandate XII, vi, 3 = James 4, 12; Vis. IV, ii, 1 = Apoc. 21, 2.

[12] The Martyrdom of Polycarp also quotes from the Gospels of St. Matthew and St. John, Acts, Epistle of St. Jude, and the Apocalypse; there seems to be an allusion to the Gospel of St. Mark and 1 Peter.

[13] St. Justin the Apologist (c. 100/110—162/163), also quotes from the Gospels of St. Matthew and St. Luke; he alludes to the Gospels of St. Mark and St. John, Acts, and to the following Epistles: Romans, 1 and 2 Corinthians, Galatians, Ephesians, Philippians, Colossians, 2 Thessalonians, 1 Peter, and 1 John. Of the deutero-canonical books he quotes from the Apocalypse (cf. *Dial. c. Tryphone*, LXXXI, 4), and alludes to the Epistle to the Hebrews (*ibid.*, XIII, 1) and the Epistle of St. James (cf. *II Apol.*, VII, 1).

[14] Cf. Lagrange, M. J., "Histoire ancienne etc.," 44-57.

ings. His limited Canon of the New Testament writings does not prove that he was unacquainted with the other sacred writings, but merely shows that Marcion rejected them, because he thought that the Apostles who wrote these Epistles were too Jewish.

The two outstanding adversaries against Marcion were St. Irenæus (who fought him from the point of view of philosophy), and Tertullian (who assailed him from the legalistic point of view). Although St. Justin Martyr wrote a treatise against Marcion, this work has been lost.

St. Irenæus (135/140—202/203) specifically proves that the writings of the New Testament were of Apostolic origin (*Adv. Hær.*, III, *Præf.*). He insists upon the fact that this Apostolic preaching is authoritative, and then speaks of the four Gospels having been written severally by St. Matthew in Hebrew, by St. Mark the disciple and interpreter of St. Peter, by St. Luke the companion of St. Paul, and by St. John the disciple of the Lord and published at Ephesus (*Adv. Hær.*, III, 1). He accepts only four canonical Gospels and rejects all apocryphal Gospels (*Adv. Hær.*, III, xi, 8). Furthermore, he shows that St. Paul's preaching coincides exactly with the witness of St. Luke in the Acts of the Apostles (*Adv. Hær.*, III, xiii, 3, and xv, 1). Besides, St. Irenæus in his many writings either quotes from or alludes to all of the Pauline writings with the exception of the Epistle to Philemon, but he does not believe the author of the Epistle to the Hebrews to have been St. Paul. He also made use of the Catholic Epistles with the exception of 2 Peter and 3 John. His witness for the Apocalypse of St. John is clear (*Adv. Hær.*, V, xxvi, 1).

Though unfortunately St. Irenæus does not give a complete list of the books of the New Testament, he made use of all the sacred books with the exception of the following three Epistles: Philemon, 2 Peter, and 3 John. Although he quotes from the Shepherd of Hermas, he did not acknowledge it as part of the Sacred Scriptures.

Tertullian (160—240/250) maintains that Marcion as a non-Christian had acquired no right to use the Christian Scriptures

(*De Præscr.*, XXXVII), and that the books of the New Testament are of Apostolic origin. He insists that Marcion had mutilated the Gospel of St. Luke, and that there are four Gospels: two by the Apostles, St. John and St. Matthew, and two by Apostolic men, St. Luke and St. Mark (*Contra Marcionem*, IV, ii and v). In his various works he also refers directly to Acts (*De Jejunio*, II and X) and to thirteen Pauline Epistles (*Contra Marcionem*, IV, v, V, xix), but he attributes the Epistle to the Hebrews to Barnabas (*De Pudic.*, XX). He also refers to 1 Peter (*De Oratione*, XX), to 1 John (*De Pudic.*, XIX), probably to the Epistle of St. James (*Scorpiace*, XII), to Jude (*De Cultu Fem.*, I, iii), and to the Apocalypse (*De Pudic.*, XX; *De Præscr.*, XXXIII). There seems to be no references to three Epistles: 2 Peter, 2 and 3 John.

From the various texts of the New Testament quoted by Tertullian and from their similarity with the Scriptural texts of later Latin writers, it seems very likely that he made use of a Latin version, which probably also contained the three deutero-canonical Epistles, although to these he does not refer.

The Montanists, so-called after its founder Montanus (c. 160) of Phrygia in Asia Minor, pretended to experience the revelation of the Advocate or Paraclete promised in the Fourth Gospel. This sect acknowledged the books of the Old and New Testaments, with the exception of the Epistle to the Hebrews. Their own revelations were collected and called the "third or newest testament." These were placed beside the canonical Scriptures and at times considered as having greater authority. Tertullian became one of the outstanding members of this sect.

Art. 3. Ecclesiastical Tradition from 210 to c. 350

During the third and early half of the fourth century the witnesses throughout the East and the West to the contents of the Canon of the New Testament are both clear and valuable.

(*a*) *At Rome.*—St. Hippolytus (170/175—235) was a recognized scholar of the Roman Church, and many of his writings are known to us. Modern scholars now ascribe to him the *Philosophoumena*, formerly declared to be the work of Origen, and the Muratorian Fragment.[15] In his writings St. Hippolytus cites all the books of the New Testament with the exception of three short Epistles: Philemon, 2 and 3 John. In the Muratorian Fragment (E.B., 1-7) five Epistles are omitted: (Hebrews, 1-2 Peter, James, and 3[?] John). Hippolytus states that some Christians did not wish to read in church the Apocalypse of Peter, and he excludes the Epistles to the Laodiceans and to the Alexandrians as well as the "Shepherd of Hermas."

Novatian (c. 250) is the first Latin writer of the Roman community known to us. In his writings he either alludes to or quotes from all of the books of the New Testament with the possible exception of the Epistle to the Hebrews.

Because of the numerous persecutions of Christians there are no further writings of importance until the middle of the fourth century. During the persecution of Diocletian (285-305) orders were given by the Emperor to destroy the Christian Scriptures by fire.

(b) *In Africa.*—St. Cyprian (210-258), Bishop of Carthage, does not speak of the Gospels or the Acts, but these books do not concern us at present. He quotes from ten Pauline Epistles (failing to mention Philemon and doubting the origin of the Epistle to the Hebrews), and from 1 Peter, 1 John, and the Apocalypse. A brief treatise called *Ad Novatianum* (c. 253), once attributed to him, cites as Scripture both the Epistle to the Hebrews and the Epistle of St. Jude. About the same time Bishop Aurelius of Chullabi quotes from 2 John. Thus, for this period there are only lacking references to the following Epistles: Philemon, 2 Peter, 3 John, and James.

In an African Canon of 359, which has been edited by
* Mommsen, mention is made of twenty-four books of the New

---

[15] Cf. Lagrange, M. J., "Histoire ancienne, etc.," 66-84. This fragment, a mutilated MS. of the eighth century, was first edited by Muratori at Milan in 1740.

Testament, the omissions being the Epistles to the Hebrews, of James, and of Jude.[16]

(c) *At Alexandria.*—Clement (150—211/216) omits references only to the Epistles to Philemon, 2 Peter, and 3 John. Origen (185/186—254/255), in his homily to Josue (VII, 1), gives the complete canon of twenty-seven books; the same may be said of Dionysius (190-265), with this reservation that he ascribed the Apocalypse to an unknown John of Ephesus.

Amongst the early manuscripts from Egypt evidence for the wide circulation of the Gospels and the Acts may be seen in the papyrus fragments. Worthy of notice is P^{52} (Papyrus Rylands of the early second century), which is the earliest known fragment of any MS. of the New Testament and an important proof for the early circulation of the Fourth Gospel in Egypt. The Chester Beatty collection contains: P^{45} of the early third century, with fragments of the four Gospels and Acts; P^{46} of the early third century, which originally contained the following ten Epistles of St. Paul—Romans, Hebrews, 1 and 2 Corinthians, Ephesians, Galatians, Philippians, Colossians, 1 and 2 Thessalonians; P^{47} of the third century with fragments of the Apocalypse. Further evidence for the usage of deutero-canonical books may be had in P^{13} and P^{17} of the fourth century for the Epistle to the Hebrews, P^{20} of the third century and P^{23} for the Epistle of St. James, P^{18} of the third-fourth century and P^{24} of the fourth century for the Apocalypse. Amongst the uncials, *Codex Sinaiticus* of the early fourth century contains the entire New Testament; *Codex Alexandrinus* of the early fifth century contains all the books of the New Testament, except that some passages in the Gospels of Matthew and John and in the second Epistle to the Corinthians have been lost by mutilation; *Codex Vaticanus* of the early fourth century contains all the books of the New Testament up to the Epistle to the Hebrews 9, 14.

(d) *In Palestine.*—Eusebius of Cæsarea (265-340) gives a

---

[16] Cf. Lagrange, M. J., "Histoire ancienne, etc.," 86-88.

complete list of twenty-seven books comprising the New Testament. He divides them into three classes: (1) *homologoumena* or universally acknowledged: 22 books, i.e., the four Gospels, Acts, fourteen Pauline Epistles, 1 Peter, 1 John, and finally the Apocalypse with the qualification "if it be thought right"; (2) *antilegomena* or disputed: 5 books, i.e., James, Jude, 2 Peter, 2 and 3 John; (3) *spurious:* Apocalypse. Thus, Eusebius is undecided where to place the Apocalypse, and he is further influenced by Dionysius in distinguishing between John the Apostle and John the Presbyter. To John the Apostle he ascribes the Gospel and the First Epistle, to John the Presbyter he ascribes the Apocalypse and the Second and Third Epistles (Eusebius, *Hist. Eccl.*, III, 25 and 39).

St. Cyril of Jerusalem (313/315—386) in his *Catechesis* (IV, 36), composed probably about the year 348, gives a complete Canon of the New Testament, omitting only the Apocalypse.

(e) *In Asia Minor.*—St. Firmillian, Bishop of Cæsarea in Cappadocia, in a letter to St. Cyprian written in 256, explicitly refers to the deutero-canonical Epistle, 2 Peter.

St. Methodius, Bishop of Olympus (d. 311), who was the relentless adversary of Origen, cites all the books of the New Testament with the exception of two Epistles, 2 Thessalonians and Philemon. He ascribes the Epistle to the Hebrews to St. Paul and the Apocalypse to St. John.

Canon 60 of the Council of Laodicea, held about 360 in Phrygia, gives a complete list of the books of the New Testament with the exception of the Apocalypse (E.B., 10), and very likely this omission was due to the influence of Eusebius and the Church of Antioch.

Of the three Cappadocian Fathers, St. Basil (330-379) admits all the books comprising the Canon of the New Testament. St. Gregory of Nazianzus (328/329—389/390), in a poem entitled "De veris libris Scripturæ divinitus inspiratæ," gives a list of all the books of the New Testament; although there is no explicit reference to the Apocalypse, it is possible that an implicit reference is contained in the line: "Joannes

omnibus præco ad cœlos usque pertingens." [17]   St. Gregory of
Nyssa (335-394) undoubtedly was influenced by his brother,
St. Basil, even though there is little evidence that he made use
of all the books of the New Testament.

St. Amphilochius (340/345—403), Bishop of Iconium, a contemporary and friend of the three Cappadocian Fathers gives
a complete Canon of twenty-seven books.

(f) *The Antiochian Church*.—For the history of the origins
of Christianity, Syria occupies the first place by reason of its
antiquity. Antioch was the place where the followers of Christ
were first called Christians. It was known for the stay of St.
Peter and St. Paul, for the activity of St. Ignatius Martyr,
and was the seat of a bishopric. In the fourth century Rome,
Alexandria, and Antioch were the three capitals of Christianity. The primacy and jurisdiction of Rome were uncon-
tested, but Alexandria and Antioch vied with each other for
the second place of honor, which, however, Constantinople
won for itself after the Council of 361.[18]

St. Theophilus (115—182/183), the sixth Bishop of Antioch,
attributes perfect equality to the books of the Old and New
Testaments (*Ad Autolycum*, III, 12), and asserts that the
Evangelists were inspired. He is the first Father to ascribe
explicitly the Fourth Gospel to John the Apostle (*ibid.*, II, 22).
St. Jerome tells us that he composed a harmony of the four
Gospels. In his work, entitled *Ad Autolycum*, he makes use of
the following Epistles: Romans, 1 Corinthians, Colossians, 1
Timothy, and, according to Eusebius (*Hist. Eccl.*, IV, 24), also
of the Apocalypse. Since some of his writings are lost, it is
impossible to know the extent of the Canon in the opinion of
St. Theophilus.

Both Serapion, Bishop of Antioch (191-212), and Paul of
Samosata (condemned in A.D. 268 for denying the divinity of
Christ) were viewed with suspicion. We know little of the
extent of their Canons.

Lucian (d. 312) revised the Greek texts of both the Old and

---

[17] Cf. Lagrange, M. J., "Histoire ancienne, etc.," 116 f.
[18] Cf. Lagrange, M. J., "Histoire ancienne, etc.," 120.

New Testaments. We do not know what books comprised his New Testament version, but it is very likely that he, like the other Syrian Fathers, acknowledged the four Gospels, Acts, the fourteen Pauline Epistles, James, 1 Peter, and 1 John— that is, twenty-two books.

(g) *The Syrian Church.*—Christianity was well established in the region about Antioch, where the Greek language was employed. But the people in the small villages and in the rural sections spoke for the most part Aramaic. This Semitic dialect had two principal centers, namely at Adiabene (the modern Mossul) and Edessa (the modern Orfa), with the neighboring town of Nisibis near Persia.

Tatian (120—after 173) of Adiabene is best known for his *Diatessaron,* a Gospel-harmony compiled from the four Gospels; but according to Eusebius (*Hist. Eccl.,* IV, 29) he altered certain expressions of the Apostles under the pretext of correcting the style.

Aphraates (275/285—356) quotes from the four Gospels (perhaps according to the *Diatessaron*), the Acts, and all the Pauline Epistles, excepting 2 Thessalonians, Titus and Philemon. He has perhaps also an allusion to the Apocalypse. It is worthy of note that he quotes from an apocryphal Epistle of St. Paul to the Corinthians, which in reality is an excerpt from the apocryphal Acts of Paul.

St. Ephraem (306-373), the deacon of Nisibis and Edessa, wrote one commentary on the *Diatessaron* of Tatian and another on fourteen Epistles of St. Paul; for the Epistle to Philemon, however, he substituted the apocryphal Epistle to the Corinthians. There is no evidence that he made use of 2 and 3 John or of Jude, since these Catholic Epistles were not as yet translated into Syriac and neither Aphraates nor St. Ephraem understood Greek.

In a Syriac Canon composed about the end of the fourth century mention is made of the four Gospels, the Acts, fourteen (canonical) Pauline Epistles. The Catholic Epistles and the Apocalypse are not mentioned, but some of these were added in the fifth century, and others even later.

The evidence for this period of ecclesiastical tradition between 210 and 350 shows that the apocryphal books were for the most part definitely excluded and never received universal recognition. Furthermore, it can be seen that at the beginning of this period a complete Canon was given by Origen, and that, in spite of the strenuous objections in the third century to the deutero-canonical books, they were not rejected but retained.

Art. 4. The First Stabilization of the Canon 350-405

Between 350 and 405 took place what is called the first stabilization of the Canon to distinguish it from its definitive stabilization wrought by the Council of Trent. During this period the complete Canon of New Testament books was established both in Egypt and in the West.

(a) *In Egypt.*—St. Athanasius (295-373), Patriarch of Alexandria, gives us in one of his festal epistles a complete Canon of twenty-seven books of the New Testament, which is the same as that proposed over a century before by Origen.

(b) *In Gaul.*—St. Hilary of Poitiers (315—367/368) did not compose a list of books comprising the New Testament Canon as he did for the Old Testament, but he undoubtedly acknowledged the proto-canonical books. He also attributed the Epistle to the Hebrews to St. Paul, and made use of the Epistle of James and 2 Peter and of the Apocalypse, which he ascribed to John. Thus, he omitted references to the three deutero-canonical books, Jude, 2 and 3 John.

(c) *In Spain.*—Priscillian, Bishop of Abila in Lusitania (c. 380), was the founder of an heretical sect, which recognized both the proto-canonical and deutero-canonical books, and failed to mention only 3 John.

(d) *In Italy.*—St. Ambrose (340-397), Bishop of Milan, made use of all the proto-canonical and deutero-canonical books. The only writings of the New Testament about which there is any doubt are 2 and 3 John. He ascribed the Epistle to the Hebrews to St. Paul and the Apocalypse to St. John.

Ambrosiaster (c. 370), whatever his identity may be, edited

a commentary to thirteen Epistles of St. Paul; he omitted the Epistle to the Hebrews, which he considered as canonical but not Pauline. In the two extant works which bear his name, he makes use of all the books of the New Testament with the exception of the Epistle of St. Jude.

(e) *In Africa.*—St. Augustine (354-430), Bishop of Hippo, in his book entitled *Doctrina Christiana* (397), gives us a complete list of New Testament books which is identical with the canonical lists of Origen and St. Athanasius. Under his influence the Council of Hippo (October 8, 393) and the two Councils of Carthage (397 and 419) repeated this same Canon (E.B., 12, 14).

(f) *At Rome.*—The so-called Gelasian Decree (492-496), attributed by some writers to Pope Damasus (c. 382), makes mention of the twenty-seven books of the New Testament (E.B., 20). The same complete Canon is given by Pope St. Innocent I in his letter written on February 20, 405, to Bishop Exsuperius of Toulouse (E.B., 16), and by Tyrannius Rufinus (345-410).

At the beginning of the fourth century, Pelagius wrote a commentary on the thirteen Epistles of St. Paul, omitting the Epistle to the Hebrews. Besides these Pauline Epistles, he recognized the Epistle of St. James and 2 Peter, and the Apocalypse.

Art. 5.   The Last Hesitations in the East

(a) *The Position of St. Jerome.*—St. Jerome (d. 420), like Clement of Alexandria, was both a priest and a scholar. At his time the complete list of twenty-seven books comprising the New Testament literature was an established fact. Being a keen critic and an observant reader, he knew the difficulties and doubts relative to some of the deutero-canonical books and greatly magnified them.

In a letter to Paulinus, written about the year 394 (M.L., XXII, 548 f), he gave a complete list of canonical books, which is identical with the list of the African churches. He does not deny the canonicity of the deutero-canonical books, and in his letter to Dardanus written about 414 (M.L., XXII, 1103) even defends the Pauline authenticity of the Epistle to the Hebrews and the Joannine authenticity of the Apocalypse, but he mentions the doubts and hesitations of some of the writers of the past.[19]

(b) *The Isolated Position and Uncertainties of the Oriental Church.*—Constantine transformed Byzantium into a second Rome, and after the Council of Constantinople in 381 this city became second in importance within the Empire, superseding both Alexandria and Antioch. In the subsequent period it was isolated from both Egypt and the West in regard to its Canon of the New Testament, and received very little support for its position. The doubts and hesitations centered chiefly about four short Catholic Epistles (2 Peter, 2 and 3 John, Jude) and the Apocalypse.

St. John Chrysostom (344-407) does not give a catalogue of sacred books, although he wrote very extensively. He seems to have followed the Lucian revision of the New Testament, which would have omitted four Epistles (2 Peter, 2 and 3 John, Jude) and the Apocalypse. Theodoret (393-457) followed the same Canon as Chrysostom.

Theodore of Mopsuestia (350-428) is unique in his position. He rejects three Catholic Epistles (James, 1 Peter, and 1 John) that had been acknowledged by other writers, and never refers to them in his writings.

In the Apostolic Constitutions (c. 400) no mention is made of the Catholic Epistles or the Apocalypse, since these books were perhaps not used in the liturgy of the Syrian churches.

Other witnesses worthy of mention are: Cosmas Indicopleustes (c. 547), who recognizes the Catholic Epistles (James, 1 Peter and 1 John) and declares the other four Epistles (2 Peter, 2 and 3 John, Jude) are controverted; the Council of

[19] For the Epistle to the Hebrews cf. *De vir. ill.*, V (M.L., XXII, 647 ff); for the Second Epistle of St. Peter, cf. *De vir. ill.*, I (M.L., XXIII, 638); for the Epistle of St. James, cf. *De vir. ill.*, II (M.L., XXIII, 639); for the Epistle of St. Jude, cf. *De vir. ill.*, IV (M.L., XXIII, 646); for the Second and Third Epistles of St. John, cf., *De vir. ill.*, IX (M.L., XXIII, 655).

116 A COMPANION TO SCRIPTURE STUDIES

Trullo (692), which insists upon no particular Canon, but ratifies the various Canons already accepted; Leontius of Byzantium (485-543), who in his Canon gives a complete list of sacred books of the New Testament; Andrew, Bishop of Cæsarea in Cappadocia (c. 600), who defends the canonicity and authenticity of the Apocalypse on the authority of the Fathers.

(c) *The Syriac Church.*—The Peshitto version was most likely the work of Rabbula, Bishop of Edessa (412-435), and originally contained the four Gospels, Acts, fourteen Pauline Epistles, 1 Peter, 1 John, and James, that is, twenty-two books. The four shorter Catholic Epistles and the Apocalypse were still missing when the Syrian Church split into two irreconcilable factions, the Nestorians and the Monophysites or Jacobites.

The Nestorians, who believed in the existence of two persons in Christ, retired to Persia and later introduced Christianity into China. They retained the Peshitto version of the New Testament with its limited Canon.

The Monophysites, who professed one nature in Christ, accepted the four shorter Catholic Epistles (2 Peter, 2 and 3 John, and Jude) and the Apocalypse after their condemnation by the Fourth General Council of Chalcedon in 451. This is evident from the New Testament version by Philoxenus of Mabbug (507), which was revised in 616 by Thomas of Harkel. The Council of Florence (1441), in its Decree for the Jacobites, ordered that the twenty-seven books of the New Testament were to be held as inspired and canonical (E.B., 32).

Art. 6. From the Sixth Century to Our Own Time

(a) *The Middle Ages (692-1517).*—Some of the Greek writers repeat certain of the ancient Canons, and leave out the Apocalypse. Nicephorus (d. 828), Patriarch of Constantinople, acknowledges all the books of the New Testament with the exception of the Apocalypse, and Photius (d. 891) most

likely held the same opinion.[20]   On the other hand, Nicephorus
Callistus of the fourteenth century has a complete Canon.   To
the inspired and canonical books of the New Testament St.
John of Damascus (d. 754) added the Canons of the Apostles.

The doubts that occur in rare instances among Latin writers
about some of the deutero-canonical books were due to the
critical remarks of St. Jerome.   Prescinding from Junilius
Africanus (c. 550), who seemed to follow the Canon of Theodore of Mopsuestia, and from St. Isidore of Seville (d. 636),
who merely repeats the doubts of St. Jerome about some
Epistles but admits their inspiration, we find only two further
witnesses worthy of mention in the West.   John of Salisbury
(d. 1183) wished to include the apocryphal Epistle of St. Paul
to the Laodiceans among the canonical Epistles of St. Paul.
Cardinal Cajetan (d. 1534) held that the Epistle to the
Hebrews and four Catholic Epistles (James, 2 and 3 John,
and Jude) were of doubtful authority.

(b) *The Council of Trent (1546)*.—The first Reformers did
not agree on the extent of the Canon of the New Testament.
Luther excluded the Apocalypse and three Epistles (Hebrews,
James, and Jude).   Zwingli rejected the Apocalypse, and
Œcolampadius eliminated all the deutero-canonical books.
The Lutheran Chemnitz (d. 1588) excluded all the deutero-
canonical books as being inferior, and this policy was followed
by the Lutherans till the seventeenth century.   Since, however,
the Calvinists did not take any decisive stand against the
seven deutero-canonical books, the Lutherans returned to the
complete Canon with this slight difference, that the four books
rejected by Luther occupied the last position in printed editions of Lutheran Bibles.

After several congregations of theologians had met and had
discussed the books and the text of the Bible, the Council of
Trent in its Decree "Sacrosancta" of April 8, 1546, formally
and definitely canonized the twenty-seven books for the first
time, and made it an article of faith for all Christians to believe in their divine inspiration (E.B., 44 f).   While the Vati-

[20] Cf. Zarb, S., *op. cit.,* 450 f.

can Council (1869-1870) did not repeat the Canon of sacred
books determined by the Council of Trent, it confirmed the
Decree "Sacrosancta."

CHAPTER III

THE UNCANONICAL OR APOCRYPHAL BOOKS
OF THE BIBLE

Besides the canonical books of the Old and New Testaments which the Church acknowledges as sacred and inspired, there is an entirely separate religious literature comprising books which were once declared to belong to the Old or New Testament, and which are called therefore *apocryphal* (lit., hidden, concealed).

Amongst the pagans the word *apocryphal* was used to designate secret books containing esoteric doctrines, known only to the initiated. The Jews distinguished between *genuzim* books and *hitsonim* books; the former were "put aside" by reason of old age and mutilation, whilst the latter represented those which were placed "outside" of the list of sacred books and thus to some degree might be considered apocryphal by the Jews.

The Fathers, apologists, and ecclesiastical writers understood the term in many ways. To some (e.g., St. Jerome, St. Augustine) apocryphal books meant books of hidden origin or false authorship. To others (e.g., Origen, St. Augustine) they designated books containing things contrary to faith or that were otherwise objectionable. To some (e.g., Rufinus, Origen) they signified books which were not allowed to be read in the public services of the Church. To others (e.g., St. Jerome) they meant books which were not canonical.

The purpose of the writers of these apocryphal books varied. Among the writers of the Old Testament apocrypha a threefold aim was possible: *halachic* (i.e., juridical), to strengthen the Mosaic Law through new regulations and interpretations; *haggadic* (i.e., moral), to adorn the biblical narrative with fictitious stories or details at times and to give advice for instilling piety; *apocalyptic* (or prophetical), to engender hope

among oppressed Jews by publicizing in the name of a patriarch or a prophet their liberation and their salvation through
the Messias. The Christian apocryphal writings were often
intended merely to satisfy the curiosity of the faithful by
supplying accounts omitted by the New Testament books, but
often they were composed by heretics and publicized under
fictitious names in support of their false and erroneous doctrines.

The severe policy of the Church in regard to the apocryphal
books explains the reason why so many of these books are
known to us at present only by name. However, many of
these books are still extant.

The apocryphal books may be studied by the biblical interpreter with great fruit. The apocryphal books of the Old
Testament throw a light on the religious and moral opinions,
messianic hopes, and historical conditions prevailing among
the Jews at the time of their composition. The apocryphal
books of the New Testament help to appraise the doctrines
and opinions prevailing amongst the faithful and the heretics
during the first centuries of Christianity. Often they contained material worthy of credence; for example, the Protoevangelium of James is the first document to mention the
parents of our Blessed Lady and her presentation in the temple.

Many of these writings were held in the greatest esteem by
the Fathers and early Christian writers. The Septuagint and
some of the MSS. of the Old Latin contain 3 Esdras. The
Sistine-Clementine edition of the Vulgate adds after the
canonical books the Prayer of Manasses, 3 and 4 Esdras, and
the Roman liturgy makes use of some of the apocryphal texts.

Art. 1.　The Apocryphal Books of the Old Testament

Bibliography: * Bousset-Gressmann, W., "Die Religion des Judentums
im späthellenistischen Zeitalter" (3rd ed., Tübingen, 1926), 6-52;
* Charles, R. H., "The Apocrypha and Pseudepigrapha of the Old Testa-
ment in English" (2 vols., Oxford, 1913); Felten, J., "Neutestamentliche
Zeitgeschichte," I (2nd and 3rd ed., Regensburg, 1925), 537-642; Frey,
J. B., in D.D.L.B., (Suppl.) s.v. *Apocryphes de l'Ancien Testament;*
* Kautzsch, E., "Die Apokryphen and Pseudepigraphen des Alten Testa-

mentes" (2 vols., Tübingen, 1900-1921); Lagrange, M. J., "Le Messianisme chez les Juifs" (Paris, 1909); Reissler, P., "Altjüdisches Schrifttum ausserhalb der Bibel" (Augsburg, 1928); *Schuerer, E., "Geschichte des Jüdischen Volkes." III (4th ed., Leipzig, 1909), 268-407, 524-528, 555-592; Székely S., "Bibliotheca Apocrypha," I (Freiburg i. Br., 1913); *Eissfeldt, O., "Einleitung in das A.T." (Tübingen, 1934), 658-692; *Bentzen, A., "Introduction to the O.T." (Copenhagen, 1948), 236-252; *Pfeiffer, R.H., "History of New Testament Times" (New York, 1949).

These books may conveniently be placed in two general categories: (a) those of Palestinian origin, and (b) those of Hellenistic origin. In both of these classes the aims of the writers are manifested by the contents of their books.

(a) THE APOCRYPHAL BOOKS OF PALESTINIAN ORIGIN

Intertestamental Period

Besides the proto-canonical books (except Esther) and commentaries (*pesharim*) to some of these books (Habakkuk, Micah, Psalms, Nahum, Isaiah) contained in the Palestinian Canon and three deutero-canonical books (Tobias, Sirach, and the Epistle of Jeremias) in the Alexandrian Canon, the Essene community of Qumran on the Dead Sea (c. 150 B.C.-A.D. 68) left behind manuscripts (some of which are now preserved in fragmentary form) not only of the commonly known apocryphal books of the Old Testament (e.g., the Books of Henoch and Jubilees; the Testaments of the Twelve Patriarchs), but also others hitherto unknown (e.g., A Description of the Heavenly Jerusalem) and their own sectarian literature (e.g., The Damascus Document; the Rule of War; the Hymns).[1]

(1) *The Book of Henoch.*[2] Apocalyptic and eschatological

[1]Cf. Frey, J.B., *op. cit.*, 357; Milik, J.T., "Ten Years of Discovery in the Wilderness of Judaea" (London, 1959); Burrows, M., "The Dead Sea Scrolls" (New York [10th printing] 1957); Vermes, G., "Discovery in the Judean Desert" (New York, 1956); * Gaster, T. H., "Dead Sea Scriptures in English Translation" (Garden City, N. Y., 1956); *Revue de Qumran* (Paris, 1958-).

[2]Cf. Vitti, A., "Ultime critiche su Enoc etiopico," in *Biblica*, 12 (1931), 316-325; Da S. Marco, E., "Il concetto di giustizia dell' Enoc Ethiopico e S. Paolo," in *Biblica*, 18 (1937), 277-302, 383-417; * Torrey, C. C., "Notes on the Greek Texts of Enoch," in J.A.O.S., 70 (1942), 52-60; *Zuntz, G., "Notes on the Greek Enoch," in J.B.L., 61 (1942), 193-204. Cf. also Gry,

in character, this work is of the greatest importance for the knowledge of Jewish theology in the second century B.C. It was used as an authoritative work by other apocryphal writers, by the Fathers, and by ecclesiastical writers. The original work was written probably in Aramaic (now represented by ten or more fragmentary manuscripts from Qumran Cave IV) and was translated into Greek. This Greek version (preserved partly in the Chester Beatty and the University of Michigan collections of the fourth or possibly fifth century A.D. [Henoch 97-107]; in an eighth century manuscript of Akhmin in Upper Egypt [Henoch 1, 1-32, 6]; and in some long quotations by Syncellus, a Byzantine writer (c. A.D. 800) served as the basis of the Ethiopic (fourth or fifth century after Christ) and Latin translations.

The Ethiopic translation of the book does not represent a literary unity. It is a redaction of various unconnected parts expressing the religious and moral opinions of the Jewish people. The Patriarch Henoch, who walked with God and was taken up to heaven by Him (Gen. 5, 24), appears throughout the work and thus confers upon it a loose unity.

The Ethiopic work consists of five sections preceded by an introduction and followed by a conclusion.

Introduction. Announcement of the Last Judgment of the World (1-5).

I. *Book of Angels and Universe* (6-36). It treats of the fall of the angels, their punishment, and of Henoch's journeys through the earth and sheol.

II. *Book of Parables and Similitudes* or the *Book of the*

L., "Hénoch X, 19 et les belles promesses de Papias," in R.B., 53 (1946), 197-206; Milik, J. T., "The Dead Sea Scrolls Fragment of the Book of Enoch," in *Biblica,* 32 (1951), 393-400; Grelot, P., "L'eschatologie des Esseniens et le livre d'Hénoch," in *Rev. de Qum.,* 1 (1958, 113-132; *idem,* La géographie mythique d'Hénoch et ses sources Orientales," in R.B., 65 (1958), 33-69; Milik, J. T., "Henoch au pays des aromates (ch. xxvii a xxxii). Fragments araméens de la grotte 4 de Qumran," in R.B., 65 (1958), 70-77.

Messias (37-69). There is a general description of the eternal mansions of the righteous and the wicked after the judgment and the development of the theme of Messias as "The Son of Man."

III. *Book of Astronomy* (72-82). It explains current ideas about the courses of the sun, moon, stars, winds, etc.

IV. *Book of Historical Visions* (83-90). It describes the history of the world (i.e., from Adam to the establishment of the Messianic Kingdom) where people are represented as different animals.

V. *Parenetic (Exhortatory) Book. Apocalypse of Weeks* (91-105). Henoch admonishes the just to remain faithful, to keep firm in their Jewish faith, and gives them a glimpse at the eternal rewards. There is also a description of the world drama in ten acts, or periods, from Henoch's birth to the Messianic judgment; of these ten periods, seven have already passed, while the other three are to come.

Conclusion. The Miracles and Signs at the Birth of Noe; The Last Admonition of Henoch (106-108).

It is important to note that sections I and IV are represented by five Aramaic manuscripts from Qumran Cave IV. Similarly section III on astronomy is exhibited by four Aramaic manuscripts from Cave IV. Finally, part of section V has been preserved by one manuscript from the same cave which seems to have contained the main library of the Essene convent (c. 150 B.C.-A.D. 68). These sections are intimately linked in the Machabean history. It is to be noted that Section II, or the "Book of Parables," i.e., the "Book of the Son of Man," is thus far missing in the Qumran library. Thus it seems very plausible that this Messianic section was added by a Jew or Jewish Christian of the late first or second century A.D., who brought these various isolated sections together and gave them their present form.[3]

---

[3] Cf. Milik, J. T., "Ten years, etc.," 33 f.

(2) *The Book of Jubilees.*[4]—This work is haggadic and halachic in character and owes its name to the fact that it arranges in a chronological order the events recorded in Gen. 1—Ex. 12, that is, the story of salvation from creation to the Sinaitic Covenant in periods of jubilees, of forty-nine years (cf. Lev. 25). The author also proposes a calendar reform based upon a special form of the solar calendar consisting of 52 weeks (364 days) divided into four seasons of 13 weeks each, and each season consisting of three months, and fixed dates for the main festivals.

The book is sometimes called *Leptogenesis* (i.e., Little Genesis) because it gives an interpretation on the Book of Genesis in accordance with the ideas of the author and his contemporaries, or the Essene community. It is likewise designated as the "Apocalypse of Moses," because it treats Moses as the recipient of divine revelations contained in the book to give greater authority to the message of the author.

It is to be carefully noted that this book is one of the rare instances of apocryphal (or pseudepigraphal) writings where there is basically the same textual form for all the texts and versions. This book has been preserved completely in an Ethiopic version and partially (i.e., about one third) in a Latin translation. Both of them were made from a Greek text which, together with a Syriac version, was translated from the Hebrew original text. The Qumran literature of this book is represented by about ten fragmentary Hebrew manuscripts from various caves (I, II, IV). From the historical allusions in the book it seems very probable that it was written before 100 B.C. (Milik).

[4]Cf. Martin, F., "Le Livre des Jubilés, but et procédés de l'auteur; ses doctrines," in R.B. 8 (1911), 321-344, 502-533; Tisserant, E. "Fragments syriaques du Livre des Jubilées," in R.B. 30 (1931), 55-86, 206-232; Vogt, E., "Kalenderfragmente aus Qumran," in *Biblica*, 39 (1958), 72-77; *Baumgarten, J. M., "The Beginning of the Day in the the Calendar of Jubilees," in J.B.L., 77 (1958), 355-360; *Zeitlin, S., "Beginning of the Day in the Calendar of Jubilees," in J.B.L., 78 (1959), 153-156; cf. also *Obermann, J., "Calendaric Elements in the Dead Sea Scrolls," in J.B.L., 75 (1956), 285-297; Jaubert, A., "La date de la céne. Calendrier biblique et liturgic chrétienne" (Paris, 1957).

(3) *The Testaments of the Twelve Patriarchs.*[5]—This work is haggadic in character, and purports to give the last words of Jacob's twelve sons to their children. In every discourse there are three parts: the autobiography of the Patriarch, a moral exhortation, and a prophecy concerning the future destiny of the tribe. The general theme of the book is ethical; thus, Ruben speaks of fornication, Simeon of envy, Levi of pride and the priesthood, Juda of bravery, avarice, and fornication, Issachar of simplicity, Zabulon of compassion and mercy, Dan of anger and lying, Nephtali of goodness, Gad of hatred, Aser of the two ways open to man, either vice or virtue, Joseph of chastity, and Benjamin of an honest mental attitude.

The book was originally written in Hebrew or Aramaic in the second half of the second century B.C. The original Semitic text has been lost, and the Greek text made from the original contains many Christian interpolations. Versions also appeared in Armenian (made from the Greek) and Old Slavic.

There is no trace of the Hebrew or Aramaic archetype in the Qumran literature as the basis for the presently known Greek text. Aramaic fragments of the *Testament of Levi* (from Caves I, IV) do not seem to have any relation to the Greek version, which is known to us, but rather is "identical with that of Aramaic fragments recovered a half a century ago from the Cairo Geniza" (Milik, J.T., *Ten Years, etc.* 34). These fragments, with some special additions (a prayer of Jacob and some liturgical prescriptions), are curiously contained in a tenth-century Greek manuscript on Mount Athos. Various Hebrew fragments of the *Testament of Nephtali* have been discovered, and their differences from the Greek version is evident.

[5]Cf. Greitemann, W., "De Messia ejusque Regno in Testamentis duodecim Patriarcharum," in V.D., 11 (1931), 156-160, 184-192; Uricchio, P., "De Lege et Messia in ordine ad justificationem in Testamentis XII Patriarcharum," in V.D., 26 (1948), 98-103, 152-162, 304-310; Milik, J. T., "Le Testament de Levi en Araméen. Fragment de la grotte 4 de Quamran," in R.B., 62 (1955), 398-406; Grelot, P., "Notes sur le Testament Araméen de Levi," in R.B., 63 (1956), 391-406.

Some scholars (e.g., Milik) on the basis of the Qumran literature maintain that our present *Testaments of the Twelve
Patriarchs* is the composition of one author because of their
uniform literary thought pattern. This author (who was acquainted with the Jewish expectations from the Old Testament
promises and who at the same time put a quasi-Christian stamp
of interpretation upon the Biblical texts) is regarded as a
Jewish Christian of the late first or early second Christian
century.

(4) *The Psalms of Solomon.*[6]—The Psalms, eighteen in
number, are haggadic in character. The author expresses his
entire confidence in the goodness and justice of God, his contempt for sinners who are trampling under their feet things
most sacred to Israel and are indulging in the most shameful
debauchery, his sorrow in view of the misfortunes that are
crushing his native country, his invincible hope of a better
future which the Messias will inaugurate. The most ardent
desire for the coming of the Messias, called "the king, the son
of David," is expressed in Psalms 17 and 18.

These Psalms were composed between the end of the reign
of Alexander Jannæus (that is, about 80 B.C.) and 40 B.C.
Specifically, however, Psalms 8 and 17 were written after the
capture of Jerusalem by Pompey (63 B.C.), and Psalm 2 after
his death in Egypt (September 28, 48 B.C.). The author (if
all were written by the same author) was a pious Jew of
Jerusalem, who composed these Psalms either in Hebrew or
Aramaic. No one can say with certainty why they are
ascribed to Solomon. Either it was the author's name, or perhaps even a title added later by a scribe.

(5-8) *Other Short Apocryphal Qumran Books.* Worthy of
mention among the shorter Dead Sea Scrolls is first of all (5)
a *Genesis Apocryphon*[7] once called the *Lamech Scroll* (because

[6]Cf. Viteau-Martin, "Les Psaumes de Salomon" (Paris, 1911); Ab Alpe,
A., "Christologia in Psalmis Salomonis," in V.D., 11 (1931), 56-59, 84-88.
[7]Cf. *Avigad, N.-*Yadin, Y., "A Genesis Apocryphon" (Jerusalem,
1956); * Kutcher, E. Y., "Dating the Language of the Genesis Apocryphon," in J.B.L., 76 (1957), 288-292; *Lignée, H., "Concordance de 1 Q
Genesis Apocryphon," in *Rev. de Qum.*, 1 (1958), 163-186; *Lehmann,

he is the narrator of a section of the partially preserved second column) containing stories and legends of the Patriarchs. The scroll orginally was about nine feet long. The beginning and end of the scroll are now missing and only three pages (Gen. 12-14) of the original eighteen are complete. This Aramaic scroll from Cave I has a great bearing on the research in the field of Biblical Aramaic and the origins of Biblical Targums. It is dated by some scholars (*Kutscher) as possibly in the first century B.C. (6) A *pseudo-Jeremianic work* is represented by several manuscripts which are loosely connected with the canonical books of the prophet or his secretary Baruch. (7) The so-called *Testimonies Document* (4 Q *Testimonia*)[8] from the fourth Qumran cave and dating from about 100-75 B.C. contains various explanations of four texts, of which all but the last are Biblical quotations (Deut. 5, 28 f and 18, 18 f; Num. 24,15-17; Deut. 33, 8-11; and a citation from an apocryphon called the *Psalms of Joshua*). (8) *The Prayer of Nabonidus*, the insane Neo-Babylonian king who spent seven years in the town of Teima is preserved in a small Aramaic scroll from Cave IV. This text helps us to correct the long suspected copyist's error in Dan. 4, 28-30 where Nabuchodonosor's name occurs.[9]

(9-12) *Qumran Sectarian Literature.*—Most important in the entire library from the viewpoint of the Essenian sect is (9) *The Rule of the Community*,[10] also frequently called *The*

M. R., "1 Q Genesis Apocryphon in the Light of Targumim and Midrashim," in *Rev. de Qum.*, 1 (1958), 249-263; Grelot, P., "Sur l'Apocryphe de la Genesis (col. XX, ligne 26)," in *Rev. de Qum.*, 1 (1958), 273-276.

[8] Cf. *Allegro, J. M., "Further Messianic References in Qumran Literature," in J.B.L., 75 (1956), 182-187; Skehan, P. W., "The Period of the Biblical Texts from Khirbet Qumran," in C.B.Q., 19 (1957), 435-440; Fitzmyer, J. A., "4 Q Testimonia and the New Testament," in *Theol. St.*, 18 (1957), 513-537.

[9] Cf. Steinmueller, J. E.-Sullivan, K., art. "Baltas(s)ar" and "Nabuchodonosor" in C.B.E.O.T.; Milik, J. T., "Prière de Nabonide, etc." in R.B., 63 (1956), 407-415; Vogt, E., "Precatio Nabonid in pia narratione Judaica," in *Biblica*, (37 (1956), 532-534.

[10] Cf. *Brownlee, W. H., "Excerpts from the Translation of the Dead Sea Manual of Discipline," in B.A.S.O.R., 121 (1951), 8-12; *idem*, "Light on the Manual of Discipline from the Book of Jubilees," *ibid.*, 123 (1951),

Manual of Discipline. It has been preserved in an almost complete scroll from Cave I (c.6 feet long and c.9 inches wide) and ten fragments from Cave IV. The author of this rule was, according to some scholars, "the Teacher of Righteousness" (e.g., Milik). Scholars are not in agreement as to its division. Broadly speaking, after a title and introduction (1, 1-15) the first part contains a liturgy for the candidates who enter the covenant and its annual renewal (1,16-3, 12); the second part is doctrinal and gives an explanation of the two spirits in man (3, 13-4, 26); the third part discusses the rules to be observed (5, 1-9, 11) and includes a penal code for the violation of good conduct (6, 24-7, 25); the fourth, or final, part considers the themes of appointed times, seasons, etc. (9, 12-11, 22). This monastic rule contains two additions in the large, fairly complete roll, namely, the *Rule of the Congregation* and a list of *Benedictions.*

(10) The *Damascus* or *Sadokite Document* is the next important one among the strictly sectarian or Essene works. It explains to some extent the origin of the Jewish sect that settled at Qumran, its relations with the Therapeutae of Egypt and the Jewish community at Damascus which is also known to us from the Acts of the Apostles. Two manuscripts of this document were discovered in 1896 in the ruins of a *genizah* (i.e., cellar repository for worn-out manuscripts) in Cairo, Egypt. These eleventh-century manuscripts in good Hebrew were published by *S. Schechter in 1910. Various copies of this document were discovered in the Qumran caves (IV, V, VI), and the oldest of them is dated between 75 and 50 B.C. The Qumran recension is substantially the same as the Cairo A copy, but it also had additions to the both Cairo recensions.

Like the *Rule of the Community,* the *Damascus Docu-*

30-32; Milik, J. T., "Manuale disciplinae," in V.D., 29 (1951), 129-158; Audet, J. P. "Affinites litteraires et doctrinales du Manuel de Discipline," in R.B., 59 (1952), 219-238, 60 (1953), 41-82; Guilbert, P., "Le plan de la Règle de la Communauté," in *Rev. de Qum.,* 1 (1958), 323-344; *idem,* "Deux écritures dans les colonnes VII et VIII de la Règle de la Communauté," *ibid.,* 1 (1958), 199-212.

ment is concerned with the practical organization of the community. The document consists of two parts. The first part (1-9; 19-20), haggadic in character, comments upon God's plan of salvation in history (i.e., in Machabean times), especially relating to the last times (i.e., "from the day when the Teacher of the community died until the rising of the Messiah from Aaron and Israel," 19, 35-20,1), in which the author's center of interest lies in the religious differences and struggles between the members of the Essene sect and the congregation of traitors "under the leadership of a certain scoffer" or "the man of lies" (1, 13-21; 20, 13 ff). The second part (10-18), halachic in character, contains the precise rules of conduct to be observed by the members of the New Covenant in their settlements about Damascus.[11]

(11) *The Rule of the War,* [12] first published as *The War of the Sons of Light against the Sons of Darkness* by E. L. Sukenik and N. Avigad (Jerusalem, 1954 [English edition, Jerusalem, 1955]), contains the greater part of the work and is supplemented by five fragmentary manuscripts from Cave IV. According to some scholars, this book, describing the apocalyptic army of the Essenes, is indirectly based upon the Roman military manual.

(12) *Thankgiving Hymns (Hodayot),* [13] consisting of about

---

[11]Cf. *Rabinowitz, I., "A Reconsideration of 'Damascus' and '390 years' in the 'Damascus ('Zadokite') Fragments," in J.B.L., 73 (1954), 11-35; Milik, J. T., "Ten Years, etc.," 38 f., 58-60, 90 f.

[12]C. Carmignac, J., "Les citations de l'Ancien Testament dans La Guerre des Fils de la luminére contre les fils des ténèbres," in R.B., 67 (1956), 234-260, 375-390; *idem,* "Concordance hebraique de la Règle de la Guerre," in *Rev. de Qum.,* 1 (1958), 7-50.

[13] Cf. Milik, J.T., "Duo cantici ex volumine hymnorum nuper invento ad Mare Mortuum," in V.D., 28 (1950), 362-371; *idem,* "Nota ad volumen hymnorum mss. Maris Mortui," *ibid.,* 29 (1951), 231 f; Bauchet, P.J.M., "Transcription and Translation of a Psalm from Sukenik's Dead Sea Scroll," in C.B.Q., 12 (1950), 331-335; Glanzman, G. C., "Sectarian Psalms from the Dead Sea," in *Theol. St.,* 13 (1952), 487-524; *Chamberlain, J. V.," Another Qumran Thankgiving Psalm," in J.O.N.E.S., 14 (1955), 32-41; Carmignac, J., "Remarques sur le texte des Hymnes de Qumran," in *Bibilica,* 39 (1958), 139-155; Delcor, M.," Cinq nouveaux psaumes esséniens?" in *Rev. de Qum.,* 1 (1958)85-102; Carmignac, J., "Localisation des fragments 15, 18 et 22 des Hymnes," in *Rev. de Qum.,* 1 (1958), 425-430; *Michaud, H., "A propos d'un passage des Hymnes" (1 Q Hodayot, II, 7-14); in *Rev. de Qum,* 1 (1958), 413-416.

twenty Essene Psalms, shows a marked contrast to the apocryphal Psalms of Solomon. This collection of hymns, found at Qumran (a long, badly damaged roll from Cave I and six fragmentary manuscripts from Cave IV), represents a high spiritual level of the relationship existing between God and man that some scholars believe it "could well be at least in part the work of 'the Teacher of Righteousness' himself, or else derived from his oral catechesis" (Milik, J.T., *Ten Years, etc.*, 40).

There are other writings which were found at Qumran, both religious and secular in character, which show the wealth of the Essene library. Worthy of mention are the so-called *mishmarot*, or courses throwing light on the Qumran calendar; an Aramaic *Description of the Heavenly Jerusalem*, [14] a detailed description based on Ezechiel; *horoscopes* and *two copper rolls*[15] describing hidden treasures.

Christian Period[16]

(13-16) There are several apocryphal writings which seemed to have emanated from Jewish Palestinian circles and which

---

[14] Cf. Baillet, M., "Fragments araméens de Qumran 2. Description de la Jérusalem Nouvelle," in R.B., 62 (1955), 22-245.

[15] *Kuhn, K. G., "Les rouleaux de cuivre de Qumran," in R.B., 61 (1954), 193-205; Milik, T., "The Copper Document from Cave III, Qumran," in B.A., 19 (1956), 60-64; *Mowinckel, S., "The Copper Scroll— An Apocryphon," in J.B.L., 76 (1957), 261-265.

[16] No detailed mention need be made of two sites near Qumran. In *Wadi Murabba'at* four caves were discovered in 1951 by Bedouins and explored in 1952 by Pére de Vaux and *G. Lankester Harding, and there were found the earliest Semitic (palimpsest) papyrus (18 x 8 cm. and dating to the eighth century B.C.) and some Biblical and non-literary documents, most of which belonged to the period of the Second Jewish Revolt (A.D. 132-135) and included two original letters of Simeon ben Kosebah (later known as Bar Kochba). Cf. R. de Vaux," Le grottes de Murabba'at et leur documents," in R.B., 60 (1953), 245-267; *idem*, "Quelques textes hebreux de Murabba'at," *ibid.*, 268-275; Milik, J. T., "Une lettre de Siméon bar Kokheba," *ibid.*, 276-294.

The site of *Khirbet Mird* (ancient Hyrcania) was explored by a Belgian expedition in 1952 which discovered fragments of Biblical codices written in Greek uncials containing the Old and New Testaments (between the fifth and eighth centuries A.D.), some parchment fragments and palimpsests of the Bible and a few non-literary texts in Christian Palestinian Aramaic (perhaps of the sixth century A.D.). The occupation of this site was not connected with the Qumran Community.

have not yet been identified with the books of the Qumran library.

(13) *The Assumption of Moses.*[17]—This work is apocalyptic in character, and is also called by scholars the Ascension of Moses or the Testament of Moses. It was first edited in 1861 by Ceriani from a sixth-century Latin MS. found in the Ambrosian library at Milan. The first three lines (which probably also contained the title), as well as the ending of the book, are missing. This book, as it stands, contains the testament of Moses to Josue. Moses before his death appoints Josue as his successor and foretells the future destinies of the people, their entrance to the Promised Land, the schism of the ten tribes, the destruction of Jerusalem and the temple, the captivity, the return of two tribes from the exile, the impiety of priests and kings, persecutions, and the heavenly judgment by which Israel will be raised to the stars from where she will look down and see her enemies in hell; finally Moses encourages his successor.

The book was composed after the deposition of Archelaus in A.D. 6. The Latin translation was based upon a Greek text, but the original book was written by a pious Palestinian Jew either in Hebrew or Aramaic.

(14) *The Ascension of Isaias.*—This work is halachic in character, and is composed of various parts: (a) the Martyrdom of Isaias, which was known to Origen and seems to have been written in the first century of our era; (b) the Testament of Ezechias, a Christian apocalypse of the end of the first century; and (c) the Vision or Ascension of Isaias of the early half of the second century. These various writings were collected and united to form one book in the third or fourth century.

In the Martyrdom of Isaias it is narrated how the prophet incurred the wrath of King Manasses and was sawed asunder at the king's command. This tradition became very prevalent

---

[17] Cf. Lattey, C., "The Messianic Expectation in The Assumption of Moses," in C.B.Q., 4 (1942), 9-21.

in the first centuries of the Christian era both amongst the Jews and the Christians. The Ascension of Isaias enjoyed great popularity with the early heretics.

The complete Ethiopic and the fragmentary Latin and Slavic versions are based upon a Greek text, which has been only partially preserved.[18]

(15) *Fourth Book of Esdras.*[19]—This work is apocalyptic in character, and was one of the most widely circulated and read of all the apocryphal books. Both Greek and Latin Fathers made use of it, and it was translated into the Syriac, Ethiopic, Arabic, Armenian, Sahidic, and Georgian languages. In the West it was widely spread by means of many Latin MSS. of the Bible, and is found at the end of our authorized edition of the Latin Vulgate. Only chapters 3 to 14 belong to the original Jewish apocryphal work, whereas chapters 1-2[20] and 15-16 are Christian additions.

The original Jewish chapters contain seven visions given to Esdras at Babylon during the exile, thirty years after the destruction of Jerusalem. The mission of the Messias and the messianic era are stressed in these visions. In the last vision Esdras is commanded to write some books of instruction for future generations, because the Law had been burnt and no one knew any longer the works of God. Then for forty days Esdras, filled with divine wisdom, dictated to five scribes and edited ninety-four books. Of these twenty-four (i.e., the canonical books) were to be published for all, and seventy books were to be restricted solely to the wise and learned.

---

[18] Cf. Tisserant, E., "Ascension d'Isaie" (Paris, 1909).

[19] Cf. Garofalo, S., "De Judæorum fatis religiosis in apocryphis Libro IV Esdræ," in V.D., 19 (1935), 280-287; Holzmeister, U., " 'Requiem aeternitatis' dona eis, Domine, et 'lux perpetua' luceat eis," in V.D., 17 (1937), 321-328; Keuler, J., "Die Eschatologische Lehre des vierten Esdrasbuches" in B.S., 20—ii (1922); Mazerski, J., "Libri IV Esdræ doctrina hamartologica," in V.D., 12 (1932), 374-376, 13 (1933), 84-90, 215-222, 247-250, 359-370; Pelaia, B. M., "Eschatalogia Messianica IV Libri Esdræ," in V.D., 11 (1931), 244-249, 310-318; Sigwalt, C., "Die Chronologie des 4 Buches Esdras," in B.Z., 9 (1911), 146-148.

[20] 2, 34 f is used for the Introitus of the Mass pro Defunctis, and 2, 37 for the Introitus of the Mass on Tuesday after the Feast of Pentecost.

Then "after having written all these things" Esdras was carried away. Nearly all scholars agree that the Jewish section was written at the end of the first century of our era by a Palestinian Jew either in Hebrew or Aramaic.

The canonical value of this book as well as that of 3 Esdras was rejected by St. Jerome: "Nec quemquam moveat, quod unus a nobis liber (Esdræ) editus est, nec apocryphorum tertii et quarti somniis delectetur."

(16) *The Syriac Apocalypse of Baruch.* [21]—This work is known to us only from one Syriac MS. of the Peshitto version, found by Ceriani and published for the first time in 1871.

The work purports to describe the revelations made to Baruch, the secretary to Jeremias, immediately before and after the destruction of Jerusalem by the Babylonians. These revelations end with the messianic period. To this Apocalypse there is added Baruch's letter to the nine and a half tribes (chs. 78-86), which occurs in many Syriac MSS.

The book was written at the beginning of the second century of our era, and after the composition of 4 Esdras. The Syriac translation was based upon a Greek text, but the original language of the Apocalypse was either Hebrew or Aramaic.

(b) THE APOCRYPHAL BOOKS OF HELLENISTIC ORIGIN [22]

Among the earliest writings in Greek by the Jews in the diaspora is the Letter of Aristeas describing the origin of the Septuagint version or the Greek translation of the Old Testament Hebrew Bible. See SEPTUAGINT.

There are several apocryphal works which originated among the Hellenistic Jews and are worthy of mention.

(1) *The Jewish Sibyls.*—This book is apocalyptic in character, and forms but a part of twelve books of sibylline oracles. The greater part of these oracles were composed by

[21] Cf. Sigwalt, C., "Die Chronologie der syrischen Baruchapokalypse," in B.Z., 9 (1911) 397 f; A Vallisoleto, X.M., "Christologia in apocalypsi Baruch Syriaca" in V.D. 11, (1931), 212-221.
[22] Cf. Frey, J. B., *op. cit.*, 357, 423-460.

Christians. Modern critics are almost unanimous in declaring that the third book is of Jewish origin, and most of them agree that the fourth and fifth books were composed by Jewish authors.

The Jews of the dispersion wished to show that they were by no means inferior to the pagans in culture and composed their sibylline works for religious propaganda.

The first and second books of sibylline oracles are a combination of Christian and Jewish elements, and treat of the period from the creation of the world to its end. The third book, the oldest Jewish part, was composed at Alexandria, Egypt, about 140 B.C. It denounces the idolaters and threatens them with all sorts of punishments; it predicts the divine punishment of the enemies of the Jewish people and the coming of the Messias as well as his ultimate victory. The fourth book foretells the punishments of Asia and Europe, and urges their inhabitants to be reconciled with God; otherwise the earth will be destroyed with fire (cf. IV. 172-179: "Dies iræ, dies illa, solvet sæclum in favilla, teste David cum Sibylla," etc.). The fifth book has manifold contents about the battle of the stars through which the world is set afire.

All of the sibylline oracles were written in Greek hexameter. The Jewish parts were composed in the second century B.C., and the Christian sections between the second and fourth century of our era.

(2) *Third Book of Machabees.*—This work is halachic in character. The title is a misnomer, since the work has nothing to do with the history of the Machabees. Its theme, however, like the canonical Books of Machabees, treats of the persecution of the Jews.

The book records that, after Ptolemy IV Philopator (221-204 B.C.) was prevented by the Jews of Jerusalem from entering the temple, he began to wreak his vengeance on the Hebrews in his dominion. He had a great number of these brought to the hippodrome of Alexandria, but through a special miracle they were saved.

The entire account is a midrashic fable. There is no trace

of such a miraculous event in any of the Jewish books. Josephus relates something similar for the reign of Ptolemy VII Physcos (170-164 and 145-117 B.C.), but the time and circumstances vary from those recorded in the apocryphal Book of Machabees (cf. *c. Apionem*, II, 5). It is possible that both accounts are based upon some actual historical event, but from their present form it is impossible to know what happened and when it happened. The author wished to console his coreligionists and strengthen their faith during the time of trials and persecutions.

The book was written either in the first century B.C. or in the first century of our era, but before the destruction of the temple. It was written in Greek, and probably at Alexandria. No trace of its contents is found in Jewish literature, but the book was accepted by some of the Greek, Syriac, and Armenian churches. None of the Latin Vulgate MSS. contain this apocryphal book.

(3) *Third Book of Esdras*.[23]—This work is halachic in character, and the title given is derived from the Vulgate MSS. It is designated as the *first (A)* book of Esdras in the Septuagint, Old Latin, and Syriac versions from its position immediately before the canonical Books of Esdras and Nehemias; the two latter are united to form one book by the Septuagint, called the *second (B)* Book of Esdras.

The entire contents of this Third Book of Esdras, with the exception of a few passages, may be found in the canonical Books of Paralipomenon, 1 Esdras and 2 Esdras (or Nehemias), and treats of the history of the temple from the rule of Josias (640-609 B.C.) to its rebuilding after the exile and to the resumption of divine services in the temple under Esdras.

The origin of this book is disputed. Some scholars hold that 3 Esdras or Esdras A was the original Septuagint version of the canonical Books of Esdras, whereas Esdras B repre-

---

[23] Cf. Bayer, E., "Das dritte Buch Esdras und sein Verhältnis zu den Büchern Esra-Nehemia," in B.S., 16 (1911); Fischer, J., "Das apokryphe und das kanonische Esdrasbuch," in B.Z., 2 (1904), 351-364; Reissler, P., "Der textkritische Wert des dritten Esdrasbuches," in B.Z., 5 (107), 146-158.

sented the Theodotion version of these books. Others maintain that 3 Esdras is merely a Greek compilation which was made in the first or second century B.C. from the canonical books mentioned above. It seems, however, more probable that this Greek version of 3 Esdras was made from a Hebrew or Aramaic text, the prototype of which differed from the Massoretic Text, and that 3, 1—5, 6 (which has no parallel in the canonical books) was taken from some other source.

The canonical value of this book offers some difficulty. Many Protestant scholars wrongly affirm that this book should be recognized as canonical, and that it was erroneously excluded from the canonical lists by St. Jerome and the Councils of the Church.

It is true that this book was listed among the canonical books in many Greek MSS. and the Old Latin, and that it was quoted as an inspired writing by some Fathers. But at the same time it should be noted that this acknowledgment was neither universal nor constant. The Fathers and ecclesiastical writers, when they officially enumerate the books received by the Church, only acknowledge the canonical books, 1 and 2 Esdras (Nehemias), and exclude 3 Esdras (thus, Melito, Origen, St. Athanasius, St. Gregory Nazianzus, St. Cyril of Jerusalem, St. Epiphanius, Rufinus, St. Jerome, St. Augustine, Leontius, and Junilius). It is also to be kept in mind that the witness of many Fathers quoted by scholars in favor of the canonicity of the book is uncertain. Thus, it followed that for a certain period the matter remained doubtful, and some of the Fathers and ecclesiastical writers attributed divine inspiration to the book. But from the fifth century on, the book was considered as apocryphal, at least by the Latin Church.

In regard to the time of composition of this book it may be said that it was written in the first century B.C. or even earlier. The author was a Jew, who probably lived at Alexandria. Catholic liturgy makes use of this book (5, 40) for the Offertory of the Mass for the election of the Roman Pontiff: "They should not participate of the holy things, till there would arise a high priest in manifestation and truth." The book is also to be found in the appendix of the Sistine-Clementine Vulgate edition.

(4) The Prayer of Manasses.—This work, haggadic in character, owes its origin to a narrative in the Book of Paralipomenon. When King Manasses was led away as captive to Babylonia, he prayed to Jahweh and repented. He entreated God and besought Him earnestly. His prayer was heard and he was allowed to return to Jerusalem and to his kingdom. "His prayers are contained in the Annals of the Kings of Israel and in the Chronicles of Hozai" (2 Par. 33, 12 f; 33, 18 f). This prayer was an attempt to supply a lacuna in the sacred text.

The prayer consisting of a divine praise (vv. 1-7), a pardon of sins (vv. 8-14), and a doxology (v. 15), is to be found in many Septuagint MSS., the Didascalia, and the Apostolic Constitutions; in the Vulgate MSS. it is placed after the Second Book of Paralipomenon. It is also to be found in the Appendix of the Sistine-Clementine Vulgate edition. The prayer seems to have been written in the Greek language by a Hellenistic Jew in the first century before the Christian era.

(5) Fourth Book of Machabees.—Haggadic in character, this work aims to show that reason directed by piety possesses the greatest power to control the passions. This theme is illustrated by facts taken from Jewish history, for example, the courage of Onias, the martyrdom of Eleazar, and the heroic sufferings of the seven brothers and their mother. The author shows his acquaintance with Greek rhetoric and Stoic philosophy. There is not sufficient reason to hold with Eusebius and St. Jerome that the author was Josephus Flavius. The book was written by a Hellenistic Jew probably at the beginning of the Christian era.

(6) The Slavic Book of Henoch (or The Secrets of Henoch).—Apocalyptic in character, this work contains sixty-eight chapters describing the various visions of Henoch, to which moral lessons are added. The original book was written either in Greek or more likely in the Semitic language (i.e., Hebrew

or Aramaic). It was written before the destruction of the temple, and thus in the earlier part of the first century of the Christian era.

(7) *Later Apocryphal Works or Fragments.*—The remaining apocryphal books and fragments are alluded to by the Fathers and ecclesiastical writers, and at times are specifically proscribed. As, however, none of them are of great importance, the mere listing of their titles will suffice:

The Paralipomenon of Jeremias (halachic);
The Testament of Job (halachic);
The Testament of Solomon (halachic);
The Apocalypse of Elias and Sophonias (apocalyptic);
The Apocryphal Book of Ezechiel (apocalyptic);
The Life of Adam and Eve (halachic);
The Apocalypse of Moses (halachic);
The Testament of Adam (halachic);
The Apocalypse of Abraham (apocalyptic);
The Testament of Abraham (apocalyptic).

Art. 2. The Apocryphal Books of the New Testament

Bibliography: Amann, E., in D.D.L.B. (Suppl.) s.v. *Apocryphes du Nouveau Testament;* *Hennecke, E.- *Schneemelcher, W., "Neutestamentliche Apokryphen" (3rd ed., Tübingen, 1959); *James, M. R., "The Apocryphal New Testament" (Oxford, repr., 1955); *idem,* "Latin Infancy Gospels" (London, 1927).

Analogous to the general division found in the canonical books of the New Testament, the apocryphal books are divided into Gospels, Acts, Epistles, and Apocalypses. The greater part of this apocryphal literature was published in the second and third centuries.

Not everything that Jesus did and taught is contained in the canonical Gospels (cf. John 20, 30; 21, 25), but there are many things, and especially sayings, which have been preserved by the Early Christians and handed down by tradition. These sayings, or *logia*, of Christ, which are not contained in

the canonical Gospels, are called *agrapha*[1] (i.e., not written).
Some of these are found as additions to the received texts of
our Gospels or as quotations in the Fathers,[2] and others have
been discovered in various papyri fragments as well as in the
Coptic *Gospel of Thomas.*

Regarding the authenticity of these sayings of Jesus, scholars
generally agree that the sayings which are identical with those
in the canonical Gospels are to be considered as authentic as
those in the New Testament; that the sayings which are paraphrases or independent variants of canonical sayings and are
found only in patristic literature are to be considered as contained in a possible different collection than the ones in the
Four Gospels; that the sayings which were previously unknown
and with a Gnostic (Manichæan) viewpoint, as the *Gospel of
Thomas*, are to be considered as unauthenticated.[3]

Among the Greek agrapha mention may be made of a very
small papyrus (8.5 x 7 cm.) of the fourth or fifth century,
Pap. Ox. 840 written in the Synoptic style;[4] two leaves and a
fragment composed before 150 *Pap. Egerton 2* with some
Johannine texts incorporated;[5] and several other small fragments, as *Oxyrhynchus Papyrus 1224* of the beginning of the

---

[1] Cf. *Resch, A., "Agrapha" (Leipzig, 1906); Vaganay, L., in D.D.L.B.
(Suppl.) s.v. *Agrapha;* Fitzmyer, J. A. "The Oxyrhynchus *Logoi* of Jesus
and the Coptic Gospel according to Thomas," in *Theol. St.*, 20 (1959),
505-556 and his extensive bibliography of the Oxyrhynchus sayings, 556-
560.

[2] Cf. *Hennecke, E.- Schneemelcher, W., *op. cit.*, 52-55; *James, M. R.,
op. cit., 33-37; Ruwet, J., "Les 'Agrapha' dans les oeuvres de Clément d'
Alexandrie," in *Biblica*, 30 (1949), 133-160; Donovan, J., "Note on the
Eusebian Use of Logia," in *Biblica*, 7 (1926), 301-310).

[3] Cf. Fitzmyer, J. A. *op. cit.*, 508-510.

[4] Cf. *Grenfell, B. P.- *Hunt, A. C., "Oxyrhynchus Papyris" (vol. V.,
London, 1908) ; *idem*, "Fragment of an Uncanonical Gospel from Oxyrhynchus" (Oxford, 1908); Jeremias, J., "Der Zusammenstoss Jesu mit
dem pharisäischen Oberpriester auf dem Tempelplatz. Zu Pap. Ox. V.
840," in Coniectanea Neotestamentica. XI in honorem A. Fridrichsen
(Lund-Köpenhamm, 1947), 97-108; *Hennecke, E.-*Schneemelcher, W.,
op. cit., 57 f.

[5] Cf. *Bell, H. I.- *Skeat, T. C., "Fragments of an Unknown Gospel"
(London, 1935); *idem,* "The New Gospel Fragments" (London, 1935);
*Hennecke, E.- *Schneemelcher, W., *op. cit.*, 58-60; *James, M. R., *op.
cit.*, 569 f.

fourth century, *Papyrus Cairensis 10735* of the sixth or seventh century, and the so-called *Fajjum fragment* of the third century.[6]

Among the most important agrapha thus far discovered are the Greek *Pap(yrcs) Ox(yrhynchus) 1, 654 and 655*, which collections of the saying of Jesus (of the second and third centuries) are very closely related and part of the recently found Coptic *Gospel of Thomas. Pap. Ox. 1*,[7] part of a codex, was found at Oxyrhynchus (modern Behnesa) in 1897 and contains eight logia, or sayings, of Jesus. *Pap. Ox. 654*,[8] part of a roll, was discovered in the same place in 1903 and contains seven logia. *Pap. Ox. 655*,[9] also part of a roll, was found in the same place and time as the preceding collection and contains five logia. These three Greek fragments are copies written at different periods from the same work, as their logia are found in the Thomas Gospel and the introduction and logia of *Pap. Ox. 654* are parallel with those in the Coptic Gospel.

A Sahidic Coptic *Gospel of Thomas* (mentioned above)[10] was found in 1945 at Nag Hamadi (ancient Chenoboskion) of Upper Egypt and is now preserved in the Coptic Museum of Old Cairo. This Gospel is in the midst of a papyrus codex (A.D. 350-400) between the *Apocryphon of John* and the *Gospel of Philip*. It is a new independent apocryphon related not with the Infancy Gospel bearing the same name, but with Gnostic and Manichæan writings. This Gospel is not in the form of a canonical Gospel, but an artificial collection or

[6] Cf. *Hennecke, E.- *Schneemelcher, W., *op. cit.,* **72-74.**

[7] Cf. *Grenfell, G. P.- *Hunt, A. S., "Logia Jesou, Sayings of Our Lord" (London, 1897); *idem,* "The Oxyrhynchus Papyri" (Part I, London, 1898); *Hennecke, E.- Schneemelcher, W., *op. cit.,* 66-70. 213.

[8] Cf. *Grenfell, G. P.- *Hunt, A. S., "The Oxyrhynchus Papyri" (vol. IV, London, 1904), 1-22; *Hennecke, E.,- *Schneemelcher, W., *op. cit.,* 61-66. 213.

[9] Cf. **Grenfell, G. P.- *Hunt, A. S., "The Oxyrhynchus Papyri" (Vol. IV, London, 1904), 22-28; *Hennecke, E.- *Schneemelcher, W., *op. cit.,* 70-72. 213.

[10] Photographs (80-99) of this Gospel were published by *Pahor Labib, "The Gospel according to Thomas" (Cairo, 1956). For an English translation consult *Guillaumont, A., etc., "The Gospel according to Thomas; Coptic Text Established and Translated" (New York, 1959).

illogical arrangement of 114 sayings attributed to Jesus according to the commonly used stereotyped formula: "Jesus has said." [11]

(a) THE APOCRYPHAL GOSPELS [12]

The apocryphal Gospels may be ranged into various groups according to the purpose of their authors: (1) rival Gospels; (2) heretical Gospels, or (3) supplementary or fictitious Gospels.

(1) *The Rival Gospels*.—Among the Gospels of the synoptic type, which were set more or less in opposition to the canonical Gospels, may be mentioned three Gospels used by the Jewish Christians (the Gospel of the Ebionites or of the Twelve Apostles, the Gospel of the Nazarenes, and the Gospel according to the Hebrews), the Gospel according to the Egyptians, and the Gospel of Peter. Of these Gospels only fragments have survived.

The Gospel of the Ebionites (also called by some the Gospel of the Twelve Apostles) was written between A.D. 150 and 200 and contained the errors of the Ebionite sect. All our knowledge of this Gospel is derived from St. Epiphanius, who says that the author of this apocryphal writing falsified the Gospel of St. Matthew. The Gospel of the Nazarenes is known only from a few allusions in the Fathers.[13]

The most important of these Jewish Christian Gospels is the Gospel according to the Hebrews.[14] This is frequently mentioned by the Fathers (e.g., St. Irenæus, Hegesippus, Clement of Alexandria, Origen, Eusebius, St. Epiphanius, and St. Jerome). It was written in Aramaic; St. Jerome translated

---

[11] Cf. *Hennecke, E.- *Schneemelcher, W., *op. cit.*, 199-223; Fitzmyer, J. A., *op. cit.*, 551-556; *Gold, V. R., "The Gnostic Library of Chenoboskion," in B.A., 15 (1952), 70-88.

[12] Cf. Vitti, A., "Evangelia apocrypha," in V.D., 3 (1923), 20-27; *Hennecke, E.- *Schneemelcher, W., *op. cit.*, 75-377; *James, M. R. *op. cit.*, 1-227.

[13] Cf. *Hennecke, E.- *Schneemelcher, W., *op. cit.*, 100-104.

[14] Cf. *Lagrange, M. J., "L'Evangile selon les Hébreux," in R.B., 31 (1922), 161-181, 321-349.

it into Greek and Latin (*De vir. ill.*), and declared that many people believed it to be the authentic Gospel of St. Matthew (*In Matt.*, 12, 13). It seems very likely that this apocryphal Gospel was a revised edition of the canonical Gospel of St. Matthew, that it received additions from the other canonical Gospels, and that it was used by the Nazarenes who fled to the Transjordanic region shortly before the destruction of Jerusalem in A.D. 70.[15]

The Gospel according to the Egyptians was composed in Egypt about 150, and is mentioned as well as condemned by Clement of Alexandria, St. Hippolytus, and St. Epiphanius. Various heretical sects (Encratites, Valentinians, Naassenes, and Sabellians) made use of this writing as the basis of their heresies.

The Gospel of Peter is mentioned by Origen (*In Matt.*, 10, 17). Eusebius places it among the apocryphal writings (*Hist. Eccl.*, III, 25), and states that Bishop Serapion of Antioch permitted the Gospel to be read by the members of the parish at Rhossus, but that, when Serapion himself afterwards read the book and found that it contained heresy (i.e., of a Docetic character), he forbade further reading of it (*op. cit.*, VI, 12). The book was composed in Syria before 150. In 1884 a manuscript of the eighth-twelfth century was found at Akmim, Egypt, and contains the greater part of the history of the Passion and Resurrection.[16]

(*2*) *The Heretical Gospels.*—These Gospels were written by heretics to defend their false teachings, and may be conveniently grouped into two classes: the pseudepigraphic Gospels and the forged Gospels.

Among the pseudepigraphic Gospels current among the Gnostics may be listed the Gospel of Thomas, the Gospel of Matthias, the Gospel of Philip, the Gospel of Judas, the Gospel of Bartholomew, and the Gospel of Barnabas.

The Gospel of Thomas (mentioned by Origen, St. Hippo-

---

[15] Cf. Höpfl, H., *op. cit.*, 100.

[16] Cf. *James, M. R., *op. cit.*, 90-94, 507-510; Vaganay, L., "L'Evangile de Pierre" (Paris, 1930).

lytus, St. Cyril of Jerusalem and St. Irenæus) seems to have been written by a Gnostic in the second century. Three forms of it are extant, two Greek texts (A and B) and one Latin. The first and longer Greek text (A) narrates the various miracles of the child Jesus from the age of five to twelve; the second Greek text (B) treats of the childhood of Our Lord from the age of five to twelve; the Latin deals with the infancy of Christ from the age of two (i.e., the flight into Egypt) to twelve (i.e., the finding of the child Jesus in the temple).[17] But none of these texts in their present form seem to be the same as the heretical Gospel attacked by the Fathers. This heretical Gospel is probably the Gospel (or *Logia*) of Thomas mentioned above at the beginning of this article.

The Gospel of Matthias, of the third century, is mentioned by Origen, Clement of Alexandria, and others. The Gospel of Philip is cited by St. Epiphanius as apocryphal; it was written about 200, since the author of the Gnostic work "Pistis Sophia" of the third century seems to allude to it. According to St. Irenæus and St. Epiphanius, the Gospel of Judas was used by the Gnostic sect, called the Cainites. The Gospel of Bartholomew [18] is mentioned by St. Jerome, and seems to have been written in Egypt during the fourth century. The Gospel of Barnabas is spoken of in the Gelasian Decree, but nothing definite is known about the writing. Other Gnostic Gospels mentioned by St. Epiphanius are: the Gospel of Perfection, the Gospel of Eve, and the Questions of Mary.

Among the forged Gospels two call for brief mention: the Gospel of Basilides and the Gospel of Marcion. The former is mentioned by Origen, but the nature of this writing is uncertain. The latter consisted of a mutilated form of St. Luke's Gospel.

(3) *Supplementary or Fictitious Gospels.*—These Gospels

---

[17] Cf. *James, M. R., *op. cit.*, 49-65.

[18] Moricca, U., "Un Nuovo Testo Dell' 'Evangelo Di Bartolomo,' " in R.B., 30 (1921), 481-516, 31 (1922), 20-30; Tisserant-Wilmart, "Fragments Grecs et Latins de l'Evangile de Barthélemy," in R.B., 10 (1913), 161-190, 321-368.

aim to fill in the gaps left in the canonical Gospels about the origin and family of Our Lord or about the circumstances of His Passion and Resurrection. They may conveniently be grouped into three classes: those dealing with the parents of Jesus, with His Infancy, or with His Passion.

Among the Gospels dealing with the parents of Our Lord the most important are the Protoevangelium of James, the Assumption of the Virgin, and the History of Joseph the Carpenter. Besides the Gospel of Thomas mentioned above, there is the Arabic Gospel of the Infancy which treats of the boyhood of Christ. Finally, the Gospel of Nicodemus is of interest for the period of Pontius Pilate.

The Protoevangelium of James [19] treats in twenty-four chapters of the period from the birth of the Blessed Virgin to the infanticide by Herod the Great. It was written by an orthodox Christian in Greek about 150, and is the first document to mention Joachim and Anna, the parents of our Blessed Lady by name. This apocryphal writing had a very wide circulation in the early Church, and was translated into many languages. On this Gospel of James depended the authors of the Gospel of Pseudo-Matthew,[20] or the Book of the Birth of the Blessed Mary and the Infancy of the Savior (fifth or sixth century) and the Book of the Nativity of Mary (tenth or eleventh century). From these latter two sources the poets and painters of the Middle Ages drew the materials for verse and canvas.

The History of the Falling Asleep and the Assumption of the Virgin [21] was composed originally in Greek in the fourth century, and at one time was ascribed by some to St. John the Apostle. Upon this book depends the standard Latin form called *Liber de transitu V.M.*, falsely attributed to Bishop Melito of Sardis, and put among the apocryphal books by the

---

[19] Cf. Amann, E., "Le Protoévangile de Jacques et ses remainiements latins" (Paris, 1910); * James, M. R., *op. cit.*, 38-49.
[20] Cf. * James, M. R., *op. cit.*, 70-79.
[21] Cf. * James, M. R., *op. cit.*, 194-227; Vitti, A., "Libri apocryphi de Assumptione B.M.V.," in V.D., 6 (1926), 225-234.

Gelasian Decree. This book was translated into many languages.

The History of Joseph the Carpenter[22] was an Egyptian book current among the Monophysites. In thirty-two chapters it treats of the life and death of St. Joseph. This book was written not earlier, and very probably later, than the fourth century.

The Arabic Gospel of the Infancy[23] treats in fifty-five chapters of the history of the Infancy of Christ from His birth to the age of twelve. This Gospel probably was written before the seventh century in Syriac, from which the Arabic version seems to be derived. It consists of a combination of the facts contained in the two canonical Gospels of St. Matthew and St. Luke and in the two uncanonical Gospels of James and Thomas.

The Gospel of Nicodemus[24] consists of two parts. The first part, called the Acts of Pilate, deals with the trials of Jesus before Pilate, His crucifixion and Resurrection, and in its present form can hardly be older than the fourth century. The second part, an addition to the Acts and called the Descent into Hell, gives an account of Christ's descent to limbo. Carinus and Leucius, sons of Simeon, who were raised from the dead at Our Lord's Resurrection, relate how, during their confinement in limbo, they witnessed His appearance there. This second part seems to have been appended to the Acts of Pilate in the fifth century.

(b) The Apocryphal Acts

Most of these apocryphal writings were composed by heretics in support of their doctrines. Some of them, however, were later revised and recast by orthodox hands.

(1) The Acts of John.[25]—According to Nicephorus, this work consisted of 2500 lines. It narrates the many miracles

[22] Cf. *James, M. R., op. cit., 84-86.
[23] Cf. *James, M. R., op. cit., 80-82.
[24] Cf. *James, M. R., op. cit., 94-146.
[25] Cf. *James, M. R., op. cit., 228-270.

performed by St. John the Apostle at Ephesus; how he cured
many sick from their illnesses and restored many dead people
to life, among whom were Callimachus and Drusiana (79 f);
finally, on a certain Sunday he gathered the faithful together
to bid them farewell (106 ff), gave them all eucharistic bread
(109 f), and then, having left the city, he ordered two men
to dig a grave for him, into which he stepped, and, after a
prayer of thanksgiving, gave up his spirit (111-115).

These Acts were composed about 150 by a certain Leucius
Charinus, a Gnostic. This writing was adopted by various
heretical sects: the Encratites, the Manichæans, and the
Priscillianists. At the beginning of the fifth century the deacon Prochorus expanded the Acts, but at the end of the sixth
century Pseudo-Abdias made a compendium of them and
removed everything from them that was heretical.

(2) *The Acts of Paul.*[26]—Nicephorus states that this work
consisted of 3600 lines. According to Tertullian, it was composed shortly before his time; the date may therefore be about
160-170, and the author was an orthodox Christian.

A complete Greek text has not yet been found, but three
principal parts of this apocryphal work are extant. (a) The
first part, consisting of the Acts of Paul and Thecla, has survived in the Greek and many versions. These Acts relate how
Thecla, at the preaching of St. Paul in Iconium, embraces
Christianity and decides to break her engagement with
Thamyris to lead a life of virginity. Because of this the
Apostle is brought to the judgment seat, and then scourged
and sent out of the city. Thecla is condemned to be burnt,
but the fire took no hold on her and she is miraculously saved.
The virgin then came to Paul at Antioch, where she refused
to marry Alexander, a Syriarch. For this reason she is condemned to the wild beasts, but they did not do her any harm.
After many more trials she is set at liberty, returns to Iconium,
and then departs for Seleucia in Isauria, where she dies.
(b) The Martyrdom of Paul, forming the second part of this

[26] Cf. *James, M. R., *op. cit.*, 270-299; Vouaux, L., "Les Actes de Paul
et ses lettres apocryphes" (Paris, 1913).

work, is preserved separately in Greek and other versions. It narrates how Paul raised to life Patroclus, a cup-bearer of Nero, and then converted him and others of Cæsar's household. For this reason Nero orders the Apostle to be beheaded. (c) The Correspondence with the Corinthians, or third part, will be treated in the next section on the Apocryphal Epistles.

(3) *The Acts of Peter*.[27]—These Acts are mentioned by Eusebius and St. Jerome as an apocryphal writing which treats of the life and martyrdom of St. Peter. From the fragments the following story may be gathered: Paul leaves Rome for Spain (1-4). Christ appears to Peter at Jerusalem and bids him to proceed to Rome to combat the errors of Simon, the magician (5-32). While at Rome, Peter's life is endangered because of his preaching. To avoid being killed, Peter leaves Rome, but has hardly left the city when the Lord appears to him. Peter says to the Lord: "Lord, whither goest thou thus?" And the Lord answers: "I am going to Rome to be crucified again." Peter then understands what he is to do; he returns in joy to Rome, where he is crucified with his head downwards (33-41).

The Acts were written in Greek by a resident in Asia Minor not later than 200. The author seems to have been acquainted with the Acts of John, and probably was a member of the Gnostic sect. The original text has been lost, but a large portion of this work has been preserved in a seventh-century Latin MS. (*Acta Vercellensia*). The Martyrdom (33-41) is extant in Greek, Latin, and many versions. Much of this material about St. Peter has also been used in the Clementine *Recognitions* and *Homilies*.

A recasting of the Acts of Peter and the Acts of Paul, together with the addition of some details, may be found in the apocryphal work called the Acts of Peter and Paul, written at the beginning of the third century.[28]

Our principal source of knowledge for another apocryphal

---

[27] Cf. *James, M. R., *op. cit.*, 300-336; Vouaux, L., "Les Actes de Pierre" (Paris, 1922).
[28] Cf. *James, M. R., *op. cit.*, 472-475.

writing called *Kerygma Petri* (i.e., the Preaching of Peter) is Clement of Alexandria, who gives a series of quotations from it. This writing was composed by an orthodox Christian in Egypt or Greece about 150.

(4) The Acts of Andrew.[29]—These Acts were accepted by the heretical Encratites, Manichæans, and Priscillianists. In his letter of February 20, 405, to Bishop Exsuperius of Tolouse, St. Innocent I mentions the philosophers Nexocharidis and Leonidas as the authors of this writing (E.B., 17), but Evodius names Leucius Charinus as its author. It seems more likely that the author of the Acts of Andrew imitated the style and composition of Leucius, who was the author of the Acts of Peter and the Acts of John (E.B., 17). The original Gnostic writing of the second century, with the exception of a few fragments, has been lost.

Many parts of these original Acts have been recast by early Catholic writers after the fifth century, and may be found in the Acts of Andrew and Matthias, in the Acts of Peter and Andrew, and in the Martyrdom of Andrew which describes his crucifixion at Patras, in Achaia.

(5) The Acts of Thomas.[30]—This work was originally written by a Gnostic, probably in Syriac during the third century. The original work has been lost, but it has been recast by a Syriac Catholic writer. The Greek text of these Acts seems to be a version from the Syriac. The other versions—the Latin, Ethiopic, and Armenian—are of little importance.

In these Acts is described the journey of St. Thomas to India, where he performs various miracles, preaches virginity and continency in particular, and is martyred. Traces of Gnostic doctrines may be found both in the Syriac and in the Greek texts, but particularly in the latter.

The above-mentioned Acts of John, Paul, Peter, Andrew, and Thomas were collected into one volume, and the Manichæans substituted them for the canonical Acts of the Apostles.

[29] Cf. *James, M. R., *op. cit.*, 337-363, 453-460.
[30] Cf. *James, M. R., *op. cit.*, 364-438.

Besides these five Acts, a few others of secondary or minor importance are mentioned in the ancient writings: the Acts of Philip,[31] the Passion of Bartholomew, the Acts of Barnabas, and the Acts of Thaddæus.

(c) The Apocryphal Epistles

Besides the apocryphal Epistle of St. Paul to the Alexandrians, mention of which is found only in the Muratorian Fragment (E.B., 5), three other Epistles are falsely ascribed to the Apostle.

(1) *The Correspondence between the Corinthians and St. Paul.*[32]—This work was occasioned by the remark of St. Paul found in the canonical First Epistle to the Corinthians 5, 9 and 7, 1, and has been inserted in the apocryphal Acts of Paul. "Stephan and the presbyters who are with him" write to Paul about two men, who arrived at Corinth and are teaching "that we must not use the prophets, and that God is not Almighty, and that there shall be no resurrection of the flesh, and that man was not made by God, and that Christ did not come down in the flesh nor was He born of Mary, and that the world is not of God, but of the angels." They therefore ask Paul to come to them and remove this scandal. Paul, then, answers them by teaching them the true Christian doctrine.

St. Ephraem wrote a commentary on this correspondence, believing it to be canonical. The Armenians received these Epistles from the Syrians, and in the fifth century placed them in their Bibles as canonical writings. This correspondence between the Corinthians and the Apostle, together with the Acts of Paul, was written about 160 to 170.

(2) *The Epistle to the Laodiceans.*[33]—This letter was occasioned by St. Paul's remark found in his canonical Epistle to the Colossians (4, 16). The Muratorian Fragment mentions that an Epistle by this name was being used by the followers

---

[31] Cf. *James, M. R., *op. cit.*, 439-453; 467 f., 470 f.
[32] Cf. *James, M. R., *op. cit.*, 289-291.
[33] Cf. *James, M. R., *op. cit.*, 478-480; Tisserant, E., "La version mozarabe de l'épître aux Laodicéens," in R.B., 7 (1910), 249-253.

of Marcion. Since the Latin text which has reached us does not contain anything heretical, it cannot be identified with the Marcionite Epistle.

The Epistle was originally written in Greek and probably in the fourth century, since it is mentioned by various writers from the fourth century onwards. Its contents have been taken from the other canonical Epistles of St. Paul, and especially from his Epistle to the Philippians.

(*3*) *The Correspondence of Paul and Seneca.*[34]—This correspondence consists of eight letters of Seneca the philosopher and six letters of Paul. The letters were composed in Latin during the fourth century, since they were in existence before the time of St. Jerome (who makes mention of them) and St. Augustine (who says that they are not worthy of any credence).

(d) The Apocryphal Apocalypses

Besides the Apocalypse of Thomas (proscribed in the Gelasian Decree and known from two recently discovered Latin MSS.) and the Apocalypse of Stephen (about which we know little beyond its condemnation in the Gelasian Decree), there are two early Apocalypses worthy of consideration: the Apocalypse of Peter and the Apocalypse of Paul.

(*1*) *The Apocalypse of Peter.*[35]—This work was written in Greek in the second century, and is mentioned by Clement of Alexandria and the Muratorian Fragment (E.B., 6). Eusebius, St. Jerome, and Sozomen declare that the Church has recognized for a long time its spurious and uncanonical character.

A complete text of this Apocalypse is now extant in the Ethiopic version, which was first published by Abbé S. Grébaut in 1910 together with a French translation. The contents is as follows: Our Lord, while He is seated upon the Mount of Olives, is entreated by His disciples to declare to them the

---

[34] Cf. *James, M R., *op. cit.*, 480-484.
[35] Cf. *James, M. R., *op. cit.*, 505-521; Prümm, K., "De genuino Apocalypsis Petri Textu," in *Biblica,* 10 (1929), 62-80.

signs of His coming and of the end of the world (cf. Matt. 24, 3). The Lord answers that His coming will be with majesty and then reminds them of the parable of the fig-tree (Matt. 24, 32 f), which He interprets for them with great detail. He furthermore predicts that Henoch and Elias will be sent to resist the Antichrist, and describes the horrible signs which will precede the resurrection and the general judgment. Then He shows His disciples the places where the sinners are condemned and the punishment meted out to various sinners; on the other hand, He describes the happiness of the elect in paradise. Finally, Our Lord, accompanied by Moses and Elias, is taken up into heaven.

(2) *The Apocalypse of Paul.*[36]—This work is mentioned by Sozomen, and condemned by St. Augustine and in the Gelasian Decree. The author pretends that the writing was found during the reign of Theodosius (379-395) in a marble chest located in the foundation of Paul's home at Tarsus. At the bidding of Our Lord, the Apostle Paul is urged to appeal to sinners to repent, since the sun, moon, stars, and waters are appealing to God to punish sinners. Twice a day, at sunrise and sunset, the angels, who are the guardians of every people and of every man, appear before God and render an account of all the deeds of mankind, whether good or bad. Paul is then shown the deaths and judgments of the righteous and the wicked, as well as paradise, the new Jerusalem, where he sees the prophets of the Old Testament, the innocent children slain by Herod, the Patriarchs, and David. Afterwards he is led to see the river of fire burning with heat and in it a multitude of men and women being punished for their sins. Special punishments are meted out to those who did not confess that Christ came in the flesh and that the Virgin did not bear Him, or who denied that the bread and the cup of blessing of the Eucharist is the body and blood of Christ. For all those in hell, Paul obtains forever a cessation of their punishments one

---

[36] Cf. *James, M. R., op. cit., 525-555.

day a year, on Easter.[37]   The Apocalypse concludes with a second vision of paradise. This book seems to have been written at the end of the fourth or the beginning of the fifth century.   This Apocalypse of Paul was translated into many languages, and was widely read in England, France, and Germany during the Middle Ages.

St. Epiphanius refers to another apocalypse, which he calls the Ascension of Paul. This writing was used by the Cainites, a Gnostic sect, in the second or third century, but it has been lost.

---

[37] The Apocalypse of the Virgin, written in the ninth century, speaks of the days of Pentecost as a season of rest to the lost. This general idea seems to have been borrowed from the rabbinical tradition, which grants the Sabbath as the day of respite for the souls in hell.

Supplementary Bibliography: Kaupel, H., "Der Herr der Geister," in B.Z., 24 (1939), 249-251; Vitti, A., "De B.V. Annuntiatione juxta evangelia Apocrypha," in V.D., 3 (1923), 67-74; *idem,* "Epistula Apostolorum apocrypha," *ibid.,* 3 (1923), 367-373, 4 (1924), 210-218; *idem,* "Apocryphorum de Magis enarrationes," *ibid.,* 7 (1927), 3-13; *idem,* "Descensus Christi ad inferos juxta Apocrypha," *ibid.,* 7 (1927), 138-144, 171-181; *idem,* "S. Familia in Aegypto ubinam juxta Apocrypha constiterit," *ibid.,* 9 (1929), 3-13.

PART III

TEXTS AND VERSIONS OF THE BIBLE

General Remarks

(1) Writing.[1]—Writing is known to have existed in the fourth millennium before the Christian era both in Egypt and Babylonia. Besides the various materials employed by the ancients to record writings—as stone (cf. Ex. 31, 18; 34, 1. 28), clay (cf. Ez. 4, 1), wood, wax, bark, linen, metals (cf. Job 19, 24), potsherds or ostraca—there are three others which play an important rôle in the history of biblical MSS.: leather, papyrus, and parchment or vellum. Paper, a Chinese invention, plays an insignificant part in the history of biblical writing, because of its late arrival in Europe and Western Asia.

Leather and skins are not expressly mentioned in the Old Testament as writing materials, but their use may be presumed. The use of the book in roll form (cf. Jer. 36, 2-4; Ez. 2, 9) and the mention of the scribe's knife (cf. Jer. 36, 23) implies either leather or papyrus. The Letter of Aristeas was written on leather; the Talmud requires all copies of the Law to be written on skins and in roll form, and this regulation is still in force for volumes intended for synagogue use. It would seem that the Old Testament Scriptures were habitually written on prepared skins, and that vellum was substituted only in the case of ordinary, private copies.

Papyrus, used as a writing material in Egypt prior to 2600 B.C., also plays an important part in the history of the Bible. The Septuagint version of the Old Testament as well as the books of the New Testament were originally written upon

---

[1] Cf. *Kenyon, F. G., in H.D.B., s.v., *Writing;* Steinmueller, J. E.- Sullivan, K., art., "Ostraca," "Papyrus," "Writing," etc., in C.B.E.O.T.

this material. The writing was arranged in columns (*selides*), with the title at the end or on a thin strip of papyrus (*sillubos*) or vellum attached to the outside of the roll. To protect the roll from damage, it might be enclosed in a cover (*phainoles*) or stored in a wooden case (*capsa*). The average life of a papyrus MS. was hardly more than two hundred years. The roll form for papyrus was the ordinary one used until the Christian era, but in the early years of the second century the codex form for papyrus made its first appearance, probably due to Christian influence. In the fourth century vellum largely superseded papyrus for sacred literature, though papyrus continued to be employed until the seventh century.

Parchment or vellum [2] was the chief material for book production from the fourth to the fifteenth century, but it was known even prior to the fourth century of our era. According to Varro, it originated at Pergamum under Eumenes (197-158 B.C.), but its adoption for general use was slow. The final victory of vellum and the codex form (i.e., the modern book form) was achieved in the fourth century. Emperor Constantine instructed Eusebius to have fifty MSS. prepared on vellum by skilled calligraphers for the churches, and Acacius and Euzoius reproduced the works of Origen in vellum codices about the middle of the fourth century.

With the spread of Christianity the demand for complete copies of the Scriptures increased. No papyrus roll of ordinary length (about 35 feet) [3] could hold more than one of the longer Gospels, and thus a set of thirty or forty rolls would be necessary for the writings of the whole Bible. On the other hand, the entire Bible could be gathered into a single codex of not an immoderate size. Examples of such MSS. are *Codex Vaticanus* and *Codex Sinaiticus*, for which the finest vellum was employed.

---

[2] Parchment differs from leather in not being tanned, but smoothed with pumice after the hairs and flesh have been removed. Strictly speaking, vellum refers to materials prepared from calves and antelopes, and parchment from sheep, etc., but, practically speaking, there is no distinction between these two materials. The sheet of vellum was folded into quires, and the writing was arranged into one, two, or more columns. Cf. Steinmueller, J. E.-Sullivan, K., art., "Parchment," "Scroll," in C.B.E.O.T.

[3] The longest papyrus roll known today is 133 feet long.

Among the implements for writing may be mentioned the stylus (a sharp, pointed metal instrument for writing on clay or wax tablets; cf. Job 19, 24; Jer. 17, 1), the reed (used on papyrus and possibly on leather; cf. 3 John 13; Ps. 44, 1), metal pens (in the shape of a reed or quill), and ink. The ink seems to have been either the juice discharged by the cuttle-fish or a mixture of soot and gum. Metallic inks were not used with the papyrus, but were adopted early in the history of the vellum; it is this element which has caused the erosion so often seen in many early vellum MSS. (e.g., in *Codex Vaticanus* and *Codex Sinaiticus*). In the Middle Ages, how-ever, a less corrosive ink was generally employed.

(2) *The Original Languages of the Bible.*—Generally speaking, it can be said that the Old Testament was written in a branch of the Semitic language and the New Testament in the Aryan or Indo-European language. Specifically, how-ever, all the books of the Bible were originally written in one of three languages. In regard to the Old Testament, all the proto-canonical books were originally written in Hebrew,[4] and of the deutero-canonical books only the Books of Wisdom and 2 Machabees were originally written in Greek; a few parts have been written in Aramaic[5] (e.g., Dan. 2, 4[b]—7, 28; 1 Esd. 4, 7-6, 18 and 7, 12-26; Jer. 10, 11; two words in Gen. 31, 47). In regard to the New Testament, all the books were originally

[4] Etymologically, the word comes from 'ibrim, and the Israelites were called by that name, either because they descended from 'Eber (Heber), the nephew of Sem, or because they came from the region across (Hebr., 'eber)—that is, from over there, from the other side of the Euphrates River to the land of Canaan. Their language is called Hebrew for the first time in the Prologue of Sirach (132 B.C.), but prior to this time it was called the Canaanite (Isa. 19, 18) or the Jewish language (4 Kgs. 18, 26; 2 Esd. 13, 24). The rabbis call it the sacred or holy language. Cf. *Kraeling, E. G., "The Origin of the Name 'Hebrews,'" in A.J.S.L.L., 58 (1941), 237-253.

[5] The Aramaic language was sometimes called the Syrian language (2 Mach. 15, 37), or the Hebrew language (John 5, 2), or even the Chaldaic language (St. Jerome). This Aramaic language (which developed into various dialects called the Syriac, the Chaldaic, the Samaritan, the Talmudic, and the Targumic) was once the international language of diplomacy (4 Kgs. 18, 26) used by the Assyrian, Babylonian, and Persian kings, when they wished to communicate with their subjects. During and after the exile the Jewish people made use of this language. Cf. Messina, G., "L'antico arameo," in *Miscellanea Biblica*, II, 69-103.

written in Greek with the exception of the Gospel of St. Matthew, which was composed in Aramaic.   However, many Aramaic words and expressions have been employed by all the sacred writers—talitha cumi (Mark 5, 41), Ephphetha (Mark 7, 34), Abba (Rom. 8, 15), Eloi, Eloi, lamma sabacthani (Mark 15, 34), corbona (Matt. 27, 6), Haceldama (Matt. 27, 8), etc.

Almost all the books of the Old Testament, therefore, were written in the Hebrew language. Like the South Canaanite (spoken in Phœnicia and Palestine), North Canaanite (spoken at Ugarit or Ras Shamra), East Canaanite (apparent from the Sinaitic texts), and Aramaic, Hebrew was a Northwest-Semitic [6] dialect. Since the differentiation between these various dialects was well under way by the middle of the second millennium before Christ, the present Hebrew text of many books of the Old Testament may show archaic words and expressions prevalent during the early development of the Hebrew language. These Northwest-Semitic dialects, together with the East-Semitic (i.e., the Assyro-Babylonian or Accadian) and the Southwest-Semitic (i.e., the Arabic and Ethiopic), are the main branches of the Semitic language.

(3) *The Origin of the Alphabet.*[6a]—The origin of the alphabet is still shrouded in a certain degree of mystery, and has not as yet been traced with certainty. The Sumerian cuneiform system, which was borrowed and modified by the Accadians, Babylonians, Assyrians, Hittites, Mitannians, and early Persians, was syllabic. The Egyptian hieroglyphic system, to which the Cretan was similar, supposed a knowledge of hundreds of signs and symbols. The Canaanites, however, intro-

[6] Cf. *Albright, W. F., "The Present State of Syro-Palestinian Archaeology," in "The Haverford Symposium" (New Haven, 1938), 1-46; *idem,* "Recent Progress in North-Canaanite Research," in B.A.S.O.R., 30 (1938), 18-24; *Flight, J. W., "The Present State of Studies in the History of Writing in the Near East," in "The Haverford Symposium" (New Haven, 1938), 111-135; *Harris, Z. S., "Development of the Canaanite Dialects" (New Haven, 1939); *Albright, W. F., "The Old Testament and the Canaanite Language and Literature," in C.B.Q., 7 (1945), 5-31; Steinmueller, J. E.—Sullivan, K., art., "Hebrew Language," in C.B.E.O.T.

[6a] Cf. Steinmueller, J. E.- Sullivan, K., art. "Alphabet," in C.B.E.O.T.

duced the alphabet and substantially their own system of writing. Some of the more important Semitic alphabetic inscriptions may be mentioned.[7]   (1) The Proto-Sinaitic Inscriptions of Serabit (nineteenth or eighteenth century B.C.) were found in 1904-1905 by * Flinters Petrie. The script is based upon the Egyptian hieroglyphics, and the Semitic language represents a dialect closely related to the East Canaanite. Some scholars maintain that these inscriptions are the true sources of the Phœnician alphabet.   (2) The Gezer Fragment (seventeenth or sixteenth century B.C.), found in 1929, shows a close similarity to the preceding inscriptions, and furnishes a connecting link between the Phœnician alphabet and the Proto-Sinaitic inscriptions.   (3) The Ras Shamra Inscriptions (sixteenth to fourteenth century B.C.), found in 1929 on the site of the ancient Ugarit, furnish us with a cuneiform alphabet of thirty characters.   Some scholars maintain that this alphabetic system was invented in competition with the Phœnician alphabet, which was by this time already in existence.   (4) Beth Shemesh Ostracon and (5) the Byblus Texts date from the fifteenth or fourteenth century B.C.   (6) The Lachis Inscriptions on a ewer and bowl (fourteenth or thirteenth century B.C.) were found on the modern site of Tell ed-Duweir. (7) The Baluah Stele (between the fourteenth and twelfth centuries B.C.) was discovered in 1931 in the region of Moab. (8) The Tell el-Hesi Inscription dates from the thirteenth or twelfth century B.C., and (9) the Yehimilk Inscription of Byblus from the twelfth.   (10) The Ahiram Inscription of Byblus (twelfth to eleventh century) is in Phœnician script closely resembling the Moabite Stone.   (11) The Roueisseh Spearhead Inscription dates from the eleventh century B.C. (12) The Gezer Calendar Tablet, (13) the Abibaal Inscription of Byblus, and (14) the Elibaal Inscription of Byblus all date

---

[7] Cf. *Flight, J. W., *op. cit.*, 123 f; *Albright, W. F., "The Early Evolution of the Hebrew Alphabet," in B.A.S.O.R., 63 (1936), 8-12; cf. also Vaccari, A., "Scriturra Fenicia-Samaritana nella Bibbia Ebraica," in *Biblica*, 19 (1938), 188-201; *Albright, W. F., "Exploring in Sinai with the University of California African Expedition," in B.A.S.O.R., 109 (1948), 5-19; *idem*, "The Early Alphabetic Inscriptions from Sinai and Their Decipherment," *ibid.*, 110 (1948), 6-22.

from the tenth century B.C., and are written in Phœnician script. (15) The Samaria Ostraca (between 833 and 775 B.C.) is also in Phœnician script. (16) The Moabite Stone of King Mesa (ninth century B.C.) was found in 1868 near Dibon in the ancient land of the Moabites and is in Phœnician script. (17) The Baal Lebanon Plate dates from the ninth century B.C. (18) The Kalamu Inscription (ninth century B.C.) was found in 1902 at Sendschirli in Northern Syria and is in Phœnician script. (19) The Zakir Stele (ninth or eighth century B.C.) is in Aramaic script. (20) The Siloam Inscription (eighth century B.C.) was found in Jerusalem in 1880 and is in Phœnician script. (21) The Jerusalem or Ophel Ostracon dates from the seventh century B.C. (22) The Lachis Letters (589/588 B.C.) consists of eighteen ink-inscribed sherds written in old Hebrew alphabetic scripts in a language representing a dialect of Juda. These letters were written from outposts to the official in command of the garrison, which was defending this city against the army of Nabuchodonosor. Since these letters are contemporaneous with the period of the prophet Jeremias, they afford important testimony regarding the real historical situation and the very language used by the prophet. (23) The Elephantine Papyri (fifth century B.C.) were discovered in 1904 to 1907 in Egypt and are in Aramaic script. (24) The Eshmunazar Sarcophagus also dates from the fifth century B.C.

The obvious conclusion from the preceding study on the origin of the alphabet is that the oldest books of the Old Testament, and the Pentateuch in particular, might have been written in a Semitic and probably a Phœnician alphabetic system.[8]

(4) *Biblical Greek.*—The Books of Wisdom and 2 Machabees were originally written in Greek, and some of the parts of Daniel and Esther have been preserved only in the Greek. All of the books of the Old Testament were translated into the Greek at Alexandria, prior to the Christian era. Then too,

[8] Cf. Haeffele, J., "Vetus Testamentum fuitne lingua accadica signisque cuneiformibus conscriptum?" in V.D., I (1921), 340-344.

all of the books of the New Testament, with the exception of St. Matthew's Gospel, were originally written in this language.

The Greek, found in these books is not the classical Greek, but is a mixture of various dialects, especially the Attic and the Ionian, with various additions, especially from the Latin and Hebrew. This language is called the common or popular language (i.e., *koiné* Greek). It was spread by the conquests of Alexander the Great through Asia Minor, Syria and Egypt.

The Seleucids, the successors of Alexander the Great, spread this language through Syria. It was used by the inhabitants of the Decapolis and the Jews of the dispersion, who likewise had their synagogues in Jerusalem and were called Hellenists (cf. Acts 6, 1). This language was also employed by the proselytes and Greek merchants trading in Palestine. The Herodian kings favored the Greek language and culture, and the Roman procurators used this Greek in their business transactions.

CHAPTER I

THE ORIGINAL TEXTS OF THE BIBLE

Art. 1. The Hebrew-Aramaic Text of the Old Testament

Bibliography: Dennefeld, L., "Critique textuelle de l' A.T.," in
D.D.L.B. (Suppl.); * Kennedy, J., "An Aid to the Textual Emendment of
the O.T." (Edinburgh, 1928); Mangenot, E., "Texte de l' A.T." in
D.D.L.B.; Vaccari, A., "De textu hebraico V.T.," in I.B.; Wutz, F., "Exegese und Textkritik," in B.Z., 23 (1935), 1-19, 129-146; *Perles, F.,
"Analekten zur Textkritik des A.T." (Leipzig, 1922); Vaccari, A., "Due
Codici del Pentateuco Samaritano," in *Biblica,* 21 (1940), 241-246; Coppens, J. "La critique du texte hebreu de l'Ancien Testament," *ibid.,* 25
(1944), 9-49; Van der Ploeg, J. "Le rôle de la tradition orale dans la
transmission du texte de l'Ancien Testament," in R.B., 54 (1947), 5-41;
Guillaume, A., "Les manuscrits Hebreux," in R.B. 59 (1952), 182-186;
Rosen, H. B., "Remarques au sujet de la phonologie de L'Hebreu Biblique," in R.B., 60 (1953), 30-40; Saydon, P. P., "Assonance in Hebrew as
a means of expressing emphasis," in *Biblica,* 36 (1955), 287-304; *Green-
berg, M., "The Stabilization of the Text of the Hebrew Bible Reviewed
in the Light of the Hebrew Materials from the Judean Desert," in
J.A.O.S., 76 (1956), 157-167; *Wernberg-Moeller, P., "Pronouns and Suf-
fixes in the Scrolls and the Masoretic Text," in J.B.L., 76 (1957), 44-49.

(a) THE HEBREW WRITING

The present form of the Hebrew-Aramaic text betrays in
many instances a different form of script from that which
must have existed in the autographs of the sacred writers.
This was the result of a long and changeable history of the
text. The original MSS. of the hagiographers have perished,
and textual alterations, though they do not affect the substantial integrity of the text, are undeniable. These alterations in
the history of the transmission of the text may be slight modifications of the original MSS., additions made to them, glosses
or explanatory notes gradually incorporated into them, ancient
and antiquated words or phrases modernized, or faulty readings which may be ascribed to careless copyists. A knowledge
of this long and changeable history of the text will aid the
scholar to attain in many instances the original, primitive text.

The Phœnician Script.—It is very likely that the Hebrews for their first biblical books made use of a system of alphabetic writing that was akin to the Phœnician system. The various ancient inscriptions, which have been noted in the last chapter, show that this is historically possible. Variant readings occurring in the present Hebrew text also prove that the Phœnician alphabet had been used, since the easily interchangeable letters or consonants readily explain some of these variant readings [1] [compare 2 Sam. 23, 32 (Jassen) with 1 Par. 11, 34 (Hassem)].

The Aramaic Script.[2]—Jewish tradition ascribes to Esdras the change from the Phœnician to the Aramaic script. However, this is not entirely accurate. It is very likely that during and after the exile the Jewish people under the leadership of Esdras began to make use of the Aramaic script, but the change was a slow process, and the new script came into general usage only about the time of Our Lord (cf. Matt. 5, 18). This Aramaic script, which the Hebrews evolved to a new and finer form of writing, is also called the *square* script[3]

Besides the two scripts, in which the books of the Old Testament were written or into which they were changed, there are other extrinsic factors which must be considered in the

[1] Cf. Vaccari, A., "Scrittura Fenica-Samaritana nella Biblica Ebraica," in *Biblica*, 19 (1938), 188-201. The oldest Semitic papyrus found at Murabba'at, Palestine, is a palimpsest in the Hebrew language and Phoenician script and dates back to the eighth century B.C.; cf. de Vaux, R., "Les grottes de Murabba'at et leurs documents," in *R.B.*, 60 (1953), 261; Milik, J. T., "Ten Years of Discovery in the Wilderness of Judaea" (London, 1959), 129.

[2] Cf. Goettsberger, J., *op. cit.*, 409-412. The majority of the almost 600 fragmentary manuscripts of the Qumran Library (c. 150 B.C.-A.D. 68) were written in the Aramaic script.

[3] We learn palaeographically from Qumran that there are four phases playing an important role in the evolution of the square script: 1) the *archaic* phase (200-150 B.C.) being similar to the Aramaic script in contemporaneous documents; 2) the *Hasmonean* phase (150-50 B.C.) representing a formative and liberal period; 3) the *Herodian* phase arriving at a uniform size and constant shape; 4) *ornamental* script (c. A.D. 50) chosen later at the Synod of Jamnia as the type for Biblical manuscripts. Besides this square script there is also evidence at the same time of an Aramaic *cursive* and *mixed* script. Cf. Milik, J. T., "Ten Years, etc." 133-136.

transmission of the Hebrew text. Although in ancient times there was a possibility of separating words from one another by various signs (e.g., Tell el-Amarna Letters, Moabite Stone, Siloam Inscription, Samaritan script), yet the Jewish tradition stating that Moses wrote the Law as one word (i.e., *scriptio continua*) has strong support. This lack of separation of individual words explains some variant readings found in the transmission of the Massoretic Text, in the Greek as well as Latin translations (compare MT, LXX, and Vulg. in 1 Sam. 1, 1; Prov. 18, 3 etc.). The final Hebrew consonants for the letters, *k, m, n, p,* and *ts,* appear rather late, perhaps in the first or second century of our era. St. Jerome and the Talmud were acquainted with these final consonants. Although the Moabite Stone and the Elephantine Aramaic Papyri make use of signs to indicate the place where a new sentence was to begin, yet the variant divisions of verses in the Massoretic Text and the Septuagint show that there was either no separation or no definite arrangement for the *separation of sentences.* The many *abbreviations* found in the post-biblical Jewish literature indicate that these also played an important part in the transmission of the Hebrew text. In fact, abbreviations are also found in the Greek Old and New Testaments and in the Latin version. The ancient Jews, like the Phœnicians, made use of special signs for *numbers* (vertical lines for units, horizontal lines for decades, circles between two vertical lines for hundreds), and this is evident from the Elephantine Aramaic Papyri. But nowhere is there evidence that these or similar figures were employed in the biblical writings. There are two other ways in which numbers were designated: either the first letter alone of the entire word was written [e.g., m (eah) = 100] or the consonants were used as numerical signs; [4] since, however, little is known of the first system and the earliest traces of the second system are first found on Machabean coins of 140 and 139 B.C., a satisfac-

---

[4] Cf. Vaccari, A., "Compendia numerorum in S. Litteris," in V.D., 9 (1929), 257-259.

tory explanation for the variant numerical readings—both in parallel passages of the Hebrew text itself and in the texts of the Massoretic Text and various versions when compared—is still to be looked for.

(b) The History of the Text

First Period: The Transmission of the Original Text to A.D. 100.—During the first period very many variant readings appeared both in the transcription and redaction of the Hebrew text, and these are evidences of the freedom with which the text has been handled.[4a]

Besides the ordinary faults of copyists, there are also other causes explaining the variant readings. Some of the authors, for example, Jeremias (36, 2-4. 32), prepared *several copies* of their writings. Certain writings, as the Psalms (2 Par. 29, 25. 30; 35, 15) and the Proverbs (Prov. 25, 1), were scattered in large and small scrolls. Since books were constantly being added to the Canon, and these were being arranged into various collections for liturgical usage, extreme care and scrupulous accuracy were not always employed by the copyists. At the time of the Babylonian exile and the persecution of Antiochus IV Epiphanes (1 Mach. 1, 56), many copies of the sacred books were destroyed or lost, so that Nehemias and Judas Machabee made every attempt to establish new libraries of the Sacred Scriptures.

The variant readings in this first period of textual transmission can be established in a threefold manner: by comparing the parallel passages which occur in the Hebrew text; by comparing the Massoretic Text with the Septuagint, and by comparing the Hebrew text with the Samaritan Pentateuch.

The Parallel Passages of the Hebrew Text.—Besides the parallel passages occurring in the Books of Samuel, Kings, and Paralipomenon, the following are the principal ones worthy of mention:

[4a] The Qumran literature shows the great freedom that was exercised between various recensions of the Old Testament. Cf. Milik, J. T., "Ten Years, etc.," 140.

Ps.[5] 14 = 53   Jer. 52 = 4 Kgs. 24, 18—25, 30

40, 14-18 = 70   1 Esd. 2, 3-63 = 2 Esd. 7, 6-73

57, 8-12 + 60, 7-14 =   1 Par. 16, 8-35 = Ps. 105, 1-
108   15 + 96, 1-13 + 107, 1 +
                                106, 47 f

18 = 2 Sam. 22

Isa. 2, 2-4 = Mich. 4, 1-3   Ex. 20 = Deut. 5, 6 ff
36—39 = 4 Kgs. 18,   Lev. 9, 2 ff = Deut. 14, 4 ff
13—20, 19

Jer. 49, 7-14 = Abd. 1-9

When these texts are carefully compared, it will be noticed that many textual changes had crept into the text during this first period. There are *confusion of consonants* (2 Sam. 22, 11 and Ps. 18, 14), *dittography* (2 Sam. 23, 8 josheb bashshebeth, i.e., sitting in the chair, for Ishbosheth), *haplography* (Ps. 18, 6 and 2 Sam. 22, 6), *homœoteleuton* (1 Par. 11, 13 and 2 Sam. 23, 10 f), *substitution of synonyms* (Ps. 18, 7 and 2 Sam. 22, 7), *bosheth* replaces *baal* in proper names (2 Sam. 2, 8 and 1 Par. 8, 33; Jdgs. 6, 32 and 2 Sam. 11, 21), *Elohim* is substituted for Jahweh (Ps. 42-84).

The Differences between the Massoretic Text and the Septuagint.—The Septuagint represents a Hebrew text that is much older than the present Massoretic Text.[6] In many instances words and expressions of the Greek version reflect a Hebrew text different from the Massoretic Text.[7] There are also some notable differences of sequence, omissions, additions, and abbreviations. Chapters 36-39 of Exodus, which deal with

[5] The Psalms here are cited according to the numbers in the Massoretic Text.

[6] Cf. Wutz, F., "Alte Stämme und Formen die von G (S) nich bezeugt werden," in B.Z., 18 (1928), 1-31.

[7] Cf. *Swete, H. B., "An Introduction to the Old Testament in Greek" (2nd ed., Cambridge, 1914), 442-444; Skehan, P. W. "Qumran and the Present State of Old Testament Text Studies: The Masoretic Text," in J.B.L., 78 (1959), 21-25; *Orlinsky, H. M., "The Septuagint Text," *ibid.*, 26-33.

the erection of the tabernacle and other things pertaining to the divine worship, have extraordinary variations in the Greek; some verses are omitted and others are transposed. The following passages are not found in the Greek: 1 Sam. 17, 12-31; 17, 55—18, 5; 1 Par. 1, 10-23. In chapters 11 and 12 of 2 Esdras there is an omission of twenty-three verses. A difference of sequence is found in 3 Kings 4—7, as well as in Proverbs 24, 23—31, 10. In the Book of Jeremias, the prophecies against the Gentiles (MT and Vulg. chs. 46-51) are placed in the Greek in the middle of the book (after 25, 14) and according to a new plan. An historical introduction is prefixed to the Book of Lamentations by the Greek translator. The deutero-canonical parts of Esther and Daniel are also contained in the Septuagint.

The Differences between the Massoretic Text and the Samaritan Pentateuch.—Although there is a substantial identity between these two texts, yet there are some notable differences in details. There are some *textual transpositions* (Ex. 30, 1-10 is placed after 26, 35 in the Samaritan Text, and Ex. 29, 21 is placed after 29, 28), and *additions* by the Samaritan Pentateuch (after Ex. 7, 18. 29; 8, 1. 19; 9, 5. 19; before Ex. 10, 3; 11, 3; Num. 31, 20 etc.). There are also some minor changes in *orthography, accidence, meaning,* and *numbers.*

As illustrative of conditions toward the end of this period, mention must be made of the entire Qumran literature, consisting of Isaias and fragmentary remains of the proto-canonical and some deutero-canonical books as well as various apocryphal and sectarian Essenian books (see above: Apocryphal Books). Secondly, there is about the same time as the Qumran literature the extensive Jewish activity in Egypt with the Greek Septuagint, and this literary activity included the copying of Hebrew Biblical texts as we know from the *Papyrus Nash*,[8] which was found in 1902 in the Fayum region of Middle Egypt. It probably belongs to the second century B.C. (thus e.g., *Albright, *Birnbaum), consists of one page of 24 lines

[8] Cf. R.B., I (1904), 242-250; Vaccari, A., "Papyri hebraicæ," in V.D., 3 (1923), 284 f.

with approximately 30 letters to a line, and contains the entire
Decalogue (Ex. 20, 2-17 or Deut. 5, 6-21) and the beginning
of the Shema. Thirdly, the textual condition of the Hebrew
Old Testament may also be obtained by taking into proper
consideration the Old Testament citations of some of the rabbis
in the Mishna and the Greek quotations not only of the Jewish
writers as Josephus Flavius of Palestine and Philo of Egypt,
but also of the Apostolic Fathers of the Church.

Second Period: From A.D. 100 to 500.—At the beginning of
this period one recension or critical text became predominant
in Jewish circles, and was preferred to all other codices. The
adoption of a MS. as the standard text seems to have been
made by the scribes at the Synod of Jamnia. This text in
regard to its consonants has remained substantially unchanged
from about A.D. 100.

Whereas the Vulgate of St. Jerome, the citations of some of
the rabbis in the Mishna, the Gemara, the Targums, and the
revisions of the Greek Text (e.g., Aquila, Symmachus, Theodotion, Quinta, Sexta, and Septima of Origen) suppose substantially the same textual form as the Massoretic Text, the
Syriac Peshitto and much more the Septuagint differ from this
Hebrew text and frequently represent a purer and a genuine
transmission of the original text.[9]

During this period the *Tannaim* (i.e., the teachers of the
Mishna) and *Amoraim,* or Talmudists, continued the work of
their immediate predecessors. They divided the text into
verses, numbered them, and put the total at the end of each
book. When there was a question of correcting errors, they
added a little circle or star over the error, and then in the
margin (but not in the text) they noted the reading which
they preferred, employing the words *Kethib* (i.e., what is
written) and *Qere* (i.e., what must be read). They also
marked with peculiar signs certain readings which seemed
doubtful to them, but made very few changes—about eighteen
in the entire text.[10]

[9] Cf. Goettsberger, J., *op. cit.,* 422.
[10] Cf. Vaccari, A., in I.B., 231 f.

Third Period: From A.D. 500 to 900.—During this period the last and most extensive activity in regard to the Old Testament text was witnessed. The Massoretes, called the collectors of tradition (Hebr., *ba'ale hammassoreth*), collected, arranged, and continued the results of the biblical criticism of the past. At the same time, to facilitate and secure the correct reading of the text, they placed in and around the consonants various signs to indicate the vowels.

The Vowel System.[11]—In the beginning the Semitic alphabet consisted solely of consonants. Gradually the necessity of using vowels was experienced, and a few consonants, called "matres lectionis" (yod, waw, he, aleph), were employed as vowels. The Greeks were the first people to isolate the vowel from the syllable, and by uniting the isolated consonants with the isolated vowels furnished the basis of exact pronunciation. The various early Greek transcriptions of the Hebrew text by the Jews of the dispersion show what attempts were made to secure the correct reading of the text. At the time of St. Jerome it does not seem that the Palestinian Jews made use of vowels, or if they did so, their use was very rare (cf. *Ep. lxxiii ad Evangelum,* 8 in M.L., XXII, 445). The Septuagint, St. Jerome, and the Talmud are acquainted with the exact pronunciation of the text but not with a vowel system. On the other hand, a Hebrew MS. of the tenth century is fully equipped with a perfect pointed text, which has all the vowels, punctuation, and accentuation.

The consonantal text equipped with vowel signs was developed in two principal systems: the school of *Tiberias* or western system (which is generally adopted today and is the infra-linear punctuation), and the school of *Babylonia* (which is supra-linear punctuation). These various systems, based upon the articulation of words known by oral tradition, give us substantially the correct pronunciation; they received their definite form during the seventh or eighth century.

[11] Cf. Goettsberger, J., *op. cit.,* 415 f; Wutz, F., "Abweichende Vokalisationsüberlieferung im hebr. Text," in B.Z., 21 (1933), 9-21.

The Writings of the Massoretes.[12]—The Massoretes by placing the vowels, punctuation, and accentuation in the consonantal text rendered the Hebrew text immutable. In addition, they numbered the verses, words, and letters of every book, indicated what verse, word, and letter was in the middle of the book, and noted the frequency of individual letters. Part of the material which they had collected was added at times to the Biblical MSS. When this was written on the upper or lower margins and spread out, it was called the *Massora marginalis magna;* when this was written next to the text and between the columns in a short and abbreviated form, it was called *Massora marginalis parva.* At other times these notes were collected in separate MSS. and kept distinct from the biblical text.

The oldest dated MS. is the Codex Petropolitanus (916), which contains the Later Prophets and the Massora, written in the Babylonian punctuation. Other codices of the tenth century are also extant.

(c) THE PRINTED TEXT

The Hebrew text of the Psalter with the commentary of * D. Kimchi was the first Hebrew book of the Bible to be printed (Bologna, 1477). This was followed by the publication of the Pentateuch with the Targum of Onkelos and the commentary of * Rabbi S. Jarchi (Bologna, 1482). Next apveared the Prophets (Socino, 1485), and the Hagiographa (Naples, 1486-1487).

The first complete edition of the entire Hebrew Bible was published at Socino in 1483 under the direction of * Abraham Chajjim. Subsequently the Hebrew Bible was printed in various places, but of the various editions which appeared one is worthy of particular attention—the *Rabbinical Bible,* edited

---

[12] Cf. Hyvernat, H., "Petite introduction a l'étude de la Massora," in R.B., 11 (1902), 551-563, 12 (1903), 529-549; *idem,* "Lexique Masorétique," in R.B., 13 (1904), 521-546, 14 (1905), 203-254, 515-542; Ramirey, A., "Un texto puntuado y Masora, etc.," in *Biblica,* 10 (1929), 200-213, 11 (1930), 108-121, 14 (1933), 303-329.

by * James ben Chajjim and printed by Daniel Bomberg at Venice in 1524-1525. The text of Chajjim represented a critical study of MSS. of the Massoretic Text and became the "textus receptus."

Critical editions to the Hebrew Old Testament were issued at Oxford in 1776-1788 by * B. Kennicot, whose critical labors were supplemented by the famous Orientalist of Parma, John Bernard de Rossi, in 1784-1788 and again in 1798.

In more recent times critical editions were published by * S. Baer and * Francis Delitzsch (Leipzig, 1869-1892), by * D. C. Ginsburg (London, 1894-1896, 1906, etc.), *R. Kittel in collaboration with many editors (4th ed., Stuttgart 1949).[12a]

The division of the Hebrew Bible into our present system of chapters was borrowed by * R. Solomon ben Ismael (1330) from the Vulgate, and occurs in the 1524-1525 Bomberg Bible. The present verse division was first introduced into the Hebrew printed text by Sabionetta for the Psalter (1556) and by Arias Montanus for the entire Bible (1571) in the Antwerp Polyglot.[13]

In these Hebrew Bibles one may also find a certain liturgical division, called *Parashah* or section, which goes back to ancient times (cf. Acts 15, 21; Josephus, *Contra Apionem*, II, 17). According to the Babylonian Jews and later the Palestinian Jews, the Sabbath lessons were divided into 54 large Parashahs for the Pentateuch, so that these readings would last for the entire year. Every Parashah is divided into smaller sections, which number 669 smaller sections for the Law; these sections were ultimately determined by Moses Maimonides. Some of these smaller sections are called *open* (Hebr. pethuhoth), and begin a new line; their number is given as 290. Other smaller sections are called *closed* (Hebr. sethumoth), and designate a sub-section which begins in the middle of a line; their number is given as 379. The sections taken from the other books of the Old Testament for liturgi-

---

[12a] For a good concordance consult * Mandelkern, S.V.T., "Concordantiae hebraicae atque chaldaicae" (2nd ed., Berlin, 1925).

[13] Cf. Goettsberger, J., *op. cit.*, 415.

cal reading are called *haphtaroth*. The modern Hebrew Bibles also contain at times the division of the Massoretes into *sedarim* or orders; for the Pentateuch there are from 154 to 167, and for the entire Old Testament 452. These *sedarim* were used for a triennial cycle of Sabbath reading by the Palestinian Jews, or served as convenient pegs for the scholar to allude to a particular passage in his explanation of the text.[14]

(d) The Critical Value of the Massoretic Text

Our Massoretic Text substantially represents the Hebrew consonantal text which was selected from the various Hebrew MSS. at the end of the first century of our era. Since, however, one textual form became predominant and was used exclusively as the standard in Jewish circles, the study of Massoretic biblical MSS., no matter how numerous they may be, will offer very few variant readings of major importance. On the other hand, the Septuagint and Syriac Peshitto at times show traces of a different Hebrew archetype, and will aid the critical scholar to obtain an accurate or fairly accurate reconstruction of the primitive text.

(1) The Massoretic Text is generally a *good critical text* and agrees substantially with the original text. In this sense it should be regarded as *authentic* and used as the basic text for Old Testament interpretation.

(2) There are, however, irrefutable signs of *textual defects* in the Massoretic Text, where the exact words of the hagiographers have not always been preserved. These corrupted or false readings, though they do not affect the substantial integrity of the text, should not be preferred to those obtained from the other versions, especially the Septuagint, when the latter are critically certain, render the meaning more intelligible, and explain satisfactorily the causes for these variant readings in the Massoretic Text.

(3) In many cases the textual corruption preceded the

---

[14] Cf. Goettsberger, J., *op. cit.*, 415.

Septuagint version, and the primitive Hebrew text must be reconstructed by means of *conjectural criticism*. Here the dangers of treating the text quite arbitrarily are increased, if we are subjectively inclined to uncertain theories; for example, if a critic accepts a doubtful metrical system as the criterion of textual criticism, or if he is a priori dominated by alleged conclusions of a literary criticism such as that proposed by the school of * Graf-Wellhausen.

Art. 2. The Greek Text of the New Testament

General Bibliography: *Westcott-Hort, "The N.T. in the Original Greek," 2 (London, 1881—); *Gregory, C. R., "Prolegomena ad N.T. græce" (Leipzig, 1884-1894); *idem,* "Textkritik des N.T." (Leipzig, 1900); *idem,* "Canon and Text of the N.T." (Edinburgh, 1907); *idem,* "Die griech. Handschriften des N.T." (Leipzig, 1908); *idem,* "Einleitung in das N.T." (Leipzig, 1909); *Von Soden, H., "Die Schriften des N.T. in ihrer ältesten erreichbaren Textgestalt," 1 (Berlin, 1902-1910); *Scrivener—Miller, "A Plain Introduction to the Criticism of the N.T." (4th ed., London, 1894); Jacquier, E., "Le N.T. dans l'Eglise chrétienne," 2 (Paris, 1913); *Kenyon, F. G., "Handbook to the Textual Criticism of the N.T." (London, 1926); *idem,* "The Text of the Greek Bible" (London, 1937); Lagrange, M. J., "Introduction à l'étude du N.T.," 2 (Paris, 1935); *Lake, K., "The Text of the N.T." (6th ed., New London, 1928); *Milligan, G., "The N.T. and Its Transmission" (London, 1932); *Robertson, A. T., "An Introduction to the Textual Criticism of the N.T." (London, 1925); Sacco, G., "La Koine del N.T. e la trasmissione del sacro testo" (Rome, 1928); *Souter, A., "The Text and Canon of the N.T." (London, 1930); Vaganay, L., "An Introduction to the Textual Criticism of the N.T." (St. Louis, 1937); Vogels, H. J., "Handbuch des Neutestamenlichen Textkritik" (Münster, 1923); Zerwick, M., "Quid cognito graecitatis biblicae ad S.Scripturam interpretandam conferat," in V.D., 23 (1943), 55-62, 89-96, 122-128, 147-158, 213-219, 245-256; *Metzger, B. M., "Recent Spanish Contribution to the Textual Criticism of the N.T.," in J.B.L., 66 (1947), 401-423; *Wilgren, A., "The Use of the Versions in N.T. Textual Criticism," in J.B.L., 67 (1948), 135-142; *Morgenthaler, R., "Statistik des Neutestamenlichen Wortschatzes" (Zürich-Frankfurt a/M, 1958).

GRAMMARS OF THE N.T.: Abel, F. M., "Grammaire du Grec biblique" (Paris, 1927); *Blass-Debrunner, "Grammatik des neutestl. Griechisch" (6th ed., Göttingen, 1931); *Moulton, I. H., "A Grammar of the N.T. Greek" (2 vols., Edinburgh, 1920); *Nunn, H. P. V., "A Short Syntax of N.T. Greek" (3rd ed., Cambridge, 1920); Idem, "The Elements of the N.T. Greek" (Cambridge, 1914); *Robertson, A. T., "A Short Grammar of the Greek N.T." (4th ed., London, 1919).

DICTIONARIES OF THE N.T. GREEK: *Bauer, W., "Griechisch-Deutsches Wörterbuch zu den Schriften des N.T." (3rd ed., Berlin, 1937); *Grimm-Thayer, "Greek-English Lexicon of the N.T." (London, 1904); *Moulton-Milligan, "The Vocabulary of the Greek Testament Illustrated from the Papyri" (London, 1929); Zorell, "Lexicon Græcum N.T." (Paris, 1930).

CONCORDANCES TO THE N.T. GREEK: *Bruder, C. H. "Concordantiæ omnium vocum N.T." (7th ed., Göttingen, 1913); *Moulton-Geden, "A Concordance to the Greek Testament" (Edinburgh, 1897); *Schmoller, "Handkonkordanz zum Griech. N.T." (5th ed., Stuttgart, 1931).

PALÆOGRAPHY: *Gardthausen, V., "Griechische Paläographie," I (2nd ed., Leipzig, 1911-1913); *Kenyon, F. G., "Books and Readers in Ancient Greece and Rome" (London, 1932); *Schubert, W., "Einführung in die Papyruskunde" (Berlin, 1918); Idem, "Griechische Paläographie" (Munich, 1925); *Thompson, E. M., "An Introduction to Greek and Latin Palæography" (Oxford, 1912); Vogels, H. I., "Codicum N.T. Specimina" (Bonn, 1929).

The MSS. of the New Testament display two forms of the letters. The *uncials,* or *majuscules,* are large capital letters, and these were employed exclusively on the vellum or parchment codices till the ninth or tenth century. The *minuscules* are small letters generally linked together by ligatures, and for this reason this kind of writing is often called *cursive* (i.e., running). From about the middle of the ninth century when they began, and almost exclusively from the eleventh century, these letters continued in use until the invention of printing.

In the uncials as well as in some of the older minuscules there was no separation made between the various words, thus giving the occasion for variant readings (cf. John 1, 3). Though punctuation and accentuation were known to the Alexandrian grammarians, they did not come into common usage until the seventh or eighth century. Then, too, in the older codices a few abbreviations occur (e.g., for Jesus, Christ, Israel, Jerusalem, etc.), and at times these gave rise to variant readings in later codices.

To supply for the lack of punctuation, a book which was meant for the public was at times divided according to the meaning. A *colon* was to show that a phrase was long, and a *comma* was to indicate that the phrase was short. These are to be distinguished from the term *stichometry,* which ordinarily consisted of sixteen syllables or thirty-six letters to the line and was used commercially to estimate the earnings of the copyist.

(a) THE GREEK TEXT OF THE NEW TESTAMENT

No *autographs* of the New Testament writers are extant. Many *apographic* MSS., however, are available and these reproduce the words of the Greek autographs. Besides the Patristic citations, which are true witnesses of the textual condition existing at the time of their writing, there are lectionaries (i.e., parts of the Scriptures employed in the liturgy) and various early versions, which represent or reproduce the meaning of the original texts into other languages.

(1) *The Number of MSS.*—Up to the present 4,288 MSS. of the Greek New Testament have been catalogued. These codices are classified under four main heads:

Papyri 67
Uncials 210
Minuscules 2,401
Lectionaries 1,610

Of these many MSS. only 53 contain the entire New Testament, while the rest have only parts of it.

(2) *The Designation of These MSS.*—The system commonly accepted today by scholars for indicating the various MSS. is that suggested by * C. R. Gregory. The papyri are denoted by *P* followed by a number. Uncials are denoted by numbers preceded by O, but for the first forty-five of them the old designations of * Wettstein and * Tischendorf by Latin, Greek capital letters, and the Hebrew letter *aleph* are retained. Minuscules are designated by Arabic numerals. For the lectionaries the letter *l* is taken followed by the Arabic numerals.

The system of * Von Soden has been abandoned by modern scholars, because it proved too cumbersome to be practical. He eliminated the distinction between the uncials and the minuscules, and indicated the MSS. by numerals preceded by the letter δ, ε, or α, which signified respectively διαθήκη (i.e., codices containing the entire New Testament), εὐαγγέλιον (i.e., codices containing the Gospels alone), and ἀπόστολος (i.e., codices containing the Apostolic writings). The Arabic numbers were not arranged in continuous succession, but were added to indicate the age of the codex (cf. Jacquier, *op. cit.*, 72 ff.).

Among the *Papyri* [14a] MSS., P [52] (Manchester, Rylands Library) of the early second century contains John 18, 31—33. 37 f. This small fragment of a code of the Fourth Gospel is the earliest known fragment of any MS. of the New Testament, and is important as evidence for the early circulation of this Gospel; in fact, within a generation after its composition it is found in a distant locality.[15] Among the newest acquisitions are the Chester Beatty Collection, P[45], P[46], and P[47]—remnants not of rolls but of codices. P[45] consists of thirty leaves of a codex, which originally contained all of the four Gospels and the Acts; it is of the early third century.[16] P[46] consists of eighty-six leaves, of which thirty are at Ann Arbor, Michigan; originally the MS. contained all of the Pauline Epistles with the possible exception of the Pastoral Epistles, and is of the early third century.[17] P[47] consists of ten leaves of a third-century codex, which originally contained the Apocalypse of St. John.[18] Written about the same time as the Chester Beatty papyri is P [66] (Papyrus Bodmer II) con-

---

[14a] *Clark, K. W., "A Descriptive Catalogue of Greek N.T. MSS. in America" (Chicago. 1937); *Maldfeld, G.-*Metzger, B. M., "Detailed List of the Greek Papyri of the New Testament," in J.B.L., 68 (1949), 359-370 (that is, Papyrus 1-62); Florit, E., "Parlano anche i Papiri" (2nd ed., Rome, 1943); *Metzger, B. M., "Recently Published Greek Papyri of the N.T.," in B.A., 10 (1947), 25-44; *idem*, "Recent Discoveries and Investigations of N.T. Manuscripts," in J.B.L., 78 (1959), 13-20.

[15] Cf. *Roberts, C. H., "An Unpublished Fragment of the Fourth Gospel" (Manchester, 1935); *Bell, H. I.-*Skeat, T. C., "Fragments of an Unknown Gospel" (London, 1935).

[16-18] Cf. * Kenyon, F. C., "Chester Beatty Biblical Papyri" (London, 1933-1936); * Sanders, H. A., "A Third-Century Papyrus Codex of the Epistles of St. Paul" (Ann Arbor, 1935); * Lietzmann, H., "Zur Würdigung der Chester-Beatty Papyrus der Paulusbriefe" (Berlin, 1934); Merk, A., in *Miscellanea Biblica* II (Rome, 1934), 375-406; Lagrange, M. J., in R.B., 43 (1934), 4-41, 161-171, 481-493.

taining two thirds of the Gospel of St. John.[19] Among the most recent additions is P [67] (Papyrus Barcinonensis I), two fragments or folios of about the second century containing a few verses from St. Matthew's Gospel.[20]

Among the principal uncials[21] may be mentioned: *Codex Sinaiticus* (א or S, or δ 2, or 01) of the early fourth century, containing the whole of the New Testament; *Codex Alexandrinus* (A, or δ 4, or 02) of the early fifth century, containing the entire New Testament with, however, some serious gaps; *Codex Vaticanus* (B, or δ 1, or 03) of the early fourth century, containing the books of the New Testament up to Hebrews 9, 14 (the rest has been lost); *Codex Ephraemi* (C, or δ 3, or 04), a palimpsest text of the fifth century, consisting originally of the entire New Testament but now containing only two-thirds (every book, excepting 2 Thess. and 2 John, is represented); *Codex Cantabrigiensis* or *Bezæ* (D, or δ 5, or 05) of the fifth or sixth century, consisting of the four Gospels and the Acts, but with gaps both in the Greek and in the Latin; *Codex Claromontanus* (D^p, or α 1026, or 06) of the sixth century, consisting of the Pauline Epistles but with some gaps both in the Greek and in the Latin.

There are about fifty minuscules which contain the entire New Testament, but among the many minuscule MSS. worthy of mention may be cited 33 (or δ 48) of the ninth century

[19] Cf. *Martin, V., "Papyrus Bodmer II. Evangile de Jean, chap. 1-14" Geneva, 1956); *idem*, "Papyrus Bodmer II, Supplement: Evangile de Jean, chap. 14-21" (Cologny-Geneva, 1958); Boismard, M.-E., "Le Papyrus Bodmer II," in R.B., 64 (1947), 363-398; Smothers, E. R., "Papyrus Bodmer II; An Early Codex of St. John," in *Theol. St.*, 18 (1957), 434-441; Collins, J. J., "Papyrus Bodmer II," in C.B.Q., 20 (1958), 281-289; Zimmermann, H., "Papyrus Bodmer II und seine Bedeutung für die Textgeschichte des Johannes-Evangeliums," in B.Z., 2 (1958), 214-243.

[20] Cf. Bartina, S., "Another New Testament Papyrus (P⁶⁷)," in C.B.Q., 20 (1958), 290 f.

[21] Cf. * Kenyon, F. G., "The Text, etc.," 75-96; * Milne, H. J. H.-* Skeat T. C., "Scribes and Correctors of the Cod. Sinaiticus" (London, 1938); *idem*, "The Codex Sinaiticus and the Codex Alexandrinus" (London, 1938); Stegmüller, O., "Zu dem Bibelorakeln in Codex Bezae," in *Biblica*, 34 (1953), 13-22; *Oliver, H. H., "A Textual Transposition in Codex C (Ephraemi Syri rescriptus)," in J.B.L., 76 (1957), 233-236; *Halch, W. H. P., "The Greek MSS. of the N.T. 1. At Mt. Sinai" (Paris, 1932); "2. At Jerusalem" (Paris, 1934).

(considered as the queen of the minuscules) and the Ferrar group [so-called after * Professor Ferrar (d. 1871) of Dublin University], which is headed by 13[21a] (of the twelfth century) and includes 69, 124, 346, 543, 713, 788, 826, 828, 983. This Ferrar group of MSS. displays various peculiarities: the passage of the adulteress (John 7, 53—8, 11) is placed after Luke 21, 38; the account of the bloody sweat (Luke 22, 43 f) is placed after Matt. 26, 39.   Critical scholars hold that this group originated in Calabria or Sicily, and is to be associated with the Cæsarean group of MSS.

The lectionaires are liturgical books containing either readings from the Gospels only (evangeliaries), or from the Acts and Epistles (epistolaries), or from both (complete lectionaries).   They are written in uncials or semi-uncials, and are generally parchment MSS. about three-fourths of them are evangeliaries, while there are only about 170 complete lectionaries; the oldest of these does not go back beyond the sixth century.[22]   Too little value is still attached to these MSS.

(3) *The Classification of These MSS.*—It is essential for clearness, simplicity, and certainty, as well as for the knowledge of the history of the text, to ascertain the mutual relationship existing between the MSS. and then to reduce all these witnesses as far as possible to individual classes or families.   This procedure has entailed long, patient, and scholarly research, and consisted first in eliminating useless codices as witnesses (when they depend upon others and lack authority for some reason or another), and secondly in reducing the useful witnesses to family classifications.

Among the scholars who have contributed most in classifying the MSS. into various families are: * J. Bengel (1734), * J.

[21a] Cf. *Lake, K. and S., "Family 13 (The Ferrar Group). The Text according to Mark. With a Collation of Codex 28 of the Gospels" (London, 1941).

[22] Cf. *Colwell, E. C.,-*Riddle, D. W., "Prolegomena to the Study of the Lectionary Text of the Gospels" (Chicago, 1933); *Branton, J. R., "The Common Text of the Gospel Lectionary in the Lenten Lections" (Chicago, 1934); *Redus, M. W., "The Text of the Major Festivals of the Menologies in the Greek Gospel Lectionary" (Chicago, 1936; *Buck, H. M., "The Johannine Lessons in the Greek Gospel Lectionary" (Chicago, 1958).

S. Semmler (1767), * J. J. Griesbach (1774-1777), L. Hug (1826), J. M. Scholz (1830), * Westcott and * Hort (1881: Alexandrian, Neutral, Western, and Syrian Families), * Von Soden [1902-1910: H(esychian), I(erusalem), and K(oine) Families], * B. H. Streeter (1924: Cæsarean Family added), and * F. G. Kenyon [1937: α (Byzantine), β (Alexandrian), γ (Cæsarean), δ (Western), and ε (Syrian) Families].

Since these various families show peculiar characteristics, it is necessary to study these qualities, if we wish to arrive at the original text of the New Testament books. The influence of these families may vary for the different books.

The Gospels.—The first family (called by scholars either Neutral, Hesychian, or Alexandrian) consists of the older uncials, at the head of which is B. It is supported by a few minuscules (33 and 157), and by the Coptic (i.e., Bohairic and Sahidic) and (to a large extent) the Vulgate versions. Of the Fathers Origen is the most important witness of this type, and at times Clement of Alexandria. Some of the chief characteristics of this family are: *brevity* (e.g., in Matt. 1, 25 it omits "suum primogenitum," in Matt. 5, 22 "sine causa," in John 3, 13 "qui est in cœlis," in Mark 16, 9 to the end, in John 7, 53-8, 11), the *common forms* of the words and orthography, and relative *immunity from harmonistic tendencies* (e.g., Matt. 5, 44 lacks the addition in Luke 6, 27 f, and Luke 11, 2 ff lacks the addition in Matt. 6, 9 ff). This textual family had its place of origin in Egypt, probably at Alexandria, and is considered by critics to have the greatest critical value.

The second family (called Western [22a] because of its wide diffusion in the West) consists of D (and W in Mark 1-5), the Old Latin, especially the African forms, and St. Cyprian. Some of the chief characteristics of this family are: *additions* (cf. Luke 11, 2-4; Matt. 20, 16), *a few significant omissions* (cf. Luke 10, 42; 24, 51 f), *paraphrases* (cf. Luke 5, 10 f. 15 f.

[22a] Cf. *Kenyon, F.G., "The Western Texts in the Gospel and Acts" (London, 1939).

27), and *harmonistic tendencies* (cf. Luke 3, 24-31 in the genealogy of Christ).

The third family (called Cæsarean or Palestinian) is the latest addition to the textual apparatus.[23]   It consists of Codices Koridethi or θ (of the eighth century), 700 (of the eleventh or twelfth century), and 565 (of the ninth or tenth century), which correspond to a text used by Origen during the latter part of his life and by Eusebius of Cæsarea. To these MSS. can be added for the Gospel of St. Mark: P^{45}, W, Famm. 1 and 13. P^{45} shows that this text was current in Egypt, and this textual form may have originated there; Cæsarea, therefore, should be regarded as the chief place of utilization. Because of its peculiarities, this Cæsarean group stands midway between the Neutral (Alexandrian) and Western texts. For the other Gospels the Cæsarean text has not yet been definitely established.

The fourth family [24] (also called Byzantine, Antiochian, or Lucian Recension) is found in the greater number of uncials (headed by A), and the great majority of minuscules; it was entrenched in print by the printed editions of Erasmus and Stephanus, and became known as the *Textus Receptus* or the Received Text. Some of the chief characteristics of this family are: *elegance of diction* (i.e., it polishes the language by bringing the forms of words and also the syntax in harmony with classical usage), *harmonistic tendencies, additions* (i.e., by adding here and there a subject or object, or

---

[23] Cf. *Streeter, B. H., "The Four Gospels" (2nd ed., London, 1927); * Lake and * Blake, "The Text of the Gospels and the Koridethi Codex," in *Harvard Theol. Rev.*, 16 (1923), 267-286; *idem*, "The Caesarean Text of the Gospel of Mark," *ibid.*, 21 (1928), 207 ff; Lagrange, M. J., "Le group dite Cesaréen des manuscrits des Evangiles," in R.B., 38 (1929), 481-512; *idem*, "Introduction, etc.," II, 144-168; * Kenyon, F. G., "Recent Developments in the Textual Criticism of the Greek Bible" (London, 1933); Ayuso, T., "Texto Cesariense e precesariense?" in *Biblica*, 16, (1935), 369-415; Stapleton, M. "Early Revisions of the Greek Gospels," in *St. Louis Proceedings* (1937), 38-57; *Metzger, B. M., "The Caesarean Text of the Gospels," in J.B.L., 64 (1945), 457-489; * Hills, E., "The Inter-Relationship of the Caesarean Manuscripts," in J.B.L., 68 (1949), 141-159.

[24] Cf. *Kenyon, F. G., "The Text, etc.," 197-203; *Lake, K. & S., "The Byzantine Text of the Gospels," in *Memorial Lagrange* (Paris, 1940), 251-258; Lattey, C., "The Antiochene Text," in Scripture, 4 (1951), 273-276.

by changing the construction for the sake of clearness), and *conflation* (i.e., by combining two variant readings: cf. Luke 24, 53 "laudantes et benedicentes"). This type of text made its first appearance about the end of the fourth century, and then became predominant in the Church of Constantinople.

The fifth family (called the Syrian) is represented in the Old Syriac version, and its Western color is due to the influence of Tatian's *Diatessaron*. The other Syriac versions, the Armenian and Georgian versions, help to reconstruct this textual type.

The Acts of the Apostles.—In regard to the Acts of the Apostles, three families of MSS. are of importance. These families may be represented by codices different from those given for the Gospels.

The first family, the Alexandrian or Neutral, is characterized by its purity and abridgment, and is represented by the manuscripts B, S, C, A, and by the Coptic Bohairic and the Latin Vulgate versions.

The second family, the Western, is represented by the Græco-Latin bilinguals D, E, with the Old Latin MSS. and P^{41}, P^{48}. The variations in additions and paraphrases are so numerous from the preceding family that scholars have offered various theories to explain these differences.[25]

Another family, the Byzantine or Antiochian, is represented by the manuscripts L, P, H, etc. It approximates the first family of MSS., but borrowed some additions from the second family of MSS.

The Pauline Epistles.—In the Pauline Epistles there are no variations in substance between the first and second families. The first family is represented by the manuscripts B, S, C, A, and the second by the Græco-Latin bilinguals D, E, G, F. Most of the variants in the second family are purely verbal, or slight expansions to clarify the reading or meaning.

The Byzantine or Antiochian text, represented principally

---

[25] Cf. *Kenyon, F. G., *ibid.*, 224-236; *idem*, "The Western Text in the Gospel and Acts" (London, 1939); Steinmueller, J. E., in C.S.S., III, 223 f.

by manuscripts K, L, is characterized by its elegance of diction and tendency at times to conflate the text.

The Catholic Epistles.—Since the manuscript D lacks by mutilation the Catholic Epistles, the Western readings for the Catholic Epistles cannot be given with certainty. Hence, these Epistles are represented by only two families of MSS.: the Alexandrian by manuscripts B, S, C, A, and the Byzantine by L and some minuscules.

The Apocalypse.—For the Apocalypse there is no Greek MS. representative of the Western family. The Latin versions have been made from the Alexandrian family, which is to be sought in S, C, A. The Byzantine text may be reconstructed from the commentary of Bishop Andrew of Cæsarea in Cappadocia.[26]

(b) The History of the Greek Text of the New Testament

During the second and third century the *Western* text (so called from its wide diffusion in the West, although it was derived from a Greek original) was spread everywhere. This type of text is found in the writings of St. Justin Martyr, St. Irenæus, and Clement of Alexandria, in P^{38} and P^{48}, in the Old Latin, and partly in the Sahidic. This textual type was also used by Marcion and Tatian in his *Diatessaron*, which Gospel Harmony influenced the Old Syriac version, where readings from the Western text are found.[27]

At the beginning of the third century there arose under editorial supervision in Egypt, probably at Alexandria, a text which is represented mainly by the two great uncials B and S, and is found in many MSS. of Egyptian origin and in the Coptic versions. Origen (d. 254-255), at least in his earlier writings, made use of MSS. predominantly of this type. Eusebius of Cæsarea, who followed the traditions of Origen,

---

[26] Cf. Schmid, J., "Untersuchungen zur Geschichte der griech. Apokalipsetextes," in *Biblica,* 17 (1936), 11-44, 167-201, 273-293, 429-460.
[27] Cf. * Kenyon, F. G., "The Text, etc.," 117-124.

introduced into the Gospels a system of sections and canons, which system of notation is still found in some of the modern editions of the Greek text (e.g., that of * E. Nestle). Some modern scholars (e.g., * Von Soden) have tried to associate the name of Hesychius (d. at the beginning of the fourth century) with this text, but this *Alexandrian* or Egyptian text had been in existence long before his time.

At the end of the third century Lucian (d. 312), a priest and the founder of the first catechetical school of Antioch, not only revised the Septuagint, but also made a recension of the New Testament text. This textual form developed into the *Byzantine* type, which acquired predominance in the Church of Constantinople, and then continued to be the current text throughout the Middle Ages. Finally by the printed editions of Erasmus [28] and Stephanus, it was entrenched in print until 1881.

From 1700 to 1830 various attempts were made to collate ancient Greek MSS. and versions, and to edit the Greek text as correctly as possible. Among the scholars worthy of mention are * John Mill (Oxford, 1707), * J. A. Bengel (Tübingen, 1734), * J. J. Wetstein (Amsterdam, 1751-1752), * J. J. Griesbach (Halle, 1774-1777; 2nd ed. Jena, 1796-1806), and the Catholic, J. M. Scholz (Leipzig, 1830).

The year 1831 marks the beginning of the modern period of textual criticism and the departure from the Received Text. Ancient MSS. according to the textual type of B and various versions were collated, and upon these the Greek text was edited. * C. Lachmann (Berlin, 1831) aimed at determining a text which was widely diffused at the end of the fourth century. * S. P. Tregelles, an English Quaker, edited a critical text based upon ancient MSS. versions and the Fathers (London, 1857-1872). * C. Tischendorf is the outstanding textual critic of the last century. His first edition appeared

---

[28] Cf. Bludau, A., "Die beiden ersten Erasmus Ausgaben des N.T. und Ihre Gegner," in B.S., 7 (1902); also Altgeier, A.. "Exegetische Beiträge zur Geschichte des Griechischen vor dem Humanismus," in *Biblica,* 24 (1943), 261-288.

at Leipzig in 1841; his last edition, the eighth, printed at Leipzig 1869-1872—to which his pupil * C. R. Gregory added the Prolegomena (1884-1894)—is his best critical edition and marks his definite departure from the Received Text. * Westcott and * Hort, after thirty years of study, published their Greek edition (1881), which followed the manuscripts B and S. * B. Weiss also followed manuscript B and those allied with it (Berlin, 1892). * E. Nestle (1898—) bases his text upon Tischendorf, Westcott and Hort, and Weiss, and gives the readings which are preferred at least by two of these scholars.

* Hermann von Soden classified into three families (Hesychian, Jerusalem, and Koine) more than 1900 MSS. which he believed were of the third or fourth century. He edited the text (Göttingen, 1913), and based his readings upon the majority vote of these three recensions, except when there was a case of a harmonistic tendency and a reading from Tatian.

Among the Catholic editions mention may be made of those by F. X. Reitmayer (Munich, 1847), V. Loch (Regensburg, 1861), G. Perin (Padua, 1890), M. Hetzenauer (Innsbruck, 1896-1898), E. Bodin (Paris, 1910—), F. Brandscheid (Freiburg, 1901; 2nd ed., 1922—), and the recent critical editions by H. I. Vogels (Düsseldorf, 2nd ed., 1922) and A. Merk (Rome, 1933—).

(c) The Critical Value of the Greek Text of the New Testament

In spite of the large number of variant readings, the Greek text has reached us *substantially unchanged and uncorrupted*.

In the modern accepted critical text there are less than 150,-000 words, and about 200,000 variant readings are distributed among 4288 MSS., some being found in one family of MSS., and some in another.

Since, however, the greater part of the text shows perfect uniformity, we can say with * Westcott and * Hort that seven-eighths of the Greek New Testament is critically certain. Of the remaining one-eighth many of the variant readings concern the same word or phrase, and most of these readings consist merely in changes of spelling or particles, in the order of words, in grammatical differences and the usage of synonyms, or in the conscious or unconscious faults of copyists. However, all of these are immaterial changes, which do not obscure the meaning of the text. Of the variants which remain, there are hardly 200 which affect the meaning of the text, and of these only 15 are of major importance.[29] Yet, these and the other variants neither add to or detract from a single dogma of the Church. Cf. Luke 22, 43 f; John 5, 3b-4; 7, 53-8, 11; 1 Cor. 15, 51; 1 John 5, 7b-8a; etc.

With these facts in mind, we can reach a genuine appraisal of the Greek text of the New Testament. No other book has been copied so diligently and been quoted so frequently in ancient times. The greater the number of MSS., their variety and independence, the greater must be the value of those readings which display harmony. Hence, where the biblical MSS. agree, no other book in the world possesses such certainty as to its real critical value. In regard to the readings where the MSS. disagree, critical scholars have reduced the question of doubtful readings to the minimum. The Greek New Testament is, therefore, not only substantially correct, but even in readings of secondary importance the variations are inconsequential.

[29] Cf. Vaccari, A., in I.B., 255.

Chapter II

THE ANCIENT VERSIONS OF THE BIBLE

The early translations of the books of the Bible from the original into another language are of importance. They help us in interpreting the meaning of the original, for we learn from them how early readers understood the meaning of the original. Besides, they enable us to determine the original text, and may at times be considered as almost equivalent to first-class MSS. of the originals. If their origin is known, they are then of great assistance in tracing the history of the original text.

But all translations are not of equal value. If a translation is made from the original, it surpasses in value a translation made from another translation. Old translations have greater weight than later ones. Likewise, literal translations deserve more consideration than free ones. Other circumstances may also be considered: whether the version belongs to the same linguistic stock as the original, and whether the translator himself was a master of both languages.

The Septuagint surpasses all the versions by reason of its antiquity and critical authority. It is also of great value in determining the history as well as the contents of the Canon of the Old Testament. During the Christian period its history is shared by the New Testament text, and many Greek MSS. furnish us with the books of both Testaments.

Art. 1. The Greek Versions of the Old Testament

General Bibliography: *Hermann and *Baumgartel, "Beiträge z. Entstehungsgeschichte der Septuaginta" (Berlin, 1923); *Kenyon, F. G., "The Text of the Greek Bible" (London, 1937); *De Lagarde, P. A., "Septuagintastudien" (Göttingen, 1891-1892); Mangenot, E., in D.D.L.B., s.v. *Version de Septante;* McGarry, W. J., "Early Revisions of the Septuagint," in *St. Louis Proceedings* (1937), 29-37; *Nestle, E., "Septuagintastudien," I-V (Ulm, 1886-1896; Stuttgart, 1899-1907); *Ottley, R. R., "A Handbook to the Septuagint" (New York, 1920); Pretzl, O.,

"Septuagintaprobleme im Buche der Richter," in *Biblica*, 7 (1926), 233-269, 353-383; *Procksch, O., "Studien zur Geschichte der Septuaginta" (Leipzig, 1910); *Rahlfs, A., "Septuagintastudien" (Göttingen, 1891-1892); *Swete, H. B., "An Introduction to the O.T. in Greek" (2nd ed., Cambridge, 1914); *Thackeray, H., "The Septuagint and Jewish Worship" (London, 1921); Vaccari, A., "Codex Melphictensis Rescriptus" (Rome, 1918); Vander Heeren, A., in C.E. s.v. *Septuagint;* Wutz, F. X., "Die ursprüngliche Septuaginta," in *Theol. Blätter* (1923), 111-117; *idem,* "Die Bedeutung der Transkriptionen in der Septuaginta, in B.Z., 16 (1924), 193-213; *idem,* "Alte hebräische Stämme im Psalmentext der Septuagints," in B.Z., 17 (1925), 1-28; *idem,* "Die Transkriptionen von der Septuaginta bis zu Hieronymus" (Stuttgart, 1925); "Ist der hebräische Urtext wieder erreichbar?" in *Zeitschrift für die alttest. Wissenschaft* (1925), 115-119; *idem,* "Systematische Wege von der Septuaginta zum hebräischen Urtext" (Stuttgart, 1937); Goettsberger, "Einleitung in das A.T." (Freiburg i. B., 1927); *Orlinksy, H. M., "On the Present State of Proto-Septuagint Studies," in J.A.O.S., 61 (1941), 81-91; *Meecham, H. G., "The Oldest Version of the Bible" (London, 1932); Ziegler, J., "Untersuchungen zur Septuaginta des Buches Isaias" (Münster, 1934); *idem,* "Die Vorlage der Isaias-Septuaginta (LXX) und die erste Isaias-Rolle von Qumran (1 Qlsa)," in J.B.L., 78 (1959), 34-59; Altgeier, A., "Beobachtungen am Septuaginta der Bücher Esdras und Nehemias," in *Biblica*, 22 (1941), 227-251; Mercati, G., "Note di letteratura biblica," in *Vivre et Penser,* 1 (1941), 5-15; *Wikgren, A., "Two Ostraca Fragments of the Septuaginta Psalter," in J.O.N.E.S., 5 (1946), 181-184; Auvray, P., "Comment se pose le probleme de l'inspiration des Septante," in R.B., 59 (1952), 321-336.

PHILOLOGY: *Hatch and *Redpath, "A Concordance to the Septuagint" (2 vols.), and Supplement (Oxford, 1897); *Helbing, R., "Grammatik der Septuaginta" (Göttingen, 1907); *Reider, J., "Prolegomena to a Greek-Hebrew and a Hebrew-Greek Index to Aquila" (Philadelphia, 1916); *Thackeray, H., "A Grammar to the O.T. in Greek," I (Cambridge, 1909).

TEXTS FOR SCHOOL USAGE: *Rahlfs, A., "Septuaginta id est Vetus Testamentum græce juxta LXX interpretes" (2 vols., Stuttgart, 1935); *Swete, H. B., "The Old Testament in Greek according to the Septuagint," I (Cambridge, 1925), II (1922), III (1912).

(a) THE MANUSCRIPTS [1]

The Greek MSS. of the Old Testament are usually classified under three heads: papyri, uncials, and minuscules. The system of *Rahlfs for listing these MSS. has now been generally accepted, and at present the actual total of MSS. is about 1560.

Among the papyri, No. 957 (John Rylands Library, Manchester) is contemporaneous with some Dead Sea Scrolls. This fragment is from the second century B.C. and contains

---

[1] Cf. *Rahlfs, A., "Verzeichnis der griech. Handschriften des A.T." (Berlin, 1914); Vaccari, A., in I.B., 258 f; *Kenyon, F. G., *op. cit.,* 36-65.

Deut. 23, 24—24, 3; 25, 1-3; 26, 12. 17-19 and 28, 31-33.[2]
Among the more important papyri may be mentioned the
Chester Beatty group Nos. 961 to 968. This collection, formerly in an early Christian community of Egypt, comprises
fragments from the Books of Genesis (961, a codex of the
fourth century, and 962, a codex of the latter part of the third
century), of Numbers and Deuteronomy (963, a codex of the
first half of the second century), of Ecclesiasticus or Sirach
(964, a codex of the fourth century), of Isaias (965, a codex
of the first half of the second century), of Jeremias (966, a
codex of the late second or third century), of Ezechiel, Daniel,
and Esther (967 and 968, a codex of the first half of the third
century)[2a].

Among the uncials the four great codices S, A, B, C, contain
both Testaments. The rest of the uncials are generally designated by Latin letters, and contain some particular division
of the Old Testament. The minuscule MSS. are designated
by Arabic numerals, and very few of them contain all the
books of the Old Testament.

Besides the citations from many Fathers, valuable evidence
for the Septuagint text may be derived from the translations
which depend directly upon it (e.g., the Old Latin, Coptic,
and Syriac versions, and the Gallican Psalter of St. Jerome).

(b) The Origin of the Septuagint

Long before the third century B.C., there were individual migrations of Jews to foreign lands, especially to Egypt. Perhaps this dispersion in Egypt began at the time of Pharao
Sesac (cf. 3 Kgs. 14, 25 f) in the tenth century B.C., but a

[2] Cf. Vaccari, A., "Fragmentum Biblicum sæc. II ante Christum," in
Biblica, 17 (1936), 501-504; *idem,* "Fragmentum V.T. vetustissimum
nuper repertum," in V.D., 16 (1936), 369-372; Algeier, A., "Deut. 25, 1-3
im Manchester Papyrus," in *Biblica,* 19 (1938), 1-18.

[2a] Cf. *Kenyon, F. G., "The Chester Beatty Biblical Papyri" (London,
1934-1937); Allgeier, A., "Die Chester Beatty-Papyri zum Pentateuch"
(Paderborn, 1938); *Johnson, A. C., etc., "The J. H. Scheide Biblical
Papyri Ezechiel" (Princeton, 1938); *Payne, B. J., "The Relationship of
the Chester Beatty-Papyri of Ezechiel to Codex Vaticanus," in J.B.L.,
68 (1949), 251-265.

migration is certain to have taken place in the sixth century
B.C., when many Jews from Jerusalem at the time of the
Babylonian exile (cf. Jer. 43, 4 ff) fled to Egypt. In the fifth
century B.C. the Jews were firmly established as a military
colony on the island of Elephantine near the modern Assuan,
where they had even their own sanctuary; this is known to us
from the Elephantine Aramaic Papyri of the Persian Period.

From the time of Alexander the Great on, Egypt came
under the influence of the Greek culture. With this cultural
expansion was also spread the koine Greek language, which
condition lasted to the beginning of the Byzantine Period
(c. A.D. 324).

During the Hellenization of Egypt the Jewish communities
living there were also affected. Hence, the Egyptian Jews
adopted the Greek language for their vernacular in social and
commercial relations as well as for their literature.

In so far as religion was concerned, the Old Testament still
played an important rôle in the lives of the Jewish people.
The desire to use their religion for propaganda purposes and
the need of the new language (the Greek) for the younger
Jewish generations were contributing factors in the origin of
a Greek text of the Old Testament. But whether there were
pre-Septuagint texts of either the whole Old Testament or
parts of it,[3] and whether there were Greek transcriptions of the
Hebrew text (as Professor Wutz maintains), are questions
still keenly debated by scholars.

The Letter of Aristeas.[4]—The oldest witness for the origin
of the Septuagint version is the Letter of Aristeas. According
to this letter, Aristeas, a Jewish offícial at the court of Ptolemy
Philadelphus (285-246 B.C.), was sent to Jerusalem with many
liberated Jews, to obtain from the High Priest Eleazar a copy

---

[3] Aristobulus of Alexandria (180-145 B.C.) believed Plato (427-347 B.C.)
knew of the Jewish laws from a Greek version; Eusebius (*Præf. Ev.,*
XIII, 12) implied the existence of some books of the Old Testament in
Greek before 400 B.C.

[4] For the Greek text of the letter consult *Swete, H. B., "An Introduction, etc.," 551-606, and *Meecham, H. G., "The Letter of Aristeas" (Manchester, 1935); for an English translation consult *Charles, R. H., "The
Apocrypha, etc.," II, 83-122, and for a German translation see *Kautzsch,
E., "Die Apokryphen, etc.," II, 1-31.

of the Jewish Law for the chief librarian of Alexandria, Demetrius Phalereus. The high priest not only sent a copy of
the Law but also seventy-two learned Hebrew scholars (six
from each tribe), and these translated the Law into the Greek
language on the island of Pharos. According to the story,
each scholar was shut up by himself, but after seventy-two
days when all the results were compared, they were found to
be exactly the same.[5]

This letter, although it is now commonly recognized as a
forgery with many legendary details, existed already about
200 B.C. It rests, however, on a foundation of fact to this
extent, that during the reign of.Ptolemy Philadelphus the Pentateuch was translated into the Greek (about 250 B.C.).

The other books of the Old Testament were gradually translated into the Greek. Even though pre-Christian authorities
do not make mention of all the Greek books of the Old Testament, we may conclude from the Prologue of Sirach (c. 130
B.C.) that almost the entire Old Testament had already been
translated into Greek by that time. For this reason most
scholars hold that the Septuagint was completed by 100 B.C.
There is no conclusive proof that this work of translating the
books of the Old Testament continued even to the beginning
of the Christian era or even beyond this.

The name *Septuagint* is taken from the number of scholars
(seventy or seventy-two) who were engaged in the translation
of the Pentateuch, the first instalment of the entire Old Testament. This term is in fact applied to the entire Old Testament in most Greek MSS., even though the individual books
were translated at different times and by various authors.

(c) The Qualities and Effects of the Septuagint

By reason of its long history, this version has no uniform
value in all its parts. The individual books of the Septuagint
give evidence of different kinds of translation, and the value

---

[5] According to Wutz this letter refers to a revision or recension of a
former imperfect Greek translation which had been previously made
according to a Hebrew consonantal text.

of the translation varies from book to book. But in general we can admit that the Pentateuch is the best translation of all. Next in merit are the Earlier Prophets, because of the simplicity of the text. The Later Prophets, because of their difficult contents, were poorly translated; thus, Isaias is very poorly rendered, and the translator of Daniel so indulged in paraphrases that the translation of Theodotion subsequently was substituted by the Church to take its place. The Kethubim are the worst of all; thus, in the Psalms there is a servile translation, in Esther there is a free translation, and in Job much is omitted because of the difficulty of the archetype. In particular, the work of different translators is evident in duplicate passages.

Even though the individual books of the Septuagint are of unequal value, there are some common peculiarities manifested in them. In many books there is the tendency to render the difficult passages more intelligible, to clarify obscure readings, to remove the unevenness of style, and to polish linguistic difficulties. Many things that were seemingly unbecoming to God in the archetype were changed. The Messianic passages were represented in a clearer light than the Jews subsequently wished to admit.

The Greek text, which the Septuagint translators wished to produce primarily for their own age and people, increased in prestige from century to century. The Egyptian Jews as well as the Hellenic synagogues in Palestine, the East as well as the West, received their religious knowledge of the Old Testament by means of this translation. The propagation of the Gospel to the Gentiles was facilitated by this translation. This version was also of great significance for primitive Christian literature. Nations to whom the Hebrew Scripture remained a closed book, became acquainted with the Old Testament writings by means of this Greek version (thus, the Armenian, Ethiopic, Coptic, Georgian, Latin and Slavic translators made use of the Septuagint); and even Semitic nations, such as the Syrians and Arabians, found their approach to the Old Testament more convenient at times through the Greek translation.[6]

[6] Cf. Goettsberger, J., *op. cit.*, 431.

(d) The Later Greek Translations of the Old Testament

The Septuagint, which originated in Jewish circles and was diligently used by their synagogues and writers (e.g., Philo and Josephus), remained an unchallenged translation until the beginning of the second century of our era. The Jews became alienated from the Septuagint after the Christian Church in her apologetical controversy with the Jewish writers pointed out the Messianic passages, which were more clearly and forcibly presented in the Greek version than in the Hebrew text. Toward the end of the first century of our era, the text and the Canon of the Old Testament were definitely fixed by the Jews in Palestine, and the Septuagint version did not seem to meet their criteria. Soon the reliability of the Septuagint was denied, and the aversion of the Jews developed into a bitter hatred, so that the day of its translation, which during the time of Philo was celebrated as a feast, became a day of fast and mourning. As a result, the Hellenized Jews had to fashion an entirely new Greek translation. This led to the production of three alternative versions and some partial ones.

The Greek Version of Aquila.—Aquila, a proselyte from Sinope in Pontus, completed about A.D. 128 a Greek translation of the proto-canonical books. It was slavishly literal, and was condemned by Christians for its textual corruptions and incomprehensible Greek. Yet, it was held in the highest esteem by the Jews for four centuries. When, in A.D. 553, Emperor Justinian ordered the Jews throughout the Byzantine Empire to study the original Hebrew text, the version of Aquila lost its authority. This version was taken by Origen in his Hexapla, and fragments of it survive in Hexaplaric MSS.[7]

The Greek Version of Theodotion. [7a]—Soon after Aquila, a second version was produced by Theodotion, a proselyte from Ephesus. He seems to have made a free revision of the Sep-

---

[7] Cf. Goettsberger, J., *op. cit.*, 434 f, footnote 9; *Silverstone, A. E., "Aquila and Onkelos" (Manchester, 1931).

[7a] Cf. *Cooper, C. M., "Theodotion's Influence on the Alexandrian Text of Judges," in J.B.L., 67 (1948), 63-68.

tuagint version rather than an entirely new translation. Besides the Book of Daniel (including the deutero-canonical parts) found in the Septuagint MSS., only some fragments survive in the Hexaplaric MSS.

The Greek Version of Symmchus. [7b]—Toward the end of the same second century the third translation appeared. It was an entirely new translation of the Old Testament by Symmachus, an Ebionite. He aimed at making his translation good Greek. This version was utilized by Origen in his Hexapla, but only isolated fragments of the translation are known to us.

Three partial versions (i.e., of the Minor Prophets and Prophetical Books) have been designated as *Quinta, Sexta,* and *Septima* by the Fathers.

(e) THE HEXAPLA OF ORIGEN (185/186—254/255)

The common usage of the Greek Bible by the Apostolic Fathers, apologists, and ecclesiastical writers gave rise to the multiplication of copies of the Septuagint. Due to the deliberate and indeliberate changes by copyists, variant textual readings developed in the course of time. To remedy this condition, Origen undertook to establish the true text.

His purpose in revising the Septuagint version was twofold. First, he wished to show Christians, who were disputing with the Jews, what was in the Hebrew text and what was not there. Secondly, he aimed at producing a uniform text that would eliminate the variant readings.

In his voluminous work, the *Hexapla,* which he produced in Palestine about A.D. 240, he placed side by side in six parallel columns:[8] (1) the Hebrew text; (2) the same transliterated

---

[7b] Cf. *Schoeps, H. J., "Mythologisches bei Symmachus," in *Biblica,* 26 (1945), 100-111; *idem,* "Symmachus und der Midrasch," in *Biblica,* 29 (1948), 31-51.

[8] Cf. *Orlinsky, H. M., "The Columnar Order of the Hexapla," in *Jewish Quarterly Review,* 27 (1936), 137-149.

in Greek characters; [9] (3) Aquila; (4) Symmachus; (5) the Septuagint; (6) Theodotion. The texts were arranged in short phrases according to the Hebrew order, and the most important column was the fifth, which Origen sought to bring in line with the original text. For this purpose he borrowed a critical system which was used by the Alexandrian philologists. Whenever he wished to indicate matter in the Septuagint but not in the original text, he made use of the obelus ($-$, $\div$, $\div$); and whenever he wished to indicate what was missing in the Septuagint but was in the original text, he added the matter and indicated it by an asterisk ($※$).

After this gigantic work, he edited a shortened edition, or *Tetrapla,* which contained only the last four columns of the Greek texts. Both works have perished (perhaps in 638 when Cæsarea was destroyed by the Arabs).

This fifty-volume work of Origen was probably never fully copied. The only extant specimens are a few verses of Psalm 45 (from the second to the sixth column) [10] and part of Psalm 22 (in all six columns). But the biblical scholars of olden times frequented the library of Cæsarea, and fortunately a great deal of this material has been preserved in the writings of the Fathers, in MSS., and in the margins of some MSS.[11]

(f) THE HEXAPLARIC GREEK TEXT AND OTHER GREEK RECENSIONS [12]

St. Jerome, writing in the year 396 (*Præf. in Paral.*), mentions the various Greek texts current in the fourth century:

[9] Cf. Pretzl, O., "Die Aussprache der Hebräischen nach der zweiten Kolumne der Hexapla des Origenes," in B.Z., 20 (1932), 4-22; *Staples, W. E., "The Second Column of Origen's Hexapla," in J.A.O.S., 59 (1939), 71-80; *Speiser, E. A., "The Pronunciation of Hebrew Based Chiefly on the Transliterations in the Hexapla," in J.Q.R., 23 (1933), 233-266, 24 (1933), 9-46; Mercati, J., "Note esaplari," in *Biblica*, 25 (1944), 1-8.

[10] Cf. *Swete, H. B., *op. cit.*, 62 f.

[11] *F. Field has published in 1871 many of these Hexaplar fragments; cf. Vaccari, A., in I.B., 266 f; Mercati G., "Il problema della colonna II dell'Esaplo," in *Biblica*, 28 (1947), 1-30, 173-215; Vosté, J. M., "La version syro-hexaplaire de la Sagesse," in *Biblica*, 30 (1949), 213-219; Gottstein, M. H., "Neue Syrohexaplafragmente," in *Biblica*, 37 (1956), 162-183.

[12] Cf. McGarry, W. J., *op. cit;* Pretzl, O., *op. cit.*

"Alexandria and Egypt praise Hesychius as the author of their Septuagint; Constantinople to Antioch approves of the exemplars of Lucian; midway between these provinces Palestinian codices are read, which were revised by Origen and published by Eusebius and Pamphilus."

The Publications of Eusebius and Pamphilus.—The fifth column of Origen was to serve the needs of scholars, and this was published in a separate form by Eusebius of Cæsarea (d. 340) and Pamphilus (d. 309). Believing that Origen had succeeded in restoring the Septuagint to its original purity, these two scholars employed many scribes to copy out this fifth column. This revised Greek text is called the Hexaplaric recension of the Septuagint, whereas the unrevised Greek text is simply called the koine text.[13]

The Hexaplaric recension as published by Eusebius and Pamphilus[14] affected the subsequent history of the Septuagint. The Hexaplaric symbols soon lost their meaning to copyists, who either mistook or omitted them. Thus, a Septuagint text was transmitted in which the original text was contaminated by readings from the other columns (especially that of Theodotion).

The Recension of Hesychius.[15]—The existence of this recension is mentioned only by St. Jerome. It is thought that Hesychius may be the Egyptian bishop mentioned by Eusebius (*Hist. Eccl.*, VIII, 13, 7) and martyred in 311. No conclusive evidence is yet available concerning this recension, but critics have identified its text with the Coptic versions, the Egyptian Fathers, especially those of Alexandria during the fourth and fifth centuries. *Codex Marchalianus*, and the uncials 26, 36, 90 f, 198, 228 and 238 present the Hesychian text.

[13] Cf. St. Jerome, *De vir. ill.*, 75, and *Ep. cvi*, 2.
[14] Cf. *Codices Coislinianus* (M of the seventh century) and *Sarravianus* (G of the fifth century); *Codex Marchalianus* (Q of the sixth century), a Hesychian text but with many readings from Origen in the margins and in the text, and therefore considered one of the principal authorities for the Hexaplaric text in the Prophets.
[15] Cf. Bardy, G., "Notes sur les recensions hésychienne et héxaplaire du livre de Neh (II Esd.)," in R.B., 15 (1918), 192-199; *Kenyon, F. G., "Hesychius and the Text of the New Testament," in *Memorial Lagrange* (Paris, 1940), 245-250.

The Recension of Lucian.[16]—Lucian (martyred 310/312) was the founder of the catechetical school at Antioch. He did not produce a new translation, but revised an already existing text, which was called by St. Jerome the koine text. Besides making emendations from the Hebrew text, he attempted to obtain clearness and ease of comprehension by polished, conflated, and at times conjectural readings.[17]   Assigned to this edition are *Codex Basilio-Vaticanus* (N-V of the eighth or ninth century), the minuscules 19, 62, 75 (in Genesis), 82, 93, 108 (of the fourteenth century containing the Octateuch and historical books), and 118 (of the thirteenth century containing the Octateuch), 308 etc. The MSS. 108 and 118 were used for the great Complutensian Polyglot. This recension of Lucian was adopted by the Antiochian Fathers, especially St. John Chrysostom and Theodoret. Some critics believe that this recension was employed also as the basis of the Philoxenian Syriac, the Ethiopic, the Gothic, and Slavic translations.

The four forms of the Septuagint revision (the pre-Hexaplaric recension, the Hexaplaric, the Hesychian, and the Lucian) were circulated in various regions; yet, in the course of time these various texts reacted on one another, so that it is now extremely difficult for textual critics to segregate these texts and to classify them in their distinctive groups.

(g) The Critical Value of the Septuagint

It is the purpose of textual critics to obtain the genuine reading of the original Septuagint version. But this is to be acquired, not by making use of one MS. or of one family of MSS., but by collating the readings of the various families. This being done, it is necessary to consider also translations from the Greek which had the pre-Hexaplaric Septuagint as their basis (e.g., the Old Latin and the Coptic-Sahidic versions), and likewise the citations dispersed in the rabbinical

---

[16] Cf. Tisserant, E., "Notes sur la recension lucianique d'Ezéchiel," in R.B., 8 (1911), 384-390; Pirot, L., "Note sur la recension de Lucien d'Antioche dans Esdras-Néhéme," in *Biblica,* 2 (1921), 356-360.

[17] Cf. Vaccari, A., in I.B., 269.

writings as well as in the Fathers who wrote before the time of Origen.

This preliminary research having been concluded, the variant readings must be carefully compared with the Massoretic Text. The readings, which are more conformable with the Hebrew, are to be rejected, and the readings, which disagree with the Hebrew, are to be retained, unless there are cases of mere consonantal confusion.

(h) THE PRINTED TEXTS OF THE SEPTUAGINT [18]

Four editions of the Septuagint text printed before the end of the eighteenth century are of importance; all the rest of the editions are based upon these four.

(1) The Septuagint of the Complutensian Polyglot was printed in 1517, published in 1520-1521, and represents the Lucian recension. This Complutensian text was followed by the four great Polyglots edited by Arias Montanus (Antwerp, 1569-1572), * B. C. Bertram (Heidelberg, 1586-1587, etc.), * D. Wolder (Hamburg, 1596), and Michael Le Jay (Paris, 1629-1645).

(2) The Aldine edition, representing the Hesychian recension, was printed at Venice in 1518. At least six editions appearing between 1524 and 1687 (printed in Germany, Switzerland and elsewhere) followed this edition.

(3) The Sistine edition, published at Rome in 1587 under the auspices of Sixtus V, is based upon the *Codex Vaticanus* and other MSS. which supply the gaps in that codex. According to some critics, this codex represents the older and unrevised text of the Septuagint. This edition was frequently reprinted (e.g., the Polyglot of * B. Walton, London, 1657).

(4) The edition of * J. E. Grabe (Oxford, 1707-1720) was based upon the *Codex Alexandrinus*.

Among the critical editions of the Septuagint there are six worthy of mention.

(1) The edition of * Holmes and * Parsons (Oxford, 1798-1827), in five volumes, gave the text of the Sistine edition;

[18] Cf. * Swete, H. B., *op cit.*, 171-194.

313 MSS., besides other versions and Patristic quotations, were collated and annotated.

(2) *A. F. C. Tischendorf edited four editions of the Septuagint (Leipzig, 1850-1869), which represented a revised Sistine text.

(3) The edition of V. Loch (Regensburg, 1866-1886) contains the *Codex Vaticanus,* and was completed by the *Codex Alexandrinus* and the Polyglot Bibles.

(4) The four editions of *H. B. Swete (Cambridge, 1887-1912) were based upon the *Codex Vaticanus* and completed by the *Codex Alexandrinus;* the variant readings from the principal uncials were added.

(5) The preceding manual was the forerunner of a larger Cambridge edition, which was published by *Brooke and *McLean. Between 1906 and 1935 eight parts have appeared (i.e., from Genesis to 2 Esdras).

(6) The Septuagint-Commission of Göttingen Institute, founded in 1908, has contemplated a large critical edition under the editorship of *A. Rahlfs. So far he has edited the Book of Ruth (Stuttgart, 1922), Genesis (1926), the Psalms with Odes (Göttingen, 1931). *W. Kappler has edited the First Book of Machabees (Göttingen, 1936), and J. Ziegler the Book of Isaias (Göttingen, 1939). As a manual for class work * Rahlfs edited the Greek text in two volumes (Stuttgart, 1935).

Art. 2. The Latin Versions

GENERAL BIBLIOGRAPHY: Stummer, E. Einführung in die lateinische Bibel" (Paderborn, 1928); Steinmueller, J. E., "The Pre-Jerome Latin Version," in H.P.R., 36 (1936), 1037-1041; idem, "The History of the Latin Vulgate," ibid., 39 (1938), 252-257, 347-361; Botte, B., "Versions latine antérieurs à St. Jerome," in D.D.L.B., 5 (Paris, 1951), 333-347); Musurillo, H., "The Problem of the Itala," in Theol. St., 17 (1956), 93-97.

OLD LATIN: Sabátier, P., "Bibliorum sacrorum latine versiones antiquae" (3 vols., Reims, 1735-1743; a new edition being prepared by the Beuron Monastery, 1951-); *Wordsworth, P.-*Sanday, W.-*White, H. J., "Old Latin Biblical Texts" (vols. I-VII, Oxford, 1883-1923); "Collectanea Biblica Latina" (vols. I-VIII, Rome, 1912-1945); *Jülicher, A., "Itala: das N.T. im altlat. Überlieferung" (I-II, Berlin, 1938-1940; revised by * W. Matzkow-* K. Aland, ibid., 1954).

During the past century Catholics as well as non-Catholics have been actively engaged in the reconstruction of Old Latin texts. Worthy of mention are in *Germany*, E. Ranke, H. Rönsch, L. Ziegler, P. Corssen, J. Haussleiter, E. von Dobschütz, A. Jülicher, H. von Soden, A. Allgeier, A. Dold, H. J. Vogels, J. Schildenberger, etc; in *France*, L. Deslisle, G. Morin, P. Battifol, S. Berger, D. de Bryne, B. Botte, etc.; in *Italy*, A. Amelli, G. Mercati, A. Vaccari; in *England*, T. K. Abbott, W. Sanday, J. Wordsworth, H. J. White, J. Gwynn, C. Burkitt, E. S. Buchanan, C. H. Milne; in *America*, K. Lake, D. Sanders; in *Spain*, T. Ayuso Marazuela; in *Norway*, J. Belsheim.

VULGATE: Allgeier, A., "Die Hexapla in den Psalmenübersetzungen des heiligen Hieronymus," in *Biblica*, 8 (1927), 450-463, 468 f, and 463-468 (A. Vaccari); *idem*, "Der Brief an Sunnia und Fretela und seine Bedeutung für die Textherstellung der Vulgata," in *Biblica*, 11 (1930), 86-107; *idem*, "Die erste Psalmenübersetzung des hl. Hieronymus und das Psalterium Romanum," in *Biblica*, 12 (1931), 447-484; *Berger, S., "Histoire de la Vulgate pendant les premieres siècls du moyen-âge" (Paris, 1893); De Bruyne, D., "Un Nouveau Document sur les Origines de la Vulgate," in R.B., 10 (1913), 5-14; Cavallera, F., "Saint Jerome, sa vie, et son œuvre" (Louvain, 1922); Dirksen, A. H., "St. Jerome's Revision of the Old Latin New Testament," in *St. Louis Proceedings* (1937), 63-74; Feder, A., "Zusätze zum Schriftstellerkatalog des hl. Hieronymus," in *Biblica*, 7 (1920), 500-513; Fonck, L., "Hieronymi scientia naturalis exemplis illustratur," in *Biblica*, 1 (1920), 481-499; Gasquet, F. A., in C.E., s.v. *Vulgate*; *idem*, "Alcuni Scritti e Brevi Saggi di Studii sulla Volgata" (Rome, 1917); * Grutzmacher, R., "Hieronymus" (3 vols., Lepzig, 1901-1908); Höpfl, H., "Kardinal Wilhelm Sirlets Annotationen zum Neuen Testament," in B.S., 13 (1908); *idem*, "Beiträge zur Geschichte der Sixto-Klementinischer Vulgata," in B.S., 18 (1913); Murillo, L., "S. Jeromimo el 'Doctor Maximo,'" in *Biblica*, I (1920), 431-456; Power, E., "The Lost Ninth Century Bible of Carcassone," in *Biblica*, 5 (1924), 197-201; *idem*, "Corrections from the Hebrew in the Theodulfian MSS of the Vulgate," in *Biblica*, 5 (1924), 253-258; Quentin, H., "Memoire sur l'etablissement du texte de la Vulgate, I, Octateuque" (Rome, 1922); *idem*, "La Vulgate a travers les siècles et sa revision actuelle" (Rome, 1926); *idem*, "Essais de Critique Textuelle (Ecdotique)" (Paris, 1926); Reilly, W. S., "The Vulgate, the Official Latin Text," in *St. Louis Proceedings* (1937), 58-62; Salmon, P., "Notes sur quelques lecons du Palimpseste de Bobbio de la Vulgate Hieronymienne," in *Biblica*, 21 (1940), 133-137; Sutcliffe-Vaccari, "De duobus exemplaribus Sixtinæ Bibliorum," in *Biblica*, 14 (1933), 348-356; Vaccari, A., "Bollettino Geronimiano," in *Biblica*, 1 (1920), 379-396, 533-562; *idem*, "I fattori dell'esegesi geronimiana," in *Biblica*, 1 (1920) 457-480; *idem*, "Frammento di un perduto Tractatus di S. Girolamo," in *Biblica*, 1 (1920), 513-517; *idem*, "Uno scritto di Gregorio d'Elvira tragli spurii di S. Girolamo," in *Biblica*, 3 (1922), 188-193; *idem*, "Sixtus V eiusque in S.Scripturam curæ," in V.D., 2 (1922), 369-374; *idem*, "Di Gobelino Larido, ottimo editore della Volgata," in *Biblica*, 6 (1925), 211-217; *idem*, "Psalterium Gallicanum' e Psalterium juxta Hebræos,'" in *Biblica*, 8 (1927), 213-215; *idem*, "Esaple ed Esaplare in S. Girolamo," in *Biblica*, 8 (1927), 463-468; *idem*, "De clementinæ 'Præfationis ad lectorem' auctoritate," in V.D., 8 (1928), 152-159; Vosté, J. M., "De Latina Bibliorum versione quæ dicitur 'Vulgata'" (Rome, 1927); Zerwick, M., "De revisione Vulgatæ," in V.D., 21 (1941), 148-154; Vogels, H. J., "Vulgatastudien" (Münster, 1928); Newton, W. L., "Influence of St. Jerome's Translation of the O.T.," in C.B.Q., 5 (1943), 17-33.

PHILOLOGY: *Harden, J. M., "Dictionary of the Vulgate N.T." (London, 1921); Peultier, Etienne, Gautois, "Concordantiarum universæ S.S. thesaurus" (Paris, 1897); *Plater and *White, "A Grammar of the Vulgate" (Oxford, 1926); Stummer, F., "Einige Beobachtungen über die Arbeitsweise des Hieronymus bei der Übersetzung des A.T., aus der hebraica veritas," in *Biblica*, 10 (1929), 3-30; *idem*, "Lexikographische Bemerkungen zur Vulgata," in "Miscellanea Biblica," II (Rome, 1934), 179-202; *idem*, "Beiträge zur Lexikographie der lateinischen Bibel," in *Biblica*, 18 (1937), 23-50; Wutz, F., "Onomastica sacra," I (Leipzig, 1914), II (Leipzig, 1915).

TEXTS: Fillion, L., "Biblia Sacra juxta Vulg. Exemplaria e Correctoria Romana" (Paris, 1887; 10th ed., 1930); Gramatica, Al., "Bibliorum sacrorum juxta Vulgatam Clementinam nova editio" (Milan, 1914; 3rd ed., Rome, 1930); Hetzenauer, M., "Biblia Sacra Vulgatæ Editionis" (Innsbruck, 1906—); * Wordsworth and * White, "Novum Testamentum D.N.I.C. latine secundum editionem S. Hieronymi" (Oxford, 1889—1934), and the pocket edition (Oxford, 1911—1920); Sulpician Fathers, "Biblia Sacra juxta Vulgatam Clementinam" (Paris, 1927; 1938).

Of all the ancient biblical versions none has had such a varied history as the Latin, and none has surpassed this version in its permanent results and universal importance. The history of the Latin text began with the Vetus Latina or Old Latin, which was subsequently replaced by the Vulgate of St. Jerome. The pre-Jerome Latin text in its various phases is both interesting and important for the history of textual criticism.

(a) THE PRE-JEROME LATIN VERSION

(1) Historical Background.—We are at a complete loss to find any direct references to the origin of the Latin translations of the Bible. The production of such translations was doubtless in answer to the needs of the various communities.

Though we have evidence of a Hebrew community living at Rome even in pre-Christian times, there are no traces of a Latin Old Testament being read there similar to the Septuagint in the dispersion. We know from the Acts of the Apostles (18, 2) that Aquila of Pontus (a Hebrew with a Latin name), together with his wife Priscilla, met St. Paul at Corinth after the Jews had been expelled from Rome by Emperor Claudius. Pontus, however, was a Hellenistic region, and the language of Aquila was undoubtedly Greek. The use of Latin names at this period does not necessarily imply the knowledge of that language. Thus, Saul is also called Paul (Acts 13, 9), and John likewise Mark (Acts 12, 12. 25; 15, 37). Even in the Christian era Latin did not become the current language of the Jews at Rome until the fourth century after Christ. Of the many inscriptions in the Jewish catacombs on Monte Verde in the Via Appia, about two-thirds are in Greek, while the rest are either in Latin or Hebrew.

The conquest of Greece and the Orient by the Roman legions brought Grecian culture and its language to the West. The Greek tongue became the general medium of contact throughout the Empire, and its influence upon the élite at Rome is commented upon by the Roman satirist, Juvenal (c. 55-125). Then, too, we know that the Roman emperor and philosopher, Marcus Aurelius (A.D. 161-180), wrote his "Meditations" in Greek. However, in the third century an anti-Hellenistic tendency arose in the Capital, and at the end of that century Latin once again became supreme at Rome.

Similar linguistic conditions prevailed in the Christian community at Rome. St. Mark, though he wrote his Gospel at Rome for the Roman community and incorporated Latin expressions and phrases in his Gospel, composed it in Greek. The same can be said of St. Paul for his Epistle to the Romans. Of the first sixteen Popes from St. Peter to St. Callistus (217-222), only three have Latin names; namely, St. Clement, St. Pius, and St. Victor. Of these St. Clement wrote his Epistle to the Corinthians in Greek. St. Victor (189-199) was the first of this community to write in Latin; however, it must be remembered that he was of African origin. During this period a member of the Roman community composed the "Shepherd of Hermas" in Greek, and St. Hippolytus likewise employed this language in his writings.

The first origins of a Latin Bible are to be found in the Christian regions that were immune from the Hellenistic influence, namely, in Southern Gaul and Africa. Eusebius (*Hist. Eccl.*, V, 1) has preserved for us a letter that the communities of Lyons and Vienne wrote to the churches in Phrygia and Asia Minor concerning the persecutions sustained in 177-178 during the reign of Marcus Aurelius. This letter is replete with biblical quotations and expressions that disagree with the Greek New Testament, and agree rather with the Latin text. Thus, it seems very probable that at this early date the New Testament either wholly or in part was known and being studied in Southern Gaul in the Latin language.

In the proconsular province of Africa and Numidia the Latin culture and language always retained its predominant influence. From this province we have the "Acta Martyrum Scillitanorum" (so-called from the martyrs of the city of Scillium) from A.D. 180, and written in Latin. These Acts reveal to us that the faithful possessed at least the Pauline Epistles. Then too the "Passio SS. Felicitatis et Perpetuæ" (A.D. 202/3), though preserved in Greek, was according to scholars written originally in Latin. The African apologist and so-called "primus Latinorum," Tertullian, wrote at the beginning of the third century, and in his writings there are traces of a Latin version of the Bible. It is, however, admitted by all scholars that St. Cyprian, Bishop of Carthage (martyred on September 14, 258), made diligent use of a Latin Bible.

From these considerations it is evident that some books of the Bible existed both in Southern Gaul and Northern Africa at the end of the second century. About the same period, or at the latest about the middle of the third century, public as well as private needs required a Latin version of the Bible at Rome, the center of Christianity, where some Greek words and expressions, however, were retained in the liturgy.

(2) *The Number of Translations and the Value of the Old Latin.*—The once almost universal opinion that there was only one Latin version (the *Itala*) prior to St. Jerome's time is now almost abandoned by scholars. Both St. Augustine (*De Doctr. Christ.*, II, 16, in M.L., XXXIV, 43) and St. Jerome (Preface to Damasus) speak of the plurality of translators and translations.

Of the Latin translations in use prior to St. Jerome there were two principal types.. In the New Testament these two are clearly distinguishable. One type, known as the *African family*, is to be found in the *Codices Bobiensis* (fifth century) and *Palatinus* (fifth century), and (amongst the Fathers) Tertullian and St. Cyprian. The other family, the *European*, was current under a twofold form, namely, the *Itala* and the *Gallican*. This latter family is represented in the *Codices Vercellensis* (fourth century), *Veronensis* (fifth century),[1] *Bezae* (sixth century), etc., and by the following Fathers, St. Ambrose, Rufinus, M. Aurelius Cassiodorus, St. Jerome (partially), and St. Augustine.

It need not surprise us to find St. Augustine's Scriptural quotations agreeing with the Fathers of the West. He had lived in Milan, was converted there by St. Ambrose, and was acquainted with the Latin text current in Italy. He expressed his preference for this textual form, when he became acquainted with the African type, and at times noted differences of meaning between the two: "In ipsis autem interpretationibus Itala ceteris præferatur, nam est verborum tenacior cum perspicuitate sententiæ" (*De Doct. Christ.*, II, 15, in M.L., XXXIV, 46).

Not only have we two general types of translations (which is evident from a careful comparison of *C. Bobiensis* with *C. Vercellensis*), but even within the same family the work of different translators is noticeable, since from several incompleted translations one or more complete versions were made that substantially were the same. Thus, the Four Gospels still read in our Vulgate—even after the revision of them by St. Jerome—show traces of three distinct translators. A comparison between MSS. *Lugdunensis*, *Wirceburgensis*, *Monacensis* and St. Augustine for the Book of Leviticus shows four different translators.

In the course of time new corruptions were added by copyists. Readings from the three Greek recensions (the Hexapla of Origen and the Hesychian and Lucian recensions) were adopted and incorporated. In the Preface of his Gospel re-

---

[1] Cf. Ongaro, G., "Saltero Veronese e revisione Agostiniana," in *Biblica*, 35 (1954), 443-474.

vision addressed to Pope Damasus, St. Jerome sharply outlines the faults of the Old Latin: "The text was either badly rendered by stupid translators, or awkardly changed by meddlesome but incompetent revisers, or either interpolated or twisted by sleepy copyists."

Though it gradually gave way to the Vulgate of St. Jerome which was officially adopted by the Council of Trent in 1546 and published in 1590-92, the Old Latin still retains great value. (a) This pre-Jerome version is of historical value for the history of the Canon. It contains not only the proto-canonical but also the deutero-canonical books, thereby showing that the Church always regarded these latter books as inspired. (b) This version is also of great linguistic value, because the many MSS. representative of this version show the evolution of the Latin language. It gives us the spoken language (or the *lingua quotidiana*) of the ancient Latins, and at the same time clearly illustrates the genesis of the Romance languages. (c) As a critical translation, the Old Latin is a faithful and indeed servile rendition of the Greek New Testament or of the Septuagint. Such Greek words as anathema, baptism, holocaust, mystery, scandal, etc., were retained, and have now become part and parcel of our own language. At the same time this version is of great value for the reconstruction of the Septuagint text, although for the New Testament it is representative of a type that is called the Western Family. (d) The exegetical value of this version, however, is very small. The translators frequently miss the mark, neglect the various shades of meaning in the Greek word, and were contented at times with giving a mere mechanical translation.

The more one studies the Old Latin [2] in its various phases, the more one learns to appreciate the slow and gradual victory of St. Jerome's Vulgate over it. While the earlier version shows the ardent desire of the Church to bring the Bible to all classes of people, it had to make place for a better translation by a more competent translator, St. Jerome.

[2] Cf. * James, L. J. H., "The Celtic Gospels. Their Story and Their Text" (London, 1934).

(b) The Latin Vulgate

(1) St. Jerome and the Latin Bible.—Eusebius Hieronymus, or St. Jerome, was born at Stridon in Dalmatia, but the year of his birth is uncertain. According to some it was 331, and according to others 340 or even 347. His father, a man of means, sent his son to Rome when his elementary education had been completed at home. In the Eternal City Jerome studied under the famous grammarian, Donatus, and specialized in rhetoric. The fruits of this literary education can be seen in his writings. He was baptized about the year 366 by Pope Liberius (352-366), and became seriously interested in religion.

Jerome left Rome about 367, and during the succeeding year he travelled to the court of Emperor Valentinianus I (364-375) at Treves. Here, where shortly before St. Athanasius of Alexandria had lived in exile and introduced monasticism into the West, Jerome made up his mind to embrace an ascetical life and became interested in theological studies. Later he settled at Aquileia, and together with his boyhood friend, Tyrannius Rufinus, and a circle of young men, followed a life of virtue and study. Unknown circumstances brought this happy ideal to an end.

About 374 he left with some companions for the East. Jerusalem was his goal, but at Antioch he was stricken with fever and was unable to continue his journey. Upon recovery of his health he attended the exegetical lectures of Apollinaris of Laodicea, the intimate friend of St. Athanasius, and later retired to the desert of Chalcis near Antioch to live the life of a hermit. Here he devoted himself to the study of ascetical writings and to manual labor, but his keen intellect gave him no peace. He, therefore, began to copy books, tried to perfect himself in Greek, and began seriously to study Hebrew under a converted Jew. After about three years, theological controversies among the monks drove him out of the desert. He returned to Antioch and was ordained priest by Bishop Paulinus.

In 379-380 he set out for Constantinople, the Roman Capital of the East, to attend the lectures of St. Gregory of Nazianzus. Finally, in 382, accompanied by Paulinus of Antioch and St. Epiphanius, he went to Rome.

Because of his knowledge of the East, Pope Damasus had invited Jerome to Rome to help settle the Meletian Schism. The Roman Synod did not accomplish its purpose, but this second Roman residence of Jerome was of the greatest importance for his literary activity. In these years he revised the Latin Gospels, and perhaps also the other books of the New Testament. Upon the death of Pope Damasus (December 10, 384) Jerome was forced to leave Rome. He now travelled to Antioch, visited the sacred shrines in Palestine, and before definitely settling in Bethlehem in the autumn of 386 made a hurried visit to Egypt. As superior of a monastery and the spiritual director of a convent at Bethlehem, he led a life of asceticism and literary activity until his death on September 30, 420.

(*2*) *The Revisions and Translations of the Bible by St. Jerome.*—Jerome's activity as a reviser and translator was threefold.

(*i*) Because of the many variant readings in the Old Latin text, Pope Damasus requested Jerome to revise the Latin translation of the Four Gospels.[2a] Hence, he did not give us a new translation, but about the year 383 revised the then current Latin text in accordance with some Greek MSS. Vogels has established that for Luke, 22, 39—24, 11 Jerome used a Latin text akin to the Old Latin MSS.—*Veronensis* (fifth century), *Palatinus* (fifth century), *Corbeiensis* (fifth century), and *Vindobonesis* (fifth-sixth century). It is still a matter of research what particular pre-Vulgate MSS. were used for the remaining parts of Luke, and for Matthew, Mark and John. Nor can it be stated definitely what Greek MSS. Jerome used, though it is generally conceded that Jerome's text very frequently is allied to the Alexandrian family of which *Codex Vaticanus* is the chief representative. It has not

[2a] Cf. Metlen, M., "The Vulgate Gospels As a Translation," in C.B.Q., 8 (1946), 83-88, 230-235, 433-437, 8 (1947), 106-110, 220-225.

yet been definitely established whether Jerome also revised the other books of the New Testament. The majority of scholars are inclined to the opinion that he made such a revision.

During this visit to Rome, Jerome also revised the Psalter according to the Septuagint. It contains Lucian readings. This Psalter was called the "Roman Psalter" because of its use in the Liturgy in the City of Rome. It was used in Italy generally until Pius V (1566), in the Doge chapel of Venice until 1808, in the Ambrosian Liturgy at Milan until Pius X (1911), and is still being used in the Basilica of St. Peter in Rome. Traces of it may still be found in the Invitatory (Ps. 94)—excepting the third nocturn for Epiphany—of this old Roman Breviary, and in the Introit, Gradual and Tract for Sundays and ancient feasts in the Roman Missal.

(ii) While at Bethlehem in 387, Jerome became interested in the Hexapla of Origen (d. 254/255), which could be easily seen and studied at Cæsarea in Palestine. He therefore determined to revise the Latin text of the Old Testament according to the Hexaplaric Septuagint. He began with the Psalter about the year 387, and based its revision upon the fifth column of the Hexapla. This was his second revision of the Psalter. It was first used for divine services in Gaul, and thus came to be called the "Gallican Psalter." By the end of the seventh century it was adopted by all churches excepting Rome, Milan, and Venice. Still later it was received in the official edition of the Vulgate text at Rome, and is one of the two texts in the Breviary that is left optional for priests of the Latin Rite to recite for the Divine Office. The other text is the New Latin Psalter according to the Hebrew prepared by the Jesuit Fathers (1945).

All of the proto-canonical books were revised according to the Hexapla. But of this immense work, which was either stolen or lost ("fraude cujusdam periit"), there are only extant the Psalter mentioned above, the Book of Job, the prefaces and a few fragments of Proverbs, Ecclesiastes and Canticles, and the preface of Paralipomenon.

(*iii*) About the year 390 Jerome began at Bethlehem a much larger project. It was the Latin translation of the Old Testament directly from the Hebrew (*Hebraica veritas*). His chief incentive to undertake this work was the calumny of the Jews, who continually declared that Christians lacked the genuine Scriptural text, and that their theological arguments, based either upon the Latin or Greek texts, were not authentic or valid (*Præfatio in librum Isaiæ*). The following are the books and the approximate time of their translation: [3]

390	Samuel, Kings
?	Tobias [4]
391	Psalter (Hebrew) [5]
392	Sixteen Books of the Prophets [6]
393	Job
395	Esdras, Nehemias
396	Paralipomenon
397	Proverbs, Ecclesiastes, Canticles
398-404	Pentateuch
405-	Josue, Judges, Ruth, Esther
?	Judith

Thus, after sixteen years Jerome completed his translation of the Old Testament, with the exception of the deutero-canonical books of Wisdom, Ecclesiasticus, Baruch and 1 and 2 Machabees.

Our modern Vulgate text is therefore composed of the following parts:

(1) The New Testament.

   (a) Gospels revised according to the original Greek.
   (b) The other books of the New Testament, which also

---

[3] Cf. Vaccari, A., in I.B., 299.

[4] The deutero-canonical Books of Tobias and Judith were translated from the Chaldaic or Aramaic at the request of friends.

[5] The Psalter and the Prophets were translated into Greek by his friend Sophronius. This Psalter was never officially used by the Church, and is not found in many MSS.

[6] The deutero-canonical parts of Daniel were translated from the Greek version of Theodotion, and those of Esther from the Septuagint.

were probably revised, but this is by no means certain.

(2) The Old Testament.

(a) The proto-canonical books, excepting the Psalter, are directly from the Hebrew (the Gallican Psalter is according to the Hexapla).

(b) The deutero-canonical books.

(i) Tobias and Judith are from the Aramaic.

(ii) Wisdom, Ecclesiasticus, Baruch and 1 and 2 Machabees were not revised by Jerome, but taken from the Old Latin, which is based upon the Septuagint.

(iii) Additions in Daniel from Theodotion and those of Esther from the Septuagint.

(3) The Qualities of St. Jerome's Version.—Three main principles guided the great biblical scholar in his Latin translation from the Hebrew; namely, to make the text intelligible, to avoid slavish renderings, and to take cognizance of the elegance of diction. His translation, therefore, has various well-known characteristics.

(*i*) Chief among these characteristics is *clarity of exposition.* Generically speaking, none of the ancient writers expressed the real meaning more accurately or better than Jerome, even though at times he missed a minor point or judged as a Christian theologian rather than as a textual critic (e.g., in some Messianic passages). To render the meaning of the text very distinct, he often added a word or phrase (Gen. 31, 47; Judges 12, 6), translated Hebrew proper names into their etymological meaning (Gen. 41, 45; Prov. 30, 1), used popular (1 Sam. 15, 12) or mythological expressions (Job 21, 33), or even Jewish fables (Jos. 14, 15).[7]

(*ii*) Another quality of Jerome's version is *fidelity of translation.* He abhorred slavish renderings of the Hebrew lest the real meaning be lost. To obtain the faithful sense of the

[7] Cf. Stummer, F., "Einführung, etc.," 110 ff.

original text he often consulted other versions. Thus, he sometimes departed from the Hebrew in favor of the Septuagint (Zach. 14, 20), its Lucian recension (2 Sam. 6, 7), Aquila (Ex. 34, 29), Symmachus (Gen. 14, 1), or Theodotion (Dan. 3, 24 ff).[8]

(*iii*) His translation shows a certain *elegance of diction*. Harsh Hebrew constructions were rendered according to the Latin syntax. Long Hebrew sentences were broken up. The same Hebrew word at times was rendered by various synonyms even in the same context. These main characteristics, however, are not everywhere prevalent to the same extent.

(*4*) *The Origin of Our Present Vulgate Text.*—Very little encouragement was given to St. Jerome during his lifetime for his translation of the Old Testament from the Hebrew. It is true that Sophronius and Lucinius Bæticus welcomed this translation, but opposition to it was more prevalent. Not only did an African community riot against its bishop because of the introduction of the new text, but also Tyrannius Rufinus stubbornly resisted it. St. Augustine, considering the practical needs of the Church, would have preferred a revision according to the Septuagint, but towards the end of his life became very sympathetic towards it, though he did not use it publicly. In time opposition gradually abated. From the fifth century on,[8a] scholars of Gaul (France) and Spain for the most part preferred Jerome's translation to the Old Latin. Towards the end of the sixth century it acquired equal footing with the Old Latin in Italy, and St. Gregory the Great (d. 604) made use of both translations. In the following century St. Jerome's text was adopted by all the churches in Spain, according to St. Isidore of Seville (d. 636). It was not, however, until the eighth and ninth centuries that it was universally adopted. St. Bede (d. 735) called it "nostra editio," but the name *"Vulgata editio,"* first applied to it probably by Roger Bacon (d. 1294), was used and sanctioned by the Council of Trent.

[8] Cf. Stummer, F., "Einführung, etc.," 99-105.
[8a] Cf. Dold, A., "Neue Teile der ältesten Vulgata-Evangelienhandschrift aus dem 5. Jhdt.," in *Biblica,* 22 (1941), 105-146.

(c) The History of the Vulgate Text to the Council of Trent (1545)

The simultaneous existence of the Old Latin and the Vulgate was not advantageous for the pure transmission of either textual form. In the course of centuries the Vulgate lost its original purity. In the same codices some books taken from the Vulgate and others from the Old Latin were to be found. For example, *Codex Monacensis* (eighth-ninth century) has Job according to the Vulgate, but Tobias, Judith and Esther according to the Old Latin. Then, too, mixed readings are at times detected in some of the old MSS. This is especially true of some of the Spanish MSS., and in particular of *Codex Cavensis* (eighth century), representing the school of Peregrinus, a Spanish bishop living between 450 and 500. An interesting example of a blended reading still to be found in the official Vulgate edition is 2 Samuel 1, 18 f; "Considera, Israel, pro his, qui mortui sunt, super excelsa tua vulnerati" is from the Old Latin, and "Inclyti, Israel, super montes tuos interfecti sunt" is from the Vulgate.

The trouble caused by blended or mixed readings was recognized very early by scholars. Time after time attempts were made to recover the true text of St. Jerome. Thus, there gradually arose definite families of MSS., distinct from one another either according to the regions where they were spread (Spain, England, France, Italy, etc.), or according to religious communities that preferred a certain textual type.

Among the first to recognize the need of a revision and to attempt to restore the original Vulgate text was Victor of Capua, Italy (d. 554). His chief work was a Gospel Harmony similar to Tatian's *Diatessaron*, and for this he used St. Jerome's text instead of the Old Latin. His work is preserved in *Codex Fuldensis*, the oldest MS. of the entire New Testament (brought to Fulda by St. Boniface, the apostle of Germany). More important is the name of M. Aurelius Cassiodorus (d. 575) of Italy, who carefully collected very old manuscripts of the Old and New Testaments according to St.

Jerome, and had them copied in one volume.[9] It is noteworthy that one of the best Latin Vulgate codices, the *Codex
Amiatinus,* has some relationship with the Cassiodorian text.
This codex, so called because it once belonged to the monastery
of Amiato near Siena, Italy, was copied about the year 700
near Jarrow, England, and intended as a papal gift by St.
Ceolfrid. This codex played an important rôle at the time of
the Sistine-Clementine revision in the sixteenth century, and
is now acknowledged as the head of the Alcuin family of MSS.
by the Benedictine Commission for the revision of the Vulgate.

At the time of Charlemagne systematic attempts were made
to revise the then current text. Bishop Theodulf of Orleans
(d. 821), in trying to reacquire the text of St. Jerome, followed an eclectic method and was largely influenced by Spanish MSS.[10] This revision exercised very little influence, and
only a few codices preserved this recension. Emperor Charlemagne in 797 invited Alcuin of York, England, to edit an
edition of the Vulgate according to the best MSS. With the
aid of English codices this task was finished in 801. This
Alcuin recension, akin to the Codex Amiatinus, was free from
the Old Latin readings, and represented a fine edition of St.
Jerome's Vulgate. It was widely spread throughout the
Middle Ages and enjoyed great authority.

But this revision of Alcuin did not have permanent results.
Due to such reasons as difficulties of international communication and a lack of a well-established book market, textual
corruptions continued. Isolated attempts were made to correct these corruptions. Noteworthy among these revisers
were: St. Peter Damian (d. 1072), Lanfranc, O.S.B., Archbishop of Canterbury (d. 1089), Stephen Harding, Abbot of
Citeaux (d. 1134), Nicolas Maniacoria, deacon of St. Damasus

[9] Very rarely before his time was the entire Latin Bible to be found
in one single volume. This accounts for MSS. having books of the Old
Latin and Vulgate bound in the same volume.

[10] In the Psalms the Theodulfian MSS. have made corrections accord-
ing to the Hebrew Texts (cf. Power, E., in *Biblica,* 5, 1924, 253-258); Cf.
* Gluntz, H. H., "History of the Vulgate in England from Alcuin to
Roger Bacon" (Cambridge, 1933).

Rome (d. 1145). Their influence, however, was locally restricted. In the twelfth century there were hardly two MSS. that were identical. The chief reasons for textual corruptions in the Vulgate were threefold: additions, changes, and omissions.

In the thirteenth century the Bible called the *Biblia* or *Exemplar Parisiense* and used at the University of Paris exercised great influence. It seems to have been derived from the Alcuin revision, but other textual forms also contributed to its contents. The most notable external qualities of this edition are the same order of books as in our modern Bibles and a convenient division of the books into chapters. This chapter division was introduced by Stephen Langton in 1214, and has been substantially retained in our present Vulgate. Its greatest critic was Roger Bacon, O.F.M. (d. 1294), who wrote thus of it: "Textus est pro majori parte horribiliter corruptus in exemplari vulgato, hoc est Parisiensi." For this reason various "Correctories" (collections or corrected readings) were made by the Dominicans and Franciscans. These attempts to restore the original Vulgate text were indeed laudable, but because of their limited influence, private authority, and at times the incompetency of some copyists, they contributed very little to the emendation of the Vulgate. Indeed, the confusion increased.

The history of the Vulgate in the latter part of the Middle Ages has not yet been carefully investigated. Yet, there is evidence that the need of a revised Vulgate text was recognized by Nicholas of Lyra (d. 1340), Peter of Alliaco (d. 1420), and the Congregation of Windesheim (early part of the fifteenth century), of which Thomas a Kempis was a member. According to Dom Quentin, O.S.B., the MSS. from the sixth-seventh to the fourteenth century can be divided into three principal families: the *Spanish* family, of which the best MS. is the *Codex Toletanus* (eighth century); the *Alcuin* family, of which the best MSS. are the *Codex Amiatinus* (eighth century) and the *Codex Vallicellianus* (ninth century); and the *Theodulfian* family, of which the best MS. is the *Codex Otto-*

bonianus (eighth century). Other MSS. (such as the *Exemplar Parisiense,* the Italian MSS. etc.) are mere modifications or mixtures of these three great family types.

The invention of printing by Gutenberg at Mayence was of the greatest importance for the history of the Vulgate. About 1452 he printed the entire Vulgate in folio (two columns and forty-two lines per folio) from some German MS. that represented the *Exemplar Parisiense.* Soon afterwards Bibles were being printed at Strassburg, Bamberg, Basle, Venice, and Rome. By the close of the fifteenth century about one hundred editions of the Vulgate had appeared. The greater number of the editions were reprints of the Parisian text.[11]

The art of printing did not immediately represent progress in the history of the Vulgate. At first, the most convenient MS. was taken and printed. The Vulgate, however, did obtain a very wide circulation, and with the appearance of the Hebrew Psalter in 1477 and the Greek Psalter in 1481 careful comparison was made between the various texts. Not only were the differences between the Vulgate texts themselves noticed, but also their relationship with the original languages and versions began to be studied, and thus many variant readings were discovered. Hence, many attempts were made to revise the Vulgate text or to edit independent Latin translations.

To appreciate the existing confusion due to the lack of a unified method and purpose, and to understand the importance of the discussions of the Tridentine Fathers and the decisions of the Council of Trent, let us briefly review the more important editions of the Latin Bible, whether entire or partial, that appeared in the first half of the sixteenth century.

(i) Critical Editions of the Vulgate with Variant Readings from Latin MSS.

[11] Editions of the Bible independent of the Parisian text were published at Vicenza (1476) by Leonard Basileensis, and at Venice (1495) by Paganinus de Paganinis.

1504   Adrian Gumelli
1511   Albert Castellanus, O.P.
1520   Complutensian Polyglot
1528–1557   Robert Stephan (Robert Estienne)
1530   Gobelinus Laridius.
1547–1583   John Henten, O.P.

(*ii*) *Corrections in the Vulgate according to Original Texts*

1522 * Osiander (1527 reprinted by the Catholic, Rudelius)
1542–1557   Isidor Clarius, O.S.B.

(*iii*) *Entirely New Latin Translation from the Original Texts*

1512   Faber Stapulensis (Jacques Lefevre d'Etaples) [12]
1515   Felix Pratensis, O.S.Aug.
1516–   Erasmus
1528   Santes Pagnini, O.P.
1530–   Cardinal Cajetan, O.P.
1532–1540 * Conrad Pellicanus
1534–1546 * Sebastian Muenster
1542 * Michael Servetus
1543 * Leo Judae
1551 * Sebastian Castellius

(d) The History of the Vulgate Text from the Council of Trent to the Present Day

On April 8, 1546, two Biblical Decrees were solemnly promulgated by the Tridentine Fathers. The first, called "Sacrosancta," declares the Catholic rule of faith in regard to the Sacred Scriptures by repeating the value of divine tradition, defining the inspiration of the Bible, and listing officially the books of the Canon. Then for the first time these books were formally canonized. This first Decree is a formal dogmatic definition of the Church (cf. E.B., 60).

---

[12] His Pauline Epistles were used by Luther. Cf. Lenhart, J. M., 'Protestant Latin Bibles of the Reformation from 1520-1570. A Biographical Account," in C.B.Q., 8 (1946), 416-432.

The second Decree, called "Insuper," refers to the editing and use of Sacred Scripture. The words of this Decree making the Vulgate authentic and official for the Latin Rite are as follows: "The same Sacred and Holy Synod, considering that it would be of no small advantage to the Church of God if it were clearly made known which of all the Latin editions of the Sacred Books in circulation is to be held as authentic, hereby declares and enacts that the same well-known Old Latin Vulgate edition, which has been approved by the long use of so many centuries in the Church, is to be held as authentic in public readings, disputations, preachings, and expositions, and that no one shall dare or presume to reject it under any pretense whatsoever" (E.B., 61).[13] This same Decree also specifies that "Sacred Scripture, especially this well-known Old Latin Vulgate edition, shall be published as correctly as possible." [13a]

It is this disciplinary Decree "Insuper" that is of greatest importance for the history of the Vulgate. To understand it fully, we must take into consideration both the preliminary discussions as well as subsequent events.

(i) The Council of Trent in declaring the Vulgate to be authentic did not reject the original texts.

On March 8-9, 1546, two congregations of theologians met to prepare their material for the next general council meeting. The following is a résumé of their discussions. The Vulgate should be taken as the authentic text of the Bible (i.e., as the source for arguments in faith and morals). The direct reason for this is, not so much its conformity with the originals, but its usage for more than a thousand years in the Church, which guarantees that the Vulgate contains the written Word of God unfalsified.[14] On March 17, 1546, this report in the

[13] The "Insuper," according to the more common opinion, is a disciplinary Decree based upon the dogmatic fact that the Vulgate conforms substantially with the originals, and therefore contains no errors in faith and morals. Cf. Vosté, J-M., "La Volgata al Concilio di Trento," in *Biblica*, 27 (1946), 301-319; *idem*, "The Vulgate at the Council of Trent," in C.B.Q., 9 (1947), 9-25.

[13a] Cf. Vosté, J-M., "De revisione textus graeci N.T. ad votum Concilii Tridentini facta," in *Biblica*, 24 (1943), 304-307.

[14] Cf. Höpfl, H., "Beiträge, etc.," 3-11.

form of the *first abuse* was presented to the Fathers of the General Council. It stated that there were various editions of the Sacred Scriptures being used as authentic in public readings, disputations, expositions, and preachings. The remedy prescribed was to declare only the Vulgate as authentic, but not to detract from the authority of the Septuagint used by the Apostles, nor to repudiate other versions.[15]

On March 23, 1546, there was a discussion of this first abuse and its remedy. The mind of the Fathers of the Council is represented in the declaration of the Bishop of Fano: "The Council does not wish to reject all the texts of Sacred Scripture with the exception of the Vulgate. Such versions as the Septuagint, Aquila, Symmachus and Theodotion are not to be rejected or frowned upon. Because of the variant readings the commission urged the acceptance of one translation as authentic and prescribed its use for the Church. The commission selected the Vulgate of St. Jerome, because it is better than the other translations and because of its long and continued usage in the Church." [16]

On April 1, 1546, there was a further discussion of the subject. Cardinal Pacheco demanded that all versions, except the Vulgate, be condemned. The Bishop of Fano replied that such an action would place too much of a restriction upon Christian freedom. Cardinal Pacheco's repeated demand two days later fell upon deaf ears. Cardinal Pole's request to have the Hebrew and Greek originals included among the authentic texts was also rejected, but indirect references to them were given in the final Decree of April 8 in the words: "Sacred Scripture, especially this well-known Old Latin Vulgate edition, shall be published as correctly as possible."

It is therefore evident that the Council of Trent in declaring the Vulgate to be authentic did not prefer it to the original texts, nor to the ancient versions. On the other hand, the Vulgate in its relation to all the *other Latin versions* was declared authentic. The original texts needed no declaration of authenticity; they were so *ipso facto.*

[15] Cf. Höpfl, H., *op. cit.,* 12.
[16] Cf. Höpfl, H., *op. cit.,* 13 ff.

(*ii*) By declaring the Vulgate to be authentic, the Council of Trent does not exclude the existence of minor errors in it, but presupposes it to be free from substantial errors, at least in matters pertaining to faith and morals.

For practical reasons the Fathers made no mention in the official Decree of the minor textual corruptions in the Vulgate manuscripts, although they had discussed the subject thoroughly and urged corrections to be made quietly to avoid scandal or casting suspicion on the Vulgate.[17] In the report of the two congregations of theologians meeting on March 8-9, 1546, it was admitted that the Vulgate does not agree with the originals in all details, but that these differences are in minor details and not in matters of faith and morals. It was furthermore proposed that the Vulgate should be revised, and the errors that had crept into the text should be corrected.[18] On March 17, 1546, this report in the form of the *second abuse* was presented to the Fathers of the General Council. It stated that there were in circulation many variant readings in the Vulgate manuscripts. To remedy this abuse it was suggested that the primitive Vulgate be restored, and that this task should be performed by the Holy See.[19]

On March 23, 1546, a long discussion was held on this subject. Cardinal Pacheco in particular raised the difficulty that it would be impossible to declare any version as authentic, and at the same time admit that it contains textual corruptions. The Bishop of Fano answered this objection by declaring that a distinction had to be made between the Vulgate as a version and the individual manuscripts or editions of the Vulgate. The Vulgate as a version is free from error, but the various manuscripts or editions of it are not necessarily free from error. The Vulgate may have some slight mistakes, but these have no bearing on faith and morals.

The word *authentic* used in the Council of Trent is to be taken in the juridical sense of *worthy of belief, reliable, credible, truthful, trustworthy, authoritative.* An authentic docu-

---

[17] Cf. Höpfl, H., *op. cit.,* 17.
[18] Cf. Höpfl, H., *op. cit.,* 3-12.
[19] Cf. Höpfl, H., *op. cit.,* 12.

ment is one that secures credence, one that merits faith so that it cannot be rejected or called into question. Since the autographic copies of the Scriptures are lost, the Church guarantees in general the fidelity and the trustworthiness, but not the philological accuracy, of the Vulgate. She guarantees its reliable argumentative force in matters pertaining to faith and morals. In other matters the Vulgate possesses no other authority than that of a good old translation.[20]

The Decree "Insuper," with the two points discussed above in (i) and (ii), has been often misunderstood. It was used for a long time by Protestants as one of their stock charges against the Church. Likewise, many Spanish theologians under the influence of Cardinal Pacheco maintained that the Vulgate was the *sole* authentic text, and represented the originals even *in minimis*. Some of them even went farther and declared that the Vulgate text was directly inspired. St. Bellarmine, however, reveals what was in the minds of the outstanding scholars of this century. He clearly proves that the Vulgate according to the intention of the Tridentine Fathers was authentic in regard to faith and morals, and that this was sufficient for the purpose of the Church. Furthermore, he stresses that the Hebrew and Greek originals are no less authentic than the Vulgate, and hence anyone who rejects the original texts should be reproved. In conclusion, he rightly adds that the Oriental Churches make use of texts and versions other than the Vulgate, and yet these must be recognized by us as authentic.[21]

(iii) The Fathers of the Council recognized the lack of conformity existing between the various manuscripts and editions of the Vulgate. They therefore decreed that "Sacred Scripture, and especially this well-known Old Vulgate, shall be published as correctly as possible." They had also urged that this task be performed by the Holy See.

Before the first Pontifical Commission for the revision of the Vulgate was appointed in 1561, there were two large under-

[20] C. Höpfl, H., *op. cit.*, 22 ff; Pius XII, in "Divino afflante Spiritu" (E.B., 549).
[21] Cf. Höpfl, H., *op. cit.*, 40 ff.

takings worthy of mention. At Rome Cardinal Marcello
Cervini, the Papal Legate to the Council and uncle of St.
Bellarmine, obtained good Greek and Latin manuscripts, and
intended to publish not only the Vulgate but also the Greek
and Hebrew texts. He entrusted the work of the New Testament to his protégé, William Sirleto, and that of the Septuagint to Nicholas Majoranus. It is unfortunate that Sirleto's
Annotations to the New Testament, in which he severely criticized the inaccuracies of Erasmus' Latin translation, and his
revised Greek New Testament were never published.[22] Likewise, Majoranus' revision of the Greek Old Testament according to the *Codex Vaticanus* (B) was never published and no
trace of his critical work remains. At Louvain the theological
faculty entrusted John Henten, O.P., with the preparation of
a critical edition of the Vulgate in accordance with the wish of
the Tridentine Decree. In 1547 he published the Vulgate,
which was based upon Robert Stephan's edition of 1540, and
compared it with 28 manuscripts and 2 incunabula. Upon the
death of Henten (1566), his critical work was continued by
Francis Lucas of Bruges and frequently reprinted. The
Louvain edition of 1583 was used by the Roman revisers. It
is noteworthy that the Henten-Stephan Bible was based upon
the *Exemplar Parisiense,* which is also the basis of our official
Vulgate text.

In 1561 the *first special commission* was appointed by Pope
Pius IV (1559-1565), who brought the Council of Trent to a
close. Four Cardinals stood at the head of this commission,
which was to publish the revision of the Vulgate and the writings of the Greek and Latin Fathers. The publication of the
Vulgate, however, came to a standstill because they had no
definite critical principles to govern their revision.[23]

In 1569 the *second commission* for the revision of the Vulgate was appointed by Pope Pius V (1566-1572). At the head
of the commission were five Cardinals, of whom the most

[22] Cf. Höpfl, H., *op. cit.,* 48-52; Idem, "Kardinal Sirlets Annotationen,
etc."
[23] Cf. Stummer, F., "Einführung, etc.," 177 f.

noted were Sirleto and his pupil, Anthony Carafa. They were
assisted by twelve consultors. The manuscripts of Rome,
Italy and Europe were collated. At Florence the Benedictines
collated twelve manuscripts, and a similar work of collecting
thirty-four Biblical manuscripts was performed at Monte
Cassino by the members of the same Order. This vast material was placed at the disposal of the commission. From
April 28, 1569, to December 7, 1569, twenty-six plenary ses-
sions were held. Again lack of definite critical principles
brought the task to a standstill.

In 1586 the *third commission* was appointed by Pope Sixtus
V (1585-1590). In the preceding period the Biblia Regia or
Polyglot had been published at Antwerp (1569-1572) under
the supervision of Arias Montanus. At Rome a special commission after ten years of intensive work published the Septuagint in 1587. This work of the Septuagint was of the
greatest utility for the revision of the Vulgate. Cardinal
Carafa was placed at the head of the new Vulgate commission.
The members of the commission had at their disposal much
collected material of variant readings, but especially the
Codices Amiatinus, Vallicellianus, Legionensis, and *Tole-*
tanus,[24] and a 1547 Louvain Bible with the marginal readings
of Cardinal Sirleto. After two years of intensive efforts the
results of the commission were handed to the Pope. Their
findings are contained in a 1583 folio edition of the Louvain
Bible, with the textual emendations proposed by the commission in the margin. The emendated critical text differed so
much from the then current text that the Pope did not give
it his approval.

Pope Sixtus V now determined to revise the Vulgate himself with the aid of the Spanish Jesuit, Toledo, and the Augustinian, Angelo Rocca. Rejecting for the most part the
proposed emendations of the Carafa commission, the Pope
returned to the Louvain text. Likewise, the conventional division of chapters into verses was altered by him. On Novem-

---

[24] Cf. Vaccari, A., in I.B., 317.

ber 25, 1589, the printing of the Vulgate was finished. The
Bible was prefaced by the Bull "Aeternus ille celestium" [24a] of
March 1, 1590, which today is commonly recognized as not
having been properly and canonically promulgated. On May
2 it was distributed to the members of the Curia and on May
31 to the Catholic princes. Copies were then also sold to the
public. But Pope Sixtus was not content with his new work.
He was preparing to print a separate copy of *corrigenda* so
that each one could make his own corrections, but died on
August 27, 1590, before completing his task. This Vulgate
of Sixtus V was not well received, because it had rejected the
advice of the Carafa commission; it had a very sloppy appearance with corrections made by erasures and slips pasted or
words stamped over the text, and had changed the conventional order of verse division. On September 5, 1590, the sale
of the Sistine Bible was forbidden and all available copies
were destroyed.

In February, 1591, Pope Gregory XIV acting upon the
advice of St. Robert Bellarmine appointed a *fourth commission,* but this time for the revision of the Sistine Bible. It
consisted of Cardinal Colonna, Prefect of the Index Congregation, six other Cardinals (including William Allen), and
eleven consultors (including St. Robert Bellarmine). They
were all agreed on the following principles of revision: (1)
what had been taken away from the text should be restored;
(2) what had been added should be removed; (3) what had
been changed should be reconsidered or corrected; (4) attention should be paid to punctuation. In the beginning the
work of revision proceeded rather slowly, so that after forty
days only the Book of Genesis was completed. A smaller
commission, therefore, was entrusted with the completion of
the task. The two Cardinals Colonna and Allen together
with eight consultors, including St. Bellarmine, retired to
Zagarola, the summer home of Cardinal Colonna, and after

[24a] Cf. Baumgarten, P. M., "Die Veröffentlichung der Bulle 'Eternus
ille celestium' von 1 März, 1590," in B.Z., 5 (1907), 189-191; *idem,* "Das
Original der Konstiution, etc.," *ibid.,* 5 (1907), 337-351.

nineteen days finished the revision on June 23, 1591.[25] Due to
the untimely death of Pope Gregory XIV the revision could
not be immediately published.

On January 30, 1592, Pope Clement VIII began his pontificate and approved the work of the Gregorian commission.
This edition of the Vulgate appeared in folio on November 9,
1592. A second edition in quarto appeared in 1593, and a
third edition in 1598. These editions appeared under the
name of Sixtus V. No Bull so extensive as the "Æternus ille
celestium" was issued, but only a short one entitled "Cum
sacrorum" and dated November 9, 1592. In 1604 the name
of Clement VIII was added by Robillius of Lyons to that of
Sixtus V, and thus our Vulgate in time came to be called the
Sistine-Clementine edition.[26]

Thus, we see that the Sistine Vulgate commission of Cardinal Carafa had as its principal purpose the publication of a
critical text carefully edited according to the best manuscripts
and original texts. On the other hand, Sixtus V preferred the
textus receptus of his time. The Gregorian-Clementine commission sought the *via media* between the strictly critical and
popular text.[27]

The editors of the Clementine Bible in their "Præfatio ad
Lectorem," [28] which appeared in the first three editions, admitted in advance that their work was not by any means
perfect, and this was also felt by learned scholars. Francis

<hr>

[25] Cf. Vosté, J. M., *op. cit.*, 30.
[26] Hetzenauer enumerates 4,900 differences between the Sistine and
Clementine versions. Cf. Vosté, J. M., *op. cit.*, 30.
[27] Cf. Höpfl, H., *op. cit.*, 172 f.
[28] The "Præfatio ad Lectorem," written according to the mind of St.
Bellarmine, states among other things that Pope Sixtus V after his Bible
had been printed and published decided and decreed that the entire
work under print should be revised (totum opus sub incudum revocan-
dum censuit atque decrevit). This sentence has been described by some
as a pious fraud and by others as objectively wrong. Under Benedict
XIV St. Bellarmine's canonization was deferred on account of this sentence. This incriminating sentence in its present form did not originate
exclusively from St. Bellarmine. His outline had received various modifications. It is evident that the redaction of a document *urbi et orbi*
would not be entrusted to an individual person, holding only a minor

Lucas of Bruges (d. 1619) highly praised the Clementine edition, but published at Antwerp in 1603 and 1618 two correctories of variant readings that were to be utilized in future revisions of the Vulgate. For two centuries there was no one who, insisting upon the readings of Lucas, edited an emendated Vulgate text. About the middle of the last century the Roman Barnabite, Ungarelli, and his pupil and successor, Vercellone, collected and published (1860-1864) vast material on the variant readings of the Vulgate as far as the Fourth Book of Kings. Among modern Vulgates we may mention Fillion, Hetzenauer, Gramatica and the Sulpician edition. In Protestant circles * Wordsworth and * White published at Oxford (1889—) a critical edition of the New Testament. Likewise worthy of mention is the Parisian Protestant theologian, * Samuel Berger, who in 1893 published a very important work on the history of the Vulgate in the early part of the Middle Ages.

A new period in the history of the Vulgate began under St. Pius X (1903-1914). It happened on April 30, 1907, that Cardinal Rampolla, the President of the Biblical Commission, sent a letter in the name of the Holy Father to the Abbot Primate Hildebrand de Hemptenne, asking whether the various Benedictine Congregations would undertake this revision of the Vulgate. The abbots, then assembled at Rome, unanimously accepted the arduous task. In the autumn of the same year a small commission under the presidency of Cardinal Francis A. Gasquet [29] began to organize the work. Their first step was the acquisition of manuscripts and the careful and accurate comparison of these with one another.

---

position in the Church, as was the case with Bellarmine at that time. He had suggested that the new Vulgate contain the names of Sixtus V and Gregory XIV, but his advice was not followed. It is true that no fully determined plan of Sixtus V to revise his Bible is known, but this does not exclude him from manifesting his desire both privately and orally. Cf. Höpfl, H. *op cit.*, 186-221; also Tromp, S., "De revisione textus N.T. facta Romae a commissione Pontificia circa a 1617 praeside S. R. Bellarmino," in *Biblica*, 22 (1941), 303-306.

[29] Cf. Weld-Blundell, A. "The Revision of the Vulgate Bible," in *Scripture*, 2 (1947), 100-105.

The scope of their work is aptly and succinctly given by Cardinal Gasquet in his article on the Vulgate contained in the "Catholic Encyclopedia" (XV, 516a): "Substantially, no doubt, the present authentic Clementine text represents that which St. Jerome produced in the fourth century, but no less certainly it, the printed text, stands in need of close examination and much correction to make it agree with the translation of St. Jerome. No copy of the actual text is known to exist; and the corruptions introduced by scribes, etc., in the centuries posterior to St. Jerome, and even the well-intentioned work of various correctors, have rendered the labors of trying to recover the exact text from existing MSS. both difficult and delicate. This, however, is the work which must be done as the first step in the revision of the Vulgate. It is consequently the aim of the present commission to determine with all possible exactitude the Latin text of St. Jerome, and not to produce any new version of the Latin Scriptures. Of course, it is altogether another matter to determine how far St. Jerome was correct in his translation: to settle this will no doubt be the work of some future commission."

In 1922 D. H. Quentin, O.S.B.,[30] published the principles which would guide them in the publication of the Octateuch (Genesis to Ruth). All of the manuscripts are divided into three families: (1) the *Spanish family*, with as principal witness the *Codex Turonensis;* (2) the *Theodulfian family*, with as principal witness the *Codex Ottobonianus;* (3) the *Alcuin family*, with as principal witness the *Codex Amiatinus.* The two subsidiary families, the Italian and that of the Parisian University, being of secondary importance, are not taken into consideration. In cases of differences between the three families the "règle de fer," or democratic method of the majority ruling, is invoked. This Octateuch has now been published: Genesis (1926), Exodus and Leviticus (1929), Numbers and Deuteronomy (1936), Josue, Judges and Ruth (1939). Subsequently there appeared Samuel (1944), Kings (1945), Parali-

[30] Cf. Quentin, D. H., "Collectanea Biblica Latina" (vol. VI. Rome, 1922); *idem,* "Essais de Critique Textuelle" (Paris, 1926).

pomenon (1948), Esdras, Tobias, Judith (1950), Esther and Job (1951), Psalms (1953), Proverbs, Ecclesiastes and Canticles (1957).

The Book of Psalms translated directly from the Hebrew has been published by the Professors of the Pontifical Biblical Institute: "Liber Psalmorum cum Canticis Breviarii Romani" (Rome, 1945).[31]

Art. 3. The Aramaic Versions

From about the fourteenth century onwards the Aramaic people with their own peculiar Semitic dialect rapidly spread over the entire Near East. The Jewish people came into direct and intimate contact with this language during the Babylonian exile, and later brought this dialect with them into Palestine. After the Jewish language became aramaicized, proper regard had to be given to this new dialect in the liturgy, and this fact led to the origin of the Targums (Hebr., *Targumim*, i.e., translations, interpretations). When, in the synagogal services, some verses had been read from the Hebrew Bible, an oral translation with a short explanation was added in Aramaic. Later these translations and explanations were written down and used for private reading. Finally they were authorized for public worship.[1]

The earliest mention of a written Targum (to Job) is for the period of Gamaliel I, the teacher of St. Paul.[2] The various individual Targums, however, do not predate the third century of our era, although it is possible that some portions of them are from an earlier period. These Targums, which are available for nearly all the proto-canonical books of the Old Testament, are distinguished from one another by their dia-

---

[31] Cf. Bea., A., "Il Nuovo Salterio Latino" (Rome, 1946; French 1947; Spanish 1947 and German 1948 translations); *idem*, "The New Psalter: Its Origin and Spirit," in C.B.Q., 8 (1946), 4-35; *idem*, "I primi dieci anni del nuovo Salterio latino." in *Biblica*, 36 (1955), 161-181.

[1] Cf. Steinmueller, J. E.-Sullivan, K., art. "Aramaeans," in C.B.E.O.T., and "Aramaic," in C.B.E.O.T. and C.B.E.N.T.

[2] Cf. * Bacher, W., in J.E., s.v. *Talmud.*

lects and also by their manner of paraphrasing the Hebrew text.

(a) THE INDIVIDUAL TARGUMS

(1) *The Pentateuch.*—There are various Aramaic paraphrases of the Pentateuch. The *Targum of Onkelos* [3] or *Babylonian Targum* was written about the third century. It was originally written in the Palestinian dialect, but redacted in Babylonia. It is more closely connected with the Hebrew archetype than the other Aramaic translations, and frequently gives a literal translation of the original text. The *Palestinian Targum* or *Targum Jerushalmi I*, also called the Targum of Pseudo-Jonathan, is composed of a mixed linguistic type, and in its present form was not used before the seventh century; it gives a free rendition of the Hebrew text. The *Targum Jerushalmi II* or *Fragment Targum* is composed of a mixed linguistic type, and may be considered as a sort of revision of Pseudo-Jonathan's Targum. The *Targum Jerushalmi III* appears as marginal readings in some of the MSS. to Targum Onkelos. The *Samaritan Targum*, according to a Samaritan tradition, was composed by a Nathanael about 20 B.C., but it surely existed at the time of Origen, because he refers to it.

(2) *The Prophets.*[3a]—The official Targum to the Prophets (i.e., the Earlier and the Later Prophets according to the Talmudic distinction) is the *Targum Jonathan* ben Uzziel, the most prominent pupil of Hillel. It is not as literal as the Targum Onkelos, but contains the same linguistic peculiarities. Although in its present form it was completed about the fourth century, there are traces of older parts.

(3) *The Hagiographa.*—Targums have been composed between the fifth and ninth centuries for nearly all the Hagi-

---

[3] This name Onkelos, which probably was applied to Aquila, was due to an error by the Babylonian rabbis (cf. *Bacher, W., *loc. cit.*).

[3a] Cf. *Churgin, P., "Targum Jonathan to the Prophets" (New York, 1928); Dies-Macho, A., "Un segundo fragmento del Targum Palestinense a los Profetas," in *Biblica,* 39 (1958), 198-205.

ographa. The Targums to Psalms and Job closely follow the Hebrew text, whereas the Targum to Proverbs was derived from the Syriac Peshitto.[4] The Targums to the five Megilloth (Canticles, Ruth, Lamentations, Ecclesiastes, and Esther) are of later origin and suggest an Aramaic Midrash. The Book of Esther, which was read on the Feast of Purim, is extant in three Targums. The Targum for the Book of Chronicles (Paralipomenon) belongs substantially to the fourth century, but it was not concluded until the ninth century. No Targums are as yet available for the Books of Daniel, and 1 and 2 Esdras. Since most of these Targums are of late origin and follow the Massoretic Text as their archetype, they are of little value for the textual criticism of the Old Testament.

(b) THE SYRIAC PESHITTO [5]

BIBLIOGRAPHY: Pigoulewski, N., "Manuscrits Syriaques bibliques de Leningrad," in R.B., 46 (1937), 83-92, 225-230, 392-400, 47 (1938), 83-88, 214-226; Vosté, J.-M., "Projet d'une édition criticoecclésiastique de la Pesitta sous Léon XIII," in Biblica, 28 (1947), 281-286; Vogel, A., "Studien zum Pesitta-Psalter," in Biblica, 32 (1951), 32-56, 198-231, 336-363, 481-502; Delekat, L., "Die Peschitta zu Jesaja zwischen Targum und Septuagint," in Biblica, 38 (1957), 321-335.

The Bible has been translated on several occasions into the Syriac language. The versions in that language are either directly from the original texts or from the Septuagint, and they have influenced, even though it be in a small degree, other versions, such as the Ethiopic, Armenian, Arabic, and perhaps even the Latin.

(1) *The Old Testament.*—We are uncertain how and when this translation originated. It seems to have been used by Bardesanes of Edessa (A.D. 154-222), but it is certain that both Aphraates and his contemporary of the fourth century, St. Ephraem, employed this version. Since this version in

---

[4] Cf. Baumstark, A., "Peshitta and palästinisches Targum," in B.Z., 19 (1931), 257-270.

[5] Peshitto is the Jacobite pronunciation, whereas the Nestorians say Peshitta. Both mean "the simple or common" translation.

many parts bears purely Jewish characteristics, many scholars maintain that it originated in Jewish circles. If this conclusion be right, it would then be plausible to hold that the Jewish dispersion in Mesopotamia, and especially at Edessa, translated even in *pre-Christian times* the books of the Old Testament into Syriac, just as the Alexandrian Jews had done.[6] Other scholars,[7] however, maintain that it originated in the *second century after Christ* from the Hebrew text.

As this version was translated directly from the Hebrew text, only the proto-canonical books appeared at first, with the exception of the Books of Paralipomenon, 1 and 2 Esdras, and Esther, which were added in the fourth century of our era. The deutero-canonical books were added still later.

Not having a uniform origin, the books have also no uniform value. The translation as a whole is excellent; it is exact and faithful without being too servile or literal.[8] Of all the books the Pentateuch is best translated.

This version shows considerable traces of the influence of the Septuagint in the Psalms, Isaias, and the Minor Prophets, so that they have many identical readings which are contrary to the Massoretic Text. This harmonization between the Septuagint and the Peshitto is explained by some textual critics (as e.g., Vaccari, * Barnes, etc.) as the result of a later Peshitto revision according to the Septuagint, and by others (e.g., Goettsberger, Wutz, etc.) by the theory that the Peshitto at times has an older and better Hebrew archetype than the Massoretic Text.

The principal MSS. of the Peshitto Old Testament are: *Codex Ambrosianus* of the sixth century (a photolithographic edition of which was made by A. M. Ceriani at Milan in 1879-1883), British Museum Add. MS. 14,425 (the Pentateuch of A.D. 464), etc., Cambridge 1, 1, 2 of the twelfth century, etc.

[6] Goettsberger, etc.
[7] Vaccari, * Kenyon, etc.
[8] Cf. Peters, C., "Zur Herkunft der Peshitta des ersten Samuel-Buches," in *Biblica*, 22 (1941), 25-34.

Thus far the printed editions of this version are based upon a few, easily accessible MSS. The first edition appeared in the Parisian Polyglot of 1645, and lacked Esther and the deutero-canonical books; this text (together with the missing books and 3 Esdras and 3 Machabees) was reprinted in the London Polyglot of 1654-1657. * S. Lee (London, 1823-1824) used the London Polyglot as his basic text, and availed himself of some recent MSS. and citations from the Syriac writers, especially from St. Ephraem and Barhebræus. These three editions present the Jacobite text. The Nestorian text, however, was printed at Urmia in 1852. The deutero-canonical books, which were missing from * Lee's Old Testament and the Urmia Bible, were edited by * P. de Lagarde (Leipzig, 1861). The last printed edition was made by the Dominican Fathers at Mossul (1871-1891) in three volumes.

(2) *The New Testament.*—The Syriac texts of the New Testament have been handed down under a triple form: Tatian's *Diatessaron,* the separate Gospels, and the Peshitto version.

Tatian's Diatessaron.—About 172 Tatian, a native of the Euphrates valley and a disciple of St. Justin Martyr, left Rome for his native land, where he died about 180. He composed a Harmony of the four Gospels, but whether this was done at Rome or in Syria is disputed. Similarly scholars are not agreed whether this Harmony was originally written in Greek [9] or more probably in Syriac.[9a]

[9] A Greek fragment of Tatian's Diatessaron found at Dura (a Roman fort on the Euphrates) was written before A.D. 256 when the town was captured by the Persians. Cf. * Kraeling, C. H., "A Greek Fragment of Tatian's *Diatessaron* from Dura" (London, 1935); Lagrange, J. M., in R.B., 49 (1935), 321 ff; Merk, A., in *Biblica,* 17 (1936), 234-241; Peters, C., in *Biblica,* 21 (1940), 51-55.

[9a] Evidence now seems to be pointing to Syriac as the original language, as we may gather from a recently discovered Syriac MS. containing about three fourths of Ephraem's commentary on the Diatessaron (cf. * Metzger, B. M., "Recent Discoveries, etc.," in J.B.L., 78 [1959], 16 f) and a Persian Gospel Harmony based upon a Syriac *Vorlage.* Cf. Messina, G., "Notizia su un Diatessaron persano tradotto dal siriaco" (Rome, 1940); *idem,* in *Biblica,* 23 (1942), 268-305, 24 (1943), 59-106, 30 (1949), 356-376; Peters, C., "Das Diatessaron Tatians, etc." (Rome, 1939); *idem,* in *Biblica* 23 (1942), 68-77, 323-332; * Metzger, B. M., "Tatian's Diatessaron and a Persian Harmony of the Gospels," in J.B.L., 59 (1950), 261-280.

The original *Diatessaron* has been lost. Besides the Dura Greek text, there is now available not only the greater part of St. Ephraem's commentary on the Diatessaron in the original Syriac, but also an Armenian translation of the latter's work. These, together with the Arabic version [10] made in the eleventh century from the Syriac and the *Codex Fuldensis,* written by Bishop Victor of Capua in A.D. 541-546,[11] help to reconstruct the Diatessaron. The lack of Syriac codices with the Tatian text is explained by the fact that, at the command of their bishops, the faithful substituted the separate Gospels for the Diatessaron.

The Separate Gospels or *Old Syriac.*[12]—These Gospels were called *Evangelion da-Mepharreshe* (i.e., the Gospel of the separate). This version is now extant in two MSS.: the *Codex Curetonianus* and the *Codex Sinaiticus.*

The *Codex Curetonianus* (Sy^c) [13] was found in 1842 by * W. Cureton in Egypt. It is a MS. of the fifth century and is now preserved at the British Museum. The *Codex Sinaiticus* (Sy^s) [14] derives its name from the Syriac MS. found on Mount Sinai in the monastery of St. Catherine by *Mrs. Lewis and *Mrs. Gibson, and is of earlier date than the former codex.

The Old Syriac was made about 200 (i.e., after the *Diatessaron*), and the Western readings found in this form of text in the Church of Edessa are due to the influence of Tatian.

The Peshitto.—The origin of the New Testament Peshitto, which became the official Bible of the Syriac Church, is probably to be attributed to Bishop Rabbula of Edessa (411-435).

[10] Cf. * Preuschen, E., "Diatessaron. Aus dem Arab. übers. mit Einleitung u textkrit. Anmerkungen" (Heidelberg, 1926).

[11] Cf. Vaccari, A., "Propaggini del Diatessaron in Occidente," in *Biblica,* 12 (1931), 326-354.

[12] Cf. Vogels, H. J., "Die altsyrischen Evangelien," in B.S., 16 (1911); *idem,* "Drei parallele Varianten in altsyrischen Evangelium," in B.Z., 9 (1911), 263-265; Lagrange, M. J., "L'ancienne version Syriaque des Evangiles," in R.B., 29 (1920), 321-352, 30 (1921), 11-44.

[13] * Cureton, W., "Remains of a Very Ancient Recension of the Four Gospels in Syriac" (London, 1858).

[14] * Lewis, A. S., "The Old Syriac Gospels or Evangelion da-Mepharreshe" (London, 1910). Cf. Vööbus, A., "A Critical Apparatus for the Vetus Syra," in J.B.L., 70 (1951), 123-128.

He not only ordered the churches to remove the *Diatessaron,* but also translated the New Testament from Greek into Syriac. His text, the Peshitto, became the accepted Syriac version. About 250 MSS. of this text are known to exist.

In its original form the Peshitto contained all the books of the New Testament, excepting the four minor Catholic Epistles (2 Peter, 2 and 3 John, Jude) and the Apocalypse. These four Epistles and the Apocalypse were added later.

(c) THE OTHER SYRIAC VERSIONS

(*1*) *The Philoxenian Version.*—The reputation and wide diffusion of the Greek text was the occasion why the Syrians tried to procure a fresh translation from the Greek; besides, the intercourse between the Syrians and the Greeks was becoming increasingly intimate. In 508 Philoxenus, Jacobite Bishop of Mabug, ordered Polycarp, his chor-bishop, to make a new translation of the New Testament and the Psalter.

Of this version only a few fragments from the Book of Isaias are extant, but this shows that the Philoxenian Version had been extended to include the other books of the Old Testament. Some scholars (e.g., * Kenyon, etc.) assert that the four minor Epistles and the Apocalypse were added to the official Peshitto from this version, but this is doubtful and denied by many (e.g., Höpfl, Vaccari, etc.). The translator of this version made use of the Lucian or Byzantine Greek recension.

(*2*) *The Syro-Hexaplar Version.*—This version was produced by Bishop Paul of Tella (near Edessa) in 616-617 at Alexandria, Egypt. It was a translation of the whole Old Testament into Syriac according to the Hexaplaric recension of Origen. Paul, together with many scholars, gave an extremely literal translation, carefully transcribed the critical symbols of Origen, and wrote down many variant readings from the other columns of the Hexapla; because of these three qualities this Syriac translation is one of the principal authorities for the text of Origen and the pre-Hexapla Septuagint.

The Syro-Hexaplar version is still extant in the second volume of a once complete MS. The first volume has been lost since the time of A. du Maes (d. 1573), but a few variant readings from this volume were given by him. The second volume containing the poetical and prophetical books is in the Ambrosian Library at Milan (a photolithographic edition of which was published by A. M. Ceriani in 1874 at Milan). Fragments of the entire Old Testament are dispersed in various MSS. and marginal readings from the same version are found in the work of the Syrian Fathers. Then too an Arabic translation of the Syro-Hexapla to the Pentateuch, Wisdom, and Job is still extant.[14a]

(1) *The Harkleian Version* (Sy[h]).[15]—About the same time and place, Thomas of Harkel revised at Alexandria the Philoxenian version of the New Testament from Greek MSS. He was extremely literal, and the MSS. employed by him were of the *Codex Bezæ* type. Added in the margins or in the text were variant readings.

(4) *The Palestinian Syriac.*[16]—The Melchites, who spoke a Syro-Palestinian dialect (sometimes called Christian-Palestinian), made their own translation of the Bible in the fifth or sixth century. They did this when they separated from the rest of the Syrians because of the various Christological disputes which raged between the fourth and sixth centuries. The translation probably included the entire Bible, but nearly all the surviving MSS. are in the form of lectionaries. In the Old Testament the version follows the Hexaplaric recension, and in the New Testament a mixed type.

[14a] Vosté, J. M., "La version syro-hexaplaire de la Sagesse," in *Biblica,* 30 (1947), 213-219; Gottstein, M. H., "Neue Syrohexaplafragmente," *ibid.,* 37 (1956), 162-183.

[15] C. Delaporte, L. J., "L'évangéliaire héraclëen, etc.," in R.B. 4 (1907), 254-258, 9 (1912), 391-402; * Hatch, W. H. P., "To what Syriac version or versions of the Gospels did Thoma of Harqel refer in his margin?" in J.B.L., 65 (1946), 371-376; Zuntz, G., "Etudes harkleenes," in R.B. 57 (1950), 550-582.

[16] Cf. Lagrange, M. J., "L'Origine de la version Syro-Palestinienne des Evangiles," in R.B., 35 (1925), 481-504.

Art. 4.   Other Oriental Versions

(a) THE COPTIC VERSIONS [17]

Coptic is the old Egyptian language, written in Greek characters with the addition of six demotic letters. The script seems to have been still in its early stages of development at the end of the second century or the beginning of the third century.

There are two main dialects in the Coptic language: *Sahidic* (the dialect spoken in Upper or Southern Egypt) and *Bohairic* (the dialect spoken in Lower or Northern Egypt). The Middle Egyptian dialects (e.g., *Akhmimic* and *Fayyumic*) are of less importance for the history of the text.

All of these Coptic versions represent translations from the Greek, and are of importance for the history and textual form of the Greek Old and New Testaments, since they were composed before the time of Origen.

The Coptic versions in the Old Testament generally follow a textual form akin to *Codex Vaticanus* or the Alexandrian type. The Sahidic version of the Old Testament, written before the end of the second century, is pre-Hexapla, and was subsequently superseded by the Bohairic. In the New Testament the Coptic versions are the main supporters of the Alexandrian type, but they have also a few Western readings, especially in the Gospels.

(b) THE ETHIOPIC VERSION

The Ethiopians or Abyssinians were converted to the faith by St. Frumentius about 320. It is not certain when the Bible

---

[17] The complete New Testament in the two main dialects and with an English translation may be found in * G. Horner, "The Coptic Version of the N.T. in Southern Dialect" (7 vols., Oxford, 1911-1924); *idem*, "...in the Northern Dialect" (4 vols., Oxford, 1898-1905). Fragments of the Old Testament representing various Coptic dialects are scattered throughout the principal libraries of the world (e.g., Vatican, Bibliothèque National of Paris, British Museum) and private collections (e.g., C. L. Freer and especially * D. M. Pierpont Morgan with a collection of fifty volumes in the Sahidic dialect). Cf. also Till., W., in *Biblica*, 20 (1939), 241-263, 361-386; Simon, J., in *Miscellanea Biblica* (Rome, 1934), 161-178.

first appeared in their language, which they called *ge'ez*, but which has been called Ethiopic since the sixteenth century. It is not likely that their version made its appearance before the fourth or fifth century. The oldest MSS. extant are of the thirteenth century and show that they were influenced by various other versions, as the Greek, Arabic, Coptic, etc. Most of these MSS. are now located in London, Rome, Paris, Berlin and Jerusalem.

Both Testaments were made from the Greek, but the Old Testament was translated from a Greek type that was closely associated with *Codex Vaticanus*.[18]

(c) THE ARMENIAN VERSION [19]

The Armenians were converted to Christianity by St. Gregory Illuminator (d. 330), and their Scriptures were translated into their language by St. Mesrop (d. 441), the inventor of the Armenian alphabet, and St. Sahak (390-440). It is generally admitted that this first translation was based upon the Syriac Peshitto. However, after the Council of Ephesus (431), at which Nestorianism was condemned, Eznik and Koriun, two pupils of St. Mesrop, made a new translation from Greek MSS. procured from Constantinople and Egypt. For the Old Testament the Hexapla of Origen served as the basis, while in the New Testament the text is akin to *Codex Koridethi* or the Cæsarean type. There are many MSS. of the Armenian version, but the oldest dates from 887.

(d) THE GOTHIC VERSION

According to ecclesiastical writers, Ulfilas (318-383), an

---

[18] The entire Old Testament was published by * A Dillmann (Leipzig & Berlin, 1853-1894). A recent non critical edition of the entire Bible was published by F. De Bassano (Asmara, 1920-1926). Cf. also Euringer, S., in *Biblica*, 17 (1936), 327-344, 479-500, 18 (1937), 257-276, 369-382, 20 (1939), 27-37.

[19] The best critical edition of the entire Bible was edited by J. Zohrab (Venice, 1805; 2nd ed., 1860). The New Testament, or the Gospels, were also printed alone (Vienna, 1864; Venice, 1877; Moscow, 1890; Paris, 1920). Cf. also Lyonnet, in R.B., 43 (1934), 69-87, 47 (1938), 355-382, in *Biblica*, 19 (1938), 121-150; Merk, A., in *Biblica*, 4 (1923), 356-374, 7 (1926), 40-71.

Arian bishop of the Mæso-Goths, translated the entire Bible into the Gothic, with the exception of the Books of Kings. The Old Testament was translated from a Lucian recension of the Septuagint, and the New Testament [20] from a text which was predominantly of the Byzantine or Antiochian type. This version only exists in fragments, and the principal MS. is the *Codex Argenteus* at Upsala of the fifth or sixth century, which contains more than half of the four Gospels.

(e) THE GEORGIAN VERSION

The Iberians or Georgians in the Caucasus received their Christianity and their early Scriptures from the Armenians. The first books of the Bible were translated from the Armenian about the fifth or sixth century. Later on, in the tenth century, the rest of the books were translated from the Greek, and the earlier translated books were revised according to the Greek by the monks of Mount Athos. The Old Testament text is based upon the Hexapla of Origen, and the New Testament text is akin to the Cæsarean recension.

(f) THE ARABIC VERSIONS

The Arabic versions of the Bible are very numerous, but all of them are relatively recent (from the eighth to the tenth century), and therefore of little importance to the textual critic. With regard to the Old Testament, there are two kinds of translations; one is based upon the Hebrew and the other upon the Septuagint. The best Hebrew-Arabic translation is attributed to * Rabbi Saadias Gaon (892-942), and includes the Pentateuch, Job, Psalms, Proverbs, and Isaias. The Greek-Arabic translation of the Prophets [21] and the Sapiential Books is found in the Parisian and London Polyglots. In

---

[20] Cf. * Friedrichsen, G. W. S., "The Gothic Version of the Gospels" (Oxford, 1926). A critical edition of the Bible may be found in * Streitberg, W., "Die gotische Bible" (Heidelberg, 1919). Cf. also Wimart, A., in R.B., 36 (1927), 46-61

[21] Cf. Vaccari, A., "Le versioni arabe dei Profeti," in *Biblica*, 1 (1920), 266-268, 2 (1921), 401-423, 3 (1922), 401-423.

regard to the New Testament [22] it suffices to mention the eleventh-century translation of Tatian's *Diatessaron*.

(g) THE SLAVONIC VERSION [23]

The first Slavonic version is attributed to the two missionary brothers, St. Cyril (d. 869) and St. Methodius (d. 885). This version did not contain all the books of the Bible, but only the Gospels, the Psalter, and those parts which occur in the liturgy. This old version has reached us under a double form: codices written in Cyrillic or Russian letters and codices in glagolitic letters. It was only at the end of the fifteenth century that a collection of all the books of the Bible was contained in the Slavonic version. When Archbishop Gennadius of Nowgorod desired a complete Bible, he found it necessary to have some books of the Old Testament translated from the Vulgate, Esther 1-10 from the Hebrew, and other books from the Greek.[24] In their liturgical books the Catholic Croats still make use of this old Slavonic version in glagolitic letters. The Gennadius Bible has remained substantially the ecclesiastical Russian Slavonic Bible, and was also accepted by the Bulgarians and Serbs. Aside from the foregoing, new translations have appeared in the vernacular among the Russians, Bulgarians, and Serbs, as well as among the other Slavonic groups which belong either to the Roman Catholic or the Protestant Church.

[22] Cf. Graf, G., "Exegetische Schriften zum Neuen Testament in arabischen Sprache bis zum 14 Jahrhundert," in B.Z., 21 (1933), 161-169; Vaccari, A., "La storia d'una Bibbia araba," in *Biblica*, 11 (1930), 350-355.

[23] Cf. Snoj, A., "Veteroslavicæ versionis Evangeliorum pro critica et exegesi textus momentum," in *Biblica*, 3 (1922), 180-187; *idem*, "Der Beitrag von Maximos Agioritis zur Verbesserung des Textes der Altslavischen Bibel," in B.Z., 23 (1935), 44-49; Schweigel, J., "La Bibbia slava del 1751 (1756)," in *Biblica*, 18 (1937), 51-73; Schweigl, J., "De textu recepto slavico Evangelii liturgici," in *Biblica*, 24 (1943), 289-303.

[24] Cf. Goettsberger, J., "Einleitung, etc.," 479.

CHAPTER III

ENGLISH VERSIONS OF THE BIBLE

Bibliography: * Allen, P. S. & H. M., "Sir Thomas More Selections from his English Works and from the Lives by Erasmus and Roper" (Oxford, 1924); * Brown, J., "The History of the English Bible" (Cambridge, 1911); * Campbell, W. E. & * Reed, A. W., "The Dialogue Concerning Tyndale by Sir Thomas More" (London, 1927); * Cotton, H., "A List of Editions of the Bible and Parts Thereof in English" (Oxford, 1821); Gasquet. F. A., "The Old English Bible and Other Essays" (London, 1897); * Hills, M. T., "A Ready Reference History of the English Bible" (American Bible Society, 1935); * Lewis, J., "A Complete History of the Several Translations of the Holy Bible and New Testament into English" (3rd ed., London, 1818); * Lupton, J. H., in H.D.B., s.v. *Versions;* * Moulton, W. F., "The History of the English Bible" (London, 1911); "Roman Catholic and Protestant Bibles Compared. The Gould Prize Essays," edited by * Melancthon Williams Jacobus (2nd ed., New York, 1908); Parsons, W., "First American Editions of Catholic Bibles," in *Historical Records and Studies,* 27; Steinmueller, J. E., "English Catholic Versions of the Bible," in H.P.R., 36 (1936), 1154-1159; *idem,* "American Catholic Versions of the Bible," in H.P.R., 36 (1936), 1268-1274; *idem,* "Early English N.T. Translations," in *St. Louis Proceedings* (1937), 75-106; *idem,* "Revisions of the English Bible," in H.P.R., 38 (1938), 826-832; * "The English Hexaplar (London, 1834); * "The Greek Testament with Readings Adopted by the Revisers of the Authorized Version" (Oxford, 1882); * Westcott-Wright, "A General View of the History of the English Bible" (3rd ed., New York, 1927); Arbez, E. P., Testament with Readings Adopted by the Revisers of the Authorized 48-75; Parochus, "The Church and the Wyclifite Bible," in *Scripture,* 6 (1954), 79-83.

Art. 1.   The Anglo-Saxon Versions

Perhaps the earliest form in which the Bible narrative was made easily accessible to English readers was the verse para‧phrase of the Book of Genesis and of parts of the books of the Old and New Testaments by the Northumbrian herdsman, Caedmon, about A.D. 670.   Of this work only fragments have survived.   At the end of the seventh century Guthlac made an interlinear Anglo-Saxon translation of the Psalter, and not long afterwards Aldhelm, Bishop of Sherborne, made another interlinear translation of the Psalter, fifty Psalms being in verse and the rest in prose.

St. Bede (d. 735) is said to have translated the entire Bible, but this version has perished. King Alfred the Great (d. 901) is also reported to have made a translation of the earlier part of the Psalter, but this has also probably perished. In the tenth century Farmer and Owen translated the Gospels, and about the beginning of the next century Archbishop Aelfric of Canterbury translated the first seven books of the Old Testament and the Book of Job.

After the Norman Conquest, translations of the Bible began to be made into early English (an intermixture of Norman-French and Anglo-Saxon). In the pre-Wyclifite period there are three names worthy of mention. Orm, an English Augustinian monk of the thirteenth century, translated parts of the Gospels and of the Acts and other parts of the Old and New Testaments. About 1320 William Shoreham, Vicar of Chart Sutton, translated the Psalter. Richard Rolle, a hermit of Hampole about the same time, also translated the Psalter and added a running commentary.

Art. 2. The Catholic Pre-Reformation English Bible

The history of the Catholic pre-Reformation Bible is still shrouded with a mysterious veil. Up until the beginning of this century it was commonly asserted that this Bible was the Wyclifite Bible. According to this assumption, * Wyclif about the year 1380 completed the New Testament, while his colleague, * Nicholas de Hereford, translated the Old Testament to Baruch 3, 20; the rest was completed either by Wyclif himself or under his supervision. A few years later, a revised edition was completed by * John Purvey, a disciple of Wyclif. Critical Protestant scholars are now beginning to incline to the view that Wyclif had little to do with the actual translation, but that the translation was begun under his influence (e.g., * Hills). Perhaps eventually all scholars will accept the thesis of Cardinal Gasquet that the two pre-Reformation vernacular versions of the Bible, proved by the numerous MSS. once in the possession of loyal sons of the Church, are in reality Catholic versions.

The pre-Reformation versions were translated from the
Latin Vulgate, perhaps from MSS. associated with the *Exemplar Parisiense,* which basically represented the Alcuin
revision of the Vulgate. Our modern division into chapters,
originating. from Cardinal Stephen Langton of Canterbury
and once Magister at Paris in 1206, generally follows the
Parisian Bible.

Art. 3. The Protestant English Bibles

(a) DURING REIGN OF KING HENRY VIII (1509-1547)

* William Tyndale [1] (1484-1536) translated the New Testament and published it in 1525 in quarto at Cologne and in
1525 in octavo at Worms. This translation exercised an influence on all subsequent Protestant English versions. It was
made from the Greek instead of the Vulgate. Of the Old
Testament he translated only the Pentateuch (1530 or 1531,
at Marburg) and the Book of Jonas (1531, probably at
Antwerp).

The following are some of the principles underlying Tyndale's New Testament translation. (a) In his prologues,
marginal notes, arrangement of books, and probably at times
in the rendition of the text itself, he was influenced by Luther.
(b) His translation represented a definite break away from
the Roman Catholic Church. (c) He used the second edition
of Erasmus and sometimes the third edition as the basis of his
translation. He thus helped to propagate the *Textus Receptus*
or Received Text, which critics now reject as an inferior
textual form. He also incorporated some of the inaccuracies
of Erasmus's Latin translation, and these mistranslations have
been followed by some of the other earlier Protestant versions.
(d) The direct influence of the Vulgate upon his translation
remains doubtful, or at least small. (e) The influence, whether
direct or indirect, of the Catholic pre-Reformation New Testament is greater than was recognized up to the present.

[1] Cf. Steinmueller, J. E., in *St. Louis Proceedings,* 76-88.

* Myles Coverdale (1488-1569), who knew neither Greek nor Hebrew, published the Bible at the request of * Thomas Cromwell. The first edition appeared on October 4, 1535, at Zurich, and, although it was dedicated to Henry VIII, it appeared without royal license. Printed in England two years later, this Bible contains "the king's most gracious license," and the name of Queen Jane (Seymour) is substituted for that of Queen Anne (Boleyn), who had been beheaded. In regard to the New Testament, Coverdale followed Tyndale and Lûther in the arrangement of the books, and used as the basis of his translation Tyndale's first edition, revised by the help of the second and by Luther's German.

* Thomas Matthew, or *John Rogers (1500-1555), published the entire Bible in 1537 at the expense of two London merchants. This was printed in folio, probably at Antwerp. Through * Thomas Cromwell the royal license was obtained for the volume, which was dedicated to Henry VIII. Neither the Old nor the New Testament represented independent translations, but were derived chiefly from Tyndale and Coverdale.

In 1539 a new translation of the Bible was published in folio by the layman * Richard Taverner (1505-1575), who in the same year issued the New Testament in quarto and octavo. Although he closely followed Tyndale in his New Testament translation, he introduced numerous changes based on the Greek and the Vulgate.

All the English Bibles thus far printed were replete with notes and prologues favorable to the cause of the Reformation and offensive to many groups. England was rapidly heading towards Protestantism, but its break with the past was as yet incomplete. * Cromwell determined to bring to a successful issue his scheme, and circumstances were favorable to him.

* Myles Coverdale was entrusted with the task of editing a new edition of the entire Bible, and Cromwell himself invested £400 in the venture. It was agreed to have this work printed by Francis Regnault of Paris, but difficulties between France and England forced the work to be discontinued in 1538. Cromwell, however, succeeded in having the type, press, and

printers brought to London, where the work was finally completed in folio in April, 1539, though it is possible that the edition was issued only several months later. This Bible was called the *Great Bible* because of its large format. The title page contains a wood cut, commonly ascribed to Hans Holbein, representing Henry with * Cranmer and * Cromwell distributing Bibles to the people. It bore no dedication, no annotations, only simple prefaces. With this Bible, Cranmer had no connection.

In April, 1540, a second edition appeared. It contained a Prologue by * Cranmer which appeared in the subsequent editions. The title page bears the words: "This is the Bible appointed to the use of the Church." In July, 1540, a third edition appeared, and in November a fourth edition. A fifth edition followed in May, 1541, a sixth in November, and a seventh and last edition in December, 1541. The Great Bible of 1539 agrees with Tyndale's 1534 edition in the translation of many individual words (e.g., ἐκκλησία, χάρις ἐπίσκοπος, etc).

Towards the end of Henry's reign there was a distinctive reaction against the Protestant Reform movement and the indiscriminate reading of the Bible by all classes of society. The reading of Tyndale's books and Coverdale's New Testament was prohibited, but the Great Bible remained unforbidden. The Reformers on the continent had set the spark to rebellion and revolution. Henry now determined to keep England free from the continental conflicts, but it was too late. In his desire for a divorce he had encouraged the anticlerical party and tolerated the doctrines of the Reformers. He had broken with the See of Peter and appointed as his counsellors the enemies of the Catholic Church.

(b) DURING REIGNS OF KING EDWARD VI (1547-1553), QUEEN MARY (1553-1558) AND QUEEN ELIZABETH (1558-1603)

During the period from King Edward VI (1547) to Queen Elizabeth (d. 1603), three new English Bible translations appeared: the Geneva and Rheims Bibles were published on the continent, and the Bishops' Bible was edited in England.

The *Geneva Bible* had its beginning with the publication of the New Testament at Geneva, Switzerland, in 1557. This translation is commonly attributed to * William Whittingham (1524-1579), a brother-in-law of * John Calvin, who wrote the Introductory Epistle. The text was abundantly furnished with marginal notes Calvinistic in tone. This edition, however, was never reprinted. In 1560 the entire Bible was printed in quarto at Geneva by * Roulan Hall. It was the joint production of several Reformers, but their names are not mentioned. However, it is commonly attributed to * William Whittingham, * Anthony Gilby, and * Thomas Sampson. It was printed in Roman type and dedicated to Queen Elizabeth. It was furnished with an Address to the Reader, chapter headings, marginal references, and notes. Though it was never officially approved for ecclesiastical use, yet about 140 editions of it were printed up to the time of the Civil War (1642-1649) because of its convenient format. It is also referred to at times as the Puritan Bible. The New Testament of the 1560 Geneva Bible does not represent an independent translation; it is a revision of * Whittingham's 1557 edition, which was based upon Tyndale's translation and Beza's Latin New Testament.

Another Bible published on the continent was the Rheims-Douay Version by Catholics in exile. We shall refer again to this later in the next article.

The *Bishops' Bible* was published in 1568. Its chief editor was * Matthew Parker, Archbishop of Canterbury, who distributed the work among a group of scholars of whom eight were bishops. This Bible was published in folio and printed at London *cum privilegio regiæ majestatis*. Although it never formally obtained royal sanction, the Constitutions and Canons Ecclesiastical of 1571 ordered that each archbishop and bishop should have a copy of this Bible at his house, and that each cathedral should likewise have a copy. The price at which the first edition was sold was about $80.00 in our currency. The Bishops' Bible taken as a whole is of unequal value. The Old Testament especially manifests many defects due to the independent methods of the individual revisers and the lack of careful final revision by the chief editor. The New Testament revision shows greater originality and scholarship. The Great Bible seems to have been taken as the basic text and compared with the Greek text and the Geneva Version. In 1572 a second revised edition of the New Testament appeared, and this was generally followed by the later editions. This second edition was the basic text used by the revisers of the King James or Authorized Version forty years later. It showed again the influence of the Geneva Version.

(c) During the Rule of King James I (1603-1625)

The King James or Authorized Version.—When James I came to the throne in March, 1603, there were chiefly three Bibles in circulation in England: namely, the Bishops' Bible, the Geneva Bible, and the Rheims New Testament. The Bishops' Bible, which took the place of the Great (Cranmer) Bible, was sanctioned by ecclesiastical authorities. The Geneva Bible, though Puritan in its notes and comments, had become very popular among the people because of its convenient form and low price. The Rheims New Testament was spread in Catholic circles.

In January, 1604, at the Hampton Court Conference remote preparations were made for a new English version that should reconcile the various Protestant religious parties. The king suggested that the new translation should be made by the learned men of both universities, reviewed by the bishops and ecclesiastics, then presented to the privy council, and finally ratified by his royal authority. In July of the same year the king drew up a list of fifty-four translators to whom the work was to be entrusted. However, little progress in this project was made for three years.

In the year 1607 earnest efforts were taken to bring the scheme into operation. Forty-seven men were entrusted with the task. The entire body was divided into six companies, four for the Old Testament and two for the New Testament, and two companies were to hold meetings respectively at Westminster, Oxford, and Cambridge. Genesis–2 Kings was assigned to Westminster, 1 Chronicles–Ecclesiastes to Cambridge, Isaias–Malachias to Oxford, the deutero-canonical books to Cambridge, the four Gospels, Acts and Apocalypse to Oxford, Romans–Jude to Westminster.

Various rules were drawn up to guide the revisers. Among the most important of these instructions may be mentioned: (1) the Bishops' Bible was to be taken as the basis of the new translation; (2) the names of the prophets, holy writers, and other names in the text were to be retained as they were vulgarly used; (3) the old ecclesiastical words were to be kept, (e.g., church *loco* congregation); (4) no marginal notes were to be affixed, except the brief explanation of some Hebrew and Greek words; (5) the translations of * Tyndale, * Matthew, * Coverdale, * Whitchurch, and * Geneva were to be used when they agreed better with the text than the Bishops' Bible.

When each company had completed its task, six delegates (i.e., two members from each company) were chosen to supervise the final preparation of the work for the press. In nine months their particular work was completed.

This revised version was published in folio and Gothic letters by * Robert Barker in London in 1611. It contained an engraved title page, a Dedication to King James, a Preface to the Reader, a Calendar, etc. There is no evidence to show that it was considered as the "Authorized Version" (i.e., publicly sanctioned by Convocation or Parliament, or by the Privy Council, or by the King), but it did contain the words "Appointed to be read in Churches."

There seems to have been a second impression of the same version issued that year by another printing office. These two are distinct, and are the parents of millions of English Protestant Bibles. Within three years fourteen editions in various formats were printed, and corrected editions were subsequently issued by the Universities of Cambridge and Oxford.

The immediate effect that this new version had was to stay the reprinting of the Bishops' Bible, though its New Testament was reprinted in 1618 or 1619. The chief rival of the new version was the Geneva or Puritan Bible, which remained in private use until the middle of the seventeenth century.

The Anglican Bishop * Lightfoot praises the grand simplicity of this version, and John Cardinal Newman speaks of the "grave majestic English" in this version. It is generally admitted that this version has exercised great influence upon English literature.

This version has many defects, making the general revision of 1881-1885 and 1901 inevitable. * Moulton states: "The execution of different parts of the work will prove to be unequal—the Epistles, for example, standing far below the Pentateuch in accuracy and felicity of rendering; many flaws and inconsistencies will reveal themselves; occasionally it will be found that better renderings have been deliberately laid aside and worse preferred." [2] Apart from the various literal and textual defects in the various editions of this version, the cardinal fault lies in its poor *apparatus criticus*, especially in regard to the New Testament.

For the Old Testament the translators used as their sources the Antwerp Polyglot with an interlinear Latin translation of the Hebrew text by Arias Montanus (1572), the Latin translation of the converted Jew, * Immanuel Tremellius (1572), and the translation of the deutero-canonical books by his son-in-law, * Francis Junius. The revisers speak also of their consulting "the Spanish, French, and Italian translators"; the English translations consulted are mentioned above. The Pre-Reformation Bibles and the Douay (1609-1610), based on the Vulgate, exercised no influence upon the new translation. Though the Bishops' Bible was nominally the basis for the new translation, there are many changes in the prophetical books due to the influence of the Geneva version. In the historical or poetical books the changes from the Bishops' Bible are fewer. In the deutero-canonical books there are

[2] Cf. * Moulton, W. F., *op. cit.*, 207 f.

many original changes, and here the revisers displayed independent freedom.

It is precisely in regard to the New Testament that the translators "suffered most from the corrupt form in which the Greek text of the New Testament was presented to them." [3] If the *apparatus criticus* used by them was poor, making the English revised version of 1881-1885 and 1901 inevitable, the editors of this new nineteenth-century revision would yet have been spared their extensive and laborious task (from a critical standpoint) had the original translators not totally neglected the Vulgate text, which was based upon more ancient Greek MSS. than they were translating. They took as their basic sources the *Textus Receptus* from the third edition of Robert Stephen and the various Greek editions of * Theodore Beza with his Latin version. Of the English versions the Geneva and the Rheims exercised the greatest influence. The Rheims enriched the vocabulary of the Authorized Version. "The Rhemish Testament was not even named in the instructions furnished to the translators, but it has left its mark on every page of their work." [4]

Among the more important translations in modern times are those of James Moffatt (N.T., 1913; O.T., 1924), * J. M. Powis Smith-Edgar J. Goodspeed (Chicago, 1935), and the *Revised Standard Version* (New York, 1952) which represents a scholarly and critical revision of the revision of the King James or Authorized Version of 1881-1885 and 1901, and, more recently, *The New English Bible: New Testament* (Oxford-Cambridge, 1961).

Art. 4.   The Catholic English Bibles

(a) THE ORIGINAL DOUAY-RHEIMS VERSION

During the religious persecutions of Queen Elizabeth (1558-1603) many Catholics were obliged to leave England. Among these scholars was Dr. William Allen (1532-1594), sometime Fellow of Oriel College, Oxford, and founder of the English

[3] Cf. * Wescott-Wright, *op. cit.*, 256.
[4] Cf. * Moulton, W. F., *op. cit.*, 207.

College at Douay in 1568, which, because of political troubles in Flanders, was transferred a few years later to Rheims. Dr. Allen subsequently became a member of the Carafa Commission at Rome for the revision of the Vulgate, and was created Cardinal in 1587.

With him was a group of scholars, who resolved to produce according to the Latin Vulgate an English Bible worthy of the Church. Among these were: Dr. Gregory Martin, formerly Fellow of St. John's, Oxford, and professor of Hebrew and Sacred Scripture at the English College; Dr. Richard Bristow, formerly Fellow of Exeter College and moderator of the newly formed English College; John Reynolds, formerly of New College, and Dr. Worthington.

The translation of the Old and New Testaments was accomplished by Gregory Martin and revised by the others. The annotations to the New Testament were prepared by Bristow and Allen, while those to the Old Testament were written by Worthington.

The New Testament was published in small quarto at Rheims in 1582 by John Fogney, and the Old Testament was printed also in quarto at Douay by Lawrence Kellan in 1609-1610. The New Testament was reprinted in folio at London in 1589 by Protestants, who likewise reprinted it in 1601, 1617, and 1633 together with the Bishops' Bible. An American Protestant reprint in octavo was also made in New York–Boston in 1834.

The following Catholic reprints are to be found: Rheims New Testament in 1600 (second edition printed at Antwerp by Daniel Veroliet with a few alterations and corrections), in 1621 (third edition), in 1633 (fourth edition); Douay Old Testament in 1635 (second edition). After one hundred years, the Rheims New Testament began to be reprinted with modernized spelling: 1738 (fifth edition), 1788 (sixth edition), 1816-1818 (seventh edition).

Both Protestant as well as Catholic scholars have highly commended this translation for its scrupulous accuracy and fidelity. The Authorized or King James Version of 1611 was greatly influenced by the vocabulary of the Rheims New Testament.

(b) THE REVISIONS OF THE DOUAY-RHEIMS VERSION

At the beginning of the eighteenth century the need was felt for a change in the English Catholic Bible. The English language had developed to such an extent that many words and expressions in the Douay-Rheims Version had become obsolete and were no longer in use. In 1718 Dr. Cornelius Nary of Dublin translated the Vulgate New Testament into more modern English, and a similar task was undertaken in 1730 by Dr. Robert Witham, president of the College of Douay, but their translations never became popular.

England.—The outstanding reviser of the eighteenth century was the Douay scholar and later Vicar-Apostolic of the London district, Bishop Richard Challoner (1741-1781), who had the Catholic Church of the United States under his jurisdiction from 1758 to 1781. Recognizing the need of a modern translation of the Bible for the people, he revised in 1749 the Rheims New Testament according to the Clementine Vulgate. This was published in duodecimo (Dublin?). In the following year, 1750, he edited in four volumes also in duodecimo (Dublin or London?) the entire Bible, which included his second edition of the New Testament. Two years later (1752), a third edition of his New Testament appeared. The entire Bible was reprinted in 1763-1764 (probably at Dublin) with American Catholics in its list of subscribers, and the New Testament in 1772 and 1777.

Dr. Challoner does not give any information as to the principles, the source, or the extent of his changes. In regard to his labors on the Old Testament as a whole, Cardinal Newman after a careful examination of some passages writes: "We may pronounce that they issue in little short of a new translation. . . . Challoner's version is even nearer to the Protestant than it is to the Douay; nearer, that is, not in grammatical structure, but in phraseology and diction" ("Tracts," 416). Again: "It is difficult to avoid the conclusion that at this day the Douay Old Testament no longer exists as a received version of the authorized Vulgate" (*ibid.*, 418 f). In regard to the first edition (1749) of the Rheims New Testament, Cardinal Newman shows the adoptions from the Protestant version (*ibid.*, 419), and concerning the other two editions he writes: "We have already implied that Dr. Challoner made corrections of his own editions of the New Testament as they successively issued from the press. The second edition (1750) differs from the first, according to the collations which Dr. Cotton has printed, in about 124 passages; the third (1752) in more than 2,000" (*ibid.*, 421 f). Dr. Challoner also revised the extensive notes found in the Douay-Rheims Bible, and those in modern editions are chiefly based on his.

The Old Testament of Dr. Challoner has remained practically unrevised during the past two hundred years, except for the revision by Archbishop Kenrick of Baltimore. The New Testament, however, has been repeatedly revised, but the basic text has almost always remained one of Dr. Challoner's three revisions.

Scotland.—The first English Catholic Bible printed in Scotland appeared at Edinburgh in 1761 (five volumes, duodecimo) through the zeal of Dr. George Hay, one of the Vicars-Apostolic in Scotland and an intimate friend of Challoner. It can hardly be considered an independent revision. This Bible was reprinted at Edinburgh in 1804-1805, and the unsold copies were published in Dublin in 1811 with new title pages. A reprint of the New Testament at Dublin in 1811 has among its subscribers Dr. Troy and Dr. Murray. This New Testament was reprinted at Dublin in 1814 and at Belfast in 1817.

Ireland.—The revisions by Bernard MacMahon, a Dublin priest, endorsed by Archbishops Carpenter (for the first edition) and Troy (for the subsequent editions), represents the continuation of Challoner's labors, or the connection of his own revision with that of Challoner. The Dublin revision of the New Testament in 1783 (in duodecimo) styles itself "the fourth edition revised and corrected anew" (i.e., of Challoner). According to * Dr. Cotton, it varies from Challoner's text in about 50 places in the Gospels, and over 500 places in the other books. In 1791 the entire Bible (in quarto) was re-edited at Dublin under the supervision of Archbishop Troy and was called the *"fifth edition,"* about 200 more changes being introduced into the New Testament. This latter edition was reprinted in folio at Dublin in 1794. The New Testament editions of 1803 and 1810 were subjected to further revisions.

Archbishop Troy of Dublin was succeeded by Dr. Daniel Murray (1823-1852), who edited the entire Bible in 1825. The text of the New Testament follows Dr. Challoner's early editions of 1749 and 1750. Five new impressions of the entire Bible appeared between 1825 and 1847. The entire Bible was reprinted at Glasgow in 1833-1836, with the approbation of the Vicars-Apostolic of England and Scotland, and the New Testament in Northern Ireland at Newry in 1838 and at Belfast in the same year. This Belfast edition bearing the approval of Dr. Denvir, Bishop of Down and Connor, was based upon Dr. Murray's revision, and was frequently reprinted with or without the Old Testament between 1836 and 1852.

Northern England.—At Manchester Oswald Syers edited the entire Bible in 1811-1813, and in his New Testament followed the early editions (1749 and 1750) of Challoner. At the same time a rival appeared that for over one hundred years retained its popularity. The edition of Rev. George Leo Haydock appeared in Manchester 1812-1814 (Dublin, 1812-1813; Edinburgh and Dublin, 1845-1848). While the Old Testament remained basically the Challoner text of 1750, as regards the New Testament he largely followed Dr. Troy's edition of 1794. The characteristic element of this edition is its abundance of extensive annotations. The two Dublin editions of 1822 and 1824 were carelessly edited and full of errors.

The Bibles of Dr. Gibson and Dr. Bramston, two Vicars-Apostolic, hardly differ from Challoner's text. Dr. Gibson, in the New Testament text of the entire Bible published in folio in 1816-1817 at Liverpool (and reprinted in 1822-1823 at London), follows Challoner's later editions, while Dr. Bramston in his edition of 1829 follows Challoner's 1763-1764 edition.

England and Ireland.—In the year 1815 the New Testament was published at Dublin with the approval of Dr. William Poynter, who had received his education at Douay and later became the Bishop of the London district (1812-1827). It closely followed Challoner's text of 1749. Subsequent editions appeared in 1818 at Cork, in 1823 at London, in 1825 at London, in 1826 at Dublin (printed with the approval of the four Archbishops of Ireland and at the expense of the Commissioners of Irish Education; reprinted in 1834, 1835, 1837, and 1840, and finally in 1842 at London).

England.—In 1847 the entire Bible was printed by Richardson of London and Derby. This revision was based upon Dr. Troy's text of 1803, with slight modifications. It had the approval of Dr. Walsh, Vicar-Apostolic, and Dr. Wiseman, his coadjutor.

During this nineteenth century Dr. Lingard edited at London in 1836 an independent translation of the Four Gospels from the original Greek. Though highly praised by Cardinals Wiseman and Newman and Archbishop F. P. Kenrick, it never became popular.

In the present century the *Westiminster Version* of the New Testament, a translation from the Greek and under the editorship of C. Lattey, S.J. and J. Keating, S.J., has been completed (1914-1935), but the translation of the Old Testament seems to have been halted. A translation from the Vulgate of the New Testament (1944), of the Psalms (1947), and of the Old Testament (vol. I, 1948; vol. II, 1950) and of the entire Bible (New York, 1956) has been published by Ronald A. Knox. It has been received favorably in many quarters for its elegant diction, but criticized severely in others for paraphrastic tendencies.

The United States.—Up until the end of the nineteenth century all of the English Catholic Bibles printed in the United States, with the possible exception of Archbishop Kenrick's

Bible, were merely reprints of English or Irish editions. According to the compilations of J. G. Shea (1859), O'Callaghan (1861), and Finotti (1872), approximately one hundred editions of the entire Bible or the New Testament were published in the period between 1790 and 1860. Some of these editions were limited to five hundred copies, while others reached the number of two thousand.

The first Catholic Bible to be printed in the United States was a reprint of Challoner's 1763-1764 revision. It was published in quarto by Carey, Steward & Co. of Philadelphia in 1790. Fifteen years later, Matthew Carey of Philadelphia published in quarto a Bible, which was a reprint of Dr. Troy's fifth Dublin edition. The following brief chronological survey will give an idea of the various types of English Bibles printed in the United States between 1790 and 1852:

1790: Challoner's second edition, 1763-1764 by Carey, Steward & Co.
1805: Troy's 1791 Dublin "fifth edition," by Carey.
1817: Hay's Dublin edition of 1811, by Duffy.
1824: Troy's fifth Dublin edition, by Cummiskey.
1825: Haydock's 1812 Challoner, by Cummiskey.
1829: Challoner's 1750 revision of the N. T., by Devereux and later by Sadlier.
1833: Murray's 1825 revision, by Doyle and later by Dunigan.
1852: Haydock's 1812 edition, by Dunigan.
1852: Haydock's edition by Husenbeth, published by Virtue & Yorston.

From this brief analysis we can see that no standard type of Catholic English Bible prevailed in the United States during the period of 1790 and 1860, and that the title "Douay-Rheims Version" is a blanket name to cover not only the original English Catholic version but also its various revisions.

The entire Bible was revised by Archbishop F. P. Kenrick between 1849 and 1860. It was not an independent translation from the Vulgate, but was declared to be "a revision of the Rhemish translation." In the Gospels Archbishop Kenrick adopted many of Lingard's readings. Of the completed work only the New Testament reached a second edition (1862).

(c) Translations from the Greek Original

A modern translation of the four Gospels by the Dominican scholar, Rev. F. Spencer, appeared in 1898. The translation was made directly from the Greek original and diligently compared with the Latin Vulgate and old Syriac Peshitto versions. The New Testament, translated into English from the Greek by Rev. F. Spencer, was edited by Rev. Charles J. Callan, O.P., and Rev. John A. McHugh, O.P., in 1937. This excellent translation was reprinted in 1940 (Macmillan Co.).

(d) The Confraternity Edition of the New and Old Testaments

For the first time in the history of the English Catholic Bible a group of scholars has collaborated in editing a new version of the Bible. After five years of intensive labor they edited the New Testament under the patronage of the Episcopal Committee of the Confraternity of Christian Doctrine (1941). This edition in modern English represents a revision of the Challoner-Rheims Version, and is based upon a critical edition of the Latin Vulgate.

Under the same Episcopal Committee various members of the Catholic Biblical Association of America are now engaged in translating the New Testament from the Greek and the Old Testament from the original languages. So far vol. I Genesis to Ruth (Paterson, N. J., 1952), vol. III Job to Sirach (*ibid.*, 1955), and vol. IV Isaia to Malachia (*ibid.*, 1961) have appeared.

PART IV

HERMENEUTICS: INTERPRETATION OF HOLY SCRIPTURE

Bibliography: Grannan, P., "A General Introduction to the Bible," IV (St. Louis, 1921); Kortleitner, F. X., "Hermeneutica Biblica" (Innsbruck, 1923); Höpfl, H., "Tractatus de Inspiratione S.S. et Compendium Hermeneuticæe Biblicæ Catholicæ" (Rome, 1923); Fernandez, A., "De Interpretatione," in I.B., 339-466; * Torm, F., "Hermeneutik des N.T." Göttingen, 1930); Wutz, F., "Exegese als textkritisches Hilfsmittel," in B.Z., 24 (1939), 365-382; Fuller, R. C., "Trends in Biblical Interpretation," in *Scripture*, 4 (1950), 175-180; Schelkle, K. H., "Über alte und neue Auslegung," in B.Z., 1 (1957), 161-177; Stuhlmueller, C., "The Influence of Oral Tradition upon Exegesis," in C.B.Q., 20 (1958), 299-326; * Muilenburg, J., "Preface to Hermeneutics," in J.B.L., 77 (1958), 18-32; McKenzie, J. L., "Problems of Hermeneutics in Roman Catholic Exegesis," J.B.L., 77 (1958), 197-204; Schnackenburg, R., "Der Weg der katholischen Exegese," in B.Z., 2 (1958), 161-176; Philbin, R. G., "Some Modern Protestant Attitudes towards Hermeneutics," in C.B.Q., 21 (1959), 115-135·

The name *hermeneutics* is derived from the Greek ἑρμηνεύειν, which means to interpret, to explain.

Inspiration teaches us that the Bible by its very nature is the Word of God and is free from error, or is inerrant. The canon brings to our attention what books are considered inspired by the Catholic Church. By the study of Biblical texts and versions, or textual criticism, we may conclude that these inspired, canonical books reached us in a substantially correct and integral condition and may arrive at fairly accurate copies of original texts. There now remains the establishment of solid norms, definite rules of interpretation, so that the exegete, expositor or interpreter may discover the genuine sense or exact meaning of the Bible and expound this. The discussion of these norms and guides in this treatise is called hermeneutics.

By Biblical hermeneutics we mean the art or the science of those rules or principles according to which the true sense of Sacred Scripture can be ascertained and expounded. Hermeneutics treats rather of the theory of Biblical explanation, whereas exegesis is the practical application of the hermeneutical rules.

The proper object of hermeneutics is to acquire the actual meaning of the Bible—of its books, passages, texts and sentences—as was originally intended by the sacred writers. It seeks to determine the writer's thought which he had in mind or what he was thinking about when he wrote and expressed under definite circumstances in words. "There is no one indeed but knows that the supreme rule of interpretation is to discover and define what the writer intended to express, as St. Athanasius excellently observes: 'Here, as indeed is expedient in all other passages of Sacred Scripture, it should be noted on what occasion the Apostle spoke; we should carefully and faithfully observe to whom and why he wrote, lest, being ignorant of these points or confounding one with another, we miss the real meaning of the author'" ("Divino afflante Spiritu," E.B., 557). The more remote the writer is in time and place from his readers, and the more the opinions and circumstances of his age and country differ from their own, the more there is need of special rules to understand his book.

Contrary to the belief of some new sectaries (e.g., Jehovah's Witnesses) who declare that the Bible is self-explanatory and easy for the average modern layman, even without any special training to understand almost everything without proper guidance, it is to be maintained that the Bible contains many obscure matters which are difficult to understand or interpret for various reasons.[1] First, the various books were written in ancient languages (Hebrew, Aramaic, Koine Greek, which in their present forms are dead or unspoken for many centuries, as Hebrew); in countries and times extensively different from our cultural levels and patterns; by authors and for readers with other educational backgrounds and psychological thought-processes. Secondly, the contents of the Bible

---

[1] Cf. Cotter, A., "The Obscurity of Scripture," in C.B.Q., 9 (1947), 453-464.

also contain at times strict revelation of the mysteries of faith which could not be explained merely by human reasoning and were not subject to the realms of purely human experience.[2]

According to St. Augustine (*De doctr. christ.*, 1, 1, 1 [P.L. 34, 19]), there are two matters about which every treatise of the Bible should revolve, namely, a way of properly understanding the Bible (i.e., *heuristics*, the discovery of the senses of the Bible) and the manner of presenting these finds when they are properly understood (i.e., *prophoristics*, i.e., the explanation of these meanings to others. However, there should be added another to these two considerations as a preface, that is *noematics*, the theory of the various senses or meanings of the Bible. It will also be very useful to add something of the history of exegesis which contains the concrete, practical and universal application of hermeneutical principles to the Old and New Testaments.

[2] Cf. Höpfl-Leloir, "Introductio generalis," etc., 403.

Chapter I

NOEMATICS:

THE VARIOUS SENSES OF SCRIPTURE

There is, strictly speaking, a technical distinction between *signification* and *sense*. The former is the meaning of *separate, detached* words, which are taken independently of their context or determined circumstances and as they are found in the dictionaries (e.g., Webster, Funk & Wagnalls in English; Gesenius in Hebrew; Grimm-Thayer in Greek) with various shades of meanings. Sense, however, is the meaning of a *collection* of words expressed in phrases, clauses, sentences, paragraphs, chapters, books by a speaker or writer under peculiarly existing or commonly flourishing historical or literary conditions. The Biblical sense is the *mens auctoris* (lit., the mind, intention of the author) and, therefore (by reason of the act of inspiration), the meaning which the Holy Spirit wished to communicate to us through the language of the sacred writer.

Man's thoughts or ideas are outwardly expressed by either words or deeds, both of which are recorded in the Bible by the sacred writers. We must also bear in mind, however, that God, being the principal Author of the Bible, may also foresee and direct, in one way or another, certain historical and human events to have not only the ordinary, but also a significant, profound, future meaning, and thus to confer upon these important religious affairs a twofold meaning, that is, the *literal* and *typical*. Hence, the literal sense would be the meaning expressed immediately and directly by the words of the sacred writers and should be the meaning which the actual Biblical words in their context convey. It is precisely this meaning that the trained interpreter or expositor tries primarily and above all to discover according to the solid rules of interpretation. The typical sense, however, is based only indirectly upon the words and directly upon things, events, or persons (either individually or collectively) used to express something else on a higher level and to foreshadow some greater truth. Let us take, for example, the text from the prophet Osee (11, 1): "I have called my son from Egypt." In the literal sense the text refers to the people of Israel returning home from Egypt; in Matthew (2, 15) it is typically applied to Jesus returning home to Palestine from Egypt.

Thus, the Bible is the only book in all literature which contains these two kinds of sense. Strictly speaking, the typical sense is not a Biblical sense because it is based mainly upon facts rather than words. However, it should be regarded *equivalently* as a Biblical sense, because it is founded indirectly upon the words of Sacred Scripture and was intended by God.[3]

The basis for this distinction between these two senses is found in the Bible itself (cf. John 3, 14; Matt. 12, 39 f; Gal. 4, 22 ff; Col. 2, 17). The Fathers of the Church, particularly those of the Alexandrian school, admit and defend this twofold meaning of the Sacred Scriptures. We must also remember that the *ecclesia orans* in its liturgy very frequently applies this dual Biblical meaning.

There are various other terms or subdivisions of this twofold sense depending upon how the Biblical subject-matter is regarded or treated. 1) Thus, if the *contents* are considered, we may speak of such meanings as the *historical* (i.e., relating to historical matters), *allegorical* (to faith), *tropological* (to morals), *existential* (to man's present life), *anagogical* (to future life), *eschatological* (to the last things), *Messianic* (to the promised Messias or His Kingdom), *prophetic* (to prophetic utterances), *theological* (to things strictly divine), etc. 2) If a *literary criterion* is referred to, we may see such meanings as *grammatical,* or *philological* (i.e., based upon the rules of grammar or speech), *logical* (upon the context according to the rules of thinking), etc. 3) If the *writer's assent* is taken into consideration, we may have such meanings as *true, prob-*

---

[3] Cf. Fernández, A., *op. cit.,* 366 f.

able or *doubtful.* 4) If there is a question of *clearness*, then the author's meaning may be *obvious* or *obscure.* 5) If the matter of *truth* is concerned, the result could be *true* or *false.* 6) If the *usage of words* is considered, then the sacred writer's meaning could be assumed as *properly literal* or *improperly literal* (see below). 7) Within recent times special attention is being paid to what is called the *plenary (sensus plenior)*, *consequent* and *accommodated* senses.[4]

Art. 1. The Literal Sense

Some other names applied by some scholars to the literal meaning are: grammatical, logical, historical; explicit and implicit, or consequent.[5]

The far-reaching importance of obtaining the literal sense of the Bible is stressed by Pius XII in his "Divino afflante Spiritu": "Let the Catholic exegete undertake the task, of all those imposed on him the greatest, that namely of discovering and expounding the genuine meaning of the Sacred Books. In the performance of this task let the interpreters bear in mind that their foremost and greatest endeavor should be to discern and define clearly that sense of the Biblical words which is called literal" (E.B., 550).

In stressing the fact that the greatest task of the Catholic interpreter is to find and expound the Bible's genuine meaning, which is the literal, His Holiness was not proclaiming a new doctrine, but was merely repeating the traditional teaching of the Church.

The literal sense, as explained above, is the message or truth which the sacred writer wished to express or convey at least in some vague or confused manner, and this is the meaning at which every interpreter must try to arrive. Thus, there must be a meeting of minds, a substantial identity, a general harmony in the ideas, thoughts, judgments between the Holy Spirit as the Inspirer, the sacred writer as the inspired person, and the Church or exegete as the interpreter.

[4] Cf. Fernández, A., *op. cit.*, 367.
[5] Cf. Höpfl, H. *op. cit.*, 91 f.

Hence, for us ultimately to obtain in this modern age the originally intended literal meaning of any passage in the Bible, three significant factors must be taken into careful consideration: *First,* did the inspiring Holy Spirit convey the message or truth either completely or only partially, distinctly or only obscurely to the inspired writer? *Secondly,* in what literary form was the hagiographer (conscious or unconscious of his inspiration, of a divine urge in him and of heavenly guidance) expressing his message? *Thirdly,* did the interpreter truly capture and correctly express the essence of the meaning of this divinely intended, identical thought-pattern between God and His hagiographer?

The literal sense is sub-divided into two varieties: (a) the *proper literal* sense, or the precise literal meaning, which is expressed by words taken in their etymological, or grammatical, or obvious, ordinary meaning (cf. Gen. 1, 1; Isa. 7, 14; Deut. 6, 5); (b) the *improper literal* or *metaphorical* sense, which is expressed by words taken in their transferred, derived, or figurative meaning.[6]

This improper literal sense can refer either to *individual words* or to the *entire sentence* or *discourse.*

The improper literal sense relating to individual words may be of various kinds. It may be a *synecdoche*—i.e., the whole used for the part, the genus for the species, the abstract for the concrete or vice versa (cf. Ps. 64, 3 "all flesh shall come to thee"; flesh stands for man). It may be a *metonomy*—i.e., one word used for another, a cause placed for the effect, the container for the things contained, the inventor for the thing made, etc. (cf. 1 Cor. 11, 26: "For as often as you shall eat this bread and drink the cup," i.e., what is contained in the cup; cf. also Matt. 10, 34; John 11, 25; 1 Pet. 2, 24). It may be a *metaphor*—i.e., a contracted simile or comparison, or a figure of speech by which a word is transferred from an object to which it properly belongs to another, in such a manner that a comparison is implied (cf. John 1, 29 "Behold the lamb of

[6] Cf. Brown, S. J., "Image and Truth. Studies in the Imagery of the Bible" (Rome, 1955).

God"; cf. also Ps. 1, 3; Matt. 5, 13 f; etc.). It may be an *emphasis*—i.e., a higher meaning than the words express (cf. Matt. 7, 22 "that day" for the day of judgment; cf. also Ez. 20, 11; Ps. 1, 6). It may be a *hyperbole*—i.e., more is said than is really meant; hyperbolic expressions are not to be taken too strictly but according to their context and the circumstances of the one speaking (cf. Gen. 13, 16; 3 Kgs. 10, 27). It may be an *ellipsis*—i.e., the omission of a word or phrase which should be supplied (cf. Gen. 3, 22; Ps. 6, 4).

The improper literal sense relating to entire sentences and passages may also be of various kinds. It may be a *parable*[7] —i.e., a developed and continued comparison or similitude (cf. 2 Sam. 12, 1-4; 14, 6 ff; 3 Kgs. 20, 38 ff; Matt. 13, 3-33). It may be an *allegory* [8]—i.e., a developed and continued metaphor or simile with the comparative words and forms left out (cf. Ps. 79; Isa. 5, 1 ff; Ez. 17, 1 ff; John 10, 11 ff). Often allegorical elements are mixed with parables or parabolic elements with allegories. It may be a *fable*—i.e., a feigned narrative, which never happened nor ever could happen, because inanimate objects or animals are introduced as animate or having the use of reason to convey some moral lesson (cf. Jdgs. 9, 8-15 and 4 Kgs. 14, 9 the only two fables in the Bible). It may be a *riddle*—i.e., a more obscure allegory, the sense of which can only be detected through subtle reasoning (cf. Jdgs. 14, 14).

The *symbolical* sense is also a species of the improper literal sense. A symbol is a thing or figurative action by which something else is signified or represented; for example, in Matt. 27, 24 the washing of hands is to signify innocence. The symbolic meaning is a truth expressed by a symbolic sign. It differs from a parable or allegory, because there is a real image by which something is represented or a truth is illustrated. There are symbolic actions (cf. 3 Kgs. 11, 29-39; Isa. 20, 2 ff; Jer. 19, 1 ff; Ez. 4, 1 ff; 5, 1 ff; 12, 3 ff), visions (cf. Ez. 37, 1 ff; Acts 10, 10 ff), objects (cf. Num. 15, 38-40), names (cf Isa. 7, 3; 8, 3; Os. 1, 4 ff), numbers (cf. Gen. 4, 15; Am. 1, 3. 6. 9; Apoc. 21, 12).

[7] Cf. Steinmueller, J. E.-Sullivan, K., art. "Parable," in C.B.E.N.T.
[8] Cf. *Idem*, art. "Allegory," in C.B.E.N.T.

It is the common opinion among Catholic scholars that every passage of the Bible has a literal sense. This is the fundamental principle of interpretation. It is very likely that there is *only one* literal sense, whether proper or improper, in each and every passage of the Bible. The few passages seemingly in favor of the multiplicity of literal senses (cf. Ps. 2, 7 with Acts 13, 13, Hebr. 1, 5 and 5, 5; Matt. 8, 17 and Isa. 53, 4; Acts 3, 22 and Deut. 18, 15-19; John 11, 49-52) can be satisfactorily explained by exegetes, so that there is no need of admitting the plurality of literal senses for any passage in the Bible.[9] These multiple meanings are so intimately connected with one another that they appear as parts of the whole and are included in the consequent sense.

Art. 2. The Typical (Spiritual) Sense

Other designations of the typical sense are: real, spiritual, mystical, allegorical, mediate, indirect, etc.

The correct usage of this typical sense is clearly brought out by Pius XII in his "Divino afflante Spiritu": "Doubtless all spiritual sense is not excluded from the Sacred Scripture. For what was said and done in the Old Testament was ordained and disposed by God with such consummate wisdom, that things past prefigured in a spiritual way those that were to come under the new dispensation of grace. Wherefore the exegete, just as he must search out and expound the literal meaning of the words, intended and expressed by the sacred writer, so also must he do likewise for the spiritual sense, provided it is clearly intended by God. For God alone could have known this spiritual meaning and have revealed it to us.

[9] Cf. Höpfl, H., *op. cit.*, 105-123; Fernández, A., in I.B., 370-377; *idem,* "De mente S. Augustini relate ad unitatem sensus literalis," in V.D., 7 (1927), 278-284; Höpfl, H.—Leloir, L., *op. cit.*, 418-430. Barrosse, T., ("The Senses of Scripture and the Liturgical Pericopes," in C.B.Q., 21 [1959], 1-23) advocates a multiple sense or a new, second, literal sense which is acquired by a reinterpretation of some Biblical texts to be found "not in an analysis of the nature of the act of inspiration but rather in the nature of the function that the inspired writings have to play in the Church or in the development of revealed religion" (p.21); such a rethinking is due to a "liturgical inspiration," that is, "the Church confers a new sense on a text with some sort of divine guidance" (p.2).

Now Our Divine Savior Himself points out to us and teaches us this same sense in the Holy Gospel; the Apostles also, following the example of the Master, profess it in their spoken and written words; the unchanging tradition of the Church approves it; finally, the most ancient usage of the liturgy proclaims it, wherever may be rightly applied the well-known principle: 'The rule of prayer is the rule of faith.' Let Catholic exegetes then disclose and expound this spiritual significance, intended and ordained by God, with that care which the dignity of the divine word demands; but let them scrupulously refrain from proposing as the genuine meaning of Sacred Scripture other figurative senses" (E.B., 552 f).

The typical sense is that meaning by which the things, signified by the word, signify according to the intention of the Holy Spirit yet other things, and which is founded upon and supposes the literal sense. The person, event, or thing which is employed by God to signify something else or foreshadow something else, is called the *type* or the exemplar. The person, event, or thing which is foreshadowed is called the *antitype;* thus, for example, Adam is a type of Christ (cf. Rom. 5, 14), and baptism is called an antitype (cf. 1 Pet. 3, 21) of the waters of the deluge.

God employed in the Old Testament persons (e.g., Adam, Melchisedech), events (e.g., various legal enactments as the bones of the passover lamb which were not to be broken, etc.), and things (manna, brazen serpent, passover lamb) to foreshadow other things. By reason of the objects foreshadowed the typical sense is divided into *Messianic,* prophetical or allegorical *types* (because they refer to the Messianic kingdom), *anagogical types* (because they prefigure the things of the world to come), and *tropological types* (because they convey lessons for our moral guidance).

There are three elements necessary for a true type. First, there must be a *real existence* of the person, event, or thing. In this manner the type differs from metaphors, allegories, or parables, which are mere images without any historical foundation. If some authors call the typical sense also the allegorical sense, this must not be confused with the improper literal sense of allegory. Secondly, there must be a *similarity* between the thing which is the type and the thing which is prefigured by the type. In other words, there should be some likeness between the type and the antitype. Thus, according to Hebrews 7, 1 ff Melchisedech is a type of the Eternal High Priest, Christ, because in the Old Testament he is referred to without any allusion to a father or mother or genealogy, although he undoubtedly had parents. Thirdly, it must be God's intention to prefigure. This divine intention must be manifested in some manner. God in His divine providence so arranges the lives of the great heroes of the Old Testament and describes them through the sacred writers in such a manner that they appear as images of the future Messias.

From the Bible and ecclesiastical tradition it is certain that the typical sense *exists* in regard to the Old Testament. The sacred books give many examples of persons, events, or things which were literally applied to the Old Testament, and then were assigned by the sacred writers of the New Testament to Christ. For example, Christ says that Jonas the prophet is an image of the Resurrection of the Messias (cf. Matt. 12, 39 ff), and that the brazen serpent is a type of the crucifixion (cf. Num. 21, 9; John 3, 14); the passover lamb (cf. Ex. 12, 46; Num. 9, 12) prefigures Christ, whose bones were not to be broken (John 19, 36); according to St. Paul, the sacrifices and institutions of the Old Testament are but the foreshadows of future blessings (cf. Col. 2, 16 ff; Hebr. 10, 1); the passage of the Red Sea is a type of Baptism (1 Cor. 10, 1-11); Agar and Sara are types of the two Covenants (Gal. 4, 22). Besides, the ecclesiastical writers and Fathers (e.g., St. Justin Martyr, Tertullian, St. Irenæus, St. Cyprian, St. Augustine and St. Jerome) believed in the typical sense. Then too, the Church has frequently made use of the typical meaning in her liturgy.

From the citations of Christ and St. Paul we may conclude that the Old Testament as a whole is a type of the New Testament. But Origen, the Alexandrian school, and the Protestant Symbolists of the seventeenth century transgressed the proper limits when they tried to find types everywhere in the Old Testament and neglected the literal meaning of the Bible. Authors are not in agreement whether types are also found in the New Testament. It may be conceded that no Messianic types will be found in the New Testament, but it is also possible that anagogical types may be found, especially in the Apocalypse.

Theoretically, the *argumentative* value is the same for the typical as for the literal sense, because both meanings are directly intended by God, and the Apostles themselves made use of both to prove their doctrine. However, for the demonstration of a theological argument the use of the typical sense is of little apologetical value. If the typical sense is certain, it is given by the sacred writers and the ecclesiastical magisterium; but whenever it is doubtful, the argument has no scientific value. Since the Bible does not teach anything through the typical sense that is not elsewhere taught literally, we can readily admit that the more powerful theological argument is to be sought in the literal meaning.

Art. 3. Plenary, Consequent and Accommodated Senses

In recent times there have been extensive, critical and fruitful discussions about these three senses and their precise relationship with the literal sense.

(a) PLENARY SENSE

Bibliography: Fernández, A., in *Institutiones Biblicae* (6th ed., Rome, 1951), 381-385; *idem*, "Sensus Typicus. Sensus Plenior," in *Biblica*, 33 (1952), 526-528; *idem*, "Nota referente a los sentidos de la S. Escriptura," in *Biblica*, 35 (1954), 72-79; Bierberg, R., "Does Sacred Scripture Have a Sensus Plenior?" in C.B.Q., 10 (1948), 182-195; Brown, R. E., "The History and Development of the Theory of a Sensus Plenior," in C.B.Q., 15 (1953), 141-162; *idem*, "The Sensus Plenior of Sacred Scripture" (Baltimore, 1955) with a full bibliography 154-161; Krumholtz, R. H., "Instrumentality and the Sensus Plenior," in C.B.Q., 20 (1958), 200-205; O'Rourke, J. J., "Marginal Notes on the Sensus Plenior," in C.B.Q., 21 (1959), 64-71; Rivera, A., "Inimicitias ponam . . . "—"Signum aparuit (Gen. 3, 15; Apoc. 12, 1)," in V.D., 21 (1941), 183-189; Coppens, J., "Les Harmonies des Deux Testaments" (Tournai & Paris, 1949); Schmid, J., "Die atl. Zitate bei Paulus und die Theorie von sensus plenior," in B.Z., 3 (1959), 161-173; Tamisier, R., "The Total Sense of Scripture," in

Scripture, 4 (1950), 141-143; Giblin, C. H., "As it is Written . . . A Basic Problem in Noematics and Its Relevance to Biblical Theology," in C.B.Q., 20 (1958), 327-353, 477-498.

The plenary, or fuller sense (*sensus plenior*), sometimes even called the evangelical sense (A. Colunga), as a principle of Biblical interpretation is now recognized by many scholars as being closely *allied to the literal sense*. It is to be regarded as having been built over or founded upon a deeper and more profound meaning of the Biblical words or message than the sacred writers understood at the time of their compositions and wished to express, but which God intended at times to develop through and beyond their words. The problem of the plenary sense *is not concerned with the possibility* of God's message, with its absolute clearness in His mind, being conveyed to the mind of the sacred writer in some form of relative, finite clearness. The question is rather this: Did God, in making use of the intellectual talents of the prophets and other sacred writers (as His weak, finite, rational instruments), allow them only (in accordance with their personal limitations, the capacity of their readers or listeners to understand their message, historical circumstances, etc.) to obtain and recognize a glimpse, a part of the entire picture of the truth or of the message in its totality; did He at the same time intend that other subsequent prophets, hagiographers, Christ and His Apostles reinterpret, rethink and add further details to that same message; and did He also intend that the living, teaching body of His New Covenant, the Church, would see the more complete picture of this divine message and teach it through her doctrines and liturgy in accordance with the historical needs of her development? In other words, the plenary sense supposes that the Holy Spirit, who conferred the inspirational light upon any sacred writer to make his infallible judgment about a divine message, did also radiate His light more clearly and more fully upon one or more subsequent hagiographers, so that this same divine message shines more progressively in greater brilliance (e.g., certain Christological and Marian doctrines).

Although our professor, the venerable Spanish Jesuit, P. A. Fernández, has popularized the term "sensus plenior," yet this concept or idea has its basis in Catholic tradition and was expressed by Leo XIII in his encyclical "Providentissimus Deus": "It must be observed that, in addition to the usual reasons which make ancient writings more or less difficult to understand, there are some which are peculiar to the Bible. For the language of the Bible is employed to express . . . many things which are beyond the power and scope of the reason of man—that is to say, divine mysteries and all that is related to them. There is sometimes in such passages a fullness and a hidden depth of meaning (*ampliore quadam et reconditiore sententia*) which the letter hardly expresses and which hermeneutical laws hardly warrant" (E.B., 108).

Every scholarly exegete or interpreter must recognize various restrictions or limitations placed upon him when he applies the plenary sense. First and above all, he must take into consideration and evaluate the context of all the Biblical passages referring to the same divine message. Hence, he will find many examples of this progressive meaning in the prophetic Messianic passages of the Old Testament (e.g., Gen. 3, 15; Isa. 7, 14 f), and because of their fulfillment known from the New Testament he should know of their fuller, or plenary, meaning of these prophetic passages than that of the prophets who first uttered and wrote them down. Secondly, the exegete must bear in mind that a fuller meaning (i.e., reinterpretation, rethinking) to Biblical passages of the Old Testamen has been authentically given by Our Lord Himself (cf. Luke 24, 27), the Apostles, the witnesses of the life and resurrection of Jesus (cf. Acts 2, 14-36) and the teaching authority of the Church "to whom it belongs to judge the true sense and interpretation of Holy Scripture" (E.B., 62). Finally, it is to be remembered that we, as faithful Christians of Christ's New Covenant, now profitably, fruitfully read many books of the Old Testament (e.g., Proverbs, Ecclesiasticus, Wisdom, etc.) with an entirely different religious conviction, attitude, thought-pattern than the first Jewish readers of these books.

After these brief observations about the plenary sense of the Bible, we agree that it may be adequately defined in the words of Father R. E. Brown: "That additional, deeper meaning, intended by God, but not clearly intended by the human author, which is seen to exist in the words of a biblical text (or group of texts, or even a whole book) when they are studied in the light of further revelation or development in the understanding of revelation" ("The Sensus Plenior," etc., 92).

(b) Consequent Sense (Theological Conclusion)

This sense, sometimes called the *implicit sense,* is that which is reached by a simple process of reasoning which began from some proposition or truth contained in the Bible or is that which contains a simple explanation and application of the Biblical text. Since this final result, especially a *theological conclusion,* is itself not formally contained in the Sacred Scriptures, this consequent sense cannot be called a divine or Biblical sense, that is, properly or precisely, but only widely or loosely so, because only one part of the divine message is divinely revealed or inspired, while the conclusion, or second part (although divinely foreseen), is left to the individual person, the theologian or the divinely guided Church to determine.[10]

The consequent sense is used in the Bible itself. Thus Our Savior at times applied Old Testament texts in this sense. For example, he concluded from the fact that God called Himself "The God of Abraham, the God of Isaac and the God of Jacob" (Ex. 3, 6) that these Patriarchs (i.e., their souls) were still alive, because "he is not the God of the dead, but of the living" (Matt. 22, 31 f). Similarly, St. Paul derived theological conclusions from some Old Testament texts, for instance, from the Deuteronomic text: "You shall not muzzle an ox when it is treading out grain" (Deut. 25, 4); he logically drew the conclusion that the Apostles had the just right to be

---

[10] Cf. De Vine, C., "The Consequent Sense," in C.B.Q., 2 (1940), 145-155; Brown, R. E., "The Sensus Plenior, etc." 22-27.

supported by the faithful, because God has a greater care for the welfare of men (i.e., the Apostolic workers) than for oxen (1 Cor. 9, 7-11).

This consequent sense is of great importance for every theologian. Having been assured of the genuine literal meaning of a Biblical text by the trained exegete, he can bring this to a legitimate conclusion. At the same time we must bear in mind that this sense helps Christians to deepen their piety. Thus, through pious meditation upon various Biblical texts and messages, theoretical and practical principles may be derived and applied to Christian living. In accordance with these principles many of the homilies and commentaries of the Fathers of the Church were written.

(c) ACCOMMODATED SENSE

By accommodated sense is meant *another meaning* given to the text by an interpreter than that intended directly or indirectly by the sacred writer. It is usually given by the reader or the preacher in his application of his Biblical sermons to present-day conditions of life.[11] This accommodation should never be used as a theological proof, but merely as an example or illustration.

This meaning is based upon a certain *resemblance* between two objects (i.e., persons, things, events in the hagiographer's mind and those in the interpreter's mind) or in a certain *analogy* between two truths (one expressed by the sacred writer and another not intended to be expressed by him). When proper and due regard for this resemblance and analogy is imprudently neglected, the Biblical meaning may be falsely and harmfully distorted by the preacher or writer.

Various general principles should be followed for the proper application of this sense.

(1) If in this likeness an accommodation is based upon the *extension of the literal* meaning, then it is to be recommended. Thus, for example, St. Paul frequently accommodates words

[11] Cf. Holzmeister, U., "De accommodatione textuum biblicorum," in V.D., 18 (1938), 272-278; Höpfl, H.—Leloir, L., *op. cit.*, 432-435.

of the Old Testament as a powerful, useful and edifying example for his readers (e.g., Ps. 18 [19], 5 in Rom. 10, 18; Ex. 16, 18 in 2 Cor. 8, 15; Jos. 1, 5 in Heb. 13, 5). Similarly, the Church in her *liturgy* often makes use of the accommodated sense (e.g., the Praise of the Fathers in Sir. 44, 1—50, 23 is applied to the Holy Confessors of the Church; Prov. 8, 1-36 and Sir. 24, 1-47 relating to divine Wisdom are applied to our Blessed Mother Mary). Similarly *modern preachers* often make practical applications of Bible stories and narratives, Biblical messages, truths and texts for the purpose of enriching the contents of their topics and of adding vitality, strength and unction to their preaching (e.g., the words of Ps. 109 [110], 4: "The Lord has sworn, and he will not repent: You are a priest forever, according to the order of Melchisedech" are applied to the priests of the New Covenant; Christ's words of commendation to Nathanael: "Behold, a true Israelite in whom there is no guile" [John 1, 47] is applied to every true, sincere and holy Christian).

(2) If in this resemblance an accommodation is based not upon the sense of the words found in their proper context, but rather upon *individual, isolated words and phrases* (as the play upon words and phrases), the interpreter must be extremely cautious, because the accommodated application may be given a false or ridiculous twist (e.g., the words of Abraham: "I am your shield, your reward shall be very great" [Gen. 15, 1] should not be applied to the eternal, heavenly rewards of the saints after their death; the words of Christ: "He who loves father and mother more than me is not worthy of me" [Matt. 10, 37] should not be quoted by a non-cloistered superior in denying a subject permission to see his or her parents during a grievous illness).

(3) *Precepts* or *proverbs* found in the Bible, even though they may be directed at times to one individual person, are not to be taken as examples of the accommodated sense when they are properly applied by the exegete or preacher to modern circumstances, but rather are applications of the real, genuine, literal sense, or examples of the consequent sense.

(4) Any accommodation by modern interpreters or preachers that is based upon a *false exegesis* of any Scriptural text cannot be approved and should be disregarded. It is self-evident that any application of a Biblical text, passage or even book based upon a false foundation cannot possibly merit abiding confidence and the approval of a deeply religious Jew or Christian (e.g., the false modern application of the Book of Job by *Archibald MacLeish in his Pulitzer Prize play *JB*).

(5) In accommodating Biblical texts or passages to present circumstances of life, to our modern Christian mode of living, the interpreter, the theologian and especially the preacher must avoid presenting the accommodated sense for the literal meaning and offering it as a *dogmatic proof* for his assertions, thereby misleading his readers and listeners. Thus his audience is led erroneously to believe that his message is God's message and the word of God.

In fine, the accommodated sense should represent a reverential regard and attitude for God's written word.

Pius XII in "Divino afflante Spiritu" gives some general directives about this accommodated sense: "It may indeed be useful, especially in preaching, to illustrate and present the matters of faith and morals by a broader use of the Sacred Text in the figurative sense, provided this be done with moderation and restraint; it should, however, never be forgotten that this use of the Sacred Scripture is, as it were, extrinsic to it and accidental, and that, especially in these days, it is not free from danger, since the faithful, in particular those who are well-informed in the sciences, sacred and profane, wish to know what God has told us in the Sacred Letters rather than what an ingenious orator or writer may suggest by a clever use of the words of Scripture" (E.B., 553).

CHAPTER II

HEURISTICS:

THE DISCOVERY OF THE SENSE OF SCRIPTURE

Heuristics is that part of Hermeneutics which tries to discover the true sense of the Bible. Since the Holy Scriptures are both human and divine documents, it is necessary to be guided by various rules, or criteria, to obtain the true meaning of the Biblical text. These rules or norms which are applied to the Bible as a human document are called the literary criteria, and those which are applied to it as a divine document are called dogmatic criteria.

Art. 1. The Literary Criteria

In the Encyclical "Providentissimus Deus," after he had discussed the utility of examining the various ancient MSS. in their original languages to discover the original or genuine reading, Pope Leo XIII mentions the canons which should guide the student in the exposition and investigation of the meaning. He says: "Hence whilst weighing the meanings of words, the connection of ideas, the parallelism of passages, and the like, we should by all means make use of such illustrations as can be drawn from apposite erudition of an external sort" (E.B., 107). Besides mentioning these internal and external criteria, Pius XII in his "Divino afflante Spiritu" (E.B., 550) also refers to the literary forms as an important aid in the discovery of the correct and genuine meaning of the Bible: "What is the literal sense of a passage is not always as obvious in the speeches and writings of the ancient authors of the East as it is in the works of the writers of our own time. For what they wished to express is not to be determined by the rules of grammar and philology alone, nor solely by the context; the interpreter must, as it were, go back wholly in spirit to those remote centuries of the East and with the aid of history, archæology, ethnology and other sciences, accurately determine what modes of writing, so to speak, the authors of that ancient period would likely use, and in fact did use (E.B., 558).

These literary criteria are the rational principles of Hermeneutics and are applied to the Bible as a human document, as a human literary production. This scientific or rational approach to the sacred books is sometimes called the grammatic-historical meaning or interpretation. The inner criteria are those which concern the biblical text, while the external criteria are the circumstances which help us to determine the mind of the sacred writer more clearly.

(a) THE INTERNAL CRITERIA

Of the internal criteria the language of the sacred writer, the context, the parallel passages and the literary forms are of greatest importance to understand the content of the Biblical text and message.

(1) *The Languages.*—[12] The principal source for searching for the literal meaning of the Bible is the language, the ordinary speech commonly used by the people. The usage of the language is the constant manner in which some definite author was accustomed to express his ideas or thoughts in writing at any given time. It is the grammatical and historical nexus between words and ideas employed by mankind to give outward expression to their thoughts.

Since the Bible was written in Hebrew, Aramaic and Greek, and since the authentic version of the Church is the Latin Vulgate, [13] it will be necessary for the scholar to master these

---

[12] Cf. Steinmueller, J. E.—Sullivan, K., in C.B.E.O.T., art. "Alphabet" (47-50), "Archæology" (96-101), "Hebrew Language" (499 f), "Writing" (1147-1150); Holzmeister, U., "Sensus exclusivus et praecisivus in S.S.," in *Biblica,* 7 (1926), 170-182, 20 (1939), 264-275; Schmidt, J., "Das Wortspiel im Alten Testamente," in B.Z., 24 (1938), 1-17; Holzmeister, U., "Termini abstracti pro concretis in S.Scriptura adhibiti," in V.D., 21 (1941), 209-218.

[13] Cf. Part III. TEXTS AND VERSIONS OF THE BIBLE.

languages (cf. "Providentissimus Deus," E.B., 106, 108) as well as to acquire some facility in the other Oriental languages. This has been stressed in recent times by Pius XII in "Divino afflante Spiritu": "In this our time, not only the Greek language, which . . . is familiar to almost all students of antiquity and letters, but the knowledge of Hebrew also and of other Oriental languages has spread far and wide among literary men. Moreover, there are now such abundant aids to the study of these languages that the Biblical scholar, who by neglecting them would deprive himself of access to the original texts, could in no wise escape the stigma of levity and sloth. For it is the duty of the exegete to lay hold, so to speak, with the greatest care and reverence of the very least expressions, which, under the inspiration of the Divine Spirit, have flowed from the pen of the sacred writer, so as to arrive at a deeper and fuller knowledge of his meaning. Wherefore let him diligently apply himself so as to acquire daily a greater facility in Biblical as well as in other Oriental languages and to support his interpretation by the aids which all branches of philology supply" (E.B., 547).

This knowledge of the Biblical and other ancient languages helps the scholar to become well acquainted with the vocabulary, grammar and style of the sacred writers, and by philological comparison of Biblical words with cognate languages and various ancient versions he will recognize whether the words are to be taken in the proper or improper literal sense.

(2) *The Context.*—The context is the connection between what precedes and what follows in the same passage or discourse. The analysis of the context will be of great assistance in determining the exact meaning of ambiguous words and phrases, if the philological study of the sacred text does not suffice. There are four kinds of contexts: logical, psychological, historical, and prophetical.

(a) The *logical context* supposes that there is some connection between the various ideas of the same author. This logical context is of two kinds: *proximate,* which consists in the relation between the subject and the predicate; and *remote*,[14] which occurs between various propositions related to one another in some manner, as premise and conclusion, cause and effect, genus and species, parts and the whole. In the loose sense of the word, the remote context can also apply to whole books, so that its principal parts enable us to discover the plan of the sacred writer.

Scholars at times also distinguish between the immediate and mediate logical context. The *immediate* context is had when the various words and propositions are intimately connected with one another. This then corresponds either with the proximate or remote context. The *mediate* context presupposes a loose connection between the various parts; for example, the idea begun by St. Paul in 2 Corinthians 2, 12 ff is continued in 7, 5 ff.

The proximate logical context—also called the grammatical context—is determined according to the rules of grammar and shows what words are to be united or separated, and how the words are to be connected with one another (cf. Greek text of John 1, 1).

The remote logical context shows the relationships existing between various sentences, and is usually determined by the use of particles.

(b) The *psychological context* arises from the association of ideas.[14a] Our mind at times connects ideas and things with one another, although they have no logical connection; yet, because the ideas are similar or contrary or because of temporal or logical circumstances, these thoughts are so associated in our minds that they cause others to flow spontaneously. Take, for example, the conversation of Christ with the Samaritan woman who came to the well to draw water. Our Lord speaks to her of the living water that will bring eternal

[14] Cf. Holzmeister, U., "De forma chiastica in N.T. adhibita," in V.D., 14 (1934), 337-341; Sutcliffe, E. F., "Effect As Purpose: a Study in Hebrew Thought Patterns," in *Biblica*, 35 (1954), 320-327.

[14a] Cf. Le Frois. B. J., "Semitic Totality Thinking," in C.B.Q., 17 (1955), 195-203; *idem*, "The Semitic Thought-Pattern in Sacred Scripture," in A.E.R., 134 (1956), 374-394.

life (John 4, 10 ff); when the Apostles offer Him food, Jesus answers: "My food is that I do the will of him who sent me" (John 4, 34). Thus the progress of the speaker's or writer's thoughts may be at times traced.

(c) The *historical context* is had when the parts of a book are chronologically connected in the order of time (e.g., the Gospels of St. Luke and St. John). But St. Matthew, whose principal dogmatical thesis is to show that Jesus was the Messias promised by the Prophets, prefers the logical order of events.

(d) The *prophetical context* signifies that the prophet foresees the chronological connection between two or more events as if they would come to pass at the same time. For example, Matt. 24 forecasts the fall of Jerusalem and the end of the world; Isa. 40 ff forecasts the liberation of the people under Cyrus, the return from the exile, and the Messianic period.

Of these four kinds of context the most important is the logical context for the determination of the meaning.

(3) *Parallelism.*[15]—Parallel passages are those which have some resemblance either between the words employed or between the subject-matter treated. The former is called *verbal,* and the latter *real* parallelism.

This verbal parallelism is perfect when the same words or grammatical constructions are found in the various passages of the Bible (cf. Matt. 8, 3 and Luke 5, 13; Matt. 9, 5 ff and Mark 2, 9-11 and Luke 5, 23-25). But when such complete conformity is lacking between the texts, this parallelism is imperfect, and of this there are numerous examples in the Synoptic Gospels. Real parallelism, where the same thought is expressed or where the same subject is discussed, is subdivided into historical and didactical or dogmatic parallelism.

Real historical parallelism records the same event or series of events. Thus, the Books of Kings frequently treat of the same events as those recorded in the Books of Paralipomenon; the Evangelists at times refer to the same miracles (e.g., the

---

[15] Cf. Bonamartini, U., "L'epesegesi nella S. Scrittura," in *Biblica,* 6 (1925), 424-444.

multiplication of loaves is narrated by the four Evangelists).

Real didactical parallelism inculcates the same truth. Thus, the Gospels frequently teach us the doctrines of Christ which are also found in the Pauline Epistles (e.g., the subject of marriage).

All of these kinds of parallelism serve a *useful purpose* in the correct understanding of the biblical text.

Verbal parallelism, which very often coincides with real parallelism, is of great assistance in the determination of the meaning of obscure words or in the confirmation of a precise meaning. Thus, for example, the meaning of 'almah (Isa. 7, 14), "virgin," is confirmed by the usage of the word in other passages of the Old Testament.[16] Whenever, therefore, some passages of the Bible seem difficult or obscure, their meaning should be sought and explained, if possible, according to the more obvious and clearer parallel passages; thus, for example, Eph. 1, 10 becomes clear in the light of Rom. 13, 9; Gen. 49, 10 is clarified when a comparison is made with Ez. 21, 32.

In the poetical books there is a kind of imperfect verbal parallelism. There is a certain rhythm between the various sentences. It consists in the equal distribution or balance of thought, so that the individual members correspond with one another. There are three recognized forms of this poetical parallelism: synonymous, antithetical and synthetical. *Synonymous parallelism* simply repeats the same thought in other words (e.g., Ps. 2, 4; 50, 9; 75, 3; Prov. 3, 13-18, etc.). *Antithetical parallelism* produces a contrast (e.g., Prov. 10, 1-4ᵃ; 10, 15. 28.29; Luke 1, 52, etc.). *Synthetical* or *progressive parallelism* occurs when the second member of the verse completes the thought of the first by adding a reason, or by a logical sequence, or by some grammatical conjunction (cf. Ps. 3, 5. 6; 68, 2; 144, 18, etc.).[17]

Historical parallelism serves a useful purpose, since very often different narratives of the same fact mutually complete

[16] Cf. Steinmueller, J. E., "The Etymology and Biblical Usage of 'almah," in C.B.Q., 2 (1940), 28-43.

[17] Cf. Steinmueller, J. E.—Sullivan, K., art. "Poetry," in C.B.E.O.T., 863-867.

one another; for example, the Fourth Gospel, particularly in regard to the Passion of Christ, completes the Synoptic Gospels. Nevertheless, we must bear in mind that similar passages do not always bespeak identity; for example, Abraham's sojourn in Egypt (Gen. 12, 11-20) must not be confused with his stay in the land of Abimelech (Gen. 20, 1-8); the curing of the servant of the centurion (Matt. 8, 5-13; Luke 7, 1-10) is not to be confounded with the curing of the son of the ruler (John 4, 46-54).

The same is also true with regard to doctrinal parallelism. The collection of parallel passages will aid the interpreters in understanding correctly the doctrines inculcated in the Bible. The general rule should be that parallel passages by the same author are to be preferred to those by different authors, because the same manner of thinking and the same language are generally retained by the same author. When two or more sacred writers treat of the same doctrine, the one should be explained in the light of the other or others; for example, the Sermon of the Mount is contained in the full form in Matthew chs. 5-7 and in an abbreviated form in Luke 6, 26-49. However, at times the true sense of a passage cannot be derived by parallel passages; then either the context or the tradition of the Church will be the determining factors.

In order to find the parallel passages in the Bible, recourse should be made to the concordances. The *verbal concordances* are those which give the individual words of the Bible in the alphabetical order; thus, * Mandelkern for the Hebrew text, * Hatch-Redpath for the Septuagint, Peultier-Etienne-Gantois for the Vulgate text of the Old and New Testament, * Moulton-Geden for the Greek New Testament, * Young for the Authorized Version and Thompson for the Douay-Rheims Version.

The *real concordances* are those which give the subject-matter of the Bible in alphabetical order; e.g., "Lexicon Biblicum," Lueg's "Biblische Realkonkordanz," Kalt's "Biblische Real-Lexikon," * Hasting's "Dictionary of the Bible," Vigouroux' "Dictionnaire de la Bible," Steinmueller, J. E.—

Sullivan, K., "Catholic Biblical Encyclopedia: Old Testament I, New Testament II;" "Bijbelsch Woordenbook"; Haag's "Bible-Lexikon."

Citations.—The New Testament contains many citations taken from Old Testament books.[18] These quotations may be regarded to some extent as parallel passages. The general principles governing these quotations, whether explicit or implicit, from the viewpoint of inspiration and inerrancy have been explained above (see Part I, chapter IV: THE EFFECT OF INSPIRATION: INERRANCY).

Since most of these citations are related to prophetical utterances, or the Psalms, the problems arises about their interpretation by the inspired New Testament writers. Perhaps the following brief summary may act as a useful guide.

(a) Whenever the *fulfillment of any prophecy* is expressed through such stereotyped formulas as: "so that it might be fulfilled" (Matt. 1, 22 f; 8, 16 f; 13, 34 f), "well did . . . prophesy concerning you" (Matt. 15, 7 f), "that the Scripture(s) might be fulfilled" (Matt. 26, 56; John 13, 18; 19, 36), "then was fulfilled what was spoken by . . ." (Matt. 2, 17; 27, 9), etc., then, after such expressions, we should accept the Biblical words or message in a literal or typical meaning, or at least as the sacred writers' theological conclusion, but not as his accommodated meaning.

(b) When a New Testament writer *adds his own inspired words* to a passage from the Old Testament, his mental attitude may vary: thus, he may use merely accommodation and intend only to illustrate his teaching through some Biblical resemblance; or he may desire to add an appealing emphasis to his teaching by repeating Biblical tradition accepted either literally or typically, or by giving his own theological conclusion.

[18] Cf. Steinmueller, J. E.—Sullivan, K., art. "Old Testament Quotations," in C.B.E.N.T., 466-471; * Metzger, B. M., "The Formulas Introducing Quotations in the N.T. and the Mishnah," in J.B.L., 70 (1951), 297-308; Carmignac, J., "Les citations de l'Ancient Testament," in R.B. 63 (1956), 234-260; 375-390.

(c) Similarly, the New Testament writers, ministering in the diaspora and quoting passages from the Septuagint Bible that differed at times from the primitive Hebrew textual form, may simply be using the Greek Old Testament and accommodating it because of some resembling thought, idea or action; if, however, they are quoting this Greek version as a strictly Scriptural proof, then their inspired reasoning or judgment must agree substantially with its main thought, but not necessarily with every particular word. We must always bear in mind that the Old Testament Bible read by most Jews (i.e., outside of Palestine) and Christians in the Roman Empire was the Septuagint and not the Hebrew Bible, and that many of the quotations from the Old Testament could have been made from memory and, if that be the case, aimed to contain principally the main thoughts, ideas of the quoted passages.

(4) *Literary Forms.*—In modern times the study of the literary forms as an internal criterion (although not without the dangers of extravagant assertions) is showing some promising results as a notable, scholarly contribution toward the doctrine of Biblical inerrancy (see Part I, BIBLICAL INSPIRATION, Chapter IV, THE EFFECT OF INSPIRATION: INERRANCY) and the correct interpretation of the Biblical meaning. See *special excursus*, p.284.

(b) THE EXTERNAL CRITERIA

The external circumstances which determine the composition of any book are called external criteria. All these circumstances can be reduced to four: namely, the author of the book, the occasion, the end or purpose, and the readers to whom the book was consigned.

These external criteria, which determine the peculiar character and proper circumstances of the hagiographer and the conditions under which the sacred books were composed, may also be great aids in the correct interpretation of the text.

(1) *The Author of the Book.*—Since every literary production shows the character and culture of the writer, it is im-

portant to know something, if possible, of the writer, his native country, environment, and literary accomplishments.

The authors of the Bible are Semites and possess very vivid imaginations; they often employ tropes or *figurative language* taken from agricultural life, herd-raising, etc. Hence, the knowledge of the flora and fauna as well as of archæology is required for understanding correctly their customs. At times they employ *very strong language,* yet this can be easily explained in the light of their culture and age.

The Semites prefer a *paratactic manner of speaking and writing;* that is, the simple coördination of sentences by the mere conjunction, "and." The usage of periods, to break the monotony of reading, is everywhere evident in the works of the classical Greek and Latin writers, but it is very seldom employed in the Bible. The Prologue of St. John is a good example of the concatenation of thoughts through the simple conjunction "and."

The Semitic *manner of thinking* is not based upon the laws of logic or philosophy. Thus, the Hebrews do not sufficiently distinguish between the various causes. Often they attribute events directly to God, and thus omit the secondary causes used by Him. They do not distinguish sufficiently between the various modes by which a cause, especially the primary cause, is related to the effect. We, however, distinguish between "wish, desire, order, permit, tolerate, not impede, etc.," but to the Hebrew mind whatever is attributed to God for any reason whatever, He simply wishes and does. With this in mind, many of the difficulties arising in the Old Testament in regard to divine causality will completely vanish (cf. Ex. 4, 21; 7, 3; Am. 3, 6, etc.).

The nature and peculiarities of the Hebrew language employed by many sacred writers must also be considered by the interpreter. It is rich in imagery but poor in abstract ideas, and has little flexibility.

The characteristic qualities of the sacred authors cannot be disregarded. In the Old Testament the prophet Amos was a shepherd; hence, the language employed by him is simple, and his ideas are principally taken from the pastoral life. The prophet Isaias, however, as a polished writer, employs the most elegant diction. In the New Testament, St. Paul, a Hellenic Jew and a Roman citizen, uses a great variety of images from social life and the Roman law. St. Luke, who was learned in Greek letters, has a Prologue similar to the classical authors, while the rest of the Gospel, in koine Greek, shows both beauty and elegance.

The sacred writers also at times made explicit or implicit usage of various sources, of which they either approve or disapprove.

(2) The Occasion.—The occasion of the book is an external circumstance, which moves the author to write. Thus, for example, the occasion for writing the First Epistle to the Corinthians was the report which messengers brought back to St. Paul about the schism in the church and about the various abuses and difficulties proposed by the faithful; the occasion for the Second Epistle to the Thessalonians was the misinterpretations of the First Epistle to them; the occasion of the Epistle to the Galatians was the teaching of Judaizers, who sought to persuade the faithful to become circumcised and accept the Mosaic Law.

Frequently within a book the occasion of a particular passage or narrative is given. Thus, for example, the question proposed by the doctor of the Law: "Who is my neighbor?" gives rise to the Parable of the Good Samaritan (Luke 10, 29 ff); the general attitude of the Pharisees towards other people was the occasion of the Parable of the Pharisee and the Publican (Luke 18, 10-14).

(3) The End, or the Purpose, of the Writer.[18]—The scope, which is intimately connected with the occasion, is that which the author intends to accomplish through his writing. It is the end, the aim, the purpose which he has in mind when

[18] Many modern scholars, instead of using the terms occasion, purpose of a book, passage, etc., prefer to speak of a Biblical *Sitz im Leben* (i.e., situation, or setting, in life), a German phrase, as an answer to practical problems anchored in actual life-situations or in living conditions prevalent in an historical period.

writing his book. This scope may be general—that which the author intends for his entire book. It may also be special— that which he wishes to convey in particular parts of his book.

The purpose of the book helps the interpreter to determine the contents of the book, the exposition as well as the reason why particular words are employed. For example, St. Matthew, wishing to demonstrate that Jesus is the Messias promised in the Old Testament by the Prophets, often alludes to the fulfillment of prophecies and treats his Gospel in a logical, dogmatical, and apologetical, rather than in an historical or strictly chronological, manner. St. John wishes to prove the divinity of Christ through His preaching and miracles; St. Luke (1, 1-4) desires to give an accurate exposition of the life of Christ; the Book of Ecclesiastes shows that man in this life cannot attain perfect and unchangeable happiness; the Book of Ruth intends to give the genealogy of King David and the history of some of his ancestors.

Sometimes the general scope is explicitly stated (cf. Prov. 1, 1-6; 2 Mach. 2, 20-33; Luke 1, 1-4; John 20, 31). At other times the purpose of the book is known from the cause of its origin; thus, for example, the false brethren, the Judaizers, taught the Galatians that circumcision and the observance of the Mosaic Law were necessary for salvation, but St. Paul in his Epistle to the Galatians insists upon the fact that the Jewish ordinances are not necessary and that such a doctrine is pernicious.

(4) *The Readers and Other Circumstances.*—It is also important that we bear in mind the readers for whom the book was destined. Thus, for example, St. Matthew wrote his Gospel for the Christian Jews and for the Jews in general; hence, many things could not be easily understood by the Gentile readers, and the Gospel supposes a knowledge of Jewish geography, history, archæology, and culture. St. Luke wrote for Gentile converts, and for this reason he selects parables and narratives of miracles that prove his thesis, namely, that the mercy of God extends to all people and that the Gentiles are called to the Church of Christ.

Closely linked to the sacred authors and the first readers of their books are the circumstances of *time and place* which must also be considered for the perfect understanding of Biblical books and passages. These sacred writers presuppose many details which must now be the object of research by interpreters through a diligent, scholarly, minute study of Biblical antiquities; as, for instance, the historical, cultural and religious conditions of the Fertile Crescent countries, especially of the Hebrews; the manners and customs of all these peoples; their religious beliefs, etc. Thus, for example, the sacrifice of the daughter of Jephte (Jdgs. 11, 30-39) can easily be explained in the light of the bloody period of the Judges. The Book of Jonas is made understandable in the light of Assyrian history. The Books of Esdras (and Nehemias) require some knowledge of the Babylonian Exile, the destruction of the Babylonian Kingdom and the rise of the Persian Empire.

(5) *Special Aids from Auxiliary Sciences.*—To assist the modern scholar or interpreter in acquiring the literal sense, there are at his disposal many Biblical periodicals, dictionaries, encyclopedias, commentaries, monographs. But these may be regarded, more or less, as general tools. Particular mention, however, must be made of the special aids which the exegete obtains from some auxiliary sciences, such as Biblical history (i.e., of the Old and New Testaments), archæology, antiquities, geography, natural history with its flora and fauna, theology (i.e., of the Old and New Testaments). Some of these special helps are included in this volume or have been discussed by us elsewhere.

(a) *Biblical History.*—The Old Testament: cf. Steinmueller, J. E.—Sullivan, K., "A Companion to the Old Testament" (New York, 1946), 54-230; *idem*, art., "Genesis 1-11" and "Israel, History of," in C.B.E.O.T. The New Testament: cf. idem, "A Companion to the New Testament" (New York, 1944), 59-152.

(b) *Biblical Archæology.*—The Old Testament: cf. Steinmueller, J. E.—Sullivan, K., "A Companion to the Old Testament," 31-53; *idem*, art., "Archæology," in C.B.E.O.T.

(*c*) *Biblical Antiquities, Geography, Natural History* (cf. this volume).

(*d*) *Biblical Chronology.*—Old Testament: cf. Steinmueller, J. E.—Sullivan, K., art., "Chronology of the O.T.," in C.B.E.O.T.; New Testament: *idem*, art., "Gospel Harmony," in C.B.E.N.T.; Steinmueller, J. E., "A Gospel Harmony" (New York, 1942).

(*e*) *Biblical Theology.*—The Old Testament: cf. Steinmueller, J. E.—Sullivan, K., art., "Religion of Israel," "Monotheism," "Messias," "Messianic Kingdom," etc. in C.B.E.O.T.; *idem*, art., "Christology," "Paulinism," "Mystical Body of Christ," etc., in C.B.E.N.T.

(c) THE LITERARY FORMS[19]
EXCURSUS

I. Definition and General Remarks.—Literary forms or genres are external patterns or kinds of speech which regulate and reflect the thoughts, feelings or actions of people and are employed by them at definite times and localities, and express the meaning intended by the author. Like styles in architecture, these forms allow us to study (besides and within the general categories of historical, prophetical and didactic literature) the development of languages, the history of laws, institutions, religious beliefs, etc., as expressions of certain cultures and periods. Our western mentality and its literature are not always a safe guide for the interpretation of the ancient literature of the Near East or Fertile Crescent, and particularly of the Bible.

Within recent times (1943) the encyclical "Divino afflante Spiritu" of Pius XII gave special prominence to ancient liter-

[19] Cf. Steinmueller, J. E.—Sullivan, K., art. "Literary Forms," in C.B.E.O.T., 637-639; Robert, A.—Tricot, A., "Guide to the Bible," vol. I, 280-346, 496 f. Legault, A., "An Application of the Form-Critique Method," in C.B.Q., 16 (1954), 131-145; Audet, J.-P., "Esquisse historique du genre littéraire de la 'Benediction' juive et de 'l'Eucharistie' chrétienne," in R.B., 65 (1958), 371-399.

ary forms of expression used "in poetic description or in the formulation of laws and rules of life or in recording the facts and events of history" (E.B., 558). The Holy Father impresses upon the Catholic commentator that the study of "the manner of expression or the literary mode adopted by the sacred writer may lead to a correct and genuine interpretation; and let him be convinced that this part of his office cannot be neglected without serious detriment to Catholic exegesis (E.B., 560). By the knowledge of such ancient modes of expression (whether of speaking or writing), which were meant for men and couched in human language, "can be solved many difficulties, which are raised against the veracity and historical value of the Divine Scriptures" and at the same time "this study contributes to a fuller and more luminous understanding of the Sacred Writer" (E.B., 560).

II. Various Kinds of Literary Forms.—Different Biblical books and passages have diverse literary forms. Besides the general traditional categories there are also specific literary genres which must be solidly based not on our western concepts of literary patterns, but upon the entire ancient Near East literature. Thus, the *historical literary forms* in ancient books and passages may be viewed as religious, moral, edifying, primitive, ancient or legal history, myth, or haggadic Midrash. The *didactic literature forms* may also include the epistolary genre, as letters, notes, etc. The *poetic literary forms* may contain fables, allegory, parables, lyric or gnomic poetry. The *prophetic literary forms* may also consist of various apocalyptic genres. Besides these commonly recognized Oriental literary forms there are a few others as pseudepigraphy, genealogy, apothegm, maxim, etc. When the interpreter or exegete has properly determined the literary genre of a Biblical book or passage, and this specific category is generally accepted by modern critical scholarship, then we have received a correct key for the genuine interpretation of the hagiographer's mind.

III. Literary Form of the Natural Sciences.—The interpretation of scientific matters in the Bible should offer no particular problem and difficulty to the exegete, if he bears in mind that the human authors of the Bible received no particular revelation concerning these matters and remained children of their period. Since the Bible does not scientifically treat of natural phenomena, it employs a literary genre that must be understood according to figurative language, the external appearances of natural objects or a popular account of the natural sciences. [20]

IV. Literary Forms of History.—History is the record of past events. To the Greeks and Romans this reconstruction and interpretation of the remembered past were based upon rigorous and methodical comparison and criticism. But their history was, for a great part, meaningless in the sense that it led to human futility, that is, the future was believed to be the result of natural fatality or repetitive patterns. [21]   The modern historian "does not believe in guidance, either by fate or providence. He fancies that the future can be created and provided by himself." [22]   These modern historians, however, are now concerned with the future of Europe and of the world and have added to their concept of history—unlike the Greeks and Romans—the future with its anxieties as something to be investigated and known as a fact. "The classic historian asks: How did it come about? The modern historian: How shall we go ahead?" [23]   Thus modern scholarship has been influenced by the futurist notion of history prevalent in the Old and New Testaments.

Bible history is primarily a salvation history. This sacred history is the medium of revelation, which does not consist merely in recording bare facts. [24] This history has a past and a meaningful future. The fulfillment of the Old and New Testament prophecies are understood quite differently from the prognostications of the ancient pagans. "The final ful-

[20] Cf. Steinmueller, J. E., "Some Problems of the Old Testament," 1-23.
[21] Cf. Löwith, K., "Meaning in History" (3rd impr., Chicago, 1955), 1-19.
[22] Cf. Löwith, K., *op. cit.*, 9-10.
[23] Cf. Löwith, K., *op. cit.*, 17.
[24] Cf. Rowley, H. H., "The Old Testament and Modern Study" (1st ed., 1951; repr., Oxford, 1956), 75.

fillment of Hebrew and Christian destiny lies in an eschatological future, the issue of which depends on man's faith and
will and not on a natural law of pragmatic history."[25]   In
this divine economy of salvation history everything comes
from God and is directed to Him through Jesus Christ as the
Mediator.   To exclude (with * Celsus, * Voltaire, etc.) this
salvation history of the world and revelation from the profane
and general history of mankind and civilization is ridiculous
and false.

In recording past events, the sacred writers, for the greater
part children of the Semitic world and thought-patterns, follow the literary forms of their times.   As Semites, they did
not employ norms conformable to and identical with modern,
Western, scientific forms.   But while they might have chosen
some particular facts and focused their attention on them, at
times might have treated them incompletely or paid little
attention to the details of chronolgy and geography ("the
eyes of history"[26]), yet they did stress religious, moral, psychological, mental or emotional factors.

Hence, it is also necessary to recognize the correct Semitic
historical forms for the discovery of the genuine meaning of
the Bible.   The Oriental garb of historical presentation or the
envelope of Eastern formalities and styles must not be mod-
elled arbitrarily, but must be accurately analyzed, critically
as well as judiciously appraised in the light of other ancient
literature, and objectively interpreted for the contents of the
divine message.

1. Religious History.—Some of the sacred writers did produce a record of past events with a direct, religious purpose
or slant (cf. 2 Tim. 3, 16).   Thus the aim of the author, for
example, of the Books of Samuel was to show that the religious institutions of the Hebrews, even the monarchy, were
of divine origin; of the Book of Kings was not to give a complete history, but a carefully selected summary of the political conditions during the monarchical period, demonstrating

25 Cf. Löwith,, K., *op. cit.*, 9.
26 Cf. McKenzie, J. L., "The Two-Edged Sword," 62.

that the fate of the nation depended upon its observance of the divinely revealed Law; of the Books of Paralipomenon was to give his co-religionists, who returned from the Babylonian Exile, a religious history of the Kingdom of Juda with emphasis upon the temple liturgy and its priesthood as well as the particular rights of the Davidic dynasty. Similarly, the religious purpose of the Four Gospels and the Acts of the Apostles is evident to every scholar.

The omission of apparently important events unsuitable for the purpose of the hagiographers; the deviation or neglect of a chronological arrangement of material; the presentation of a telescopic or abridged version of many events into one account, even short abstracts of important incidents, discourses or speeches—all of these conditions cannot be said to sacrifice historical truth or objective reality. Modern editorial or journalistic policies of the larger cities follow similar policies along political lines and community needs, and these newspapers can hardly be condemned by their readers or even scholarly historians for wilfully distorting the truth.[26a]

2. *Pre-History and Ancient History.*—By pre-history is meant the entire material contained in the first eleven chapters of Genesis. These chapters include the answers to man's age-old, ever troublesome problems about various origins: cosmic, human, national. Besides pre-history (A. Bea, J.-M. Vosté, E. P. Arbez),[27] other terms are used to designate these

[26a] R. A. MacKenzie proposes a novel theory which can throw confusion into the religious history of the Old Testament. He maintains that the Susanna Story in the Book of Daniel is not based upon any historical reality, but as a Jewish *haggadah,* which emphasizes faith (*quid credendum est*), adapts the general theme of marital faithfulness, borrows the general ideas (a faithful wife, calumniation, and then vindication by a wise child) from a secular or pagan *folklore,* but dramatizes this theme as a religious story. Hence, as a literary form, this religious story should be classified among the *martyr legends* of the Old Testament just like Dan. 1, 1 ff; 3, 1 ff; 6, 1 ff ("The Meaning of the Susanna Story," in *Canadian Journal of Theology,* 3 [1957]) 211-218.

[27] Cf. Bea, A., "Il problema del Pentateuco e della storia primordiale," extract from *La Civiltà Cattolica* (April 17, 1948); Vosté, J.-M., "The Pontifical Biblical Commission on the Pentateuch" and "Letter of the Pontifical Biblical Commission," in H.P.R., 48 (1948), 567-574; Arbez, E. P., "Genesis I—XI and Prehistory," A.E.R., 123 (1950), 81-92, 202-213, 284-294.

origins: for instance, *primitive history* (Pere Lagrange);[28] *folklore* (J. Feldmann);[29] or *mythology* (J. L. McKenzie).[30]

It is true that neither Gen. 1—11 nor the ancient Semitic literature may be accepted in the strict, scientific sense of history, which is today defined as the recording of a past event, being based on documents or sources relating the fact accurately, being placed in its proper time and place, and described or interpreted exactly as it really happened. Although ancient, profane literature of the Fertile Crescent cannot be called history in this strict meaning, yet it had rendered a great deal of historical material from which scientific history can be reconstructed.[31]

[28] Cf. Lagrange, J. M., "Historical Criticism and the Old Testament" (London, 1905), 180-213.

[29] Cf. Feldmann, J., "Paradise u Sündenfall' (Münster, 1913), 602.

[30] Here it is not the question of the adoption of mythological words, phrases, clauses or even elements which have been carefully stripped of any polytheistic flavor by a monotheistic writer (cf. Ez. 1; 10), but of the incorporation of myths as such and of its ideas in the commonly accepted meaning. The "Humani Generis" of Pius XII (Aug. 12, 1950) warns that "whatever of the popular narrations have been inserted into the Sacred Scriptures must in no way be considered on a par with myths . . . the product of an extravagant imagination" (E.B., 618). Many years before the encyclical, Père Lagrange decided to avoid the term "mythology" because of its association in the popular mind "with the idea of a false or even childish religion" (*op. cit.*, 195 f). On the contrary, J. L. McKenzie, by denying the conventional definition of myth and by advocating a newer definition with some modern scholars, concludes that it "is possible to accept myth as a vehicle of truth and as such it is not by definition excluded from the literary forms of the Bible ("Myth and the Old Testament," in C.B.Q., 21 [1959] 267) and that "surely there now ought to be little room for timidity and misunderstanding if we call Hebrew literature in some passages mythical, or wisdom discourses couched in mythopoeic patterns" (*ibid.*, 282).

In applying rationalistic, existential norms to the origin of Christianity, * Rudolf Bultmann, as the principal and most influential representative of Form-Criticism, teaches that we know little of the historical Jesus and, therefore, must carefully peel off the sheath of myth enveloping the message in the New Testament and must lay bare the true meaning of revelation. This process Bultmann calls demythologizing the New Testament. Cf. Steinmueller, J. E., in C.S.S., vol. III.

[31] Cf. Bea, A., for a fine summary of the subject: "Whoever is familiar with the literature of the ancient Semitic peoples and of the Egyptians will easily see that among these peoples one cannot speak of 'history' in this strict sense; here it is rather a question of the transmission of particular facts in the form of annals, or of a mingled presentation of facts and legends or myths, or of popular traditions transmitted orally and not by writing or by authentic documents. But even these accounts contain a

If such reconstruction has been made possible in profane history, so that we can read, for instance, the real history of Egypt, Assyria, etc., with a great deal of confidence and accuracy, so, too, it should be done with the religious history of the Sacred Scriptures, whether this be pre-history or ancient history.   Such history contains the description of events and conveys various teachings according to literary patterns known and used by the sacred writers. Thus, the historical elements are to be rediscovered if we wish to construct a history of the Old Testament in our sense of history.

The proper determination and accurate interpretation of such literary forms as pre-history, ancient or other subordinate ones cannot be taken for granted, but must be solidly based upon various important factors. 1) A critical, comparative study of the Bible and the profane ancient literature of the East regarding various origins (as cosmological, human, racial), languages, first civilizations, etc. 2) A proper analysis of ancient Oriental style as the non-logical, psychological approach to a subject, the embellishment of ideas with concrete and lively colors and the gradual development of one's thoughts as if in concentric circles. 3) An accurate evaluation of the ancient Oriental mentality and formulation of historical truth.

3. Mosaic Law.[32]—The main body of laws regulating the conduct of the Hebrew state or society is found in the Mosaic Code, which is arranged or distributed according to various historical contexts and may be favorably compared with the codes of the cultured peoples of the ancient Oriental nations,

---

valuable amount of 'historical' material. In fact, no one would want to deny that events can be transmitted even in such a form, events which really happened in the past, and which are determined in regard to time and space. If such were not the case, all the efforts of our learned experts to construct on such a basis a 'history' (in the modern sense) of the ancient Orient world, from the very beginning, would be in vain" ("Il problema, etc.," 124 [our translation]).

[32] Cf. Van der Ploeg, J., "Studies in Hebrew Law," in C.B.Q., 12 (1950), 248-259, 416-427; 13 (1951), 28-43, 164-171, 296-307; Steinmueller, J. E.— Sullivan, K., art. "Law and Legal Practice of Israelites," in C.B.E.O.T., 624-626; *idem*, art., "Crimes and Punishments," in *ibid.*, 246-248.

as, for instance, the Sumerians, Babylonians, Assyrians, etc.[33]

The contents of the revealed Israelite Laws shows a stylistic resemblance with the common law practised in the ancient Near East. Different juridical styles are found intermingled through the Pentateuch. a) *Casuistic laws*, commencing with the word "if," are found in Ex. 21-22 (the Covenant Code) and Deuteronomy. The stereotyped "if" juridical formula is found in the Code of Hammurabi (c. 1690 B.C.), whose work as a great Babylonian lawgiver had a great influence, both directly and indirectly, upon subsequent generations of people and other racial groups throughout the Near East. b) A combination of *casuistic* and *jussive* styles (i.e., "if" and "thou," or "you") is often found in the Book of Deuteronomy and elsewhere. c) *Absolute, categorical* or *apodictic* formulas are found throughout the entire Pentateuch (cf. the Decalogue in Ex. 20, 1-17 and Deut. 5, 6-21; Lev. 18, 6; 19, 15; Num. 28, 16; Deut. 23, 3). These and other styles show the various literary forms that could be used by the sacred writers to express the Hebrew Law of the Old Testament.

V. Didactic Literary Form.—The didactic literature of the Old Testament (comprising the Books of Job, Psalms, Proverbs, Ecclesiastes, Canticle of Canticles, Wisdom and Sirach) is intended to instruct or edify. This literary form in general offers no particular difficulties. It has at times historical elements or backgrounds with a poetical presentation.

The *Book of Job* may be pointed out as possessing the combination of three literary forms, that is, the didactic, poetical and historical, but it is from the standpoint of its historical literary form that it is called at times *edifying history*.

Perhaps no other didactic book has been so thoroughly studied and analyzed as the *Psalter*. This may be due to the fact that the Psalms are being used to this day and accommodated or applied to various circumstances of modern living by Jews, Protestants and Catholics. Some scholars believe that *cultic categories* (as their usage in the temple or syna-

---

[33] Cf. section "Collections of Laws from Mesopotamia and Asia Minor," in * Pritchard's A.N.E.T., 159-198.

gogues) were to be the decisive factors in determining the literary forms of the Psalms. Other scholars strongly defend the *Sitz im Leben* theory (i.e., the setting in life or the actual, real-life situations or conditions), or the answer to man's problems and anxieties, and this answer becomes firmly anchored in the belief and spirit of the average man. It seems very likely that literary forms based upon cultic and historical needs are determining factors in the specific classification of some Psalms. As these Psalms now play an important role in Jewish and Christian prayers, so, too, they must have had a leading role in the Hebrew and Jewish liturgy. Many of the Psalms were also based upon ancient events of divine actions with individuals or nations in the history of the Israelites (e.g., Exodus, the Mosaic Law given on Mount Sinai, etc.) and these stories were recalled, relived, reinterpreted or accommodated to the spiritual needs of the people.[34]

In the Sapiential Books (Proverbs, Ecclesiastes, Canticle of Canticles, Wisdom and Sirach) religious wisdom (Heb., *chokhmah*) is constantly stressed. Within recent times *Gattungsforschung* (i.e., methodical type-analysis) has been extended from the Psalms to the wisdom literature (including Job). The single *mashal* (i.e., proverb, adage) is regarded as having developed into groups of *aphorisms* (i.e., from Greek, meaning pointed definitions or pithy sayings) or *apothegms* (i.e., from Greek meaning teresely applied and concretized aphorisms), *extended maxims* (i.e., from Latin, meaning a saying with the greatest authority, and commonly a short precept related to life and living) and *didactic poems* of still greater length which may result in a poem of such lengths as the Book of Job. This wisdom literature of the Old Testament is not isolated, but has its counterpart among such neighbors as the Edomites, Arabs, but especially the Egyptians.[35]

---

[34] Cf. * Gunkel, H., "Einleitung in die Psalmen" (Göttingen, 1933); Descamps, A., "Pour un classement litteraire des Psaumes," in Melanges . . . A. Robert (Paris, 1957), 187-196; Murphy, R., "A New Classification of Literary Forms in the Psalms," in C.B.Q., 21 (1959), 83-87.

[35] Cf. * Rowley, H. H., "The Old Testament and Modern Study" (reprint of 2nd impr., Oxford, 1956).

The commonly called didactic literature of the New Testament consists of the fourteen Pauline Epistles and the seven Catholic Epistles. a) Most of these Epistles follow the three-fold external form usual in ancient profane writings of the Græco-Roman world: first, a prologue which includes the name of the writer, the name of the person (individual or moral, as the Church), the greeting and, at times, a blessing, or *baruch* (missing in profane literature); secondly, the body of the letter; and thirdly, the conclusion. b) We may roughly distinguish between a letter and an epistle.[36] The *former* is something non-literary, a private communication between two persons, the substitute for a modern telephone conversation, but neither the contents nor the form are decisive factors in determining the characteristic nature of a letter. In the category of letters may be placed the Pauline writings (except Hebr.), 2 and 3 John. The *latter*, that is, the epistle, is a work of literature, a composition destined for the general public (i.e., Catholic) or a particular public (church). It assumes the form of a treatise or essay, and in this class may be placed the Epistles to the Hebrews, of James, Peter, Jude (1 John ?). This distinction between letter and epistle by *A. Deissmann, based upon texts of the Græco-Roman world, also offers for the New Testament didactic literature an *intermediate zone* in which some special contents of a private letter addressed to a particular individual or a small group of choice readers may be intended by the sacred writers to be the standard for a wider or the widest circle of readers; for instance, their answers to particular problems was to be applied to the entire church (e.g., the case of the Pauline privilege).[37]

VI. Poetic Literary Form.—This literary form, which appears occasionally in the historical books and almost exclusively in the didactic books, does not follow the same rules, norms and patterns of the literal interpretation as the historical narratives. The Hebrew poet, like the western bard,

---

[36] Cf. * Deissmann, A., "Light from the Ancient East" (London, 1910), 217-238.
[37] Cf. Robert A.—Tricot, A., "Guide to the Bible," vol. I, 327-330.

exercises a richly gifted, lively and creative imagination that often results in the usage of figurative, symbolic, expressive language given in various kinds of parallelisms or balanced thoughts and full of striking figures of effective speech (e.g., contrasts, comparisons, etc.), distinctive allusions (e.g., to divine attributes, natural objects), sound suggestions, etc. Thus, by employing decorative arrangements of his subject-matter and various external and internal stylistic devices, the inspired Old Testament poet produced a very proper, pleasing and popular expression of the Semitic thought-pattern.

Although the poetical books and passages of the Old Testament consist mainly of *lyric* and *didactic* poems, yet *epic* and *dramatic* characteristics are not completely lacking. Thus the Song of Debbora (Jdgs. 5, 1-31) is considered one of the earliest and finest examples of Hebrew epic poetry; Job may be regarded as a didactic poem planned in the form of a dramatic dialogue; Proverbs may be held to be didactic lyrics, and the Psalms as purely devotional lyrics or hymns; the Canticle of Canticles is viewed by many scholars to be a lyric with a dramatic form of dialogue; the Lamentations of Jeremias consists of five lyric poems, the first four of which are alphabetic acrostics written in *qinah* (elegiac) verse in which the second line is shorter than the first; Ecclesiasticus, or Sirach, is a didactic lyric; Ecclesiastes and Wisdom are reflective lyrics.[38]

VII. Prophetic Literary Form.—Some of the principal prophetic forms may be found in various, commonly employed, characteristic formulas or accepted methods of presentation of revealed truth. 1) In regard to the *outward form*, various formulas are used as stereotyped expressions. There are some to express the origin or the authenticity of the divine message: for instance, "Yahweh says" (lit., "the utterance" or "declaration of Yahweh" [ne'um yahweh], Isa. 14, 22; Ez. 13, 6 f; Os. 2, 15; Mal. 1, 2; cf. Apoc. 1, 8; etc.), "the word of

---

[38] Cf. Steinmueller, J. E.—Sullivan, K., art. "Hebrew Poetry," in "A Companion to the Old Testament" (New York, 1946), 276-300; *idem*, art. "Poetry," in C.B.E.O.T., 863-867.

Yahweh" came to . . . (*debhar yahweh*: Jer. 1, 4; Ez. 3, 16; Jon. 1, 1; Zach. 4, 8). There is also the formula with Messianic and eschatological implications (*be'acharith hayyomim*, i.e., "in the latter days," Gen. 49, 1; Isa. 2, 2; Jer. 23, 20; Ez. 38, 16; Os. 3, 5). 2) In regard to the *grammatical method* of presenting prophetical truths it is carefully to be noted that future events are often described in the present (also past [Vulg.]) tense because the prophets have a current, mental picture of what will happen after a long time. 3) In regard to the *message* itself we may expect a necessary bond between the future event and the actual moral condition of the prophet's audience or readers. *Per modum unius* he may describe together two or three future events (e.g., the advent of Cyrus, the return from the Babylonian Exile, the Messianic Age in Isa. 40 ff; the destruction of Jerusalem and the Second Coming of Christ in Matt. 24). In exhorting his audience or giving them a severe lecture, the prophet very often calls his earnest attention to the sad, unhealthy, unhappy *moral state* of his people, especially of their rulers, by the usage of imperative tenses (sg. or pl.) usually introduced by the verb *shem'a* (i.e., hear, listen, pay attention [to what I have to say]) or something similar (Isa. 32, 9 ff; Jer. 13, 15 f). This general formulary pattern occurs under various literary forms. a) It appears under a soul-probing formula of questions and answers (sometimes implied), like the modern Catholic catechism (Isa. 28, 23-29; Jer. 2, 4 ff; Ez. 18, 25 ff; Amos 3, 1 ff). b) It also occasionally appears under a conditional form, the "if formula," the outcome of which will be (depending upon the decision of the human will) a divine blessing or punishment (Jer. 22, 2 ff). c) It may be given under the guise of a judge pronouncing a medicinal sentence upon the criminal nation or some of its citizens (Isa. 1, 10 ff; Jer. 44, 24 ff; Os. 4, 1 ff; 5, 1 ff; Joel 1, 2 ff) or upon the enemies of the Chosen People (Isa. 51, 21-23; Jer. 28, 15 f).

VIII. Other Literary Forms.—One of the literary forms is

pseudepigraphy, that is, the use of a fictitious name, or a pen name (e.g., Solomon as the author of Proverbs or Ecclesiastes). This literary device offers no difficulty, if the first readers, from the contents of the book and other circumstances, know that the real author is using a pen name. Other literary forms are allegory, parable, proverb and symbolism.

Art. 2. The Authentic Interpretation

Exegesis is more than a mere philological, critical, and historical examination of the Biblical text. It is, in particular, an exploration into the Bible for its spiritual message; to find out what dogmatic and moral truths are contained therein. By reason of this fact we have various dogmatic principles of hermeneutics.

Commentators "should set forth in particular the theological doctrine in faith and morals of the individual books or texts, so that their exposition may not only aid the professors of theology in their explanations and proofs of the dogmas of faith, but may also be of assistance to priests in their presentation of Christian doctrine to the people, and, in fine, may help all the faithful to lead a life that is holy and worthy of a Christian" ("Divino afflante Spiritu," E.B., 551).

(a) THE CHURCH, THE AUTHENTIC INTERPRETER OF HOLY SCRIPTURE[39]

The authentic interpretation is that given by the infallible teaching authority of the Church, to whom the deposit of faith was entrusted so that she would guard, explain, and expound it to the faithful. For this reason the Council of Trent in its disciplinary Decree "Insuper" states: "No one . . . shall

---

[39] Cf. Lattey, C., "De Ecclesia et Scriptura," in V.D., 8 (1928), 119-126; Siegman, E. F., "The Use of Scripture in Textbooks of Dogmatic Theology," in C.B.Q., 11 (1949), 151-164; Burke, L. G., "Holy Scripture as a Locus Theologicus," in C.B.Q., 11 (1949), 351-359; Geiselmann, J. R., "Scripture and Tradition in Catholic Theology," in *Theol. Dig.,* 6 (1958), 73-78; Michl, J., "Dogmatischer Schriftbeweis and Exegese," in B.Z., 2 (1958), 1-14.

presume to interpret Sacred Scripture contrary to the sense which Holy Mother the Church held and holds, to whom it belongs to judge the true sense and interpretation of Holy Scripture" (E.B., 62). Although this law is proposed under the negative form, yet it contains a positive precept, because, if it is forbidden to explain the Bible contrary to the sense which the Church held and holds, it is immediately evident that the books must be interpreted according to the meaning proposed by the Catholic Church. The positive form of this regulation was given shortly after the Council of Trent by Pope Paul IV (1564) and was repeated by the Vatican Council (E.B., 78).

It may be legitimately asked *to what extent does the Church enjoy this prerogative of authentically interpreting the Holy Scriptures.* The Council of Trent and the Vatican Council answer in a general manner by stating: ". . . in things of faith and morals, belonging to the building up of Christian doctrine." In interpreting this sentence Catholic scholars differ. Some defend the rigid opinion by maintaining everything (i.e., every single passage, whether it relates to faith and morals or not) in the Bible is subject to the positive interpretation of the Church. Others defend the lax opinion by restricting the right of the Church strictly to matters of faith and morals. The more probable opinion is the *via media*, that which stands between them. The authority of the Church *per se* extends to dogmatic passages of the Bible, where it can positively, directly, and infallibly determine the sense that must be held by all. The other truths come under her jurisdiction only in so far as they are intimately connected with matters of faith and morals. In regard to those things which do not pertain to faith and morals in any way (e.g., the natural sciences), the right of the Church is only *indirect* and *negative*. Subjects, therefore, that are strictly scientific (e.g., mathematics, geology, geography, which have no connection with man's eternal salvation), but not necessarily outside of her interests, are outside of the jurisdiction of the Church. When, however, the profane sciences propose an opinion that is contrary to a teaching of the Church, she can reject that explanation, and indirectly and negatively explain the sense of Holy Scripture.

From these considerations it follows that the Catholic scholar must follow the authentic interpretation which the Church proposes for any Biblical book or passage. Aside from this special guidance he is at liberty and is positively encouraged to pursue his field of research. "The Church by no means prevents or restrains the pursuit of Biblical science, but rather protects it from error, and largely assists its real progress. A wide field is still left open to the private student . . ." ("Providentissimus Deus," E. B., 109). "Quite wrongly, therefore, do some pretend that nothing remains to be added by the Catholic exegete of our time to what Christian antiquity has produced" ("Divino afflante Spiritu", E.B., 555).

(b) The Sources of Authentic Interpretation

There are various sources from which we may gather that the mind of the Church has given or wishes to give us her authentic interpretation or wishes us to regard it as having been handed down to us.

(1) *The Decisions of the Teaching Authority of the Church.* —The real, important, Catholic source for the genuine interpretation of the Bible is not the individual interpreter, but the magisterium (i.e., the teaching authority) of Christ's Church. This authority teaches *directly* or *indirectly* at all times and everywhere the same doctrinal and moral message based upon the spiritual contents of the Bible and, in some rare instances, has defined the precise meaning of some Biblical passages.

Historically speaking, the Church has very rarely exercised her right to *propose directly* (through a positive or negative formula) to her members what they must *de fide* believe to be the genuine meaning intended by the sacred writer. Thus, the Council of Trent *positively* declared John 3, 5 to mean the Sacrament of Baptism, John 20, 22 f to signify the Sacrament of Penance, and James 5, 14 f to refer to the Sacrament of Extreme Unction. Similarly, the Vatican Council authentically interpreted Matt. 16, 16-19 and John 21, 15-17 to mean the promise and institution of the primacy of Peter or the Holy Father. There are instances in which the Church *negatively* explains her position by declaring what is false. Thus, for instance, she condemned J. L. Isenbiehl's book (1774) in which the author maintained Isa. 7, 14 to be a mere allusion to the Emmanuel prophecy and not a literal or typical reference to Christ's virginal birth (E.B., 74).

The Church more frequently uses an *indirect* method of explaining the meaning of a Biblical passage. Thus, for example, the Council of Trent quotes Rom. 5, 12 to strengthen the belief in original sin, and the Vatican Council cites Luke 22, 32 to confirm the truth about the infallibility of the Pope. Although both texts are merely cited as proofs and not as infallible interpretations of the Biblical sense, yet it seems very likely that both Councils intended to give us the authentic meaning of these passages.

In various decrees of the Councils or in papal encyclicals [40]

[40] The following papal encyclicals were issued containing important Biblical teachings: (1) "Providentissimus Deus" (see appendix for text). Cf. Collins, J. J., "Providentissimus Deus," in H.P.R., 44 (1943), 112, 117; Cotter, A. C., "The Antecedents of the Encyclical Providentissimus Deus," in C.B.Q., 5 (1943), 117-124; Murphy, R .T., "The Teachings of the Encyclical Providentissimus Deus," *ibid.*, 125-140; Hartegen, S., "The Influence of the Encyclical Providentissmus Deus," *ibid.*, 141-159. (2) "Pascendi Domini Gregis" (Feeding the Flock of Christ) by St. Pius X on Sept. 8, 1907 (E.B., 257-282). This encyclical condemned the false doctrines of Modernists. Cf. Bea, A., "L'enciclica Pascendi e gli studi biblici," in *Biblica,* 39 (1958), 121-138. (3) "Spiritus Paraclitus" (see appendix for text). (4) "Divino affante Spiritu" (see appendix for text). Cf. Bea., A., "Divino affante Spiritu. De recentissimis Pii PP.XII litteris encyclicis," in *Biblica,* 24 (1943), 313-322; Ahern, B., "Textual Directives of the Encyclical Divino affante Spiritu," in C.B.Q., 7 (1945), 340-347. (5) "Humani Generis" (The Human Race) by Pius XII on August 12, 1950 (E.B., 611-620). It points out some false opinions threatening to undermine Catholic doctrine and discusses in particular such problems as evolution, polygenism and the free interpretation of the historical books of the Old Testament. Cf. Vollert, C., "Humani Generis and the Limits of Theology," in *Theol. St.,* 12 (1951), 3-23; Weigel, G., "Gleanings from the Commentaries on Humani Generis," in *Theol. St.,* 129 (1951), 520-549; De Fraine, J., "Humani Generis and Sacred Scripture," in *Theol. Dig.,* 11 (1954), 155-158.

there are numerous Biblical citations which are applied to *illustrate* (i.e., by a complementary or concrete clarification) a doctrinal teaching and *not to prove it*. In these cases the last word has not been given and the interpretation must not be regarded as infallibly defined (e.g., the encyclical of Pope Pius IX on Dec. 8, 1854 concerning the text of Gen. 3, 15: "She shall crush thy head and thou shalt lie in wait for her heel").

Less solemnly than through her councils, the Church through her *extraordinary magisterium* (i.e., various Sacred Congregations and her Pontifical Biblical Commission) may declare by decrees or decisions the meaning of the Bible.

In this century the *Pontifical Biblical Commission* has played an important role in the history of the Catholic Bible. It was instituted on Oct. 30, 1902 by Leo XIII to promote and direct Biblical studies (E. B., 137-148). About five years later (Nov. 18, 1907) St. Pius X in his *Motu Proprio* determined the authority of its decisions (E.B., 283-288). From these it follows: (1) that its decrees are neither infallible nor unchangeable; (2) that they enjoy the same authority as the other Sacred Congregations; (3) that external as well as internal consent is required; (4) that this assent need not be absolute and irreformable; (5) that the formal object of these decrees is the security or non-security of any doctrine, that is, it does not stress so much the truth or falseness of a Biblical interpretation as it safeguards a revealed doctrine by declaring such and such an interpretation is unproven, untimely, and tends to weaken the teaching of the Church.[41]

The *Enchiridion Biblicum*, containing some important ecclesiastical documents which relate to Biblical interpretation, was first published under the authority of the Pontifical Biblical Commission in 1927. The second edition (1954) brought these documents up to date.[42]

[41] Cf. Stanley, Ahern, Murphy, "The Interpretation of the Pontifical Decrees," in C.B.Q., 17 (1955), 50-53.

[42] On the occasion of the second edition of the *Enchiridion Biblicum* there appeared two articles, one by A. Miller, Secretary of the Commission, in *Benediktinische Monatschrift,* 31 (1955), 49 f, and the other by

Whenever the Church has not authentically defined the meaning and interpretation of Biblical books and passages, the scholar should follow the *traditional explanation of the ordinary teaching office* in regard to faith and morals.

(2) *The Authority of the Fathers.*[43]—The Council of Trent states: ". . . it is not lawful for the exegete to interpret contrary to the unanimous consent of the Fathers," that is, the interpretation which the Fathers by unanimous consent either received or rejected must be received or rejected. This interpretation must be restricted to the spiritual message of the Bible, that is, its doctrinal and moral meaning, because, in regard to the natural sciences, philology (to a large extent) and profane history, they also remained children of their times. The Patristic period is usually considered from the time of St. Clement of Rome at the end of the first century to St. Bernard of Clairvaux in the twelfth century.

In regard to this unanimity various factors must be taken into consideration. (1) Mathematical uniformity is not required, but moral unanimity suffices. Hence, if a great number of Fathers, the others being silent, agree in the explanation of a Biblical passage, there is true harmony (e.g., Mal. 1, 10 ff concerning the Eucharist; Isa. 7, 14 ff concerning the virgin birth of Christ). This agreement is also had when a few Fathers of different churches and possessing great authority within their respective communities have a similar explanation of any text, while the others do not contradict their meaning. It is also had when relatively few Fathers of great

---

A. Kleinhans, Under-secretary of the Commission, in *Antonianum*, 30 (1955), 63 f. In these two discussions the authors maintain the continued validity of the decrees, but suggest that secondary elements proposed in them, which are of a purely scientific nature and have no relationship, either direct or indirect, with the truths of faith or morals, are left to the commentator who may pursue with perfect freedom the scientific research on the subject "salva semper auctoritate magisterii Ecclesiae." From these two discussions a few scholars falsely concluded that the decissions have been tacitly revoked and are now only of historical interest. Cf. Dupont, J., "A propos du nouvel Enchiridion Biblicum," in R.B., 62 (1955), 414-419; Siegman, E. F., "The Decrees of the Pontifical Biblical Commission," in C.B.Q., 18 (1956), 23-29.

[43] Cf. Sutcliffe, E. F., "De arte heuristica in re patristica," in V.D., 5 (1925), 314-318.

authority explain the sense of the Bible in times of serious religious crises, when the doctrines of the Church are being attacked (e.g., 1 Cor. 4, 7 is explained by St. Augustine, St. Jerome, etc., against the Pelagians to mean the gratuity of the divine election and of supernatural gifts). (2) Occasionally the Fathers agree in repudiating a meaning that may have been given to a Biblical passage, but then disagree as to its true meaning. In this case it is not lawful to retain the sense rejected by them, but we may seek another explanation (e.g., in Phil. 2, 5-8 all Fathers agree that the text refers to the pre-existing Christ, but differ in their explanation of the various words). (3) When there is no agreement among the Fathers on some question of faith or morals, their opinion has not the weight of very great authority; yet, it should not be spurned. (4) In matters not relating to faith and morals, the Catholic interpreter enjoys perfect freedom to arrive at his own conclusions, provided these are not against the meaning that is commonly and traditionally held by the Church. (5) Those books should be consulted in which the Fathers, as the standard bearers and staunch defenders of an unwavering faith, officially comment upon the Bible, and likewise those books in dogmatic theology in which their works are cited, analyzed, explained and defended.

(3) *The Analogy of Faith.*[44]—In an analogy there is implied a related likeness between various objects. By analogy of faith is meant the harmony or agreement which exists between all the truths of revealed religion. In those passages where there is neither an authentic interpretation of the Church nor the unanimous consent of the Fathers the analogy of faith should be followed.

The analogy of faith is sometimes applied negatively. If an interpretation suggested by any exegete is opposed to the doctrine of the Church, it is to be rejected as false. "In the other passages the analogy of faith should be followed, and Catholic doctrine, as authoritatively proposed by the Church,

[44] Cf. Rom. 12, 6.

should be held as the supreme law; for, seeing that the same God is the Author both of the sacred books and of the doctrine committed to the Church, it is clearly impossible that any teaching can, by legitimate means, be extracted from the former, which shall in any respect be at variance with the latter. Hence, it follows that all interpretation is foolish and false which either makes the sacred writers disagree one with another, or is opposed to the doctrine of the Church" ("Providentissimus Deus," in E.B., 109). We know from the analogy of faith that the text: "And the Word was made flesh" (John 1, 14) means that the Word assumed human nature, that the washing of the feet of the Apostles (John 13, 9 ff) was not a sacrament, that the phrase "brethren of the Lord," often used in the New Testament, does not refer to Christ's actual brothers, but to cousins or other relatives.

A meaning, therefore, that is contrary to the analogy of faith is false. Similarly, that meaning which alone is in accordance with the analogy of faith must be considered as true. If, however, many interpretations can correspond with this analogy of faith, then the true sense must be sought from the context, parallel passages, etc.[45]

[45] Cf. Höpfl, H. *op. cit.*, 198 f; also Lattey, C., "De regula fidei," in V.D., 7 (1927), 210-217.

Chapter III

PROPHORISTICS:
THE EXPLANATION OF THE TEXT OF
SCRIPTURE

Prophoristics treats of the manner in which the Bible can be explained to others, and this explanation or exposition of the text is exegesis or applied hermeneutics.

Incomplete explanations of the Bible may be found in various vernacular versions, paraphrases, glosses, scholia, postillæ and catenæ. Complete and scientific explanations of the Bible are contained in commentaries.

(a) Incomplete Explanations of the Bible

(1) Vernacular Versions.[1]—These versions are translations of the Bible into the modern spoken languages, and do not include the ancient versions employed by the Oriental churches.

A version into any modern language should be faithful and clear. It should be *faithful;* that is, the translator must render the original text as accurately as possible, neither adding nor subtracting anything. He must also try to imitate the style of the original, retain the figurative and poetic language, and never take away or obscure the dogmatical and moral truths contained in the text. It is not necessary, however, to give a servile rendition of the original text, but the interpreter should try to render faithfully the text and aim at elegance without violating the rules of grammar. A version should be *clear;* that is, the translator must render the text in such a manner that it is easily understood by the reader. It is necessary, therefore, that the interpreter be fully equipped with the

---

[1] Cf. * Goodspeed, E. J., "Problems of New Testament Translation" (Chicago, 1945); Arbez, E. P., "Translating the O.T. out of the Original Languages," in C.B.Q., 7 (1945), 48-75.

knowledge of Biblical philology, theology, philosophy, history, archæology, etc.

(*2*) *Paraphrases.*—A paraphrase (from the Greek *para-phrasis*, i.e., circumscription) is a restatement of the meaning of the original text, but in clearer words and in greater detail than is found in the original. It clarifies vague and ambiguous words, which are only implicitly contained in the sacred writer's book. A good paraphrase should be faithful; that is, it must not change the true meaning of the sacred writer, and should not be too lengthy or verbose.

Examples of these paraphrases are found in the Aramaic Targums of the Old Testament (as the Targum Onkelos of the Pentateuch, Targum Jonathan of the Earlier Prophets, etc.), in Ecclesiastes by St. Gregory Thaumaturgus (d. 270), and in the New Testament by Desiderius Erasmus (d. 1536) and Bernardinus a Piconio (d. 1709).

(*3*) *Glosses.*—The gloss is the explanation of an obscure, rare, or foreign word in the text. At present the term is applied to those words or explanations which crept into the biblical text.

These glosses, properly so-called, are either marginal (as in the case of Walafrid Strabo, who died in 849) or interlinear (as in the books of Anselm of Laon, who died in 1117). Worthy of note are also the glosses by St. Bede (d. 735), Alcuin (d. 804), and Rhabanus Maurus (d. 856).

These glosses were collected in alphabetical order in the so-called *glossaries*, which became the basis of our modern dictionaries. The most important are those of Hesychius (c. 380), Photius (d. 891), the "Etymologicum magnum" (of the eleventh or twelfth century) in Greek, and that of St. Isidore of Seville in Latin.

(*4*) *Scholia.*—Scholia are short explanations of not single words but of obscure passages. They differ from the glosses, which single out for explanation only particular words, and from commentaries by their brevity and conciseness. Origen is perhaps the first author to have written scholia, having composed these to the Proverbs of Solomon.

(5) Postillæ.—The postillæ (i.e., from *post* = after and *illæ* = those things) are short explanations placed after the text. They are brief, running commentaries to the text. The most outstanding of these is that of Nicholas of Lyra (d. 1340) on the books of the Old and New Testaments.

(6) Catenæ.—The name is derived from the "Catena Aurea" of St. Thomas Aquinas. They are Patristic scholia combined into collective commentaries so as to form a *chain.* The most famous of all the catenæ is that of St. Thomas (d. 1274). Worthy of mention are also the catenæ of Procopius of Gaza (c. 528), the first writer of catenæ on a large scale, Andrew (c. 520), Nicetas (eleventh century) and Œcumenius (eleventh century).

(b) Complete and Scientific Explanations of the Bible

A complete and scientific explanation of the Bible is to be had in a commentary, which is a solid, systematic, and continuous explanation of any book or of the entire Bible. A commentary is distinguished from an exegetical dissertation or monograph, which exhaustively treats of a particular text or doctrine. The arrangement of a commentary on the Bible should be as follows: (1) the commentary should be preceded by a special introduction to the book, treating of the author, the time of writing, the occasion, the purpose, the contents, the sources of the book, the readers, the historical conditions, and the textual condition of the book; (2) for the sake of clearness, the text to be explained should be divided into larger and smaller sections, with an analysis of the subject-matter as a preface to each section; (3) the commentary may be arranged in a twofold manner: one method is to give a section of the text and then its explanation, as in the "Cursus Sacræ Scripturæ," or Fonck's "Parables and Miracles"; the second method is to place the text on the upper part of the page and the commentary on the lower part of the page, as in the "Etudes Bibliques," the "Bonner Bibel," and Grimmelsman's "Book of Ruth," * "The Interpreter's Bible"; (4) in this commentary proper, the Catholic commentator must have due regard for textual criticism; that is, he must try to reproduce as far as possible the original text, where variant readings occur. He must also avail himself of all the resources of scholarship in the domains of philology, history, theology, etc., for the purpose of elucidating obscure passages. He should not avoid true difficulties, but must try to explain the difficult passages as far as he is able and refute the chief explanations put forward by others with whom he does not agree.

At times a one-volume commentary follows the same procedure as above, but omits the text (e.g., *A Catholic Commentary on Holy Scripture,* * J. R. Dummelow, * C. Gore, etc., to the entire Bible; *A Catholic Commentary on the New Testament* [Confraternity]).

Appendix

(a) *The Bible and Liturgy.*—The temple, synagogue and Church always made use of the Bible in its liturgy. The liturgy of the Church largely draws its text from the books of the Sacred Scriptures. Many elements of our public and official cult are of Biblical origin and may be found to prevail predominantly in the texts of the Mass, Canonical Hours and of the administration of the sacraments.[1] The application of the Biblical passages was made in various senses (see Chapter I).[2]

Some scholars follow the leadership of * Hermann Gunkel[3] whose *Gattungen* (different types) of Psalms were based upon the conclusions of the *religionsgeschichtliche Schule* (i.e., re-

---

[1] Cf. Lallou, W. J., "The Bible and Liturgy," in C.B.Q., 4 (1942), 210-217; *Worship* (Collegeville, Minn., 1926-).

[2] For the usage and explanation of Biblical texts in the liturgy of the Church by A. G. Fonseca, A. G. H. Liese, U. Holzmeister, C. Rösch, etc., see V.D., 5 ff (1925 ff); cf. also Ruwet, J., "Lecture liturgique et livres saints du N.T.," in *Biblica,* 21 (1940), 378-405; Hennig, J., "The First Chapter of Genesis in the Liturgy," in C.B.Q., 10 (1948), 360-375; Barrosse, T., "The Senses of Scripture and the Liturgical Pericopes," in C.B.Q., 21 (1959), 1-23.

[3] * Gunkel, H., "Die Psalmen" (Göttingen, 1926). Cf. McKenzie, J. L., "The Two-Edged Sword," 267 ff.

ligious, historical school, so called from the comparative study of religion or history of religion), but were claimed to have originated to meet the needs of a *Sitz im Leben* (i.e., a life or historical situation). On the other hand, * S. Mowinckel [4] returned to the philological method and maintained that nearly all the Psalms were *cult poems* and *cultic* in origin and, as ritual poems, served primarily as a song-book of the temple. Among recent studies of Catholics there are to be found discussions concerning not only literary forms, but also the *cultic Sitz im Leben* needs of the primitive Christian Church being fulfilled by some New Testament writings.[5]

(b) *The Bible and Preaching.*[6]—Popes, especially those in recent times, have stressed the importance of the Bible being used as the principal source of preaching by the priest. Leo XIII refers to this thought in the "Providentissimus Deus": "It is this peculiar and singular power of Holy Scripture, arising from the inspiration of the Holy Spirit, which gives authority to the sacred orator, fills him with Apostolic liberty of speech and communicates force and power to his eloquence" (E.B., 87). Benedict XV in his "Spiritus Paraclitus," written on the occasion of the fifteenth centenary of St. Jerome's death, reminds us that if Bible students and preachers diligently studied their Bible "they would, too, derive abundant help from the infinite treasury of facts and ideas in the Bible, and would thence be able to mould firmly but gently the lives and characters of the faithful" (E.B., 486). Within recent times Pius XII in the "Divino afflante Spiritu" points out most clearly the duty of the priest to preach the Bible or the gospel of Jesus Christ: "Let priests . . . after they have themselves by diligent study perused the sacred pages and

[4] * Mowinckel, S., "Psalmenstudien" II. III (Christiania, 1922. 1923).

[5] Cf. Stanley, D. M., "Liturgical Influences in the Formation of the Four Gospels," in C.B.Q., 21 (1959), 24-38; Orlett, R., "An Influence of Early Liturgy upon the Emmaus Account," *ibid.*, 21 (1959), 212-219.

[6] Cf. Da Fonseca, L. G., "Praedicatio et Sacra Scriptura," in V.D., 7 (1927), 193-196; Vargha, T., "S. Scripturae est fons principalis praedicationis," in V.D., 15 (1935), 22-25; Renehan, J. F., "How to Present Catholic Views on the Bible to Non-Catholics," in C.B.Q., 9 (1947) 199-205.

made them their own by prayer and meditations, assiduously distribute the heavenly treasures of the divine word by sermons, homilies and exhortations; let them confirm the Christian doctrine by sentences from the Sacred Books and illustrate it by outstanding examples from sacred history and in particular from the Gospel of Christ Our Lord . . . let them set forth all this with such eloquence, lucidity and clearness that the faithful may not only be moved and inflamed to reform their lives, but may also conceive in their hearts the greatest veneration for the Sacred Scripture" (E.B., 566).

(c) *Reading the Bible.*[7]—The Holy See has always permitted the faithful to read *approved versions* or translations of the Bible, and this attitude was followed generally by the hierarchy, or bishops of the Church. To encourage Catholics throughout the world to read the Bible, the Church at various times has even granted her members spiritual blessings, such as various indulgences. The Popes not only encouraged the faithful to read the Bible, but also urged them to form Biblical associations, as the St. Jerome Society and others, to distribute to the ordinary faithful and to the poor copies of the Bible, but especially the New Testament or the Gospels and Psalms. We may say to the credit of the Diocese of Brooklyn, New York, that the Confraternity of the Precious Blood, under its able director, Msgr. Joseph Frey, has fulfilled this papal directive in the most perfect and laudatory manner.

In recent times Pius XII urged the hierarchy of the world to bring their faithful closer not only to the Bible, but also to its inspired, spiritual, vivifying message: "The same venera-

[7] Cf. Rosman, H., "Tolle, lege," in V.D., 20 (1940), 33-43, 116-123, 151-155; Schumacher, M., "Tolle, lege," in C.B.Q., 6 (1954), 53-60; Smith, E., "The New Testament in Our Colleges," in C.B.Q., 4 (1942), 37-44; Monro, M. T., "Enjoying the New Testament" (London, 1945); * Love, J. P., "How to Read the Bible" (New York, 1945); Smith, I., "Sacred Scripture and Catholic Living," in C.B.Q., 9 (1947), 59-64; Zerwick, M., "Quomodo oporteat nos legere Sacram Scripturam," in V.D., 25 (1947) 3-11; Nober, P., "Lectio Vere Divina," in V.D., 31 (1953), 193-208; Pagano, S., "Public Bible Readings," in C.B.Q., 16 (1954), 20-32; Avery, B. R., "Daily Bible Reading with the Church," in *Scripture*, 7 (1955), 77-83, 119-128; Charlier, C., "The Christian Approach to the Bible" (Westminster, Md., 1958); Sullivan, K., "God's Word and Work" (Collegeville, Minn., 1958); Daniélou, J., "Living the Faith," in *Theol. Dig.*, 7 (1959), 41-46.

tion (which priests in their preaching should try to inculcate in the hearts of the faithful) the Bishops should endeavor daily to increase and perfect among the faithful committed to their care, encouraging all those initiatives by which men, filled with apostolic zeal, laudably strive to excite and foster among Catholics a greater knowledge of and love for the Sacred Books. Let them favor, therefore, and lend help to those pious associations whose aim it is to spread copies of the Sacred Letters, especially of the Gospels, among the faithful, and to procure by every means that in Christian families the same be read daily with piety and devotion; let them efficaciously recommend by word and example, whenever the liturgical laws permit, the Sacred Scriptures translated, with the approval of the ecclesiastical authority, into modern languages; let them themselves give public conferences or dissertations on Biblical subjects, or see that they are given by other public orators well versed in the matter" ("Divino afflante Spiritu," E.B., 566).

(d) *The Bible and Its Various Effects.*[8]—There are many results that are ascribed (i.e., with the aid of divine grace), either directly or indirectly, to the Bible as its rich spiritual fruitage: for instance, a deeper spiritual life of a Christian soul; a clearly defined division in history, as the Old and New Testaments or the calculation of time as B.C. or A.D., as the important effect of one sole incident (i.e., the salvific death of Jesus Christ on the cross of Calvary) with future and eternal implications; the cultural division and progress of the world based upon the preaching of the gospel message and its effectiveness (e.g., western and eastern cultures); the important role of every individual person as a free being in the affairs of his government, etc.

---

[8] Cf. Closen, G. E., "De Sacra Scriptura et vita orationis Christian-orum," in V.D., 23 (1942), 103-116; Rost, H., "The Cultural Influence of the Bible," in C.B.Q., 11 (1949), 120-132; * Herberg, W., "Biblical Basis of American Democracy," in *Theol. Dig.*, 4 (1956), 28-30.

PART V

THE HISTORY OF EXEGESIS

Bibliography: Bardy, G., "La litterature patristique des 'Quæstiones et responsiones' sur l'Ecriture Sainte," in R.B., XLI (1932), 210-236, 341-369, 515-537, XLII (1933), 14-30, 211-229; Devreesse, R., "Anciens commentaires grecs de l'Octateuque," in R.B., 44 (1935), 166-191, 45 (1936), 201-220, 364-384; Höpfl, H., "Tractatus de Inspiratione, etc.," 222-279; Vaccari, A., in I.B., 467-522; *idem,* "Esegesi antica ed esegesi nuova," in *Biblica,* 6 (1925), 249-274; * Goodspeed, E. J., "A History of Early Christian Literature" (Chicago, 1942); * Grant, R. M., "The Bible in the Church. A Short History of Interpretation" (New York, 1948); Spicq, L., Robert, A., Vaganay, L., "Interpretation," in D.D.L.B. Suppl. 4 (1949), 561-646.

In the preceding part we have seen the basic principles underlying Hermeneutics. It remains to be seen how these principles have been applied in the history of biblical interpretation.

Chapter I

THE ANCIENT PERIOD
(From the first to the tenth century A.D.)

Art. 1. The Interpretation of the Jews

(a) THE HELLENIC JEWS

The Hellenistic Jews of Alexandria borrowed the allegorical system of interpretation from pagan writers, who toned down the fables of the various gods and goddesses by trying to discover a deeper meaning in the writings of Homer (thus, e.g., * Cornutus, * Heraclitus, * Cicero, etc.).

The Jews of Alexandria tried to reconcile the revealed doctrine of the Old Testament with Greek philosophy. In the pre-Christian period both * Aristeas, in his letter to Philocrates, and * Aristobulus (c. 175-150 B.C.) made use of the allegorical interpretation. The outstanding Jew of this Alexandrian school was * Philo.[1]

The exegetical works of Philo may be divided into three parts. (1) In his book, *Sacrarum legum allegoria*, he indulges in the allegorical system. Thus, for example, he explains Adam to mean spirit, Eve to mean sensation, the serpent to be a symbol of sensuality, the brazen serpent to be a symbol of temperance, etc. (2) In his books, *De opificio mundi, Vitæ Patriarcharum, De Decalogo, De specialibus legibus,* the literal explanation predominates. (3) In his book, *Quæstiones et solutiones,* which is a catechetical explanation of the Pentateuch, he employs a mixture of literal and allegorical explanations. Philo states that there are three kinds of Jewish interpreters. The first class rejects the allegorical interpretation, and this class he despises. He condemns the second class of interpreters who explain everything allegorically, but

---

[1] Cf. * Bentwich, N., "Philo-Judæus of Alexandria" (Philadelphia, 1940).

agrees with a third class who combine the literal with the allegorical interpretation.

The Jews of Alexandria employed this method of interpretation with an apologetical purpose. They wished to make various passages and ordinances of the Old Testament appear as worthy of God—for example, anthropomorphisms, many rites of ablution, Sabbatical laws, regulations about food, etc. Being superior to the Gentiles in doctrinal and moral truths, they also sought to surpass them in culture and philosophy.

(b) The Palestinian Jews

To understand the customs and mentality of the Jews living at the time of Christ, it is necessary to study the *Talmud* (which, with the *Targums,* is the oldest form of exegesis of the non-Hellenistic Jews) and the *Midrashim.*

The Palestinian Jews were, above all, casuists. For this reason casuistry predominates in the Talmud and various rules of interpretation were made (e.g., the seven rules of Hillel), in which the literal sense mostly prevails.[2] The Midrashim are exegetical commentaries on the various books of the Old Testament, and in these the literal meaning does not always predominate.

The object and scope of Jewish interpretation are twofold: halachic and haggadic. The *halaka* explains the Law, sets the norm of life, tells "quid agendum est"; the *haggada* is something speculative, explains the history of the people, and tells "quid credendum est." In the Talmud the halaka predominates, whereas in the Midrashim the halaka prevails in the Mechilta to Exodus, Siphra to Leviticus, Siphre to Num-

---

[2] Cf. Vaccari, A., in I.B., 478 f; also * Schürer, E., "Geschichte des jüdischen Volkes" I (5 ed., Leipzig, 1920), 111-161; * Strack, H., "Einleitung in Talmud u. Midrasch" (Munich, 1921); Bonsirven, J., "Le Judaisme palestinien au temp de Jésus-Christ. Sa Théologie" (Paris, 1935); *idem,* "Exégèse rabbinique, exégèse paulienne" (Paris, 1939); *idem,* "Exégèse juive," in D.D.L.B. Suppl. 4 (1949), 562-569; *idem,* "Interpretatio Agadica (Heinemann)", in V.D., 30 (1952), 349-352; * Moore, G. F., "Judaism" vol. I, II (4th impr., 1944, Cambridge, Mass); vol. III (2nd pr., 1930 *ibid.*).

bers and Deuteronomy, but the haggada predominates in the other books such as the Midrash Rabboth to the Pentateuch and the five Megilloth, Tanchuma or Jelamdenu to the Pentateuch, Pesikta to the biblical readings, Pirke de Rabbi Elieser or Baraita de Rabbi Elieser to Bible History, and Jalkut Shimoni to various passages of Scripture.

Art. 2. The Apostolic Fathers and Apologists

Bibliography: *Lake, K., "The Apostolic Fathers" (2 vols., London-New York, 1912-1913); Kleist, J. A., "The Epistles of St. Clement of Rome and St. Ignatius of Antioch" (Westminster, Maryland, 1946); Glimm, F. X., Matique, J. M., Walsh, G. G., "The Apostolic Fathers" (New York, 1947).

For St. Clement of Rome: cf. Boismard, R. P. M., in R.B., 55 (1948), 376-387; *Young, F. W., in J.B.L., 67 (1948), 339-346.

For St. Ignatius of Antioch: cf. Fonck, L., in *Biblica*, 2 (1921) 342-347; Burghardt, W. J., in *Theol. St.*, 1 (1940), 1-26, 130-156; Hochbau, J. T., in *Theol. St.*, 7 (1946), 525-557.

For the Didache: cf. Stanley, D. M., in C.B.Q., 17 (1955), 216-228; Audet, J.-P., "La Didaché. Instructions des Apôtres" (Paris, 1958); Bligh, J., in V.D., 36 (1958), 350-356.

For the Letter of Barnabas: cf. Cadbury, H. J., in J.Q.R., 26 (1936), 403-407; Holzmeister, U., in V.D., 21 (1941), 69-73.

For the Shepherd of Hermas: cf. Bardy, G., in R.B., 8 (1911), 391-407; Mercati, S. G., in *Biblica*, 6 (1925), 336-338.

For Papias: cf. Lgf., in V.D., 3 (1934), 93 f; Vaccari, A., in *Biblica*, 20 (1939), 413 f; Gry, L., in *Vivre et Penser*, 3 (1945), 112-124.

For St. Theophilus of Antioch: cf. Richard, M., in R.B., 47 (1938), 387-397; *Grant, R. M., in J.B.L., 66 (1947), 173-196.

For St. Irenæus: cf. Smith, J., in *Biblica*, 38 (1957), 24-34.

The first traces of biblical interpretation are found in the Apostolic Fathers and apologists of the second century, who wrote no exegetical commentaries, but often quote from or allude to the Bible to show that the Messianic prophecies were fulfilled in Christ (e.g., St. Justin Martyr), or to refute heretics (e.g., St. Irenæus), or to increase the religious devotion of the faithful (e.g., St. Clement of Rome, St. Ignatius of Antioch, St. Polycarp). As a rule, these writers explained the Bible in the literal sense, but they also made use of the typical and allegorical meanings.

Amongst the Apostolic Fathers and apologists, Pseudo-Barnabas made use of types and gematria, that is, a method of interpreting the Scriptures based upon the numerical value of the letters in the words (cf. IX. 9). St. Clement of Rome (I Cor., XII, 7, 8) allegorically interpreted the scarlet cord which Rahab hung from her window to save herself and her family from destruction (Jos. 2, 21), to mean the redemption through the blood of Christ. St. Justin Martyr frequently used the typical sense in his writings; thus, the twelve bells worn by the high priest on his vestments were signs of the twelve Apostles; the manner of roasting the passover lamb was taken to be a sign or symbol of the Cross, etc. St. Theophilus of Antioch frequently indulged in allegorical explanations of the Bible, and apparently St. Irenæus at times had recourse to allegorism.

Art. 3.   The School of Alexandria

Bibliography: Bardy, G., "Pour l'histoire de l'école d'Alexandrie," in *Vivre et Penser,* 2 (1942), 80-109.

For Clement of Alexandria: cf. Camelot, T., in R.B., 53 (1946), 242-248; Ruwet, J., in *Biblica,* 29 (1948), 77-99, 240-268, 391-408.

For Origen: cf. Bardy, G., in R.B., 16 (1919), 106-135, 34 (1925), 217-252; Ruwet, J., in *Biblica,* 23 (1942), 18-42, 24 (1943), 18-58, 25 (1944), 143-166, 311-334.

For Eusebius of Caesarea: cf. *Murphy, H. S., in J.B.L., 73 (1954), 162-168; Penna, A., in *Biblica,* 36 (1955), 1-19.

For Cyril of Alexandria: cf. Reuss, J., in *Biblica,* 25 (1944), 207-209.

The school of Alexandria was the first Christian school to be founded. It was established at first as a catechetical school for the instruction of neophytes, but later it embraced all the branches of Christian knowledge. Hence, it can be rightly called the first Christian theological school or seminary.

Pantænus is commonly considered the founder of this school. Towards the end of the second century (c. 180) he taught there. He had been born in Sicily and was converted from the Stoic philosophy to Christianity (cf. Eusebius, *Hist. Eccl.,* V, 10). Clement of Alexandria (150—215) succeeded his master, and professed that there were three senses in the Bible: the literal, the moral, and the prophetical or allegorical. He further asserted that all the Scriptures were to be interpreted allegorically (cf. Eusebius, *Hist. Eccl.*, V, 11). This manner of interpretation he developed and explained in the entire fifth book of *Stromata,* which showed that he was practically enslaved to Philos's allegorical method.

The greatest master and chief pride of the school of Alexandria was Origen (186—254/255), the pupil of Clement. Because of his immense patience and energy he is frequently called "the man of iron" (*Adamantius*). His *Hexapla* and *Tetrapla* made him the father of textual criticism; his scholia gave us the first examples of marginal readings; his homilies served as models for popular sermons; his commentaries were the first continuous exegesis to the Scriptures.

In his book of First Principles (*Peri Archon*), Origen gave an outline of the hermeneutical principles for the interpretation of the Bible. His principles may be briefly summarized as follows. (a) The primary purpose of the Bible is to teach the profound mysteries relating to God and man, but the secondary purpose is the historical and obvious meaning for those who are unable to grasp these mysteries. (b) Because of man's threefold constitution according to Platonic philosophy (the *soma* or body, the *psyche* or soul, and the *pneuma* or spirit; cf. also 1 Thess. 5, 23), he distinguishes between three senses in the Bible. (1) The corporal or obvious meaning is the lowest and is expressed without literary figures or metaphors. It is roughly equivalent to the literal proper sense. This meaning, says Origen, is meant for beginners. (2) The psychic sense is for the more learned. Although he does not give any explanation of this, from the various examples given it would correspond to a moral sense. (3) The deepest meaning in the Bible is found in the spiritual sense, which may be also called the anagogical, mystical, or metaphorical sense. Hence, this spiritual sense not only comprises our typical but also our improper literal sense. This pneumatical sense being the most profound of all, it can only be understood by the most learned people. Origen elsewhere combines both the psychic and pneumatic sense under the name "higher sense," which he places in opposition to the first. (c) Everything in the Bible has a higher meaning, but not everything has a literal or obvious (i.e., corporal) meaning. (d) Many passages do not have the literal sense; otherwise there would be in the Bible absurdities, scandalous sayings unworthy of God. Hence, these things were written with the avowed purpose of avoiding the corporal sense, and must be interpreted in the higher sense. (e) Historical events are not types of historical events, nor are corporal things types of corporal things, but both the corporal and historical are mere types or prefigurations of mystical things. Herein lies the entire allegorical principle of the Alexandrian school.

Origen is rightly criticized for his underlying principles of exegesis. But he is not to be judged too harshly or too severely, because the literal sense among the Alexandrians is more restricted than our modern connotation of the word, because in his zeal he was defending the Church against the Jews, the heretics and ignorant brethren, because he always acknowledged the Church as the court of last appeal in all controversies and as the authentic interpreter of the Scriptures. Yet, in spite of his hermeneutical principles he did not fail to study the literal meaning of words.

The Followers of Origen.—The influence of Origen was felt throughout the Orient and many followed his footsteps; for example, St. Gregory Thaumaturgus (d. after 270) in his paraphrastic book of Ecclesiastes, Theognostus, the successor of Dionysius the Great as president of the catechetical school, and Pierius.

Eusebius of Cæsarea (d. 340), as a great historian, should have preferred the literal meaning and did so in his historical books. But in the rest of his writings he bowed to the influence of Origen and indulged in allegorical interpretations— for example in his *Demonstratione evangelica,* in his commentaries to the Psalms, and in the greater part of his commentary to the Book of Isaias.

St. Athanasius (d. 375) follows the simple, literal meaning in his dogmatic and polemical works, but in the exegetical commentaries to the Canticle of Canticles, Job, and Psalms the allegorical interpretation prevails.

Didymus the Blind (313-398), for many years the president of the catechetical school, followed the exegetical principles of Origen and developed principally the spiritual meaning of the text.

St. Cyril of Alexandria (d. 444), the great opponent of Nestorianism, explained nearly all the books of the Old and New Testaments. In his writing, *De adoratione et cultu in spiritu et veritate* (M.G., LXVIII), he shows that the Mosaic Law was abrogated according to the letter, but remains according to the spirit. In his work, *Glaphyra* (i.e., Polished Explanations, M.G., LXIX), he explains selected passages from the Pentateuch typically and mystically. But in his commentaries on the Minor Prophets and Isaias, Psalms, Canticle of Canticles, Luke, John, Romans, 1 and 2 Corinthians, and Hebrews, he adheres rather to the literal sense.

Hesychius, a priest of Jerusalem (d. after 451), was also a follower of the school of Alexandria. He wrote commentaries to Leviticus and Psalms, homilies to Job, scholia to the Psalms, Isaias, Daniel and Minor Prophets.

The Adversaries of Origen and Allegory.—Even during the lifetime of Origen and more so after his death, opposition to his hermeneutical principles arose. Nepos, an Egyptian bishop, wrote a work *Contra allegoristas,* in which he defended the literal interpretation of Apoc. 20, 4-22 in defense of the millennium. Dionysius, the successor of Origen at the school of Alexandria, wrote two volumes against Nepos' interpretation (*De promissionibus*).

Among the adversaries of Origen and the strict allegorical method may also be mentioned St. Methodius (d. 311) and St. Epiphanius (d. 403), Bishop of Salamis, on the island of Cyprus.

Art. 4.   The School of Antioch

Bibliography: Vaccari, A., "La 'teoria' nella scuola esegetica di Antiochia," in *Biblica,* 1 (1920), 3-36; *idem,* "La 'teoria' esegetica Antiochena," *ibid.*, 15 (1934), 93-101; Ternant, P., "La theoria d'Antioch dans le cadre des sens de l'Ecriture," *ibid.*, 34 (1953), 135-158, 354-383, 456-486.

(a) First Period. For Titus of Bosra: cf. Baumstark, A., in *Biblica*, 16 (1935), 257-299, For the Nicene Council (A.D. 325): cf. Vaccari, A., in V.D., 5 (1925), 344-351.

(b) Second Period. For St. John Chrysostom: cf. Batiffol, P., in R.B., 8 (1899), 566-572; Fabbi, F., "La condiscendenza divina nell' inspirazione biblica," in *Biblica*, 14 (1933), 330-347; *Dicks, C. D., in J.B.L., 67 (1948), 365-376; Prümm, K., in *Biblica*, 30 (1949), 161-196, 377-400. For St. Nilus, his disciple: cf. Sovic, A., in *Biblica*, 2 (1921), 45-52. For Theodore of Mopsuestia: cf. Pirot, L., "L'oeuvre exégétique de Théodore de Mopsueste" (Rome, 1913); Vosté, J. M., in R.B., 34 (1925), 54-81, 38 (1929), 382-395, 542-554; Devresse, P. in R.B., 37 (1928), 340-366, 38 (1929), 35-62, 41 (1932), 261-263; *idem,* "Le commentaire de Théodore de Mopsueste sur les Psaumes" (1-80; Rome, 1939); *idem,* in R.B., 53 (1946), 207-241; *idem,* "Essai sur Théodore de Mopsueste" (Vatican City, 1948); Vaccari, A., in *Biblica*, 23 (1942), 1-17; Sullivan, F. A., in *Theol. St.,* 12 (1951), 179-207; McKenzie, J. L., in *Theol. St.,* 19 (1958), 345-373. For his Nestorian Followers: cf. Vosté, J.-M., in R.B., 27 (1928), 221-232, 386-419. For the Arian Aristerius of Cappadocia (c. 400): cf. Richard, M., in R.B., 44 (1935), 548-558.

(c) Third Period. For Theodoret of Cyrus; cf. Macel, R., in R.B., 43 (1934), 88-96. For Adrian: cf. Mercati, G., in R.B., 11 (1914), 246-255.

This school was founded at the end of the third century by Lucian, a priest of Antioch, who was martyred in 312 at the time of Emperor Maximianus. He wrote no exegetical commentaries, but edited the Greek text of the Old and New Testaments.

The history of this school can be conveniently divided into three periods: (a) its rise from Lucian to Diodorus of Tarsus (excl.), that is, from about 280 to 360; (b) its glory under Diodorus and Theodore of Mopsuestia, that is, from 360 to 430; (c) its decline, that is, from 430 to 500.

The Principles of This School.—This school insisted upon the grammatical and historical meaning, and was opposed to the allegorical system of interpretation. It admitted the typical sense of the Bible, by what they called technically *theory,* and which they applied prudently. Due consideration was given to the history of revelation, so that the Old and New Testaments were carefully distinguished. It examined carefully passages from the point of view of philology and took the context as well as the various consequences into consideration.

(a) The First Period 280-360

Eustathius of Antioch (d. after 330) sharply rebuked Origen for his allegorical method of interpretation in the book, *De pythonissa,* which is still extant. Theodore of Harkel (d. 355), Eusebius of Emesa (d. about 359), and Titus of Bostra (d. after 364) are also representatives of this first period.

(b) The Second Period 360-430

Diodorus of Tarsus (d. before 394) was one of the most important members of this school. Both St. John Chrysostom and Theodore of Mopsuestia were his pupils. He wrote many commentaries on the Old and New Testaments, but only a few of them are extant. Since his orthodoxy was questioned during the period of the Nestorian controversies, his books were destroyed.

In the fragment extant on the Psalms he gives the differences existing between history, theory, allegory, tropology, and parable. According to Diodorus, theory is founded upon an historical fact, upon an event which really took place and whereby this was indicative of something greater and more perfect in the future. He asserts that many of these types are found in the Old Testament. This theory differs from the allegory of the Alexandrians, who either deny or prescind from the literal and historical reality of the event. On the other hand, theory always supposes the actual occurrence of the fact. Just as allegory was proper to the Alexandrians, theory was peculiar to the Antiochians.

St. John Chrysostom (344-407) was a prolific writer and an unexcelled orator. Most of the Scriptures were explained by him through homilies, which was the only method employed by him. Many of his writings are still extant (e.g., homilies to Genesis, Psalms, Matthew, John, and the Pauline Epistles).

The principle which he employs in his interpretation is called "condescension"—that is, God, in manifesting His mind to the sacred writers, condescends to the usages of human languages and adapts Himself to the intelligence of man. This condescension, however, places truth in the Scriptures.

In regard to various senses employed in the Bible he follows the following principles: he prudently rejects allegory and admits the typical meaning; he distinguishes three kinds of meanings in the Scriptures, the literal, the allegorical (i.e., improper literal sense), the anagogical sense (i.e., typical sense).

Theodore of Mopsuestia (d. 428) was a prodigious worker, and his exegetical works are enumerated by Ebediesu. Of his many writings are still extant his commentary on the Minor Prophets, a large part of his commentary on the Pauline Epistles preserved in Latin, a commentary on St. John, and fragments of various other works (cf. M.G., LXVI). He was the most daring of all the Antiochian writers and the most tenacious in his historical interpretation. Thus, he denied the inspiration of Job, Canticle of Canticles, Paralipomenon, Esdras, Nehemias, and also of the deutero-canonical books of the Old Testament, as well as of James, 2 Peter, 2 and 3 John, Jude, and the Apocalypse of the New Testament; he reduced the number of Messianic types to the minimum and only acknowledged four Psalms (2; 8; 44; 109) as Messianic; he declared that Solomon possessed the gift of wisdom but not of prophecy, thus probably distinguishing between various degrees of inspiration.

Theodore was called the father of Nestorianism by St. Cyril of Alexandria. He taught that no nature is complete without a person, so that therefore in Christ there were two persons with only a moral unity existing between them, just as existed between man and wife. Because of his errors he was condemned by the Council of Constantinople IV.

(c) The Third Period 430-500

Polychronius of Apamea (d. about 430) was almost as clever as his brother Theodore of Mopsuestia, but surpassed him in prudent judgment. He avoided the extremes of his brother, but followed the general historical method of the school. It seems that he was the first to make use of the Hebrew text for the Old Testament in explaining the prophecies. Only a few fragments of his commentaries on Job, Jeremias, and Daniel are now extant.

Theodoret, Bishop of Cyrus (c. 390-458), was the most prominent member of this school during its declining period. He is noted not so much for his originality as for his prudent selection of things written by his predecessors. In his *Quæstiones in libros historicos* he sought out the most difficult passages of the Scriptures, as well as the apologetical reasons why some opponents vilified the Scriptures. In his commentary on the Psalms he presents an exegesis that stands midway between the allegorical and literal senses. His commentaries on the Prophets are noted for their fine exegesis, while those on the New Testament are outstanding. He is ranked second to St. John Chrysostom for his clear analysis of the Pauline Epistles.

Adrian the Monk of the fifth century closes the series of Antiochian writers. He depended upon the writings of Theodore of Mopsuestia and Theodoret, and composed a work called "An Introduction to the Sacred Scriptures" in which he explained the exegetical principles of the Antiochian school (M.G., XCVIII).

Even though Antioch soon declined in importance, its principles of biblical interpretation have remained to the present time as the foundation of hermeneutical studies. Though several of its members by reason of their excessive adherence to the literal sense seemed to ignore the axiom "virtus stat in medio," the remainder wisely interpreted Holy Writ according to the mind of the sacred writers, literally or typically.

Despite the fact that this school gave the opportunity to Theodore of Mopsuestia to sow the seeds of heresy in his pupil, Nestorius, the school as a whole always remained loyal and faithful to the Church. The orthodox members of this school condemned the writings of Theodore, long before Emperor Justinian in the sixth century.

Art. 5. The Latin Fathers

Bibliography: For St. Ambrose: cf. Wilbrand, W., in B.Z., 12 (1912), 337-350; Caragliano, T., in *Biblica*, 27 (1946), 30-64, 210-240; Ambrogio, S., *ibid.*, 26 (1945), 238-276, 27 (1946), 3-17.

For Julian of Eclanum: cf. Vaccari, A., in *Biblica*, 4 (1923), 337-355; Bouwman, G., in V.D., 36 (1958), 284-291.

For St. Jerome: cf. Vulgate above; also Stummer, F., in *Biblica*, 18 (1937), 174-181; Abel, F. M., in *Vivre et Penser*, 1 (1941), 94-119, 213-230; Sutcliffe, E. F., in *Biblica*, 29 (1948), 112-125, 195-204; *idem* in C.B.Q., 11 (1949), 139-143; *Cooper, C. M., in J.B.L., 59 (1950), 233-244; Loewe, R., in *Biblica*, 34 (1953), 44-77, 159-192; Rehm, M., *ibid.*, 35 (1954), 174-197; Sutcliffe, E. F., *ibid.*, 36 (1955), 213-222.

For St. Augustine: cf. Costello, C. J., "St. Augustine's Doctrine on the Inspiration and Canonicity of Scripture" (Washington, D.C., 1930); Vitti, A., in V.D., 10 (1930), 87-95, 145-152, 193-200; Lobignac, M., *ibid.*, 10 (1930), 368-373; De Bryne, D., in R.B., 41 (1932), 550-560; Fischer, B., in *Biblica*, 23 (1942), 139-164, 241-267; Perrella, G., *ibid.*, 26 (1945), 277-302; Most, W. G., in C.B.Q., 13 (1951), 284-295; Gallus, T., in V.D., 32 (1954), 129-141.

St. Hippolytus (170/175—236) of Rome was a contemporary of Origen and a man of great talent. He wrote many works in Greek, but only a few of these are extant. Although he was not dependent upon the Alexandrian school, he resembled Origen in his preference for allegorical interpretation.

Tertullian (d. about 240) and St. Cyprian (d. 258) did not write commentaries on the Sacred Scriptures, but in their writings they frequently explained Biblical passages, usually in the literal sense.

Because of the various dogmatic difficulties raging in Asia Minor, many Latin writers of the fourth century followed the Alexandrian school of interpretation.

St. Victorinus (d. 303), Bishop of Pettau in Styria (now Hungary), wrote many commentaries, but only that on the Apocalypse remains. He believed firmly in the millennium.

St. Hilary (315-367) of Poitiers, in Gaul, in his commentary on St. Matthew, made use of both the allegorical and typical senses, and in his commentary on the Psalms closely followed Origen.

St. Ambrose (340-397) depended upon Philo, Origen, and at times on St. Basil for his homilies.

Gregory of Eliberis (d. about 392) was the author of twenty

homilies, edited by Batiffol and Wilmart under the title "Tractatus Origenis de Libris SS. Scripturarum."

Apponius (fifth century) explained the Canticle of Canticles typically and made use of the Vulgate edition.

Tychonius, a Donatist composed (about 382) a *Liber Regularum,* which contained the general principles of Hermeneutics. This work was praised by St. Augustine. There are also references to his commentary on the Apocalypse, which was a definite break from the literal interpretation.

There was also an author of commentaries on the Minor Prophets, Job, and the Psalms, who followed the Antiochian exegetical principles. He is commonly supposed to be Julian, Bishop of Eclanum, a follower of the Pelagian heresy.

Independent methods were followed by three Latin writers: Ambrosiaster, St. Jerome, and St. Augustine.

Ambrosiaster, so called by Erasmus, was the unknown author of a commentary on thirteen Epistles of St. Paul, once attributed to St. Ambrose. He is also the author of the *Quæstiones Veteris et Novi Testamenti,* which were once published under the name of St. Augustine.

St. Jerome (342-420) in his method of interpretation wished to steer a middle course between the historical and allegorical senses. He preferred the allegorical meaning of Origen whenever the proper literal sense seemed to him to render a text unbecoming or ridiculous. In his later works he insisted more upon the literal meaning.

St. Augustine (354-430) ranks immediately after St. John Chrysostom in his homiletical explanations, but he might have not lacked philological training. In his homilies he indulged in allegories, the mystical interpretation of numbers, and moral applications. In his theological works he adhered to the literal sense.

Art. 6. The Cappadocian Fathers

These Asiatic Fathers do not represent a dependence upon either the Alexandrian or Antiochian School, but remained neutral in the face of these two systems of exegesis.

The Cappadocian triumvirate comprises St. Basil the Great, St. Gregory of Nazianzus, and St. Gregory of Nyssa. These Greek Fathers represent a school of thought which prevailed at Cæsarea in Cappadocia.

St. Basil the Great (330-379), together with St. Gregory of Nazianzus, was an admirer of Origen, and they both collected the works of this great Alexandrian. He, however, rejected allegories as mere dreams and old ladies' fables. He wrote nine homilies to the Hexaëmeron (M.G., XXIX, 3-208), which he explained in the literal sense. His homilies on the Psalms were written in the moral sense.

St. Gregory of Nyssa (335-395) was the younger brother of St. Basil. He wrote eight homilies on Ecclesiastes in the literal sense, fifteen homilies on the Canticle of Canticles, and an apologetical explanation of the Hexaëmeron. But in his book on the life of Moses he employed the boldest allegory.

St. Gregory of Nazianzus (328/9—389) interpreted Matthew 19, 1-17, and explained the Scriptures in some of his poems.

Two other Asiatic Fathers worthy of note are Apollinarius of Laodicea (310-390) and St. Epiphanius of Constantia (315-403).

Art. 7. The Syrian Fathers

Bibliography: For St. Ephraem; cf. Mercati, S.J., "Ephraem Syri Opera" (Rome, 1915); Riccioti, G. (Turin-Rome, 1925); Vaccari, A., in V.D., 1 (1921), 240-244.

St. James Aphraates (275/285—340) wrote twenty-three letters which are sometimes called homilies, discourses, or demonstrations. His episcopal see was perhaps at Mar

St. Ephraem (306-373) was born at Nisibis, probably of Christian parents. Here he was a doctor and pillar of strength to the faithful during the years when the city was besieged by the armies of the Persians. When the city was taken by the Persians (363), he withdrew with a mass of Christians to the Roman territory at Edessa, where he taught and wrote to the end of his life. He always remained in deacon's orders. It seems that he interpreted the entire Bible, but very few of his books are extant. Of these some are in Syriac, some in Armenian, and others in Latin. He surpassed the Greek Fathers in this fact, that he explained the Syriac version (Peshitto), an Oriental language closely related to the Hebrew, which, however, he did not understand. Thus, he was able to penetrate more deeply into the sense of the Old Testament. He followed the principles of the Antiochian school, avoided allegories, and frequently, especially in his homilies, admitted types. In the rest of his works he adhered to the literal and historical meanings.

Art. 8. The Late Patristic Period

Bibliography: Cordoliana, A., "Le texte de la Bible en Irlande du V au IX siècle," in R.B., 57 (1950), 5-41; Bieler, L., "Der Bibeltext des hl. Patrick," in *Biblica,* 28 (1947), 31-58, 236-263; Vaccari, A., "La Bibbia nell'ambiente di S. Benedetto," *ibid.,* 29 (1948), 321-344; Staab, K., "Die griechischen Katenenkommentare zu den katholischen Briefen," *ibid.,* 5 (1924), 296-353; Sutcliffe, E. F., "Some Footnotes to the Fathers," *ibid.,* 6 (1925), 205-210; Graf, G., "Exegetische Schriften zum N. T. in Arabischer Sprache bis zum 14 Jahrhundert," in B.Z., 21 (1933), 22-40.

For Ischodad: cf. Vosté, J.-M., in *Biblica,* 25 (1944), 261-296, 26 (1945), 12-36, 182-202, 303-306, 29 (1948), 169-194, 313-320, 30 (1949), 1-9, 305-313.

For Barhebræus: cf. Goettsberger, J., in B.S., 5 (1900).

For St. Bede: cf. Sutcliffe, E. F., in *Biblica,* 7 (1926), 428-439, 16 (1935), 300-306; Vaccari, A., *ibid.,* 5 (1924), 369-373; Weisweiler, H., *ibid.,* 18 (1937), 197-204; Hablitzel, J., in B.Z., 24 (1939), 357-359; Laistner, M. L. W., "Bedae Venerabilis expositio Actuum Apostolorum et retractatio" (Cambridge, Mass., 1939).

For Rhabanus Maurus: cf. Hablitzel, J., in B.Z., 19 (1931), 215-227.

The age of productivity in biblical exegesis ceased in the fifth century, and in the sixth century various attempts were made to compile excerpts from the earlier interpreters. In this manner the writings of the Fathers were collected. They were called *catenæ* (i.e., running commentaries on the books of the Bible from the citations of the Fathers). At the end of each excerpt the name of the author was given.

Procopius (465-528) of Gaza is the first author or compiler of these excerpts, which are extant for the Pentateuch, historical books, Books of Solomon, and Isaias. He drew his material from St. Cyril of Alexandria, St. Basil, and St. Gregory of Nazianzus.

Other compilations were edited by Philotheus (seventh century) for the Minor Prophets; Polychronius the deacon (ninth century) for the Books of Solomon; Nicetas of Harkel (eleventh century) for Job, Psalms, the Major Prophets, Matthew, Luke, John and the Pauline Epistles; Macarius Chrysocephalus (fourteenth century) for Genesis, Matthew, Luke.

These compilations of the Fathers were also edited in commentaries by Greek as well as Latin Fathers.

Greek Authors.—Olympiodorus, a deacon of Alexandria (c. 505-516), composed commentaries on Ecclesiastes, Jeremias, Lamentations, Job, Proverbs, Esdras, and Canticle of Canticles. Gregory (c. 600), Bishop of Girgenti (Agrigentum in Sicily), is the author of a lengthy commentary on Ecclesiastes. Œcumenius (c. 600), Bishop of Tricca in Thessaly, wrote a commentary to the Apocalypse. Andrew, Archbishop of Cæsarea in Cappadocia, also composed a commentary on the Apocalypse before 637, and Anastasius Sinaita (c. 640-700) interpreted the Hexaëmeron. St. John Damascene (d. 750) has left behind commentaries on the Pauline Epistles, and was largely dependent upon St. John Chrysostom, Theodoret, and Cyril of Alexandria for his material.

Photius (d. 891) composed *Quæstiones et diatribæ ad Amphilochium,* in which he discussed many biblical questions. In his great work, *Bibliotheca,* he preserves many excerpts from exegetical books which have perished. Besides, he wrote a commentary on St. Luke's Gospel.

Theophylactus, Archbishop of Achridis in Bulgaria (d. 1107), composed commentaries on the Minor Prophets and on all the books of the New Testament. In his explanation of the Pauline Epistles he quoted from Clement of Alexandria, Methodius, St. Basil, St. Cyril of Alexandria, and in particular from St. John Chrysostom.

Euthymius Zigabenus (d. c. 1118) interpreted the Psalms, the Four Gospels, and the Pauline Epistles according to the mind of St. John Chrysostom.

Amongst the Syrians Ischodad, Bishop of Hadatha (c. 850), composed commentaries on various books, and depended upon

the writings of Theodore of Mopsuestia. Gregory Abulfar-
agius, commonly called *Barhebraeus* (d. 1286), composed
various commentaries on the books of the Old and New
Testaments in the form of scholia.

Latin Authors.—Aurelius Cassiodorus (477-570), of the
monastery of Viarium in Calabria, Italy, collected a library
of all the books which he could find. His voluminous commentary on the Psalms was based upon St. Augustine. He
also edited commentaries on the Epistles, the Acts, and the
Apocalypse.

St. Gregory the Great (540-604) in his explanation of the
Bible followed a practical end, and thus often neglected the
literal meaning for the allegorical. He commented upon the
Book of Job and composed homilies on the Gospels.

St. Isidore of Seville (d. 636) collected many excerpts from
the Fathers, and interpreted many passages both typically
and allegorically.

St. Bede (674-735) wrote commentaries on the Pentateuch, the historical books of the Bible, Proverbs, the Canticle of Canticles, and explained these allegorically. His
commentaries on the Gospels, Acts, Catholic Epistles, and
Apocalypse were explained both literally and morally.

Alcuin (735-804) composed brief commentaries on the
Penitential Psalms, Ecclesiastes, the Canticle of Canticles, St.
John's Gospel, the Epistles to Titus and the Hebrews, and the
Apocalypse. He depended upon the writings of St. Ambrose,
St. Jerome, St. Augustine, St. Gregory, and St. Bede, and often
indulged in the mystical sense.

Rhabanus Maurus (c. 784-856), a pupil of Alcuin, com-
mented upon the Pentateuch, the historical books, Proverbs,
Wisdom, Ecclesiastes, Jeremias, Ezechiel, Matthew, and the
Pauline Epistles.

Walafrid Strabo (c. 808-849), a pupil of Rhabanus Maurus,
was the celebrated author of the *Glossa Ordinaria*. It was the
ordinary exegetical handbook for centuries. With him the
ancient period of exegesis can be considered as closed.

CHAPTER II

THE SCHOLASTIC PERIOD

"With the age of the scholastics came fresh and welcome progress in the study of the Bible. That the scholastics were solicitous about the genuineness of the Latin version is evident from the *Correctoria Biblica,* or lists of emendations, which they have left. But they expended their labors and industry chiefly on interpretation and explanation. To them we owe the accurate and clear distinction, such as have not been given before, of the various senses of the sacred words; the assignment of the value of each 'sense' in theology; the division of books into parts, and the summaries of the various parts; the investigation of the objects of the writers; the demonstration of the connection of sentence with sentence, and clause with clause; all of which is calculated to throw much light on the more obscure passages of the sacred volume. The valuable work of the scholastics in Holy Scripture is seen in their theological treatises and in their Scripture commentaries; and in this respect the greatest name among them all is St. Thomas Aquinas" ("Providentissimus Deus," cf. E.B., 81).

Art. 1.   The Jewish School

Bibliography: Landgraf, A. M., "Ein frühscholastischer Traktat zur Bibelexegese der Juden," in *Biblica,* 37 (1956), 403-409.

The founder of philology and rational exegesis amongst the Jews was * Saadias al Fayyumi (892-942), also called Gaon (i.e., the doctor). His grammatical and lexicographical works were printed in Arabic, and he translated many books of the Old Testament into Arabic and added commentaries. There were other Jews who followed these principles of Saadias—for

example, in Spain, * Abi-'L Walidi Ibn Ganah (985-1050),
* Moses Ibn Giquitilla (eleventh century), * Abraham Ibn
Esra (1092-1167). These authors combined the literal sense
with the grammatical or philological meaning.

In France a new method was initiated by the exegete
* Rabbi Salomon Ishaki (1040-1105), also called Rashi from
the initials of his name. He laid particular stress upon the
literal sense. His commentaries bore an influence upon subsequent Christian and Jewish exegetes.

The family of * Kimchi, from Toulouse, united the good
points of these two schools. This family included the father,
Joseph (1110-1175), one son Moses (d. 1190), who surpassed
all in knowledge and fame, and another son David (1160-
1235), also called Radak, whose grammar (*Sepher miklol*) and
lexicon (*Sepher shorashim*) became the basis of our Hebrew
studies. These three wrote commentaries on the books of the
Old Testament and interpreted them in the literal sense.

* Moses Maimonides or Rambam (1135-1204) explained the
Scriptures according to philosophical principles. * Levi Ben
Gerson (1288-1344) followed the footsteps of Maimonides
and interpreted the Scriptures according to the principles of
Aristotle.

The commentaries of these authors were printed in the
various rabbinical Bibles which were edited at Venice, Basle,
Amsterdam, and Warsaw. Some of these were translated into
Latin—for example, the Book of Proverbs by A. Giggei
(Milan, 1620), the Canticle of Canticles by G. Genebrard
(Paris, 1585), the Psalms by * A. Janvier (Paris, 1660),
Ecclesiastes by * P. Costo (Lyons, 1554), Isaias by * Mal-
anima (Florence, 1774), etc.

In the eighth century arose a Jewish sect which believed
only in the authority of the Scriptures and ignored the traditions of their Fathers. They were called the *Karaites*. The
following authors of this sect are worthy of mention: * Iaphet
ben Ali (tenth century), * Jacob ben Ruben (twelfth century),
* Aaron ben Joseph (d. 1294), and * Aaron ben Elias (fourteenth century).

The commentaries produced by the mystical schools are of little practical value. These schools originated in Spain in the thirteenth century and then spread to Germany, where the principal teacher of mystical interpretation was * Moses Ben Nachman (1194-1280). Four senses of the Bible were admitted: the literal, the allegorical, the tropological, and mystical sense. Their doctrine reached its culmination in a celebrated book called *Zohar* (thirteenth century), which is a commentary on the Pentateuch, is full of theosophical speculations, and became the codex for the *Kabalists*.

The Italian Jews followed a more reasonable mystical and philosophical exegesis. The principal authors were * Isaias a Trani (d. c. 1250) and * Emmanuel Romanus (1270-1330).

Also worthy of mention is the school called *darshanim* (investigators), which produced the famous collection *Jalcut Shimoni* (thirteenth century), a haggadic commentary on the entire Old Testament from old Midrashim and various writers.

Art. 2. The Christian Latin School

Bibliography: *Smalley, B., "The Study of the Bible in the Middle Ages" (Oxford, 1952); Landgraf, A., "Zur Methode der biblischen Textkritik im 12 Jahrhundert," in *Biblica*, 10 (1929), 445-474; *idem, ibid.*, 18 (1937), 74-94; Rost, H., "Die Bibel im Mittelalter" (Augsburg, 1939); Kleinhans, A., "Der Studiengang der Professoren der Hl. Schrift im 13 u 14 Jahrhundert," in *Biblica* 14 (1933), 381-399; Spicq, C., "Esquisse d'une histoire de l'exégèse latin au Moyen Age" (Paris, 1944); Garofalo, S., "Gli Umanisti italiani del sec. XV e la Bibbia," in *Biblica*, 27 (1946), 338-375; Vosté, J.-M., "Medieval Exegesis," in C.B.Q., 10 (1948), 229-246; Schneider, H., "Die biblischen Oden in Jerusalem und Konstantinopel," in *Biblica*, 30 (1949), 432-452; *idem*, "Die biblischen Oden im Mittelalter," *ibid.*, 30 (1949), 479-500; Wilmart, A., "Un repertoire d'exégèse composé en Angleterre vers le début du XIII siècle," in *Memorial Lagrange* (Paris, 1940), 307-346.

For Anselm of Laon: cf. Landgraf, A., in *Biblica*, 23 (1942), 170-174.

For Hugo of St. Cher: cf. Sutcliffe, E., in V.D., 6 (1926), 149-156.

For St. Albert the Great: cf. Vaccari, A., in *Biblica*, 13 (1932), 257-272, 369-384; *idem*, in V.D., 12 (1932), 337-344.

For St. Thomas Aquinas: cf. Pelster, F., in *Biblica*, 3 (1922), 328-338, 4 (1923), 300-311, 5 (1924), 64-72; Vitti, A., in V.D., 4 (1924), 153-159; Synave, P., in R.B., 35 (1926), 40-65; Kürzinger, J., in *Biblica*, 23 (1942), 306-317; Vosté, J.-M., in V.D., 24 (1944), 97-99; Lonergan, B., in *Theol. St.*, 7 (1947), 35-79; Callan, C. J., in C.B.Q., 9 (1947), 33-47.

For Nicholas of Lyra: cf. *Halperin, H., "Nicolas of Lyra and Rashi: The Minor Prophets" (New York, 1941).

At the beginning of the twelfth century a new fervor began to manifest itself amongst the Latins in regard to theological studies, and this new spirit also influenced the interpretation of the Scriptures. Imbued by the study of the Fathers and the philosophy of Aristotle, the Christians began to write commentaries on the books of the Bible.

In the pre-scholastic period lived many scholars worthy of mention: Anselm of Laon (d. 1117), the author of an interlinear glossary or commentary; Bruno of Astensis, who explained the Pentateuch, Job, Proverbs, Canticles, the Psalms, four Gospels, and the Apocalypse; Rupert of Deutz (d. 1135), who wrote commentaries on many books of the Old and New Testaments; Hugh of St. Victor (d. 1141), Peter Abelard (d. 1142), St. Bernard, Abbot of Clairvaux (d. 1153), and the gifted and celebrated Peter Comestor (d. 1179), whose *Historia Scholastica* remained a biblical manual of the historical books for many centuries.

The scholastics of the thirteenth century, who had built up an admirable construction of scientific dogmatic theology, considered the Scriptures as the foundation and culmination of all wisdom. They indicated clearly the nexus and progress of ideas in the Scriptures, accurately weighed and discussed the individual sentences, and evolved various dogmatical truths with the aid of Aristotelian logic. Although they lacked the philological and historical background which is required for a complete explanation of the Bible, their commentaries are very practical and useful.

While the scholastics followed the division of senses given by Cassianus and Bede—namely, the literal, allegorical, tropological (moral), and anagogical senses,—they considered these last three as species of one genus, the spiritual sense. Hence, they practically admitted only two senses, the literal and the typical.

There are four outstanding exegetes of this period, of whom three were Dominicans.

Hugh of St. Cher, O.P. (d. 1263), composed verbal concordances to the Scriptures and then, later, *Postillæ* to the whole Bible.

St. Albert the Great, O.P. (d. 1280), wrote commentaries on Job, the Psalms, Lamentations, Baruch, the Prophets, the four Gospels, and the Apocalypse. He followed principally the literal sense, but did not entirely despise the allegorical meaning.

St. Thomas Aquinas, O.P. (d. 1274), wrote commentaries on Job, the Psalms (1-50), Isaias, Jeremias (1-32), Lamentations. He left a running commentary to the four Gospels called the *Catena Aurea,* which consists of excerpts taken from the Fathers. He also wrote his own commentaries on Matthew and John.

St. Bonaventure, O. F. Min. (d. 1274), called *Doctor seraphicus,* composed a few commentaries on Ecclesiastes, Wisdom, Luke and John, in which, besides the literal sense, he freely applied the mystical sense.

Other exegetes of this period are, Nicholas of Gorham, O.P. (d. 1295), Duns Scotus, O. F. Min. (d. c. 1308), Ægidius Columna (d. 1316), the best pupil of St. Thomas, Albertus Patavinus (d. 1328), Robert Holcot (d. 1349), Michael Aiguanus (d. 1400).

In the fourteenth century the study of the Oriental languages began to flourish. The Council of Vienne (1311-1312) urged that the Oriental languages should be taught at the universities of Paris, Oxford, Bologna, and Salamanca.

Raymond Martini, O.P. (d. 1290), was a converted rabbi and had been acquainted with the rabbinical traditions. He wrote a noted work entitled *Pugio fidei adversus Judæos et Mauros,* in which he showed that Christ was the Messias.

Nicholas of Lyra, O. F. Min. (d. 1340), a Norman, is known for his *Postilla* (i.e., a brief commentary to all the books of the Bible). In this work he followed the literal meaning and very rarely employed the mystical sense. For nearly three centuries this remained a popular commentary, and even after the invention of the printing press was frequently edited.

Paul a S. Maria (d. 1435) was the Christian name of the Jewish convert, Salomon Ben Levi. He wrote *Additiones* to the *Postilla* of Nicholas of Lyra, in which he further amplified the text and at times corrected the explanation.

In the following century many interpreters edited long commentaries on moral, dogmatic, and polemical subjects. Of these the most famous are: Alphonse Tostatus of Spain (d. 1455), the Carthusian S. Dionysius de Ryckel of Belgium (d. 1471), the Augustinian James Perez of Valencia, Spain (d. 1490).

Chapter III

THE MORE RECENT PERIOD

Bibliography: Crump, F. J., "The Gutenberg Bible," in C.B.Q., 14 (1952), 213-218.
For Santes Pagnini: cf. Gauthier, J. D., in C.B.Q., 7 (1945), 175-190.
For Francis Vatablus: cf. *Hubbard, A. P., in J.B.L., 66 (1947), 197-209.
For Card. Cajetan: cf. Vaccari, A., in V.D., 14 (1934), 321-327; Collins, T. A., in C.B.Q., 17 (1955), 363-378.

In the fifteenth century the knowledge of the Greek language, ancient culture, and history started a new period for exegesis. This movement began in Italy and then spread to the rest of Europe. At that time Greek MSS. of the New Testament as well as of the Septuagint became more accessible to the West. Besides the study of Greek and Hebrew, the invention of printing aided immeasurably in the diffusion of the biblical text. Then too, the defection brought about by Protestantism divided the Christian world into two hostile camps.

Amongst the first to apply the knowledge of the Greek language to the Scriptures was the Italian, Laurentius Valla (d. 1457), in his *Annotationes in N.T.*, which consisted of critical and grammatical remarks on the text. Afterwards Faber of Estaples (d. 1536) edited commentaries on the four Gospels, all the Pauline Epistles, and the Catholic Epistles. Erasmus of Rotterdam (d. 1536) also edited the Greek New Testament, with his own Latin version and notes.

Amongst those who devoted themselves to the study of Hebrew and the Old Testament may be mentioned Santes Pagnini (d. 1541), Francis Vatablus (d. 1547), Jerome Oleaster (d. 1563), and Rudolph Baynus (d. 1560).

Some authors employed both the Hebrew and Greek languages in their commentaries—for example, Card. Thomas de Vio Cajetan, O.P. (d. 1535), Isidore Clarius (d. 1555), Adam Sasbout (d. 1553), and Francis Titelmann (d. 1557).

Art. 1. From the Council of Trent to 1650

Bibliography: Vaccari, A., "Esegesi ad Esegeti al Concilio di Trento," in *Biblica,* 27 (1946), 320-337; Grabka, G., "Cardinal Hosius and the Council of Trent," *Theol. St.,* 7 (1946), 558-576.

For St. Robert Bellarmine: cf. Tromp, S., "Opera oratoria postuma" (2 vols., Rome, 1943-1944); Bea, A., *Biblica,* 13 (1932), 1-5.

For Maldonatus: cf. Deville, R., in V.D., 29 (1951), 107-111.

For Cornelius a Lapide: cf. Galdos, R., in V.D., 17 (1937), 39-44, 88-95, 146-152, 166-172, 212-218, 234-241, 18, (1938), 82-92.

For John Mariana: cf. De Los Rios, E., in V.D., 16 (1936), 267-278.

For St. Lawrence of Brindisi: cf. Andreas ab Alpe, in V.D., 22 (1942), 152-158, 183-189; Gumbinger, C., in C.B.Q., 8 (1946), 265-280.

Catholic Exegesis.—This was a period of the most fruitful activity, and it is called the second "golden age of Catholic exegesis." This activity was the result of the great zeal amongst the Catholics against the Protestant Reformers and of the particular encouragement given by the Decrees of the Council of Trent.

A new way was paved for the study of *introduction* by Sixtus Senensis, O.P. (d. 1569), in his work entitled "Bibliotheca Sancta." The introductory questions to Scripture were also treated by Ludwig de Tena (d. 1622) and Francis Pavone (d. 1637).

Biblical Criticism.—Besides the editors of the Sistine and Clementine Bibles, the following were noteworthy workers in this field: Francis Lucas of Bruges (d. 1619), John Morinus (d. 1659), Peter Carbo (d. 1590), Marius a Calasio (d. 1620).

Biblical Geography.—This was treated by Christian Adricomius (d. 1585), Abraham Ortelius (d. 1598), James Bonfrerius (d. 1642), and Francis Quaresmius (d. 1656).

Biblical Archeology.—This was treated by Arias Montanus in the Antwerp Polyglot, Charles Sigonius (d. 1584), Fort. Schacchi (d. 1643), Mar. Mersennius (d. 1649), and Cœl. de Monte Marsano (d. 1659).

Commentaries.—The following are the more important scholars who wrote commentaries on individual books, on the Old or New Testaments, or on the entire Bible: James Bonfrerius, S.J. (d. 1642), Nicholas Serarius, S.J. (d. 1609), Benjamin Pererius, S.J. (d. 1610), Gaspar Sanctius (d. 1628),

Anthony Agellius, Ord. Theat. (d. 1608), Gilbert Genebrard, O.S.B. (d. 1597), St. Robert Bellarmine, S.J. (d. 1621), Simon de Muis (d. 1644), John Pineda, S.J. (d. 1637), Michael Ghislerius, O. Theat. (d. 1646), Cornelius Jansenius, Bishop of Ghent (d. 1576), John Maldonatus, S.J. (d. 1583), John Lorinus (d. 1634), William Estius (d. 1613), Benjamin Justinianus, S.J. (d. 1622), L. ab Alcasar, S.J. (d. 1613), F. Ribera, S.J. (d. 1591), Cornelius a Lapide, S.J. (d. 1637), John de la Haye, O.F.M. (d. 1661), who collected and edited the commentaries of Emmanuel Sa (d. 1596), John Mariana (d. 1624), Thomas Mavenda (d. 1628), James Tirinus (d. 1636), John Gordon (d. 1641), and Stephen Menochius (d. 1655). St. Lawrence of Brindisi (d. 1619) was also very active in the production of Biblical works.

Protestant Exegesis.—The Protestants of the sixteenth century declared that the Bible was the only source of faith. Having rejected the Vulgate version, they returned to the original texts and immediately devoted themselves wholeheartedly to the Bible. Their work represents chiefly extension rather than real exegetical progress. To the principles of rational Hermeneutics they added nothing new which had not already been taught by the humanists and the scholastics. Even though they severely attacked the allegorical meaning of the preceding ages, their doctrine of the biblical meanings does not substantially differ from the scholastics.

* Flacius Illyricus and * Sal. Glassius were the chief exponents of systematical presentations of hermeneutical problems. * Luther explained much by types, and this method of interpretation reached its culmination at the end of this period in * John Koch (1603-1669), who together with his followers are commonly called the Symbolists. * Calvin and his followers held to the literal meaning.

Having rejected the authority of the Church, the Protestants in regard to the principles of supernatural interpretation made their own analogy of faith. When they accepted their dogmas of faith, as in their symbols of faith, they appointed themselves or their synods as the sole judges of interpretation.

The first scholar to prepare the way for the critics of a later period was * Hugo Grotius (1583-1645), in his "Annotationes in V. et N.T.," which for the greater part was a philological treatise on the Bible.   * Matthew Pole in his "Synopsis criticorum sacrorum" (London, 1660) collected the principal commentaries of this period.   But of greater value are the archæological and philological writings of Protestants during this period—for example, those of * Samuel Bochart (London, 1663), * John Drusius (d. 1616), and * Ludwig de Dieu (d. 1642).

Art. 2.   The Beginning of Biblical Criticism (1650-1800)

Bibliography: For John Bernard de Rossi: cf. Vaccari, A., in V.D., 11 (1931), 349-352.
For Jean Astruc: cf. O'Doherty, E., in C.B.Q., 15 (1953), 300-304.

The critical approach to the Bible began with * Ludwig Cappelus in 1650 among the Protestants and with Richard Simon in 1678 among the Catholics.

Catholic Exegesis.—During this period the following writers are worthy of mention: Bernard Lamy (d. 1715) and Cherubinus a St. Joseph (d. 1716) in biblical introduction; Bartolocci-Imbonati (1675-1693) and James Lelong (d. 1723) in bibliography and literary history; Fr. Houbigant, S.J. (d. 1753), and John Bernard de Rossi (1784-1798) in textual criticism; Bl. Ugolini (1744-1769) in archæology; John J. Berryer (d. 1758) and Natalis Alexander (d. 1722) in bible history; James B. Bossuet (d. 1704), Bernard a Piconio (d. 1709), and August Calmet (d. 1757) for their commentaries; Jean Astruc (1753) for higher or literary criticism.

Protestant Exegesis.—During this period mention may be made of * I. G. Carpzovius (d. 1767) in introduction; * H. Relandus (d. 1718) in geography; * John Lightfoot (d. 1675) and * Christian Schöttgen (d. 1751) in archæology; * John J. Wetstein (d. 1754), * John Bengel (d. 1752), and * Albert Schultens (d. 1750) in philology; * I. A. Ernesti (d. 1781) in hermeneutics; * M. Geier (d. 1680), * C. Vitringa (d. 1722),

* I. Cleric (d. 1736), * John H. Michaelis (d. 1738), and
* Christian B. Michaelis (d. 1764) in exegesis proper.

Art. 3   The Nineteenth and Twentieth Centuries

Bibliography: *Willoughby, H. R. (Editor), "The Study of the Bible
Today and Tomorrow" (Chicago, 1947); *Rowley, H. H. (Editor), "The
Old Testament and Modern Study" (Oxford, 1951); * "The Interpreter's
Bible" (vol. I: New York-Nashville, 1952), 127-141; Bea, A., "Bible
Studies Today," in *Theol. Digest,* 3 (1955), 51-54; Philbin, R. G., "Some
Modern Protestant Attitudes towards Hermeneutics," in C.B.Q., 21
(1959), 115-135.

The second golden age of Biblical studies which was
marked by outstanding accomplishments until about the end
of the seventeenth century was followed generally by over a
century (c. 1800-1918) of great decline.   The outstanding
reasons for this scholarly and popular inactivity were the
reign of rationalism (with modern Communism as its by-
product), the supreme attraction of the natural or physical
and social sciences, the unusual stress placed upon historical
and patristic studies, and the deplorable neglect of scholarly
Biblical studies.   All of these causes contributed to the decline, disregard or destruction of the authority of the Bible
in the religious life of people or in other fields.   This period
may be termed the least fruitful and the most unsatisfactory
in the history of exegesis.

Rationalism, which was the result of Deism in England, was
applied to the Old Testament by * Baruch Spinoza (d. 1677)
and * H. S. Reimarus (d. 1768) to the New Testament. Its
principles were applied to hermeneutics by * John S. Semmler (d. 1791); to the Old Testament by * J. G. Eichorn
(d. 1827), * John Sev. Vater (d. 1826), * M. L. De Wette
(d. 1849); to the New Testament by * H. E. Paulus (d. 1851),
* Ferdinand Chr. Bauer (d. 1860), and especially by * D.
Fried. Strauss (d. 1875), and * E. Renan (d. 1892).

Rationalists do not recognize the divine origin and authority
of the Bible, but regard the books as mere profane or secular
documents and often maintain that they are erroneous. They

deny the existence of a supernatural order or anything supernatural, and explain whatever appears miraculous as a myth
or fable. Hence, in their interpretation of the books of the
Bible they apply the system of evolution, deny the authenticity
of the books, and frequently ascribe to the books or parts of
them a very late date of composition.

The new compromising approach by *J. Wellhausen (1844-
1918) and the School of Higher (or Literary) Criticism, being
based upon rationalistic and subjective principles, became
popular, ruled the non-Catholic academic world for over a
century, and then had to be abandoned because of its apparent weaknesses. Against this approach were Catholic, Orthodox Protestant and Jewish scholars who kept on the defensive
by stressing the genuineness, credibility and authority of the
Bible, but hardly had the time to develop the religious and
theological teaching of the Biblical books.

The modern approach to Biblical studies began after World
War I (1914-1918) and is based upon the great advances
made in archæology, the ancient history and literature of the
entire Fertile Crescent.[1] As the result of these archæological
discoveries and their objective evaluation, rigid interpretation,
the Biblical literature must no longer be considered as an
isolated library, but rather as a vital part of the entire Fertile
Crescent pattern of culture and writings. Furthermore, these
Biblical writings, because of their inspired character, now also
stand out more clearly for their uniqueness, that is, their
religious and literary peculiarities (e.g., compare the Mosaic
Code with ancient Semitic law codes, as the Code of Hammurabi); the writings of the prophets with the Babylonian
incantations; the wisdom literature of the Old Testament

---

[1] Cf. Steinmueller, J. E. — Sullivan, K., art. "Archaeology," in
C.B.E.O.T.; *Albright, W. F., "Archæology and the Religion of Israel"
(2nd ptg., Baltimore, 1941); *Finegan, J., "Light from the Ancient East"
(2nd ed., Princeton, 1959); Parrot, A., "Studies in Biblical Archæology"
(New York, 1955-); *Pritchard, J. B., "Ancient Near East in Pictures"
(Princeton, 1955); *idem*, "Ancient Near Eastern Texts" (2nd ed., Princeton, 1955): *idem*, "Archæology and the Old Testament" (Princeton,
1958); Simons, J., "Jerusalem in the Old Testament" (Leiden, 1952);
*Wright, G. E., "Biblical Archæology" (Philadelphia, 1957).

with that of Egypt and elsewhere; the Gospels with the historical writings of some Greek and Roman authors; the Epistles of St. Paul with various Roman and Greek letters; etc.).

The modern approach to Biblical studies has been very fruitful among scholars.

(1) The modern non-Catholic approach is *pneumatological*, or theological. It abandons the sterile Wellhausian evolutionary approach to the Bible (i.e., the so-called historicism) because it left the individual soul in a vacuum and was unable to satisfy the permanent, religious needs of devout people. This theological approach stresses the doctrinal and religious elements (*fides et mores*) of the Bible. This approach was first sponsored by *Karl Barth in 1919 (Römerbrief) and, later, on a wider and more scholarly basis by * Gerhard Kittel in his *Theologisches Wörterbuck* (vol. I, Stuttgart, 1933; vol. VI, *ibid.*, 1954-1959), still to be completed. In this monumental work, which international scholars of all creeds admire, we find that the Old and New Testaments are definitely linked together and that Christianity is not treated or regarded as a mere offshoot of Qumran, Gnostic, Manichæan or Persian religions.

Less successful, but more compromising, is the approach of the liberal existentialist * Rudolf Bultmann, one of the most influential German thinkers of modern Protestantism. His basic problem, like that of many other Protestant theologians, is to distinguish between the historical Jesus and the Christ of faith, as if kerygmatically these two were distinct. Bultmann's method is to de-mythologize the New Testament, that is, to strip the gospel message of alleged mythological thought-patterns. "For the Catholic exegete . . . the problem of demythologizing, as understood by Bultmann, does not exist" (Bea, A., *op. cit.*, 54). However, Bultmann stresses another element, namely, the adaption, application of the New Testament thought-pattern to *modern man*. From this secondary, practical approach scholars may fruitfully learn and apply the great Biblical lessons: What is the theological and moral content of the Bible? How does it apply to man under present living conditions? *And* (what is disregarded in Bultmann theology) how does man's present theological and moral conduct become decisive for his future life in heaven or hell?

(2) The modern Catholic approach to the Bible was inaugurated by Pope Leo XIII in his encyclical "Providentissimus Deus" (Nov. 18, 1893), which laid the foundation for a renewed Catholic scholarly research in Biblical studies. Mention may be made of two outstanding pioneers of this movement: the Jesuit, Rudolph Cornely (1830-1908), who edited and guided the commentaries of the *Cursus Scripturae Sacrae,* and the Dominican Père M.-J. Lagrange, the founder of the Ecole Biblique of Jerusalem, of the *Revue Biblique* and of the *Etudes Bibliques.*

Other papal encyclicals issued for positive guidance in Biblical research and for the formation of Biblical scholars are: "Pascendi Domini Gregis" by St. Pius X (Sept. 8, 1907), "SpiritusParaclitus" by Pope Benedict XV (Sept. 15, 1920), "Divino afflante Spiritu" by Pope Pius XII (Sept. 30, 1943), and "Humani Generis" by the same Pontiff.[2]

Besides these encyclicals the Holy See encouraged specialized Biblical studies and scholarship by positive action. Thus, Leo XIII established the Pontifical Biblical Commission (Oct. 30, 1902), and St. Pius X declared that its decisions bind Catholcis in conscience (Nov. 18, 1907). The same saintly Pontiff established the Pontifical Biblical Institute at Rome (May 7, 1909), placing Leopold Fonck, S.J., of the University of Innsbruck, Austria, in charge.

From these papal writings and actions we may gather that modern Catholic Biblical scholarship has its own particular characteristics and function. (1) Its primary aim is to obtain the *literal meaning* of the Biblical words, expressions and passages which was intended by the sacred writer. (2) Then, too, the mode of expression or *literary form* adapted by the

---

[2] Cf. Steinmueller, J. E.—Sullivan, K., art., "Encyclicals, Pontifical Biblical," in C.B.E.O.T.

sacred writer should be studied and determined. (3) Finally, God's message and preaching (*kerygma*) through the prophets and Apostles to mankind is to be properly presented. This *Biblical theology* (unlike that of non-Catholics who constantly begin anew) should be based upon sound, solid, traditional interpretation of the Church and will be a little different from the current approach found in dogmatic and moral theology. "Biblical theology as understood today . . . [consists] in setting forth systematically the whole doctrinal content of both Old and New Testaments, from its earliest beginnings through its gradual development and enlargement as one period of revelation followed another. Thus, it is nothing less than the crown and completion of all the individual contributions of exegetes" (Bea, A., *op. cit.*, 54).[3]

For the richness of modern scholarly Catholic and non-Catholic literature on the Bible, that is, books and periodicals, confer the "Elenchus Bibliographicus Biblicus" in *Biblica* (Rome, 1920-).

[3] Cf. Steinmueller, J. E., "Eran, Philein, Agapan in extra-Biblical and Biblical sources," in *Studia Anselmiana* (Rome, 1951), 404-423; *idem*, "Sacrificial Blood in the Bible," in *Biblica*, 40 (1959), 422-433; Spicq, C., "Agapé dans le Nouveau Testament" (3 vols., Paris, 1958-1959).

PART VI

SACRED ANTIQUITIES

Bibliography: Kortleitner, F. X., "Archæologia Biblica" (new ed., Innsbruck, 1917); * Watzinger, C., "Denkmäler Palästinas" (2 vols., Leipzig, 1933, 1935); * Barrois, A.-G., "Manuel d'Archeologie Biblique" (2 vols., Paris, 1939, 1953); * Pritchard, J. B., "Ancient Near East in Pictures" (Princeton, 1954) fig., 574 ff.

CHAPTER I

SACRED PLACES

Art. 1.   The Tabernacle (Ex. 25-27; 30; 36-40) [1]

Bibliography: Lesêtre, H., in D.D.L.B., s.v. *Tabernacle;* * Kennedy, A. R. S., in H.D.B., s.v. *Tabernacle;* * Schick, C., "Die Stifshütte, der Tempel in Jerusalem und der Tempelplatz der Jetztzeit" (Berlin, 1896); * Cross, F. M., "The Tabernacle," in B.A., 10 (1947), 45-68.

The tabernacle consisted of two parts: (a) a court; (b) the tabernacle proper.

(a) THE COURT OF THE TABERNACLE (Ex. 27, 9-19; 38, 9-20)

This court (Hebr., hatser), with entrance on the east side, formed a sacred rectangular enclosure, 100 cubits long and 50 cubits wide (about 150 x 75 feet), and fenced off from the rest of the encampment with linen curtains.   These curtains (Hebr., qelaim) probably numbered 15 (since we know that the special curtain at the gate of the court measured 20 cubits, Ex. 27, 16), and were made of fine twisted linen.   The special curtain, however, was woven in the four sacred colors: violet, purple, scarlet, and white.   The curtains were fastened upon 60 posts or pillars, and were so arranged that on the north and south sides stood 20, and on the east and west sides 10. These pillars, made of acacia wood (Hebr., shittim wood), stood on bronze bases and had silver capitals, which were

---

[1] Various names have been given to the tabernacle: the dwelling (Hebr., mishkan), the dwelling of the witness (Hebr., mishkan ha'eduth), the dwelling of Jahweh (Hebr., mishkan Jahweh), the sanctuary (Hebr., miqdash), the tent or tabernacle of the witness (Hebr., ohel ha'eduth), etc.   This tabernacle, however, must be carefully distinguished from "the tent of meeting" (Hebr., ohel mo'ed), which seldom means the sacred sanctuary of Jahweh (cf. Ex. 30, 36; Num. 3, 7), but rather refers to the tent of Moses (cf. Ex. 33, 7-11; Num. 11, 16; 12, 4; Deut. 31, 14), placed outside of the camp.   Here Moses consulted the will of God and employed Josue, the Ephraimite, as his minister.

furnished with fillets or bands of silver. The pillars were kept in their position by means of cords fastened to bronze pegs driven into the ground.

Furniture in the Court.—In the court stood the altar of holocausts or burnt-offerings and the bronze laver.

The *altar of holocausts* (Ex. 27, 1-8; 38, 1-7) consisted of a framework of acacia wood, 5 cubits square and 3 cubits high, and stood in the center of the first eastern square. The hollow framework was filled up with earth and stones, so that the latter formed the altar proper. The wood was sheathed with bronze plates, and provided at the corners with four bronze horns. Half-way between the top and the base of the altar a projecting ledge about 1½ cubits wide surrounded the altar, so that the priests could more easily perform their sacred duties. A bronze screen or lattice work covered the outer lower half of the altar to serve as an ornamentation, to prevent profane hands from touching the altar, and to provide a place where the blood of the victims could be spilled at the base of the altar. The altar was carried by means of two poles of acacia wood overlaid with bronze, and these poles were attached by means of rings or bands to the upper extremities of the lattice work. In conjunction with the altar various instruments were required: forks and spits to turn the victims over in the fire; pots to receive the ashes; shovels to remove the ashes; bowls or basins to receive and scatter the blood; fire-pans and knives for the sacrifice. The fire on this altar was never allowed quite to die out (Lev. 6, 12 f), and was miraculously lit at the first sacrifice (Lev. 9, 24).

The *bronze laver* (Ex. 30, 17-21; 38, 8) stood between this altar of holocaust and the tabernacle proper, a little to the south, and was made of the bronze "mirrors of the women who served at the gate of the meeting" (Ex. 38, 8). No clear description of this laver is given in the Bible, but on the analogy of the brazen sea in the temple, it seems to have consisted of two parts: the upper part was shaped like a cauldron to hold the water, and the lower part served as a

basin that could be used by the priests to wash their hands
and feet before entering the tabernacle, and also to cleanse
the flesh of the sacrificial victims and the sacrificial vessels
and garments, if they happened to be stained. The upper
part probably had two openings or taps to let out the water;
the base was either square or round and of a moderate height.

(b) THE TABERNACLE PROPER (Ex. 26; 36)

The tabernacle was situated in the center of the western
square of the enclosure and formed a long quadrangle. Its
length (interior) was 30 cubits and its width (interior) 10
cubits. It was made of a wooden framework, composed of
48 strong planks or beams of acacia wood. Each plank was
covered with gold and measured 10 cubits in length, 1½
cubits in width, and about ½ cubit in thickness. This wooden
frame surrounded the interior on three sides, but on the fourth
side were columns and a curtain. The two longitudinal walls
contained 20 planks each; the shorter end (or western wall)
only 8, of which the two in the corners measured only half a
cubit. At the lower end of each plank were two projections
which fitted into silver sockets, and on the outer side were
golden rings, five on each beam, through which were passed
the gilded bars that kept all the planks in place, and so kept
the whole structure together.

The space enclosed in this wooden framework was divided
into two parts: the Most Holy Place or the Holy of Holies
and the Holy Place or the Holy. (1) The *Most Holy Place*
measured 10 cubits in length, width, and height, and contained
the ark of the covenant. A special curtain of violet, purple,
scarlet, and white colors separated both Places, and was decorated with golden threads and figures of cherubim. It hung
down from four posts of acacia wood covered with gold and
placed at equal distances from one another. These pillars
had bases of silver and capitals of gold. (2) *The Holy Place*
measured 20 cubits in length and 10 cubits in width and
height, and contained the altar of incense, showbread table,

and golden lampstand. The curtain or portière at the opening of the tabernacle was of the same kind as in the Most Holy Place, but was not decorated with cherubim. It hung down from five posts of acacia wood covered with gold and resting in five bronze bases or sockets. The high priest alone entered the Most Holy Place on the Feast of Expiation, but the ministering priests entered daily the Holy Place.

The tabernacle did not have any wooden roof, but its place was taken by *coverings* stretched over the framework. These coverings were four in number (Ex. 26, 1-14; 36, 8-19). (1) The lowest or inner covering consisted of ten cloths or curtains woven in four colors (violet, purple, scarlet and white) with figures of cherubim. Each of the ten curtains was 28 cubits long and 4 wide, and they were joined together in two sets of five, so as to form two large curtains each measuring 28 by 20 cubits, and the whole covering that they formed together was 40 cubits long and 28 wide. We are not told how the five separate parts of each half were composed; but we know that each of these two sets of five at the end of the curtains had 50 violet loops, placed opposite to one another, and fastened together by means of 50 golden hooks or clasps. (2) The second covering was less precious. It was woven of goats' hair and composed not of 10, but of 11 curtains, each of which was 30 cubits long and 4 wide. Its total extent, therefore, was 30 by 44 cubits. It, too, consisted of two parts, the front one being made of 6 curtains and the back one of only 5. These two parts were fastened together by means of 150 loops and 50 brass hooks, so as to form one whole. It should be noted that half a curtain hung down at the front and rear of the tabernacle (Ex. 26, 9. 12). This covering was longer and wider to protect the innermost one. (3) The third covering consisted of rams' skins dyed red. No size or description is given, but it probably served to protect the other two coverings. (4) The fourth covering consisted of *tahash* skins. The word tahash seems to refer to some marine animal as the seal or the halicore (dugong) that is found in the Red Sea, and not to the badger which lives in holes in the earth. No size or description of this outer covering is given.

Those who maintain that the tabernacle had a flat roof (e.g., * Kennedy) insist that the first covering was placed on the roof lengthwise so that 10 cubits hung over the western wall and reached the ground. Of the width, 10 cubits formed the roof, leaving 18 cubits to hang down the sides. But because of the numerous difficulties caused by such an hypothesis many scholars prefer the interpretation of * Schick that the roof was oblique. The middle bar (Ex. 26, 28; 36, 23) is interpreted as the ridge pole, extending 5 cubits in the front and 5 in the back of the tabernacle, thus being 40 cubits long and 15 cubits above the ground. In the front or eastern side, where there were five pillars placed 5 cubits from each other and supporting the portière, the central pillar, 15 cubits high, supported the ridge pole and was flanked by two pillars 10 cubits high, which in turn were flanked by two pillars 5 cubits high. Thus, a small vestibule stood at the entrance to the Holy Place. A similar arrangement of five pillars, though not mentioned in the Bible, is assumed for the western wall. The inner covering would then have stretched across the entire ridge pole for a distance of 40 cubits. Along the northern and southern sides, 5 cubits from the tabernacle, were placed pillars 5 cubits high attached to the ground by means of cords and pegs. The various coverings hung obliquely on both sides of the tabernacle until they reached these pillars and formed a covered passageway along the sides (cf. 1 Sam. 3, 3).

Furniture in the Holy Place.—Three articles of furniture stood in the holy place: the altar of incense, the table for the loaves of proposition or showbread, and the golden lampstand.

(1) The *altar of incense* (Ex. 30, 1-10; 37, 25-29), also called the golden altar, occupied a position in the middle before the inner curtain. It was four-cornered and made of acacia wood, measuring 2 cubits in height and 1 cubit in length and width. It had a so-called "roof" (*gag*); that is, a raised edge ran all round the flat upper surface, and a golden garland was fastened to the edge, as in the table of the showbreads. Below the garland on each side were two golden rings, through which poles were passed for carrying the altar.

Horns were fastened to the four corners. The whole was overlaid with gold. Incense was offered on this altar daily, both morning and evening. The ritual was as follows. A priest took some glowing charcoal from the altar of holocausts and carried it in a golden vessel into the tabernacle, whilst another carried the incense. The first priest scattered the charcoal on the altar, and the second laid the incense upon it. Meanwhile the people stood in the court, engaged in prayer, and then they received the priest's blessing. The incense consisted of four ingredients: stacte (Hebr., nataf), onycha, galbanum, and pure incense (Ex. 30, 34-38), which were called collectively *sammim* (i.e., sweet perfumes). It had to be salted, and had to be clean and holy (i.e., some salt was strewed over it, as over everything offered in sacrifice); it was not to contain any foreign ingredients, and after it was mixed, was to be used only in the sanctuary. It was forbidden, under the penalty of death, to use incense mixed in this particular manner for any profane purpose.

(2) The *table for the loaves of proposition* or showbreads (Ex. 25, 23-30; 37, 10-16) stood on the north side of the Holy Place, and to the right of the entrance. It was of acacia wood, measuring 2 cubits long, 1 cubit wide, and 1½ cubits high, and was completely covered with sheets of gold. At the top was a projecting ledge of gold (*misgereth*, i.e., enclosure) as wide as a man's hand, so that the surface of the table lay below it, and round about this margin ran a golden garland. To the legs of the table four rings were fastened, through which poles could be passed so that it might be carried. These poles also were of acacia wood, overlaid with gold. Upon the table lay always twelve thin loaves of the finest wheat flour, called showbread, perpetual bread, holy bread, or bread of God. They were arranged in two rows of six, and Josephus Flavius assures us that they were unleavened. Every Sabbath they were taken away and replaced by fresh ones; the priests ate the stale bread within the sanctuary (Lev. 24, 5-9). At this ceremony the incense near the loaves was burned (perhaps on the altar of incense). The loaves were carried in on (probably

two) shallow dishes and set in order; the incense was placed
in little bowls. Wine also was brought in (perhaps only on
the Sabbath) in special jugs, poured into bowls and then
offered as libations, being thrown out on the ground. All the
accessory vessels were of pure gold.

(3) The *golden lampstand* (Ex. 25, 31-40; 37, 17-24)
stood sideways on the south side of the Holy Place, opposite
the showbread table, and to the left of the entrance. A talent
of gold was used in its construction. It was of beaten work
or repoussé of finest gold; it had seven branches, the one in
the middle rising straight up from the base, and the others
being in pairs on either side of it. The central shaft rested
upon a pedestal called in Holy Scripture *jarek* (i.e., hip or
loin); the name seems to have been selected because there
were probably feet lower down, whilst the upper part suggested a body with outstretched arms. On the branches were
ornaments like the cup of a flower, consisting of a knob and a
blossom. These were placed on the central shaft below the
points where the arms branched off, and also at the place
where the shaft joined its pedestal. Moreover, each side-
branch bore three such ornaments, so that there were twenty-
two in all. At the upper ends were lamps, but these did not
actually form part of the lampstand, and only rested on the
seven branches. In shape they probably resembled the ordinary lamps of antiquity; that is to say, they were oval, having
at one end a projecting wick and at the other a handle by
which they could be carried. At the ends of the seven arms
were slight depressions to hold the lamps. The lamps cast
their light inwards, towards the showbread table on the north.
Every morning they had to be taken down to be cleaned, and
then replaced. The purest olive oil was burned in these lamps.
As accessories are mentioned (Ex. 25, 38) golden snuffers and
dishes to hold the snuffers and wicks.

Furniture in the Most Holy Place. —The *ark of the covenant* or of the witness stood in the Most Holy Place (Ex.
25, 10-22; 37, 1-9). It was a chest of acacia wood, covered
with gold both inside and outside. Its length was 2½ cubits,

its width and height 1½ cubits. Round the middle of it ran a garland of pure gold. At the four corners were golden rings, through which gilded poles were passed along the shorter sides (cf. 3 Kgs. 8, 8) to enable the ark to be carried; these poles were never to be removed. Inside the ark was nothing but the two stone tables, on which the Ten Commandments were inscribed (Ex. 25, 16; Deut. 10, 4 f). According to Hebrews 9, 4, beside the holy ark were kept Aaron's rod and a vessel of manna. In Deuteronomy 31, 25 f we read that the Book of the Law also lay beside the ark.

Over the ark was the *kapporeth* (i.e., a cover of pure gold). It was by no means intended merely to close the ark, but had a far higher purpose. This is implied by the fact that it was of solid gold, whilst the ark was only of wood overlaid with sheets of gold, and also by the command that the kapporeth should be as long and as broad as the ark (Ex. 25, 17); if it were only a cover, this would be a matter of course. Its true purpose is suggested by the Holy of Holies being called the house of the kapporeth. The word *kapporeth* (i.e., propitiatory or place of atonement) is derived from the verb "kipper" meaning "to expiate or atone." The kapporeth may be explained as God's resting place. At either end of it, and inseparable from it was a cherub of beaten gold, undoubtedly in human form, but with wings which were stretched inwards over the ark. The two cherubim on the kapporeth formed the throne of God (cf. 1 Sam. 4, 4), of which the ark was the footstool. It was therefore called the *shekina* (i.e., dwelling). From this spot God made answer to Moses and other leaders of the people, when they consulted Him on important matters (cf. Ex. 25, 22). If the question is asked how we are to imagine this presence of God, whether it was perceptible to the senses or only perceptible intellectually, we may reply that the object of the Holy of Holies was to perpetuate the memory of the events on Sinai, and that for this reason we may believe the presence of God to have been perceptible in clouds and fire (Lev. 16, 2; Isa. 37, 14; 1 Par. 13, 6). It is, however, improbable that this presence could always be per-ceived; as a rule, it was latent, and became visible only on important occasions.

The History of the Ark.[2]—After the Israelites crossed the Jordan the ark was placed by Josue at Galgal (Jos. 4, 19). Shortly afterwards it was used in the siege of Jericho (Jos. 6, 4 ff) and on Mount Ebal (Jos. 8, 33). After the permanent occupation of the Promised Land it was placed most likely at Silo with the tabernacle (Jos. 18, 1), where it was still to be found 300 to 350 years later at the time of Samuel (1 Sam. 3, 3). By way of exception it was brought to Bethel during the war of the Israelites with the tribe of Benjamin (Jdgs. 20, 27).

During the Philistine wars the Israelites brought it to Aphec (1 Sam. 4), but it was captured by the Philistines and taken by them to Azotus, Geth, and Accaron (1 Sam. 5). After nine months it was returned and brought to Bethsames, where it remained but a brief time (1 Sam. 6, 12 ff). Subsequently it was transferred to Cariathiarim (1 Sam. 7, 1), where it remained for nearly 80 years.

Though the tabernacle was situated at Nobe under the high priest Achimelech (1 Sam. 21), yet the ark remained at Cariathiarim until King David, having defeated the Jebusites, transferred it (2 Sam. 6, 3; 1 Par. 13, 6) to the house of Obededom the Gethite, where it remained for three months (2 Sam. 6, 11; 1 Par. 13, 14). Finally it was brought by David to Mount Sion, Jerusalem, and placed in a special tent or tabernacle (2 Sam. 6, 12 ff; 1 Par. 15-16), and here it remained until King Solomon constructed the temple.

The History of the Tabernacle.—After the occupation of the Promised Land by the Israelites the tabernacle had three permanent sites. (1) It was transferred from Galgal to *Silo* (Jos. 18, 1), where Josue distributed the land by lot to the Israelites "before the Lord at the door of the tabernacle of the witness" (Jos. 19, 51). Here it remained during the period of the Judges (cf. Jdgs. 18, 31; 21, 19; 1 Sam. 1, 9; 3, 3) until

[2] Cf. Worden, T., "The Ark of the Covenant," in *Scripture*, 5 (1952), 82-90.

after the death of Heli, when Silo was destroyed probably by the Philistines (cf. Jer. 7, 12; 26, 6; Ps. 77, 60). (2) At the time of King Saul and David's flight from his court it was situated at *Nobe*, where the high priest Achimelech and 85 priests ministered, and where the ephod, loaves of proposition, and the sword of Goliath were to be found (1 Sam. 21-22). (3) Solomon offered various sacrifices on the altar of holocausts in *Gabaon*, where the tabernacle was situated (2 Par. 1, 3; 3 Kgs. 3, 4). Here Sadoc, of the Aaronic line of Eleazar, and his brethren priests ministered (1 Par. 16, 39), while Abiathar, the friend of David, of the Aaronic line of Ithamar, and his brethren priests ministered at the ark and its special tabernacle on Mount Sion (cf. 1 Par. 16, 37). At the time of the dedication of the temple by Solomon the remnants of the tabernacle together with its furniture and vessels were stored in one of the chambers of the temple (3 Kgs. 8, 4; 2 Par. 5, 5).

The Modern Critical School.—The modern critical school, outside the Church, declares that the Pentateuch does not favor a uniform place of worship but rather gives evidence of an evolutionary historical process. Exodus 20, 24-26, taken from the Book of the Covenant and called E (i.e., Elohistic document), is alleged to be the oldest of the laws and to date from the ninth century B.C. (i.e., many centuries after the activity of Moses). It is maintained that this law permits a multiplicity of sanctuaries. Deuteronomy 12, 4-28, called D (i.e., Deuteronomistic document), these critics say, is an attempt made towards centralization of worship at the time of King Josias (622 B.C.). Leviticus 17, called P (i.e., Priestly document), represents the final stage in the evolutionary process of worship, and demands the absolute centralization of worship before the tabernacle, which is supposed never to have existed. This law, they assert, was enacted in the sixth century B.C., after the time of the prophet Ezechiel or the Babylonian exile.

This evolutionary historical process supposed by modern rationalistic critics cannot be sustained. Ex. 20, 24-26 is primarily concerned with the form and quality of the altar and secondarily supposes the possibility of numerous sanctuaries in the future. But whether this multiplicity is simultaneous or successive is not indicated in the text. According to this law given in the first year of the forty years of Hebrew nomadic life, no individual was to erect altars anywhere on his own responsibility, but only in those places designated by God. In the year's sojourn on Mount Sinai, while the tabernacle with its altar of holocausts was being constructed, sacrifices were offered to God. Even after the completion of the tabernacle, sacrifices could be offered in individual cases on altars of unhewn stones (Ex. 20, 25 f) and on those sites revealed by God. The fact that the quality of this altar was different from that of the altar of holocausts shows that provision was being made for extraordinary sacrifices. There can be no contradiction in this that God, who made a general law for the people to observe, ordered at times individuals to sacrifice. In spite of the fact that Ex. 20, 24 permits some sort of multiplicity of worship, whether successive or simultaneous, yet this same law of the Covenant inculcates some kind of unity of worship when it commands every male Israelite to appear three times a year before Jahweh their God (Ex. 23, 17). This may be considered as a preparatory step for the localized unity of worship.

Leviticus 17 forbids any animal to be slaughtered outside of the camp and tabernacle. Every butchering must at the same time be a sacrifice before the door of the tabernacle, the only place of worship for the nomadic Hebrews. The law, therefore, advocates the centralization of worship. The text supposes the existence of the tabernacle, and it is preposterous to assume that the priests during the period of the Babylonian exile gave such a detailed description of the tabernacle to a fictitious object. The tabernacle was an historical reality, and its existence in the pre-Davidic period is clearly borne out by the historical books of the Old Testament, archæology, and other secular documents.

This law of Leviticus, restricting worship to a determined

place, could be easily observed by the Hebrews living closely together in the desert, but it would be impractical for the people in the Promised Land. To provide for this future contingency, when the twelve tribes would be settled in their territories, Moses gave the law contained in Deuteronomy 12, 4-28. It mitigated the requirement of bringing all animals before the tabernacle to be slaughtered as sacrifices, but even this was later practised as a pious custom (cf. 1 Sam. 14, 32 ff). It specified that there would be one centralized place of worship for all in one of the tribes (Deut. 12, 14). Thus, Deuteronomy 12 is a logical sequence to Leviticus 17, rather than the reverse as critics hold. Frequently the authors of the Books of Kings indicate that the plurality of sanctuaries was contrary to the law.

Art. 2   The Temple of Solomon[3]

(3 Kgs. 6-8; 2 Par. 3-5; Ez. 40-42; 46; Josephus, *Antiq.*, VIII. 3)

When the Israelites took Jerusalem from the Jebusites and obtained complete possession of the city, it was proposed to build a temple to the Lord on Mount Moria, according to the same plan as the tabernacle (cf. Wisd. 9, 8). King David collected a great quantity of materials for this purpose (1 Par. 29, 2 ff), and gave them and the designs that he had prepared according to divine inspiration (1 Par. 28, 19) to his son Solomon, who faithfully carried out his father's wishes. He began to build the temple in the fourth year of his reign (968 B.C.) and completed it in seven years (3 Kgs. 6).

The site was first chosen by David (1 Par. 22, 1 f) and later actually by his son Solomon (2 Par. 3, 1). Here on Mount Moria, on the threshing floor of Ornan, the Jebusite, David had seen an angel standing and built an altar (2 Sam. 24, 16 ff; 1 Par. 21, 20 ff). This mountain now artificially levelled contains the celebrated Mohammedan shrine "Haram esh-

[3] Cf. * May, H. G., in B.A.S.O.R.. 88 (1942), 19-27; * Waterman, L., in J.O.N.E.S., 2 (1943), 284-294; * Garber, P. L., in B.A., 14 (1951), 2-24; *idem*, in J.B.L., 77 (1958), 123-129; * Wright, G. E., in B.A., 18 (1955), 43 f.

Sherif" (i.e., the chief sanctuary). Its outer walls total about 5,000 feet in length and give an area of almost 468,000 square feet. Almost within the center of this rectangle there is another levelled space with an area of about 79,500 square feet, but this construction is posterior to the destruction of the temple by Titus; within this area and almost in the center there is today a building called "Kubbet es-Sakhra" (i.e., Dome of the Rock),[4] which corresponds with the altar of holocausts of the Solomon temple.

(a) DESCRIPTION OF THE TEMPLE [5]

The temple building consisted of four parts. (1) The *Holy of Holies* (Hebr. debir) was 20 cubits in length, width and height (3 Kgs. 6, 20; 2 Par. 3, 8). (2) The *Holy Place* (Hebr. hekal) was 40 cubits long, 20 cubits broad, and 30 high. These two places comprised "the house, which King Solomon built to the Lord," and were 60 cubits in length, 20 in width, and 30 in height (3 Kgs. 6, 2; 2 Par. 3, 3). An upper chamber, 10 cubits in height, was situated over the Holy of Holies (cf. 1 Par. 28, 11; 2 Par. 3, 9). (3) In front of the house of the temple was a *porch* (Hebr., ulam or elam) 10 cubits in depth (east to west), and running along the whole width of the building (20 cubits); nothing is stated as to its height in the Third Book of Kings, but in 2 Par. 3, 4 we are told that it was 120 cubits high. This reading may perhaps be due to a copyist's mistake, and varies from the Septuagint, Syriac and Arabic readings. It seems very likely that the height of the porch was the same as that of the house (i.e., 30 cubits). (4) All round the outside of the temple, except at the east or front, ran an *annex* (Hebr., jazua, i.e., spread out) containing three stories of chambers for the things used in the temple worship and for storage of supplies. The beams supporting

---

[4] Cf. * Dalman, G., "Neue Petra-Forschungen und der heilige Felsen von Jerusalem" (Leipzig, 1912).

[5] Cf. Seisenberger, *op. cit.*, 81 ff. Vincent, H., "La description de Temple de Solomon," in R.B., 4 (1907), 515-542; * Davies, T. W., in H.D.B., s.v. *Temple*.

these stories rested on rebatements in the temple wall, on which the floor joists rested so as not to penetrate into the wall. The thickness of the wall is not given, but the first story had its full thickness so that the chambers on the first floor were 5 cubits wide. The temple wall receded on either side ½ cubit, so that the chambers of the second floor were 6 cubits wide. In like manner another ½ cubit was added on either side of the temple wall for the flooring of the third story, so that the chambers here were 7 cubits wide (3 Kgs. 6, 5 f). The height of each story was 5 cubits (3 Kgs. 6, 10). If the ceilings and floor joists are included, we may assume that the whole annex was about 18 cubits in height; the house of the temple itself, being 30 cubits high, rose considerably above it. All these are the inside measurements and do not include the thickness of the walls.

The Holy Place, but not the Holy of Holies, had *windows* (3 Kgs. 6, 4) along the wall of the house and above the chambers of the third story. The term window must not be understood in our modern sense. They were either latticed openings, like most windows in the Orient, or broad within and narrow without.

Both the Holy of Holies and the Holy Place had *doors* (3 Kgs. 6, 31. 34). The dimensions for Solomon's temple are not given, but in Ezechiel's temple they were 6 and 10 cubits wide respectively (Ez. 41, 2 f). The door of the Holy of Holies was pentagonal, of olive wood and divided into two halves. The Holy Place was entered by folding doors of cypress wood, which folded back in two pieces on each side. The posts for both Places were of olive wood. Upon both doors were carved figures of cherubim, palm trees, and open flowers, overlaid with gold. The Holy of Holies also had a curtain (2 Par. 3, 14) similar to that which hung formerly in the tabernacle, and hence it is very likely that both halves of the door were always open.

It is commonly assumed that the *roof* was flat (not oblique or gabled) from the fact that altars were erected there by idolatrous kings (cf. 4 Kgs. 23, 12).

The temple had two *courts* (cf. 4 Kgs. 23, 12). Round the temple was the *inner court* with the altar of holocausts, also called "the court of the priests" (2 Par. 4, 9). It was enclosed by a wall of hewn stone, covered with cedar wood (3 Kgs. 7, 12), and was paved with stones (4 Kgs. 16, 17). The extent of this court is not given. In the temple of Ezechiel the court of the priests was 100 cubits long and 100 wide (Ez. 40, 47), while the outer court was 500 cubits long and 500 wide (Ez. 42, 20). The *outer* or *great court* was distinct from the court of the priests or "the inner court of the house of the Lord" (3 Kgs. 7, 12). It was paved with stones (2 Par. 7, 3) and surrounded by a wall of hewn stone covered with cedar wood. This court, however, enclosed Solomon's palace and other royal buildings.

The courts had *gates* covered with brass (2 Par. 4, 9); these were at least three in number (cf. Jer. 38, 14; 52, 24 and 4 Kgs. 25, 18, which refer to the three doorkeepers). The principal entrance was the *northern gate* (Ez. 8, 3; 9, 2), which was probably identical with "the upper gate of Benjamin" (Jer. 20, 2), "the upper gate of the house of Jahweh" (4 Kgs. 15, 35), and the "gate of the altar" (Ez. 8, 5). A *western gate* is mentioned in 1 Par. 26, 16. A *southern gate,* later called "new gate," stood between the royal palace and the temple (Jer. 26, 10; 36, 10; cf. also 1 Par. 9, 18).

(b) The Decoration and Furniture of the Temple

The entire walls of the temple were made of great hewn stones (3 Kgs. 6, 7). The interior walls were lined with cedar boards so that no stone could be seen (3 Kgs. 6, 15 f. 18). The roof was also made of the same wood, and perhaps covered with stone to protect the building from the rain (3 Kgs. 6, 9). The stone floors of the house were covered with cypress wood (3 Kgs. 6, 15).

The inner walls of the Holy of Holies and the Holy Place were adorned with gourds and open flowers (3 Kgs. 6, 18), cherubim and palm trees (3 Kgs. 6, 29 f), carved in relief and profusely overlaid with gold (3 Kgs. 6, 20 ff). Even the floor itself in both Places was covered with gold (3 Kgs. 6, 30). According to 2 Paralipomenon 3, 8, the amount of gold used for the Holy of Holies was equivalent to 600 talents.

In the porch stood two *bronze pillars*. The one at the right of the entrance to the temple was called *Jachin*, that is, "He (God) will establish"; and the other at the left *Booz*, that is, "In Him (God) is strength" (3 Kgs. 7, 21; 2 Par. 3, 17). They were cast in the Jordan valley at the ford of Adamah between Succoth and Sartham (3 Kgs. 7, 46) by Hiram Abi, whose father was a Tyrian artificer (3 Kgs. 7, 14) and mother a Danite (2 Par. 2, 14) living in the tribe of Nephtali (3 Kgs. 7, 14). These two pillars of molten brass were 18 cubits high (3 Kgs. 7, 15; a copyist's error in 2 Par. 3, 15 has 35 cubits) and 12 in circumference (3 Kgs. 7, 15). They were hollow within (not like the bronze pillars of the Assyrians, which were filled with tree trunks), but the metal was four fingers in thickness (Jer. 52, 21). Both of them were surmounted by capitals 5 cubits high (3 Kgs. 7, 16; 2 Par. 3, 15), but there is no mention of a base or pedestal. Each capital, globular in shape (3 Kgs. 7, 42), was richly adorned with net work and two rows of one hundred pomegranates so arranged that four pomegranates were firmly attached to the capitals, while the rest in four groups of twenty-four hung loosely like a chain (3 Kgs. 7, 16-19; 2 Par. 3, 16; Jer. 52, 23). Their tops were fashioned in the shape of a lily, an ornament 4 cubits high (3 Kgs. 7, 19. 22). From the text it cannot be clearly determined whether this lily ornamentation was to be considered the upper part of the capital or merely an addition placed upon it.

The *brazen sea* (3 Kgs. 7, 23-26; 2 Par. 4, 2-6) was a very large cylindric vessel or round basin situated in the court between the temple and the altar, towards the south. The basin itself was 5 cubits high, 10 in diameter, and 30 in circumference. This laver was a palm or handbreadth in thickness, and its rim curved outwards in the shape of a lily (3 Kgs. 7, 26; 2 Par. 4, 5). The manner in which the water was

permitted to flow out is not mentioned in the text. Below the
rim were two rows of pomegranates in relief, cast at the same
time as the basin; there were ten pomegranates to every cubit
around the circumference of the sea (3 Kgs. 7, 24; 2 Par. 4,
3). This vessel was used either directly or indirectly by the
priests to wash their hands and feet, and also the flesh of victims. The capacity of this laver was 2,000 baths of water (3
Kgs. 7, 27, but 2 Par. 4, 5 has 3,000 baths), that is, about
19,600 gallons or 72,800 liters. This brazen sea rested upon
twelve brazen oxen which stood in four groups facing the cardinal points (3 Kgs. 7, 25; 2 Par. 4, 4). King Achaz (736-
728 B.C.: 4 Kgs. 16, 17) removed the brazen oxen because of
their value, and placed the "sea" on the stone pavement.

There were ten *brazen lavers* (3 Kgs. 7, 27-39; 2 Par. 4, 6),
five of which were placed on the right wing and the other five
on the left wing of the temple (3 Kgs. 7, 39). These lavers
consisted of three parts: the base or stand, the wheels, and
the basin. The base was a four-cornered box, 4 cubits square
at the top and 3 cubits in height (3 Kgs. 7, 27), and was made
of panels or horizontal borders and ledges or vertical cross-
pieces, both of which were decorated with lions, oxen, cherubim, and embossed wreaths (3 Kgs. 7, 28 f). On the top of
this base was a round compass (3 Kgs. 7, 35), or a mouth
cylindric in form (3 Kgs. 7, 31); the outside measurement of
this was 1½ cubits across, and the inside measurement 1 cubit,
while it was raised ½ cubit above the base proper (3 Kgs. 7,
31. 35). At the corners were undersetters or pillars, the lower
extremities of which formed the feet in which the axles of the
wheels were set (3 Kgs. 7, 30). The second part of the laver
consisted of four brass wheels (3 Kgs. 7, 30) 1½ cubits high
(3 Kgs. 7, 32), which were completely under the base of the
laver. Thus, the lavers could be moved to and fro when required, and convey the flesh to the brazen sea and the altar.
The third part consisted of the basin, 4 cubits in diameter (3
Kgs. 7, 38) and a little more than 1 cubit in height; this had
a capacity of 40 baths (i.e., 392 gallons). These lavers were
employed for washing the flesh of victims (2 Par. 4, 6). Even

though they were constructed of brass, this does not exclude the possibility that the greater part of the interior consisted of wood, since King Achaz removed the brass panels without destroying the lavers.

In the inner court was also to be found the *brazen altar of holocausts,* 20 cubits in length and width and 10 cubits in height (3 Kgs. 8, 64; 4 Kgs. 16, 14; 2 Par. 4, 1). In design it resembled that of Moses, and was filled up inside with earth and stones. It probably had several projecting ledges, on the uppermost of which the officiating priests stood. It must also have had steps, at least on the east side (cf. Ez. 43, 17).

In the Holy Place stood: (1) the *altar of incense* near the curtain, which was of cedar wood overlaid with gold; (2) *ten golden lampstands,* bearing seven lamps each, arranged in fives along the north and south walls respectively; (3) *ten tables of showbreads,* five on each side. We have no information regarding the size and shape of all these furnishings; they no doubt differed only in size from those in the tabernacle.

In the Holy of Holies stood the *ark of the Covenant.* Apparently no new one was made, but Moses' ark with the kapporeth and the two cherubim upon it were transferred to the temple (3 Kgs. 8, 1 ff; 2 Par. 5, 2 ff). Near the ark, however, were stationed two large cherubim (3 Kgs. 6, 23-28), that is, figures of angels in human form, made of olive wood overlaid with gold, keeping watch over it. Each figure was 10 cubits high and had wings 5 cubits long. One wing was stretched out backward and touched the wall; the other was lifted forward so as to meet the corresponding wing of the other cherub above the kapporeth. The figures stood upright with their faces turned towards the entrance (2 Par. 3, 13). The poles for carrying the ark, which were never removed, projected so that their ends could be recognized through the curtain (3 Kgs. 8, 8).

Solomon's temple stood for 375 years (961-586 B.C.), and was used as intended during the whole time of the kings of Juda. In 586 B.C. it was plundered by the Babylonians and burned with the city of Jerusalem. The holy vessels and furniture, in so far as they were of precious materials, were taken to Babylon.

Art. 3. The Temple of Zorobabel

(1 Esd. 1; 3; 6)

The temple erected by the Jews after their return from the Babylonian exile is called "the temple of Zorobabel." In 536 B.C. Cyrus, the king of the Persians, issued a royal decree in favor of the Jews. It contained the following important clauses: (a) permission was granted to all Jews in the Persian Empire to return to their native country; (b) the Jews were allowed to rebuild their temple (1 Esd. 1, 2 ff; 6, 2); (c) the measurements and materials were specified (1 Esd. 6, 3 f); (d) the expenses for the construction of the temple were to be paid for by the Persian royal treasury (1 Esd. 6, 4); (e) all the golden and silver vessels removed by the Babylonians were to be restored to the Jews (1 Esd. 6, 5); (f) all Jews were to contribute freely to the temple (1 Esd. 1, 4).

Having returned to their home land under the leadership of Zorobabel (1 Esd. 2, 2), of the royal family of David, many Jews at once restored the altar of holocausts on its former base and renewed the daily sacrifices from the first day of Tishri—that is, September/October (1 Esd. 3, 1-6). In the second year of their return they began to gather materials for the construction of the temple (1 Esd. 3, 8). They had hardly laid the foundations (1 Esd. 3, 9-13), when the Samaritans, whose coöperation had been refused, succeeded in hindering the completion of this work (1 Esd. 4, 1-5). After fifteen years Zorobabel, encouraged by the prophets Aggeus and Zacharias (1 Esd. 5, 1), succeeded in resuming the construction of the temple during the reign of King Darius I (521-486 B.C.). The work was then carried on with great zeal, and after four and a half years the temple was ready for consecration (516 B.C.: 1 Esd. 6, 14-18).

From Esdras 6, 3 it appears that the new temple, 60 cubits high and 60 wide, was larger in extent than Solomon's, but less beautiful. The Holy of Holies was empty, since the ark of the covenant was missing (cf. 2 Mach. 2, 4-7). A stone was placed over the spot where the ark once stood, and on it the high priest set the censer on the Day of Atonement. In the Holy Place were an altar of incense, a golden lampstand, and a table for showbreads (1 Mach. 1, 23; 4, 49). In the court of the priests were an altar of holocaust built of stone (1 Mach. 4, 38 ff) and a laver (Sir. 50, 3). This court was surrounded by a larger court of the people (1 Mach. 4, 38. 48), which in time was fortified (Sir. 50, 1 f; 1 Mach. 6, 7. 51 ff; 13, 52).

In the year 169 B.C., Antiochus IV Epiphanes plundered the temple of Jerusalem (1 Mach. 1, 21-29; 2 Mach. 5, 11-21) and desecrated it by the worship of false gods (1 Mach. 1, 62; 2 Mach. 6, 2 ff). Judas Machabeus, after driving out the Syrians, repaired the buildings, replaced some of the furniture that had been destroyed, and had the temple reconsecrated on the twenty-fifth of Casleu (December; cf. 1 Mach. 4, 36 ff; 2 Mach. 10, 1 ff). This was the origin of the feast of Encænia or Dedication (cf. John 10, 22). At this time strong fortifications were added to the temple, but nevertheless it was again captured by the Romans under Pompey (63 B.C.), and also by Herod the Great, who with the aid of Roman troops captured Jerusalem and stormed the temple (37 B.C.)

Art. 4. The Temple of Herod

(Josephus, *Antiq.*, XV, 11; *idem, Bella Jud.*, V, 5; tract *Middoth*)

Cf. Vincent, L. H., "Le temple hérodien d'après la Misnah," in R.B., 61 (1954), 5-35, 398-418; *idem,* "Jerusalem de l'Ancient Testament" (vol. II, Paris, 1959).

In the eighteenth year of his reign (20-19 B.C.), Herod the Great began to restore the temple of Zorobabel, and in a year and a half the whole house of the temple was finished by the priests. The courts took eight years, but the work on the surrounding buildings was still going on during Our Lord's lifetime and was finally completed at the time of the procurator

Albinus (A.D. 62-64). It was hardly finished when it was destroyed by Titus in A.D. 70, thus fulfilling the prophecy of Our Lord.

The area of Herod's temple corresponded essentially with the present Haram esh-Sherif, and was surrounded by a high wall. There were various *gates* that led to this enclosure. On the eastern side there was the one gate, called Susan (cf. 4 Kgs. 11, 6; 2 Par. 23, 5; 2 Esd. 3, 31), and erroneously identified with the modern Golden Gate. It was through this gate that the scapegoat was released, and that Christ entered the temple area on Palm Sunday. On the northern side there was one gate, called Taddi. On the western side there were four gates: the first towards the north, the second called Kiponos (now Bab es-Silseleh, of which there remains "Wilson's Arch"), the third (now called Barclay's Gate) which led to a road that descended to the Tyropœon valley, the fourth near the south-west corner (now called Robinson's Arch) which led to the king's palace. On the southern side were the two Hulda gates—one, a double gate, towards the west, and the other, a triple gate, towards the east. Remnants of these last gates are still to be found in the vaulted substructures beneath the south side of the Haram.

The *outer court* is commonly known as "the Court of the Gentiles," because both Gentiles and Jews legally unclean were allowed to enter it. This court was paved with stones of various colors, and its walls were surrounded by porticoes or cloisters. The royal portico on the south was the most precious. The south colonnade was quadruple and consisted of 162 columns. Three aisles were formed by these columns— a middle aisle 45 feet wide and 100 feet high, and two side aisles 30 feet wide and 50 feet high. The columns with their bases and Corinthian capitals were 27 feet high and so thick that it took three men to span them. Along the eastern side was the Portico of Solomon (cf. John 10, 23; Acts 3, 11; 5, 12), so called because it either contained parts of his porch or had been built upon the same site. This portico and those on the north and west sides had two aisles, with two rows of columns.

The roofs of these cloisters were covered with cedar wood. In these cloisters various small rooms were placed; here the people were instructed, and buyers, sellers, and money-changers erected their booths (cf. John 2, 14; Matt. 21, 12).

A stone *balustrade* (Hebr., soreg), 3 cubits high, enclosed a forecourt, lying higher, where notices in Greek and Latin were placed forbidding any foreigner under the penalty of death from entering the inner court (cf. Acts 21, 26 ff).

Fourteen steps led up to the level area (Hebr. hel, i.e., small fortress, wall), which formed a terrace 10 cubits wide. This *forecourt* surrounded the walls of the inner court.

The *inner court* was surrounded by a wall 40 cubits high on the outside, and 25 cubits on the inside, as the ground inside was raised. Five steps and an inclined walk led from the lower to the higher ground. This wall had nine gates, of which six led into the inner western court and three into the inner eastern court, or court of women. On the north side three led into the men's court and one into the women's. A similar arrangement of four gates was had on the south side. On the east side this court was entered by Nicanor's Gate, also called the Gate Beautiful (Acts 3, 2. 10). The other gates had doors 30 cubits high and 15 cubits wide; the Nicanor Gate, however, was 50 cubits high and 40 cubits wide, and was made of Corinthian brass. These portals had large spaces within of 30 cubits and rooms on each side. Over the gates there were upper rooms, which made these gates look like towers. Before the actual gates were two pillars, 12 cubits in circumference.

The inner court was divided into two parts by a wall. The eastern part was the *court of the women,* 135 cubits in length and width, into which women as well as men were admitted. In the four corners of this court were four cells, and thirteen boxes (corbona) were distributed within this court to receive contributions for the temple (cf. Luke 21, 1; John 8, 20). Fifteen steps led from the western side of the women's court to another gate, which was on the level of the western inner court. This western portion, 187 cubits in length (east to

west) and 135 cubits in width, included the men's court and
the priests' court.

The *court of the men or Israelites* was 11 cubits wide, and
surrounded the priests' court on all but the west side. In this
area the Levite singers and musicians stood; here the
Israelites, who represented the nation at the sacrifices, also
took their station. The first-born (cf. Luke 2, 22) and the
first fruits were also offered here. Various cells were placed
in this court for storing essentials necessary for the sacrifice.

The *court of the priests* was separated from the men's court
by a stone wall 1 cubit in height, and was 176 cubits long and
135 wide. Within this area stood the altar of holocaust and
the brazen sea. The *altar of holocausts,* 50 cubits in length
and width and 15 cubits high, was made of unhewn stones and
had corners like horns. To the north of this altar were twenty-
four rings fixed in the ground to tie the animals destined for
sacrifice, eight marble tables to wash the parts of the victims,
and eight pillars to flay the victims. Towards the south west
of the altar the *brazen sea* was situated and was filled with
the waters coming from the pools of Solomon.

The *temple* proper, situated on higher ground, was reached
by means of twelve steps. It was built of immense blocks,
and was richly gilded both inside and outside. It consisted of
a porch, the Holy Place, the Holy of Holies, and an annex.
The *porch* was 100 cubits in both height and width and 11
cubits deep (from east to west); the entrance was 70 cubits
high and 20 wide. Over this entrance Herod placed a golden
eagle, a Roman emblem. The *Holy Place* was 40 cubits long,
20 wide, and 60 high; it contained the altar of incense, one
table for showbread, and one lampstand—the latter two taken
back to Rome by Titus as trophies of war. Its golden doors,
consisting of two parts, were 45 cubits high and 16 wide; they
were left open. But before these doors was a beautifully em-
broidered Babylonian curtain. The *Holy of Holies* was 20
cubits long, 20 wide, and 60 high, and was empty except for
the stone that marked the site where the ark once stood.
Separating this from the Holy Place was a precious curtain,

which was torn in two at the death of Christ (Matt. 27, 51).
Around the outside of the temple, except at the east or front,
ran an *annex* containing three stories of small rooms, thirty-
eight in number. The height of this annex was 60 cubits.
The roof was probably a low gable, with gilded spikes on the
gable to prevent birds from polluting it.

Art. 5.   Other Temples Dedicated to Yahweh

The Samaritan Temple.—The Samaritans and their sect
originated with the fall of Samaria in 722 B.C., when this city
was destroyed by Sargon II and the majority of the inhabitants of the northern kingdom were taken into the Assyrian
captivity. The land was then colonized by foreigners (4 Kgs.
17, 24), but a priest of Israel was sent back to teach the
people how to worship Yahweh (4 Kgs. 17, 27 f; cf. also
Josephus, *Antiq.*, IX, 14, 3). During the rule of Zorobabel
(536-516 B.C.) this mixed population, the Samaritans, wished
to show their religious solidarity with the Jews by offering to
help rebuild the temple of Jerusalem, but their help was
refused (1 Esd. 4, 1 ff). It was at the time of Nehemias (c.
430 B.C.) that certain abuses arising from mixed marriages
had to be remedied and he expelled from the community the
brother of the high priest Jaddua, Manasses, who had married
the daughter of the Persian satrap, Sanballat II, and had
refused to leave her (2 Esd. 13, 28; Josephus, *Antiq.*, XI, 7-8).
Manasses thereupon built a temple on Mount Garizim [6] near
Sichem, which the Machabean king, John Hyrcannus (135-
104 B.C.), destroyed in 129 B.C.

Jewish Temples in Egypt.—In the sixth and fifth centuries
B.C. there was a Jewish military colony in the fortress Jeb on
the island of *Elephantine* near modern Assuan. Here the Jews
erected a sanctuary with an altar which was spared by the
Persian Cambyses when he invaded Egypt (525 B.C.). It was
called "the sanctuary of the God Jaho (Yahweh) in the city of
Jeb." During the absence of the Persian satrap Arsames, a

---

[6] Josephus (*Antiq.*, XIII, 9, 1) intimately links the construction of this
temple with Alexander the Great, about one hundred years after Nehemias.

Persian minor official, at the instigation of the Egyptian priests of Chnub, destroyed the temple (411/410 B.C.).

In the second century B.C., Ptolemy VI Philometer (180-170 B.C.) permitted Onias, the son of the Jewish high priest Onias (2 Mach. 3-4), and his followers, who had been driven from Jerusalem, to erect a temple at *Leontopolis,* in the vicinity of Heliopolis near modern Cairo. Here a formal religious cult was established which lasted until A.D. 73, when the temple was ordered closed by Vespasian, who tried to prevent the Jews from assembling anywhere in large numbers.

Art. 6.   The Synagogues

Bibliography: Felten, J., "Neutestamentliche Zeitgeschichte," I (3rd ed., Regensburg, 1925), 384-400; * Schürer, E., "Geschichte des jüdischen Volkes im Zeitalter Jesu Christi," II (4 ed., Leipzig, 1907), 498-536; * Kohl-Watzinger, "Antike Synagogen in Galiläa" (Leipzig, 1916); * Bacher, W., in H.D.B., s.v. *Synagogue;* * Kohler, K., "The Origins of Synagogue and Church" (New York, 1929); * Sukenik, E. L., "Ancient Synagogues in Palestine and Greece" (Oxford, 1934); Fonseca, L. G., "De antiquis Synagogis in Galilæ," in V.D., 8 (1928), 93-96.

The word *synagogue* is derived from the Greek meaning "a bringing or assembling together (of men)," and in the Septuagint stands for the Hebrew "qahal or edah." It seems very likely that the synagogue did not exist in pre-exilic times, but that its history is dependent to some extent upon the Scribes. It originated in the Babylonian exile, when the Jews, separated from the temple and its sacrifices, began to study zealously the Law and live as far as possible according to its enactments (cf. Ez. 8, 1; 14, 1; 20, 1). This movement undoubtedly received a great encouragement from Esdras in Palestine (cf. 2 Esd. 8, 1 ff; 9, 1 ff; 13, 1 ff).

The synagogues were built at the expense of the Jewish community or represented a pious donation (cf. Luke 7, 5). At the time of Our Lord they were found throughout Palestine— at Nazareth, Capharnaum, Dora, Cæsarea, Tiberias, etc. Immediately before the destruction of Jerusalem by Titus this city was said to have had 394 (Babylonian Talmud) or 480 (Jerusalem Talmud). Outside of the Holy Land they were erected in Babylonia, Syria,[7] Asia Minor, Alexandria, and Rome. Hence, Philo hardly exaggerates when he writes that there was a Jewish place of prayer in every city (*Vita Mosis*, 3, 27).

From the ruins of the synagogues of Galilee, which do not go back beyond the second century A.D., it seems that they were quadrangular in form. There was one principal entrance and two smaller side-doors. Some also had porticoes. The interior was divided into various aisles by rows of pillars.

The most important furnishing of the synagogue was the *press* (Hebr., tebah) or chest, in which the parchment rolls of the Sacred Scriptures, wrapped in cloths, were kept. In the center of the synagogue there was an elevated lectern or pulpit from which the Scriptures were read. For the congregation there were seats, some of which were more prominent than others (cf. Matt. 23, 6). The Talmud also makes mention of a special reading desk, lamps and oil.

The most important official was "the ruler of the synagogue" (Mark 5, 22). He was responsible for the maintenance of order (Luke 13, 14), and determined who was to conduct the public worship (Acts 13, 15). Excommunication from the community, either temporal or perpetual (Luke 6, 22; John 9, 22; 12, 42; 16, 2), and the punishment of scourging (Matt. 10, 17) seem to have been determined by the elders. Every synagogue had its attendant (Hebr., hazzan), whose duty it was to fetch the Scriptures to the readers and bring the parchment rolls back to the press (Luke 4, 20). He called upon the priest at the proper moment to pronounce the blessing. He could either read the Scripture or give it to some one else to read. Sometimes he acted as leader in prayer, though this

---

[7] Recent excavations at Dura-Europos have brought to light a synagogue of A.D. 245-256 with mural paintings of biblical scenes and persons. Cf. * Rostovtzeff, * Bellinger, * Hopkins, and * Welles, "The Excavations at Dura-Europos conducted by Yale University and the French Academy of Inscriptions and Letters" (New Haven, 1936); Du Mesnil du Buisson, in R.B., 45 (1936), 72-90, and in *Biblica*, 18 (1937), 153-173, 458 f; *idem*, "Les Peintures de la Synagogue de Doura-Europos 245-256 après J.-C." (Rome, 1939); Fischer, J. A., "The Synagogue Paintings at Dura Europos," in C.B.Q., 17 (1955), 69-75.

function could be performed by any qualified member of the congregation. He was the schoolmaster or his assistant, and had to carry out the sentence of scourging.

Public worship was regularly held in the mornings of the Sabbath and feast days, also on Mondays and Thursdays. At least ten male members were required for religious service, which consisted chiefly in the reading of the Law and its interpretation. The Mishna mentions that the divine service consisted of the recitation of the Shema (Deut. 6, 4-9; 11, 13-21; Num. 15, 37-41), of the prayer (Shemone-Esre, i.e., eighteen benedictions), the reading of the Law and Prophets (followed by an exposition of the text or sermon), and the blessing.

Chapter II

SACRED PERSONS

Bibliography: Linder, J., "Geschichte des Alten Bundes" (Klagenfurt, 1913); Seisenberger, M., "Practical Handbook for the Study of the Bible" (New York, 1933), 90-105.

Art. 1. The Old Testament Priesthood in General

The priest is the mediator between God and man. He is chosen by God to offer the gifts and sacrifices of people to God and to obtain graces and blessings from the Almighty for the people (Hebr. 5, 1-4). Whoever is divinely called for this sublime mission is taken from among men, becomes in a special manner the property of God, and is destined for His ministry. The priest alone is empowered to act as mediator between God and man (Hebr. 5, 4). When, therefore, Core and his rebellious followers wished to assume the priestly mission without being lawfully called, they were severely punished (Num. 16).

Some sort of priesthood existed before the Mosaic period. Originally, everyone was the minister of his own sacrifice; thus, Cain and Abel (Gen. 4, 3 f), Noe (Gen. 8, 20), Jacob (Gen. 33, 20; 35, 1), and Moses (Ex. 17, 15; 24, 6 ff; 29, 1 ff). Of the Patriarchs we read that Abraham, Isaac, and Jacob built altars, and it is explicitly stated that both Abraham and Jacob sacrificed. The son could only begin to sacrifice after he had become the head of a family (compare Gen. 28, 18 with 31, 15) or tribal chief (e.g., Meichisedech and Jethro), and traces of this may be found even after the institution of the levitical priesthood, when the head of the family was ordered to slay the paschal lamb (Ex. 12, 3).

Israel was to represent itself as a united people and worship God with sacrifices and gifts. For His service He elected the tribe of Levi, and from this tribe the family of Aaron was chosen for His priesthood. The reason for the choice of this tribe depended upon God's free will (Num. 18, 6 f), and this tribe showed itself worthy of its call when its members joined Moses to suppress the golden calf worship (Ex. 32).

Not all the members of the tribe of Levi were to participate in an equal degree in the divine services. The priesthood was conferred exclusively on Aaron and his male descendants (Ex. 28, 1); the other members of the tribe were to serve as ministers of the priests. In addition, however, Aaron and his successors were appointed to the high priesthood, and thus there arose a threefold distinction within the tribe. First, there were the *Levites*, that is, the non-priestly members of the tribe, who were to act as assistants to the priests. Secondly, there were the *priests*, that is, all the male descendants of Aaron and their sons. Thirdly, there was the *high priest*, that is, the first-born of Aaron and his successor according to the right of the first-born.

This tripartite hierarchical division also corresponded with the threefold division of the tabernacle; the Levites were only allowed to enter the inner court, whereas the priests could also function in the Holy Place. The high priest alone could enter the Holy of Holies.

(a) THE LEVITES

Election.—Levi, the founder of the tribe, Jacob's third son by Lia, had three sons, Gerson, Caath, and Merari (Ex. 6, 16-25; Num. 26, 57-61), so that the tribe was divided into three parts: the Gersonites, the Caathites, and the Merarites. They were selected to take the place of the first-born sons of the Israelites, to become in a peculiar way God's property (Num. 3, 41), and to look after His service. By reason of the death of the first-born of the Egyptians and the rescue of the first-born of the Israelites, God had obtained a particular right to Israel's first-born, and consequently demanded their dedication and sanctification (Num. 3, 13; 8, 17). Possible disturbances in the maintenance of families may have been the reason why the tribe of Levi was substituted to take the place of the first-born. Moses accordingly was ordered to take a census of all male Levites, from one month and upward. The number of first-born non-Levites totalled 22,273 and the number of the Levites 22,000 (Num. 3, 39-43). These Levites were to take the place of the first-born, and the 273 excess had to be redeemed at 5 shekels apiece; this price of redemption, 1,365 shekels, was to be given to Aaron and his sons (Num. 3, 46-51). Of these Levites those who were between the ages of 30 and 50, numbering 8,580 (2,750 Caathites, 2,630 Gersonites, and 3,200 Merarites), were selected for the ministry (Num. 4, 34-49).

Consecration.—Before the Israelites left Mount Sinai, the Levites were solemnly consecrated to the Lord (Num. 8, 5-22). They were sprinkled with the water of purification and had to shave off their hair and wash their clothes. After they were cleansed, the representatives of the people laid their hands upon the Levites as a sign that the nation was offering the Levites to God as His possession. The actual presentation to the Lord was made by Aaron himself (Num. 8, 11). The rite of consecration was concluded with the sacrifice of two bullocks and a meal-offering. The Levites were to lay their hands upon the heads of the bullocks, which were then sacrificed, one being a sin-offering and the other a burnt-offering or holocaust. After this ceremony the Levites entered on their duties.

The consecration of the Levites on Mount Sinai seems to have held good for all times, and no mention is made in the Bible of a renewed consecration. The ministry of the Levites at the sanctuary was hereditary.

Duties.—The Levites were to perform all duties that were not reserved for the priests. They were to assist the priests in their duties and perform the more menial labor in the sanctuary (Num. 3, 6-8). During the wanderings of the Israelites in the desert, they encamped nearest to the tabernacle, on the west, south, and north sides of it (Num. 3, 23. 29. 35), whilst Moses, Aaron, and the priests were stationed on the east side near the entrance (Num. 3, 38). They had to erect the tabernacle, and take it down when the march was resumed; they carried parts of it on the march, as well as the sacred furniture (Num. 3, 26. 31. 36 f). At the time of David they were completely reorganized (1 Par. 23-26), and of the 38,000 Levites who were thirty years and upward four distinct classes were formed. (a) 24,000 were chosen as ministers of the priests. These were the Levites, strictly so called. They were in charge of the sacred vessels and treasures (1 Par. 9, 26-29), brought in the first fruits and tithes (2 Par. 31, 12), flayed the victims (2 Par. 29, 34: since there were not a sufficient number of priests at that period), handed the blood of victims to the priests (2 Par. 30, 16), prepared the show-breads and the cakes used at sacrifices (1 Par. 9, 31 f), and at times killed the paschal lamb for those who were legally unclean (2 Par. 30, 17). (b) There were 6,000 overseers and judges; (c) 4,000 porters, and (d) 4,000 singers and musicians. No distinctive clothing is mentioned for them in the Mosaic Law.

Besides the Levites, there were other men employed to do the more menial labors around the tabernacle and temple, such as cutting wood and carrying water. They were called Nathinites (Hebr., nethinim, i.e., given ones, bondmen: cf. Num. 31, 47; Jos. 9, 23 ff; 1 Par. 9, 2; 1 Esd. 2, 43. 70; 8, 20).

The *period of service* for the Levites began at 30 years of age for the heavy work of carrying the parts of the tabernacle (Num. 4, 3. 23. 30. 35. 39. 43. 47), and at the age of 25 years for the lighter tasks (Num. 8, 24); their service lasted till the age of 50 years (Num. 4, 3 ff), when they were to retire, but might volunteer to do certain kinds of work to assist their younger brethren (Num. 8, 25 f).

Income.—Since the tribe of Levi belonged to God, He was their portion and inheritance (Num. 18, 20). For this reason no territorial boundaries were assigned to it after the conquest of Canaan. But to the entire tribe were allocated 48 towns, 13 to the priests and 35 to the Levites; these towns were distributed through the territories of the other tribes (Num. 35, 1-8; Jos. 21). As a means of livelihood they had, besides the produce of their herds, a tithe of all the produce of the fields, gardens, and cattle of all Israel (Num. 18, 24), but they had to surrender a tenth of this tithe to the priests (Num. 18, 26). They were invited to take part in the sacrificial meals and were free from military service and taxation.

(b) THE PRIESTS

Election.—Aaron and his descendants were chosen by God to be priests even before the worship of the golden calf (Ex. 28, 1; 32, 1 ff). Aaron belonged to the Caath branch of the tribe of Levi, and had four sons (Ex. 6, 23). Two of his sons, Nadab and Abiu, were killed for their carelessness in the service of God (Lev. 10, 1 ff), so that only the two remaining sons, Eleazar and Ithamar, could pass on the priestly office to their descendants. Every other Israelite and every other Levite not belonging to the family of Aaron, and even the descendants of Moses (1 Par. 23, 14 ff) because they were not pure Hebrews, were excluded from the priesthood. When subsequently King Ozias usurped some functions of the priestly office, he was struck with leprosy (2 Par. 26, 16-21). The election of the family of Aaron was.divinely confirmed by two outstanding miracles: the punishment of Core and his followers (Num. 16) and the blooming of Aaron's rod (Num. 17).

Requirements.—The first requirement of every priest serving in the sanctuary of the Old Testament was that he be a descendant of Aaron. For this purpose priestly registers or lists were carefully compiled and preserved. When, after the exile, certain priests could not prove their priesthood through these written registers, they were excluded from the priesthood (1 Esd. 2, 62; 2 Esd. 7, 64). No fixed age is prescribed in the Mosaic Law, but it is very likely that the age appointed for priests to function was the same as that for the Levites. The descent from Aaron in the Old Testament was of such a nature that the coming of the High Priest, Jesus Christ, of the tribe of Juda, meant the abrogation of the Aaronic priesthood and the institution of a new order of things (Hebr. 7, 12). In this new Messianic period even the Gentiles were to be taken as priests and Levites (Isa. 66, 21).

Other requirements, both physical and moral, were necessary for the proper performance of their sacerdotal functions. They were to be physically fit, and any one who had any bodily defect was to be excluded from priestly duties but not from his income (Lev. 21, 16-24). Moral integrity was also demanded of the priests. They were to marry Hebrew virgins or widows (Lev. 21, 7), and the high priest was to marry only a virgin (Lev. 21, 14). During the time that they were engaged in the service at the sanctuary, they were to refrain from wine and intoxicating beverages (Lev. 10, 9), and remain apart from their wives (cf. Lev. 15, 16-18; 22, 3). Since any contact with a corpse caused legal uncleanness, they were forbidden to touch any corpses, except those of their nearest relatives (Lev. 21, 1-4), but the high priest was forbidden to touch any corpse (Lev. 21, 11) because he represented the perfection of the priesthood. They were forbidden to show immoderate signs of mourning, especially by imitating pagan funeral rites (Lev. 21, 5).[1] They were to observe carefully the regulations concerning food, and had to be legally clean to eat parts of the victims used in sacrifices.

Consecration.—The priestly consecration or "sanctification" of Aaron and his sons by Moses (Ex. 29; 40, 12-15; Lev. 8) consisted of two principal acts. (a) The first part was accomplished by bathing the body, putting on priestly garments, and anointing. A specially prepared oil was poured on the head of Aaron (Ex. 29, 7; Lev. 8, 12; 21, 10), but only the forehead of his sons was anointed according to rabbinical sources. (b) The second part of the consecration ceremonies consisted in offering a threefold sacrifice: a young bull as a sin offering, a ram as a holocaust, and another ram as a peace offering. The right ear lobe, the thumb of the right hand, and the big toe of the right foot, of both Aaron and his sons were smeared with the blood of this third sacrifice by Moses; then its fatty tissues and the right shoulder were placed into the priests' hands and later burnt upon the altar of holocaust. Finally, Aaron and his sons and their garments were sancti-

[1] Cf. Steinmueller, J. E., "Primitive Hebrew Religion," in H.P.R., **40** (1940), 1186 f.

fied by sprinkling them with blood mixed with oil. This consecration of the priests was repeated for seven days, and on the eighth day the priests entered upon their office.

Whether this rite of consecration was repeated in the case of subsequent priests is uncertain. It is, however, certain that in the pre-exilic period each high priest, before he could assume the office of his predecessor, was anointed with oil and invested with his pontifical robes (Ex. 29, 29; Lev. 21, 10; Num. 20, 26-28; 1 Par. 29, 22). Since the oil of anointing[2] was lacking after the exile, the high priests were no longer anointed; they simply had to put on the pontifical robes and offer a sacrifice.

Dress.—The priests, when engaged in their sacred duties, wore four special garments. (a) They wore a linen loin-cloth to cover the middle of the body, from the hips to the thighs (Ex. 28, 42). (b) A long tunic, resembling a modern alb, reached from the neck to the ankles; it was woven of various colors, and was provided with sleeves (Ex. 28, 39). (c) The girdle or sash was woven of the four sacred colors, and was so long that it could be wound several times round the body and its ends hung down below the knees. (d) A white linen turban was wound around the head. The priests wore no sandals, as unshod feet were a sign of reverence due to places dedicated to divine worship (cf. Ex. 3, 5; Jos. 5, 16).

Duties.—The duties of the priests were of a threefold nature. (a) In the Holy Place they had to remove the old loaves of proposition and substitute fresh ones every Sabbath, put incense on the altar of incense every morning and evening, and trim the lamps on the golden lampstand. (b) In the court of the temple they were to offer the various sacrifices on the altar of holocausts, keep the fire burning day and night, sprinkle the blood of the sacrificial victims, and bless the people after the morning sacrifice (Num. 6, 23-26). (c) Outside of the tabernacle and temple they were to distinguish between the sacred and the profane, the pure and the impure; thus, they had to inspect and judge cases of leprosy, purifica-

---

[2] Cf. Steinmetzer, F., "Das heilige Salböl des Alten Bundes," in B.Z., 17 (1909), 17-29.

tions of women either after childbirth or hemorrhages, vows, divorce, jealousy, etc. They were to act as interpreters and teachers of the law of God, and because of their frequent neglect of this duty the prophets before the exile and the Scribes after the exile assumed this obligation. They were to act as judges in the more difficult civil and religious trials (Deut. 17, 8-12). Together with the Levites, they were to keep a watch over the temple. They were to blow the silver trumpets, etc.

Lest the sacred service be interrupted at any time, King David divided the priestly families into twenty-four classes, sixteen from the Aaronic line of Eleazar and eight from the Aaronic line of Ithamar (1 Par. 24, 3-19). Each class had to take a week's turn at the temple—that is, from Sabbath to Sabbath.

Income.—The maintenance of the priests was provided for in various ways. (a) Of the sacrificial victims they received the meat of most sin offerings and trespass offerings, the breast and the right shoulder of peace offerings, the skins in holocausts or burnt offerings, parts of the unbloody sacrifices, and the loaves of proposition. (b) Of the fruits of the earth they received the first-fruits of field and garden produce, tithes which the Levites had to hand over to them from their tithes, etc. (c) Of the herds they received the meat of the first-born males of all clean beasts and the price for the redemption of the first-born male of unclean beasts; they received also part of the wool from sheared sheep. (d) Finally, they received the money paid for the redemption of the first-born of man, everything dedicated to Yahweh by a vow, etc.

(c) The High Priest

Name.—At the head of the entire priesthood stood the high priest, who is also called "the chief priest," "the chief," "the anointed priest," or simply "the priest" *par excellence.*

Duties.—Besides those functions which he shared in common with all priests, the high priest was assigned to the following exclusive duties: he was to enter the Most Holy Place once a year, on the Feast of Atonement, and expiate for the sins of the entire nation (Lev. 16); he was to ascertain the will of God by means of the Urim and Thummim; he was to watch over everything connected with the divine worship, and over the priests and Levites; in the administration of justice he was to give the final judgment, and at a later period of history he presided over the Sanhedrin; he was to anoint the new king.

Dress.—The exalted dignity of the high priest was also manifested in his official dress, which he wore over his usual priestly attire (Ex. 28, 4-39; 39, 1-30) when exercising his priestly office, except on the Day of Atonement. It consisted of the following parts: (a) an *overgarment* (Hebr., meil: Ex. 28, 31-35) made of dark bluish purple. This had an opening on the top so that it could be passed over the head and was without sleeves. A border of pomegranates and little bells adorned it (Sir. 49, 10 f). This garment probably reached to the knees, so that the white tunic could be seen below it. (b) The *superhumeral* or scapular (Hebr., ephod: Ex. 28, 6-8), made of white linen interwoven with gold, violet, purple, and scarlet. This consisted of three parts: (1) two squares of cloth, one covering the breast and the other the back; (2) two shoulder straps of gold to hold these squares in place; and (3) a girdle of the same material as the squares to fasten the lower part of the superhumeral to the body. On the golden shoulder straps two onyx stones were mounted, on which were engraved the names of the twelve tribes, six upon each stone. The superhumeral in its size and shape resembled a dalmatic. (c) The *breastplate* (Hebr., hoshen: Ex. 28, 15-30). This was a square of one span (c. 10 inches), was doubled to form a pocket or burse, and was made of the same material as the superhumeral. On the outer side were set four rows of precious stones, three to a row, and on each stone was engraved the name of one of the twelve tribes. At each corner of the breastplate was a golden ring. To the rings at the two upper corners were attached two twisted chain cords of pure gold, having at their extremities golden clasps, by means of which they were tied to the shoulder straps of the superhumeral. Violet bands or cords were passed through the rings at the two lower corners, and also through two other rings which were sewn on to the edge of the shoulder straps of the superhumeral below the arms.[3]   In this way the breastplate was kept in place. Inside the breastplate were placed the *Urim* (i.e., light or doctrine) and the *Thummim*[4] (i.e., perfection or truth). These were some objects which God designated as instruments of His infallible answers to questions of importance. They constituted a sacred oracle placed in the breastplate, by means of which Yahweh, when consulted by the high priest in matters of moment, manifested His will. The material and shape of these two objects, and the manner in which they were used, are unknown. (d) The *head-covering* (Hebr., mitsnepheth). This tiara was higher than that worn by the priests; furthermore, it was ornamented with a violet or blue purple ribbon, to which a golden plate was fastened on his forehead. Upon this plate was engraved the words: "Holiness to Yahweh."

Art. 2. The Modern Critical School

The modern critical school, outside of the Church, maintains that in the earliest period of Hebrew history no distinction existed between priests and laymen. At the time of Moses laymen assumed the obligations of the priesthood. With the enactment of the Deuteronomistic code (D) at the time of the religious reform of King Josias (623/622 B.C.) there was a second development, because the tribe of Levi was selected for the priesthood (Deut. 18, 1-5), which, however, remained something indefinite. Finally during the reforms of Ezechiel, who labored as a prophet (592-567 B.C.) among the Hebrews in the Babylonian captivity, a group of priests within the tribe of Levi were degraded to the menial offices (Ez. 44, 9-15), and

[3] Cf. Seisenberger, *op. cit.,* 98.
[4] Cf. Mangan, E. A., "The Urim and Thummim," in C.B.Q., 1 (1939), 133-138; Olivera, B. S., "Urim et Tummim," in V.D., 7 (1927), 181-185.

were now called simply Levites. This distinction between non-priestly and priestly Levites was therefore first made by Ezechiel, but it was then developed by the priestly code (P) into the three orders of high priest, Aaronic priests, and Levites—a threefold order which is taken for granted after the time of Esdras. To support this evolutionary development of the priesthood, these critics cite Biblical texts outside of the Pentateuch to prove that the levitical and priestly offices, with the exclusive right to conduct religious worship, did not exist as yet in the early period of the kings, and that consequently the Law giving the Levites and the priests that right did not emanate from Moses.

Catholic scholars [5] point out that the Biblical texts cited by critics admit other explanations. Some of these sacrifices by laymen were due to theophanies (cf. Jdgs. 13, 19); others were merely sacrificial banquets (1 Sam. 9, 12 ff). Some of these sacrifices were undoubtedly offered through priests (2 Sam. 24, 26); others were true sacrifices but contrary to the Law (2 Par. 26, 16). It is also possible that in some cases the sprinkling of the blood on the altar, the essential part of the sacrifice, was conducted by the priest, and that the Biblical account makes no mention of this. Finally, extraordinary powers were at times conferred upon individuals by God, as in the cases of the prophets Samuel, Elias, Eliseus, etc.

These reasons are sustained by other historical facts that prove the preëminence of the tribe of Levi in early Hebrew history. The house of Heli of the tribe of Levi had already been elected in Egypt by Jahweh to offer sacrifices (1 Sam. 2, 27 f). At the time of the Judges, Michas sought for a Levite to take care of his local shrine (Jdgs. 17, 7-13), and having found one he exclaimed: "Now I know God will do me good, since I have a priest of the race of the Levites" (v. 13). This same Levite was taken by the tribe of Dan, when it migrated to the north (Jdgs. 18). The Levite mentioned in the Book of Judges 19 went to the house of God, because he

[5] Cf. Goettsberger, J., "Einleitung in das A.T." (Freiburg i.B., 1928), 105-109.

was obliged to liturgical service there (v. 18). After the division of the kingdom, Jeroboam I (932-912 B.C.) was accused of having erected shrines on the high places and of having taken for their service laymen of the lowest classes, "who were not of the sons of Levi" (3 Kgs. 12, 31). King Ozias of Juda (779-740 B.C.) was vigorously reproved by a priest, because he dared to enter the temple of God and offer incense: "It does not belong to thee, Ozias, to burn incense to the Lord, but to the priests, that is, to the sons of Aaron, who are consecrated for this ministry" (2 Par. 26, 18). From these historical facts it is evident that the priesthood within the tribe of Levi had an intimate relation with the divine worship, and that the priesthood of the Old Testament existed before the time assigned by critics to the priestly code (P).

These critics also maintain that no distinction existed between Levites and priests before the time of Ezechiel (Ez. 44, 6 ff). But this distinction can be proved to have existed even before his time. Even before the text cited by the critics, Ezechiel distinguishes between priests, who are guardians of the sanctuary, and priests, the sons of Sadoc, who are of the sons of Levi and minister to God (Ez. 40, 45 f; cf. also 42, 13; 43, 19). The prophet Jeremias also makes mention of various grades of priests: "the ancients of the priests" (Jer. 19, 1) and "the chief in the house of the Lord" (Jer. 20, 1; 29, 25 f). It is also evident from the Books of Kings that the tribe of Levi was organized; they are called "the ancients of the priests" (4 Kgs. 19, 2; Isa. 37, 2), doorkeepers of the temple (4 Kgs. 12, 9; 22, 4; 23, 4; 25, 18). It was to this last menial task of doorkeepers that the degraded priests, who had practised idolatry, were relegated.

Art. 3.   The Sanhedrin and the Jewish Sects

1. THE SANHEDRIN

Bibliography: Felten, J., "Neutestamentliche Zeitgeschichte," I (3rd ed., Regensburg, 1925), 313-328; * Schürer, E., "Geschichte des Jüdischen Volkes im Zeitalter Jesu Christi," II (4th ed., Leipzig, 1907), 237-267.

Name.—The word Sanhedrin (Hebr., Sanhedrim) is a Greek word Aramaicized, and means "sitting together." It is applied by Greek authors to any assembly, whether convened to deliberate or to pass judgment (Vulg. concilium); Greek-speaking Jews also used the term "gerousia" while the Rabbis often speak of "beth din" (i.e., the house of judgment).

History.—During the time of Esdras (1 Esd. 10, 8) there existed a body of elders with executive powers. In the period of the Seleucids (*Antiq.,* XII, 3, 3) and the Machabees (1 Mach. 14, 28; 2 Mach. 1, 10) it was identified with the Gerousia. Under Alexandra (76-67 B.C.) it obtained jurisdiction to do whatever was necessary for the welfare of the state; Gabinius (57 B.C.) limited the jurisdiction of the Jerusalem Gerousia to the city and its neighboring district, but Julius Cæsar (47 B.C.) restored to it its former prestige. Its first important act was to condemn Herod for his conduct in suppressing a Galilean rebellion. Upon his accession to the throne Herod allowed it to function, but put forty-five of its members to death and appointed the high priests at will. After the death of Herod the Great and the deposition of Archelaus (A.D. 6), the Sanhedrin was considered the supreme council and the supreme court of justice, in which were vested the legislative, civil and ecclesiastical powers.

Jurisdiction.—In matters purely Jewish the authority of the Sanhedrin, even during the Roman period, extended beyond the confines of Judea (cf. John 1, 19-28; Acts 9, 2; 22, 5; 26, 12). Before it as the supreme religious tribunal of the Jews stood Our Lord, Peter, John, Stephen and Paul. It could have Jews arrested and could inflict corporal punishment (e.g., scourging) upon them. Whether it retained under the procurators the power of carrying the death sentence into execution is disputed. Some scholars hold its death sentence needed the ratification of the procurator (cf. John 18, 31); others maintain that only the death penalty by means of crucifixion was reserved to the procurator, and thus Stephen was stoned to death by order of the Sanhedrin (Acts 7) and James by order of the high priest, Ananus. The high priest ordinarily invited the members of the council to convene, but in the case of St. Paul it was convoked at the instigation of the tribune, the representative of the procurator. On the Sabbath and on religious feasts no judicial trial was to take place.

Membership.—The Sanhedrin consisted of seventy-one members, including the president or high priest. It included not only the aristocratic sacerdotal class of Sadducees but also the Pharisees, many of whom were Scribes. The New Testament refers to this assembly as "the chief priests, the Scribes and the ancients," or simply as "the ancients of the people."

(a) The Chief Priests.—According to Josephus and the Bible, it seems that the acting high priest was the president of the Sanhedrin. In the widest sense of the word, not only were the former high priests included in this term, but also the chiefs and representatives of the twenty-four priestly families. All of them belonged to the Sadducean party.

(b) Scribes.—At the time of Our Lord most of the Scribes were Pharisees, and since they were skilled in the law and its interpretation, they exercised a great influence in the Sanhedrin.

(c) Ancients (elders).—Whenever these were distinguished from the two other classes, they probably comprised members of the priestly families or representatives of the nobility.

End of the Sanhedrin.—At the beginning of the Judæo-Roman war the Sanhedrin played a leading rôle, but soon the zealots seized the government and put this assembly out of the way. With the destruction of Jerusalem (A.D. 70), the Roman privileges conferred upon the Jewish people were revoked, and the Sanhedrin disappeared forever. The later rabbinical schools at Jamnia and Tiberias were only nominal resurrections.

2. The Jewish Parties or Sects [1]

(Josephus, *Antiq.*, XVIII, 1, 2-6, XIII, 5, 9; Acts 15, 5; 26, 5)

Josephus mentions three sects or parties in Palestine: the Pharisees, the Sadducees and the Essenes. The New Testament speaks only of two (the Pharisees and the Sadducees), but also refers to the Herodians as the enemies of Our Lord.

(a) *The Pharisees.*[2]—The Pharisees were not, strictly speaking, a political party, but inasmuch as they assumed to be the supreme and perfect expression of religious life, we may call them a sect.

Name.—The name Pharisees is derived from the Aramaic, Parishim (i.e., the separated ones), because they separated themselves from their own coreligionists, who did not follow their doctrines and mode of living. This name appears for the first time during the rule of John Hyrcannus I (135-105 b.c.). Another name applied to them was "Haberim" (i.e., neighbors), because they considered only Jews legally clean as their neighbors. A third name used was "Hassideans" (i.e., the pious ones: cf. 1 Mach. 2, 42; 2 Mach. 14, 6), but these were the precursors of the Pharisees. The fourth name applied to them was "Scribes," because nearly all the Scribes were Pharisees, although not all Pharisees were Scribes.

Origin and History.—In the second century b.c. a twofold religious party system became predominant in Jewish life. The one, the priestly aristocracy, favored Hellenization, while the other, the Hassideans, were opposed to the introduction of Hellenic culture. The latter were strict observers of the Law, gathered a large group of followers about them, and appointed Mathathias as their leader. These two parties, the Hellenizers and the Hassideans, though as yet not identified with the Sadducees and Pharisees, became their progenitors. The two opposing parties, the Pharisees and Sadducees, are mentioned for the first time by name during the rule of John

---

[1] Cf. Felten, *op. cit.*, 402 ff; * Schürer, *op. cit.*, 447 ff, 651 ff.

[2] Cf. Reilly, W. S., "Our Lord and the Pharisees," in C.B.Q., 1 (1939), 64-68; * Herford, R. T., "Pharisaism. Its Aim and Its Method" (London, 1912); *idem*, "The Pharisees" New York, 1924); * Finkelstein, L., "The Pharisees" (2 vols., Philadelphia, 1946).

Hyrcannus I (135-105 B.C.). Since the Machabean rulers now entered alliances with the world powers, the Hellenizers fully sympathized with the new order of things and became allied to Hyrcannus under the name of Sadducees. They were primarily a political party. On the other hand, the Pharisees, the new successors of the Hassideans, opposed this new tendency. As a religious party they demanded complete segregation from all foreign alliances and culture, and sought the faithful observance of the Law. During the rule of Alexander Jannæus (104-78 B.C.) open conflict arose between these two parties, but his wife Alexandra (78-69 B.C.) became the protectress of the Pharisees. By the time of Herod the Great, the Sadducees ceased to be a political power, and differed only from the Pharisees in their religious tenets. Herod was favorable to the Pharisees, who urged the people to be submissive to his rule. At the time of Our Lord, the high priests belonged to the Sadducean party, and the Sadducees as aristocrats had regained part of their power under the Roman procurators. As the Pharisees were the popular party, their opponents had to follow them as a matter of necessity and prudence in many details of the Law. With the destruction of Jerusalem by Titus there disappeared forever the temple, the Sanhedrin, and the Sadducees, but not the Pharisees. They are still with us under the name of rabbis.

Doctrine.—The Pharisees believed in the immortality of the soul, the freedom of the will, the resurrection of the body, future retribution, the existence of the angels, and divine providence. They also awaited a Messias, the Son of David, who would establish a temporal or earthly kingdom, free them from the Roman yoke, and subject all nations to Jerusalem. These beliefs were also current among the majority of the people.

Characteristic Peculiarities.—As their name implied, they separated themselves from all legal uncleanness, whether this be a person, place, or thing. Hence, external purity was overaccentuated. According to Josephus, they were skilled in the laws of their fathers (*Antiq.*, XVII, 2, 4), followed these with precision (*Antiq.*, XVIII, 1, 3), and held them to be as binding as the written word (*Antiq.*, XIII, 10, 6). The New Testament confirms this by stating that they followed the traditions of men in the washing of pots and cups, in giving tithes, in fasting and observing the Sabbath. Leaving the commandments of God, they followed the traditions of men (Mark 7, 8). The effects of this legalism led to hypocrisy and pride. They tried, alike in social and private life, to maintain with accurate precision the unwritten law. Hence, their legalistic, external, and often fanatical piety impressed the people, even though the latter could not follow them in practice. There was admiration rather than imitation.

Number.—At the time of Herod the Great they numbered about 6,000. This was indeed a small number. But if we consider their mode of living, we can easily conclude that the ordinary Jew found it difficult to observe all their rules and regulations.

(b) *The Sadducees.*—The name Sadducees is commonly derived from Saddok, who had been high priest at the time of David and Solomon. The high priesthood remained in this line until the time of the Machabees. Then this aristocratic family supported John Hyrcannus I and his successors. At the time of the New Testament all the chief priests belonged to this party. Other scholars derive this name from the Hebrew word "sadiq" (i.e., just), either because they upheld the written Law alone in opposition to the Pharisees, or because they acted with severity as judges.

The origin and history of the Sadducees were inextricably linked with those of the Pharisees as has been described above.

Doctrines.—The Sadducees were almost indifferent to religion. Though they were of the priestly nobility, yet they sought a purely secular state. They believed in God, but rejected the traditions of their elders and denied the freedom of the will, the immortality of the soul, the resurrection of the body, future retribution, the existence of angels, and divine providence. Together with the Pharisees they sought from

Christ a sign from heaven (Matt. 16, 1 ff). Their influence with the people being little, they seldom came into conflict with Our Lord. But in the Passion of Christ, they are also found to be His active opponents. Later they persecuted the Apostles (Acts 4, 1 ff) and put James, "the brother (cousin) of Jesus," to death (*Antiq.*, XX, 9, 1).

(c) *The Herodians.*[3]—The Gospels mention, besides the Pharisees and Sadducees, also the Herodians as the enemies of Our Lord. They were not only in Galilee (Mark 3, 6) but also in Jerusalem (Matt. 22, 16). They are to be regarded not so much as particular followers of Herod Antipas, tetrarch of Galilee, but rather as adherents of the Herodian dynasty who were trying to restore all Palestine to the rule of the Herods. They succeeded for a short time under King Agrippa I. During the Passion of Christ they united with the Pharisees and Sadducees. As long as the Herodian dynasty existed, they could exert some influence.

(d) *The Essenes.*—The Essenes are mentioned by Josephus Flavius (*W.J.*, 2, 8, 2-14; *Antiq.* 18, 1, 5), Philo (*Quod omnis probus liber*, n. 12, 12), Pliny the Elder (*Historia Naturalis*, 5, 17, 73) and Eusebius (*Preparatio Evangelica*, 8, 11) who describe them as a religious, eschatologically minded Jewish sect, which is confirmed in recent times by the Qumran literature.

Name.—Their name is derived from the Greek "hosios" (i.e., a devout, religious person) or, more probably, from the Aramaic "chassai," pl., "chassaim" (i.e., the silent ones).

Number and Headquarters.—The Essenes had, according to Philo and Josephus, about 4,000 members (i.e., most likely those living at the time of their writings or lives) and were distributed throughout various towns and villages of Palestine and in certain districts near Damascus and perhaps in Egypt. Every settlement had one particular person chosen to act as host and to offer complete hospitality to "strangers" (i.e., travelling or refugee sectarians: Josephus, *W. J.*, 2, 8, 4). One

---

[3] Bickerman, E., "Les Hérodiens," in R.B., 47 (1938), 184-197.

of their principal settlements was *near Engaddi* (thus Pliny) or the monastery of Qumran.

At Qumran: Ascetical Life and Occupation.—The Qumran monks numbering about 150 to 200 in each of the six generations lived a way of life which included duties resembling the three vows of religion and the early Christian cenobites. They practised *poverty* (i.e., their goods were held in common), *chastity* (i.e., stress was laid upon ritual purity and celibacy or the unmarried state)[4] and *obedience* (i.e., by carefully observing the "Rule of the Community" and its interpretation by their lawful superiors). Like the Benedictan dictum, *ora et labora*, the Qumranites spent a great part of their time, both during the day and at night, in common and private prayer, as well as in meditation upon the Scriptures, and earned their livelihood in farming, pottery-making and manuscript-copying.[5]

Qumran Peculiarities.—The Qumranites followed their own calendar and liturgical rites of purification. At the monastery a candidate had to follow a strict prescribed course of conduct before he became a full member of the community. A one-year postulancy, or probation, and a two-year novitiate were required of each candidate. Before full membership the novice was obliged to swear that he would honor God, hate iniquity, show fidelity to his superiors, avoid stealing, always tell the truth, never communicate their doctrines to others even under the penalty of death, preserve the books of the sect and the names of the angels (*W. J.* 2, 8, 7).

They were strict in the observance of the Sabbath. They would send their gifts to the temple, but would not offer any bloody sacrifices, because they did not recognize the non-Sadokite high-priests at Jerusalem.

---

[4] Pliny the Elder (d. A.D. 79) described them as "an eternal race and yet not one is born in it." The three cemeteries of Qumran, containing about 1,200 adult burials, also have a few graves of women (but not in the *main* cemetary) who might have been benefactors of the monks or, more likely, prominent religious women in the Sadokite priestly family, who had reguested a Qumran burial near their relatives.

[5] Cf. Brisebois, G., "De momento regulae Communitatis seu Unionis Qumran ad originem vitae religiosae," in *Antonianum*, 34 (1959), 3-31.

Tertiaries.—The other Essenes outside Qumran tried, like Tertiaries, to follow the Qumran model of life, as far as possible, and pursued various peaceful occupations, as farming, cattle breeding, shepherding, producers of honey, craftsmen, etc. They also strictly observed the Sabbath, when they assembled in their syngaogues and read the Bible which was explained to them chiefly through symbolism.

Relation with Jewry.—After God the Jewish monks of Qumran had the greatest veneration for Moses. They recognized the canonical books of the Palestinian Canon and held in reverence some of the deutero-canonical and apocryphal books of the Old Testament as well as their own literature. Unlike the political Sadducees, their relatives, they were essentially religious. Like the Pharisees they followed their own interpretation of purification.

Doctrines.—They believed in the immortality of the soul, in the reward or punishment of the soul in the next world. For them God was the cause of all good, but not of evil, and everything depended upon His determination. They were Messianists and awaited the imminent Coming of Two Messiahs.

Origin and History.—The Essenes originated from the same religious and political crises that produced the Pharisees. Both were offshoots of Hassideans (Heb., *chassidim*, i.e., the pious) who were among the first to join the army of Mathathias to resist Hellenization, to punish apostate Jews and to reacquire independence (1 Mach., 2, 42-48). Whereas the Pharisees were mainly a lay organization, the Essenes represented a priestly movement described as the "sons of Sadoc"[6] in the Qumran literature and broke away from the militant Machabees when Jonathan—an ordinary Aaronite priest of the course of Joarib

---

[6] Although they called themselves "sons of Sadoc," in their own Qumran literature, yet they are to be distinguished from their political confreres of the same name, that is, the Sadducees of Josephus and of the Gospels. The latter represented the worldly and liberal-minded "sons of Sadoc" who tolerated a compromise between Judaism and Hellenism and tried to remain friendly with the Jewish ruling power. This split among the real and liberal "sons of Sadoc" was very probably due to their attitude of non-acceptance or acceptance of the Machabees as legitimate high-priests.

(cf. 1 Mach., 2, 1) and not of the Aaronite-Eleazar-Sadokite line—accepted the high priesthood (1 Mach. 10, 15-21) from the Seleucid Alexander I Balas (c. 152 B.C.) and his brother Simon was acknowledged by both people and some priests to be "their prince and high priest forever until there should arise a faithful prophet" (1 Mach. 14, 41).

As a silent protest and passive resistence against the Machabean non-Sadokite high priesthood, the Essenes were founded by the "Teacher of Righteousness" and some of their number completely abandoned the world and public life, established the Qumran monastery near the Dead Sea and lived there for a little more than two centuries (150 B.C.—A.D. 68).

In the first phase of their existence at Qumran (150-110 B.C.) pure Essenism was represented with special rules of conduct, their own liturgy and official cultic calendar and an ardent desire for two Messiahs, an anointed civil ruler and an anointed priest. In the second phase (110-40 B.C.) some of the Pharisee laymen persecuted especially by the Machabean John Hyrcanus I (134-104 B.C.), sought refuge and peace among the Essenes and also exerted their influence upon various Essenian settlements in Palestine, Damascus and Egypt. In the third phase under the anti-Machabean Herod the Great (40/37-4 B.C.) the Essenes everywhere enjoyed a favorable position, even though the Qumran monastery for one reason or another (e.g., earthquake, Parthian invasion, etc.) was abandoned. In the fourth and last phase (4 B.C.—A.D. 68) Essenism was tinged with anti-Herodian and anti-Roman tendencies. From the Qumran book, "Rule of War," we learn of the zealot tendencies and warlike preparations against the "Kittim" (i.e., the Romans). They participated in the First Jewish Revolt (A.D. 66-70) as John the Essene was appointed one of the Jewish generals (W. J., 2, 20, 4). Qumran was destroyed by the Roman army in A.D. 68 and it became a Roman fort until the end of the first century. Thereafter the Essenes disappear as a sect from Jewish history. Either they were absorbed by official Judaism or they embraced Christianity or some form of Gnosticism. There is no trace of them among the Jewish Christian sects.

Although some non-essential similarities exist between the Essenes and the primitive Christians (and it is very likely that John the Baptist was an Essene or had some contact with the Qumran community; that Jesus was acquainted with members of this sect and its teachings; that among the early Christians found at Damascus by Saul some were Essene Messianists; that the Epistle to the Hebrews was addressed to them), yet there is no historical evidence to prove that Christianity was a further development of the Qumran sect or that the essential doctrines taught by Jesus and His Apostles (e.g., Jesus as Messias, His Messianic Kingdom or Church, His redemptive blood shed for the sins of entire mankind, the sacraments, grace, world mission of Christianity, etc.) were based upon Qumran theology.

CHAPTER III

SACRED RITUAL

Bibliography: Medebielle, A., "L'expiation dans l'ancien et le nouveau Testament" (Rome, 1924); *idem,* "Le symbolisme du sacrifice expiatoire en Israel," in *Biblica,* 2 (1921), 141-169, 273-302; *idem,* "De sacrificii Israelitici origine et natura," in V.D., 6 (1926), 214-219, 238-244, 266-272; Coleran, J. A., "Origins of the Old Testament Sacrifice," in C.B.Q., 2 (1940), 130-144; *idem,* "The Sacrifice of Melchisedech," in *Theol. St.,* 1 (1940), 27-36; McHugh, J. A., "The Essence of the Sacrifice of the Mass and Scripture," in C.B.Q., 1 (1939), 15-43; Metzinger, A., "Die Substitutionstheorie und das alt. Opfer mit besonderer Berücksichtigung von Lev. 17, 11," in *Biblica,* 21 (1940), 159-187, 247-272 353-377; Steinmueller, J.E., "Sacrificial Blood in the Bible," in *Biblica,* 40 (1959), 422-433.

Art. 1. Sacrifices

(a) SACRIFICES IN GENERAL

The most important reason for sacrifice is based upon man's intimate relationship with Almighty God, who is the Creator and first cause of all things. All created things are dependent upon Him. Since man, however, is endowed with an intellect and free will, he must acknowledge God's absolute majesty and manifest this submission through voluntary acts. This acknowledgment and this submission constitute the essence of religion, which is practised by honoring God through acts of adoration, thanksgiving, petition, and since the fall of our first parents by atonement.

These four acts are by their nature internal acts. Since man, however, is not a pure spirit but a rational animal, his nature requires that this internal worship of God find some outward or external expression. When this worship is performed in a private capacity, the worship is private, but when this is performed in the name and authority of the community, the worship is public.

External acts of worship fall into two classes: they may consist either in words as the adequate expression of thought (and this is prayer), or in symbolical actions through which

394

the inner acts of man are to some degree represented. These symbolical actions may be either signs (e.g., genuflections, folding of hands, nodding of the head, etc.), or gifts (e.g., offerings and sacrifices).

The greatest expression of divine worship is found in a sacrifice, understood in the proper sense of the term.[4] Such a sacrifice consists in this, that man offers some befitting concrete gift to God (sacrificial oblation) and makes it a victim in place of himself (immolation) to acknowledge God's absolute majesty. "Sacrifice is not oblation plus immolation, but immolative oblation."[5]

In a sacrifice man gives to God something of his own property, and this surrender occurs through real or symbolical destruction whereby the gift is taken away from its usefulness to man. In this manner man recognizes that God is the Lord of everything he has, and this homage always constitutes the latreutical element of worship, or the act of adoration. This surrender of something from one's own goods through the symbol of sacrifice is also the best means to express one's thanks to God for His beneficent action (thanksgiving offering) and to request Him to continue His goodness (impetrative offering). Then, too, sacrifice is suitable to represent the expiatory element of worship, since the destruction of the gift expresses man's consciousness of his being worthy of death and of his need of repentance, without which reconciliation with God would be impossible (propitiatory sacrifice). But all these forms of sacrifices are only types of the one true sacrifice, the sacrificial death of Christ on the cross.

(b) The Division of Sacrifices in the Old Testament

The sacrifices of the Old Testament were divided into bloody and unbloody. The material of the unbloody sacrifices was grain (which included ears of grain, flour and cakes), garden produce (as fruit, especially grapes, wine, and olive

[4] In the wide or improper sense, sacrifice may mean prayer, works of mercy, a holy life, mortification, contrition, etc.
[5] Cf. McHugh, J. A., *op. cit.*, 23.

oil), incense, and salt. The material of the bloody sacrifices was the animals of the herd, such as cattle, sheep, and goats; in some special cases doves were also allowed. In general, animals of either sex could be used for sacrifices; however, the Law prescribed special occasions when the one or the other had to be offered. Animals from the herd had to be at least eight days old, before they could be sacrificed (Lev. 22, 27); sheep and goats were generally sacrificed when a year old, and bullocks when three years old. In general, the victim was to be without blemish and should not bear any sign of weakness; only in the cases of voluntary peace offerings was any mitigation allowed (Lev. 22, 19-25).

Unsuitable material for sacrifices were all animals that could not be eaten by the Hebrews and also wild game, although considered legally clean, as deer, gazelles, and antelopes. The sacrificial material was intimately connected with the life and activity of the Israelites, and therefore aptly represented an act of abnegation and a substitute of the offerer.

Human sacrifice [6] was forbidden by the Law under the heaviest penalties (Lev. 18, 21; 20, 1-5; Deut. 12, 31; 18, 10). Among the Hebrews this pagan practice was introduced during the royal period (3 Kgs. 16, 34), but it was vigorously condemned by the prophets.

(c) The Bloody Sacrifices

According to the reasons for offering, the sacrifices are divided into (1) holocausts or burnt offerings, (2) sin and guilt offerings, and (3) peace offerings.

The common ritual for the bloody sacrifices consisted in the following five main actions. (a) The sacrificial animal was brought by the offerer himself to the court of the tabernacle or temple, where it was received by the priest and then

---

[6] Cf. Mader, E., "Die Menschenopfer der alten Hebräer und der benachbarten Völker," in B.S., 14 (Freiburg i.B., 1909); Bea, A., "Kinderopfer für Moloch oder für Jahwe?" in *Biblica*, 18 (1937), 95-107.

examined. (b) In most sacrifices the imposition of hands followed; in private sacrifices the person offering the animal laid his hands on its head (Lev. 1, 4; 3, 2. 8. 13), but in public expiatory sacrifices this was done by the elders (Lev. 4, 15). The meaning of this ceremony was that the sin of the offerer was passed over to the victim, which was to die in place of the sinful man. (c) The victim, laden with the sins of the offerer, was slain on the north side of the altar of holocausts. (d) The blood of the victim was received in a dish by the priest, who applied it according to the kind of sacrifice intended. He sprinkled part of the blood either on the side of the altar of holocausts or on its four horns, or on the altar of incense, or even towards the kapporeth in the Holy of Holies. The propitiatory element is clearly shown in the sprinkling of blood in every sacrifice, for the blood was the ordinary means of expiation (cf. Hebr. 9, 12 ff). (e) The last act of the sacrificial ritual was the burning of the flesh of the victim on the altar, after it had been skinned and cut to pieces. Either all the flesh was burnt, or only some of the fat was consumed by the altar fire, and the flesh that remained was cooked and eaten by the priests, or used by the offerer for a sacrificial feast, or burnt outside of the encampment or city.

(1) Holocausts or Burnt Offerings.—These were called in Hebrew *'olah* (that which goes up) and in Latin *holocaustum*, because the whole victim was burnt. The blood was poured round about the altar (Lev. 1). The latreutical element is emphasized through the total burning of the victim. Since the holocaust serves in a most excellent manner the highest purpose of divine adoration, the honor of God, it takes the first place among sacrifices, and therefore only male animals could be used. This sacrifice was to be uninterrupted, because twice daily, in the morning and in the evening, a lamb had to be offered; the fire on this altar was to burn day and night (Lev. 6, 9-13). With every holocaust was connected an unbloody addition, a meal and drink offering, the materials and quanti-

ties of which varied in accordance with the animal sacrificed (Num. 15, 1-12).

(2) Sin and Guilt Offerings.—Both of these sacrifices are embraced by the common name of expiatory sacrifices. The reason for the difference between these two sacrifices is difficult to determine with certainty. Aside from certain fixed times (e.g., the Passover, Pentecost, Feast of Tabernacles, Day of Atonement, New Year's festival, the New Moons), when a he-goat had to be sacrificed for the sins of the whole people, it seems that the *sin offering* (Hebr., hattath) had to be offered by individual Israelites to remove certain legal uncleannesses (e.g., the purification of women after childbirth or of a leper), or to atone for personal sins committed unintentionally and indeliberately (Num. 15, 24-29), since deliberate grievous sins were punishable with death (Num. 15, 30 f; Lev. 24, 10-23). The *guilt offering* (Hebr., asham), in distinction to the sin offering, was made when there was a question of some injury committed to the property or the rights of God Himself or of a man's neighbors. The damage had to be repaired, a fifth of the value being paid in addition, and a sacrifice offered (Lev. 5, 14-16; 6, 2 ff).

The sacrificial victim in sin offerings varied according to the position of the offerer, his wealth, and the sin to be atoned for (Lev. 4, 1-5, 13). The high priest and the whole community offered a young bullock, the head of a tribe or of a family a he-goat, the ordinary Israelite a she-goat; the poor were allowed to offer two doves. Since in these sacrifices the propitiatory element was the most important, the disposition of the blood was of special significance. The blood was not merely spilled round about the altar of holocausts as in the burnt or peace offerings, but its disposition was carefully prescribed for different places in accordance with the importance of the offering and offerer. In the private sacrifices of the individual Israelites, part of the blood was rubbed on the horns of the altar of holocausts by the priest and the rest was poured out at the foot of the altar (Lev. 4, 27-30). In the sacrifices of the whole people or of the priests, the blood was brought into the Holy Place, sprinkled seven times towards the curtain of the Holy of Holies, and rubbed on the altar of incense (Lev. 4, 3 ff). In the sin offering on the Day of Atonement, the high priest brought the blood into the Holy of Holies, poured it out seven times on the floor before the kapporeth and once on the kapporeth itself. In these sin offerings only the fat of the victims (cf. Lev. 4, 8-10) was burnt upon the altar; the rest of the meat was burnt outside of the encampment or city, if the blood of the victims was carried inside the Holy Place or Holy of Holies, but it was eaten by the priests within the sacred precincts if the blood of the victims was only taken to the altar of holocausts.

The guilt offerings were only private sacrifices, and the ritual was almost the same as that of the private sin offerings. The blood was sprinkled at the foot of the altar of holocausts, the fat was burnt on that altar, and the rest of the meat was eaten by the priests within the sacred precincts. The victim of this offering was usually a ram with a value of at least two shekels (Lev. 5, 15; 7,1-7; 14, 13). Cf. Saydon, P.B., "Sin-Offering and Trespass-Offering," in C.B.Q., 8 (1946), 393-398.

(3) *Peace Offerings.*—A peace offering (Hebr., zebah shelamim) is a general name, and appears as a thanks or praise offering (Hebr., zebah hattodah), a votive offering (Hebr., zebah neder), and freewill offering (Hebr., zebah nedabah). Every unblemished animal, male or female, of the flock or herd regarded as fit for sacrifice might be used (Lev. 3, 1.6. 12).

The blood was sprinkled round about the altar of holocausts as in the burnt offerings. Of the victim only the fatty parts (Lev. 3, 3 ff), together with a meal and drink offering (Lev. 7, 11 ff), were burnt. Then the breast and the right (hind) leg were separated from the rest of the flesh. The breast was offered to God through a ceremony called "waving." The priest placed this breast on the hands of the man offering the sacrifice, and then made a horizontal movement forwards towards the sanctuary and back again. Then it seems that another movement, from below upwards and then down again, was made with the right leg. These two pieces were given to the priests as their share of the sacrifice. The remaining meat was used by the offerer and his family for a sacrificial banquet, to which the Levites or even widows, orphans, and the poor were invited.

This sacrificial banquet was celebrated near the sanctuary (Deut. 12, 7. 12. 18; 14, 26), and represented God as the host and all partaking of the meal as His guests; it was a symbol and pledge of their mutual friendship. It served also as a type of another banquet so often mentioned in the Bible, the banquet that God was preparing for man in the Messianic kingdom. Just as the burnt offering and the sin offering were types of Christ's sacrificial death on the cross, so too the peace offering was a type of the Blessed Eucharist.

(d) THE UNBLOODY SACRIFICES

The gifts of grain and wine were to the unbloody sacrifices what the flesh and blood of victims were to the bloody sacrifices. As the material of the bloody sacrifices was taken from the Hebrews and represented their activity as cattle breeders, the material of the unbloody sacrifices was taken from their agricultural life. In addition to grain and wine, oil, salt, and incense were also used as offerings.

The grain (meal offering) was offered in various forms: as pure flour, crushed and roasted ears of grain, unleavened bread, and cakes. Of the unbloody sacrifices only the incense was totally burnt. Of the rest of the solids only a small part was burnt on the altar together with the incense, as a reminder (Hebr., azkarah) that it rendered the offerer pleasing to God (Lev. 2, 2; 5, 12); what remained belonged to the priests. The wine offering or libation was simply poured out at the foot of the altar.

The unbloody sacrifices were either supplementary to the holocausts and peace offerings or independent sacrifices, and were offered partly in the court on the altar of holocausts and partly in the Holy Place. In the Holy Place were offered the daily incense sacrifice, the light of the golden lampstand, and the showbreads with additional incense and wine offerings. On the Sabbath when these showbreads were consumed by the priests, incense was burnt and wine was thrown out on the ground as a libation. In the court were offered in particular: the meal offering (1/10 ephah of flour) which the high priest had to offer twice a day, in the morning and in the evening, for himself and the entire priesthood (Lev. 6, 12-16); secondly, the first sheaves of grain on the second day within the octave of the Passover (Lev. 23, 10-14); thirdly, two loaves of bread from the flour of the new harvest on Pentecost (Lev. 23, 15-20).

Art. 2. Laws of Purification

Almighty God had imposed upon His elected people, Israel, a particular obligation: "Be holy, because I am holy" (Lev. 11, 46). The sacred Covenant which God concluded with Israel demanded, above all, inner moral purity of the nation as well as of the individual. But Israel was also to represent itself externally as a pure and holy nation. The preservation of or restoration to this external, levitical or legal cleanness that was demanded by God, was to be accomplished by the various regulations concerning purification in the Mosaic Law.[7] No kind of laws influenced so extensively and generally the entire life of the Hebrew people as the regulations about cleanness and uncleanness, and the distinction between the clean or lawful and the unclean or unlawful food. Through these regulations the Law invaded the very homes of the Jews, checked man in his eating and drinking, restricted his activity, and made him responsible even for actions done in his sleep.

(a) THE LEVITICAL PURIFICATIONS

According to the Law, certain corporal conditions and functions defiled man before God. Anyone who was thus afflicted

[7] Cf. Linder, *op. cit.*, 570.

was unclean or impure, and hence was to be excluded from approaching the pure and holy God. Defilement was transmitted to people and even to lifeless things (e.g., a house, its utensils, etc.). These things became defiled through contact with unclean people and unclean things. To free oneself from this uncleanness and to remove the barriers that prevented man from approaching God, various ritual cleansings were prescribed. These varied for different cases, and, because of their religious character, were called "levitical purifications." These regulations are contained chiefly in the Book of Leviticus (chs. 11-15) and Numbers (ch. 19).

There were different degrees of defilement according to their causal differences; thus, the exclusion from approaching God could be larger or smaller both in regard to distance and duration. The degree of uncleanness was also made to correspond with the ceremonial purification. The slightest uncleanness prevented a man from entering the court of the tabernacle or of the temple until the evening of that day. This defilement was removed by simply taking a bath and washing one's clothes. But this defilement might also last for seven or fourteen days, or even longer. When it lasted at least seven days, a sacrifice had to be combined with the purification.

The Law distinguished between three kinds of uncleanness: (a) *Uncleanness of the Human Corpse and Animal Carcass.*— The human corpse defiled the house or tent, in which it lay, the people in it, the utensils found there as well as all open vessels, and the clothes that touched the corpse. All of these objects were considered unclean for seven days. For the removal of this defilement persons and things had to be sprinkled with the water of purification specially prepared from the ashes of the red cow (Num. 19). An animal carcass defiled anyone who touched, carried or ate it, but only until evening.   (b) *Uncleanness Due to Leprosy.*—An individual suffering from leprosy was considered unclean for the whole duration of his sickness. Dressed in mourning clothes, he had to remain away from human society and outside of the camp or city, and warn others aproaching him with the word: "Unclean!" Once he was cured in the judgment of the priest, he had to undergo a complicated ritual purification. The Law also recognized a leprosy affecting houses (a sort of corrosive action on the walls) and clothes (a sort of mold caused by dampness and want of air). (c) *Sexual Uncleanness.*—Uncleanness produced by normal or sickly functions of sexual life (e.g., the performance of marital obligations, the issue of seed and blood, menstruation, birth, etc.).

(b) THE SIGNIFICANCE AND PURPOSE OF THESE REGULATIONS [8]

Levitical defilement should not be mistaken for moral uncleanness or sin, because it was contracted independently of a man's free will. It did not, therefore, put an end to a man's internal communion with God, but only brought about a separation from the external and theocratical community. Yet, an intimate relationship existed between levitical and moral defilement. Certain conditions and functions of the body are declared as unclean, not because they are sinful in themselves, but because they are associated with sin. This also appears from the fact that the consequences of levitical uncleanness are of a religious nature (as the exclusion from approaching God), and that the purifications had a religious character and in many cases had to be performed with sacrifices.

The connection between levitical and moral defilement consists in this, that in certain conditions and functions there appear especially the consequences of sin in regard to a man's body, even independently of his will. The death of man is a punishment and picture of sin; leprosy is a decomposition of a living body, a half-dead man. But in sexual life a man is particularly subjected to the influence of sin, since especially in this sphere the evil appetites, one of the main results of original sin, manifest themselves. Because of this intimate association with sin levitical uncleanness was suitable as a

[8] Cf. Schoepfer, A., "Geschichte des A.T.," I (6 ed., Munich, 1923), 258 f.

symbol of sin and as a reminder of the general sinfulness of
the human race. On the other hand, legal or levitical purification was a symbol of the purification of the soul. The
intended purpose of these regulations about uncleanness and
purification is, therefore, evident. It was to keep alive the
consciousness of sin and the longing to be freed from sin—in
a word, to foster moral purity.

This part of the Law also throws a light on the relationship
existing between the Old and New Testaments. As sin de-
stroys internal communion with God, so levitical uncleanness
excluded a man from the external, theocratical communion
with God. As the various purifications and the sacrifices
associated with them restored corporal cleanness and theocratical communion, so also, but in a greater measure, the
blood of Jesus Christ and the Sacraments instituted by Him
effect the purification of the soul from dead works (Hebr.
9, 13 f).

(c) Laws Concerning Food

A distinction between clean and unclean beasts—that is,
what beasts were allowed and prohibited for nourishment—
was known already at the time of Noe (Gen. 7, 2; 8, 20).
Through the Mosaic Law a significant limitation was placed
upon the Israelites regarding their selection of flesh food.
These regulations regarding food had a great practical significance, because every Israelite came in contact with them
daily and was reminded continually of his particular election
by God and of his segregation from the Gentiles (Lev. 20,
24-26). Through these food regulations in the Old Testament
a separating wall was erected between the Israelites and the
Gentiles. This wall was to be razed when the Gentiles were
admitted into the Messianic kingdom. Hence, this call of
the Gentiles to the Church of Christ was revealed to St.
Peter through the vision of the abrogation of these food regulations (Acts 10, 11-17).

Four kinds of animals are distinguished by the biblical
writers: four-footed beasts, birds, fishes, and creeping beasts.

This division is not based upon a strict zoological classification but rather upon popular tradition.

The four-footed beasts were restricted to the larger quadrupeds. Of these the Mosaic Law (Lev. 11, 2-8. 26-28; Deut. 14, 3-8) reckoned as clean all those that chew the cud and have divided hoofs (as oxen, sheep, goats), and animals resembling them (as gazelles, wild goats, stags, and fallow deer). On the contrary, it was forbidden to eat beasts that lacked the two characteristics of chewing the cud and having the hoofs divided, or even lacked one of these. For these reasons it was prohibited to eat dogs, wolves, foxes, and lions, because they walk on paws; likewise camels (because not all their hoofs are divided), rabbits (which apparently chew the cud but do not have divided hoofs), and the swine (because they do not chew the cud).

In the Pentateuch no particular stress was laid upon the prohibition to eat swine's flesh, but in the course of time the eating of it was equivalent to apostasy from Judaism (cf. Isa. 65, 4; 66, 3; 1 Mach. 1, 50; 2 Mach. 6, 18). The main reason why such an aversion was shown to this meat was because the swine were used by the pagans, and especially by the Canaanites, in their idolatrous sacrifices and sacrificial banquets.

The genus "birds" comprises not only birds proper, but also the bats and grasshoppers. Of birds (Lev. 11, 13-19; Deut. 14, 11-19) about twenty species are declared to be unclean (mostly birds of prey and bats). On the other hand, pigeons, turtle-doves, quails, and other birds not expressly forbidden were clean. Four kinds of grasshoppers were also allowed.

The genus "fish" included everything that either lived or moved about in water. Of the aquatic animals (Lev. 11, 9-12; Deut. 14, 9 f) only those that had fins and scales could be eaten. Everything else was unclean (e.g., eels; testaceous or crustaceous animals such as clams, oysters, lobsters, crabs, etc.; amphibians, such as frogs, etc.).

The genus "creeping things" or reptiles also included the

mouse, the mole, the weasel, and lizard (Lev. 11, 29 f). Of the reptiles all kinds were considered unclean, whether they crept on their bellies (as snakes or worms) or moved about on four or more legs (as lizards, weasels, rats, insects; cf. Lev. 11, 41-43).

But it was not allowed to eat even clean beasts indiscriminately. Thus, it was forbidden to consume the blood and portions of flesh containing blood (Lev. 7, 26 f). It was prohibited to eat the flesh of any beast that had died a natural death or that had been killed by some wild animal. It was forbidden to eat the flesh of any beast sacrificed to a heathen god (Ex. 34, 15; 1 Cor. 10, 20-33; Acts 15, 29). Certain fatty parts of oxen, sheep, and goats were not to be eaten, because they were destined for the altar of sacrifice; thus, they were considered sacred, even apart from a sacrifice (Lev. 3, 16 f; 7, 23. 25). Finally, a kid was not to be boiled in its mother's milk (Ex. 23, 19; 34, 26; Deut. 14, 21).[9]

[9] This pagan rite is mentioned in the Ras Shamra (Ugarit) tablets of the 15th/14th centuries B.C.; cf. Casey, A., in V.D., 16 (1936), 142-148, 174-183.

CHAPTER IV

SACRED SEASONS

Art. 1. The Calendar [1]

The Israelites followed, not a solar, but a lunar year; in other words, their calendar was governed by the moon. The natural day (i.e., the period of twenty-four hours) was reckoned from sunset to sunset,[2] and consisted of two periods, that of light (day) and that of darkness (night). The term "day" is employed in the Bible both in the sense of twenty-four hours and daytime. The civil day (i.e., the period of daylight) was divided into six unequal parts: morning dawn (Hebr. shahar, cf. Gen. 19, 15, or nesheph, cf. 1 Sam. 30, 17), morning (boqer), heat of the day (Hebr. hom hajjom; it began about 9 A.M.; cf. Gen. 18, 1; 1 Sam. 11, 11), noon (Hebr. zaharajim, cf. Gen. 43, 16. 25), twilight (Hebr. nesheph, cf. 4 Kgs. 7, 5. 7), and evening (Hebr. 'erebh, cf. Gen. 19, 1). Later, on returning from the Babylonian captivity, the Jews divided the period of daylight into four parts, each of which had three hours; these parts were called first (6 A.M.-9 A.M.), third (9 A.M.-12 A.M.), sixth (12 A.M.-3 P.M.), and ninth hour (3 P.M.-6 P.M.). The night was divided at first into three watches (cf. Ex. 14, 24; Jdgs. 7, 19), and afterwards into four watches of three hours each according to the Roman system, called evening, midnight, cock-crow, and morning.

The week consisted of seven days and was based on the story of creation, as God created the world in six days and rested on the seventh day. With the exception of the seventh,

[1] Cf. Seisenberger, *op. cit.*, 139-141; Kortleitner, *op. cit.*, 663-675; * Friedländer, M., in J.E., s.v. *Calendar*. Jaubert, A., "La Date de la Cène. Calendrier biblique et liturgie chrétienne" (Paris, 1957); Milik, J. T., "Ten Years of Discovery in the Wilderness of Judaea" (London, 1958), 107-113.

[2] This division of time from sunset to sunset has been adopted by the Church, as festivals and days begin with first vespers and end with second vespers.

407

the days of the week had no particular names; they were
called simply the first, second, etc. The seventh was the Sabbath (i.e., rest). In the new dispensation Sunday, the day of
Our Lord's Resurrection, has become the day of rest.

The Hebrew month was intimately connected with the
moon, as the same word "hodesh" was used to express "new
moon" and "month." The month corresponds with the duration of the moon's circuit round the earth, and astronomically
this takes 29 days, 12 hours, 44 minutes, and 3 seconds. But
the Hebrews basing their calculations upon the visibility of
the new moon had months of either 29 or 30 days. In the
pre-exilic period special names were given only to four months:
the month of the ears of corn (Hebr., hodesh abib, i.e., the
first month; cf. Ex. 13, 4; 23, 15), the month of splendor of
flowers (Hebr., ziv, i.e., the second month; cf. 3 Kgs. 6, 1. 37),
the month of steady flowing rivers (Hebr., haethanim, i.e.,
the seventh month; cf. 3 Kgs. 8, 2), the month of increase
(Hebr., bul, i.e., the eighth month; cf. 3 Kgs. 6, 38). After
the exile the Assyro-Babylonian names came into use and are
still retained by the Jews. They are: [3]

I (7)   Nisan (March/April) with 30 days. The Passover
was celebrated on the 14th of Nisan.

II (8)   Ijjar (April/May) with 29 days.

III (9)   Sivan (May/June) with 30 days. Pentecost fell on
the 6th of this month.

IV (10)   Tammus (June/July) with 29 days.

V (11)   Ab (July/August) with 30 days.

VI (12)   Elul (August/September) with 29 days.

VII (1)   Tishri (September/October) with 30 days. On the
1st fell the civil New Year's festival, on the 10th
the Day of Atonement, on the 15th the Feast of
Tabernacles.

VIII (2)   Marheshwan (October/November) with 29 days.

IX (3)   Kislev (November/December) with 30 days. The

[3] Roman numerals represent the months of the sacred year; Arabic
numerals the months of the civil year.

Feast of the Dedication of the Temple was celebrated on the 25th (John 10, 22).

X (4)   Tebeth (December/January) with 29 days.
XI (5) Shebat (January/February) with 30 days.
XII (6) Adar (February/March) with 29 days.

To make up the difference between the lunar and solar year
a thirteenth intercalary month, called Veadar, was added
every second or third year. The determination of this intercalary month was based upon the growth of the barley, i.e.,
whether it would be ripe by the middle of the month of Nisan,
so that the harvest could be begun with the ceremony of offering the first sheaf at the Passover.

Art. 2.   The Sabbath and Sabbath Feasts

Every morning and evening a one-year-old lamb was sacrificed as a burnt offering on the altar of holocausts in the
court (Ex. 29, 38; Num. 28, 3), and at the same time fragrant
incense was laid on the altar of incense in the Holy Place.
Every pious Israelite honored God at home with his prayers
or by attending these sacrifices. But this worship of God
was to be increased from time to time by means of prescribed
sacred seasons and feasts. The cycle of feasts combined three
classes: the Sabbath feasts, the three great feasts of joy (Passover, Pentecost, and Tabernacles), the Day of Atonement.
These festive periods were ruled by the holy number seven.
The seventh day of the week was the Sabbath, the seventh
month was the Sabbath month, the seventh year was the Sabbath year, the year following seven times seven years was the
Jubilee year. The Feasts of Tabernacles and Atonement occur
in the seventh month. Pentecost was celebrated seven times
seven days from the Passover. The two principal feasts Passover and Tabernacles lasted for seven days.

(a) *The Sabbath.*—The most important of all feast days
was the seventh day of the week, the Sabbath, the day of
rest (cf. Ex. 20, 8-11; 31, 13-17), which began at sunset on

Friday. It was celebrated with complete rest. The Israelites had to refrain from all work under the penalty of lapidation (Num. 15, 36). The kinds of work forbidden are mentioned in the Bible: the collecting of manna (Ex. 16, 26 f), cooking and baking (Ex. 16, 23), the lighting of a fire (Ex. 35, 3), plowing and reaping (Ex. 34, 21), the gathering of wood (Num. 15, 32-36), the carrying of bundles (Jer. 17, 21), selling and trading (2 Esd. 10, 31; 13, 15-18). Food for the Sabbath was prepared on the preceding day (parasceve). This precept even obliged the pagan slaves of an Israelite, nor could beasts of burden be used for work. In the post-exilic period the Sabbatical rest was interpreted rather severely. The prohibition of leaving the encampment (Ex. 16, 29) was fixed to mean that no Jew could go farther than 2,000 cubits (i.e., about a quarter of an hour's walk), the distance of the Mount of Olives from Jerusalem (Acts 1, 12). Even self-defense was considered at first during the early Machabean period as a violation of the Sabbath (1 Mach. 2, 36-38: 2 Mach. 6, 11), until Mathathias ordered the contrary (1 Mach. 2, 41). At the time of Our Lord the observance of the Sabbath rest had degenerated into a burdensome and ridiculous pedantry as is known from the Gospels.

The positive side of the celebration consisted in doubling the burnt offerings in the morning and evening sacrifice (Num. 28, 9 f), in providing fresh loaves of showbread (Lev. 24, 8), and in religious assemblies for the edification of the community (Lev. 23, 2 f).

The historical basis for the Sabbath celebration is God's rest on the Sabbath after the creation of the world; the Sabbath was to be an imitation of this arrangement. The Israelite, by directing his life according to this divine plan of work and rest, was to acknowledge himself as God's possession. The Sabbath, according to St. Thomas (*Summa*, 1. 2, q. 100; art. 5, ad 2), is also a type of eternal rest destined for man after his long day's work on earth. Cf. North, R., "The Derivation of Sabbath," in *Biblica*, 36 (1955), 182-201.

(*b*) *The New Moons.*—The beginning of the month was

also celebrated with additional sacrifices (Num. 28, 11-15), and even more sacrifices were offered on the first day of Tishri, the seventh month, and the day observed with complete rest (Lev. 23, 23-25; Num. 29, 1-6). After the Babylonian captivity the civil year began with the first day of this seventh month.

(c) *The Sabbatical Year.*—Analogous with the weekly Sabbath, every seventh year was dedicated to rest (Ex. 23, 10 f; Lev. 25, 1-7; Deut. 15, 1-11). (1) Beginning in the autumn, it meant a year's rest for the entire land. No field was to be cultivated or sown; no garden and no fruit tree was to receive attention. Whatever grew without any action on the part of man, became common property. The poor and strangers and even the beasts shared in these crops. To insure the observance of this law, God promised a superabundance of crops in the sixth year (Lev. 25, 20-22). (2) During this year no debtor could be forced to pay his debt. (3) On the Feast of Tabernacles the Law was read to the assembled people.

The celebration of the Sabbatical year was to remind the Israelites that the land belonged to God, and that in the eyes of God they were living there only as strangers. The reading of the Law was to teach the Hebrews to fear God and observe the enactments of the Law. The rest from work associated with the rest of the land gave the people ample opportunity to understand the contents of the Mosaic Law. Cf. North, R., "Maccabean Sabbath Year," in *Biblica*, 34 (1953), 501-515.

(d) *The Year of Jubilee* [4] (Hebr., shanath hajjobel).—It was probably so-called from the sound of the trumpets which proclaimed its beginning on the 10th of Tishri, that is, the Day of Atonement (Lev. 25, 8-55). As in the Sabbatical year, the whole land rested and was not to be cultivated. Thus, there was no agriculture for two successive years, but God promised to provide a superabundance of crops in the years previous to these, so that there would be no reason to

[4] Cf. Power, E., "Annus Jubilæus," in V.D., 4 (1924), 353-358; Milik, J. T., "De vicissitudinibus notionis et vocabuli Jubilaei," in V.D., 28 (1950), 162-167; North, R., "Sociology of the Biblical Jubilee" (Rome, 1954).

fear a famine. The rest affected only agriculture; cattle breeding and other business went on as usual. There were two other important laws to be observed in the year of the jubilee. (1) All landed property as well as the houses of the Levites which had changed hands, reverted to the original owners or to their descendants without payment. The sale, therefore, had been merely a lease on the property, and the price varied according to the space of time to the next jubilee year. (2) All Hebrews who had been reduced to slavery were set at liberty. Because of these two laws this year was also called the year of freedom.

By returning the landed property to its original owners or their descendants, the division of the land according to God's plan was being retained for future times and God's ownership stressed. The freedom from slavery was to remind the Hebrews that not only the land but also the people belonged to God. The year of jubilee is a type of "the restoration of all things" (Acts 3, 21) at the end of the world, when the children of God will receive their entire heritage and full freedom.

Art. 3.   The Three Great Feasts of the Year

Three times a year every male Israelite (it was optional for women and children) had to make a pilgrimage to Jerusalem and appear before the sanctuary to celebrate the important feasts in common (Ex. 23, 17; 34, 23).

(a) *The Feast of the Passover* (Ex. 12).—The first and most important of the yearly recurring feasts was the Passover. The feast began on the 14th of the first month of the ecclesiastical year, that is, on the evening of the 14th of Nisan and lasted till the 21st of that month. The real first day of the feast (i.e., the 15th of Nisan) and the last day of the feast (i.e., the 21st of Nisan) were observed with Sabbatical rests and assemblies. As only unleavened bread could be eaten during this entire octave, it was also called the "Feast of the Unleavened Bread" (solemnitas azymorum).

On the 10th day of Nisan a male lamb, one year old and

free from blemish, was set aside for each family. On the 14th, "between the two evenings" (Ex. 12, 6 MT),[5] the head of the household slaughtered the lamb. If any family was too small to eat a whole lamb, two families might unite for that purpose. A bundle of hyssop was dipped into the blood as it flowed out, and some was smeared on the two doorposts and on the lintel of the house. No bone of the animal was to be broken, nor was it to be cut up, but after the skin and fat had been removed, it was roasted whole at the fire. When it was cooked through, it had to be eaten the same night with unleavened bread and bitter herbs. All of the household took part in the meal, and only the uncircumcised were excluded. As the ceremony commemorated the exodus from Egypt, all present had to have their loins girt, sandals on their feet, and a staff in their hand. The head of the house had to explain the reason for the feast. What could not be eaten had to be burnt on the following morning.[6]

When settled conditions prevailed after the occupation of Palestine by the Hebrews, slight changes were made in the ceremony, and all full-grown males were required to attend in the sanctuary. The lambs had to be killed and eaten near the tabernacle or temple. Some of the blood was sprinkled on the altar and the fatty parts were burnt. Pilgrims who came to Jerusalem to celebrate the feast received the necessary accommodations gratis from the inhabitants, but it was usual to present the host with the lambs' skins and the vessels used. As the number of strangers was very great, many spent the nights in the open air, and ate the lambs in tents.[7]

Whoever was prevented from keeping the feast on the 14th of Nisan by reason either of legal defilement or some other

[5] The Vulgate and Septuagint read "in the evening." The strictest interpretation of the Hebrew text is between twilight and complete darkness. The rabbis interpreted the expression as meaning after the evening sacrifice that took place between 1.30 and 2.30 p.m. (Pesahim 5, 1). Josephus indicated that in A.D. 66 the sacrifice of 256,500 lambs took place within the hours of 3 and 5 p.m. (?). Philo, a contempory of Our Lord, stated that the lambs were slaughtered in the temple from noon to evening; this seems to be the more probable view.

[6] Cf. Seisenberger, *op. cit.*, 146 f.

[7] Cf. Seisenberger, *op. cit.*, 147.

impediment, was bound to keep the Passover on the 14th of the following month, under the pain of death.

According to the Mishna (tract Pesahim) the Passover rites were performed as follows: At the beginning of the meal the head of the household blessed the first cup (calix qiddush), and all drank from this cup or from their own cups. After he had washed his hands, a table was brought in with the roasted lamb, unleavened bread (matsoth), bitter herbs, haroseth, a dish of vinegar or salt water. After a short prayer the head of the household took some bitter herbs and ate them, and all the rest followed his example. A second cup of wine (calix haggada) was poured out, mixed with water and then blessed. Thereupon a son of the householder, or one of the guests, was to inquire about the reasons for the ceremony and for the differences of this night from all other nights (cf. Ex. 12, 26). The head of the family then explained fully that it was held in remembrance of the delivery from Egypt and the sparing of the first-born among the Israelites. After this exhortation the first part of the hymn "Hallel" was recited or sung (Ps. 112-113, 8, i.e., Laudate pueri and In exitu Israel). After this prayer, the second cup of wine was drunk. After the master of the house washed his hands, he took a matsoth, broke it, blessed it, and then distributed the bread to the guests to eat. Now the principal part of the meal was served. This ended, a third cup of wine (calix benedictionis) was filled, and mixed with water, blessed, and drunk by all. Thereupon the second part of the hymn "Hallel" was recited or sung (Ps. 113, 9—117, i.e., In exitu Israel continued; 114 Dilexi; 115 Credidi; 116 Laudate Dominum; 117 Confitemini Domino). Towards the end of this hymn (Ps. 117, 26) a fourth cup of wine (calix hallel) was poured out, and then drunk after the conclusion of the hymn. Here the formal service ends.

During the week of the festival there were offered as a burnt offering, besides the daily sacrifice, two bullocks, one ram, seven he-lambs of the first year together with their meal and drink offering, and as a sin offering one he-goat to make atone-

ment for the people (Num. 28, 16-25). On the second day of
the festival, i.e., on the 16th of Nisan (Lev. 23, 10-14), a sheaf
of barley was offered; before this offering was made, none of
the new harvest could be used.[7a]

(b) *Pentecost*.[8]—This feast is usually called in the Old
Testament the Feast of Weeks (Ex. 34, 22; Lev. 23, 15-22;
Deut. 16, 9-12), because from the second day of the Passover
week, i.e. from the 16th of Nisan, seven weeks were reckoned
and on the next day the feast was celebrated. The English
term "Pentecost" is derived from the Greek (cf. Acts 2, 1),
which means fiftieth (day). Another name was the Feast of
the Harvest (Ex. 23, 16), because as the harvest was then
over, it was regarded as a thanksgiving festival. It was also
called the Feast of the First Fruits (Num. 28, 26), because
two loaves of leavened bread were then offered as the first
bread baked from the new harvest.

According to the Fathers and Jewish tradition, this feast co-
incided with the day when the Law was given on Mount
Sinai, fifty days after the exodus of the Israelites from Egypt.
In the Bible this feast only appears as a harvest festival. We
are therefore forced to assume that, because of this intimate
connection between the Feast of Weeks and the Feast of the
Passover, Pentecost had a double significance. This feast
lasted only one day, and was celebrated as a day of rest with

[7a] As the name Passover indicates, the feast commemorates the deliv-
erance of the Israelites from the Egyptians at the time of the exodus,
when all the first-born of the Egyptians were slain. The unleavened
bread, also called "bread of affliction," was to remind them of the haste
with which they departed from Egypt, and the bitter herbs were to
make them recall their bitter sufferings. In God's design these historical facts connected with the Passover were intended to symbolize
higher thoughts. The unleavened bread was a symbol of moral purity,
and was to remind the people that they were a holy people and should
be free from moral corruption (1 Cor. 5, 7). The lamb was a type of
Jesus Christ as victim. In the Bible He is called the lamb (John 1, 29;
1 Cor. 5, 7, etc.) and this refers to His innocence, to the command that
no bone was to be broken (John 19, 36), to the institution of the unbloody sacrifice, the Blessed Eucharist, after the passover supper, and to
the bloody sacrifice on the cross. The passover lamb was a real sacrifice,
a combination of sin and peace offering; similarly, Our Lord died for us
as a sin offering on the cross, and gives Himself to us as a peace offering
in the Blessed Eucharist.
[8] Cf. Olivera, B. Santis, "Pentecoste," in V.D., 3 (1923), 132-135.

religious assemblies and special sacrifices (Num. 28, 27-31). On this day the Israelites were expected to make free-will offerings according to the abundance of the harvest.

(c) *The Feast of Tabernacles* (Hebr. hag hassukoth).— This feast was celebrated in the autumn, in the month of Tishri, at the end of the fruit, oil, and wine harvest. It began five days after the Feast of Atonement, and lasted from the 15th to the 21st of the month. During the entire week the Israelites had to dwell in tents of tree twigs erected in the streets and open spaces, and also on the roofs and in the court-yards of the houses (Lev. 23, 42 f). Many free-will offerings and others prescribed by the Law were made during the festival. The first day was celebrated with Sabbath rest and religious assemblies. In the Sabbath year the Law was also read. The eighth day was also a holyday and called "at-sereth" (i.e., conclusion, because it concluded the Feast of Tabernacles and the feasts of the year); it also was celebrated with Sabbath rest and religious assemblies (Lev. 23, 36. 39; Num. 29, 35-38). The Feast of Tabernacles was a thanksgiving feast for the completed oil and wine harvest, and for the entire harvest of the year. At the same time it was to remind the Israelites of the time when their ancestors dwelt in tents, after their departure from Egypt. This feast, therefore, was a special feast of joy, and was also called simply "the feast" (3 Kgs. 8, 2; 12, 32).

In the post-exilic period this feast received two ceremonial additions. (1) The water libation based on Isaias 12, 3 was offered. A priest on each one of the seven days, at the time of the morning sacrifice, fetched water in a golden vessel from the fountain of Siloe, brought it to the altar of holocausts, and poured it with the wine into the pipes near the altar. Music and singing accompanied this ceremony, which perhaps gave Our Lord the occasion of applying the image of the "rivers of living water" to the sending of the Holy Spirit (John 7, 2. 37-39). (2) The illumination and torch dance took place in the evening of the first day in the women's court.

Art. 4. The Day of Atonement

On the 10th day of the 7th month (Tishri) and five days before the Feast of Tabernacles, Israel celebrated every year its reconciliation with God (Lev. 16; 23, 26-32). All work was forbidden on this day, and the entire nation was required to observe a strict fast (i.e., to take no food at all) from the evening of the 9th to the evening of the 10th of Tishri.

On this day the high priest himself had to officiate at the religious service, the principal part of which was the ceremony of the atonement. After he had kept awake during the whole preceding night and had taken a ritual bath in the morning, he offered the morning sacrifice. Then he took off his high priest's dress, took a second bath, and vested himself with the simple white garment of a priest. In this attire, without any sign of his rank, he appeared as a sinner and conducted the ritual of the atonement.

At first he brought to the sanctuary two animals for sacrifice: a young bullock as a sin offering and a ram as a burnt offering for himself and his house (i.e., for the entire priesthood). From the people he received two he-goats, the one to be a sin offering and the other to be turned loose into the desert, and also a ram to be a burnt offering. Lots were cast for the two goats, to decide which should be dedicated to Jahweh and which to Azazel. The one on whom the lot first fell for the Lord was destined to be slain as a sin offering; the other on whom the lot fell for Azazel was to be removed forever from the midst of Israel (Lev. 16, 8-10).

After casting these lots the high priest began to make atonement for himself and for the entire priesthood. He laid his hands upon the bullock destined for a sin offering, and made a confession of his sins and those of the priesthood. The bullock was then slain. He next took the censer, filled it with live coals from the altar, and taking incense with him entered the Holy of Holies, and strewed the incense on the coals immediately, so that the cloud of smoke would envelop the kapporeth. Then he came out again and, taking with him some of the blood of the bullock, he re-entered the Holy of Holies, and with his finger sprinkled once the kapporeth and seven times on the ground in front of the ark of the covenant. Again coming out, he sacrificed in the court the goat destined for Jahweh, as a sin offering on behalf of the people. Thereupon he re-entered the Holy of Holies for the third time with the blood of this victim, and performed the same sprinklings as before with the blood of the bullock (Lev. 16, 11-15). With these sprinklings of blood, atonement was made for the sins of the high priest, of the priesthood, and of the whole people.

The high priest then purified the Holy Place by taking the mingled blood of the bullock and goat, and rubbing it on the horns of the altar of incense and sprinkling it seven times with blood (Lev. 16, 18 f). The same ritual was then performed in the court on the altar of holocausts (Lev. 16, 20). After the sanctuary also was cleansed from defilement, the he-goat on whom fell the lot for Azazel was brought forth. The high priest, then, laid both his hands upon its head and pronounced upon it all the transgressions and sins of Israel. Thus laden with the sins of the nation, it was ready to be driven into the desert, that it might die or be lost there.

The flesh of the two sin offerings (the bullock and he-goat) with which the sprinklings of atonement were made was carried, after the fat had been burnt on the altar, outside the encampment or city, and was there destroyed by fire. In conclusion, the two rams were sacrificed as burnt offerings and other special sacrifices were offered (Num. 29, 7-11).

Significance of the Atonement Celebration.—The significance of this feast was immediately evident to the Israelites from the penitential character of the day, the repeated confession of sins by the high priest, and the various sprinklings with blood. Not only the sins of the priests and the people, committed during the entire year, had to be expiated, but even the sanctuary and the court had to be cleansed from all defilement. This atonement reached its height when the blood of the sin offerings was brought by the high priest into the Holy of Holies, before the earthly throne of God, and sprinkled on the kapporeth. The legal or levitical purification obtained through this atonement was also impressed upon the people in the ceremony of the sin-goat. Azazel refers either to the goat itself (Lev. 16, 9: Vulg., caper emissarius, emissary or scape goat), because it was driven away from the encampment or city, or to an evil spirit, or prince of the devils, to whom the he-goat laden with the sins of the nation was sent. All of these rites must have taught the people the sanctity of God and His laws, as well as their own sinfulness and punishability.

According to St. Paul, this feast was a type of the great atonement accomplished by Our Lord for the sins of the whole world (Hebr. 9-10). The Apostle points out the relationship between the type and the anti-type. (1) The high priest of the Old Testament, who entered with the blood of sin offerings into the Holy of Holies, is a weak type of Jesus Christ, who by virtue of His own blood entered the Holy of Holies of heaven to present to the Father His blood as the price for the redemption of mankind (Hebr. 9, 11 f). (2) The high priest had to atone year after year for his own sins as well as those of the entire nation with the blood of sin offerings. But Jesus Christ, the High Priest of the New Testament, has effected atonement once and forever, not for Himself, but for the sins of all men of all times (Hebr. 9, 28). (3) The blood of these sin offerings could only effect "the cleansing of the flesh," whereas the blood of Jesus Christ cleanses our conscience from dead works, so that we as children of God may serve the living God (Hebr. 9, 14). (4) As the high priest of the Old Testament with the blood of the sin offerings could not effect the forgiveness of sins, "the way into the Holy of Holies" remained closed for the public (Hebr. 9, 8); but Jesus Christ by His own blood had only to enter the Holy of Holies once, in order to open "the way to the Holy of Holies" of heaven forever. (5) In another passage (Hebr. 13, 11 f) the Apostle points out that the flesh of those sin offerings was burnt outside of the encampment or city, and "so Jesus also, that He might sanctify the people by His blood, suffered outside the gate."

Appendix

Festivals Instituted After the Captivity [9]

After the return of the Jews from the Babylonian captivity
(536 B.C.) several festivals were added to those prescribed by
the Mosaic Law, and some of those then introduced are still
observed.

(1) *The Feast of Purim.*—The name comes from the Persian word *pur* (plural *purim,* i.e., lots). The Persian governor,
Aman, had determined to put to death all the Jews in the Persian Empire, and the 13th of Adar (Feb./March) had been
chosen by lot as the day for this massacre. The murderous
plan was frustrated through Queen Esther, and her kinsman,
Mardochai. In remembrance of this event, the Jews, first in
Persia but afterwards also in Palestine and elsewhere, celebrated a festival on the 14th and 15th of Adar, keeping the
13th as a fast. The feast was celebrated by reading the Book
of Esther aloud in the synagogues; joyful feasts were held in
the houses (cf. Book of Esther).

(2) *The Feast of the Dedication of the Temple* [10].—This
feast, which is also called Encænia (John 10), was kept every
year in commemoration of the purification of the temple from
the idolatrous worship of the Syrians, and its re-dedication by
Judas Machabee in 165 B.C. On the 25th of Kislev (Novem-
ber-December) and on the following seven days the houses in
Jerusalem and other places were illuminated; hence, Josephus
calls the feast "Lights." There seems to have been no special
ceremony in the temple, but perhaps more sacrifices than
usual were offered.

(3) *The Feast of Rejoicing of the Law.*—This feast was
held on the 23rd of Tishri (September-October). On the last
day of the Feast of Tabernacles every year the reading of the
Pentateuch was concluded, and on the following day again
begun.

[9] Cf. Seisenberger, *op. cit.,* 154 f.
[10] Cf. Höpfl. H., "Das Chanukafest," in *Biblica,* 3 (1922), 165-179; Abel,
F. M., "La fête de la Hanoucca," in R.B., 53 (1946), 538-546.

(4) The Feast of Wood Carrying.—According to Josephus
(*Bella Jud.*, II, 17, 6) this feast was celebrated on the 14th of
Ab (July-August), but the Talmud does not mention it. It
appears that all who wished to do so carried wood to the
temple on this day, for the maintenance of the fire on the altar
of holocausts.

According to 2 Esdras 10, 34, certain families were appointed by lot (at least in the period immediately after the
captivity) to supply wood, and the days on which they performed this duty were, for the persons concerned, days of
rejoicing and honor.

Modern Jews observe the following festivals:

(1) The Passover, 15th to 22nd of Nisan (March/April).
(2) Lag Beomer, 18th of Ijjar (April/May) to commemo-
     rate the cessation of a pestilence.
(3) Pentecost, or Feast of Weeks, 6th and 7th of Sivan
     (May/June).
(4) New Year, 1st and 2nd of Tishri (September/October).
(5) Day of Atonement, 10th of Tishri.
(6) Feast of Tabernacles, 15th to 22nd of Tishri.
(7) Rejoicing of the Law, 23rd of Tishri.
(8) Dedication of the Temple, 25th of Kislev (November/
     December).
(9) Feast of Purim, 14th and 15th of Adar (February/
     March).
(10) All the Sabbaths of the year.

Chapter V

MEASURES, WEIGHTS AND MONEY

Bibliography: Metrology. Barrois, A., in R.B., 40 (1931), 185-213, 41 (1932), 50-76; * *idem*, "Manuel d'Archéologie Biblique" 2nd vol., Paris, 1953), 243-258; * Lewy, H., in J.A.O.S., 64 (1944), 65-73; * Segrè, A., *ibid.*, 73-81; *idem*, in J.B.L., 64 (1945), 357-375; * Sachs, A. J., in B.A.S.O.R., 96 (1944), 29-39; Wambacq, B. N., in V.D., 29 (1951), 341-350, 32 (1954), 266-274, 325-334; * Scott, R. B. Y., in J.B.L., 77 (1958), 205-214; *idem*, in B.A., 22 (1959), 22-39; *idem*, in B.A.S.O.R., 153 (1959), 32-34; * Glueck, N., in B.A.S.O.R., 153 (1959), 35-37.

Money: Pink, K., in *Biblica*, 20 (1939), 408-412; * Miles, G.C., in A.J.S.L.L., 56 (1939), 244-250; * Boneschi, J., in J.A.O.S., 62 (1942), 262-266; Van der Vliet, N., in R.B., 57 (1950), 110-129, 243-259, 430-442; * Barrois, A.-G., "Manuel d'Archéologie Biblique" (2nd vol., Paris, 1953), 258-273; * Kanael, B., in B.A.S.O.R., 129 (1953), 18-20; De Guglielmo, A., in C.B.Q., 16 (1954), 171-188; Spijkerman, A.-* Starkey, J., in R.B., 65 (1958), 568-584.

Linear Measures

The principal unit was the *cubit*, that is, the length of the forearm from the elbow to the extremity of the middle finger. This cubit has four different lengths.

Egyptian System

1 small "common" cubit	= 17.91 inches
1 large "royal" cubit	= 20.67 inches
1 small cubit = 6 palms	= 24 fingers
1 large cubit = 7 palms	= 28 fingers

1 small "common" cubit = 2 spans	= 6 palms	= 24 fingers	= 17.91 inches
	1 span = 3 palms	= 12 fingers	= 8.96 inches
		1 palm = 4 fingers	= 2.99 inches
			1 finger	= 0.75 inch

Babylonian System

1 small "common" cubit	= 19.49 inches
1 large "royal" cubit	= 21.65 inches
1 small cubit	= 30 fingers
1 large cubit	= 33 fingers

1 small "common" cubit = 30 fingers	= 19.49 inches
1 finger	= 0.65 inch

The Hebrews did not always make use of the same linear measurements. Their early ancestors, who lived in Mesopotamia, employed the Babylonian system. Later, when they as a nation left Egypt, they used the Egyptian system. Still later, when the greater part of the Near East came under the influence or dominion of the Assyrians or Babylonians, the Hebrews made use of the Babylonian system.

The cubit is mentioned in the ante-diluvial period in the measurements of the ark (Gen. 6, 15). Evidence for the usage of two kinds of cubits is found in the Bible. 2 Paralipomenon 3, 3, in describing the measurements of the temple of Solomon, states that "the ancient measurement" (MT) was employed, that is, probably the royal Egyptian cubit of 20.67 inches. We know that at the time of Ezechiel a cubit of another length was used (Ez. 40, 6); this cubit consisted of a cubit and a palm (Ez. 43, 13), and the reed consisted of 6 cubits (Ez. 41, 8); most probably Ezechiel is alluding to the royal Babylonian cubit of 21.65 inches.

Other units of measurement are found in the Bible. The *fathom* (Acts 27, 28) represented a space of 4 cubits or about 6 feet. The *stadium* (2 Mach. 12, 9; Luke 24, 13; John 6, 19) was a Greek measure 606¾ feet. The *mile* (Matt. 5, 41) was a Roman measure equivalent to .92 American mile. The *Sabbath day's journey* (Acts 1, 12) was by Hebrew tradition equivalent to 2,000 cubits. In measuring the fields the Hebrews employed two methods: one unit was taken as the amount of land a *yoke of oxen* could plow in a day (1 Sam. 14, 14), and the other was based on the amount of *seed* necessary to sow an area of land (Lev. 27, 16).

Measures of Capacity

Hebrew Dry Measures:

1 *Homer* =	1 *Kor* =	2 Letech =	10 Ephah =	30 Seah =	100 Gomer
	½ Kor =	1 *Letech* =	5 Ephah =	15 Seah =	50 Gomer
		1/10 Kor =	1 *Ephah* =	3 Seah =	10 Gomer
			1/3 Ephah =	1 *Seah* =	3 1/3 Gomer
				1/10 Ephah =	1 *Gomer*

100 Gomer (=	100 Issaron) =	180 Cab =	10.48 bushels
50 Gomer (=	50 Issaron) =	90 Cab =	5.24 bushels
10 Gomer (=	10 Issaron) =	18 Cab =	1.05 bushels
3 1/3 Gomer (=	3 1/3 Issaron) =	6 Cab =	1.40 pecks
1 *Gomer* (=	1 Issaron) = 1 4/5 Cab =	0.42 pecks
	1/6 Seah	=	1 Cab =	1.86 quarts

Hebrew Liquid Measures:

1 *Kor* =	10 Bath =	60 Hin =	720 Log =	97.5 gallons
	1 *Bath* =	6 Hin =	72 Log =	9.8 gallons
		1 *Hin* =	12 Log =	1.62 gallons
			1 *Log* =	0.54 quart

According to the Mishna, 1 Log is equivalent to 6 hens' eggs, which would be equivalent to smaller measures of capacity given by Germer Durand for the dry and liquid measures. But since it is difficult to know when such a change was made from the standard system, we have omitted the relative values ascribed to these measures by Germer Durand.

The Bible makes mention of other measures of capacity. The *measure* (John 2, 6) was a Greek measure roughly corresponding to the Hebrew bath. The *artaba* (Dan. 14, 2) was a Persian measure containing 1.85 bushels. The *choinix* (Apoc. 6, 6) was a Greek measure equivalent to .03 bushel.

Weights

(1) Babylonian "royal standard"

			heavy	light
1 Talent =	60 Minas =	3,600 Shekels =	133.56 lbs.	66.78 lbs.
	1 Mina =	60 Shekels =	2.23 lbs.	1.11 lbs.
		1 Shekel =	259.72 grs.	129.86 grs.

(2) Babylonian "common standard"

			heavy	light
1 Talent =	60 Minas =	3,600 Shekels =	129.9 lbs. =	65 lbs.
	1 Mina =	60 Shekels =	2.16 lbs. =	1.08 lbs.
		1 Shekel =	252.66 grs. =	126.3 grs

(3) Hebrew "common standard"

1 Talent =	30 Minas =	3,000 Shekels =	55.6 lbs.
	1 Mina =	100 Shekels =	1.8 lbs.
		1 Shekel =	130 grs.

Hebrew "sanctuary standard"
1 Shekel = 16.83 grams = 260 grains
½ Shekel = 1 Beka = 8.41 grams = 130 grains
1/20 Shekel = 1 Gerah = .841 gram = 13 grains

The greatest unit in the system of weights was the talent, which was divided into minas and shekels. The Israelitic talent had 30 minas and 3,000 shekels [cf. Ex. 38, 25-28; 3 Kgs. 10, 17 (MT) and 2 Par. 9, 16]. The same system was prevalent among the Canaanites, and was based on the decimal system (cf. Jos. 7, 21; also Gen. 23, 16). The Babylonian talent was based on the sexagesimal system (cf. 4 Kgs. 5, 5). This Babylonian system was only accepted by the Hebrews during the exile, and not before.

The New Testament (John 12, 3; 19, 39) makes mention of the Roman *libra* or pound, which was equivalent to .718 or .722 American pound, and was subdivided into 12 ounces.

Money

Gold:

1 Talent = 60 Minas =	3,000 Shekels =	108 lbs. av. =	$ 55,050.00
1 Mina =	50 Shekels =	1.8 lbs. av. =	917.50
	1 Shekel =	252.6 grs. =	18.35

These figures are based upon the modern gold value of $35 per fine troy ounce. The relative value of silver to gold among the Israelites and Babylonians was 1 to 13.3, which was adjusted so that one gold shekel of 252⅔ grains was equal in value to fifteen silver shekels of 224½ grains.

Silver:

1 Talent = 60 Minas =	3,000 Shekels =	96.2 lbs. av. =	$ 3,660.00
1 Mina =	50 Shekels =	1.6 lbs. av. =	61.00
	1 Shekel =	224.5 grs. =	1.22

Before the Babylonian exile there were no minted coins in Palestine. Bartering was practised (cf. Isa. 55, 1), and metallic weights of gold or silver were used for monetary transactions (Gen. 23, 15 f). After the exile money proper was circulated in Palestine. The invention of coins is commonly attributed to Crœsus, the king of Lydia (561-546 B.C.), but the first true coins circulated in Palestine were Persian and were minted by Darius I (521-485 B.C.). This Persian *darag* or daric (Hebr., darkemon; Vulg., solidus, drachma) is often mentioned in the First and Second Books of Esdras; it weighed 130 grains and was equivalent to $\frac{1}{60}$ mina. During the Grecian period the usual money of exchange in Palestine was the Phœnician *drachma* of 55 grains and the tetradrachma or stater, which was equivalent to the shekel of 224½ grains. During the Hellenistic period the Machabees minted bronze coins (1 Mach. 15, 6), but avoided placing any human image on them according to a strict interpretation of Exodus 20, 4, which, however, only speaks of the divine image.

At the time of Our Lord three kinds of money are mentioned in the New Testament as being used in Palestine: Jewish, Greek and Roman.

(1) *Jewish Money.*—The *shekel* was a money of account, and not an actual coin, because silver shekels made their first appearance at the time of the first revolt in A.D. 66-70. The silver money mentioned in Matthew 26, 15 and 28, 12 ff was either Roman, or Grecian, or Phœnician.

(2) *Greek Money.*—All of the Greek coins were of silver. The unit was the *drachma,* the weight of which varied at various periods and for different localities. The Attic drachma, which originally weighed 4.25 grams (65⅗ grains), had at the time of Christ fallen to 3.9 grams (60⅕ grains). It was therefore heavier than the Phœnician drachma mentioned above, which most likely was current in Palestine (cf. Luke 15, 8 ff).

The multiples of the drachma were the *didrachma* (Matt. 17, 23), or two drachmas, and the *stater,* the tetradrachma (Matt. 17, 26) or four drachmas. The Phœnician stater corresponded with the Hebrew shekel.

Two copper coins are mentioned in the New Testament: the *chalkus* and the *lepton.* The chalkus (Mark 12, 41) represented ⅛ obolus and was almost equivalent to the lepton; two lepta were equivalent to a Roman quadrans (Mark 12, 42).

The *mina* and the *talent* were moneys of account. The mina

(Luke 19, 13 ff) was equivalent to 100 drachmas, while the talent consisted of 60 minas, 1,500 staters, 3,000 didrachmas, or 6,000 drachmas.

(3) Roman Money.—The Romans reserved for themselves the right to mint gold and silver coins, but they allowed vassal princes, like Herod the Great, to mint copper coins. The money system of the Romans, like other peoples, was based upon weights. At Rome the unit of weight was the *libra* or pound (about 5,046 grains). The bimetal system was regulated by Julius Cæsar, who introduced the golden *aureus*. Between the period of Augustus and Nero the following fixed values predominated: the gold *aureus* weighed $\frac{1}{42}$ libra or 120.3 grains; the silver *denarius* weighed $\frac{1}{84}$ libra or $60\frac{1}{5}$ grains (the same weight as the Attic didrachma of this period) and represented $\frac{1}{25}$ of the value of the aureus.

Modern Values of Coins.[11]—The gold *aureus* was worth $8.77. The *denarius* often mentioned in the New Testament and the Attic *drachma* were worth about 35 cents. Among the copper coins were the *as* (= *assarion*, cf. Matt. 10, 29), $\frac{1}{16}$ denarius, which was equivalent to 2 cents, the *dupondius* or two asses (cf. Luke 12, 6), the *quadrans* or $\frac{1}{4}$ as (cf. Matt. 5, 26), and the *lepton* or $\frac{1}{8}$ as (cf. Luke 21, 2). All of these coins were based upon the Roman mintage.

The silver coins current in Palestine were principally of Phœnician standard and minted at Tyre. They were slightly lighter than the Attic coins. In ordinary transactions the Attic and Greek *drachma*, as well as the Roman *denarius*, were considered as having the same value (about 35 cents). Hence, the *didrachma* and the *stater* or *shekel* were equivalent to about 70 cents and $1.40, respectively. The *mina*, being equivalent to 100 drachmas, was equivalent to about $35.00, and the Roman-Attic *talent*, being equal to 6,000 drachmas or denarii, was equivalent to about $2,100.00.

[11] These values are based on the present value of gold of $35.00 per troy ounce or $0.729 per grain.

Part VII

GENERAL ANTIQUITIES

ARCHAEOLOGY*

Bibliography: * Albright, W. F., "The Archæology of Palestine and the Bible" (2nd ed., New York, 1935) ; *idem,* "Archæology and the Religion of Israel" (2nd ed., Baltimore, 1946) ; *idem,* "From the Stone Age to Christianity" (2nd ed., Baltimore, 1946) ; *idem,* "The Archæology of Palestine" (Repr., London, 1956) ; * Burrows, M., "What Mean These Stones?" (New Haven, 1941) ; * Finegan, J., "Light from the Ancient East" (2nd ed., Princeton, 1959) ; * Galling, K., "Biblisches Reallexikon" (Tübingen, 1934-1937) ; * Grant, E., "The Haverford Symposium on Archæology and the Bible" (New Haven, 1938) ; * Kenyon, Sir F., "The Bible and Archæology" (New York-London, 1940) ; * Kenyon, K. M., "Beginning in Archæology" (London, 1952) ; * Maisler, B., "History of Archæological Exploration in Palestine" (Jerusalem, 1936) ; * McCown, C. C., "The Ladder of Progress in Palestine" (New York, 1943) ; Parrot, A., "Archéologie mésopotamienne. I. Les Etapes. II. Technique et Problèmes" (Paris, 1946-1953) ; *idem,* "Studies in Biblical Archæology" (New York, 1955-) ; * Pritchard, J. B., "Ancient Near Eastern Texts" (2nd ed., Princeton, 1955) ; *idem,* "Ancient Near East in Pictures" (Princeton, 1954) ; *idem,* "Archæology and the Old Testament" (Princeton, 1958) ; * Watzinger, C., "Denkmäler Palästinas" (vol. I, Leipzig, 1933; vol. II, *ibid,* 1935) ; *Wright, G. E., "Biblical Archaeology" (Philadelphia, 1957) ; *Harding, G. L., "The Antiquities of Jordan" (New York, 1959).

The systematic study of written and unwritten material remains from ancient times.

I. *Introduction.*—Of the more recent historical sciences, none has developed more rapidly and contributed more substantially to a better understanding of the history, literature and religions of the Near East (including Egypt) than archæology. It not only discovers much about primitive man and ancient cultures, but also throws new light on many Biblical passages.

There can be no conflict between the truths discovered by

*This chapter is a reprinting of the article "Archæology" from our C.B.E.O.T. The asterisk preceding proper name throughout this volume and denoting non-Catholic scholars, appears in the present bibliography, but not in the text of this chapter.

archæology and the truths contained in the Bible. Any apparent conflict results either from a faulty interpretation of the material remains discovered by the archæologist (e.g., stone pillars, buildings, inscriptions) or from an inadequate understanding of the Biblical text.

The *importance* of archæology for Biblical studies is stressed by Pope Pius XII in his Encyclical letter "Divino afflante Spiritu" of September 30, 1943. "Let those who cultivate Biblical studies," he writes, "turn their attention with all due diligence towards this point [a correct and genuine interpretation] and let them neglect none of those discoveries, whether in the domain of archæology or in ancient history or literature, which serve to make better known the mentality of the ancient writers, as well as their manner and art of reasoning, narrating and writing. . . . For all human knowledge, even the non-sacred, has indeed its own proper dignity and excellence, being a finite participation of the infinite knowledge of God."

II. *Techniques and Palestinian Excavations.*—By its rigid methods of analyzing and interpreting more carefully factual data, modern archæologists have succeeded not only in sifting, controlling and amalgamating the specialized researches of the past, but also in paving the way for a newer and better reconstruction and understanding of the history and religion of the Near East. For example, prehistory, which in the nineteenth century was represented almost solely in Europe, has shifted to Palestine as the focus of pre-historic culture. Another example may be cited. The once despised potsherd found in every ancient *tell* (Arab. for "mound") has become one of the essential keys to all archæological research. By analyzing the form, ingredients and decoration of pottery and by comparing such with that found in other excavated sites, the archæologists can assign fairly accurate dates to a building or stratum.

These mounds which were built up by the accumulation of dirt, bricks, etc., and represent the results of centuries or millennia of various occupied settlements over one another, reach a very imposing height at times; for instance, in Palestine at

Bethshan (or Bethsan) there was a depth of about 85 feet in the debris of occupation and at Megiddo (or Mageddo) about 70 feet; at Tepe Gawra in Mesopotamia (15 miles northeast of modern Mossul) the mound rose some 75 feet above the surrounding plain.

Three important techniques are employed by modern archæologists in their excavations: stratigraphic excavation, accurate and meticulous recording, and comparative interpretation.

(1) In the stratigraphic excavation of a site, each stratum is entirely removed down to its foundations; the walls, rooms, etc., are carefully traced and all important objects are photographed *in situ*, before the next lower stratum or level is cleared away. When lack of sufficient funds prevent the removal of the entire mound, a definite area is chosen, then cleared away, stratum after stratum, until the virgin soil or bedrock is reached.

(2) Accurate and meticulous recording of all objects in every stratum follows. This includes an exact record of all things by means of maps, plans, drawings and photographs.

(3) A comparative interpretation is then made of all objects, especially pottery, which have been found. By comparing these objects with their similarities in the same country and in various other lands, possible cultural movements and relationships may be traced.

Modern archæology in Palestine may be divided roughly into two periods: that between 1890 and World War I, and the period between the two World Wars.

(a) The history of modern archæology began in 1890 when the British Palestine Exploration Fund sent Flinders Petrie to Palestine to locate Lachish (or Lachis). He (erroneously) selected Tell el-Hesi for his six weeks' excavation, which was continued by F. J. Bliss. During the next twenty years this Fund organized eight excavations at various sites, including Tell Zakariya (O. T. Azekah, or Azeca) by Bliss in 1898 and Gezer by R. A. S. Macalister in 1902-1905 and 1907-1909. At the same time G. Schumacher of the Deutsche Pälastinaverein dug an exploratory trench into Tell el-Mutesellim (Megiddo)

in 1903-1905, and Ernst Sellin excavated at first in 1901 at
Taanach (or Thanach), where he discovered some important
tablets, and later in the name of the Deutsche Orientgesellschaft
at Jericho in 1908-1909. Excavations were carried out at
Samaria from 1908 to 1910 by Harvard University under the
direction of G. A. Reisner. The results of these excavations
brought conflicting views regarding both philology and history.

(b) The period between the two World Wars is marked by
the greatest progress in archæological methods employed in
Palestine under the British mandate. In 1920 the British administration organized a Department of Antiquities headed by
John Garstang. In the following year the British School of
Archæology was established and in 1922 the American School
of Oriental Research in Jerusalem undertook the first in a long
series of excavations.

The British continued the archæological researches of the
preceding period in the Sephela. Garstang made exploratory
soundings at Ascalon and Gaza in 1920 and at Dor in 1923.
On the other hand Petrie, excavating for the British School of
Archæology in Egypt, made important discoveries at Tell
Jemme, south of Gaza, in 1927, at Tell el-Far'ah in 1928-1929,
and at Tell el-'Ajjul near Gaza in 1930. On the Ophel hill in
Jerusalem several campaigns were undertaken by Macalister,
J. Garrow Duncan and J. W. Crowfoot between 1923 and 1928.
The excavations at Jericho first attempted by Sellin in 1908-
1909 were continued by Garstang from 1930 to 1936 and by
American and British archæologists from 1950-55. Lachish,
first sought for at Tell el-Hesi by Petrie, was identified at Tell
ed-Duweir, excavated by the Wellcome-Marston Archæological
Expedition in 1933 under the direction of J. L. Starkey until
his murder by Arabs, January 10, 1938, and thereafter under
the direction of C. H. Inge and L. Harding.

The American School of Oriental Research in Jerusalem
under the able direction of Albright undertook a series of excavations, some of which grew to great importance: for instance, at Tell el-Ful (the site of Gabaa or Gibeah, the home
and capital of King Saul) in 1922, 1923 and 1933; at Tell Beit

Mirsim (perhaps the ancient town of Dabir or Kiriath-sepher [or Cariath-sepher]) in 1929-1936, and at Bethel in 1934 in conjunction with the Pittsburgh-Xenia Theological Seminary; at Bethzur (or Bethsur) in 1931. At Tell en-Nasbeh (identified with Mizpah [or Maspha] of Samuel, or Ataroth-Addar, or Beeroth) excavations were conducted by the Pacific School of Religion of the University of California under the direction of W. F. Bade for five seasons between 1926 and 1935, and subsequently for three seasons by J. C. Wampler. At Beth-shemesh (or Beth-sames) the excavations begun by Duncan Mackenzie in 1911-1912 were continued by E. Grant of Haverford College through five seasons between 1928 and 1933.

The most extensive excavations were conducted at Megiddo in 1925-1936 by the Oriental Institute of the University of Chicago under the direction of C. S. Fisher, P. L. O. Grey and G. Loud; at Bethshan (or Bethsan) in 1921-1933 by the University of Pennsylvania under the direction of C. S. Fisher, A. Rowe and G. M. Fitzgerald; at Samaria the previous splendid work of Reisner was continued in 1931-1935 under the direction of J. W. Crowfoot as a joint enterprise of British-American-Hebrew Universities. Between 1933 and 1943 a systematical survey of Transjordan was made by Nelson Glueck, who also directed (1937-1940) diggings at the refineries of Tel el-Kheleiteh, the ancient Ezion-Geber (or Asiongaber).

Work on a smaller scale was conducted at Mambre near Hebron by A. E. Mader in behalf of the Görres-Gesellschaft in 1926 and 1927; at Silo (Shiloh) by a Danish expedition in 1926 and 1929; at Ai by Mme. Judith Marquet-Krause in 1933-1934. At Tell el-Far'ah near Nabulus important excavations have been conducted by the French Dominican Fathers under the direction of Père R. de Vaux and Père A. M. Steve since 1946.

A protohistorical culture of the Chalcolithic Period was discovered at Teleilat el-Ghassul (1928-1938) by the Pontifical Biblical Institute under the direction of Père A. Mallon, S. J., Robert Koppel, S. J., and others. Species like the Neanderthal man have been found in Palestine: the Galilee skull discovered by Turville-Petre in 1925; remains of seven individuals discovered at Mugharet el-Qafseh south of Nazareth in 1934 by R. Neuville; the bodies of a dozen persons uncovered in or about the cave of Mugharet et-Tabun and a neighboring one near Athlit at the foot of Mount Carmel by Dorothy Garrod in 1929-1934.

This period between the two World Wars would be incomplete without a very special mention being made of Père Vincent, O. P., of Jerusalem, known to specialists as one of the foremost authorities on Palestinian archæology and topography and called by the distinguished archæologist Albright "the tutor of all."

Among the important excavations of the Jewish Palestine Exploration Society, mention may be made of Beth-yerah (mod., Khirbet Kerah, southwest corner of the Sea of Galilee) in 1944 by M. Stekelis and B. Maisler.

More extensive archæological excavations have been undertaken in Mesopotamia and Egypt where epigraphic evidence is much richer than in Palestine. All the evidence, whether written or unwritten, from the entire Near East will be briefly summarized in the following paragraphs.

III. *Levels of Civilization.* — Many millennia before man invented a system of writing and of recording human activity in written documents, he left traces of his unwritten cultures. These prehistorical and protohistorical cultures have been demonstrated by archæology in a threefold way: by remains left behind by early man (e.g., his tools, and other artifacts), by other traces of his industrial activity (e.g., buildings, rock carvings, and paintings) and by human fossil remains.

No certain eolithic remains (with the traits of crude, shapeless stones) have been discovered. But various methods have been employed to determine the early cultures, especially the Palæolithic culture (the Old Stone Age). Most important in recent years for relative dating has been the system of *geochronology* by the Swedish scholar Count de Geer (i.e., the enumeration of annual varves or layers of sediment left by the melting waters of a receding ice sheet) and of *solar radia-*

tion by Friedrich Zeuner (since 1935), which has been correlated with the glacial oscillations. Other scholars for relative dating depend upon the system of geology (i.e., the comparative study of various strata of the earth), stratigraphy (i.e., the definite arrangement of the earth's stratum at a given site), typology (i.e., a comparative study of objects found at different sites), palæontology (i.e., the presence of animal fossils), palæobotony (i.e., the presence of plants), climatic sequences (i.e., the record of climatic changes such as pluvial or dry periods in an area), etc. Hence all dates assigned to prehistoric cultures by conscientious scientists are not to be considered final, but are a matter of rough estimate, since there are no certain scientific means of measuring exactly the duration of the Palæolithic Age.

Ordinarily, however, prehistory is dated according to some geological formation of the Ice Age, the names of which are taken from various European Alpine sites where these phenomena were first observed. Thus, the duration of the four glacial stages: I. Günz; II. Mindel; III. Riss Saale; IV. Würm glaciations, that were interrupted by three interglacial stages: 1) Günz-Mindel; 2) Mindel-Riss; 3) Riss-Würm interglaciations. This entire geological period is known as the Early and Middle *Pleistocene,* which are related to a corresponding human culture called *Palæolithic.* The palæolithic cultural remains were ordinarily arranged in the general series: Chellean—(Levalloisian, Clactonian)—Acheulian—Mousterian—Aurignacian—Solutrian—Magdalenian, and allocated to various geologic Alpine formations.

Late Pleistocene or Upper Palæolithic
(Modern Man) (Aurignacian, Solutrian, Magdalenian)
Middle Pleistocene or Middle Palæolithic
IV. Ice Age: Würm-Wisconsin
3) Riss-Würm
(Archeulian, Mousterian)
III. Ice Age: Riss Saale

Early Pleistocene or Lower Palæolithic
(Heidelberg Man)
2) Mindel Riss
(Chellean, Levalloisian, Clactonian)
II. Ice Age: Mindel
1) Günz-Mindel
(Pre-Chellean)
I. Ice Age: Günz

(These periods may be read upwards for the oldest temporal sequence.)

This outline, once generally recognized for Europe, is no longer universally applicable. Thus there is no definite correlation between the successive Alpine glaciations followed by corresponding interglaciations and the Nile terraces, the raised Mediterranean beaches and the pluvial phases of the Jordan Valley. Then, too, flint artifacts of various kinds have been found in the geological formations of various terraces in the Nile Valley as well as on the surface stations of Palestine and the highland regions of western Asia.

Hence, H. Obermaier, Abbé H. Breuil and O. Menghin, considered among the foremost anthropologists, now propose two series of stone cultures for the Lower and Middle Palæolithic cultures, namely, (1) the *flake* or *blade* culture (=Clactonian; Levalloisian; Mousterian; Aurignacian; Solutrian; Magdalenian; Azilian; Tardenoisian), (2) the *hand-axe* or *fist-pick* culture (=Pre-Chellean; Chellean; Acheulian; Campignian). Mention might also be made of the Maglemosian bone culture.

(1) *The Prehistorical Period of Man* (?-5000 B.C.)

(a) *The Palæolithic Period* (?-c.8300/8000 B.C.)

Scholars are generally agreed that the Pleistocene and, with it, the last phases of the Palæolithic (i.e., Upper Palæolithic) came to an end in Europe about 8300/8000 B.C.

Besides the discovery of various types of human artifacts mentioned above, human fossils also have been found.

(i) Lower Palæolithic

Heidelberg Man (only lower jaw and all its teeth; discovered in Germany in 1907).

Piltdown Man (fragments of a skull and a single canine tooth; discovered in England from 1911-1915). It is now acknowledged as a clever scientific hoax in support of the Darwinian Theory.

Java Man (*homo modjokertensis*: a skull cap of an infant; found at Modjokerto, Dutch East Indies, in 1936).

(ii) Middle Palæolithic

Neanderthal Man (fossilized skull and limb bones of a man; discovered in the Neanderthal cave near Düsseldorf, Germany, in 1857).

From 1857 to 1934 between seventy and eighty individuals of this type enjoying a so-called Mousterian culture were discovered at twenty-six different sites in Europe and especially in the Near East, that is, in Galilee and Mount Carmel.

Pithecanthropus (a skull cap of an adult; formerly called ape-man; found in Java in 1891).

Peking Man (*Sinanthropus pekinensis:* is represented by fragments of about twenty-four individuals found between 1921 and 1936 in China).

Rhodesian Man (a skull; discovered in South Africa in 1921).

(iii) Upper Palæolithic.

In this period the so-called *homo sapiens* (modern or Neanthropic man) makes his appearance. To this type belong the Europeans (e.g., Cro-Magnon and Grimaldi in France), Negroes, Mongolians and also the primitives, such as pygmies, Bushmen, Nigritos, Australian aborigines and Tasmanians.

From the above analysis two important questions arise; namely, the exact relationship among the human fossils in the entire Palæolithic Period, and the age of man.

No definite conclusion has been reached by outstanding scholars regarding the exact relationship among human fossils in the entire Stone Age or Palæolithic Period. The few cranial remains of the Lower Palæolithic furnish no evidence that these primitive men were *genetically* related to any species of anthropoids and do not allow us to form an entirely objective and physical reconstruction of these individuals, or to make a comparison among them or even with the Neanderthal race. Nor is the relationship between the Neanderthal man and the so-called *homo sapiens* settled. Older anthropologists, such as A. Keith and H. F. Osborn, insisted upon the Neanderthals as representatives of a distinct species of the human race now wholly extinct. Modern anthropologists, such as F. Weidenreich, A. Hrdlicka and H. Weinert, maintain that these Neanderthals are the ancestors of the primitive forms in the Upper Palæolithic and that even in our modern age some Neanderthal characters may be found.

The problem of the age of mankind is difficult to answer definitely. We have no reliable chronometer, no certain scientific means of measuring exactly the duration of the Pleistocene Age either in whole or in part. Hence, all that may be said is that the Palæolithic Age represents a long stretch of time and that from the Proto-historical period to our own times is a relatively short period. We are only on solid ground when we reach the Early Bronze Age from which sufficiently probable conclusions for dating may be reached by reason of various archæological discoveries in the Near East. Consequently, it is fantastic to speak of any period from 1,500,000 to 500,000 years for the antiquity of man. Some scholars suggest 50,000 or 100,000 or even 200,000 years. But the actual fact is we do not know. Wide divergences may also be observed among modern archæologists for dating the Neanderthal man living in Palestine: Albright suggests 100,000 years, while Burrows, 30,000 years ago.

(b) *The Mesolithic Period* (c. 8300/8000-5000 B.C.)

The Mesolithic culture is a new type of culture that has been discovered to exist between the Palæolithic and Neolithic Periods. This type of culture which showed its preference for small flints (*microliths*) is marked by great migrations of different races (e.g., Baltics, American Indians, etc.), some of uncertain origin, in various parts of the world.

This culture is represented in Europe by the *Tardenoisian* (so called from the pygmy flints found at Fère-en Tardenois, in France) which was closely related to cultures in Africa and Spain. It is also found in Egypt, where it is called *Sebilian* culture, and possibly in Asia (e.g., Siberia, Manchuria, etc.).

The most adequate representation of Mesolithic culture in the Near East is the *Natufian* culture first discovered in 1928 by Miss Dorothy A. E. Garrod at Shuqbah in Wad'en Natuf (northwest of Jerusalem) and subsequently by her at Mugnaret el-Wad (i.e., the cave of the gorge) at the foot of Mount Carmel near Athlit. The Natufians had passed from the food-gathering economy to the food-producing economy. Theirs was a culture with agriculture and probably the domestication of animals, but as yet without pottery and metals. At both sites about 110 individuals were represented. They belonged to the white or Caucasian race and are the oldest race of modern man yet found in Palestine living there about 6000-5000 B.C.

(2) *The Protohistorical Period* (c. 5000—3000 B.C.)

The Protohistorical Period in the Near East marks the age when man first experimented with community life in fixed sites, such as villages and towns, invented pottery, and discovered the use of the more important metals, such as copper and gold. This period includes two cultural phases: the Neolithic or New Stone Age (c. 5000-4000 B.C.) and the Chalcolithic or Copper Age (c. 4000-3000 B.C.). These two cultures were widely distributed over the whole world with variations of time due to a steady or slow cultural development, as, for instance, Armenia and Transcaucasia, Persia and Russian Turkestan, India, Siberia and Manchuria, Central Asia, China, Japan and Korea (a Neolithic culture before 200 B.C.), southern Asia, Europe, Crete, Aegean Area and Greece, Russia, Central Europe, Italy, Malta and Sardinia, Spain, Western Europe, British Isles, Baltic Region), Africa, Oceania, America (Indians, fifteenth century A.D., still in a Neolithic

stage of culture) and especially the *Fertile Crescent,* which
region extends from the Nile Valley through Palestine and
northern Syria to the Mesopotamian Valley and where the
most rapid cultural strides in the history of civilization were
made.

(a) *The Neolithic Period* (c 5000—4000 B.C.)

The Neolithic or New Stone Age was the period when men
had no metals, but polished, instead of chipped, stone tools,
engaged in agriculture, domesticated animals and manufac-
tured pottery.

Of the Neolithic cultures in the Fertile Crescent mention
may be made of Egypt, with its Fayumian-Merimdean stage
(the earliest culture thus far known to have existed in Egypt);
of Palestine in the lowest pre-ceramic occupied levels of
Jericho (stratum IX to XVIII); of Syria, at Tell Judeideh in
the Plain of Antioch (stratum XIV) and Ras Shamra
(stratum V); and of Mesopotamia at Nineve, Tepe Gawra,
Arpachiya, Chagar Bazar, Tell Halaf, etc.

A well-developed architecture for houses, including the arch,
has been developed at this period at Tepe Gawra. Pottery,
which shows its great importance for the dating of occupa-
tional levels and for the discovery of cultural relationships,
begins with monochrome burnished wares in Egypt, Syria and
Mesopotamia. Besides pre-ceramic Jericho, the Tahunian
culture (so called from Wadi Tahumeh near Bethlehem, a surface station discoverd in 1928 by Père D. Buzy) is without
pottery and represents the early phase of the Neolithic Period.
Megaliths (i.e., dolmens, menhirs and cromlechs) of huge flat
stones and the forerunners of the Egyptian mastabas and
pyramids, may be assigned to this period, and, incidentally,
they stress the belief of the immortality of the soul.

(b) *The Chalcolithic Period* (c. 4000-3000 B.C.)

The Chalcolithic (lit., copper-stone) Age is also called

Eneolithic, or Cyprolithic, or even Copper Age. This period marks the usage of copper (not bronze) and even gold and the development of ceramic art into painted pottery.

In Egypt this period is represented by various pre-Dynastic cultural phases: the Tasian, Bedarian, Amratian, Gerzean and Semainean. In Palestine the Chalcolithic culture found its greatest expression in the *Ghassulian culture* (so called from Teleilat el-Ghassul, "little mounts of the washing plant"), also at Jericho (stratum VIII), Bethshan (stratum XVIII) and in the Esdraelon culture. In Syria the Chalcolithic is known from various objects found in the early cemetery of Byblos. It is, however, in Mesopotamia that the richest and most extensive phases of the Chalcolithic culture have been found at various excavated sites; these are designated today *Hassunan* (so called from Tell Hassunah, south of Nineve), as *Halafian* (so called from Tell Halaf, the ancient Gozan, where the earliest examples of worked gold were uncovered), *Obeidian* so called from Tell-el-Obeid or al-'Ulbaid), *Warkan* (so called from Uruk or Warka, the Biblical Erech; it was at Uruk where the first known cylinder seals were discovered and where we have the first evidence of a crude pictographic script to express human language) and *Jemdet Nasr* (the culture from which we have the earliest stone sculpture that represents a human being and the development of the script into Sumerian phonetic and word values).

All the settlements of the Fertile Crescent during this period were largely irrigation cultures. The art of building was well developed. At Teleilat el-Ghassul the rectangular shaped houses of mud brick had foundations of uncut stones, stone pavements and mural paintings with elaborate designs and fresco figures on a lime surface; one picture in particular showed a lifelike bird. Painted pottery with polychrome geometric and floral designs reached its highest level at Tell Halaf. Temple buildings are known to have existed during this period (e.g., stratum XIII at Tepe Gawra in Assyria).

(3) *The Historical Period* (c. 3000—)

History, strictly so called, being largely dependent on written documents, is not possible until such documents appear. In the Late Chalcolithic we have among the Sumerians the first evidence of pictographic script at Jemdet Nasr. But from the beginning of the Dynastic Periods of southern Babylonia and Egypt we pass from protohistory to history proper. From that time on to the present day we have recorded history. But we are here only interested in the period of the O.T., and this entire period has been enriched by archæology with its immense historical, literary and religious source material. In terms of metallic development we may give the following brief outline.

Early Bronze	3000-2100 B.C.
Middle Bronze	2100-1500 B.C.
Late Bronze	1500-1200 B.C.
Early Iron	1200- 900 B.C.
Middle Iron	900- 530 B.C.
Late Iron (or Persian) . . .	530- 330 B.C.
Hellenistic	330- 100 B.C.
Hellenistic-Roman	100 B.C.-A.D. 100

The panorama of the Fertile Crescent has been widened by the epoch-making archæological discoveries of the past century. The history of the ancient peoples and their dynasties shows a highly developed culture but a religious retrogression. Such peoples are the Sumerians (c. 2800-2300 B.C.; c. 2070-1960 B.C.), the old Accadians (c. 2360-2180 B.C.) and old Babylonians (c. 1830-1550 B.C.), the Egyptians (c. 2900-332 B.C.), the Assyrians (c. 1700-612 B.C.), the Persians (539-331 B.C.), to whom may be added the Canaanites and Phœnicians (c. 3000-332 B.C.) and the Hittites (c. 1900-1200 B.C.).

Archæological materials or sources which serve as a background for the study of the O. T. are of two kinds: unwritten and written.

(a) Among the non-literary archæological materials mention

may be made of places of worship (temples, shrines and sanctuaries), cult objects (altars, sacred pillars, incense and libation bowls), figurines and plaques with representations of objects, individuals or deities. Pottery represents the largest class of objects found on excavated sites.

From Syria and Palestine rich data has been uncovered by archæological undertakings. Places of worship going back to the Bronze Age have been found at Ugarit, Tainat, Qatna and Byblos in Syria, at Ai, Bethshan, Lachish and Megiddo in Palestine; a stone lion and libation bowl at Tell Beit Mirsim; steles representing deities or mythological scenes at Ugarit, Tell Beit Mirsim and Bethshan; small bronze images, clay plaques or nude figurines, mostly representing female deities, at many Canaanite sites. *From Mesopotamia* there is a wealth of religious temples and cultic objects. There are scores of examples of elaborate temple architecture extending from the fourth millennium at Tepe Gawra to the second century B.C. at Erech (Warka), as at Ur, Mari, Babylon, Assur, Nineve, etc. *From Egypt* important material comes for the proper understanding of the material progress and wealth of this country. Thus, for instance, there are the tombs of the early dynasties at Abydos and Saqqarah, as well as the three great pyramids at Gizeh belonging to the Fourth Dynasty (c. 2550-2450 B.C.); the fabulously rich tomb of Tutankhamun discovered in 1922 by Howard Carter; the temples at Deir el-Bahri, Karnak and Medinet Habu.

(b) The written or literal materials originating from the Fertile Crescent are so extensive that only a slight reference is possible to some of the evidence which has some bearing on the archæological background of the O. T.

IV. *Various Forms of Ancient Near Eastern Literature.*— The various categories of ancient Near Eastern literature not only casts a light upon the ancient past, but also serves as an archæological background for the Hebrew religion and history.

A. *Syria and Palestine.*—From and about Syria and Palestine there is vast documentary evidence that covers the O. T. period.

(1) The most important epigraphic evidence is the Ugarit or Ras Shamra inscriptions (sixteenth to fourteenth century B.C.) excavated by C. F. A. Schaeffer between 1929 and 1939. They consist of several hundred clay tablets and fragments that have enriched our religious and mythological knowledge of the Northern Canaanites and have clarified many O. T. references to the religious beliefs and practices of the Canaanites. They are written in a cuneiform alphabet and in a dialect closely akin to ancestral Hebrew. Among the Ugaritic myths, epics and legends mention must be made of the Poems about Baal and Anath, the Legend of King Keret, and the Tale of Aqhat (cf. H. L. Ginsberg in ANET, 129-155).

(2) The Accadian (Assyro-Babylonian) syllabic cuneiform records are also of importance.

(a) The Assyrian historical texts (c. 900-640 B.C.) point out in particular the struggle of the Assyrian kings for their conquest and maintenance of Syria and Palestine as tributary states (cf. A. Leo Oppenheim in ANET, 276-301). Some of these records confirm the historicity of the Biblical accounts. (i) An inscription of *Salmanasar II* (859-824 B.C.) lists (among the kings conquered at the Battle of Karkar in 845 B.C.) Achab of Israel and Adad-Idri (Bibl., Benadad). The Bible speaks of the alliance between Achab and Benadad in 3 Kings 20, 34. A black obelisk of the same Assyrian king records that in his eighteenth year (842) he received tribute from Jehu, son of Omri. (ii) In the annals of *Theglath-Phalasar III* (745-727) we read that he received tribute in 738 B.C. from Rasin of Damascus and Manahem of Samaria (cf. 4 Kgs. 15, 17-21); and in the campaigns led by the same Assyrian monarch in the years 734, 733 and 732 B.C. are recorded the defeat of Rasin (king of Damascus), the death of his ally, Phacee (king of Israel), the Assyrian enthronement of Osee as Phacee's successor, and the tribute received from King Achaz of Juda (cf. 4 Kgs. 15, 29; 16). (iii) The inscriptions of *Sargon II* (721-705 B.C.) record the siege of Samaria, the capital of the Northern Kingdom of Israel in 722 B.C., and the capture of 27,290 men who were settled in the region of Media (cf. Kgs. 17, 1 ff). (iv) According to the Taylor cylinder, *Sennacherib* (704-681 B.C.) in his third military campaign of 701 B.C., conquered 46 fenced cities of Juda, and carried away 200,150 inhabitants as prisoners of war; in regard to King Ezechias of Juda he writes: "Himself I made a prisoner in Jerusalem, his royal residence, like a bird in a cage." But there is no mention of Ezechias being taken prisoner (cf. 4 Kgs. 18, 13—19, 37).

(b) The records of the Neo-Babylonian Empire (626-539 B.C.) also shed light upon Biblical history. The Babylonian chronicle of *Nabopolassar* (625-605 B.C.), the founder of the Neo-Babylonian Empire, describes the events that took place between 616 and 609 B.C.: the fall of Nineve, the capital of the Assyrians in 612, and the opposition of the Egyptian army in 609, which came to the support of the Assyrians (cf. 4 Kgs. 23, 29 f relating the death of King Josias of Juda at Megiddo in 609, when he tried to impede the Egyptian army of Nechao).

(c) Not only the Assyrian and Neo-Babylonian historical records, but also their contract tablets shed some light on the practice of law during this period.

(d) The *Tell el-Amarna tablets*, discovered in Egypt in 1887, describe the chaotic conditions prevailing in Canaan. These letters in the Accadian language with occasional Canaanite words were written during the period of *Amenophis III* (1413-1377 B.C.) and his son, *Amenophis IV* (1377-1360), when the Egyptian influence upon Canaan and Syria was very weak. There were appeals for aid from the Canaanite princes, especially Abd-hiba of Jerusalem for help against the invading Habiru (Hebrews) which remained ineffective.

(e) Of the Accadian tablets found in excavations at Ugarit, Qatna (el-Mishrifeh) and Alakh (Tell 'Atshanah) in Syria, and at Taanach, Sichem, etc., in Palestine from the period between 1500 and 1200 B.C. the temple inventories of Qatna are of some importance.

(f) The *Mari tablets*, over 20,000 in number, discovered since 1935, are of great importance for approximately dating events in Mesopotamian history during the second millennium. Mari (modern Tel el-Harri) was the ancient Amorite capital in the eighteenth century B.C. The language of this nomadic West-Semitic people was almost identical with that spoken by the Hebrew patriarchs.

(g) The *Cappadocian tablets,* consisting of more than three thousand business letters and contracts of Assyrian colonists among the Hittites of Asia Minor, date back to the twentieth and nineteenth centuries B.C. and seem to mention Haran, the junction of a great caravan route, to which Abraham migrated from Ur.

(3) Several of the Egyptian hieroglyphic texts from the period of the New Kingdom (Eighteenth to Twentieth Dynasty: c. 1570-1150 B.C.) and of the early part of the Twenty-second Dynasty have a direct bearing on Syria and Palestine.

During the Middle Kingdom (Twelfth Dynasty: c. 1989-1776 B.C.) the Egyptians had already established important contacts in Syria (e.g., Ugarit, Byblos, Beirut, Qatna) as well as in Palestine (e.g., Megiddo) and continued to explore the copper mines at Serabit el-Khadem in Sinai. After the domination of the Hykos (c. 1750—1560 B.C.) and their expulsion from Egypt, a very brilliant period of Egyptian history began with the Eighteenth Dynasty (cf. John A. Wilson in ANET, 228-264.)

Queen Hatshepsut (c. 1490 B.C.), identified by some as Pharao's daughter who adopted Moses, records in an inscription the expulsion of the Hyksos. Egyptian history records the brilliant campaigns of Thutmosis III (c. 1469-1436 B.C.) against Asiatic countries (i.e., Syria and Palestine) and in particular the Battle of Megiddo. On the walls of the Amon temple at Karnak he initiated the custom of placing the names of Asiatic and African towns conquered by him (cf. ANET, 242 f). His successor, Amenophis II (c. 1436-1413), continued this Asiatic campaigning. The *Tell el-Amarna tablets* mentioned above were of the period of his successor, Amenophis III (c. 1413-1377), and, in particular, the latter's son,

Amenophis IV (c. 1377—1360 B.C.), when the Egyptian influence upon their Asiatic province was weak. It was during the Nineteenth Dynasty that military activity against Asia was renewed by Seti I (1319-1301 B.C.) and especially by Ramesses II (1301-1234) who, after his pyrrhic victory over the Hittites at Kadesh on the Orontes, concluded a treaty with King Hattusilis of the Hittites, and by Merneptah (1234-1222 B.C.). It was during either of these two Dynasties (Eighteenth and Nineteenth) that the Exodus of the Israelites from Egypt took place.

The records of the New Kingdom also throw particular light upon the O. T. (i) The *Asaru* (most probably the tribe of Aser) are mentioned among the conquered nations on the desert temple of Redesieh during the ninth year of the reign of Seti I (c. 1310 B.C.), and the name is frequently found on the walls of Karnak (Thebes) in the inscriptions of Ramesses II. (ii) The so-called *Israel Stele* of Merneptah makes the first mention in secular history of the name *Israel* and briefly describes its desolation. (iii) During the period of Egyptian decline (c. 1085-332 B.C.) King Sheshonk I (Vulg., *Sesac;* M. T., *Shishak*: 945-924: Twenty-second Dynasty) invaded Palestine during the fifth year of Roboam (928 B.C.; cf. 3 Kgs. 14, 25 f). On the walls of the Amon temple of Karnak various Palestinian towns are listed as being captured, namely Aduram, Gabaon, Ajalon, Bethhoron, Taanach, Shumen, Bethshan, Megiddo, Socho, etc. (iv) Mention may also be made of the *instruction of Amenemopet* (twelfth century B.C.) which is frequently compared to the Book of Proverbs (22, 17-24, 22).

(4) There are several Canaanite and Phœnician (late Canaanite) inscriptions written according to an alphabetic system, which served as immediate progenitors of the Hebrew, Greek and other alphabets. Although the earliest attempts of the alphabetic form of writing are traceable to Serabit el-Khadem in Sinai (called *Proto-Sinaitic* inscriptions and dated in the nineteenth or eighteenth century B.C.) and were first discov-

ered in 1904-1905 by Flinders Petrie, other later examples of the same or closely related form of the alphabet have been found in Canaan (i.e., Palestine); thus, for example, at Sichem, Gezer, Tel el-Hesy, Beth-shemesh, and Lachish for the sixteenth or seventeenth century B.C. Thus, in the pre-Mosaic period the Canaanites of Palestine had two or three alphabetic systems of their own.

Besides the Ugarit or Ras Shamra inscriptions (sixteenth to fourteenth century B.C.) there are also important documents discovered since 1923 at Byblos, including the sarcophagus of Ahiram (eleventh or twelfth century B.C.). Most of the Canaanite inscriptions after 900 B.C. have come from Cyprus, Sardinia, Carthage and other Phoenician colonies.

(5) Aramaic inscriptions have originated from two principal sources. From Syria come royal documents inscribed in stone and found at Shamal (Zendjirli), Sudjin, Ofls and Nerab. Later we have the *Aramaic Papyri* of *Elephantine*, near modern Assuan (fifth century B.C.), describing the conditions prevailing there among a Jewish military colony.

(6) Various Palestinian inscriptions in Hebrew are also worthy of note (cf. W. F. Albright in ANET 320-322). Thus, for example, the Gezer Calendar (c. 925 B.C.), the Moabite Stone of King Mesa (c. 830 B.C.; cf. 4 Kgs. 3, 4 ff), the Ostraca of Samaria (during the reign of Jeroboam II: 783-743 B.C.), the Siloam Inscription (during the reign of Ezechias: 727-699 B.C.; cf. 4 Kgs. 20, 20; 2 Par. 32, 30), and the Lachish Ostraca (589/588 B.C.), which consist of twenty-one ink-inscribed sherds, mostly letters, and shed light upon the invasion of Nabuchodonosor and the period of Jeremias.

B. *Mesopotamia and Persia.*—Israel, in a great part of its history, came into contact with the people of the Mesopotamian Valley and of Persia. Abraham came from the Sumerian city of Ur; the Northern Kingdom of Israel was overthrown by the Assyrians and the Southern Kingdom by the Neo-Babylonians. Finally, the Jews of the captivity were freed by the Persians.

There is an embarrassing wealth of material from the ancient

Sumerians, Babylonians, Assyrians, Neo-Babylonians, etc., which represents various types of literary expression, such as religious, legal, historical, didactic that may illustrate various passages of the O. T. Thus, from the Sumerians there are several hundred clay tablets from Ur; about one thousand from Shuruppak (modern Tell Farah); several thousand tablets from the Lagash period; thousands of tablets from Nippur. The plethora of documents may also be shown by a reference to twenty thousand tablets discovered at Mari of the Amorites, by the library of Assurbanipal (668-626 B.C.) discovered at Nineve.

(1) Among the *Sumerian religious myths and epic tales* mention may be made of the following: Enki and Ninhursag: a Paradise Myth; Dumuzi and Enkimdu: the Dispute between the Shepherd-God and the Farmer-God; the Deluge; Gilgamesh and Agga; Gilgamesh and the Land of the Living; the Death of Gilgamesh; Inanna's Descent to the Nether World; the Duties and Powers of the Gods (cf. S. N. Kramer in ANET. 37-59). The following *Accadian religious myths and epics* are worthy of mention: The Creation Epic (so-called *Enuma Elish* from the first two words on the seven tablets; this epic is often compared with the Biblical account of creation in Genesis); the Epic of Gilgamesh (tablet XI with its account of the Flood is often compared with the Biblical Deluge story in Genesis); Creation of Man by the Mother Goddess; Adapa; Descent of Ishtar to the Nether World; A Vision of the Nether World; etc. (cf. E. A. Speiser in ANET, 60-119). It might also be added that Sumero-Accadian hymns and prayers have also been found to be numerous (cf. Ferris J. Stephens in ANET, 383-392).

(2) Among the more important *collection of laws* are the Sumerian law-code of Lipit-Ishtar (c. 1875 B.C.), the Accadian law code of Eshnunna (c. 1925 B.C.), the famous Babylonian Code of Hammurabi (c. 1690 B.C.; this code has many Biblical parallels) and the Middle Assyrian laws of the twelfth century (cf. S. N. Kramer, Albrecht Goetze and Theophile J. Meek in ANET, 159-188).

(3) *Historical documents* are extant for the entire period of Sumero-Accadian culture. We have already cited above the historical texts referring to the history of Syria and Palestine for the period of the Assyrians and Neo-Babylonians. Some of the more ancient historical records of the Sumerians and Early Babylonians are of interest to students of the Bible. The Sumerian King List gives a number of pre-Diluvial and post-Diluvial kings with fantastic numbers for the years of their reign. From various Accadian texts it is possible to give most of the royal names from the First Babylonian Dynasty to the end of the Assyrian rule in Babylonia.

C. *Egypt.*—The oldest corpus of Egyptian religious literature is exemplified by the so-called *Pyramid Texts* which were written on the interior walls of royal pyramids toward the close of the Old Kingdom (c. 2350-2200 B.C.), consisting of about seven hundred magic spells relating to the future life of the Pharao and contain names of two hundred gods (cf. John A. Wilson in ANET, 3, 32 f). In the Middle Kingdom (c. 1989-1776 B.C.) the Pyramid Texts were replaced by what is known as Coffin Texts, that is, the magical texts were written on the inside of the coffin of the aristocracy (cf. John A. Wilson in ANET, 7, 10, 11 f [The Repulsing of the Dragon], 33 [The Fields of Paradise]). Under the New Kingdom (c. 1560-1085 B.C.) such mortuary texts to obtain eternal happiness for the deceased were generally on papyrus and are now entitled the *Book of the Dead* (cf. John A. Wilson in ANET, 3 f [Of the Creation by Atum], 9 f [The Primeval Establishment of Order], 11 f [The Repulsing of the Dragon], 34-36 [The Protestation of Guiltlessness]). This *Book of the Dead,* written on papyrus rolls, remained popular down to Roman times and either in whole or in part could be placed in the tomb of every individual. Outside of these mortuary texts there is an abundance of hymns and prayers on papyri, temple walls, etc. (cf. John A. Wilson in ANET, 365-381).

Many of the *historical documents* relating to the **Asiatics** (i.e., Palestine and Syria) and the Hittites already **have been**

mentioned above. However, from this type of historical literature must be carefully distinguished biographies that are substantially historical and true (e.g., the story of Sinuhe of the
twentieth century B.C. who went into voluntary exile beyond
Byblos, yearned to return home and received a royal invitation
to come back to Egypt and join the court; the journey of Wen-
Amon to Phœnicia in the eleventh century B.C. as an Egyptian
envoy: cf. John A. Wilson in ANET, 18-22; 25-29) and
romantic, fictitious tales (e.g., the Story of Two Brothers, one
of whom was falsely accused of suggesting adultery to the wife
of his elder brother, after he had actually rejected her advances:
cf. John A. Wilson in ANET, 23-25).

There is an abundance of *didactic and wisdom literature*
among the Egyptians. The instructions of the Vizier Ptah-
Hotep may go back to the Fifth Dynasty (c. 2450 B.C.); the
instruction for King Merikare by his father (end of the twenty-
second century B.C.); the instruction of King Amenemhet I
(died about 1960 B.C.; this text was very popular as a writing
exercise for students); the instruction of Ani and the proverbs
of Amenemopet (ath the end of the first millennicm). Cf. John
A. Wilson in ANET, 412-425.

D. *Hittites.*—The Hittite hieroglyphs have been only partially deciphered up to this time, whereas their cuneiform texts,
in use from c. 1900-1100 B.C., can be read with a degree of
certainty.

The *religious culture* of the Hittites was highly syncretistic,
that is, it was composed of various religious elements borrowed
from other nations. Of their myths, epics and legends worthy
of mention are: The Moon that Fell from Heaven; Kingship
in Heaven; The Song of Ullikummis; The Myth of Illuyankas;
The Telepinus Myth (cf. Albrecht Goetze in ANET, 120-128).
Prayers and hymns (cf. *idem* in ANET, 393-401), as well as
rituals, incantations and description of festivals (cf. *idem* in
ANET, 346-361) were practised or found among them.

Among the Hittite *legal documents* may be mentioned the
treaty of Peace between Hattusilis and Ramesses II (c. 1301-

1234 B.C.); the treaty between Mursilis (c. 1600 B.C.) and
Duppi-Tessub of Amurru; the treaty between Suppiluliumas
(c. 1370 B.C.) and Mattiwaza (cf. *idem* in ANET 201-206).
The *historical texts* record in particular the destruction of the
Kingdom of the Mitanni by Suppiluliumas about 1370 B.C.

Part VIII

THE GEOGRAPHY OF THE HOLY LAND

Chapter I

PHYSICAL GEOGRAPHY OF PALESTINE

Bibliography: (a) *General:* * Adams, J. McKee, "Biblical Backgrounds" (Nashville, 1934); Legendre, Mgr., "The Cradle of the Bible" (St. Louis, Mo.—London, 1929); Szczepanski, L., "Geographia Historica Palæstinæ Antiquæ" (Rome, 1928); * Smith, G. A., "Historical Geography of the Holy Land" (25th ed., London, 1931); Abel, F. M., "Géographie de la Palestine," I (Paris, 1933), II (Paris, 1938).

(b) *Atlases:* * Dalman, G., "Hundert Deutsche Fliegerbilder aus Palästina" (Gütersloh, 1925); * Guthe, H., "Bibelatlas" (2nd ed., Leipzig, 1926); * Philip, G., "Bible Lands" (Comparative Series of Wall Atlases); Riess, R., "Atlas Scripturæ Sacræ" (3rd ed., by Heidet, Freiburg i. B., 1925); Seraphin and Kelly, "Maps of the Land of Christ" (Paterson, 1938); * Wright, G. E.-* Filson, F. V., "The Westminster Historical Atlas to the Bible" (rev. ed., Philadelphia, 1956); * Kraeling, E., "Rand McNally Bible Atlas" (2nd ed., New York, 1957); * Scripture Atlas. "The Biblical World" (Hammond, New York, 1957); Grollenberg, L. H., "Nelson's Atlas of the Bible" (London, 1957); *idem,* "Shorter Atlas of the Bible" (London, 1959); *Kee, H. C., and Young, F. W., "The Living World of the New Testament" (London, 1960).

Art. 1. General Remarks

Extent.—The natural and political boundaries of Palestine are not coëxtensive. In regard to the former, the geographical extent varied at different times. In its widest meaning Palestine designates the territory that extends from Tyre and Mount Hermon to the Sinai peninsula (inclusive), and from the Mediterranean to the Syrian deserts. The total area of this territory is about 62,000 square miles. In its strictest meaning, Palestine designates the territory that extends from the region of Tyre to the Negeb—that is, from about latitude 33° N. to 31° N. and from longitude 34° 15′ E. to beyond 36° 30′ E. This territory is divided into two parts: Western Pales-

tine (Cisjordan) and Eastern Palestine (Transjordan). The area
of the country west of the Jordan is about 9,700 square miles,
or about the size of New Hampshire or Vermont, and the area
of the country east of the Jordan, excluding Damascus, is
about 5,900 square miles. The total area of Palestine is thus
about 15,600 square miles (about one-third the size of Pennsylvania or New York); its length from north to south is approximately 150 miles, while its width from east to west is
125 miles.

The modern political boundaries do not correspond with its
natural boundaries. Part of the territory west of the Jordan
with an area of 7,984 square miles is called Israel. The total
population estimated for Israel on December 31, 1956 was
1,872,390 (1953: Jewish, 88.9%; Moslem, 7.6%; Christian,
2.5%; others, 1.0%). The Hashemite Kingdom of Jordan with
land on both sides of this river is approximately 37,264 square
miles (i.e., including Arab Palestine with an area of 2,125
square miles and with a population of 745,786 in 1953) and an
estimated population of 1,471,000 (92% Moslem; 8% Christian) in 1956.

Position.[1]—The natural position of Palestine made it a suitable habitation for Israel, which was divinely chosen to preserve the true religion and to be instrumental in the salvation
of mankind. For several reasons this country was uniquely
adapted to this twofold purpose. First of all, Palestine resembled a mighty fortress, isolated and protected on all sides
from hostile invasions. In the north the Lebanon and Anti-
Lebanon ranges formed a strong boundary; on the west was
the Mediterranean, the stormy breakers of which made approach on that side almost impossible; the south and the east
were protected by deserts. The Hebrews were thus cut off
from intercourse with the world and its errors, and were able
to live in peace and to serve God undisturbed. Secondly, Palestine lay in the center of the ancient civilized world. Its se-
clusion, however, was not absolute, for it was surrounded by
civilized countries; for example, Assyria and Babylonia, Phœ-

[1] Cf. Seisenberger, *op. cit.,* 4 f.

nicia and Egypt, Greece and Italy. Jerusalem lay midway between Babylonia and Athens, and between Nineve and the mouth of the Nile. The chief trading routes skirted the boundaries of Palestine and the great trading cities of Tyre and Sidon, Damascus, Nineve, and Babylon were all in its neighborhood. Thus, it was possible for God's chosen people to enjoy all the benefits of civilization without being forced to share its disadvantages. Thirdly, the position of Palestine was favorable to its future mission. Its central situation between the three continents of the ancient world was carefully adapted by Providence for the speedy dissemination amongst all countries of the Gospel of the Messianic kingdom, when the time for redemption should come.

Geology.[2]—The formation of entire Syria is due to geological convulsions, which occurred in the early Tertiary epoch. During the Eocene period Syria, Mesopotamia, and Egypt were still submerged. Gradually during the Miocene period the general outlines of the land surfaces of these countries were determined, and the relative areas of land and sea were made as they exist to this day. During the diluvial period of the Quaternary epoch all Syria became divided by earthquakes into two parallel parts separated by a deep fissure or fault, which extended from Antioch to Akabah, and was surrounded on both sides by various mountain chains. There are three rivers which flow through this fissure: the Orontes, the Leontes, and the Jordan. To the east of this central depression there is a high plateau or tableland, which widens out into the Syrian desert, and has various mountain peaks: for example, Mount Hermon (9,052 feet), the culminating point of the Anti-Lebanon range; Hauran (6,000 feet); Galaad

---

[2] Cf. Köppel, R., "Palästina (Tübingen, 1930); *idem,* "Ultimæ investigationes de ætate generis humani," in *Biblica,* 15 (1934), 419-436; * Hull, E., in H.D.B., s.v. *Geology of Palestine;* Leferrière, D., in R.B., 33 (1924), 85-106; Szczepanski, L., "Historia geologica planitiei Ierichuntinæ," in V.D., 1 (1921), 336-339; Steinmueller, J. E.—Sullivan, K., art. "Geology of Palestine," in C.B.E.O.T.; Abel, J. M., in R.B., 36 (1927), 571-578, 37 (1928), 420-424, 38 (1929), 513-541; Buzy, D., in R.B., 36 (1927), 90-92, 37 (1928), 559-578, 38 (1929, 364-381; De Vaumas, E., "La fracture syrienne et le fossé palestinien," in R.B., 54 (1947), 370-387.

and Moab (3,600 to 4,000 feet); Esh Shera near Petra (5,360 feet), and the Madian Mountains (6,500 feet). To the west of the central depression are a series of mountain ranges: for example, Amanus (6,000 feet), Cassius (3,340 feet), Lebanon (11,024 feet), the Mountains of Galilee (3,933 feet), of Samaria (3,077 feet), of Judea (3,270 feet), Negeb (4,450 feet), and Sinai (8,551 feet).

In prehistoric times various regions had been formed by volcanic eruptions: Jaulan (Hebr. Golan), Trachonitis, Auranitis, sections around Safed, Tiberias, and Naim, the country about the Yarmuk River and to the east of the Dead Sea (e.g., Callirrhoe). The geological characteristics therefore vary for the different districts of the land. The mountains of Palestine consist mainly of strata of cretaceous formation. The volcanic regions consist of crystalline slate, porphyritic, and basaltic rock. The soil of the coastal plain is in some parts clayish or blackish, and in other parts sandy.

Physical Conditions: Temperature, Winds, Rainfall, Seasons.—The temperature of Palestine varies according to the period of the year and the different regions. Three zones can be distinguished. (a) In the Jordan valley the average temperature for the year is 77° F., and the normal in the winter is from 59° to 71.6°. In May 104° in the shade and in July 122° in the shade may be experienced. The harvest is much earlier here than elsewhere; at Jericho the barley harvest is completed about April 20 and the wheat harvest about May 15, whereas around the shores of Tiberias the wheat harvest is about a month later. (b) On the maritime plain the average temperature for the year is 72° F. The average temperature in February for Beirut is 59° and for Gaza 62°; in August for Beirut 84° and for Gaza 90°. Ordinarily the wheat harvest is completed by the beginning of June. (c) In the highlands [3] the average temperature throughout the year at Jerusalem is 62° F. January, the coldest month, averages 46° at the capital, and August, the hottest month, 77°. The difference in temperature between day and night sometimes

[3] Cf. Köppel, "Palästina," 40.

amounts to 52°. Though the temperature at times even drops below freezing point, yet the frost and snow do not last long. These variations are even sharper in the mountains of the Transjordan (cf. Gen. 31, 40; Jer. 36, 40), where snow sometimes lasts for several days.

The trade-winds and the regular system of land and sea winds influence the direction and character of the winds in Palestine. In general, it may be said that the north wind is cold, the south wind warm, the east wind dry, and the west wind damp. On the average, the following scale prevails: [4]

Winds from:	Days per year:	Quality:
North	30	Dry and cold (cf. Job 37, 9); they prevail in the summer.
South	11	Always warm.
East	49	Bring dryness and are frequent in autumn, winter, and spring, but rare in summer.
West	59	Bring moisture, cool breezes and rains.
Northwest	114	Moist; they prevail 79 days from May to October.
Northeast	33	Dry.
Southeast	23	Called Sirocco (Hebr., qadim); the air becomes very dry and lacks ozone; they usually occur in May and October.
Southwest	67	They prevail between October and May.

Nearly all of the rain [5] falls in the winter months. The autumn rains or "early rains" (Hebr., joreh, moreh), occurring at the end of October or the beginning of November, soften the ground and allow the farmer to sow his winter crops

[4] Cf. Szczepanksi, *op. cit.*, 37 f; Shalen, N., "La stabilité du climat en Palestine," in R.B., 58 (1951), 54-74.

[5] Cf. Sonnen, J., "Landwirtschaftliches vom See Genesareth," in *Biblica*, 8 (1927) 66-70.

(barley and wheat). Heavy rains (Hebr., geshem, sagrir) continue to fall intermittently from December until February, and it is during this season that the ground is thoroughly saturated, and the cisterns and springs are filled. The spring rains or "later rains" (Hebr., malqosh) occur in March and April. Differences in the amount of rainfall and the number of wet days exist in the various regions of Palestine.[6] During the summer season rain hardly ever falls, and the entire country is arid, but plants are kept alive by the heavy dews brought by the west wind.

In the Bible mention is only made of two seasons, summer (Hebr., qaits) and winter (Hebr., horeph, sethav). The former represents the dry season lasting from May to October, while the latter represents the wet season lasting from November to April.

Storms do not ordinarily occur during the summer months, but rather in the rainy seasons. Besides, the Bible and history record a great number of earthquakes that affected Palestine, the last being in July, 1927.

Art. 2.   Flora and Fauna

Flora.—Within the confines of Palestine vegetation is found that is in keeping with the conditions of its varied climate.[7] The whole of the coast region belongs to the Mediterranean flora. The mountain ranges have their characteristic flora. The Negeb or South Country and the wilderness belong to the desert flora. The chasm of the Jordan and the Dead Sea belong to the tropical flora.[8]

The fertility of the soil in Palestine varies. Galilee and Jaulan with the plain En-Nukra are most fertile; Samaria,

---

[6] Cf. Legendre, *op. cit.,* 210 f.

[7] Cf. Fonck, L., "Biblische Flora," in B.S., 5 (Freiburg i. B., 1900); Sonnen, *op. cit.,* 65-87, 188-208, 320-337; Planès, J., "Noms de plantes recueillies en Arabie Pétrée et dans le pays de Moab," in R.B., 2 (1905), 400-410; Ha-Reubeni, E., "Recherches sur les plantes de l'Evangile," in R.B., 42 (1933), 229-234; * Crowfoot, G. M.—* Baldensperger, L., "From Cedar to Hyssop" (London, 1932).

[8] Cf. Legendre, *op. cit.,* 221-224.

Galaad, and Moab are fertile; Judea is less fertile, but well adapted for vineyards and pasturage.[9]

Of the trees and shrubs worthy of mention are: the cedar, the oak, the terebinth, the pine, the plane, the tamarisk, the oleander, the acacia, the poplar, the storax, the castor-oil, the retama.

Amongst the fruit trees that are native to the country mention may be made of: the olive, the fig, the almond, the pomegranate, the juniper, the pistachio, the carob, the syca-more, the apple, the pear, the walnut, the apricot, the palm, and the vine. Amongst those introduced from other countries are: the banana-palm, the mulberry, the cactus, and the orange.

Amongst the principal cereals may be included wheat, barley, spelt, also millet and maize of foreign origin. The vegetables native to the country are: beans, lentils, peas, garlic, onion, leek, lettuce, etc.; those of foreign origin are: cucumbers, melons, and watermelons.

Palestine abounds in beautiful flowers. Those most frequently found are: the anemone, the crowfoot, the narcissus, the crocus, the tulip, the iris, etc.

Fauna.[10]—The fauna of Palestine, though predominantly Palearctic, contains a number of Ethiopian and Indian species, and some peculiar to its own soil.

The number of mammals in the Holy Land is estimated to be about 115, and not all of these are mentioned in the Bible. Of the domestic animals mention may be made of sheep and goats, classified as small cattle; cows, oxen and buffaloes (indigenous of India), classified as larger cattle; the ass, the mule, the camel, the horse, the swine. Cats and dogs are rarely quite tame and are usually masterless. Among the undomesticated animals may be classified the jackal, the fox,

[9] Cf. Szczepanski, *op. cit.*, 41 f.

[10] Cf. Legendre, *op. cit.*, 226-235; * Post, G. E., in H.D.B., s.v. *Natural History;* * Haas, G., "On the Occurrence of the Hippopotamus in the Iron Age, etc.," in B.A.S.O.R., 132 (1953), 30-34; * Dodge, B., "Elephants in the Bible Lands," in B.A., 18 (1955), 17-20; Benoit, P., "Un curieux ruminant biblique," in R.B., 44 (1935), 581-606; * Godbey, A. H., "The Unicorn in the Old Testament," in A.J.S.L.L., 56 (1939), 256-296.

the wolf, the lion, the leopard, the hyena, the wild boar, the bear, the deer, the gazelle, the ibex, the hare, the mouse, the mole, etc.

Due to the varied climatic conditions Palestine contains a wealth of birds and more than 350 species have been collected. Among the passeres [11] may be mentioned the thrushes, the warblers, the swallows, the honey-suckers, the finches, the sparrows, the crows, the larks, the kingfishers, the cuckoos, the woodpeckers, etc. The birds of prey [12] include the owl, the vulture, the eagle, the kite, the falcon, the hawk. To these should be added the heron, the stork, the crane, the pelican, the raven, the geese, the ducks, the swan, the pigeons, the turtle-doves, the partridges, the quails, etc.

Of reptiles [13] there are no less than 100 species in Palestine and Syria. The four orders of reptiles—the snakes, the lizards, the tortoises, and the crocodiles—are found in the Holy Land. The frog is the only member of the amphibians mentioned in the Bible, although toads, newts, and salamanders are represented.

The Jordan and its affluents, the Lake of Tiberias, and the streams that empty into the Mediterranean abound in many species of fishes, all of which are expressed by a single Hebrew term "dag." Of the 43 species found in the inland waters, 14 are peculiar to the Jordan valley.

Thousands of species of insects are represented in Palestine. There are more than 400 kinds of coleoptera, yet not one of them is mentioned in the Bible. Of the orthoptera four species were allowed by the Mosaic Law to be eaten (Lev. 11, 22); even today the Beduins eat grasshoppers or locusts. Among the hymenoptera mention may be made of the bee, the ant, and the hornet. The fly, the flea, the spider, and the scorpion also abound.

[11] Cf. Wright, M. O., "Birdcraft" (9 ed., New York, 1936), 43 ff.; Szczepanski, *op cit.*, 46.

[12] Cf. Schmitz, E., "Oiseaux repaces nocturnes de Palestine," in R.B., 11 (1914), 255-264.

[13] Cf. * Ditmars, R. L., "Reptiles of the World" (New York, 1937); *idem*, "Snakes of the World" (New York, 1937); Joüon, P., in *Biblica*, 21 (1940), 152-158.

Art. 3.   Orographic and Hydrographic Description
of Palestine

In describing the mountain system and waterways of Palestine three zones are distinguished: (1) the Jordan depression, which includes the Jordan valley, the Dead Sea, and the Arabah valley; (2) Western Palestine, and (3) the Transjordan. To these may be added: (4) the adjacent regions as Edom, Negeb, and the Sinai peninsula.

(1) *The Jordan Depression.*[14]—As a section of the Syrian depression, this extends from the sources of the Jordan to the Gulf of Akabah, and is about 275 miles long and 12½ miles wide in some places. At its starting point, Hasbeya, it is 1,847 feet above the Mediterranean and descends to 1,292 feet below sea level at the Dead Sea.

The Jordan valley may be divided into three sections: (a) the upper Jordan running through Cœlosyria to Lake Huleh; (b) the middle Jordan from Lake Huleh to Lake Tiberias; (c) the lower Jordan from Lake Tiberias to the Dead Sea.

(a) The Jordan has three sources: the Nahr el-Hasbani near Hasbeya, the Nahr Leddan near Tell el-Kadi (the ancient site of the town of Lais or Dan and 500 feet above sea level), and the Nahr Banias near the town of Banias, the ancient Paneas or Cæsarea Philippi and 1,079 feet above sea level. The union of these three sources forms the upper Jordan River. Of these three the first furnishes ⅛, the second ⅝, and the third ¼ of the water. The waters of the upper Jordan, after flowing about 6 miles through the plain of Huleh, reach the lake bearing the same name.

Lake Huleh (Lake Semachonitis of Josephus) measures about 3 miles east to west and 4 miles north to south.   It is

---

[14] Cf. Mallon, A., in *Biblica*, 10 (1929), 94-99, 214-232, 11 (1930), 3-22, 129-148, 12 (1931), 257-270, 13 (1932), 194-201, 273-283, 15 (1934), 1-7; Semkowski, L., in V.D., 9 (1933), 281-283, 17 (1937), 219-224; Köppel, R., in *Biblica*, 12 (1931), 157-167, 16 (1935), 241-256, 17 (1930), 393-406, 18 (1937), 443-449, 19 (1938), 260-266; * Glueck, N., "The River Jordan" (Philadelphia, 1946); *idem,* in B.A.S.O.R., 90 (1943), 2-23, 92 (1943), 26 f; Wand, A., in C.B.Q., 5 (1943), 430-444; * Mowry, L., in B.A., 15 (1952), 26-42.

only about 6 feet above sea level and 10-16 feet in depth. Dense thickets of reeds and papyrus surround the lake.

(b) The middle Jordan River covers a distance of about 10 miles and its fall is very rapid—from 6 feet above sea level to 682 feet below. About 2 miles south of Lake Huleh is "the Bridge of the Daughters of Jacob" (Jisr Benat Jakub), where from time immemorial there had been a ford across the Jordan on the caravan route connecting Egypt with the Mesopotamian countries. At this bridge the river is about 80 feet wide and is 42 feet below sea level.

The Lake of Tiberias [15] was anciently called the "Sea of Kinnereth" (or "Kinnerot"), the "Lake of Gennesar" (or "Gennesareth"), the "Sea of Galilee," the "Sea of Tiberias," or simply "the Sea." Today it is called by the Arabs Bahr Tabariyeh. It resembles an irregular oval, or is pear-shaped with its stalk pointing downwards. The lake is 13 miles long, and its greatest width is 7 miles. Its surface is 682 feet below the Mediterranean; its greatest depth is 154 feet. The mountains surrounding the lake are of moderate height (from 1,000 to 1,300 feet), and various wadys intersect them. In the north-west is the fertile plain of Gennesar, called today El-Ghuweir, about 3 miles long and 1 mile wide. In ancient times many towns were situated on the lake—Tiberias, Magdala, Capharnaum, Corozain, Bethsaida-Julias, etc. Of these Tiberias is the only town that remains. The lake has sweet water and abounds in fish. Due to its peculiar situation violent tempests sometimes suddenly disturb its waters.

(c) The lower Jordan valley extends from the Lake of Tiberias to the Dead Sea, and is called today El-Ghor (i.e., the depression). The direct distance between the two lakes is 65 miles. The width of the valley varies; south of the Lake of Tiberias it is almost 3½ miles, at Beisan 8 miles, but somewhat below the town it contracts to 2 miles; at the approach

---

[15] Cf. Vincent, H., in R.B., 30 (1921), 438-442, 31 (1922), 115-122; Mader, A. E., "Die Ausgrabungen auf dem Deutchen Besitz Tabgha am See Genesareth," in *Biblica*, 13 (1932), 293-297; Köppel, R., in *Biblica*, 13 (1932), 298-308; * Albright, W. F., in B.A.S.O.R., 89 (1943), 7-17.

to the Dead Sea the width is from 11½ to 14 miles. This valley is flanked by high mountains, and the lowest of its three terraces, called Ez-Zor (the cutting), serves as a bed for the Jordan River.

The lower Jordan River because of its numerous windings covers a distance of about 190 miles. As the fall between the two lakes is 610 feet, the river averages a fall of 9.3 feet per mile. Of its tributaries from the east worthy of mention are the Yarmuk (the ancient Hieromax), which has its head waters in the Hauran, Nahr ez-Zerka or the biblical Jaboc,[16] Wady Nimrim, and Wady Hesban. The principal tributaries from the west are Nahr Jalud, which passes down the valley of Esdraelon, Wady Farah, which rises on the north-east of Ebal and Garizim, and Wady Kelt. The Jordan pours c. 1½ million gallons of water into the Dead Sea daily. Before the Roman era there were no bridges spanning the river, and the word for bridge does not occur in the Old Testament. Between the two lakes, however, there are more than fifty fords. In this valley two important towns were and are situated, Bethsan [17] and Jericho.[18] Others of lesser importance were Archelais, Phasaelis, Bethnemra, Betharan, etc.

The Dead Sea [19] is also called the "Salt Sea," the "Lake of Asphalt." The Arabs usually call it Bahr Lut, or "Sea of Lot." It lies 1,292 feet below the Mediterranean Sea, and is 47 miles long and 10 miles wide. Its surface is calculated to be about 357 square miles. Its greatest depth, (1,310 feet), in the northerly part, reaches a point about 2,600 feet below the level of the Mediterranean Sea. It is flanked on the east and west by two high chains of mountains. A few small plains skirt its shores. About two-thirds of its waters is received from the Jordan river, and the rest from Engaddi in the west, Wady

[16] Cf. Mallon, A., "Les Tells riverains du Jabboq inférieur," in *Miscellanea Biblica,* II (Rome, 1934), 57-68.

[17-18] Cf. Steinmueller, J. E.—Sullivan, K., art., "Archæology," "Bethsan," "Jericho," in C.B.E.O.T.; * Kenyon, K. M., "Digging up Jericho" London, 1957).

[19] Cf. Koeppel, R., in *Biblica,* 13 (1932) 6-27; Ubach, P. B., in R.B., 53 (1946), 249-259. For discussion on Pentapolis: cf. Lagrange, M. J., in R.B., 41 (1932), 489-514; Power, E., in *Biblica,* 30 (1930), 23-62, 149-182.

Zerka Main, the Arnon, Wady el-Kerak, Wady Nemeira, and Wady el-Kerahy in the east. Making due allowances for seasonal risings of the water from 13 to 20 feet, it can be said that most of the water flowing into the Dead Sea from the various rivers and wadys evaporates daily. By reason of this extraordinary evaporation the water is impregnated with mineral substances. The water contains 25% mineral salt, of which 7% is chloric natrium, 16½% chloric magnesium, and 1% chloric calcium. As a result, the water is of a greater specific gravity than the human body. Fish, coming into this lake from the Jordan, do not survive very long. The five towns of Sodom, Gomorrah, Seboim, Adama, and Segor, mentioned in Genesis 19, were located on a fertile plain near the Dead Sea.[20]

Formerly the valley extending from the Lake of Tiberias to the Gulf of Akabah was called El Arabah (i.e., the desert region), but this term is now restricted to the region south of the Dead Sea. This valley is 115 miles long and ranges from 5½ to 12½ miles in width. It is flanked by two high plateaux. About 65 miles from the Dead Seá there is situated Rishet el Hauwar, the watershed, which stands 982 feet above the level of the Mediterranean.

(2) *Western Palestine*.[21]—The physical features of Western Palestine consist of two longitudinal divisions: (a) the maritime plain, and (b) the Western plateau.

(a) The maritime plain extends from Nahr el-Kasimiyeh to Wady el-Arish, the ancient "Torrent of Egypt." The length of this strip is about 140 miles, and is interrupted by the *Scala*

---

[20] For evidence of civilization and culture prevailing near the Dead Sea during the fourth millennium or Chalcolithic Age consult the excavations at Tuleilat el Ghassul by Père Mallon and Père Koeppel 1929-1938, and described in various articles of the *Biblica*, 11 (1930-). Cf. also Mallon. Koeppel, Neuville, "Teleilat I. Compte rendu des fouilles de l'Institut biblique Pontifical 1929-1932" (Rome, 1934); Senes, H., Murphy, J. W., Mahan, G. S., "Teleilat Ghassul II. Compte rendu . . . 1932-1936" (Rome, 1940); Vincent, H., "Les fouilles de Teleilat Ghassul," in R.B., 44 (1935), 69-104, 220-244; Cerny, E., Teleilat Ghassul," in C.B.Q., 2 (1940), 264-266.

[21] Cf. Legendre, *op. cit.*, 22-91; * Adams, *op. cit.*, 139 ff; Abel, F. M., "Le littoral palestinien et ses portes," in R.B., 11 (1914), 556-590; * Glueck, N., in B.A.S.O.R., 131 (1953), 6-15.

Tyriorum (the "Ladder of Tyre") and Mount Carmel. The northern section of this plain, extending to Mount Carmel and interrupted by the *Scala Tyriorum,*[22] has a width varying from 1¼ to 3½ miles. Several streams cross this unfertile region, the most important of which is the famous torrent, Cison. Of the ports worthy of mention are Tyre (an island until the time of Alexander the Great), Acre, and Haifa.

The southern section of this plain begins to cut into the interior. Thus, the plain from Mount Carmel to Jaffa, about 50 miles in length, reaches a breadth of about 12 miles in the region of Jaffa, and is called the Plain of Saron, extolled in the Bible for its beauty and fertility. Of the various ports (e.g., Athlit, Dor, Cæsarea) the most important is Jaffa. Several streams cross the Saron, as Nahr ez-Zerka (the only river in Palestine having crocodiles) to the north of Cæsarea, Nahr el-Auja to the north of Jaffa, etc. From Jaffa to Wady el-Arish, a distance of about 70 miles, lies the fertile lowland called the Sephela. This region is also called the Plain of Philistia, and reaches a maximum width of 30 miles towards Bersabee. The only perennial stream is Nahr Rubin, whereas Wady Ghazzeh (below Gaza) contains water only during the rainy season. In this plain were situated the towns of Sarea, Azeca,[23] Ceila, and the five fortified towns of the Philistines: Accaron, Ascalon,[24] Azotus, Gaza and Geth.

(b) The Western plateau may be considered as a continuation of the Lebanon and consists of three great divisions: the Galilean, the Samaritan, and the Judean mountain systems.

The Galilean system of mountains is made up of two groups, Upper and Lower Galilean. In Upper Galilee the hills rise to a high elevation (2,000 to 4,000 feet), Jebel Jermak being the highest peak (3,933 feet above the Mediterranean). These hills are for the most part wooded. Since this region is well supplied with rivers and springs, its plains are fertile. In Lower

---

[22] Now the political boundary between the Syrian and Palestinian countries.

[23] Identified with Tell Zachariya and excavated by * Bliss and Macalister in 1898.

[24] Excavated by * J. Garstang during 1921-2.

Galilee the hills are only half as high; thus, Nebi Dahi, also
called Little Hermon (1,690 feet); to the north-west of Nazareth, Nebi Sain (1,610 feet); to its north-east, Jebel Turan
(1,794 feet) and Ras Kruman (1,845 feet); and to its south-
east, Tabor (1,843 feet). Several fertile plains and torrents
are also situated in this region.

Separating the Galilean and Samaritan mountain systems is
the Plain of Esdraelon (260 feet above the Mediterranean),
so called from the ancient royal city of Jezrael. Its shape is
that of an irregular triangle, with its points at Mount Carmel,
Jenin, and the foot of Tabor. This plain is remarkable for its
fertility, and is drained by the Cison (which flows into the
Mediterranean) and the Nahr Jalud (which flows into the
Jordan). The towns of importance for secular and biblical
history are: Mageddo,[25] Thanach,[26] Jenin, Jezrael,[27] Sunem,[28]
Naim, and Endor.[29] This great plain was a constant meeting-
place and battle-field for nations.[30]

The central system of the Western plateau is made up of
two principal mountain chains of Samaria. In the Bible these
hills are called the "Mountains of Ephraim" or the "Mountains of Israel." The northern mountains have the shape of a
fork with Mount Ebal (3,077 feet) acting as the pivot. To
the north-east it terminates with Jebel Fukua, the Gelboe of
the Bible, with its highest point 1,692 feet above the Mediterranean, and small lateral ranges drop towards the Jordan; to
the north-west, it reaches Mount Carmel with its highest point
1,810 feet, and small lateral ranges drop towards the Plain of
Saron. Mount Carmel, which is rich in vegetation, is extolled

[25] Identified with modern Tell el-Mutesellim. The first excavations
were undertaken by * G. Schumacher (1903-05) for the German Palestine
Society. Work was resumed in 1925 for the University of Chicago by
* C. Fisher (1925-26), * P. Guy (1927-34), and * G. Loud (1935—).
[26] Excavations were made here by * E. Sellin in 1901-1904.
[27] Identified with the present little village of Zerin. Cf. Jos. 17, 15;
1 Sam. 29, 1; 3 Kgs. 18, 45; 21, 1; 4 Kgs. 8, 29; 9, 10, etc.
[28] Today Solam. It was the home of Abisag (3 Kgs. 1, 3) and of the
hostess of Eliseus (4 Kgs. 4, 8 ff).
[29] The place where King Saul went to consult the witch before the battle of Gelboe (1 Sam. 28, 7 ff).
[30] Cf. Jdgs., 4, 7. 13; 5, 21; 3 Kgs. 18, 40; also Jdgs. 1, 27 f; 5, 19-22;
4 Kgs. 9, 27 f; 23, 29 f.

for its beauty in the Old Testament. The southern mountains reach their highest point with Mount Garizim (2,850 feet). Samaria is studded with numerous valleys and plains, and worthy of mention are the fertile plain of Dothain and to its south-east the grass land, or Merj el-Gharak. The towns that play an important part in history are Dothian, Sichem[31]; Thersa,[32] and Samaria[33] (Sebaste).

The Judean system includes the tableland from about Bethel to Bersabee, i.e., approximately 60 miles. Its elevation at Tell Asur (Baal-hasor) is 3,316 feet. This together with other high hills serve as the outposts of Jerusalem, which is set on an eminence that reaches at its highest point 2,591 feet and is surrounded by Mount Scopus in the north (2,726 feet) and the Mount of Olives in the east (2,683 feet). After passing Bethlehem (2,549 feet), the plateau rises again to the Hebron hills, several peaks of which tower above 3,000 feet. A slow descent is then made until, south of Bersabee (787 feet), the plateau stretches out to the Negeb region.

The characteristic features of Judea make it a closed country. From Jericho only three great passes lead into the interior of Judea. The first, in a northwesterly direction, proceeds towards Machmas (Hebr., Mikmas), Ai, and Bethel.[34] The second, approaching the highlands towards the south-west of the town, is the biblical "Ascent of Adommin," [35] and the road mentioned in the Parable of the Good Samaritan; [36] the distance between Jericho and Jerusalem is approximately 18 miles with an average road-grade of 190 feet per mile. The

[31] Excavations were started by * E. Sellin in 1913 and after many interruptions brought to a provisional close by * H. Steckeweh in 1934. It is identified with the modern Balata, about a mile east of Nabulus.

[32] Soon after the division of the kingdom by Jeroboam I, Thersa became the capital of the northern kingdom till the time of King Omri.

[33] Samaria was made the capital of the northern kingdom by King Omri. Excavations were conducted here by Harvard University (1908-10), then again in 1931-33 and 1935 by the same University in conjunction with several archæological associations. Cf. * Reisner, Fisher, and Lyon, "The Harvard Expedition at Samaria" (2 vols., Cambridge, 1924).

[34] It was along this pass that Josue led the Israelites in his southern campaign (cf. Jos. 7).

[35] Jos. 15, 7; 18, 18.

[36] Luke 10, 30; cf. Beauvery, R., in R.B., 64 (1957), 72-101.

third takes a more southerly direction and then forks, one branch leading to Jerusalem and the other to Bethlehem. From the Sephela four important passes lead into the interior. The first is the valley of Ajalon, which begins at Gabaon, 5 miles north-west of Jerusalem. The second is the valley of Sorec, which lies west of Jerusalem, and is the road taken by the modern railroad from Lydda to Jerusalem. The third is the valley of Elah [37] or the biblical "Terebinth Valley," which leads to the south of Bethlehem. The fourth is the valley of Zaphathah, which begins at Beit Jibrin [38] (Eleutheropolis). The southern frontier offers an easy access, but can be considered closed by the Negeb region. The northern frontier is protected by its high hills that served as outposts.

Judea has very few springs and the rain water is collected in cisterns. Near Jerusalem there are the fountains of Gihon,[39] En Rogel,[40] and Ain Karim.[41] Near Bethlehem there are several fountains, the waters of which are brought to Jerusalem by an aqueduct.

Jerusalem itself was a sort of fortress and very difficult to capture. It is situated on an uneven slope, divided from northwest to southeast by a depression (which Josephus calls the Tyropœon), and surrounded on three sides by deep ravines. In the east is the valley of Cedron, or Josaphat; to the south and west the valley of Hinnom. Thus, the only easy approach is from the north. To its north is Mount Scopus, to its east the Mount of Olives, and to its south the fertile plain of Raphaim.[42]

(3) *The Transjordan.*[43]—This immense Eastern plateau, which extends from Mount Hermon in the north to Wady el-Hesa in the south and from the Jordan river in the west to

---

[37] 1 Sam. 17, 2.
[38] Cf. Abel, F. M., in R.B., 33 (1924), 583-604.
[39] 3 Kgs. 1, 33. 38. 45.
[40] 3 Kgs. 1, 9.
[41] Jos. 15, 60; the traditional birthplace of John the Baptist.
[42] 2 Sam. 5, 18. 22.
[43] Cf. Legendre, *op. cit.,* 148-194; * Glueck, N., "The Other Side of the Jordan" (New Haven, 1940); *idem,* in B.A.S.O.R., 64 (1936), 9 f, 65 (1937), 8-29, 66 (1937), 27 f, 67 (1937), 19-26, 68 (1937), 13-21, 86 (1942), 14-24, 91 (1943), 7-26; De Vaux, E., in *Vivre et Penser,* 1 (1941), 16-47; Benoit, P., in R.B., 56 (1949), 295-299.

the Syrian desert in the east, is divided into three main parts
by two deep ravines forming the beds of the Yarmuk and
Jaboc rivers.

(a) The northern part between Mount Hermon and the
Yarmuk River forms a high plateau, characterized by extinct
volcanoes. On account of the deposits of lava and ashes the
soil is very rich. This entire region, corresponding to the
ancient kingdom of Basan [44] with its capitals at Edrai and
Astaroth, may be subdivided into three parts.

(1) The Jaulan, the ancient Gaulanitis, stretched along the
Jordan valley from Hermon to Yarmuk and in the east to
Nahr el-Allan. This plateau has an altitude of from 2,290 to
2,620 feet above the Mediterranean. Due to its numerous
springs and many streams as well as its extremely rich soil,
this region has always been an attractive area for farmers
and herdsmen. Among the towns worthy of mention are
Gaulon,[45] Cæsarea Philippi,[46] Aphec, Hippos, and Bethsaida-
Julias.[47]

(2) The Hauran, the ancient Auranitis, is the region east of
the Jaulan and south of Damascus. It includes the plain
En-Nukra (which has an average altitude of 2,000 to 2,300
feet), the J. Hauran (the highest peak of which is Tell Jena
(6,033 feet), and the Leja or the Trachon (Trachonitis) of
Josephus. Towns worthy of mention in this region are Edrai
and Astaroth, the two capitals of King Og,[48] Raphon, Alimis,
Bosor, Bostra,[49] Salecha,[50] and Canath.[51]

(3) The region to the east of Damascus is called Diret et-
Tulul, and between it and the foothills of Hermon lies the
great fertile plain of Damascus.

(b) The land of Galaad (Hebr., Gilead) extends from the
Yarmuk to Wady Hesban, and is divided by the Jaboc River
into two parts: [52] Upper Galaad or Ajlun, and Lower Galaad

[44] Cf. Num. 21, 33-35; the Greco-Roman province of Batanea formed
only a part of it.

[45] Cf. Jos. 20, 8.
[46] Cf. Matt. 16, 13-19.
[47] Luke 9, 10.
[48] Cf. Deut. 1, 4; Jos. 12, 4.

[49] Cf. 1 Mach. 5, 26.
[50] Cf. Deut. 3, 10.
[51] Cf. Num. 32, 42.
[52] Deut. 3, 12 f; Jos. 12, 2; 13, 31.

or el-Belka. It represents a strip of land about 62 miles long and from 21 to 24 miles broad. This region has always been noted for its unusual pastures, and in ancient times was the home of mighty forests.

The high plateau consists of mountains ranging from 2,000 to 2,500 feet above the Mediterranean. Of the various torrents that flow through this plateau the most important is the Nahr ez-Zerka (the "Blue River") or the Jaboc, famous in its connection with the history of the Patriarch Jacob.[53] In this district flourished the towns of Gadara, Pella, Jerash, Amman or Rabbath-Ammon (the old capital of the Ammonites),[54] Mahanaim, Ephron, Jegbaa, Jazer, Bethnemra, Ramoth-Galaad, etc.

(c) The land of Moab extends from Wady Hesban to Wady el-Hesa (that is, it includes the region east of the Dead Sea), and is divided by the deep chasm of the River Arnon into two parts: Upper and Lower Moab. This entire strip of land is 65 to 68 miles long and 24 to 27 miles wide. Though there are no trees and springs are few in this district, yet it is a land traversed by streams, contains many cisterns, and has a soil that is fertile and suitable for grazing land. The high plateau reaches an elevation of more than 3,000 feet above the Mediterranean, or about 4,300 feet above the Dead Sea. To the north of the Arnon is situated Jebel Neba (2,644 feet) or Mount Nebo, from which Moses viewed the Promised Land, and Machærus (2,425 feet), where St. John the Baptist was imprisoned and beheaded; to the south of the river is El-Kerak (3,113 feet), the ancient Kir of Moab, which is the headquarters of this district. Worthy of mention is Wady Zerka Main, close to which are the sulphureous thermal baths of Callirrhoe with a temperature of 140° F. In this region of Moab flourished the towns of Kir of Moab, Ar-Moab, Aroer, Dibon,[55] Bosor, Madaba,[56] Hesebon, etc.

[53] Gen. 32, 22. 32.
[54] 2 Sam. 12, 26-29.
[55] Here in 1869 the Moabite Stone was discovered.
[56] The famous mosaic map of Palestine was discovered here in December, 1896.

(4) The Adjacent Regions.—(a) Edom,[57] the "Red Land" (so called from the red color of its cliffs), embraces the region on the east side of El Arabah, and stretches to the headwaters of the Gulf of Akabah. This entire region is composed of the massive range of Mount Seir, the principal peak of which is Mount Hor (4,430 feet).[58] The Edomite cities and towns mentioned in biblical or secular history are Petra (or Sela),[59] Thophel, Bosra, Phunon, Asiongaber,[60] Elath,[61] etc.

(b) The Negeb,[62] or South Country, is bounded on the east by the Arabah, on the south by Jebel et-Tih, on the west by the Suez Canal, and on the north by Judea and Philistia. The entire region is mountainous, rises to approximately 3,000 feet above the sea, and is intersected by various valleys, the most important of which is the Wady el-Arish, the ancient "Torrent of Egypt." The land is practically barren. Various wildernesses are mentioned in the Old Testament: the wilderness of Sur on the borders of which was Etham,[63] the wilderness of Pharan,[64] the desert of Sin near to which was Cadesbarne.[65] In the northern section there are ruins of towns that flourished during the Græco-Roman period.

(c) The Sinai peninsula,[66] triangular in form, begins at the Isthmus of Suez [67] and projects into the Red Sea after being

[57] Cf. * Kennedy, A., "Petra, Its History and Monuments" (London, 1925) ; * Robinson, G. L., "The Sarcophagus of an Ancient Civilization, Petra, Edom and the Edomites" (New York, 1930) ; Abel, F. M., in R.B., 46 (1937), 373-391.

[58] Jebel Haroun or "the Mount of Aaron," where according to an Arabic tradition Aaron died and was buried; cf. Num. 20, 29.

[59] Cf. 4 Kgs. 14, 7.

[60] Deut. 2, 8; 3 Kgs. 9, 26; for results of latest excavations consult * N. Glueck, "The Other Side, etc.," 89-113; *idem*, in B.A.S.O.R., 71 (1938), 72 (1938), 75 (1939), 79 (1940).

[61] Cf. Deut. 2, 8; 3 Kgs. 9, 26; * Glueck, N., in B.A.S.O.R., 80 (1940), 3-10.

[62] Cf. *Glueck, N., in B.A.S.O.R., 131 (1953), 152 (1958), 18-38.

[63] Cf. Num. 33, 8; Ex. 15, 22.

[64] Cf. Num. 10, 12.

[65] Cf. Num. 34, 3 f; also * Woolley and Lawrence, "The Wilderness of Zin" (New York, 1936); Vaux—Savignac, in R.B., 47 (1938), 89-100.

[66] Cf. Closen, G., in V.D., 15 (1935), 121-127, 149-159, 187-191, 213-214.

[67] Cf. Bourdon, C., "Note sur l'isthme de Suez," in R.B., 37 (1928), 232-256.

bounded by the Gulf of Suez on the west and the Gulf of Akabah on the east. This region played an important rôle in the social and religious history of the Hebrews. In the southern part of the peninsula are massive granite elevations that form the Mount Sinai group (probably the Mount Horeb of ancient times), culminating in Jebel Katherin (8,551 feet), the highest mountain in the peninsula, Jebel Musa (7,519 feet), where according to tradition the Law was given to Moses, and Jebel Serbal (6,759 feet). On the slopes of Jebel Musa is situated the famous Monastery of St. Catherine.

Chapter II

HISTORICAL GEOGRAPHY
PALESTINE OF THE OLD TESTAMENT

The Names of Palestine.—The oldest name occurring for the country west of Mesopotamia to the Mediterranean is *Amurru*,[1] found in the cuneiform records of the third millennium B.C. In the Tell el-Amarna letters of the fourteenth century B.C. the same name is used for this region. In the Egyptian records of about 1300 B.C., the "Land of the Amorites" refers to northern Palestine with its capital at Kadesh on the Orontes. In the Old Testament the phrase, "the land of the Amorites," is also used (Jos. 24, 8; Amos 2, 10). Another name applied to this region is Canaan. This name occurs in the Tell el-Amarna letters, probably for the region south of the Lebanon. Though the term appears rarely in Egyptian records, it is mentioned in Phœnician and Grecian records, and most frequently in the Bible for the entire region west of the Jordan (Ex. 15, 15). Other names mentioned in the Bible are: the Land of Israel, Land of the Hebrews, Land of Jahweh (Lord), Holy Land, the Promised Land, and Judea. Lastly, the name Palestine comes from Pelishtim, "the Philistines," and this name was originally given only to the strip of coast inhabited by the Philistines, but from the fourth or fifth century A.D. it was applied to the whole country.

The Early Inhabitants of Palestine.[2]—Among the peoples mentioned in the Bible as living in Palestine at the time of Abraham are: the Kenites, the Kenizzites, the Kadmonites,

---

[1] * Dhorme, P., "Les Amorrhéens," in R.B., 37 (1928), 63-79, 161-180, 39 (1930), 161-178, 40 (1931), 161-184; * Gelb, I. J., "Studies in the Topography of Western Asia," in A.J.S.L.L., 55 (1938), 66-85; * Lacheman, E. R., "Nuzi Geographical Names," in B.A.S.O.R., 78 (1940), 18-23; Zerwick, M., in V.D., 20 (1940), 156-159, 190-192.

[2] Skrinjar, A., "De incolis Terræ promissæ Abrahæ æqualibus," in V.D., 17 (1937), 268-279.

the Hittites, the Perizzites, the Raphaim, the Amorites, the Canaanites, the Girgashites, the Jebusites (Gen. 15, 19 f), the Horites (Gen. 14, 6) and the Hivites (Gen. 10, 17; 34, 2). Of these the more important are the Canaanites, the Amorites, and the Hittites.

The Canaanites were descendants from Ham (Gen. 10, 6), and were called by the Greeks from Homeric times the *Phœnicians*, but they themselves referred to their country as the land of Canaan. These Canaanites settled about 3000 B.C. in Syria, and then established cities at Sidon, Tyre, Simyra, etc.

The Amorites are listed in the table of nations as Hamites, descendants of the fourth son of Canaan (Gen. 10, 16). In a Sumerian text from Nippur, written about 2700 B.C., their nomadic life is described: they eat uncooked meat, do not live in houses, and do not bury their dead. At a very early period they migrated to Palestine and settled chiefly in the highlands (Gen. 14, 7. 13; Num. 13, 30).

The Hittites [3] represent an Indo-European group that invaded Asia Minor along the Halys river and settled there before the twentieth century B.C. By the middle of the second millennium they constituted a very formidable empire in Asia Minor and Syria, and had their capital at Boghaskoi. For two centuries they were the powerful enemies of the Egyptians, and it was only after the Battle of Kadesh, in which they almost broke the power of Ramses II (1292-1225 B.C.), that a treaty of peace was concluded. [4] At Carchemish they were defeated by Sargon II of Assyria in 717 B.C. and disappeared from history. When Abraham wandered through Canaan, the Hittites had already occupied Hebron (Gen. 23). His grandson Esau married two Hittites (Gen. 26, 34). It is very likely that the Hittites established new colonies in the land, so that at the time of Moses they are described as dwelling in the mountains (Num. 13, 30).

[3] Deimel, A., in V.D., 8 (1928), 189-192, 218-222, 250-254, 281-285; Cerny, E. A., "Hittites," in C.B.Q., 2 (1940), 71 ff.

[4] Steinmueller, "Some Problems, etc., 150 f.

The Horites [5] are described in the Bible as having occupied the mountains of Seir (Gen. 14, 6), and as having been dispossessed from there by the Edomites (Deut. 2, 12. 22). Some scholars maintain that in Gen. 34, 2 (cf. also Jos. 9, 7; 11, 3: Jdgs. 3, 3) Hivite stands in place of Horite. If this is the case,[6] then there would be biblical evidence for the presence of Horites in Sichem at the time of Abraham, and at Gabaon, Hermon and Lebanon in the period of Josue. It is now believed that these Horites are to be identified with an ethnical group called the Hurrians, who at a very early period settled in northern Iraq and Syria, and are related in some way to the Hyksos groups that dominated Egypt for almost a century until they were dispossessed by Ahmose I, the founder of the eighteenth dynasty.

The Raphaim are classed amongst the earliest inhabitants of Palestine. They live mainly in the Transjordanic region, in the territory of Moab, where they were called Emim (Deut. 2, 9-11), in the confines of Ammon, where they were called Zuzim or Zamzummim (Gen. 14, 5; Deut. 2, 18-21), and in the region of Basan (Gen. 14, 5; Deut. 3, 10-13; Jos. 12, 4; 13, 12). Some of them also lived in Western Palestine (Jos. 17, 15) and in the valley of Raphaim south of Jerusalem (Jos. 15, 8). Among these Raphaim are to be counted the Anakim (Deut. 2, 11), who lived in Kiriath-arba near Hebron (Jos. 14, 15; cf. also Gen. 23, 2. 19).[7]

Very little is known of the other early peoples of Palestine. The Girgashites were inhabitants of Western Palestine. The Hivites are probably to be identified with the Horites mentioned above. The Jebusites, perhaps allies of the Hittites, lived in and around Jerusalem, which at that time was called Jebus (Num. 13, 30; Jdgs. 19, 10). The Kadmonites (literally "Men of the East") were the inhabitants of the Syrian desert.

---

[5] Cerny, E. A., "Hurrians," in C.B.Q., 2 (1940), 179-181.
[6] The Septuagint has Horites for Gen. 34, 2 and Jos. 9, 7; Gen. 36, 2 calls Sebeon a Hivite, but in verses 20 and 29 a Horite.
[7] Cf. Mader, E. A., "Ausgrabung bei Hebron," in *Biblica*, IX (1928), 120-126; Idem, "Mambre, eine Stätte der Biblischen Uroffenbarung im Lichte der neuesten Ausgrabungen," in *Miscellanea Biblica* (Rome, 1934), 37-56.

Little is known of the Kenizzites. The Kenites lived in the southeast, but now and then were in alliance with the Amalakites, whose lands lay still farther south. The Perizzites during the period of the Patriarchs lived around Bethel and Sichem (Gen. 13, 7; 34, 30), and may be considered among the earliest inhabitants of Palestine.

Besides these early inhabitants of Palestine, the Philistines, whose place of origin was the island of Crete (Caphtor of Jer. 47, 4 and Amos 9, 7, and the same as the Egyptian term Keftyu), invaded the country during the period of Ramses III (1198-1167 B.C.) and settled in the Sephela plain. They formed a confederation of five cities, each of which was governed by its own ruler. Besides their own deities which they brought with them, they adopted those of the Canaanites (v.g., Dagon, Beelzebub, Astart-Derketo, etc.). Being a warlike race and armed with chariots and heavy armor, they harassed the Hebrews and ruled them for about forty years. The guerilla warfare in the period of the Judges and Samson is evidence for this, but David finally subjugated them and made them tributary.

Boundaries of the Promised Land.—When the Hebrews entered the Promised Land under Josue, the previous settlers were either conquered or driven out, while some were exterminated by God's command. Then the country was divided among the twelve tribes as their possession. The possessions of Ruben, Gad and half the tribe of Manasses, beyond the Jordan, were promised them by Moses (Num. 32) and confirmed by Josue (Jos. 13). In Galgal the possessions of Juda, Ephraim, and half the tribe of Manasses were distributed to them by Josue (Jos. 14-17). At the assembly of Silo the other seven tribes received their tribal possessions (Jos. 18-19). Within these tribes six towns of refuge (Jos. 20, 1-9) and forty-eight towns for the Levites were designated (Jos. 21, 1-43). In this territorial division the descendants of Joseph received two portions, as Ephraim and Manasses had been adopted by Jacob (Gen. 48, 5); the tribe of Levi, whose duty it was to attend to the worship of God, received no land, but the members of this tribe were distributed over the whole country. (1) The territory assigned to the tribe of *Juda* lay in the south and consisted of about eighty towns [8] (cf. Jos. 15). (2) Southward of it in the Negeb was that belonging to *Simeon*, the weakest of the tribes, with seventeen towns (Jos. 19, 1-9; 1 Par. 4, 28-33). (3) To the north of Juda lay *Benjamin* with twenty-six towns mentioned (Jos. 18, 11-28). (4) The tribe of *Dan*, with eighteen towns, lived at first to the north of Juda and west of Benjamin (Jos. 19, 40-48), but as its territory was too small and constant fighting was required for its defense, part of the tribe migrated northwards and settled near the town of Lais, which was thenceforth called Dan (Jos. 19, 47; Jdgs. 18). (5) *Ephraim* occupied the center of the country (Jos. 16, 5-9). (6) To the north of Ephraim dwelt half the tribe of *Manasses* [9] (Jos. 17, 1-13), but they were at first unable to capture the towns of Bethsan, Jeblaam, Dor, Endor, Thanac, and Mageddo; later, however, these were made tributary to the tribe (Jos. 17, 11 f); the other half of the tribe settled in the northern part of the country east of the Jordan (Jos. 13, 29-31; Num. 32, 33. 39 ff). (7) The tribe of *Issachar* lived round the plain of Esdraelon (Jos. 19, 17-23). (8) The tribe of *Zabulon* settled to the west of the Lake of Tiberias (Jos. 19, 10-16). (9) The tribe of *Aser* lived along the maritime plain of Galilee (Jos. 19, 24-31; Jdgs. 1, 31 f). (10) The tribe of *Nephtali* occupied the northernmost part of the country (Jos. 19, 32-39). (11) The tribe of *Ruben* dwelt

[8] Though one hundred and thirty-four towns were assigned to it, those occupied by Simeon, Dan, and the Philistines must be deducted. Cf. Szczepanski, *op. cit.*, 127. Among the towns mention is made of Lachis (Jos. 15, 39), which is identified with the present Tell el-Duweir, where important excavations were begun by * J. L. Starkey in 1935. Among the important finds are eighteen ostraca that date to a period shortly before the first destruction of Jerusalem (586 B.C.). Cf. articles by * Albright, W. F., * Gordon, C. H. and * Ginsberg, H. L., in B.A.S.O.R., 61 (1932)—80 (1940); also *Albright, W. F., in A.N.E.T. (2nd ed., Princeton, N. J., 1955), 321 f; Vincent, L. H., in R.B., 48 (1939), 250-277, 406-433, 563-582; * Obermann, J., in J.A.O. *Suppl.* (1938); Vaccari, A., in *Biblica*, 20 (1939), 180-199.

[9] Cf. Fernandez, A., "Los Limites de Efrain y Manasés," in *Biblica*, 14 (1933), 22-40, *idem*, "El limite septentrional de Benjamin," *ibid.*, 13 (1932), 49-60.

in the south of the district east of the Jordan (Jos. 13, 15-23; Num. 32, 34-38). (12) The tribe of *Gad* settled to the north of Ruben (Jos. 13, 24-28).

During the reign of King David (1012-972 B.C.) the Israelites had obtained their greatest territorial expansion. David had conquered the Amalekites, the Philistines, the Moabites, the Arameans, the Ammonites, and the Edomites, and made them tributary to him. The twelve tribes were united under his rule and their people enumerated (2 Sam. 24, 1-9). Jerusalem,[10] which had been considered impregnable by the Jebusites, was captured by David and made his capital (2 Sam. 5, 6-9).

After the death of King Solomon [11] (932 B.C.) the kingdom was divided into two parts: the kingdom of Juda and the kingdom of Ephraim or Israel. The former included the territory of the southern tribe of Juda, together with the tributary province of Edom; it also embraced the tribe of Simeon, which had practically lost its tribal identity, and a small part of the tribe of Benjamin. The latter included the territories of ten tribes (3 Kgs. 11, 31), that is, the entire Transjordanic region and the greater part of Western Palestine.

[10] Vincent, L.-H., "Jerusalem de l'Ancien Testament" (vol. I, Paris, 1954; vol. II, *ibid.*, 1956).

[11] Cf. * Garstang, J., "The Heritage of Solomon" (London, 1934); Heidet, L., in *Biblica*, 7 (1926), 83-87; Power, E., *ibid.*, 87-95; * Cross, F. M.—* Wright, G. E., in J.B.L., 75 (1956), 202-226.

CHAPTER III

HISTORICAL GEOGRAPHY

PALESTINE OF THE NEW TESTAMENT

Bibliography: * Dalman, G., "Orte und Wege Jesu" (Gütersloh, 1924);
Hoade, E., "Guide to the Holy Land" (Jerusalem, 1946).

Herod the Great [1] was the first ruler since the days of Solomon who was able to reunite all Palestine under one rule. His kingdom included nearly all of Western Palestine with the provinces of Idumea, Judea, Samaria, and Galilee, excepting Ascalon and Scythopolis. In the Transjordan he ruled Batanea (with Ulatha, Gaulanitis, Trachonitis, and Auranitis) and Perea. The adjoining regions were held by the Phoenicians, Itureans, Nabateans, and Greek colonists of the Decapolis. Upon his death in 4 B.C. his kingdom was divided into four parts: his son Archelaus became tetrarch (4 B.C.-A.D. 6) of Idumea, Judea, and Samaria;[2] his son Antipas became tetrarch (4 B.C-A.D. 39) of Galilee and Perea;[2] his son Philip became tetrarch (4 B.C.-A.D. 34) of Batanea; his sister Salome obtained the towns of Phasaelis, Archelais, Azotus, and Jamnia. The maritime plain was added to the Syrian province.

A description of the important places in these provinces will aid in the fuller understanding of the New Testament.

(1) JUDEA

(a) *Jerusalem.*[3]—After Herod the Great, with the aid of the Romans, had captured Jerusalem in 37 B.C., he embellished and fortified the city. In the eighteenth year of his reign (20/19 B.C.) he began to rebuild the temple, but this work

[1] For the boundaries of Palestine in the pre-Herodian period consult F. M. Abel in R.B., 48 (1939), 207-236, 530-548.

[2] Cf. Haefeli, L., "Samaria und Peräa bei Flavius Josephus," in B.S., 18 (Freiburg i. B., 1913).

[3] Cf. Vincent-Abel, "Jérusalem Nouvelle," II (Paris, 1914, 1922, 1926).

was not completed until shortly before the Jewish-Roman war of A.D. 66-70. He also refortified the Akra and named it Antonia [4] in honor of his Roman patron; it was probably here that Our Lord was brought before Pilate, and from this place of His condemnation that He carried the cross to the place of His execution outside the city. After the death of Christ, Herod Agrippa I (A.D. 41-44) erected a third wall (cf. Josephus, *Bella Jud.*, V, 4, 2-4), which is usually identified with the present northern wall [5] and enclosed the entire new northern suburb and the hill of Golgotha. During the Jewish rebellion, Titus laid siege to the city (A.D. 70) and after five months razed both city and temple. Only parts of the walls of the city were allowed to remain as a protection for the Roman garrison.

The following places in and near Jerusalem are familiar to us, as their names occur in the New Testament.

Golgotha, literally "skull," and "Calvaria" in Latin, does not derive its name from skulls of malefactors executed there. The spot probably bore some resemblance to a skull, and must have been bare and somewhat raised. It was here that Jesus redeemed us by His death on the cross. The place has been marked by an unbroken tradition, and the Church of the Holy Sepulchre has been erected there.[6]

On the southwestern plateau of Jerusalem is Mount Sion [7] with various Christian monuments and places of historical

[4] Cf. Vincent-Abel, "Jerusalem Nouvelle," II (Paris, 1922), 562-586; Vincent, H., "L'Antonia et le Prétoire," in R.B., 42 (1933), 83-113.

[5] Cf. Vincent H., "La troisième Enceinte de Jerusalem," in R.B., 36 (1927), 516-548, 37 (1938), 80-100, 321-339; 54 (1947), 90-126. In 1925 the remains of a fourth wall were found, parallel to the existing wall and about one-quarter of a mile north of it. Père Vincent assigns this to the period of Bar Cochba's revolt in A.D. 132. Other scholars maintain that it belongs to the time of Agrippa I. Cf. Mallon, A., "Le mur d'Agrippa," in Biblica, 8 (1927), 123-128; * Albright, W. F., "New Light on the Walls of Jerusalem in the New Testament Age," in B.A.S.O.R., 81 (1941), 6-10; Cerny, C.A., "The North Wall of Jerusalem," in C.B.Q. 3, (1941), 266 f; * Fisher, C. S., "The Third Wall of Jerusalem," in B.A.S.O.R., 83 (1941), 4-7.

[6] For the history of the Church of the Holy Sepulchre consult Vincent-Abel, "Jérusalem," II (Paris, 1914) 89-300.

[7] Cf. Rückert, K., "Die Lage des Berges Sion," in B.S., 3 (Freiburg i. B., 1898).

importance,[8] for example, the Cenacle,[9] Mary's Dormition,[10] St. Peter in Gallicantu, the House of Caiphas,[11] the House of Annas, etc.

The Pool of Bethesda (Vulg., Bethsaida), mentioned in John 5, 2, was situated just north of the site of the temple, outside the city. Such a pool with porches may be seen near the Church of St. Anne.[12]

The Mount of Olives [13] was so called from the numerous olive trees with which it was once covered. It lies a short distance to the east of the city, from which it is separated by the valley of Cedron.

Gethsemani [14] (the oil press) was a farm on the western foot of the Mount of Olives, beyond the brook of Cedron. Beside it was a garden to which Jesus withdrew before His Passion and in which He was betrayed by Judas.

On the eastern slope of the Mount of Olives lay the little villages of Bethphage (house of figs) and Bethany (home of sadness or of dates), both familiar to us from the life of Christ.

(b) *Bethlehem* [15] (house of bread).—This little town, the birthplace of David and of Christ, lies 5½ miles to the south of Jerusalem, and is situated on the northern slope of a hill

---

[8] Cf. Vincent-Abel, "Jérusalem," II (Paris, 1914), 421-481.

[9] Cf. Power, E., "Cénacle," in D.D.L.B. (Suppl.).

[10] Cf. Lagrange, M. J., in R.B., 8 (1899), 589-600.

[11] Cf. Marchet, X., "La Véritable Emplacement du Palais de Caïphe et l'Eglise Saint-Pierre" (Paris, 1927); Power, E., "Eglise Saint-Pierre et Maison de Caïphe," in D.D.L.B. (Suppl); *idem, in Biblica*, 9 (1928), 167-186, 10 (1929), 275-303, 394-416, 12 (1931), 411-446.

[12] Cf. Steinmueller, J. E.-Sullivan, K., art., "Bethsaida," and "Probatica," in C.B.E.N.T.

[13] For the early Christian sanctuaries of the Eleona and of the Ascension on the Mount of Olives consult Vincent-Abel, "Jérusalem," II (Paris, 1914), 337-419; Pirot, L., "Ascension," in D.D.L.B. (Suppl.).

[14] Cf. Vincent-Abel, "Jérusalem," II (Paris, 1914), 301-337); Power, E., "Gethsemani," in D.D.L.B. (Suppl.).

[15] Cf. Vincent-Abel, "Bethleheém, La Sanctuaire de la Nativité" (Paris 1914); Vincent, H., "Bethleém, La Sanctuaire de la Nativité." in R.B. 45 (1936), 544-574, 46 (1937), 93-121; Fonck, L., "De Antro Nativitatis Bethlehemitico," in V.D., 12 (1932), 11-15, 48-53; Barrois, A., "Bethleém," in D.D.L.B. (Suppl.).

running east and west. The Grotto and Basilica of the Nativity lie to the east, at a little distance from the town.

(c) *Jericho.*—This town is approximately 18 miles to the east of Jerusalem, and some distance from the Jordan. The old Canaanite and Israelitish town was in ruins at the time of Our Lord, but in its stead there stood a little to the south of the old town the new Jericho of Herod the Great.[16]

(d) *Emmaus.*[17]—This town is described in Luke 24, 13 (according to the best MSS.) as being 60 stadia (that is, about 7 miles) from Jerusalem, and is identified by some scholars with El-Kubeibeh. Others, following Eusebius and St. Jerome, prefer Nicopolis and find support in *Codex Sinaiticus* and a small number of Greek and Latin MSS. which read, "one hundred and sixty stadia."

(e) *Lydda.*—This town, now known as Ludd, is mentioned in Acts 9, 32 as the seat of an early Christian community. It was here that St. Peter healed Æneas.

(f) *Arimathea.*[18]—This was the home of the councillor Joseph (Matt. 27, 57). It was situated near Lydda. Some scholars identify it with the present town of Ramle, others with Remphtis or Rentis near the northern border of Judea.

(g) *Jaffa.*—This town, which is also called Joppa, was the seat of an early Christian community. It was here that Tabitha lived (Acts 9, 36), that Peter resided for a time at the house of Simon a tanner (Acts 9, 43), where, after his vision, the Prince of the Apostles received the messengers of Cornelius (Acts 10, 17 ff).

(2) SAMARIA

The central portion of Western Palestine derives its name

---

[16] Szczepánski, L., "Historia urbis Jericho a IV sæc. a Ch. ad nostra tempora," in V.D., 3 (1923), 121-128; Ketter, P., "Zur Lokalisierung der Blindheilung bei Jericho." in *Biblica* 15 (1934), 411-418; Steinmueller, J. E.-Sullivan, K., art. "Jericho," in C.B.E.N.T.

[17] Cf. Abel, F. M., "La distance de Jérusalem à Emmaus." in R.B., 35 (1925), 347-367; Pirot, L., "Emmaus," in D.D.L.B. (Suppl.).

[18] Cf. Heidet, L., "Arimathie," in D.D.L.B. (Suppl.).

from the town that was once the capital of the northern kingdom.   Three Samaritan towns merit some notice.

Samaria was rebuilt and refortified by Herod the Great, and called Sebaste in honor of the Emperor Augustus.   Christianity was introduced here by Philip the deacon (Acts 8, 5), and both Peter and John went there to confer the Sacrament of Confirmation (Acts 8, 14-17).

Sichar, the present Askar, is only mentioned in John 4, 5. It was situated at the foot of Mount Ebal and close to Sichem (Nabulus) and the Well of Jacob.

Cæsarea was situated on the west coast, and was therefore known as Maritima, to distinguish it from Cæsarea Philippi. It was built by Herod the Great, and raised by Emperor Augustus to the dignity of an imperial city.   In Roman times the procurator of the province generally lived here.   It was here that St. Peter baptized Cornelius and his household (Acts 10, 24 ff), and St. Paul was a prisoner here for two years (Acts 23, 33 ff).   After the destruction of Jerusalem in A.D. 70, Cæsarea was regarded as the capital and very early became a bishop's see.

(3) GALILEE

In the north of Canaan the Israelites lived in the midst of pagans, and hence this part of the country received the name *gelil haggojim* (the heathen district).   In Greek the territory was known as Γαλιλαία τῶν ἐθνῶν, or simply Γαλιλαία (Isa. 8, 23; I Mac. 5, 15; Matt. 4, 15).   Many of its towns figure prominently in the Biblical narrative.

(a) Nazareth [19] (from nezer, shoot, flower), the town of the hidden life of Jesus (Luke 2, 51), is mentioned neither in the Old Testament, nor in Josephus, nor in the Talmud.   It lies on a hill in southern Galilee, about 20 miles southwest of Tiberias and 87 miles north of Jerusalem.   Here lived our Blessed Mother (Luke 1, 26) and St. Joseph (Luke 2, 4), and

---

[19] Cf. * Dalman, G., "Orte und Wege Jesu," 61-88; Semkowski, L., in V.D., 6 (1926), 89-96, 185-190.

here Jesus preached at the beginning of His public ministry (Luke 4, 16 ff).

(b) The small village of Naim lay on the southern boundary of Galilee at the foot of Mount Tabor. It is famed as the scene of the raising of the widow's son (Luke 7, 11-15).

(c) Cana, the home of Nathanael (John 21, 2), the scene of Christ's miracle of changing water into wine (John 2, 1 ff) and of the healing of the royal official's son (John 4, 46 ff), is commonly identified with the present Kafr Kenna.

(d) Tiberias, on the southwest shore of the lake, was founded by Herod Antipas in A.D. 18 in honor of the Emperor Tiberius and replaced Sepphoris as the capital of Galilee. As the city was established over a burial place, very few Jews could be persuaded to live in the place, and it seems most likely that Jesus never visited it. The city is mentioned only once in the New Testament (John 6, 23).

(e) Not far away, and also on the west coast of the lake, was the village of Magdala, which is thought to have been the birthplace of Mary Magdalene.

(f) Capharnaum [20] was on the northwest shore of the lake, and probably is to be identified with the ruins at Tell-Hum. Although the town is not mentioned in the Old Testament, yet it is frequently referred to in the life of Our Lord and is called "his town" (Matt. 9, 1). It lay on the main caravan route leading from the maritime plain to Damascus and had a custom-house (Matt. 9, 9). Here St. Peter lived with his mother-in-law (Matt. 8, 14). This town was also a witness of many miracles that Jesus performed and in its synagogue He gave the eucharistic promise (John 6, 24 ff).

(4) The Country East of the Jordan

In the tetrarchy of Philip are two towns best known to us from the life of Christ.

[20] Cf. Dalman, "Orte und Wege Jesu," 146-163; Meistermann, B., "Capharnaüm et Bethsaïde" (Paris, 1921); Orfali, G., "Capharnaum et ses Ruines" (Paris, 1922); Abel, F. M., "Capharnaum," in D.D.L.B. (Suppl.).

Bethsaida-Julias,[21] situated at the head of Lake Tiberias, was built by Philip about A.D. 3. It was named in honor of Julia, the daughter of Emperor Augustus. The town was the home of the Apostles Peter, Andrew, and Philip (John 1, 44), the witness of many miracles (cf. Mark 8, 22), and the scene of the multiplication of the loaves and fishes (Mark 6, 45).

Cæsarea Philippi, at the foot of Mount Hermon, was originally called Paneas. Herod the Great received the town and its district from Emperor Augustus and erected a temple there in honor of his Roman patron. Philip, Herod's son, enlarged and embellished the town and gave it the name Cæsarea Philippi, to distinguish it from Cæsarea Maritima. It was in this region that Christ promised the primacy to Peter after the Apostle's profession of faith in His divinity (Matt. 16, 13 ff).

Outside of the jurisdiction of Philip was the Decapolis,[22] which consisted of ten towns bearing the stamp of Græco-Roman civilization: Scythopolis (Bethsan), Pella, Gadara, Hippos, Dium, Gerasa, Philadelphia (Rabbath Ammon), Raphana, Kanatha, and Damascus. All of these, excepting Scythopolis, lay in the region east of the Jordan. They were independent and had the right to mint coins, but had to pay taxes to Rome and levy troops. For their mutual welfare they were organized into a confederacy. The term Decapolis occurs three times in the New Testament (Matt. 4, 25; Mark 5, 20; 7, 31).

[21] Cf. Steinmueller, J. E.-Sullivan, K., art., "Bethsaida-Julias," in C.B.E.N.T.

[22] Cf. * Schürer, E., "Geschichte des Jüdischen Volkes im Zeitalter Jesu Christi," II (4th ed., Leipzig, 1907), 148-193.

APPENDIX

APPENDIX 1

I. THE MURATORIAN FRAGMENT
(SECOND CENTURY)

1 . . . quibus tamen interfuit et ita posuit. Ter-
tium Evangelii librum secundum Lucam.
Lucas iste medicus, post ascensum Christi,
cum eum Paulus quasi itineris studiosum
[5] secum adsumpsisset, nomine suo
ex opinione conscripsit, Dominum tamen nec ipse
vidit in carne, et ideo, prout assequi potuit,
ita et a nativitate Iohannis incipit dicere.

2 Quartum Evangeliorum Iohannes ex discipulis.
[10] Cohortantibus condiscipulis et episcopis suis,
dixit: « Conieiunate mihi hodie triduo et quid
cuique fuerit revelatum, alterutrum
nobis enarremus ». Eadem nocte revelatum Andreae ex Apostolis, ut recognos-
[15] centibus cunctis Iohannes suo nomine
cuncta describeret. Et ideo, licet varia singulis Evangeliorum libris principia
doceantur, nihil tamen differt creden-
tium fidei, cum uno ac principali spiritu de-
[20] clarata sint in omnibus omnia de nativitate, de passione, de resurrectione,
de conversatione cum discipulis suis
ac de gemino eius adventu,
primo in humilitate despecto, quod fu-
[25] it, secundo in potestate regali prae-
claro, quod futurum est. Quid ergo
mirum, si Iohannes tam constanter
singula etiam in epistulis suis proferat
dicens in semetipsum: *Quae vidimus oculis*

---

[1] The unbracketed marginal numbers refer to those given in the *Enchiridion Biblicum,* the official collection of biblical documents issued by the Pontifical Biblical Commission. The numbers given in square brackets refer to the lines of the Muratorian Fragment. The captions and subcaptions in brackets are given for a better understanding of the text and are not part of the original Encyclical.

[30] *nostris et auribus audivimus et manus*
nostrae palpaverunt, haec scripsimus vobis.
Sic enim non solum visorem se et auditorem,
sed et scriptorem omnium mirabilium Domini per ordinem profitetur. Acta autem omnium Apostolorum   3
[35] sub uno libro scripta sunt. Lucas optimo Theophi-
lo comprendit, quae sub praesentia eius singula
gerebantur, sicuti et semota passione Petri
evidenter declarat, sed et profectione Pauli ab Urbe ad Spaniam proficiscentis. Epistulae autem   4
[40] Pauli quae a quo loco vel qua ex causa directae
sint, volentibus intellegere ipsae declarant.
Primum omnium Corinthiis schismae haereses in-
terdicens, deinceps Galatis circumcisionem,
Romanis autem ordinem Scripturarum, sed et
[45] principium earum esse Christum intimans
prolixius scripsit. De quibus singulis neces-
se est a nobis disputari, cum ipse beatus
Apostolus Paulus sequens predecessoris sui
Iohannis ordinem non nisi nominatim septem
[50] ecclesiis scribat, ordine tali: ad Corinthios
prima, ad Ephesios secunda, ad Philippenses ter-
tia, ad Colossenses quarta, ad Galatas quinta, ad Thessalonicenses sexta, ad Romanos
septima. Verum Corinthiis et Thessalonicen-
[55] sibus licet pro correptione iteretur, una
tamen per omnem orbem terrae Ecclesia
diffusa esse dinoscitur; et Iohannes enim in A-
pocalypsi licet septem ecclesiis scribat,
tamen omnibus dicit. Verum ad Philemonem una
[60] et ad Titum una et ad Timotheum duae pro affec-
tu et dilectione, in honore tamen Ecclesiae ca-
tholicae, in ordinatione ecclesiasticae
disciplinae sanctificatae sunt. Fertur etiam ad   5
Laodicenses, alia ad Alexandrinos Pauli no-
[65] mine finctae ad haeresem Marcionis et alia plu-
ra, quae in catholicam Ecclesiam recipi non
potest; fel enim cum melle misceri non con-
gruit. Epistula sane Iudae et superscripti   6
Iohannis duae in catholica habentur et Sapi-
[70] entia ab amicis Solomonis in honorem ipsius
scripta. Apocalypses etiam Iohannis et Petri tantum recipimus, quam quidam ex nostris legi in Ecclesia nolunt. Pastorem vero
nuperrime temporibus nostris in urbe   7

[75] Roma Hermas conscripsit sedente cathedra urbis Romae ecclesiae Pio episcopo fratre
eius; et ideo legi eum quidem oportet, se pu-
blicare vero in Ecclesia populo neque inter
prophetas completo numero, neque inter
[80] Apostolos in fine temporum potest.
Arsinoi autem seu Valentini vel Miltiadis
nihil in totum recipimus; qui etiam novum
psalmorum librum Marcioni conscripse-
runt una cum Basilide Asiano Cataphry-
[85] gum constitutore.

II. OFFICIAL DECISIONS AND DECREES

(1) The Decree "Sacrosancta" of the Council of Trent
(Fourth Session, April 8, 1546)

The Sacred and Holy, Œcumenical, and General Synod of Trent **57**
. . . keeping this always in view, that errors being removed, the
purity itself of the Gospel be preserved in the Church . . . and seeing clearly that this truth . . . is contained in the written books
. . .; following the examples of the orthodox Fathers receives and
venerates with an equal feeling of piety and reverence all the books
of the Old and of the New Testament, seeing that God is the Author
of both. . . .

And it has thought it meet that a list of the sacred books be inserted in this Decree, lest a doubt may arise in anyone's mind, which
are the books that are received by this Synod.

They are as set down here below: *Of the Old Testament;* The five **58**
books of Moses, i.e., Genesis, Exodus, Leviticus, Numbers, Deuteron-
omy; Josue, Judges, Ruth, four Books of Kings, two of Paralipomenon, the first Book of Esdras, and the second which is entitled
Nehemias, Tobias, Judith, Esther, Job, the Davidic Psalter of one
hundred and fifty Psalms, the Proverbs, Ecclesiastes, the Canticle of
Canticles, Wisdom, Ecclesiasticus, Isaias, Jeremias with Baruch,
Ezechiel, Daniel; the twelve minor prophets, i.e., Osee, Joel, Amos,
Abdias, Jonas, Micheas, Nahum, Habacuc, Sophonias, Aggeus,
Zacharias, Malachias; two Books of the Machabees, the first and the
second.

Of the New Testament: The four Gospels, according to Matthew, **59**
Mark, Luke, and John; the Acts of the Apostles written by Luke the
Evangelist; fourteen Epistles of Paul the Apostle: to the Romans,
two to the Corinthians, to the Galatians, to the Ephesians, to the
Philippians, to the Colossians, two to the Thessalonians, two to Timothy, to Titus, to Philemon, to the Hebrews; two Epistles of Peter
the Apostle; three Epistles of John the Apostle; one Epistle of James
the Apostle; one Epistle of Jude the Apostle, and the Apocalypse of
John the Apostle.

But if anyone does not receive, as sacred and canonical, the said **60**
books entire with all their parts, and as they have been used to be
read in the Catholic Church and as they are contained in the Old
Latin Vulgate edition . . . let him be anathema.

(2) The Decree "Insuper" of the Council of Trent
(Fourth Session, April 8, 1546)

61   Besides, the same Sacred and Holy Synod, considering that it would be of no small advantage to the Church of God if it were clearly made known which of all the Latin editions of the Sacred Books in circulation is to be held as authentic, hereby declares and enacts that the same well-known Old Latin Vulgate edition, which has been approved by the long use of so many centuries in the Church, is to be held as authentic in public readings, disputations, preachings, and expositions, and that no one shall dare or presume to reject it under any pretense whatever.

62   Moreover, in order to restrain turbulent spirits, the Council declares that no one, relying on his own skill and distorting the sense of Scripture to suit himself, in matters of faith and morals, belonging to the building up of Christian doctrine, shall presume to interpret Sacred Scripture contrary to the sense which Holy Mother Church—to whom it belongs to judge of the true sense and interpretation of Holy Scripture—both held and continues to hold; nor (shall any one dare to interpret) Sacred Scripture contrary to the unanimous consent of the Fathers, even if interpretations of this kind are never published.

(3) Encyclical Letter of Leo XIII, "Providentissimus Deus" (November 18, 1893)

[THE TEACHING OF THE CHURCH]

The God of all providence, who in the adorable designs of His love **81** at first elevated the human race to the participation of the divine nature, and afterwards delivered it from universal guilt and ruin, restoring it to its primitive dignity, has, in consequence, bestowed upon man a splendid gift and safeguard—making known to him, by supernatural means, the hidden mysteries of His divinity, His wisdom and His mercy. For although in divine revelation there are contained some things which are not beyond the reach of unassisted reason, and which are made the objects of such revelation in order "that all may come to know them with facility, certainty, and safety from error, yet not on this account can supernatural revelation be said to be absolutely necessary; it is only necessary because God has ordained man to a supernatural end." [1] This supernatural revelation, according to the belief of the universal Church, is contained both in unwritten tradition and in written books, which are, therefore, called sacred and canonical because, "being written under the inspiration of the Holy Spirit, they have God for their author, and as such have been delivered to the Church." [2] This belief has been perpetually held and professed by the Church in regard to the Books of both Testaments; and there are well-known documents of the gravest kind, coming down to us from the earliest times, which proclaim that God, who spoke first by the prophets, then by His own mouth, and lastly by the apostles, composed also the canonical Scriptures,[3] and that these are His own oracles and words [4]—a Letter written by our Heavenly Father and transmitted by the sacred writers to the human race in its pilgrimage so far from its heavenly country.[5] If, then, such and so great is the excellence and dignity of the Scriptures, that

---

[1] Conc. Vat., sess. iii, cap. ii, *de revel.*
[2] *Ibid.*
[3] S. Aug., *De civ. Dei,* xi, 3.
[4] S. Clem. Rom., *I ad Cor.,* 45; S. Polycarp, *Ad Phil.,* 7; S. Iren., *Contra hær.,* ii, 28, 2.
[5] S. Chrys., *In Gen. hom.,* 2, 2; S. Aug., *In Ps. xxx,* serm. 2, 1; S. Greg. M., *Ad Theo. ep.,* iv, 31.

God Himself has composed them, and that they treat of God's marvelous mysteries, counsels and works, it follows that the branch of sacred theology which is concerned with the defense and elucidation of these divine books must be excellent and useful in the highest degree.

[The Intention of the Holy Father]

82   Now We, who by the help of God, and not without fruit, have by frequent Letters and exhortation endeavored to promote other branches of study which seem capable of advancing the glory of God and contributing to the salvation of souls, have for a long time cherished the desire to give an impulse to the noble science of Holy Scripture, and to impart to Scripture study a direction suitable to the needs of the present day. The solicitude of the apostolic office naturally urges, and even compels us, not only to desire that this grand source of Catholic revelation should be made safely and abundantly accessible to the flock of Jesus Christ, but also not to suffer any attempt to defile or corrupt it, either on the part of those who impiously or openly assail the Scriptures, or of those who are led astray into fallacious and imprudent novelties.

83   We are not ignorant, indeed, Venerable Brethren, that there are not a few Catholics, men of talent and learning, who do devote themselves with ardor to the defense of the sacred writings and to making them known and better understood. But whilst giving to these the commendation they deserve, We cannot but earnestly exhort others also, from whose skill and piety and learning We have a right to expect good results, to give themselves to the same most praiseworthy work. It is Our wish and fervent desire to see an increase in the number of the approved and persevering laborers in the cause of Holy Scripture; and more especially that those whom divine grace has called to Holy Orders should, day by day, as their state demands, display greater diligence and industry in reading, meditating, and explaining it.

[Benefit of Bible Study]

[A. *In General*]

84   Among the reasons for which the Holy Scripture is so worthy of commendation—in addition to its own excellence and to the homage which we owe to God's Word—the chief of all is, the innumerable benefits of which it is the source, according to the infallible testimony of the Holy Spirit Himself, who says: *All Scripture inspired of God is profitable to teach, to reprove, to correct, to instruct in justice: that the man of God may be perfect, furnished to every good work.*[1]

---

[1] 2 Tim., 3, 16. 17.

That such was the purpose of God in giving the Scripture to men is shown by the example of Christ our Lord and of His apostles. For He Himself who "obtained authority by miracles, merited belief by authority, and by belief drew to himself the multitude" [1] was accustomed, in the exercise of His divine mission, to appeal to the Scriptures. He uses them at times to prove that He is sent by God, and is God Himself. From them He cites instructions for His disciples and confirmation of His doctrine. He vindicates them from the calumnies of objectors; He quotes them against Sadducees and Pharisees and retorts from them upon Satan himself when he dares to tempt Him. At the close of His life His utterances are from the Holy Scripture, and it is the Scripture that He expounds to His disciples after His resurrection, until He ascends to the glory of His Father.

Faithful to His precepts, the apostles, although He Himself granted **85** *signs and wonders to be done by their hands,*[2] nevertheless used with the greatest effect the sacred writings, in order to persuade the nations everywhere of the wisdom of Christianity, to conquer the obstinacy of the Jews, and to suppress the outbreak of heresy. This is plainly seen in their discourses, especially in those of St. Peter; these were often little less than a series of citations from the Old Testament making in the strongest manner for the new dispensation. We find the same things in the Gospels of St. Matthew and St. John and in the Catholic Epistles; and, most remarkable of all, in the words of him who "boasts that he learned the law at the feet of Gamaliel, in order that, being armed with spiritual weapons, he might afterwards say with confidence, 'the arms of our warfare are not carnal but mighty unto God.' " [3]

Let all, therefore, especially the novices of the ecclesiastical army, **86** understand how deeply the sacred books should be esteemed, and with what eagerness and reverence they should approach this great arsenal of heavenly arms. For those whose duty it is to handle Catholic doctrine before the learned or the unlearned will nowhere find more ample matter or more abundant exhortation, whether on the subject of God, the supreme Good and the all-perfect Being, or the works which display His glory and His love. Nowhere is there anything more full or more express on the subject of the Saviour of the world than is to be found in the whole range of the Bible. As St. Jerome says, *to be ignorant of the Scripture is not to know Christ.*[4] In its pages His Image stands out, living and breathing; diffusing everywhere around consolation in trouble, encouragement

---

[1] S. Aug., *De util. cred.,* xiv, 32.
[2] Acts 14, 3.
[3] St. Hier., *De stud. Script. ad Paulin. ep. liii,* 3.
[4] *In Isaiam, Prol.*

to virtue, and attraction to the love of God. And as to the Church, her institutions, her nature, her office and her gifts, we find in Holy Scripture so many references and so many ready and convincing arguments that, as St. Jerome again most truly says, "A man who is well grounded in the testimonies of the Scripture is the bulwark of the Church." [1] And if we come to morality and discipline, an apostolic man finds in the sacred writings abundant and excellent assistance; most holy precepts, gentle and strong exhortation, splendid examples of every virtue, and finally the promise of eternal reward and the threat of eternal punishment, uttered in terms of solemn import, in God's name and in God's own words.

[B. *For the Pulpit Orator*]

87   And it is this peculiar and singular power of Holy Scripture, arising from the inspiration of the Holy Spirit, which gives authority to the sacred orator, fills him with apostolic liberty of speech, and communicates force and power to his eloquence. For those who infuse into their efforts the spirit and strength of the Word of God speak *not in word only, but in power also, and in the Holy Spirit, and in much fullness.*[2] Hence, those preachers are foolish and improvident who, in speaking of religion and proclaiming the things of God, use no words but those of human science and human prudence, trusting to their own reasonings rather than to those of God. Their discourses may be brilliant and fine, but they must be feeble and they must be cold, for they are without the fire of the utterance of God [3] and they must fall far short of that mighty power which the speech of God possesses: *for the Word of God is living and effectual, and more piercing than any two-edged sword; and reaching unto the division of the soul and the spirit.*[4] But, indeed, those who have a right to speak are agreed that there is in the Holy Scripture an eloquence that is wonderfully varied and rich and worthy of great themes. This St. Augustine thoroughly understood and has abundantly set forth.[5] This, also, is confirmed by the best preachers of all ages, who have gratefully acknowledged that they owed their repute chiefly to the assiduous use of the Bible, and to devout meditation on its pages.

88   The Holy Fathers well knew all this by practical experience, and they never cease to extol the sacred Scripture and its fruits. In innumerable passages of their writings we find them applying to it such phrases as *an inexhaustible treasury of heavenly doctrine,*[6] *or an*

---

[1] *In Isaiam*, 54, 12.   [3] Jer. 23. 29.
[2] 1 Thess. 1, 5.   [4] Hebr. 4, 12.
[5] *De doctr. chr.*, iv, 6, 7.
[6] S. Chrys., *In Gen.*, hom. xxi, 2; hom. lx, 3; S. Aug., *De Disc. Christ.*, ii.

overflowing fountain of salvation,[1] or putting it before us as fertile pastures and beautiful gardens in which the flock of the Lord is marvelously refreshed and delighted.[2] Let us listen to the words of St. Jerome, in his Epistle to Nepotian: "Often read the divine Scriptures; yea, let holy reading be always in thy hand; study that which thou thyself must preach. . . . Let the speech of the priest be ever seasoned with Scriptural reading."[3] St. Gregory the Great, than whom no one has more admirably described the pastoral office, writes in the same sense. "Those," he says, "who are zealous in the work of preaching must never cease the study of the written Word of God."[4]

St. Augustine, however, warns us that "vainly does the preacher **89** utter the Word of God exteriorly unless he listens to it interiorly";[5] and St. Gregory instructs sacred orators "first to find in Holy Scripture the knowledge of themselves, and then carry it to others, lest in reproving others they forget themselves."[6] Admonitions such as these had, indeed, been uttered long before by the apostolic voice which had learned its lesson from Christ Himself, who "began to do and teach." It was not to Timothy alone, but to the whole order of the clergy, that the command was addressed: *Take heed to thyself and to doctrine; be earnest in them. For in doing this thou shalt both save thyself and them that hear thee.*[7] For the saving and for the perfection of ourselves and of others there is at hand the very best of help in the Holy Scriptures, as the Book of Psalms, among others, so constantly insists; but those only will find it who bring to this divine reading not only docility and attention but also piety and an innocent life. For the Sacred Scripture is not like other books. Dictated by the Holy Spirit, it contains things of the deepest importance, which in many instances are most difficult and obscure. To understand and explain such things there is always required the "coming"[8] of the same Holy Spirit; that is to say, His light and His grace; and these, as the royal psalmist so frequently insists, are to be sought by humble prayer and guarded by holiness of life.

[THE SOLICITUDE OF THE CHURCH]

It is in this that the watchful eye of the Church shines forth conspicuously. By admirable laws and regulations, she has shown herself solicitous that "the celestial treasure of the sacred books, so bountifully bestowed upon man by the Holy Spirit, should not lie

---

[1] S. Athan., *Ep. fest.*, xxxix.
[2] S. Aug., *Serm. xxvi*, 24; S. Ambr., *In Ps. cxviii. serm.* xix, 2.
[3] S. Hier., *De vita cleric. ad Nepot.*
[4] S. Greg. M., *Regul. past.*, ii, 11 (al. 22); *Moral.*, xvii, 26 (al. 14).
[5] S. Aug., *Serm. clxxix*. 1.   [7] I Tim. 4, 16.
[6] S. Greg. M., *Regul. past.*, iii, 24 (al. 14).   [8] S. Hier., *In Mic.*, i, 10.

neglected."[1] She has prescribed that a considerable portion of them shall be read and piously reflected upon by all her ministers in the daily office of the sacred psalmody. She has ordered that in cathedral churches, in monasteries, and in other convents in which study can conveniently be pursued, they shall be expounded and interpreted by capable men; and she has strictly commanded that her children shall be fed with the saving words of the Gospel at least on Sundays and solemn feasts.[2]   Moreover, it is owing to the wisdom and exertions of the Church that there has always been continued, from century to century, that cultivation of Holy Scripture which has been so remarkable and has borne such ample fruit.

[A. *In the Early Times*]

91   And here, in order to strengthen Our teaching and Our exhortations, it is well to recall how, from the beginning of Christianity, all who have been renowned for holiness of life and sacred learning have given their deep and constant attention to Holy Scripture. If we consider the immediate disciples of the apostles, St. Clement of Rome, St. Ignatius of Antioch, St. Polycarp,—or the apologists, such as St. Justin and St. Irenæus,—We find that in their letters and books, whether in defense of the Catholic faith or in its commendation, they drew faith, strength, and unction from the Word of God. When there arose, in various sees, catechetical and theological schools, of which the most celebrated were those of Alexandria and of Antioch, there was little taught in those schools but what was contained in the reading, the interpretation, and the defense of the divine written word. From them came forth numbers of Fathers and writers whose laborious studies and admirable writings have justly merited for the three following centuries the appellation of the golden age of biblical exegesis.

92   In the Eastern Church the greatest name of all is Origen—a man remarkable alike for penetration of genius and persevering labor; from whose numerous works and his great *Hexapla* almost all have drawn who came after him. Others who have widened the field of this science may also be named as especially eminent; thus, Alexandria could boast of St. Clement and St. Cyril; Palestine, of Eusebius and the other St. Cyril; Cappadocia, of St. Basil the Great and the two Gregories, of Nazianzus and Nyssa; Antioch, of St. John Chrysostom, in whom the science of Scripture was rivaled by the splendor of his eloquence.

93   In the Western Church there are as many names as great: Tertullian, St. Cyprian, St. Hilary, St. Ambrose, St. Leo the Great, St.

---

[1] Conc. Trid. sess. v, *decret. de reform.*, 1.   [2] *Ibid.*, 1, 2.

Gregory the Great; most famous of all, St. Augustine and St. Jerome, of whom the former was so marvelously acute in penetrating the sense of God's Word and so fertile in the use that he made of it for the promotion of the Catholic truth, and the latter has received from the Church, by reason of his pre-eminent knowledge of Scripture and his labors in promoting its use, the name of the "great Doctor." [1]

[B. *In the Middle Ages*]

From this period down to the eleventh century, although biblical 94 studies did not flourish with the same vigor and the same fruitfulness as before, yet they did flourish, and principally by the instrumentality of the clergy. It was their care and solicitude that selected the best and most useful things that the ancients had left, arranged them in order, and published them with additions of their own—as did St. Isidore of Seville, Venerable Bede, and Alcuin, among the most prominent; it was they who illustrated the sacred pages with "glosses" or short commentaries, as we see in Walafrid Strabo and St. Anselm of Laon, or expended fresh labor in securing their integrity, as did St. Peter Damian and Blessed Lanfranc.

In the twelfth century many took up, with great success, the alle- 95 gorical exposition of Scripture. In this kind, St. Bernard is pre-eminent; and his writings, it may be said, are Scripture all through.

With the age of the scholastics came fresh and welcome progress 96 in the study of the Bible. That the scholastics were solicitous about the genuineness of the Latin version is evident from the *Correctoria Biblica*, or list of emendations, which they have left. But they expended their labors and industry chiefly on interpretation and explanation. To them we owe the accurate and clear distinction, such as had not been given before, of the various senses of the sacred words; the assignment of the value of each "sense" in theology; the division of books into parts, and the summaries of the various parts; the investigation of the objects of the writers; the demonstration of the connection of sentence with sentence, and clause with clause; all of which is calculated to throw much light on the more obscure passages of the sacred volume. The valuable work of the scholastics in Holy Scripture is seen in their theological treatises and in their Scripture commentaries; and in this respect the greatest name among them all is St. Thomas Aquinas.

When Our predecessor, Clement V, established chairs of Oriental 97 literature in the Roman College and in the principal universities of Europe, Catholics began to make more accurate investigation on the original text of the Bible as well as on the Latin version. The revival

---

[1] See the Collect on his feast, September 30.

amongst us of Greek learning, and, much more, the happy invention
of the art of printing, gave a strong impetus to biblical studies. In a
brief space of time, innumerable editions, especially of the Vulgate,
poured from the press and were diffused throughout the Catholic
world; so honored and loved was Holy Scripture during that very
period against which the enemies of the Church direct their calumnies.

[C. *In Modern Times*]

98   Nor must we forget how many learned men there were, chiefly
among the religious orders, who did excellent work for the Bible between the Council of Vienne and that of Trent; men who, by the
employment of modern means and appliances, and by the tribute of
their own genius and learning, not only added to the rich store of
ancient times but prepared the way for the succeeding century, the
century which followed the Council of Trent, when it almost seemed
that the great age of the Fathers had returned. For it is well known,
and We recall it with pleasure, that Our predecessors, from Pius IV
to Clement VIII, caused to be prepared the celebrated editions of the
Vulgate and the Septuagint, which, having been published by the
command and authority of Sixtus V, and of the same Clement, are
now in common use. At this time, moreover, were carefully brought
out various other ancient versions of the Bible, and the Polyglots of
Antwerp and of Paris, most important for the investigation of the
true meaning of the text; nor is there any one book of either Testament which did not find more than one expositor, nor any grave question which did not profitably exercise the ability of many inquirers,
among whom there are not a few—more especially of those who made
most use of the Fathers—who have acquired great reputation. From
that time downwards the labor and solicitude of Catholics have never
been wanting; for, as time went on, eminent scholars have carried on
biblical studies with success, and have defended Holy Scripture
against *rationalism* with the same weapons of philology and kindred
sciences with which it had been attacked.

99   The calm and fair consideration of what has been said will clearly
show that the Church has never failed in taking due measures to
bring the Scriptures within reach of her children, and that she has
ever held fast and exercised profitably that guardianship conferred
upon her by Almighty God for the protection and glory of His Holy
Word; so that she has never required, nor does she now require, any
stimulation from without.

[RULES FOR THE PRESENT TIME]

We must now, Venerable Brethren, as Our purpose demands, im- **100** part to you such counsels as seem best suited for carrying on success- fully the study of biblical science.

But first it must be clearly understood whom we have to oppose and contend against, and what are their tactics and their arms. In earlier times the contest was chiefly with those who, relying on pri- vate judgment and repudiating the divine traditions and teaching office of the Church, held the Scriptures to be the one source of reve- lation and the final appeal in matters of faith. Now we have to meet the rationalists, true children and inheritors of the older heretics, who, trusting in their turn to their own way of thinking, have re- jected even the scraps and remnants of Christian belief which had been handed down to them. They deny that there is any such thing as revelation or inspiration, or Holy Scripture at all; they see, in- stead, only the forgeries and falsehoods of men; they set down the Scripture narratives as stupid fables and lying stories: the prophecies and oracles of God are to them either predictions made up after the event or forecasts formed by the light of nature; the miracles and wonders of God's power are not what they are said to be, but the startling effects of natural law, or else mere tricks and myths; and the apostolic Gospels and writings are not the work of the Apostles at all.

These detestable errors, whereby they think they destroy the truth **101** of the divine books, are obtruded on the world as the peremptory pronouncements of a newly invented *free science;* a science, however, which is so far from final that they are perpetually modifying and supplementing it. And there are some of them who, notwithstanding their impious opinions and utterances about God, and Christ, the Gospels and the rest of Holy Scripture, would fain be considered both theologians and Christians and men of the Gospel, and who at- tempt to disguise by such honorable names their rashness and their pride. To them we must add not a few professors of other sciences who approve their views and give them assistance, and are urged to attack the Bible by a similar intolerance of revelation. And it is de- plorable to see these attacks growing every day more numerous and more severe. It is sometimes men of learning and judgment who are assailed; but these have little difficulty in defending themselves from evil consequences. The efforts and arts of the enemy are chiefly di- rected against the more ignorant masses of the people. They diffuse their deadly poison by means of books, pamphlets, and newspapers; they spread it by addresses and by conversation; they are found everywhere; and they are in possession of numerous schools, taken by violence from the Church, in which, by ridicule and scurrilous jesting, they pervert the credulous and unformed minds of the young to the contempt of Holy Scripture.

102   Should not these things, Venerable Brethren, stir up and set on fire the heart of every pastor, so that to this *knowledge, falsely so-called*,[1] may be opposed the ancient and true science which the Church, through the apostles, has received from Christ, and that Holy Scripture may find the champions that are needed in so momentous a battle?

103   Let our first care, then, be to see that in seminaries and academical institutions the study of Holy Scripture is placed on such a footing as its own importance and the circumstances of the time demand. With this view, the first thing which requires attention is the wise choice of professors. Teachers of sacred Scripture are not to be appointed at haphazard out of the crowd; but they must be men whose character and fitness are proved by their love of, and their long familiarity with, the Bible, and by suitable learning and study.

It is a matter of equal importance to provide in time for a continuous succession of such teachers; and it will be well, wherever this can be done, to select young men of good promise who have successfully accomplished their theological course, and to set them apart exclusively for Holy Scripture, affording them facilities for full and complete studies. Professors thus chosen and thus prepared may enter with confidence on the task that is appointed for them; and that they may carry out their work well and profitably, let them take heed to the instructions We now proceed to give.

[INTRODUCTION]

104   At the commencement of a course of Holy Scripture, let the professor strive earnestly to form the judgment of the young beginners so as to train them equally to defend the sacred writings and to penetrate their meaning. This is the object of the treatise which is called "Introduction." Here the student is taught how to prove the integrity and authority of the Bible, how to investigate and ascertain its true sense, and how to meet and refute objections. It is needless to insist upon the importance of making these preliminary studies in an orderly and thorough fashion, with the accompaniment and assistance of theology; for the whole subsequent course must rest on the foundation thus laid and make use of the light thus acquired.

---

[1] 1 Tim. 4, 20.

[INTERPRETATION]

Next, the teacher will turn his attention to that more fruitful **105** division of Scripture science which has to do with interpretation, wherein is imparted the method of using the Word of God for the advantage of religion and piety. We recognize, without hesitation, that neither the extent of the matter nor the time at disposal allows each single book of the Bible to be separately gone through. But the teaching should result in a definite and ascertained method of interpretation—and, therefore, the professor should equally avoid the mistake of giving a mere taste of every book, and of dwelling at too great a length on a part of one book. If most schools cannot do what is done in large institutions—take the students through the whole of one or two books continuously and with a certain development—yet at least those parts which are selected should be treated with suitable fullness, in such a way that the students may learn from the sample that is put before them to love and use the remainder of the sacred book during the whole of their lives.

The professor, following the tradition of antiquity, will make use **106** of the Vulgate as his text; for the Council of Trent decreed that "in public lectures, disputations, preaching, and exposition,"[1] the Vulgate is the "authentic" version; and this is the existing custom of the Church. At the same time, the other versions, which Christian antiquity has approved, should not be neglected, more especially the more ancient MSS. For, although the meaning of the Hebrew and Greek is substantially rendered by the Vulgate, nevertheless wherever there may be ambiguity or want of clearness, the "examination of older tongues,"[2] to quote St. Augustine, will be useful and advantageous. But in this matter we need hardly say that the greatest prudence is required, for the "office of a commentator," as St. Jerome says, "is to set forth not what he himself would prefer but what his author says."[3]

The question of "reading" having been, when necessary, carefully **107** discussed, the next thing is to investigate and expound the meaning. And the first counsel to be given is this: that the more our adversaries contend to the contrary, so much the more solicitously should we adhere to the received and approved canons of interpretation. Hence, whilst weighing the meaning of words, the connection of ideas, the parallelism of passages, and the like, we should by all means make use of such illustrations as can be drawn from apposite erudition of an external sort; but this should be done with caution, so as

---

[1] Sess. iv, *decr. de edit. et usu sacr. libror.*
[2] *De doctr. chr.*, iii, 4.
[3] *Ad Pammachium.*

not to bestow on questions of this kind more labor and time than are spent on the sacred books themselves, and not to overload the minds of the students with a mass of information that will be rather a hindrance than a help.

108   The professor may now safely pass on to the use of Scripture in matters of theology. On this head it must be observed that, in addition to the usual reasons which make ancient writings more or less difficult to understand, there are some which are peculiar to the Bible. For the language of the Bible is employed to express, under the inspiration of the Holy Spirit, many things which are beyond the power and scope of the reason of man—that is to say, divine mysteries and all that is related to them. There is sometimes in such passages a fullness and a hidden depth of meaning which the letter hardly expresses and which the laws of interpretation hardly warrant. Moreover, the literal sense itself frequently admits other senses, adapted to illustrate dogma or to confirm morality.

[Sensus, quem tenet Ecclesia]

Wherefore, it must be recognized that the sacred writings are wrapped in a certain religious obscurity, and that no one can enter into their interior without a guide; [1] God so disposing, as the holy Fathers commonly teach, in order that men may investigate them with greater ardor and earnestness, and that what is attained with difficulty may sink more deeply into the mind and heart, and, most of all, that they may understand that God has delivered the Holy Scripture to the Church, and that in reading and making use of His Word they must follow the Church as their guide and their teacher. St. Irenæus long since laid down that where the *chrismata* of God were, there the truth was to be learned, and the Holy Scripture was safely interpreted by those who had the apostolic succession.[2] His teaching and that of other holy Fathers is taken up by the Council of the Vatican, which in renewing the decree of Trent declared its "mind" to be this—that "in things of faith and morals, belonging to the building up of Christian doctrine, that it is to be considered the true sense of Holy Scripture, which has been held and is held by our Holy Mother the Church, whose place it is to judge of the true sense and interpretation of the Scriptures; and, therefore, that it is permitted to no one to interpret Holy Scripture against such sense or also against the unanimous agreement of the Fathers." [3]

---

[1] S. Hier., *Ad Paulin. de studio Script. ep. liii*, 4.

[2] *Contra hær.*, iv, 26, 5.

[3] Sess. iii, cap. ii, *de revel.*; cf. Conc. Trid., sess. iv, *decret. de edit. et usu sacr. libror.*

[No Restraint]

By this most wise decree the Church by no means prevents or re- **109** strains the pursuit of biblical science, but rather protects it from error, and largely assists its real progress. A wide field is still left open to the private student, in which his hermeneutical skill may display itself with signal effect and to the advantage of the Church. On the one hand, in those passages of Holy Scripture which have not as yet received a certain and definite interpretation, such labors may, in the benignant providence of God, prepare for and bring to maturity the judgment of the Church; on the other, in passages already defined, the private student may do work equally valuable, either by setting them forth more clearly to the flock or more skillfully to the scholars, or by defending them more powerfully from hostile attack. Wherefore the first and dearest object of the Catholic commentator should be to interpret those passages which have received an authentic interpretation either from the sacred writers themselves, under the inspiration of the Holy Spirit (as in many places of the New Testament), or from the Church, under the assistance of the same Holy Spirit, whether by her solemn judgment or by her ordinary and universal *magisterium* [1]—to interpret these passages in that identical sense, and to prove by all the resources of science that sound hermeneutical laws admit of no other interpretation. In the other passages the analogy of faith should be followed, and Catholic doctrine, as authoritatively proposed by the Church, should be held as the supreme law; for, seeing that the same God is the author both of the sacred books and of the doctrine committed to the Church, it is clearly impossible that any teaching can, by legitimate means, be extracted from the former which shall, in any respect, be at variance with the latter. Hence it follows that all interpretation is foolish or false which either makes the sacred writers disagree one with another, or is opposed to the doctrine of the Church.

[Commentaries of the Fathers]

The professor of Holy Scripture, therefore, amongst other recom- **110** mendations, must be well acquainted with the whole circle of theology and deeply read in the commentaries of the holy Fathers and Doctors, and in other interpreters of mark.[2] This is inculcated by St. Jerome, and still more frequently by St. Augustine, who thus justly complains: "If there is no branch of teaching, however humble and

---

[1] Conc. Vat., sess. iii, cap. 11, *de fide*.
[2] *Ibid.*

easy to learn, which does not require a master, what can be a greater
sign of rashness and pride than to refuse to study the books of the
divine mysteries by the help of those who have interpreted them?" [1]
The other Fathers have said the same, and have confirmed it by their
example, for they "endeavored to acquire the understanding of the
Holy Scriptures not by their own lights and ideas but from the writing and authority of the ancients, who, in their turn, as we know,
received the rule of interpretation in direct line from the apostles." [2]

111   The holy Fathers "to whom, after the Apostles, the Church owes
its growth—who have planted, watered, built, governed, and cherished it"; [3] the holy Fathers, We say, are of supreme authority,
whenever they all interpret in one and the same manner any text of
the Bible, as pertaining to the doctrine of faith and morals; for their
unanimity clearly evinces that such interpretation has come down
from the apostles as a matter of Catholic faith. The opinion of the
Fathers is also of very great weight when they treat of these matters
in their capacity of Doctors unofficially; not only because they excel
in their knowledge of revealed doctrine and in their acquaintance
with many things which are useful in understanding the apostolic
books, but because they are men of eminent sanctity and of ardent
zeal for the truth, on whom God has bestowed a more ample measure
of His light. Wherefore the expositor should make it his duty to follow their footsteps with all reverence, and to use their labors with
intelligent appreciation.

112   But he must not on that account consider that it is forbidden, when
just cause exists, to push inquiry and exposition beyond what the
Fathers have done; provided he carefully observes the rule so wisely
laid down by St. Augustine—not to depart from the literal and obvious sense, except only where reason makes it untenable or necessity
requires; [4] a rule to which it is the more necessary to adhere strictly
in these times, when the thirst for novelty and the unrestrained freedom of thought make the danger of error most real and proximate.
Neither should those passages be neglected which the Fathers have
understood in an allegorical or figurative sense, more especially when
such interpretation is justified by the literal, and when it rests on the
authority of many. For this method of interpretation has been received by the Church from the apostles, and has been approved by
her own practice, as the holy Liturgy attests; although it is true that
the holy Fathers did not thereby pretend directly to demonstrate
dogmas of faith, but used it as a means of promoting virtue and

---

[1] *Ad Honorat. de util. cred.*, xvii, 35.
[2] Rufinus, *Hist. eccl.*, li, 9.
[3] S. Aug., *Contra Julian*, ii, 10, 37.
[4] *De Gen. ad litt. lviii*, c. 7, 13.

piety, such as, by their own experience, they knew to be most valuable.

[OTHER INTERPRETERS]

The authority of other Church interpreters is not so great; but the **113** study of Scripture has always continued to advance in the Church, and, therefore, these commentaries also have their own honorable place, and are serviceable in many ways for the refutation of assailants and the explanation of difficulties. But it is most unbecoming to pass by, in ignorance or contempt, the excellent work which Catholics have left in abundance, and to have recourse to the work of non-Catholics—and to seek in them, to the detriment of sound doctrine and often to the peril of faith, the explanation of passages on which Catholics long ago have successfully employed their talent and their labor. For although the studies of non-Catholics, used with prudence, may sometimes be of use to the Catholic student, he should, nevertheless, bear well in mind—as the Fathers also teach in numerous passages [1]—that the sense of Holy Scripture can nowhere be found incorrupt outside the Church, and cannot be expected to be found in writers who, being without the true faith, only know the bark of Sacred Scripture, and never attain its pith.

[THE PLACE OF SCRIPTURE RESEARCH AMONG THEOLOGICAL STUDIES]

Most desirable is it, and most essential, that the whole teaching of **114** theology should be pervaded and animated by the use of the divine Word of God. That is what the Fathers and the greatest theologians of all ages have desired and reduced to practice. It is chiefly out of the sacred writings that they endeavored to proclaim and establish the Articles of Faith and the truths therewith connected, and it was in them, together with divine tradition, that they found the refutation of heretical error, and the reasonableness, the true meaning, and the mutual relation of the truths of Catholicism. Nor will any one wonder at this who considers that the sacred books hold such an eminent position among the sources of revelation that without their assiduous study and use theology cannot be placed on a true footing, or treated as its dignity demands. For although it is right and proper that students in academies and schools should be chiefly exercised in acquiring a scientific knowledge of dogma, by means of reasoning from the Articles of Faith to their consequences, according to the rules of approved and sound philosophy—nevertheless the judicious and instructed theologian will by no means pass by that method of

---

[1] Cfr. Clem. Alex., *Strom.*, vii, 16; Orig., *De princ.*, iv, 8; *In Levit. hom.*, 48; Tertull., *De præscr.*, 15ff; S. Hilar. Pict., *In Matt.*, 13, 1.

doctrinal demonstration which draws its proof from the authority of
the Bible; "for theology does not receive her first principles from
any other science, but immediately from God by revelation. And,
therefore, she does not receive of other sciences as from a superior,
but uses them as her inferiors or handmaids."[1] It is this view of
doctrinal teaching which is laid down and recommended by the
prince of theologians, St. Thomas of Aquin;[2] who moreover shows—
such being the essential character of Christian theology—how she can
defend her own principles against attack: "If the adversary," he
says, "do but grant any portion of the divine revelation, we have an
argument against him; thus, against a heretic we can employ Scripture authority, and against those who deny one article we can use
another. But if our opponent reject divine revelation entirely, there
is no way left to prove the Articles of Faith by reasoning; we can
only solve the difficulties which are raised against them."[3]

115 Care must be taken, then, that beginners approach the study of
the Bible well prepared and furnished; otherwise, just hopes will be
frustrated, or, perchance, what is worse, they will unthinkingly risk
the danger of error, falling an easy prey to the sophisms and labored
erudition of the rationalists. The best preparation will be a conscientious application to philosophy and theology under the guidance
of St. Thomas of Aquin, and a thorough training therein—as We Ourselves have elsewhere pointed out and directed. By this means, both
in biblical studies and in that part of theology which is called *positive,* they will pursue the right path and make satisfactory progress.

[AUTHORITY OF THE BIBLE]

116 To prove, to expound, to illustrate Catholic doctrine by the legitimate and skillful interpretation of the Bible is much; but there is a
second part of the subject of equal importance and equal difficulty—
the maintenance in the strongest possible way of its full authority.
This cannot be done completely or satisfactorily except by means of
the living and proper *magisterium* of the Church. The Church, by
reason of her wonderful propagation, her distinguished sanctity, and
inexhaustible fecundity in good, her Catholic unity, and her unshaken
stability, is herself a great and perpetual motive of credibility, and
an unassailable testimony to her own divine mission."[4] But, since
the divine and infallible *magisterium* of the Church rests also on
Holy Scripture, the first thing to be done is to vindicate the trustworthiness of sacred records, at least as human documents, from

[1] S. Greg. M., *Moral.,* xx, 9 (al. 11).
[2] *Summ. Theol.,* 1, q. 1, art. 5, ad 2.
[3] *Ibid.,* a. 8.
[4] Conc. Vat., sess. iii, c. ii, *de fide.*

which can be clearly proved, as from primitive and authentic testimony, the divinity and the mission of Christ our Lord, the institution of a hierarchical Church and the primacy of Peter and his successors.

[Defenders of the Bible]

It is most desirable, therefore, that there should be numerous members of the clergy well prepared to enter on a contest of this nature, and to repulse hostile assaults, chiefly trusting in the armor of God recommended by the Apostle,[1] but also not unaccustomed to modern methods of attack. This is beautifully alluded to by St. John Chrysostom, when describing the duties of priests: "We must use every endeavor that the 'Word of God may dwell in us abundantly'; [2] not merely for one kind of a fight must we be prepared—for the contest is many-sided and the enemy is of every sort; and they do not all use the same weapons nor make their onset in the same way. Wherefore it is needful that the man who has to contend against all should be acquainted with the engines and the arts of all—that he should be at once archer and slinger, commandant and officer, general and private soldier, foot-soldier and horseman, skilled in sea-fight and in siege; for unless he knows every trick and turn of war, the devil is well able, if only a single door be left open, to get in his fierce bands and carry off the sheep." [3] The sophisms of the enemy and his manifold arts of attack we have already touched upon. Let us now say a word of advice on the means of defense.

[Means of Defense]

[A. *Ancient Languages*]

The first means is the study of the Oriental languages and of the **118** art of criticism. These two acquirements are in these days held in high estimation, and, therefore, the clergy, by making themselves fully acquainted with them as time and place may demand, will the better be able to discharge their office with becoming credit; for they must make themselves *all to all*,[4] always *ready to satisfy every one that asketh them a reason for the hope that is in them*.[5] Hence it is most proper that professors of sacred Scripture and theologians should master those tongues in which the sacred books were originally written; and it would be well that Church students also should cultivate them, more especially those who aspire to academic degrees. And endeavors should be made to establish in all academic institu-

117

---

[1] Eph. 6, 13ff.
[2] Cfr. Coloss. 3, 16.
[3] *De Sacerdotio*, iv, 4.

[4] 1 Cor. 9, 22.
[5] 1 Peter 3, 15.

tions—as has already been laudably done in many—chairs of the other ancient languages, especially the Semitic, and of subjects connected therewith, for the benefit, principally, of those who are intended to profess sacred literature.

[B. *Criticism*]

119   These latter, with a similar object in view, should make themselves well and thoroughly acquainted with the art of true criticism. There has arisen, to the great detriment of religion, an inept method, dignified by the name of the "higher criticism," which pretends to judge the origin, integrity and authority of each book from internal indications alone. It is clear, on the other hand, that in historical questions, such as the origin and handing down of writings, the witness of history is of primary importance, and that historical investigation should be made with the utmost care; and that in this manner internal evidence is seldom of great value, except as confirmation. To look upon it in any other light will be to open the door to many evil consequences. It will make the enemies of religion much more bold and confident in attacking and mangling the sacred books; and this vaunted "higher criticism" will resolve itself into the reflection of the bias and the prejudice of the critics. It will not throw on the Scripture the light which is sought, or prove of any advantage to doctrine; it will only give rise to disagreement and dissension, those sure notes of error which the critics in question so plentifully exhibit in their own persons; and seeing that most of them are tainted with false philosophy and rationalism, it must lead to the elimination from the sacred writings of all prophecy and miracle, and of everything else that is outside the natural order.

[C. *Natural Sciences*]

120   In the second place, we have to contend against those who, making an evil use of physical science, minutely scrutinize the sacred book in order to detect the writers in a mistake, and to take occasion to villify its contents. Attacks of this kind, bearing as they do on matters of sensible experience, are peculiarly dangerous to the masses, and also to the young who are beginning their literary studies; for the young, if they lose their reverence for the Holy Scripture on one or more points, are easily led to give up believing in it altogether. It need not be pointed out how the nature of science, just as it is so admirably adapted to show forth the glory of the Great Creator, provided it is taught as it should be, may, if it be perversely imparted to the youthful intelligence, prove most fatal in destroying the principles of true philosophy and in the corruption of morality. Hence, to the professor of Sacred Scripture a knowledge of natural science will be of very great assistance in detecting such attacks on the sacred books, and in refuting them.

There can never, indeed, be any real discrepancy between the the- **121** ologian and the physicist, as long as each confines himself within his own lines, and both are careful, as St. Augustine warns us, "not to make rash assertions, or to assert what is not known as known." [1] If dissension should arise between them, here is the rule also laid down by St. Augustine, for the theologian: "Whatever they can really demonstrate to be true of physical nature we must show to be capable of reconciliation with our Scriptures; and whatever they assert in their treatises which is contrary to these Scriptures of ours, that is to Catholic faith, we must either prove it as well as we can to be entirely false, or at all events we must, without the smallest hesitation, believe it to be so." [2] To understand how just is the rule here formulated we must remember, first, that the sacred writers, or, to speak more accurately, the Holy Spirit "who spoke by them, did not intend to teach men these things [that is to say, the essential nature of the things of the visible universe], things in no way profitable unto salvation." [3] Hence they did not seek to penetrate the secrets of nature, but rather described and dealt with things in more or less figurative language, or in terms which were commonly used at the time, and which in many instances are in daily use at this day, even by the most eminent men of science. Ordinary speech primarily and properly describes what comes under the senses; and somewhat in the same way the sacred writers—as the Angelic Doctor also reminds us—"went by what sensibly appeared," [4] or put down what God, speaking to men, signified, in the way men could understand and were accustomed to.

The unshrinking defense of the Holy Scripture, however, does not **122** require that we should equally uphold all the opinions which each of the Fathers or the more recent interpreters have put forth in explaining it; for it may be that, in commenting on passages where physical matters occur, they have sometimes expressed the ideas of their own times, and thus made statements which in these days have been abandoned as incorrect. Hence, in their interpretations, we must carefully note what they lay down as belonging to faith, or as intimately connected with faith—what they are unanimous in. For "in those things which do not come under the obligation of faith, the saints were at liberty to hold divergent opinions, just as we ourselves

---

[1] *In. Gen. op. imperf.*, ix, 30.   [2] *De Gen. ad litt.*, 1, 21. 41.
[3] S. Aug., *ibid.*, ii. 9, 20.
[4] *Summa Theol.*, 1, q. 80, art. 1, ad 3.

are," [1] according to the saying of St. Thomas. And in another place he says most admirably: "When philosophers are agreed upon a point, and it is not contrary to our faith, it is safer, in my opinion, neither to lay down such a point as a dogma of faith, even though it is perhaps so presented by the philosophers, nor to reject it as against faith, lest we thus give to the wise of this world an occasion of despising our faith." [2] The Catholic interpreter, although he should show that those facts of natural science which investigators affirm to be now quite certain are not contrary to the Scripture rightly explained, must, nevertheless, always bear in mind that much which has been held and proved as certain has afterwards been called in question and rejected. And if writers on physics travel outside the boundaries of their own branch, and carry their erroneous teaching into the domain of philosophy, let them be handed over to philosophers for refutation.

[D. *History*]

123   The principles here laid down will apply to cognate sciences, and especially to history. It is a lamentable fact that there are many who with great labor carry out and publish investigations on the monuments of antiquity, the manners and institutions of nations, and other illustrative subjects, and whose chief purpose in all this is to find mistakes in the sacred writings and so to shake and weaken their authority. Some of these writers display not only extreme hostility but the greatest unfairness; in their eyes a profane book or ancient document is accepted without hesitation, whilst the Scripture, if they only find in it a suspicion of error, is set down with the slightest possible discussion as quite untrustworthy.

124   It is true, no doubt, that copyists have made mistakes in the text of the Bible; this question, when it arises, should be carefully considered on its merits, and the fact not too easily admitted, but only in those passages where the proof is clear. It may also happen that the sense of a passage remains ambiguous, and in this case good hermeneutical methods will greatly assist in clearing up the obscurity.

[INSPIRATION]

But it is absolutely wrong and forbidden either to narrow inspiration to certain parts only of Holy Scripture or to admit that the sacred writer has erred. For the system of those who, in order to rid themselves of those difficulties, do not hesitate to concede that divine inspiration regards the things of faith and morals, and nothing beyond, because (as they wrongly think) in a question of the truth or

---

[1] *In Sent.*, II. Dist., q. 1, art. 3.   [2] *Opusc. x.*

falsehood of a passage we should consider not so much what God has said as the reason and purpose which He had in mind when saying it —this system cannot be tolerated. For all the books which the Church receives as sacred and canonical are written wholly and entirely, with all their parts, at the dictation of the Holy Spirit; and so far is it from being possible that any error can co-exist with inspiration, that inspiration not only is essentially incompatible with error, but excludes and rejects it as absolutely and necessarily as it is impossible that God Himself, the Supreme Truth, can utter that which is not true.

This is the ancient and unchanging faith of the Church, solemnly **125** defined in the Councils of Florence and of Trent, and finally confirmed and more expressly formulated by the Council of the Vatican. These are the words of the last: "The books of the Old and New Testament, whole and entire, with all their parts, as enumerated by the decree of the same Council (Trent) and in the ancient Latin Vulgate, are to be received as sacred and canonical. And the Church holds them as sacred and canonical not because, having been composed by human industry, they were afterwards approved by her authority, nor only because they contain revelation without error, but because, having been written under the inspiration of the Holy Spirit, they have God for their Author." [1] Hence, because the Holy Spirit employed men as His instruments, we cannot, therefore, say that it was these inspired instruments who, perchance, have fallen into error, and not the primary author. For, by supernatural power, He so moved and impelled them to write—He was so present to them —that the things which He ordered, and those only, they, first, rightly understood, then willed faithfully to write down, and finally expressed in apt words and with infallible truth. Otherwise, it could not be said that He was the Author of the entire Scripture.

Such has always been the persuasion of the Fathers. "There- **126** fore," says St. Augustine, "since they wrote the things which He showed and uttered to them, it cannot be pretended that He is not the writer; for His members executed what their head dictated." [2] And St. Gregory the Great thus pronounces: "Most superfluous it is to inquire who wrote these things—we loyally believe the Holy Spirit to be the author of the Book. He wrote it who dictated it for writing; He wrote it who inspired its execution." [3] It follows that those who maintain that an error is possible in any genuine passage of the sacred writings either pervert the Catholic notion of inspiration or make God the author of such error.

And so emphatically were all the Fathers and Doctors agreed that **127**

---

[1] Sess. iii, c. ii, *de Rev.*
[2] *De consensu Evangel.*, I, c. 35.   [3] *Praef. in Job*, n. 2.

the divine writings, as left by the hagiographers, are free from all error, that they labored earnestly, with no less skill than reverence, to reconcile with each other those numerous passages which seem at variance—the very passages which in a great measure have been taken up by the "higher criticism"; for they were unanimous in laying it down that those writings, in their entirety and in all their parts were equally from the *afflatus* of Almighty God, and that God, speaking by the sacred writers, could not set down anything that was not true. The words of St. Augustine to St. Jerome may sum up what they taught: "On my own part I confess to your charity that it is only to those books of Scripture which are now called canonical that I have learned to pay such honor and reverence as to believe most firmly that none of their writers has fallen into any error. And if in these books I meet anything which seems contrary to truth I shall not hesitate to conclude either that the text is faulty, or that the translator has not expressed the meaning of the passage, or that I myself do not understand." [1]

[CATHOLIC SCHOLARS]

128   But to undertake fully and perfectly, and with all the weapons of the best science, the defense of the Holy Bible is far more than can be looked for from the exertions of commentators and theologians alone. It is an enterprise in which we have a right to expect the co-operation of all those Catholics who have acquired reputation in any branch of learning whatever. As in the past, so at the present time, the Church is never without the graceful support of her accomplished children; may their service to the Faith grow and increase! For there is nothing which We believe to be more needful than that truth should find defenders more powerful and more numerous than the enemies it has to face; nor is there anything which is better calculated to impress the masses with respect for truth than to see it boldly proclaimed by learned and distinguished men. Moreover, the bitter tongues of objectors will be silenced, or at least they will not dare to insist so shamelessly that faith is the enemy of science, when they see that scientific men of eminence in their profession show towards faith the most marked honor and respect.

129   Seeing, then, that those can do so much for the advantage of religion on whom the goodness of Almighty God has bestowed, together with the grace of the faith, great natural talent, let such men, in this bitter conflict of which the Holy Scripture is the object, select each of them the branch of study most suitable to his circumstances, and

---

[1] *Ep. lxxvii, 1,* et crebrius alibi.

endeavor to excel therein, and thus be prepared to repulse with credit and distinction the assaults on the Word of God.

And it is Our pleasing duty to give deserved praise to a work **130** which certain Catholics have taken up—that is to say, the formation of societies and the contribution of considerable sums of money for the purpose of supplying studies and learned men with every kind of help and assistance in carrying out complete studies. Truly an excellent fashion of investing money, and well suited to the times in which we live! The less hope of public patronage there is for Catholic study, the more ready and the more abundant should be the liberality of private persons—those to whom God has given riches thus willingly making use of their means to safeguard the treasure of His revealed doctrine.

[CAUTION IN DOUBT]

In order that all these endeavors and exertions may really prove **131** advantageous to the cause of the Bible, let scholars keep steadfastly to the principles which We have in this Letter laid down. Let them loyally hold that God, the Creator and Ruler of all things, is also the Author of the Scriptures—and that, therefore, nothing can be proved either by physical science or archæology which can really contradict the Scriptures. If, then, apparent contradiction be met with, every effort should be made to remove it. Judicious theologians and commentators should be consulted as to what is the true or most probable meaning of the passage in discussion, and hostile arguments should be carefully weighed. Even if the difficulty is after all not cleared up and the discrepancy seems to remain, the contest must not be abandoned; truth cannot contradict truth, and we may be sure that some mistake has been made either in the interpretation of the sacred words or in the polemical discussion itself; and if no such mistake can be detected, we must then suspend judgment for the time being. There have been objections without number perseveringly directed against the Scripture for many a long year, which have been proved to be futile and are now never heard of; and not infrequently interpretations have been placed on certain passages of Scripture (not belonging to the rule of faith or morals) which have been rectified by more careful investigations. As time goes on, mistaken views die and disappear; but *truth remaineth and groweth stronger forever and ever.*[1] Wherefore, as no one should be so presumptuous as to think that he understands the whole of the Scripture, in which St. Augustine himself confessed that there was more that he did not know than that he knew,[2] so, if he should come on anything that seems incapable of solution, he must take to heart the cautious rule

---

[1] 3 Esdr., 4, 38.   [2] *Ad Ianuar. ep. lv*, 21.

of the same holy doctor: "It is better even to be oppressed by un-known but useful signs than to interpret them uselessly, and thus to throw off the yoke only to be caught in the trap of error."[1]

132   As to those who pursue the subsidiary studies of which We have spoken, if they honestly and modestly follow the counsels We have given—if by their pen and their voice they make their studies profit-able against the enemies of truth, and useful in saving the young from the loss of their faith—they may justly congratulate themselves on their worthy service to the sacred writings, and on affording to Catholicism that assistance which the Church has a right to expect from the piety and learning of her children.

[CONCLUSION]

133   Such, Venerable Brethren, are the admonitions and the instruc-tions which, by the help of God, We have thought it well, at the present moment, to offer to you on the study of Holy Scripture. It will now be your province to see that what We have said be observed and put in practice with all due reverence and exactness; that so We may prove our gratitude to God for the communication to man of the words of His wisdom, and that all the good results so much to be desired may be realized, especially as they affect the training of the students of the Church, which is our own great solicitude and the Church's hope. Exert yourselves with willing alacrity, and use your authority and your persuasion in order that these studies may be held in just regard and may flourish in seminaries and in educational in-stitutions which are under your jurisdiction. Let them flourish in completeness and in happy success, under the direction of the Church, in accordance with the salutary teaching and example of the Holy Fathers, and the laudable traditions of antiquity; and, as time goes on, let them be widened and extended as the interests and glory of truth may require—the interests of that Catholic truth which comes from above, the never-failing source of man's salvation.

134   Finally, We admonish with paternal love all students and ministers of the Church always to approach the sacred writings with rever-ence and piety; for it is impossible to attain to the profitable under-standing thereof unless the arrogance of "earthly" science be laid aside, and there be excited in the heart the holy desire for that wis-dom "which is from above." In this way the intelligence which is once admitted to these sacred studies, and thereby illuminated and strengthened, will acquire a marvelous facility in detecting and avoid-ing the fallacies of human science, and in gathering and using for eternal salvation all that is valuable and precious; whilst, at the same

[1] *De doctr. chr.*, iii, 9, 18.

time, the heart will grow warm, and will strive, with ardent longing, to advance in virtue and in divine love. *Blessed are they who examine His testimonies; they shall seek Him with their whole heart.*[1]

And now, filled with hope in the divine assistance, and trusting to your pastoral solicitude—as a pledge of heavenly grace, and a sign of Our special good-will—to you all, and to the clergy, and to the whole flock intrusted to you, We lovingly impart in Our Lord the Apostolic Benediction.

Given at St. Peter's, Rome, November 18, 1893, the sixteenth year of our Pontificate.

LEO PP. XIII.

---

[1] Ps. 118, 2.

Bibliography: Collins, J. J., "Providentissimus Deus," in H.P.R. 44 (1943); 112-117; Cotter, A. C., "The Antecedents of the Encyclical Providentissimus Deus," in C.B.Q., 5 (1943) 117-124; Hartegen, S., "The Influence of the Encyclical Providentissimus Deus," in C.B.Q., 5 (1943), 141-159; Murphy, R. T., "The Teachings of the Encyclical Providentissimus Deus," in C.B.Q., 5 (1943), 125-140.

(4) The Decree "Lamentabili," Syllabus of Errors Condemned by the S. Congr. of the Inquisition, July 3, 1907

190   With truly lamentable results, our age, intolerant of all check in its investigations of the ultimate causes of things, not unfrequently follows what is new in such a way as to reject the legacy, as it were, of the human race, and thus fall into the most grievous errors. These errors will be all the more pernicious when they affect sacred disciplines, the interpretation of the Sacred Scripture, the principal mysteries of the faith. It is to be greatly deplored that among Catholics also not a few writers are to be found who, crossing the boundaries fixed by the Fathers and by the Church herself, seek out, on the plea of higher intelligence and in the name of historical considerations, that progress of dogmas which is in reality the corruption of the same.

191   But lest errors of this kind, which are being daily spread among the faithful, should strike root in their minds and corrupt the purity of the faith, it has pleased His Holiness Pius X, by Divine Providence Pope, that the chief among them should be noted and condemned through the office of this Holy Roman and Universal Inquisition.

Wherefore, after a most diligent investigation, and after having taken the opinion of the Reverend Consultors, the Most Eminent and Reverend Lords Cardinals, the general inquisitors in matters of faith and morals, decided that *the following propositions are to be condemned and proscribed, as they are, by this general Decree, condemned and proscribed:*

192   1. The ecclesiastical law, which prescribes that books regarding the Divine Scriptures are subject to previous censorship, does not extend to critical scholars or students of the scientific exegesis of the Old and New Testament.

193   2. The Church's interpretation of the Sacred Books is not indeed to be condemned, but it is subject to the more accurate judgment and to the correction of the exegetes.

194   3. From the ecclesiastical judgments and censures passed against free and more scientific (*cultiorem*) exegesis, it may be gathered that the faith proposed by the Church contradicts history and that the Catholic dogmas cannot be reconciled with the true origins of the Christian religion.

4. The magisterium of the Church cannot, even through dogmatic 195 definitions, determine the genuine sense of the Sacred Scriptures.

5. Since in the deposit of the faith only revealed truths are con- 196 tained, under no respect does it appertain to the Church to pass judgment concerning the assertions of human sciences.

6. In defining truths the Church learning (*discens*) and the Church 197 teaching (*docens*) collaborate in such a way that it only remains for the Church *docens* to sanction the opinions of the Church *discens*.

7. The Church, when it proscribes errors, cannot exact from the 198 faithful any internal assent by which the judgments issued by it are embraced.

8. Those who treat as of no weight the condemnations passed by 199 the Sacred Congregation of the Index or by the other Roman Congregations are free from all blame.

9. Those who believe that God is really the author of the Sacred 200 Scripture display excessive simplicity or ignorance.

10. The inspiration of the books of the Old Testament consists in 201 the fact that the Israelite writers have handed down religious doctrines under a peculiar aspect, either little or not at all known to the Gentiles.

11. Divine inspiration is not to be so extended to the whole of 202 Sacred Scriptures that it renders its parts, all and single, immune from all error.

12. The exegete, if he wishes to apply himself usefully to Biblical 203 studies, must first of all put aside all preconceived opinions concerning the supernatural origin of the Sacred Scripture, and interpret it not otherwise than other merely human documents.

13. The evangelists themselves and the Christians of the second 204 and third generation arranged (*digesserunt*) artificially the evangelical parables, and in this way gave an explanation of the scanty fruit of the preaching of Christ among the Jews.

14. In a great many narrations the evangelists reported not so 205 much things that are true as things which even though false they judged to be more profitable for their readers.

15. The Gospels until the time the canon was defined and consti- 206 tuted were increased by additions and corrections; hence in them there remained of the doctrine of Christ only a faint and uncertain trace.

16. The narrations of John are not properly history, but the mys- 207 tical contemplation of the Gospel; the discourses contained in his Gospel are theological meditations, devoid of historical truth concern- the mystery of salvation.

17. The Fourth Gospel exaggerated miracles not only that the 208 wonderful might stand out but also that they might become more suitable for signifying the work and the glory of the Word Incarnate.

209   18. John claims for himself the quality of a witness concerning Christ; but in reality he is only a distinguished witness of the Christian life, or of the life of Christ in the Church, at the close of the first century.

210   19. Heterodox exegetes have expressed the true sense of the Scriptures more faithfully than Catholic exegetes.

211   20. Revelation could be nothing but the consciousness acquired by man of his relation with God.

212   21. Revelation, constituting the object of Catholic faith, was not completed with the Apostles.

213   22. The dogmas which the Church gives out as revealed, are not truths which have fallen down from heaven, but are an interpretation of religious facts, which the human mind has acquired by laborious effort.

214   23. Opposition may and actually does exist between the facts which are narrated in Scripture and the dogmas of the Church which rest on them; so that the critic may reject as false facts which the Church holds as most certain.

215   24. The exegete is not to be blamed for constructing premises from which it follows that the dogmas are historically false or doubtful, provided he does not directly deny the dogmas themselves.

216   25. The assent of faith rests ultimately on a mass of probabilities.

217   26. The dogmas of faith are to be held only according to their practical sense, that is, as preceptive norms of conduct, but not as norms of believing.

218   27. The Divinity of Jesus Christ is not proved from the Gospels; but is a dogma which the Christian conscience has derived from the notion of the Messias.

219   28. Jesus, while He was exercising His Ministry, did not speak with the object of teaching that He was the Messias, nor did His miracles tend to prove this.

220   29. It is lawful to believe that the Christ of history is far inferior to the Christ who is the object of faith.

221   30. In all the evangelical texts the name *Son of God* is equivalent only to Messias, and does not at all signify that Christ is the true and natural Son of God.

222   31. The doctrine concerning Christ taught by Paul, John, the Councils of Nicea, Ephesus and Chalcedon, is not that which Jesus taught, but that which the Christian conscience conceived concerning Jesus.

223   32. It is not possible to reconcile the natural sense of the Gospel texts with the sense taught by our theologians concerning the conscience and the infallible knowledge of Jesus Christ.

224   33. It is evident to everybody who is not led by preconceived opinions that either Jesus professed an error concerning the immediate

Messianic coming, or that the greater part of His doctrine as contained in the Gospels is destitute of authenticity.

34. The critic cannot ascribe to Christ a knowledge circumscribed **225** by no limits except on a hypothesis which cannot be historically conceived and which is repugnant to the moral sense, viz., that Christ as man had the knowledge of God and yet was unwilling to communicate the knowledge of a great many things to His Disciples and to posterity.

35. Christ had not always the consciousness of His Messianic dig- **226** nity.

36. The Resurrection of the Saviour is not properly a fact of the **227** historical order, but a fact of merely supernatural order, neither demonstrated nor demonstrable, which the Christian conscience gradually derived from other facts.

37. Faith in the Resurrection of Christ was in the beginning not so **228** much in the fact itself of the Resurrection, as in the immortal life of Christ with God.

38. The doctrine of the expiatory death of Christ is not Evangeli- **229** cal but Pauline.

39. The opinions concerning the origin of the sacraments with **230** which the Fathers of Trent were imbued and which certainly influenced their dogmatic canons are very different from those which now rightly obtain among historians who examine into Christianity.

40. The sacraments had their origin in the fact that the Apostles **231** and their successors, swayed and moved by circumstances and events, interpreted some idea or intention of Christ.

41. The sacraments are merely intended to bring before the mind **232** of man the ever-beneficent presence of the Creator.

42. The Christian community imposed (*iuduxit*) the necessity of **233** baptism, adopting it as a necessary rite, and adding to it the obligations of the Christian profession.

43. The practice of conferring baptism on infants was a disciplinary **234** evolution, which became one of the causes why the sacrament was divided into two, viz.: baptism and penance.

44. There is nothing to prove that the rite of the sacrament of **235** confirmation was employed by the Apostles: but the formal distinction of the two sacraments, baptism and confirmation, does not belong to the history of primitive Christianity.

45. Not everything which Paul narrates concerning the institution **236** of the Eucharist (1 Cor. 11, 23-25) is to be taken historically.

46. In the primitive Church the conception of the Christian sinner **237** reconciled by the authority of the Church did not exist, but it was only very slowly that the Church accustomed itself to this conception. Nay, even after penance was recognized as an institution of the

Church, it was not called a sacrament, for it would be held as an ignominious sacrament.

238   47. The words of the Lord: *Receive ye the Holy Ghost; whose sins ye shall forgive they are forgiven them, and whose sins ye shall retain they are retained* (John 20, 22. 23) do not at all refer to the sacrament of penance, whatever the Fathers of Trent may have been pleased to say.

239   48. James in his Epistle (v. 14 and 15) did not intend to promulgate a sacrament of Christ, but to commend a pious custom, and if in this custom he happens to distinguish (*cernit*) a means of grace, it is not in that rigorous manner in which it was received by the theologians who laid down the notion and the number of the sacraments.

240   49. The Christian Supper gradually assuming the nature of a liturgical action, those who were wont to preside at the Supper acquired the sacerdotal character.

241   50. The elders who filled the office of watching over the gatherings of the faithful, were instituted by the Apostles as priests or bishops to provide for the necessary ordering (*ordinationi*) of the increasing opportunities, not properly for perpetuating the Apostolic mission and power.

242   51. It is not possible that matrimony could have become a sacrament of the new Law until later in the Church; for in order that matrimony should be held as a sacrament it was necessary that a full theological development (*explicatio*) of the doctrine of grace and the sacraments should first take place.

243   52. It was foreign to the mind of Christ to found a Church as a Society which was to last on the earth for a long course of centuries; nay, in the mind of Christ the Kingdom of Heaven together with the end of the world was about to come immediately.

244   53. The organic constitution of the Church is not immutable; but Christian society, like human society, is subject to perpetual evolution.

245   54. Dogmas, sacraments, hierarchy, both as regards the notion of them and the reality, are but interpretations and evolutions of the Christian intelligence which by external increments have increased and perfected the little germ latent in the Gospel.

246   55. Simon Peter never even suspected that the primacy in the Church was intrusted to him by Christ.

247   56. The Roman Church became the head of all the churches not through the ordinance of Divine Providence but through merely political conditions.

248   57. The Church has shown herself to be hostile to the progress of natural and theological sciences.

249   58. Truth is not any more immutable than man himself, since it is evolved with him, in him, and through him.

59. Christ did not teach a determinate body of doctrine applicable 250
to all times and to all men, but rather inaugurated a religious movement adapted or to be adapted for different times and place.

60. Christian doctrine in its origin was Judaic, but through suc- 251
cessive evolutions became first Pauline, then Joannine, and finally
Hellenic and universal.

61. It may be said without paradox that there is no chapter of 252
Scripture, from the first of Genesis to the last of the Apocalypse,
which contains a doctrine absolutely identical with that which the
Church teaches on the same matter, and that, therefore, no chapter
of Scripture has the same sense for the critic and for the theologian.

62. The chief articles of the Apostolic Symbol had not for the 253
Christians of the first ages the same sense that they have for the
Christians of our time.

63. The Church shows itself unequal to the task of efficaciously 254
maintaining evangelical ethics, because it obstinately adheres to immutable doctrines which cannot be reconciled with modern progress.

64. The progress of science involves a remodeling (*ut reformen-* 255
tur) of the conceptions of Christian doctrine concerning God, Creation, Revelation, the Person of the Incarnate Word, Redemption.

65. Modern Catholicism cannot be reconciled with true science un- 256
less it be transformed into a non-dogmatic Christianity, that is into a
broad and liberal Protestantism.

And on the following Thursday, the fourth day of the same month
and year, an accurate report of all this having been made to Our
Most Holy Lord Pope Pius X, His Holiness approved and confirmed
the Decree of the Most Eminent Fathers, and ordered that the propositions above enumerated, all and several, be held by all as condemned and proscribed.

PETER PALOMBELLI,
Notary of the H. R. U. I.

(5) From the Motu Proprio "Præstantia Scripturæ Sacræ" of Pope Pius X

ON THE DECISIONS OF THE BIBLICAL COMMISSION AND ON THE CENSURES AND PENALTIES AFFECTING THOSE WHO NEGLECT TO OBSERVE THE PRESCRIPTIONS AGAINST THE ERRORS OF THE MODERNISTS

283 In his Encyclical Letter *Providentissimus Deus,* given on November 19, 1893, our predecessor, Leo XIII, of immortal memory, after describing the dignity of the Sacred Scripture and commending the study of it, set forth the laws which govern the proper study of the Holy Bible; and having proclaimed the divinity of these books against the errors and calumnies of the rationalists, he at the same time defended them against the false teachings of what is known as the *higher criticism,* which, as the Pontiff most wisely wrote, are clearly nothing but the *commentaries of rationalism derived from a misuse of philology and kindred studies.*

284 Our predecessor, too, seeing that the danger was constantly on the increase, and desiring to provide against the consequences of the propagation of rash and erroneous views, by his Apostolic Letters *Vigilantiæ studiique memores,* given on October 29, 1902, established a Pontifical Council, or Commission on Biblical Matters, composed of a number of cardinals of the Holy Roman Church, distinguished for their learning and prudence, adding to these, under the title of *consultors,* a considerable body of men in sacred orders, chosen from among the learned in theology and in the Holy Bible, of various nationalities and differing in their methods and views concerning exegetical studies. In this the Pontiff had in mind, as an advantage admirably adapted for the promotion of study and for the time in which we live, that in this commission there should be the fullest freedom for proposing, examining, and judging all opinions whatsoever; and the letter also ordained that the cardinals of the commission were not to come to any definite decision until they had taken cognizance of and examined the arguments on both sides, omitting nothing which might serve to show in the clearest light the true and genuine state of the Biblical questions proposed for solution; and when all this had been done, that the decisions reached should be submitted for approval to the Supreme Pontiff, and then promulgated.

285 After mature examination and the most diligent consultations, certain decisions have been happily given by the Pontifical Commission on the Bible, and these of a kind very useful for the proper promotion and direction on safe lines of Biblical studies. But we observe that some persons, unduly prone to opinions and methods tainted by pernicious novelties, and excessively devoted to that principle of false liberty, which is really immoderate license, and in sacred studies proves itself to be most insidious and a fruitful source of the worst evils against the purity of the faith, have not received and do not receive these decisions with the proper obedience.

Wherefore we find it necessary to declare and prescribe, as we do **286** now declare and expressly prescribe, that all are bound in conscience to submit to the decisions of the Biblical Commission, which have been given in the past and which shall be given in the future, in the same way as to the Decrees which appertain to doctrine, issued by the Sacred Congregations approved by the Sovereign Pontiff; nor can those escape the stigma of disobedience and temerity, and consequently of grave guilt, who in speech or writing impugn these decisions; and this besides the scandal they give and the other reasons for which they may be responsible before God, for other temerities and errors usually accompanying such opposition.

Moreover to check the daily increasing audacity of a great many **287** modernists who are endeavoring by all kinds of sophistry and devices to detract from the force and efficacy not only of the Decree *Lamentabili sane exitu,* issued, by our order, by the Holy Roman and Universal Inquisition of July 3 of the present year, but also of our Encyclical Letters *Pascendi dominici gregis* given on September 8 of this same year, we do by our Apostolic authority repeat and confirm both that *Decree* of the Supreme Sacred Congregation and those *Encyclical Letters* of Ours, adding the penalty of excommunication against contradictors; and this we declare and decree, that should anybody, which may God forbid, be so rash as to defend any one of the propositions, opinions or teachings condemned in these documents, he falls *ipso facto* under the censure contained under the Chapter *Docentes* of the Constitution *Apostolicæ Sedis,* which is first among the excommunications *latæ sententiæ* simply reserved to the Roman Pontiff. This excommunication is to be understood as *salvis pœnis,* which may be incurred by those who have violated in any way the said documents, as propagators and defenders of heresies, when their propositions, opinions or teachings are heretical, as has happened more than once in the case of the adversaries of both these documents, especially when they advocate the errors of modernism, that is *the synthesis of all heresies.*

Wherefore, we again and most earnestly exhort the ordinaries of **288** the dioceses and the heads of religious congregations to use the utmost vigilance over teachers, and first of all in the seminaries; and should they find any of them imbued with the errors of the modernists, and eager for what is new and noxious, or lacking in docility to the prescriptions of the Apostolic See, no matter how they may be published, let them absolutely forbid the teaching office to such; so, too, let them exclude from sacred orders those young men who give the very faintest reason for doubt that they hold the condemned doctrines and the pernicious novelties. We exhort them also to take diligent care to put an end to those books and other writings, now growing exceedingly numerous, which contain opinions or tendencies of the kind condemned in the Encyclical Letters and Decree above mentioned; let them see to it that these publications are removed from Catholic publishing houses, and especially from the hands of students and the clergy. By doing this they will at the same time be promoting real and solid education, which should always be a subject of the greatest solicitude for those who exercise sacred authority.

All these things we will and order to be sanctioned and established by our Apostolic authority, aught to the contrary notwithstanding.

Given at Rome at St. Peter's November 18, 1907, in the fifth year of our Pontificate.

PIUS X, POPE.

(6) Encyclical Letter of Pope Benedict XV, "Spiritus Paraclitus," on the Fifteenth Centenary of the Death of St. Jerome

Since the Holy Spirit, the Comforter, had bestowed the Scriptures **444** on the human race for their instruction in Divine things, He also raised up in successive ages saintly and learned men whose task it should be to develop that treasure and so provide for the faithful plenteous "consolation from the Scriptures." [1] Foremost among these teachers stands St. Jerome. Him the Catholic Church acclaims and reveres as her "Greatest Doctor," divinely given her for the understanding of the Bible.

And now that the fifteenth centenary of his death is approaching we would not willingly let pass so favourable an opportunity of addressing you on the debt we owe him. For the responsibility of our Apostolic office impels us to set before you his wonderful example and so promote the study of Holy Scripture in accordance with the teaching of our predecessors, Leo XIII. and Pius X. which we desire to apply more precisely still to the present needs of the Church.

For St. Jerome—"strenuous Catholic, learned in the Scriptures," [2] "teacher of Catholics," [3] "model of virtue, world's teacher" [4]—has by his earnest and illuminative defence of Catholic doctrine on Holy Scripture left us most precious instructions. These we propose to set before you and so promote among the children of the Church, and especially among the clergy, assiduous and reverent study of the Bible.

[I. LIFE AND LABORS OF ST. JEROME]

No need to remind you, Venerable Brethren, that Jerome was born **445** in Stridonia, in a town "on the borders of Dalmatia and Pannonia"; [5] that from his infancy he was brought up a Catholic; [6] that after his baptism here in Rome [7] he lived to an advanced age and devoted all his powers to studying, expounding, and defending the Bible.

At Rome he had learned Latin and Greek, and hardly had he left the school of rhetoric than he ventured on a Commentary on Abdias

[1] Rom. **15**, 4.
[2] Sulpicius Severus, *Dial.*, i, 7.
[3] Cassian, *De inc.*, vii, 26.
[4] S. Prosper, *Carmen de Ingratis*, v. 57.

[5] *Vir. Ill.*, cxxxv.
[6] *Epist. lxxxii*, 2.
[7] *Epist. xv*, 1, *xvi*, 2.

the Prophet. This "youthful piece of work,[8] kindled in him such love of the Bible that he decided—like the man in the Gospel who found a treasure—to spurn "any emoluments the world could provide," [9] and devote himself wholly to such studies.

Nothing could deter him from this stern resolve. He left home, parents, sister, and relatives; he denied himself the more delicate food he had been accustomed to, and went to the East so that he might gather from studious reading of the Bible the fuller riches of Christ and true knowledge of his Saviour.[10] Jerome himself tells us in several places how assiduously he toiled: "An eager desire to learn obsessed me. But I was not so foolish as to try and teach myself. At Antioch I regularly attended the lectures of Apollinarius of Laodicea; but while I learned much from him about the Bible, I would never accept his doubtful teachings about its interpretation." [11]

From Antioch he betook himself to the desert of Chalcis, in Syria, to perfect himself in his knowledge of the Bible, and at the same time to curb "youthful desires" by means of hard study. Here he engaged a convert Jew to teach him Hebrew and Chaldaic. "What a toil it was! How difficult I found it! How often I was on the point of giving it up in despair, and yet in my eagerness to learn took it up again! Myself can bear witness of this, and so, too, can those who had lived with me at the time. Yet I thank God for the fruit I won from that bitter seed." [12]

446   Lest, however, he should grow idle in this desert where there were no heretics to vex him, Jerome betook himself to Constantinople, where for nearly three years he studied Holy Scripture under St. Gregory the Theologian, then Bishop of that See and in the height of his fame as a teacher. While there he translated into Latin Origen's *Homilies on the Prophets* and Eusebius' *Chronicle;* he also wrote on Isaias' vision of the Seraphim.

He then returned to Rome on ecclesiastical business, and Pope Damasus admitted him into his court.[13] However, he let nothing distract from continual occupation with the Bible,[14] and the task of copying various manuscripts,[15] as well as answering the many questions put to him by students of both sexes.[16]

Pope Damasus had entrusted to him a most laborious task, the correction of the Latin text of the Bible. So well did Jerome carry this out that even today men versed in such studies appreciate its value more and more.

447   But he ever yearned for Palestine, and when the Pope died he re-

---

[8] *Praef. in Abdiam.*
[9] *In Matt.,* 13:14.
[10] *Epist. xxii,* 30.
[11] *Epist. lxxxiv,* 3.
[12] *Epist. cxxv,* 12.

[13] *Epist. cxxiii,* 9, *cxxvii,* 7.
[14] *Epist. cxxvii,* 7.
[15] *Epist. xxxvi,* 1; cf. *xxxii,* 1.
[16] *Epist. xlv,* 2; cf. *cxxvi,* 3, *cxxvii,* 7.

tired to Bethlehem to a monastery nigh to the cave where Christ was born. Every moment he could spare from prayer he gave to Biblical studies. "Though my hair was now growing gray and though I looked more like professor than student, yet I went to Alexandria to attend Didymus' lectures. I owe him much. What I did not know I learned. What I knew already I did not lose through his different presentation of it. Men thought I had done with tutors; but when I got back to Jerusalem and Bethlehem how hard I worked and what a price I paid for my night-time teacher Baraninus! Like another Nicodemus he was afraid of the Jews!" [17]

Nor was Jerome content merely to gather up this or that teacher's words; he gathered from all quarters whatever might prove of use to him in his task. From the outset he had accumulated the best possible copies of the Bible and the best commentators on it, but now he worked on copies from the synagogues and from the library formed at Cæsarea by Origen and Eusebius; he hoped by assiduous comparison of texts to arrive at greater certainty touching the actual text and its meaning.

With this same purpose he went all through Palestine. For he was thoroughly convinced of the truth of what he once wrote to Domnio and Rogatian: "A man will understand the Bible better if he has seen Judæa with his own eyes and discovered its ancient cities and sites either under the old names or newer ones. In company with some learned Hebrews I went through the entire land the names of whose sites are on every Christian's lips." [18]

He nourished his soul unceasingly on this most pleasant food: he explained St. Paul's Epistles; he corrected the Latin version of the Old Testament by the Greek; he translated afresh nearly all the books of the Old Testament from Hebrew into Latin; day by day he discussed Biblical questions with the brethren who came to him, and answered letters on Biblical questions which poured in upon him from all sides; besides all this, he was constantly refuting men who assailed Catholic doctrine and unity. Indeed, such was his love for Holy Scripture that he ceased not from writing or dictating till his hand stiffened in death and his voice was silent for ever.

So it was that, sparing himself neither labour nor watching nor expense, he continued to extreme old age meditating day and night beside the Crib on the Law of the Lord; of greater profit to the Catholic cause by his life and example in his solitude than if he had passed his life at Rome, the capital of the world.

---

[17] *Epist. lxxxiv, 3.*   [18] *Praef. in 1 Paral.*

[II St. Jerome's Teaching Regarding Holy Scripture]

[1. *Plenary Inspiration of Holy Scripture*]

448   After this preliminary account of St. Jerome's life and labours we may now treat of his teaching on the divine dignity and absolute truth of Scripture.

You will not find a page in his writings which does not show clearly that he, in common with the whole Catholic Church, firmly and consistently held that the Sacred Books—written as they were under the inspiration of the Holy Spirit—have God for their Author, and as such were delivered to the Church. Thus he asserts that the Books of the Bible were composed at the inspiration, or suggestion, or even at the dictation of the Holy Spirit; even that they were written and edited by Him. Yet he never questions but that the individual authors of these Books worked in full freedom under the Divine afflatus, each of them in accordance with their individual nature and character.

Thus he is not merely content to affirm as a general principle—what indeed pertains to all the sacred writers—that they followed the Spirit of God as they wrote, in such sort that God is the principal cause of all that Scripture means and says; but he also accurately descries what pertains to each individual writer. In each case Jerome shows us how, in composition, in language, in style and mode of expression, each of them uses his own gifts and powers; hence he is able to portray and describe for us their individual character, almost their very features; this is especially so in his treatment of the prophets and of St. Paul.

This partnership of God and man in the production of a work in common Jerome illustrates by the case of a workman who uses instruments for the production of his work; for he says that whatsoever the sacred authors say "Is the word of God, and not their own; and what the Lord says by their mouths He says, as it were, by means of an instrument." [19]

If we ask how we are to explain this power and action of God, the principal cause, on the sacred writers we shall find that St. Jerome in no wise differs from the common teaching of the Catholic Church. For he holds that God, through His grace, illumines the writer's mind regarding the particular truth which, "in the person of God," he is to set before men; he holds, moreover, that God moves the writer's will—nay, even impels it—to write; finally, that God abides with him unceasingly, in unique fashion, until his task is accomplished. Whence the Saint infers the supreme excellence and dig-

---

[19] *Tract. in Ps. lxxxviii.*

nity of Scripture, and declares that knowledge of it is to be likened to the "treasure" [20] and the "pearl beyond price," [21] since in them are to be found the riches of Christ [22] and "silver wherewith to adorn God's house." [23]

[2. *Authoritative Character of Holy Scripture*]

Jerome also insists on the supereminent authority of Scripture. **449** When controversy arose he had recourse to the Bible as a storehouse of arguments, and he used its testimony as a weapon for refuting his adversaries' arguments, because he held that the Bible's witness afforded solid and irrefutable arguments.

Thus, when Helvidius denied the perpetual virginity of the Mother of God, Jerome was content simply to reply: "Just as we do not deny these things which are written, so do we repudiate things that are not written. That God was born of a Virgin we believe, because we read it. That Mary was married after His birth we do not believe because we do not read it." [24]

In the same fashion he undertakes to defend against Jovinian, with precisely the same weapons, the Catholic doctrines of the virginal state, of perseverance, of abstinence, and of the merit of good works: "In refuting his statements I shall rely especially on the testimony of Scripture, lest he should grumble and complain that he has been vanquished rather by my eloquence than by the truth." [25] So, too, when defending himself against the same Helvidius, he says: "He was, you might say, begged to yield to me, and be led away as a willing and unresisting captive in the bonds of truth." [26]

Again, "We must not follow the errors of our parents, nor of those who have gone before us; we have the authority of the Scriptures and God's teaching to command us." [27] Once more, when showing Fabiola how to deal with critics, he says: "When you are really instructed in the Divine Scriptures, and have realized that its laws and testimonies are the bonds of truth, then you can contend with advérsaries; then you will fetter them and lead them bound into captivity; then of the foes you have made captive you will make freedmen of God." [28]

---

[20] *Comment. in Matt.*, 13, 4.
[21] *Ibid.*, 13, 45.
[22] *Quaest. in Genesim, Prologus.*
[23] *Comment. in Aggœum,* 2, 1; cf. *In Gal.,* 2, 10.
[24] *Adv. Helvid.*, 19.
[25] *Adv. Fovin.*, i, 4.
[26] *Epist. xlix*, 48, *xiv,* 1.
[27] *Comment. in Jer.*, 9, 12.
[28] *Epist. lxxviii*, 30.

[3. *Biblical Inerrancy*]

450   Jerome further shews that the immunity of Scripture from error or deception is necessarily bound up with its Divine inspiration and supreme authority. He says he had learnt this in the most celebrated schools, whether of East or West, and that it was taught him as the doctrine of the Fathers, and generally received.

Thus when, at the instance of Pope Damasus, he had begun correcting the Latin text of the New Testament, and certain "manikins" had vehemently attacked him for "making corrections in the Gospels in face of the authority of the Fathers and of general opinion," Jerome briefly replied that he was not so utterly stupid nor so grossly uneducated as to imagine that the Lord's words needed any correction or were not divinely inspired.[29] Similarly, when explaining Ezechiel's first vision as portraying the *Four Gospels*, he remarks: "That the entire body and the back were full of eyes will be plain to anybody who realizes that there is nought in the Gospels which does not shine and illumine the world by its splendour, so that even things that seem trifling and unimportant shine with the majesty of the Holy Spirit." [30]

What he has said here of the Gospels he applies in his Commentaries to the rest of the Lord's words; he regards it as the very rule and foundation of Catholic interpretation; indeed, for Jerome, a true prophet was to be distinguished from a false by this very note of truth: [31] "The Lord's words are true; for Him to say it means that it is." [32] Again, "Scripture cannot lie"; [33] it is wrong to say Scripture lies,[34] nay, it is impious even to admit the very notion of error where the Bible is concerned.[35]

451   "The Apostles," he says, "are one thing; other writers"—that is, profane writers—"are another"; "the former always tell the truth; the latter—as being mere men—sometimes err," [36] and though many things are said in the Bible which seem incredible, yet they are true [37] in this "word of truth" you cannot find things or statements which are contradictory, "there is nothing discordant nor conflicting"; [38] consequently, "when Scripture seems to be in conflict with itself both passages are true despite their diversity." [39]

Holding principles like these, Jerome was compelled, when he discovered apparent discrepancies in the Sacred Books, to use every

---

[29] *Epist xxvii,* 1.
[30] *In Ezech.,* 1, 15.
[31] *In Mich.,* 2, 11; 3, 5.
[32] *In Mich.,* 4, 1.
[33] *In Jer.,* 31, 35.
[34] *In Nah.,* 1, 9.

[35] *Epist. lvii,* 7.
[36] *Epist. lxxxii,* 7.
[37] *Epist. lxxii,* 2.
[38] *Epist. xviii,* 7; cf. *xlvi,* 6.
[39] *Epist. xxxvi,* 11.

endeavour to unravel the difficulty. If he felt that he had not satis-factorily settled the problem, he would return to it again and again, not always, indeed, with the happiest results. Yet he would never accuse the sacred writers of the slightest mistake—"that we leave to impious folk like Celsus, Porphyry, and Julian." [40]

Here he is in full agreement with Augustine, who wrote to Jerome that to the Sacred Books alone had he been wont to accord such honour and reverence as firmly to believe that none of their writers had ever fallen into any error; and that consequently, if in the said books he came across anything which seemed to run counter to the truth, he did not think that that was really the case, but either that his copy was defective or that the translator had made a mistake, or again, that he himself had failed to understand. He continues: "Nor do I deem that you think otherwise. Indeed, I absolutely de-cline to think that you would have people read your own books in the same way as they read those of the Prophets and Apostles; the idea that these latter could contain any errors is impious." [41]

St. Jerome's teaching on this point serves to confirm and illustrate **452** what our predecessor of happy memory, Leo XIII., declared to be the ancient and traditional belief of the Church touching the absolute immunity of Scripture from error:

"So far is it from being the case that error can be compatible with inspiration, that, on the contrary, it not only of its very nature pre-cludes the presence of error, but as necessarily excludes it and forbids it as God, the Supreme Truth, necessarily cannot be the Author of error." Then, after giving the definitions of the Councils of Florence and Trent, confirmed by the Council of the Vatican, Pope Leo con-tinues:

"Consequently it is not to the point to suggest that the Holy Spirit used men as His instruments for writing, and that therefore, while no error is referable to the primary Author, it may well be due to the inspired authors themselves. For by supernatural power the Holy Spirit so stirred them and moved them to write, so stood by them as they wrote, that their minds could rightly conceive only those and all those things which He Himself bade them conceive; only such things could they faithfully commit to writing and aptly express with unerring truth; else God would not be the Author of the entirety of Sacred Scripture." [42]

---

[40] *Epist. lvii*, 9.
[41] *Inter Epp. S. Hier.*, 116, 3.
[42] Ency., "Providentissimus Deus."

[III MODERN VIEWS COMPARED WITH ST. JEROME'S TEACHING]

453   But although these words of our predecessor leave no room for doubt or dispute, it grieves us to find that not only men outside, but even children of the Catholic Church—nay, what is a peculiar sorrow to us, even clerics and professors of sacred learning—who in their own conceit either openly repudiate or at least attack in secret the Church's teaching on this point.

We warmly commend, of course, those who, with the assistance of critical methods, seek to discover new ways of explaining the difficulties in Holy Scripture, whether for their own guidance or to help others. But we remind them that they will only come to miserable grief if they neglect our predecessor's injunctions and overstep the limits set by the Fathers.

[1. No Distinction of Primary and Secondary Elements]

454   Yet no one can pretend that certain recent writers really adhere to these limitations. For while conceding that inspiration extends to every phrase—and, indeed, to every single word of Scripture—yet, by endeavouring to distinguish between what they style the primary or religious and the secondary or profane element in the Bible, they claim that the effect of inspiration—namely, absolute truth and immunity from error—are to be restricted to that primary or religious element. Their notion is that only what concerns religion is intended and taught by God in Scripture, and that all the rest—things concerning "profane knowledge," the garments in which Divine truth is presented—God merely permits, and even leaves to the individual author's greater or less knowledge. Small wonder, then, that in their view a considerable number of things occur in the Bible touching physical science, history and the like, which cannot be reconciled with modern progress in science!

Some even maintain that these views do not conflict with what our predecessor laid down since—so they claim—he said that the sacred writers spoke in accordance with the external—and thus deceptive—appearance of things in nature.

455   But the Pontiff's own words show that this is a rash and false deduction. For sound philosophy teaches that the senses can never be deceived as regards their own proper and immediate object. Therefore, from the merely external appearance of things—of which, of course, we have always to take account as Leo XIII., following in the footsteps of St. Augustine and St. Thomas, most wisely remarks—we can never conclude that there is any error in Sacred Scripture.

Moreover, our predecessor, sweeping aside all such distinctions between what these critics are pleased to call primary and secondary elements, says in no ambiguous fashion that 'those who fancy that when it is a question of the truth of certain expressions we have not got to consider so much what God said as why He said it," are very far indeed from the truth. He also teaches that Divine inspiration extends to every part of the Bible without the slightest exception, and that no error can occur in the inspired text: "It would be wholly impious to limit inspiration to certain portions only of Scripture or to concede that the sacred authors themselves could have erred." [43]

[2. *No Distinction of Relative and Absolute Truth*]

Those, too, who hold that the historical portions of Scripture do **456** not rest on the absolute truth of the facts but merely upon what they are pleased to term their relative truth, namely, what people then commonly thought, are—no less than are the aforementioned critics —out of harmony with the Church's teaching, which is endorsed by the testimony of Jerome and other Fathers. Yet they are not afraid to deduce such views from the words of Leo XIII. on the ground that he allowed that the principles he had laid down touching the things of nature could be applied to historical things as well. Hence they maintain that precisely as the sacred writers spoke of physical things according to appearances, so, too, while ignorant of the facts, they narrated them in accordance with general opinion or even on baseless evidence; neither do they tell us the sources whence they derived their knowledge, nor do they make other peoples' narrative their own.

Such views are clearly false, and constitute a calumny on our pred- **457** ecessor. After all, what analogy is there between physics and history? For whereas physics are concerned with "sensible appearances" and must consequently square with phenomena, history on the contrary, must square with facts, since history is the written account of events as they actually occurred. If we were to accept such views, how could we maintain the truth insisted on throughout Leo XIII.'s Encyclical— viz. that the sacred narrative is absolutely free from error?

And if Leo XIII. does say that we can apply to history and cog- **458** nate subjects the same principles which hold good for science, he yet does not lay this down as a universal law, but simply says that we can apply a like line of argument when refuting the fallacies of adversaries and defending the historical truth of Scripture from their assaults.

---

[43] Ency., "Providentissimus Deus."

[3. Historical Truth in the Bible]

459   Nor do modern innovators stop here: they even try to claim St. Jerome as a patron of their views on the ground that he maintained that historic truth and sequence were not observed in the Bible, "precisely as things actually took place, but in accordance with what men thought at that time," and that he even held that this was the true norm for history.[44]

A strange distortion of St. Jerome's words! He does not say that when giving us an account of events the writer was ignorant of the truth and simply adopted the false views then current; he merely says that in giving names to persons or things he followed general custom. Thus the Evangelist calls St. Joseph the father of Jesus, but what he meant by the title "father" here is abundantly clear from the whole context. For St. Jerome "the true norm of history" is this: when it is question of such appellatives (as "father," etc.), and when there is no danger of error, then a writer must adopt the ordinary forms of speech simply because such forms of speech are in ordinary use.

460   More than this: Jerome maintains that belief in the Biblical narrative is as necessary to salvation as is belief in the doctrines of the faith; thus in his Commentary on the Epistle to Philemon he says: "What I mean is this: Does any man believe in God the Creator? He cannot do so unless he first believe that the things written of God's Saints are true." He then gives examples from the Old Testament, and adds: "Now unless a man believes all these and other things too which are written of the Saints he cannot believe in the God of the Saints." [45]

Thus St. Jerome is in complete agreement with St. Augustine, who sums up the general belief of Christian antiquity when he says: "Holy Scripture is invested with supreme authority by reason of its sure and momentous teachings regarding the faith. Whatever, then, it tells us of Enoch, Elias and Moses—that we believe. We do not, for instance, believe that God's Son was born of the Virgin Mary simply because He could not otherwise have appeared in the flesh and 'walked amongst men'—as Faustus would have it—but we believe it simply because it is written in Scripture; and unless we believe in Scripture we can neither be Christians nor be saved." [46]

---

[44] *In Jer.*, 28, 10; *in Matt.*, 14, 8; *Adv. Helvid.*, 4.
[45] *In Phil.*, iv.
[46] *Contra Faustum*, xxvi, 3, 6.

[4. No "Tacit Quotations"]

Then there are other assailants of Holy Scripture who misuse prin- **461** ciples—which are only sound, if kept within due bounds—in order to overturn the fundamental truth of the Bible and thus destroy Catholic teaching handed down by the Fathers.

If Jerome were living now he would sharpen his keenest controversial weapons against people who set aside what is the mind and judgment of the Church, and take too ready a refuge in such notions as "implicit quotations" or "pseudo-historical narratives," or in "kinds of literature" in the Bible such as cannot be reconciled with the entire and perfect truth of God's word, or who suggest such origins of the Bible as must inevitably weaken—if not destroy—its authority.

What can we say of men who in expounding the very Gospels so **462** whittle away the human trust we should repose in it as to overturn Divine faith in it? They refuse to allow that the things which Christ said or did have come down to us unchanged and entire through witnesses who carefully committed to writing what they themselves had seen or heard. They maintain—and particularly in their treatment of the *Fourth Gospel*—that much is due of course to the Evangelists —who, however, added much from their own imaginations; but much, too, is due to narratives compiled by the faithful at other periods, the result, of course, being that the twin streams now flowing in the same channel cannot be distinguished from one another.

Not thus did Jerome and Augustine and the other Doctors of the Church understand the historical trustworthiness of the Gospels; yet of it one wrote: "He that saw it hath given testimony, and his testimony is true. And he knoweth that he saith true that you also may believe" (Jn. 19:35). So, too, St. Jerome: after rebuking the heretical framers of the apocryphal Gospels for "attempting rather to fill up the story than to tell it truly," [47] he says of the Canonical Scriptures: "None can doubt but that what is written took place." [48] Here again he is in fullest harmony with Augustine, who so beautifully says: "These things are true; they are faithfully and truthfully written of Christ; so that whosoever believes His Gospel may be thereby instructed in the truth and misled by no lie." [49]

[47] *Prol. in Comment, in Matt.*   [49] *Contra Faustum,* xxvi, 8.
[48] *Epist. lxxviii,* 1.

*[5. Modern Views Incompatible with Tradition and with
Christ's Method]*

463   All this shows us how earnestly we must strive to avoid, as children
of the Church, this insane freedom in ventilating opinions which the
Fathers were careful to shun. This we shall more readily achieve if
you, Venerable Brethren, will make both clergy and laity committed
to your care by the Holy Spirit realise that neither Jerome nor the
other Fathers of the Church learned their doctrine touching Holy
Scripture save in the school of the Divine Master Himself.

We know what He felt about Holy Scripture: when He said, "It
is written," and "the Scripture must needs be fulfilled," we have
therein an argument which admits of no exception and which should
put an end to all controversy.

Yet it is worth while dwelling on this point a little: when Christ
preached to the people, whether on the Mount by the lake-side, or in
the synagogue at Nazareth, or in His own city of Capharnaum, He
took His points and His arguments from the Bible. From the same
source came His weapons when disputing with the Scribes and Pharisees. Whether teaching or disputing He quotes from all parts of
Scripture and takes his example from it; He quotes it as an argument which must be accepted. He refers without any discrimination
of sources to the stories of Jonas and the Ninivites, of the Queen of
Sheba and Solomon, of Elias and Eliseus, of David and of Noe, of Lot
and the Sodomites, and even of Lot's wife. (Cf. Mt. 12:3, 39-42;
Lk. 17:26-29, 32).

How solemn His witness to the truth of the sacred books: "One jot,
or one title shall not pass of the Law till all be fulfilled" (Mt. 5:18);
and again: "The Scripture cannot be broken" (Jn. 10:35); and consequently: "He therefore that shall break one of these least commandments, and shall so teach men shall be called the least in the
kingdom of heaven" (Mt. 5:19). Before His Ascension, too, when
He would steep His Apostles in the same doctrine: "He opened their
understanding that they might understand the Scriptures. And He
said to them: thus it is written, and thus it behoved Christ to suffer,
and to rise again from the dead the third day" (Lk. 24:45).

In a word, then: Jerome's teaching on the superexcellence and
truth of Scripture is Christ's teaching. Wherefore we exhort all the
Church's children, and especially those whose duty it is to teach in
seminaries, to follow closely in St. Jerome's footsteps. If they will
but do so they will learn to prize as he prized the treasure of the
Scriptures, and will derive from them most abundant and blessed
fruit.

[IV PRACTICAL COUNSELS]

[*1. On the Love of the Bible*]

Now, if we make use of the "Greatest of Doctors" as our guide and **464**
teacher we shall derive from so doing not only the gains signalised
above, but others too, which cannot be regarded as trifling or few.
What these gains are, Venerable Brethren, we will set out briefly.

At the outset, then, we are deeply impressed by the intense love
of the Bible which St. Jerome exhibits in his whole life and teaching:
both are steeped in the Spirit of God. This intense love of the Bible
he was ever striving to kindle in the hearts of the faithful, and his
words on this subject to the maiden Demetrias are really addressed
to us all: "Love the Bible and wisdom will love you; love it and it
will preserve you; honour it and it will embrace you; these are the
jewels which you should wear on your breast and in your ears." [50]

His unceasing reading of the Bible and his painstaking study of **465**
each book—nay, of every phrase and word—gave him a knowledge
of the text such as no other ecclesiastical writer of old possessed. It
is due to this familiarity with the text and to his own acute judgment
that the Vulgate version Jerome made is, in the judgment of all capable men, preferable to any other ancient version, since it appears
to give us the sense of the original more accurately and with greater
elegance than they.

The said Vulgate, "approved by so many centuries of use in the **466**
Church," was pronounced by the Council of Trent "authentic," and
the same Council insisted that it was to be used in teaching and in
the liturgy. If God in His mercy grants us life, we sincerely hope to
see an amended and faithfully restored edition. We have no doubt
that when this arduous task—entrusted by our predecessor, Pius X.,
to the Benedictine Order—has been completed it will prove of great
assistance in the study of the Bible.

But to return to St. Jerome's love of the Bible: this is so conspicu- **467**
ous in his letters that they almost seem woven out of Scripture texts;
and, as St. Bernard found no taste in things which did not echo the
most sweet Name of Jesus, so no literature made any appeal to
Jerome unless it derived its light from Holy Scripture. Thus he
wrote to Paulinus, formerly senator and even consul, and only recently converted to the faith: "If only you had this foundation
(knowledge of Scripture); nay, more—if you would let Scripture give
the finishing touches to your work—I should find nothing more beautiful, more learned, even nothing more Latin than your volumes. . . .
If you could but add to your wisdom and eloquence study of and real

---

[50] *Epist. cxxx*, 20.

acquaintance with Holy Scripture, we should speedily have to acknowledge you a leader amongst us." [51]

[2. Need of Preparation]

468   How we are to seek for this great treasure, given as it is by our Father in heaven for our solace during this earthly pilgrimage, St. Jerome's example shows us.

First, we must be well prepared and must possess a good will. Thus Jerome himself, immediately on his baptism, determined to remove whatever might prove a hindrance to his ambitions in this respect. Like the man who found a treasure and "for joy thereof went and sold all that he had and bought that field" (Mt. 13:44), so did Jerome say farewell to the idle pleasures of this passing world; he went into the desert, and since he realised what risks he had run in the past through the allurements of vice, he adopted a most severe style of life.

With all obstacles thus removed he prepared his soul for "the knowledge of Jesus Christ" and for putting on Him Who was "meek and humble of heart." But he went through what Augustine also experienced when he took up the study of Scripture. For the latter has told us how, steeped as a youth in Cicero and profane authors, the Bible seemed to me unfit to be compared with Cicero. "My swelling pride shrank from its modest garb, while my gaze could not pierce to what the latter hid. Of a truth Scripture was meant to grow up with the childlike; but then I could not be childlike; turgid eloquence appealed mightily to me." [52]

So, to, St. Jerome; even though withdrawn into the desert he still found such delight in profane literature that at first he failed to discern the lowly Christ in His lowly Scriptures: "Wretch that I was! I read Cicero even before I broke my fast! And after the long night-watches, when memory of my past sins wrung tears from my soul, even then I took up my Plautus! Then perhaps I would come to my senses and would start reading the Prophets. But their uncouth language made me shiver, and, since blind eyes do not see the light, I blamed the sun and not my own eyes." [53]

But in a brief space Jerome became so enamored of the "folly of the Cross" that he himself serves as a proof of the extent to which a humble and devout frame of mind is conducive to the understanding of Holy Scripture.

469   He realized that "in expounding Scripture we need God's Holy

[51] *Epist. lviii*, 9, 11.   [53] *Epist. xxii*, 30.
[53] *Confessiones*, iii, 5; cf. viii, 12.

Spirit"; [54] he saw that one cannot otherwise read or understand it "than the Holy Spirit by Whom it was written demands." [55] Consequently, he was ever humbly praying for God's assistance and for the light of the Holy Spirit, and asking his friends to do the same for him. We find him commending to the Divine assistance and to his brethren's prayers his Commentaries on various books as he began them, and then rendering God due thanks when completed.

[3. Need of Lively Catholic Faith]

As he trusted to God's grace, so too did he rely upon the authority **470** of his predecessors: "What I have learned I did not teach myself—a wretchedly presumptuous teacher!—but I learned it from illustrious men in the Church." [56] Again: "In studying Scripture I never trusted to myself." [57] To Theophilus, Bishop of Alexandria, he imparted the rule he had laid down for his own student life: "It has always been my custom to fight for the prerogatives of a Christian, not to overpass the limits set by the Fathers, always to bear in mind that Roman faith praised by the Apostle." [58]

He ever paid submissive homage to the Church, our supreme **471** teacher through the Roman Pontiffs. Thus, with a view to putting an end to the controversy raging in the East concerning the mystery of the Holy Trinity, he submitted the question to the Roman See for settlement, and wrote from the Syrian desert to Pope Damasus as follows: "I decided, therefore, to consult the Chair of Peter and that Roman faith which the Apostle praised; I ask for my soul's food from that city wherein I first put on the garment of Christ. . . . I, who follow no other leader save Christ, associate myself with Your Blessedness, in communion, that is, with the Chair of Peter. For I know the Church was built upon that Rock. . . . I beg you to settle this dispute. If you desire it I shall not be afraid to say there are Three Hypostases. If it is your wish let them draw up a Symbol of faith subsequent to that of Nicæa, and let us orthodox praise God in the same form of words as the Arians employ." [59] And in his next letter: "Meanwhile I keep crying out, 'Any man who is joined to Peter's Chair, he is my man.'" [60]

Since he had learnt this "rule of faith" from his study of the Bible **472** he was able to refute a false interpretation of a Biblical text with the simple remark: "Yes, but the Church of God does not admit that." [61]

---

[54] *In Mich.*, 1, 10, 15.
[55] *In Gal.*, 5, 19.
[56] *Epist. cviii*, 26.
[57] *Praefat. in* 1 *Paral.*
[58] *Epist.* lxiii, 2.
[59] *Epist. xv,* 1.
[60] *Epist. xvi.*, 2.
[61] *In Dan.*, 3, 37.

When, again, Vigilantius quoted an Apocryphal book, Jerome was content to reply: "A book I have never so much as read! For what is the good of soiling one's hands with a book the Church does not receive?" [62]

473   With his strong insistence on adhering to the integrity of the faith, it is not to be wondered at that he attacked vehemently those who left the Church; he promptly regarded them as his own personal enemies. "To put it briefly," he says, "I have never spared heretics, and have always striven to regard the Church's enemies as my own." [63] To Rufinus he writes: "There is one point in which I cannot agree with you: you ask me to spare heretics—or, in other words—not to prove myself a Catholic." [64]   Yet at the same time Jerome deplored the lamentable state of heretics, and adjured them to return to their sorrowing Mother, the one source of salvation; [65] he prayed, too, with all earnestness for the conversion of those "who had quitted the Church and put away the Holy Spirit's teaching to follow their own notions." [66]

474   Was there ever a time, Venerable Brethren, when there was greater call than now for us all, lay and cleric alike, to imbibe the spirit of this "Greatest of Doctors"?   For there are many contumacious folk now who sneer at the authority and government of God, Who has revealed Himself and of the Church which teaches.   You know—for Leo XIII. warned us—"how insistently men fight against us; you know the arms and arts they rely upon."

It is your duty, then, to train as many really fit defenders of this holiest of causes as you can.   They must be ready to combat not only those who deny the existence of the Supernatural Order altogether, and are thus led to deny the existence of any divine revelation or inspiration, but those, too, who—through an itching desire for novelty —venture to interpret the sacred books as though they were of purely human origin; those, too, who scoff at opinions held of old in the Church, or who, through contempt of its teaching office, either reck little of, or silently disregard, or at least obstinately endeavour to adapt to their own views, the Constitutions of the Apostolic See or the decisions of the Pontifical Biblical Commission.

Would that all Catholics would cling to St. Jerome's golden rule and obediently listen to their Mother's words, so as modestly to keep within the bounds marked out by the Fathers and ratified by the Church.

---

[62] *Adv. Vigil.*, 6.
[63] *Dial. contra Pelagianos, Prol.*, 2.
[64] *Contra Rufin.*, 3, 43.

[65] *In Mich.*, 1, 10.
[66] *In Isa.*, 16, 1-5.

[4. Piety and Humility]

To return, however, to the question of the formation of Biblical 475 students. We must lay the foundations in piety and humility of mind; only when we have done that does St. Jerome invite us to study the Bible.

In the first place, he insists, in season and out, on daily reading of the text. "Provided," he says, "our bodies are not the slaves of sin, wisdom will come to us; but exercise your mind, feed it daily with Holy Scripture." [67] And again: "We have got, then, to read Holy Scripture assiduously; we have got to meditate on the Law of God day and night so that, as expert money-changers, we may be able to detect false coin from true." [68]

For matrons and maidens alike he lays down the same rule. Thus, writing to the Roman matron Laeta about her daughter's training, he says: "Every day she should give you a definite account of her Bible-reading. . . . For her the Bible must take the place of silks and jewels. . . . Let her learn the Psalter first, and find her recreation in its songs; let her learn from Solomon's Proverbs the way of life, from Ecclesiastes how to trample on the world. In Job she will find an example of patient virtue. Thence let her pass to the Gospels; they should always be in her hands. She should steep herself in the Acts and the Epistles. And when she has enriched her soul with these treasures she should commit to memory the Prophets, the Heptateuch, Kings and Chronicles, Esdras and Esther; then she can learn the Canticle of Canticles without any fear." [69]

He says the same to Eustochium: "Read assiduously and learn as much as you can. Let sleep find you holding your Bible, and when your head nods let it be resting on the sacred page." [70] When he sent Eustochium the epitaph he had composed for her mother Paula, he especially praises that holy woman for having so whole-heartedly devoted herself and her daughter to Bible study that she knew the Bible through and through, and had committed it to memory. He continues:

"I will tell you another thing about her, though evil-disposed people may cavil at it: she determined to learn Hebrew, a language which I myself, with immense labour and toil from my youth upwards, have only partly learned, and which I even now dare not cease studying lest it should quit me. But Paula learned it, and so well that she could chant the Psalms in Hebrew, and could speak it, too, without any trace of a Latin accent. We can see the same thing even now in her daughter Eustochium." [71]

---

[67] *Comment in Tit.*, 3, 9.
[68] *Comment. in Eph.*, 4, 31.
[69] *Epist. cvii*, 9.
[70] *Epist. xxii*, 17, 29.

He tells us much the same of Marcella, who also knew the Bible exceedingly well.[72]

476   And none can fail to see what profit and sweet tranquillity must result in well-disposed souls from such devout reading of the Bible. Whosoever comes to it in piety, faith and humility, and with a determination to make progress in it, will assuredly find therein and will eat the "Bread that cometh down from heaven"; he will, in his own person, experience the truth of David's words: "The hidden and uncertain things of Thy Wisdom Thou hast made manifest to me!" For this table of the "Divine Word" does really "contain holy teaching, teach the true faith, and lead us unfalteringly beyond the veil into the Holy of holies." [73]

477   Hence, as far as in us lies, we, Venerable Brethren, shall, with St. Jerome as our guide, never desist from urging the faithful to read daily the Gospels, the Acts and the Epistles, so as to gather thence food for their souls.

[5. Society of St. Jerome]

478   Our thoughts naturally turn just now to the Society of St. Jerome, which we ourselves were instrumental in founding; its success has gladdened us, and we trust that the future will see a great impulse given to it. The object of this Society is to put into the hands of as many people as possible the Gospels and Acts, so that every Christian family may have them and become accustomed to reading them. This we have much at heart, for we have seen how useful it is. We earnestly hope, then, that similar Societies will be founded in your dioceses and affiliated to the parent Society here.

479   Commendation, too, is due to Catholics in other countries who have published the entire New Testament, as well as selected portions of the Old, in neat and simple form so as to popularize their use. Much gain must accrue to the Church of God when numbers of people thus approach this table of heavenly instruction which the Lord provided through the ministry of His Prophets, Apostles and Doctors, for the entire Christian world.

---

[71] *Epist.* cviii, 26.   [73] *Imitatio Christi,* 4, 11.
[72] *Epist. cxxvii,* 7.

[V THE BIBLE AND PRIESTLY EDUCATION]

[1. Need of Biblical Learning]

If, then, St. Jerome begs for assiduous reading of the Bible by the **480**
faithful in general, he insists on it for those who are called to "bear
the yoke of Christ" and preach His word.
His words to Rusticus the monk apply to all clerics: "So long as
you are in your own country regard your cell as your orchard; there
you can gather Scripture's various fruits and enjoy the pleasures it
affords you. Always have a book in your hands—and read it; learn
the Psalter by heart; pray unceasingly; watch over your senses lest
idle thoughts creep in." [74] Similarly to Nepotian: "Constantly read
the Bible; in fact, have it always in your hands. Learn what you
have got to teach. Get firm hold of that 'faithful word that is according to doctrine, that you may be able to exhort in sound doctrine
and convince the gainsayers.' " [75]
When reminding Paulinus of the lessons St. Paul gave to Timothy
and Titus, and which he himself had derived from the Bible, Jerome
says: "A mere holy rusticity only avails the man himself; but however much a life so meritorious may serve to build up the Church of
God, it does as much harm to the Church if it fails to 'resist the
gainsayer.' Malachi the Prophet says, or rather the Lord says it by
Malachi: 'Ask for the Law from the priests.' For it is the priest's
duty to give an answer when asked about the Law. In Deuteronomy
we read: 'Ask thy father and he will tell thee; ask the priests and
they will tell thee. . . .' Daniel, too, at the close of the glorious vision, declares that 'the just shall shine like stars and they that are
learned as the brightness of the firmament.' What a vast difference,
then, between a righteous rusticity and a learned righteousness! The
former likened to the stars; the latter to the heavens themselves!" [76]
He writes ironically to Marcella about the "self-righteous lack of
education" noticeable in some clerics, who "think that to be without
culture and to be holy are the same thing, and who dub themselves
'disciples of the fisherman'; as though they were holy simply because
ignorant!" [77]
Nor is it only the "uncultured" whom Jerome condemns. Learned
clerics sin through ignorance of the Bible; therefore he demands of
them an assiduous reading of the text.

---

[74] *Epist. cxxvii*, 7, 11.
[75] *Epist. lii, 7; cf.* Tit. 1, 9.
[76] *Epist. liii*, 3.
[77] *Epist. xxvii*, 1.

[2. Pontifical Biblical Institute]

481   Strive, then, Venerable Brethren, to bring home to your clerics and priests these teachings of the Sainted Commentator. You have to remind them constantly of the demands made by their divine vocation if they would be worthy of it: "The lips of the priest shall keep knowledge, and men shall ask the Law at his mouth, for he is the Angel of the Lord of hosts" (Mal. 2:7).

They must realise, then, that they cannot neglect study of the Bible, and that this can only be undertaken along the lines laid down by Leo XIII. in his Encyclical *Providentissimus Deus*.[78]

They cannot do this better than by frequenting the Biblical Institute established by our predecessor, Pius X., in accordance with the wishes of Leo XIII. As the experience of the past ten years has shown, it has proved a great gain to the Church. Not all, however, can avail themselves of this. It will be well, then, Venerable Brethren, that picked men, both of the secular and regular clergy, should come to Rome for Biblical study.

All will not come with the same object. Some, in accordance with the real purpose of the Institute, will so devote themselves to Biblical study that "afterwards, both in private and in public, whether by writing or by teaching, whether as professors in Catholic schools or by writing in defence of Catholic truth, they may be able worthily to uphold the cause of Biblical study."[79]   Others, however, already priests, will obtain here a wider knowledge of the Bible than they were able to acquire during their theological course; they will gain, too, an acquaintance with the great commentators and with Biblical history and geography. Such knowledge will avail them much in their ministry; they will be "instructed to every good work."[80]

[VI PURPOSE OF BIBLICAL KNOWLEDGE]

[1. Spiritual Perfection]

482   We learn, then, from St. Jerome's example and teaching the qualities required in one who would devote himself to Biblical study. But what, in his view, is the goal of such study?

First, that from the Bible's pages we learn spiritual perfection. Meditating as he did day and night on the Law of the Lord and on His Scriptures, Jerome himself found there the "Bread that cometh down from heaven," the manna containing all delights.[81]   And we

---

[78] "Rome and the Study of Scripture," pp. 8-15.
[79] Pius X., "Vinea electa," May 7, 1909.
[80] 2 Tim. 3, 17.   [81] *Tract. in Ps. cxlvii.*

certainly cannot do without that bread. How can a cleric teach others the way of salvation if through neglect of meditation on God's word he fails to teach himself? What confidence can he have that, when ministering to others, he is really "a leader of the blind, a light to them that are in darkness, an instructor of the foolish, having the form of knowledge and of truth in the law," if he is unwilling to study the said Law and thus shuts the door on any divine illumination on it? Alas! many of God's ministers, through never looking at their Bible, perish themselves and allow many others to perish also. "The children have asked for bread, and there was none to break it to them" (Lam. 4:4); and "With desolation is all the land made desolate, for there is none that meditateth in the heart" (Jer. 12:11).

[2. Defense of Catholic Truth]

Secondly, it is from the Bible that we gather confirmations and il- **483** lustrations of any particular doctrine we wish to defend. In this Jerome was marvellously expert. When disputing with the heretics of his day he refuted by singularly apt and weighty arguments drawn from the Bible. If men of the present age would but imitate him in this we should see realised what our predecessor, Leo XIII., in his Encyclical, *Providentissimus Deus*, said was so eminently desirable: "The Bible influencing our theological teaching and indeed becoming its very soul."

Lastly, the real value of the Bible is for our preaching—if the **484** latter is to be fruitful. On this point it is a pleasure to illustrate from Jerome what we ourselves said in our Encyclical on "preaching the Word of God," entitled *Humani generis*. How insistently Jerome urges on priests assiduous reading of the Bible if they would worthily teach and preach! Their words will have neither value nor weight nor any power to touch men's souls save in proportion as they are "informed" by Holy Scripture: "Let a priest's speech be seasoned with the Bible," [82] for "the Scriptures are a trumpet that stirs us with a mighty voice and penetrates to the soul of them that believe," [83] and "nothing so strikes home as an example taken from the Bible." [84]

[3. Rules of Interpretation]

These mainly concern the exegetes, yet preachers, too, must always **485** bear them in mind. Jerome's first rule is careful study of the actual words so that we may be perfectly certain what the writer really does say.

---

[82] *Epist. lii*, 8. [84] *In Zach.*, 9, 15.
[83] *In Amos*, 3, 3.

He was most careful to consult the original text, to compare various versions, and, if he discovered any mistake in them, to explain it and thus make the text perfectly clear.

The precise meaning, too, that attaches to particular words has to be worked out, for "when discussing Holy Scripture it is not words we want so much as the meaning of words."[85] We do not for a moment deny that Jerome, in imitation of Latin and Greek doctors before him, leaned too much, especially at the outset, towards allegorical interpretations. But his love of the Bible, his unceasing toil in reading and re-reading it and weighing its meaning, compelled him to an ever-growing appreciation of its literal sense and to the formulation of sound principles regarding it. These we set down here, for they mark out a safe path for us if we would discover the Bible's meaning.

In the first place, then, we must study the literal or historical meaning: "I earnestly warn the prudent reader not to pay attention to superstitious interpretations such as are given cut and dried according to some interpreter's fancy. He should study the beginning, middle, and end, and so form a connected idea of the whole of what he finds written."[86] Jerome then goes on to say that all interpretation rests on the literal sense,[87] and that we are not to think that there is no literal sense merely because a thing is said metaphorically, for "the history itself is often presented in metaphorical dress and described figuratively."[88] Indeed, he himself affords the best refutation of those who maintain that he says that certain passages have no historical meaning: "We are not rejecting the history, we are merely giving a spiritual interpretation of it."[89]

486   Once, however, he has firmly established the literal or historical meaning, Jerome goes on to seek out deeper and hidden meanings, so as to nourish his mind with more delicate food. Thus he says of the Book of Proverbs—and he makes the same remark about other parts of the Bible—that we must not stop at the simple literal sense: "Just as we have to seek gold in the earth, for the kernel in the shell, for the chestnut's hidden fruit beneath its hairy coverings, so in Holy Scripture we have to dig deep for its divine meaning."[90] When teaching Paulinus "how to make true progress in the Bible," he says: "Everything we read in the Sacred Books shines and glitters even in its outer shell; but the marrow of it is sweeter. If you want the kernel you must break the shell."[91]

At the same time, he insists that in searching for this deeper

---

[85] *Epist. xxix*, 1.
[86] *In Matt.*, 25, 13.
[87] Cf. *In Ezech.* 38, 1; 41:23; *In Marc.*, 1, 13-31; *Epist. cxxix*, 6.
[88] *In Hab.*, 3, 14.   [90] *In Eccles.*, 12, 9.
[89] *In Marc.*, 9, 1-7; cf. *In Ezech.*, 40, 24-27.   [91] *Epist. lix*, 9.

meaning we must proceed in due order, "lest in our search for spiritual riches we seem to despise the history as poverty-stricken." [92] Consequently he repudiates many mystical interpretatations alleged by ancient writers; for he feels that they are not sufficiently based on the literal meaning: "When all these promises. of which the Prophets sang are regarded not merely as empty sounds or idle tropological expressions, but as established on earth and having solid historical foundations, then, and only then, can we put on them the copingstone of a spiritual interpretation." [93]

On this point he makes the wise remark that we ought not to desert the path mapped out by Christ and His Apostles, who, while regarding the Old Testament as preparing for and foreshadowing the New Covenant, and whilst consequently explaining various passages in the former as figurative, yet do not give a figurative interpretation of all alike. In confirmation of this he often refers us to St. Paul, who, when "explaining the mystery of Adam and Eve, did not deny that they were formed, but on that historical basis erected a spiritual interpretation, and said: 'Therefore shall a man leave,' etc." [94]

[4. True Pulpit Oratory]

If only Biblical students and preachers would but follow this example of Christ and His Apostles; if they would but obey the directions of Leo XIII., and not neglect "those allegorical or similar explanations which the Fathers have given, especially when these are based on the literal sense, and are supported by weighty authority"; if they would pass from the literal to the more profound meaning in temperate fashion, and thus lift themselves to a higher plane, they would, with St. Jerome, realize how true are St. Paul's words: "All Scripture inspired of God is profitable to teach, to reprove, to correct, to instruct in justice" (2 Tim. 3:16). They would, too, derive abundant help from the infinite treasury of facts and ideas in the Bible, and would thence be able to mould firmly but gently the lives and characters of the faithful.

As for methods of expounding Holy Scripture—"for amongst the **487** dispensers of the mysteries of God it is required that a man be found faithful"—St. Jerome lays down that we have got to keep to the "true interpretation, and that the real function of a commentator is to set forth not what he himself would like his author to mean, but what he really does mean."[95] And he continues: "It is dangerous to speak in the Church, lest through some faulty interpretation we make Christ's Gospel into man's Gospel." [96]

---

[92] *In Eccles.*, 2, 24.
[93] *In Amos*, 9, 6.
[94] *In Isa.*, 6, 1-7.

[95] *Epist. xlix (xlviii)*, 17.
[96] *In Gal.*, 1, 11.

And again: "In explaining the Bible we need no florid oratorical composition, but that learned simplicity which is truth." [97]   This ideal he ever kept before him; he acknowledges that in his Commentaries he "seeks no praise, but so to set out what another has well said that it may be understood in the sense in which it was said." [98] He further demands of an expositor of Scripture a style which, "while leaving no impression of haziness . . . yet explains things, sets out the meaning, clears up obscurities, and is not mere verbiage." [99]

And here we may set down some passages from his writings which will serve to show to what an extent he shrank from that declamatory kind of eloquence which simply aims at winning empty applause by an equally empty and noisy flow of words. He says to Nepotian: "I do not want you to be a declaimer or a garrulous brawler; rather be skilled in the Mysteries, learned in the Sacraments of God. To make the populace gape by spinning words and speaking like a whirlwind is only worthy of empty-headed men." [100]   And once more: "Students ordained at this time seem not to think how they may get at the real marrow of Holy Scripture, but how best they may make peoples' ears tingle by their flowery declamations! [101]   Again: "I prefer to say nothing of men, who, like myself, have passed from profane literature, to Biblical study, but who, if they happen once to have caught men's ears by their ornate sermons, straightway begin to fancy that whatsoever they say is God's law. Apparently they do not think it worth while to discover what the Prophets and Apostles really meant; they are content to string together texts made to fit the meaning they want. One would almost fancy that instead of being a degraded species of oratory, it must be a fine thing to pervert the meaning of the text and compel the reluctant Scripture to yield the meaning one wants! [102]   "As a matter of fact, mere loquacity would not win any credit unless backed by Scriptural authority, when, that is, men see that the speaker is trying to give his false doctrine Biblical support" (Tit. 1:10).

Moreover, this garrulous eloquence and wordy rusticity "lacks biting power, has nothing vivid or life-giving in it; it is flaccid, languid and enervated; it is like boiled herbs and grass, which speedily dry up and wither away." On the contrary the Gospel teaching is straightforward, it is like that "least of all seeds"—the mustard seed— "no mere vegetable, but something that 'grows into a tree so that the birds of the air come and dwell in its branches.' " [103]

The consequence is that everybody hears gladly this simple and

[97] Præf. in Amos.
[98] Præf. in Gal.
[99] Epist. xxxvi, 14; cf. cxl, 1.
[100] Epist. lii, 8.
[101] Dialogus contra Luciferianos, xi.
[102] Epist. liii, 7.
[103] Comment. in Matt., 13, 32.

holy fashion of speech, for it is clear and has real beauty without artificiality: "There are certain eloquent folk who puff out their cheeks and produce a foaming torrent of words; may they win all the eulogiums they crave for! For myself, I prefer so to speak that I may be intelligible; when I discuss the Bible I prefer the Bible's simplicity. . . .[104] A cleric's exposition of the Bible should, of course, have a certain becoming eloquence; but he must keep this in the background, for he must ever have in view the human race and not the leisurely philosophical schools with their choice coterie of disciples." [105]

If the younger clergy would but strive to reduce principles like these to practice, and if their elders would keep such principles before their eyes, we are well assured that they would prove of very real assistance to those to whom they minister.

[VII FRUITS OF BIBLICAL STUDY]

[1. The Soul's True Delight]

It only remains for us, Venerable Brethren, to refer to those "sweet **488** fruits" which Jerome gathered from "the bitter seed" of literature. For we confidently hope that his example will fire both clergy and laity with enthusiasm for the study of the Bible.

It will be better, however, for you to gather from the lips of the saintly hermit rather than from our words what real spiritual delight he found in the Bible and its study. Notice, then, in what strain he writes to Paulinus, "my companion, friend, and fellow-mystic": "I beseech you to live amidst these things. To meditate on them, to know nought else, to have no other interests, this is really a foretaste of the joys of heaven." [106]

He says much the same to his pupil Paula: "Tell me whether you know of anything more sacred than this sacred mystery, anything more delightful than the pleasure found herein? What food, what honey could be sweeter than to learn of God's Providence, to enter into His shrine and look into the mind of the Creator, to listen to the Lord's words at which the wise of this world laugh, but which really are full of spiritual teaching? Others may have their wealth, may drink out of jewelled cups, be clad in silks, enjoy popular applause, find it impossible to exhaust their wealth by dissipating it in pleasures of all kinds; but our delight is to meditate on the Law of the Lord day and night, to knock at His door when shut, to receive our food from the Trinity of Persons, and, under the guidance of the Lord, trample under foot the swelling tumults of this world." [107]

---

[104] *Epist. xxxvi*, 14.
[105] *Epist. xlviii (xlix)*, 4.
[106] *Epist. liii*, 10.
[107] *Epist. xxx*, 13.

And in his Commentary on the Epistle to the Ephesians, which he dedicated to Paula and her daughter Eustochium, he says: "If aught could sustain and support a wise man in this life or help him to preserve his equanimity amid the conflicts of the world, it is, I reckon, meditation on and knowledge of the Bible." [108]

[2. Zeal for the Cause of Christ]

And so it was with Jerome himself: afflicted with many mental anxieties and bodily pains, he yet ever enjoyed an interior peace. Nor was this due simply to some idle pleasure he found in such studies: it sprang from love of God and it worked itself out in an earnest love of God's Church—the divinely appointed guardian of God's Word.

489   For in the Books of both Testaments Jerome saw the Church of God foretold. Did not practically every one of the illustrious and sainted women who hold place of honour in the Old Testament prefigure the Church, God's Spouse? Did not the priesthood, the sacrifices, the solemnities, nay, nearly everything described in the Old Testament, shadow forth that same Church? How many Psalms and Prophecies he saw fulfilled in that Church? To him it was clear that the Church's greatest privileges were set forth by Christ and His Apostles. Small wonder, then, that growing familiarity with the Bible meant for Jerome growing love of the Spouse of Christ.

We have seen with what reverent yet enthusiastic love be attached himself to the Roman Church and to the See of Peter, how eagerly he attacked those who assailed her. So when applauding Augustine, his junior yet his fellow-soldier, and rejoicing in the fact that they were one in their hatred of heresy, he hails him with the words: "Well done! You are famous throughout the world. Catholics revere you and point you out as the establisher of the old-time faith; and—an even greater glory—all heretics hate you. And they hate me too; unable to slay us with the sword, they would that wishes could kill." [109] Sulpicius Severus quotes Postumianus to the same effect: "His unceasing conflict with wicked men brings on him their hatred. Heretics hate him, for he never ceases attacking them; clerics hate him, for he assails their criminal lives. But all good men admire him and love him." [110]

And Jerome had to endure much from heretics and abandoned men, especially when the Pelagians laid waste the monastery at Bethlehem. Yet all this he bore with equanimity, like a man who would not hesitate to die for the faith: "I rejoice when I hear that my children are fighting for Christ. May He in whom we believe con-

---

[108] *Prol. in Eph.*   [110] *Dial.*, 1, 9.
[109] *Epist. cxli*, 2.

firm our zeal so that we may gladly shed our blood for His faith.
Our very home is—as far as worldly belongings go—completely
ruined by the heretics; yet through Christ's mercy it is filled with
spiritual riches. It is better to have to be content with dry bread
than to lose one's faith."[111]

And while he never suffered errors to creep in unnoticed, he like-   **490**
wise never failed to lash with biting tongue any looseness in morals,
for he was always anxious "to present," unto Christ "a glorious
Church, not having spot or wrinkle or any such things, but that it
should be holy and without blemish" (Eph. 5:27). How terribly he
upbraids men who have degraded the dignity of the priesthood!
With what vigour he inveighs against the pagan morals then infecting
Rome!

But he rightly felt that nothing could better avail to stem this
flood of vice than the spectacle afforded by the real beauty of the
Christian life; and that a love of what is really good is the best
antidote to evil. Hence he urged that young people must be piously
brought up, the married taught a holy integrity of life, pure souls
have the beauty of virginity put before them, that the sweet austerity
of an interior life should be extolled, and since the primal law of
Christian religion was the combination of toil with charity, that if
this could only be preserved human society would recover from its
disturbed state.

Of this charity he says very beautifully: "The believing soul is
Christ's true temple. Adorn it, deck it out, offer your gifts to it, in
it receive Christ. Of what profit to have your walls glittering with
jewels while Christ dies of hunger in poverty?"[112] As for toil, his
whole life and not merely his writings afford the best example. Postumianus, who spent six months with him at Bethlehem, says: "He
is wholly occupied in reading and with books; he rests neither day
nor night; he is always either reading or writing something."[113]

[3. Love of Christ]

Jerome's love of the Church, too, shines out even in his Commentaries wherein he lets slip no opportunity for praising the Spouse of
Christ: "The choicest things of all the nations have come and the
Lord's House is filled with glory: that is, 'the Church of the Living
God, the pillar and the ground of truth.' . . . With jewels like these
is the Church richer than ever was the synagogue; with these living
stones is the House of God built up and eternal peace bestowed
upon her."[114]

[111] *Epist. cxxxiv.*   [113] Sulpicius Severus, *Dial.*, 1:9.
[112] *Epist. lviii,* 7.   [114] *In Agg.*, 2, 1.

"Come, let us go up to the Mount of the Lord: for we must needs go up if we would come to Christ and to the House of the God of Jacob, to the Church which is 'the pillar and ground of truth.' "[115]

"By the Lord's voice is the Church established upon the rock, and her hath the King brought into His chamber, to her by secret condescension hath He put forth His hand through the lattices."[116]

491   Again and again, as in the passages just given, does Jerome celebrate the intimate union between Christ and His Church. For since the Head can never be separated from the mystical body, so, too, love of Christ is ever associated with zeal for His Church; and this love of Christ must ever be the chiefest and most agreeable result of a knowledge of Holy Scripture.

So convinced indeed was Jerome that familiarity with the Bible was the royal road to the knowledge and love of Christ that he did not hesitate to say: "Ignorance of the Bible means ignorance of Christ."[117] And "what other life can there be without knowledge of the Bible wherein Christ, the life of them that believe, is set before us?"[118]

Every single page of either Testament seems to centre round Christ: hence Jerome, commenting on the words of the Apocalypse about the river and the Tree of Life, says: "One stream flows out from the throne of God, and that is the Grace of the Holy Spirit, and that grace of the Holy Spirit is in the Holy Scriptures, that is in the stream of the Scriptures. Yet has that stream twin banks, the Old Testament and the New, and the Tree planted on either side is Christ."[119]

Small wonder, then, if in his devout meditations he applied everything he read in the Bible to Christ: "When I read the Gospel and find there testimonies from the Law and from the Prophets, I see only Christ; I so see Moses and the Prophets that I understand them of Christ. Then when I come to the splendour of Christ Himself, and when I gaze at that glorious sunlight, I care not to look at the lamplight. For what light can a lamp give when lit in the daytime? If the sun shines out, the lamplight does not show. So, too, when Christ is present the Law and the Prophets do not show. Not that I would detract from the Law and the Prophets; rather do I praise them in that they show forth Christ. But I so read the Law and the Prophets as not to abide in them but from them to pass to Christ."[120]

Hence was Jerome wondrously uplifted to love for and knowledge of Christ through his study of the Bible in which he discovered the

[115] *In Mich.* 4:1.
[116] *Prol. in Comment. in Matt.*
[117] *Prol. in Comment. in Isa.;* cf. *Tract. de Ps. lxxvii.*
[118] *Epist. xxx*, 7.
[119] *Tract. de Ps. i.*
[120] *Tract. in Marcum,* 9, 1-7.

precious pearl of the Gospel: "There is one most priceless pearl: the knowledge of the Saviour, the mystery of His Passion, the secret of His Resurrection." [121]

Burning as he did with the love of Christ we cannot marvel that, poor and lowly with Christ, with soul freed from earthly cares, he sought Christ alone, by His spirit was he led, with Him he lived in closest intimacy, by imitating Him he would bear about the image of His sufferings in himself. For him nought more glorious than to suffer with and for Christ. [492]

Hence it was that when on Damasus' death he left Rome wounded and weary from evil men's assaults, he wrote just before he embarked: "Though some fancy me a scoundrel and guilty of every crime—and, indeed, this is a small matter when I think of my sins—yet you do well when from your soul you reckon evil men good. Thank God I am deemed worthy to be hated by the world. . . . What real sorrows have I to bear—I who fight for the Cross? Men heap false accusations on me; yet I know that through ill report and good report we win to the kingdom of heaven." [122]

In like fashion does he exhort the maiden Eustochium to courageous and lifelong toil for Christ's sake: "To become what the Martyrs, the Apostles, what even Christ Himself was, means immense labour—but what a reward! . . . What I have been saying to you will sound hard to one who does not love Christ. But those who consider worldly pomp a mere offscouring and all under the sun mere nothingness if only they may win Christ, those who are dead with Christ, have risen with Him and have crucified the flesh with its vices and concupiscences—they will echo the words: 'Who shall separate us from the charity of Christ?'" [123]

Immense, then, was the profit Jerome derived from reading Scripture; hence came those interior illuminations whereby he was ever more and more drawn to knowledge and love of Christ; hence, too, that love of prayer of which he has written so well; hence his wonderful familiarity with Christ, Whose sweetness drew him so that he ran unfalteringly along the arduous way of the Cross to the palm of victory. [493]

Hence, too, his ardent love for the Holy Eucharist: "Who is wealthier than he who carries the Lord's Body in his wicker basket, the Lord's Blood in his crystal vessel?" [124] Hence, too, his love for Christ's Mother, whose perpetual virginity he had so keenly defended, whose title as God's Mother and as the greatest example of all the virtues he constantly set before Christ's spouses for their imitation. [125]

---

[121] *In Matt.*, 13, 45.
[122] *Epist. xlv*, 1.
[123] *Epist. xxii*, 38.
[124] *Epist. cxxv*, 20.
[125] *Epist. xxii*, 38.

No one, then, can wonder that Jerome should have been so power-fully drawn to those spots in Palestine which had been consecrated by the presence of our Redeemer and His Mother. It is easy to rec-ognise the hand of Jerome in the words written from Bethlehem to Marcella by his disciples, Paula and Eustochium: "What words can serve to describe to you the Saviour's cave? As for the manger in which He lay—well, our silence does it more honour than any poor words of ours. . . . Will the day ever dawn when we can enter His cave to weep at His tomb with the sister (of Lazarus) and mourn with His Mother; when we can kiss the wood of His Cross and, with the ascending Lord on Olivet, be uplifted in mind and spirit?" [126]

Filled with memories such as these, Jerome could, while far away from Rome and leading a life hard for the body but inexpressibly sweet to the soul, cry out: "Would that Rome had what tiny Beth-lehem possesses!" [127]

[VIII St. Jerome's Labors Continued]

494   But we rejoice—and Rome with us—that the Saint's desire has been fulfilled, though far otherwise than he hoped for. For whereas David's royal city once gloried in the possession of the relics of "the Greatest Doctor" reposing in the cave where he dwelt so long, Rome now possesses them, for they lie in St. Mary Major's beside the Lord's Crib.

His voice is now still, though at one time the whole Catholic world listened to it when it echoed from the desert; yet Jerome still speaks in his writings, which "shine like lamps throughout the world." [128] Jerome still calls to us.

His voice rings out, telling us of the super-excellence of Holy Scrip-ture, of its integral character and historical trustworthiness, telling us, too, of the pleasant fruits resulting from reading and meditating upon it.

His voice summons all the Church's children to return to a truly Christian standard of life to shake themselves free from a pagan type of morality which seems to have sprung to life again in these days.

His voice calls upon us, and especially on Italian piety and zeal, to restore to the See of Peter divinely established here that honour and liberty which its Apostolic dignity and duty demand.

The voice of Jerome summons those Christian nations which have unhappily fallen away from Mother Church to turn once more to her in whom lies all hope of eternal salvation. Would, too, that the East-ern Churches, so long in opposition to the See of Peter, would listen

[126] *Epist. xlvi,* 11.   [128] Cassian, *De Incarnatione,* 7:26.
[127] *Epist. liv,* 13.

to Jerome's voice. When he lived in the East and sat at the feet of Gregory and Didymus, he said only what the Christians of the East thought in his time when he declared that "If anyone is outside the Ark of Noe he will perish in the overwhelming flood." [129]

To-day this flood seems on the verge of sweeping away all human institutions—unless God steps in to prevent it. And surely this calamity must come if men persist in sweeping on one side God the Creator and Conserver of all things! Surely whatever cuts itself off from Christ must perish! Yet He Who at His disciples' prayer calmed the raging sea can restore peace to the tottering fabric of society.

May Jerome, who so loved God's Church and so strenuously defended it against its enemies, win for us the removal of every element of discord, in accordance with Christ's prayer, so that there may be "one fold and one shepherd."

Delay not, Venerable Brethren, to impart to your people and clergy **495** what on the fifteenth centenary of the death of "the Greatest Doctor" we have here set before you. Urge upon all not merely to embrace under Jerome's guidance Catholic doctrine touching the inspiration of Scripture, but to hold fast to the principles laid down in the Encyclical *Providentissimus Deus,* and in this present Encyclical.

Our one desire for all the Church's children is that, being saturated with the Bible, they may arrive at the all-surpassing knowledge of Jesus Christ. In testimony of which desire and of our fatherly feeling for you we impart to you and all your flocks the Apostolic blessing.

Given at St. Peter's, Rome, September 15, 1920, the seventh year of our Pontificate.

BENEDICTUS PP. XV.

---

[129] *Epist.* 15:2.

(7) Encyclical Letter of Pope Pius XII, "Divino Afflante Spiritu," on Promotion of Biblical Studies

INTRODUCTION

538 1. Inspired by the Divine Spirit, the Sacred Writers composed those books, which God, in His paternal charity towards the human race, deigned to bestow on them in order "to teach, to reprove, to correct, to instruct in justice: that the man of God may be perfect, furnished to every good work." [1] This heaven-sent treasure Holy Church considers as the most precious source of doctrine on faith and morals. No wonder therefore that, as she received it intact from the hands of the Apostles, so she kept it with all care, defended it from every false and perverse interpretation and used it diligently as an instrument for securing the eternal salvation of souls, as almost countless documents in every age strikingly bear witness. In more recent times, however, since the divine origin and the correct interpretation of the Sacred Writings have been very specially called in question, the Church has with even greater zeal and care undertaken their defence and protection. The sacred Council of Trent ordained by solemn decree that "the entire books with all their parts, as they have been wont to be read in the Catholic Church and are contained in the old vulgate Latin edition, are to be held sacred and canonical." [2] In our own time the Vatican Council, with the object of condemning false doctrines regarding inspiration, declared that these same books were to be regarded by the Church as sacred and canonical "not because, having been composed by human industry, they were afterwards approved by her authority, nor merely because they contain revelation without error, but because, having been written under the inspiration of the Holy Spirit, they have God for their author, and as such were handed down to the Church herself." [3] When, subsequently, some Catholic writers, in spite of this solemn definition of Catholic doctrine, by which such divine authority is claimed for the "entire books with all their parts" as to secure freedom from any error whatsoever, ventured to restrict the truth of Sacred Scripture solely to matters of faith and morals, and to regard other matters, whether in the domain of physical science or history,

[1] II *Tim*. III, 16 f.
[2] Sessio IV, decr. 1; *Ench. Bibl.* n. 60. (3rd edition, Rome, 1956).
[3] Sessio III, Cap. 2; *Ench. Bibl.* n. 77.

as "obiter dicta" and—as they contended—in no wise connected with faith, Our Predecessor of immortal memory, Leo XIII in the Encyclical Letter *Providentissimus Deus,* published on November 18th in the year 1893, justly and rightly condemned these errors and safeguarded the studies of the Divine Books by most wise precepts and rules.

2. Since then it is fitting that We should commemorate the fiftieth anniversary of the publication of this Encyclical Letter, which is considered the supreme guide in biblical studies, We, moved by that solicitude for sacred studies, which We manifested from the very beginning of Our Pontificate,[4] have considered that this may most opportunely be done by ratifying and inculcating all that was wisely laid down by Our Predecessor and ordained by His Successors for the consolidating and perfecting of the work, and by pointing out what seems necessary in the present day, in order to incite ever more earnestly all those sons of the Church who devote themselves to these studies, to so necessary and so praiseworthy an enterprise.

I

HISTORICAL PART

WORK OF LEO XIII AND OF HIS SUCCESSORS IN FAVOR OF BIBLICAL STUDIES

§ 1—WORK OF LEO XIII

3. The first and greatest care of Leo XIII was to set forth the **539** teaching on the truth of the Sacred Books and to defend it from attack. Hence with grave words did he proclaim that there is no error whatsoever if the sacred writer, speaking of things of the physical order "went by what sensibly appeared" as the Angelic Doctor says,[5] speaking either "in figurative language, or in terms which were commonly used at the time, and which in many instances are in daily use at this day, even among the most eminent men of science." For "the sacred writers, or to speak more accurately—the words are St. Augustine's—[6] the Holy Ghost, Who spoke by them, did not intend to teach men these things—that is the essential nature of the things of the universe—things in no way profitable to salvation:"[7] which

[4] *Address to the Ecclesiastical students in Rome* (June 24, 1939); *Acta Ap. Sedis* XXXI (1939), p. 245-251.
[5] Cf. I³, q. 70, art. I ad 3.
[6] *De Gen. ad litt.* 2, 9, 20; *PL.* XXXIV, col. 270 s.; *CSEL.* XXVIII (Sectio III, pars. 2), p. 46.
[7] LEONIS XIII *Acta* XIII, p. 355; *Ench. Bibl.* n. 121.

principle "will apply to cognate sciences, and especially to history," that is, by refuting, "in a somewhat similar way the fallacies of the adversaries and defending the historical truth of Sacred Scripture from their attacks." [8] Nor is the sacred writer to be taxed with error, if "copyists have made mistakes in the text of the Bible," or, "if the real meaning of a passage remains ambiguous." Finally it is absolutely wrong and forbidden "either to narrow inspiration to certain passages of Holy Scripture, or to admit that the sacred writer has erred," since divine inspiration "not only is essentially incompatible with error but excludes and rejects it as absolutely and necessarily as it is impossible that God Himself, the supreme Truth, can utter that which is not true. This is the ancient and constant faith of the Church." [9]

540 4. This teaching, which Our Predecessor Leo XIII set forth with such solemnity, We also proclaim with Our authority and We urge all to adhere to it religiously. No less earnestly do We inculcate obedience at the present day to the counsels and exhortations which he, in his day, so wisely enjoined. For whereas there arose new and serious difficulties and questions, from the wide-spread prejudices of rationalism and more especially from the discovery and investigation of the antiquities of the East, this same Our Predecessor, moved by zeal of the apostolic office, not only that such an excellent source of Catholic revelation might be more securely and abundantly available to the advantage of the Christian flock, but also that he might not suffer it to be in any way tainted, wished and most earnestly desired "to see an increase in the number of the approved and persevering laborers in the cause of Holy Scripture; and more especially that those whom Divine Grace has called to Holy Orders, should day-by-day, as their state demands, display greater diligence and industry in reading, meditating and explaining it." [10]

Impulse given to biblical studies

541 5. Wherefore the same Pontiff, as he had already praised and approved the school for biblical studies, founded at St. Stephen's, Jerusalem, by the Master General of the Sacred Order of Preachers— from which, to use his own words, "biblical science itself had received no small advantage, while giving promise of more" [11]—so in the last year of his life he provided yet another way, by which these same

[8] Cf. BENEDICTUS XV, Enc. *Spiritus Paraclitus, Acta Ap. Sedis* XII (1920), p. 396; *Ench. Bibl.* n. 458.
[9] LEONIS XIII *Acta* XIII, p. 357 sq.; *Ench. Bibl.* n. 124 sq.
[10] LEONIS XIII *Acta* XIII, p. 328; *Ench. Bibl.* n. 82 sq.
[11] Apostolic Letter *Hierosolymae in cœnobio*, Sept. 17, 1892; LEONIS XIII *Acta* XII, pp. 239-241; v. p. 240.

studies, so warmly commended in the Encyclical Letter *Providentissimus Deus*, might daily make greater progress and be pursued with the greatest possible security. By the Apostolic Letter *Vigilantiae*, published on October 30 in the year 1902, he founded a Council or Commission, as it is called, of eminent men, "whose duty it would be to procure by every means that the secred texts may receive everywhere among us that more thorough exposition which the times demand, and be kept safe not only from every breath of error, but also from all inconsiderate opinions." [12] Following the example of Our Predecessors, We also have effectively confirmed and amplified this Council using its good offices, as often before, to remind commentators of the Sacred Books of those safe rules of Catholic exegesis, which have been handed down by the Holy Fathers and Doctors of the Church, as well as by the Sovereign Pontiffs themselves.[13]

§ 2—WORK OF THE SUCCESSORS OF LEO XIII

6. It may not be out of place here to recall gratefully the principal **542** and more useful contributions made successively by Our Predecessors towards this same end, which contributions may be considered as the complement or fruit of the movement so happily initiated by Leo XIII. And first of all Pius X, wishing "to provide a sure way for the preparation of a copious supply of teachers, who, commended by the seriousness and the integrity of their doctrine, might explain the Sacred Books in Catholic schools . . ." instituted "the academic degrees of licentiate and doctorate in Sacred Scripture . . . ; to be conferred by the Biblical Commission"; [14] he later enacted a law "concerning the method of Scripture studies to be followed in Clerical Seminaries" with this end in view viz: that students of the sacred sciences "not only should themselves fully understand the power, purpose and teaching of the Bible, but should also be equipped to engage in the ministry of the Divine Word with elegance and ability and repel attacks against the divinely inspired books"; [15] finally "in order that a center of higher biblical studies might be established in Rome, which in the best way possible might promote the study of the Bible and all cognate sciences in accordance with the mind of the Catholic Church" he founded the Pontifical Biblical Institute, en-

[12] Cf. LEONIS XIII *Acta* XXII, p. 232 ss.; *Ench. Bibl.* n. 137-148 ;v. nn. 137-139.
[13] Letter of the Pontifical Biblical Commission to their Excellencies the Archbishops and Bishops of Italy, Aug. 20, 1941; *Acta Ap. Sedis* XXXIII (1941), pp. 465-472.
[14] Apostolic Letter *Scripturae Sanctae*, Feb. 23, 1904; PII X *Acta* I, pp. 176-179; *Ench. Bibl.* nn. 149-157; v. nn. 150-151.
[15] Cf. Apostolic Letter *Quonian in re biblica*, March 27, 1906; PII X *Acta* III, pp. 72-76; *Ench. Bibl.* nn. 162-180; v. n. 162.

trusted to the care of the illustrious Society of Jesus, which he wished endowed "with a superior professorial staff and every facility for biblical research"; he prescribed its laws and rules, professing to follow in this the "salutary and fruitful project" of Leo XIII.[16]

Pius XI: *Academic degrees prescribed*

543   **7.** All this in fine Our immediate Predecessor of happy memory Pius XI brought to perfection, laying down among other things "that no one should be appointed professor of Sacred Scripture in any Seminary, unless, having completed a special course of biblical studies, he had in due form obtained the academic degrees before the Biblical Commission or the Biblical Institute." He wished that these degrees should have the same rights and the same effects as the degrees duly conferred in Sacred Theology or Canon Law; likewise he decreed that no one should receive "a benefice having attached the canonical obligation of expounding the Sacred Scripture to the people, unless, among other things, he had obtained the licentiate or doctorate in biblical science." And having at the same time urged the Superiors General of the Regular Orders and of the religious Congregations, as well as the Bishops of the Catholic world, to send the more suitable of their students to frequent the schools of the Biblical Institute and obtain there the academical degrees, he confirmed these exhortations by his own example, appointing out of his bounty an annual sum for this very purpose.[17]

8. Seeing that, in the year 1907, with the benign approval of Pius X of happy memory, "to the Benedictine monks had been committed the task of preparing the investigations and studies on which might be based a new edition of the Latin version of the Scriptures, commonly called the Vulgate," [18] the same Pontiff, Pius XI, wishing to consolidate more firmly and securely this "laborious and arduous enterprise," which demands considerable time and great expense, founded in Rome and lavishly endowed with a library and other means of research, the monastery of St. Jerome, to be devoted exclusively to this work.[19]

[16] Apostolic Letter *Vinea electa*, May 7, 1909; *Acta Ap. Sedis* I (1909), pp. 447-449; *Ench. Bibl.* nn. 297-310; v. nn. 300 et 298.

[17] Cf. Motu proprio *Bibliorum scientiam*, April 27, 1924; *Acta Ap. Sedis* XVI (1924), pp. 180-182; *Ench. Bibl.* nn. 505-512.

[18] Letter to the Most Rev. Abbot Aidan Gasquet, Dec. 3, 1907; Pii X *Acta* IV, pp. 117-119; *Ench. Bibl.* n. 289 sq.

[19] Apostolic Constitution *Inter praecipuas*, June 15, 1933; *Acta Ap. Sedis* XXVI (1934), pp. 85-87.

§ 3—Solicitude of Sovereign Pontiffs

9. Nor should We fail to mention here how earnestly these same **544** Our Predecessors, when the opportunity occurred, recommended the study or preaching or in fine the pious reading and meditation of the Sacred Scriptures. Pius X most heartily commended the society of St. Jerome, which strives to promote among the faithful—and to facilitate with all its power—the truly praise-worthy custom of reading and meditating on the holy Gospels; he exhorted them to persevere in the enterprise they had begun, proclaiming it "a most useful undertaking, as well as most suited to the times," seeing that it helps in no small way "to dissipate the idea that the Church is opposed to or in any way impedes the reading of the Scriptures in the vernacular." [20] And Benedict XV, on the occasion of the fifteenth centenary of the death of St. Jerome, the greatest Doctor of the Sacred Scriptures, after having most solemnly inculcated the precepts and examples of the same Doctor, as well as the principles and rules laid down by Leo XIII and by himself, and having recommended other things highly opportune and never to be forgotten in this connection, exhorted "all the children of the Church, especially clerics, to reverence the Holy Scripture, to read it piously and meditate it constantly"; he reminded them "that in these pages is to be sought that food, by which the spiritual life is nourished unto perfection," and "that the chief use of Scripture pertains to the holy and fruitful exercise of the ministry of preaching"; he likewise once again expressed his warm approval of the work of the society called after St. Jerome himself, by means of which the Gospels and the Acts of the Apostles are being so widely diffused, "that there is no Christian family any more without them and that all are accustomed to read and meditate them daily." [21]

§ 4—Fruits of Manifold Initiative

10. But it is right and pleasing to confess openly that it is not only **545** by reason of these initiatives, precepts and exhortations of Our Predecessors that the knowledge and use of the Sacred Scriptures have made great progress among Catholics; for this is also due to the works and labors of all those who diligently cooperated with them, both by meditating, investigating and writing, as well as by teaching and preaching and by translating and propagating the Sacred Books. For from the schools in which are fostered higher studies in theological and biblical science, and especially from Our Pontifical Biblical

[20] Letter to the Most Eminent Cardinal Cassetta *Qui piam*, Jan. 21, 1907; Pii X *Acta* IV, pp. 23-25.
[21] Encyclical Letter *Spiritus Paraclitus*, Sept. 15, 1920; *Acta Ap. Sedis* XII (1920), pp. 385-422; *Ench. Bibl.* nn. 444-495; v. nn. 444, 482, 484, 478.

Institute, there have already come forth, and daily continue to come forth, many students of Holy Scripture who, inspired with an intense love of the Sacred Books, imbue the younger clergy with this same ardent zeal and assiduously impart to them the doctrine they themselves have acquired. Many of them also, by the written word, have promoted and do still promote, far and wide, the study of the Bible; as when they edit the sacred text corrected in accordance with the rules of textual criticism or expound, explain, and translate it into the vernacular; or when they propose it to the faithful for their pious reading and meditation; or finally when they cultivate and seek the aid of profane sciences which are useful for the interpretation of the Scriptures. From these therefore and from other initiatives which daily become more wide-spread and vigorous, as, for example, biblical societies, congresses, libraries, associations for meditation on the Gospels, We firmly hope that in the future reverence for, as well as the use and knowledge of, the Sacred Scriptures will everywhere more and more increase for the good of souls, provided the method of biblical studies laid down by Leo XIII, explained more clearly and perfectly by his Successors, and by Us confirmed and amplified—which indeed is the only safe way and proved by experience—be more firmly, eagerly and faithfully accepted by all, regardless of the difficulties which, as in all human affairs, so in this most excellent work will never be wanting.

II

DOCTRINAL PART

BIBLICAL STUDIES AT THE PRESENT DAY

546   11. There is no one who cannot easily perceive that the conditions of biblical studies and their subsidiary sciences have greatly changed within the last fifty years. For, apart from anything else, when Our Predecessor published the Encyclical Letter *Providentissimus Deus*, hardly a single place in Palestine had begun to be explored by means of relevant excavations. Now, however, this kind of investigation is much more frequent and, since more precise methods and technical skill have been developed in the course of actual experience, it gives us information at once more abundant and more accurate. How much light has been derived from these explorations for the more correct and fuller understanding of the Sacred Books all experts know, as well as all those who devote themselves to these studies. The value of these excavations is enhanced by the discovery from time to time of written documents, which help much towards the knowledge of the languages, letters, events, customs, and forms of worship of most ancient times. And of no less importance is the discovery and investigation, so frequent in our times, of papyri which have contributed so much to the knowledge of letters and institutions, both public and private, especially of the time of Our Saviour.

12. Moreover ancient codices of the Sacred Books have been found and edited with discerning thoroughness; the exegesis of the Fathers of the Church has been more widely and thoroughly examined; in fine the manner of speaking, relating and writing in use among the ancients is made clear by innumerable examples. All these advantages which, not without a special design of Divine Providence, our age has acquired, are as it were an invitation and inducement to interpreters of the Sacred Literature to make diligent use of this light, so abundantly given, to penetrate more deeply, explain more clearly and expound more lucidly the Divine Oracles. If, with the greatest satisfaction of mind, We perceive that these same interpreters have resolutely answered and still continue to answer this call, this is certainly not the last or least of the fruits of the Encyclical Letter *Providentissimus Deus*, by which Our Predecessor Leo XIII, foreseeing as it were this new development of biblical studies, summoned Catholic exegetes to labor and wisely defined the direction and the method to be followed in that labor.

13. We also, by this Encyclical Letter, desire to insure that the work may not only proceed without interruption, but may also daily become more perfect and fruitful; and to that end We are specially intent on pointing out to all what yet remains to be done, with what spirit the Catholic exegete should undertake, at the present day, so great and noble a work, and to give new incentive and fresh courage to the laborers who toil so strenuously in the vineyard of the Lord.

§ 1—RECOURSE TO ORIGINAL TEXTS

14. The Fathers of the Church in their time, especially Augustine, 547 warmly recommended to the Catholic scholar, who undertook the investigation and explanation of the Sacred Scriptures, the study of the ancient languages and recourse to the original texts.[22] However, such was the state of letters in those times, that not many,—and these few but imperfectly—knew the Hebrew language. In the middle ages, when Scholastic Theology was at the height of its vigor, the knowledge of even the Greek language had long since become so rare in the West, that even the greatest Doctors of that time, in their

---

[22] Cf. ex. gr. St. JEROME, *Praef. in IV Evang. ad Damasum; PL.* XXIX, col. 526-527; St. AUGUSTINE, *De Doctr. christ.* II, 16; *PL.* XXXIV, col. 42-43.

exposition of the Sacred Text, had recourse only to the Latin version, known as the Vulgate.

15. On the contrary in this our time, not only the Greek language, which since the humanistic renaissance has been, as it were, restored to new life, is familiar to almost all students of antiquity and letters, but the knowledge of Hebrew also and of other oriental languages has spread far and wide among literary men. Moreover there are now such abundant aids to the study of these languages that the biblical scholar, who by neglecting them would deprive himself of access to the original texts, could in no wise escape the stigma of levity and sloth. For it is the duty of the exegete to lay hold, so to speak, with the greatest care and reverence of the very least expressions which, under the inspiration of the Divine Spirit, have flowed from the pen of the sacred writer, so as to arrive at a deeper and fuller knowledge of his meaning.

16. Wherefore let him diligently apply himself so as to acquire daily a greater facility in biblical as well as in other oriental languages and to support his interpretation by the aids which all branches of philology supply. This indeed St. Jerome strove earnestly to achieve, as far as the science of his time permitted; to this also aspired with untiring zeal and no small fruit not a few of the great exegetes of the sixteenth and seventeenth centuries, although the knowledge of languages then was much less than at the present day. In like manner therefore ought we to explain the original text which, having been written by the inspired author himself, has more authority and greater weight than any even the very best translation, whether ancient or modern; this can be done all the more easily and fruitfully, if to the knowledge of languages be joined a real skill in literary criticism of the same text.

Importance of textual criticism

548 17. The great importance which should be attached to this kind of criticism was aptly pointed out by Augustine, when, among the precepts to be recommended to the student of the Sacred Books, he put in the first place the care to possess a corrected text. "The correction of the codices"—so says this most distinguished Doctor of the Church —"should first of all engage the attention of those who wish to know the Divine Scripture so that the uncorrected may give place to the corrected." [23] In the present day indeed this art, which is called textual criticism and which is used with great and praiseworthy results in the editions of profane writings, is also quite rightly employed in the case of the Sacred Books, because of that very rever-

[23] *De doctr. christ.* II, 21; *PL.* XXXIV, col. 40.

ence which is due to the Divine Oracles. For its very purpose is to insure that the sacred text be restored, as perfectly as possible, be purified from the corruptions due to the carelessness of the copyists and be freed, as far as may be done, from glosses and omissions, from the interchange and repetition of words and from all other kinds of mistakes, which are wont to make their way gradually into writings handed down through many centuries.

18. It is scarcely necessary to observe that this criticism, which some fifty years ago not a few made use of quite arbitrarily and often in such wise that one would say they did so to introduce into the sacred text their own preconceived ideas, today has rules so firmly established and secure, that it has become a most valuable aid to the purer and more accurate editing of the sacred text and that any abuse can easily be discovered. Nor is it necessary here to call to mind—since it is doubtless familiar and evident to all students of Sacred Scripture—to what extent namely the Church has held in honor these studies in textual criticism from the earliest centuries down even to the present day.

19. Today therefore, since this branch of science has attained to such high perfection, it is the honorable, though not always easy, task of students of the Bible to procure by every means that as soon as possible may be duly published by Catholic editions of the Sacred Books and of ancient versions, brought out in accordance with these standards, which, that is to say, unite the greatest reverence for the sacred text with an exact observance of all the rules of criticism. And let all know that this prolonged labor is not only necessary for the right understanding of the divinely-given writings, but also is urgently demanded by that piety by which it behooves us to be grateful to the God of all providence, Who from the throne of His majesty has sent these books as so many paternal letters to His own children.

Meaning of Tridentine decree

20. Nor should anyone think that this use of the original texts, 549 in accordance with the methods of criticism, in any way derogates from those decrees so wisely enacted by the Council of Trent concerning the Latin Vulgate.[24] It is historically certain that the Presidents of the Council received a commission, which they duly carried out, to beg, that is, the Sovereign Pontiff in the name of the Council that he should have corrected, as far as possible, first a Latin, and then a Greek, and Hebrew edition, which eventually would be pub-

[24] *Decr. de editione et usu Sacrorum Librorum; Conc.* Trid. ed. Soc. Goerres, t. V, p. 91 s.

lished for the benefit of the Holy Church of God.[25]   If this desire could not then be fully realized owing to the difficulties of the times and other obstacles, at present it can, We earnestly hope, be more perfectly and entirely fulfilled by the united efforts of Catholic scholars.

21. And if the Tridentine Synod wished "that all should use as authentic" the Vulgate Latin version, this, as all know, applies only to the Latin Church and to the public use of the same Scriptures; nor does it, doubtless, in any way diminish the authority and value of the original texts. For there was no question then of these texts, but of the Latin versions, which were in circulation at that time, and of these the same Council rightly declared to be preferable that which "had been approved by its long-continued use for so many centuries in the Church." Hence this special authority or as they say, authenticity of the Vulgate was not affirmed by the Council particularly for critical reasons, but rather because of its legitimate use in the Churches throughout so many centuries; by which use indeed the same is shown, in the sense in which the Church has understood and understands it, to be free from any error whatsoever in matters of faith and morals; so that, as the Church herself testifies and affirms, it may be quoted safely and without fear of error in disputations, in lectures and in preaching; and so its authenticity is not specified primarily as critical, but rather as juridical.

22. Wherefore this authority of the Vulgate in matters of doctrine by no means prevents—nay rather today it almost demands—either the corroboration and confirmation of this same doctrine by the original texts or the having recourse on any and every occasion to the aid of these same texts, by which the correct meaning of the Sacred Letters is everywhere daily made more clear and evident. Nor is it forbidden by the decree of the Council of Trent to make translations into the vulgar tongue, even directly from the original texts themselves, for the use and benefit of the faithful and for the better understanding of the divine word, as We know to have been already done in a laudable manner in many countries with the approval of the Ecclesiastical authority.

§ 2—INTERPRETATION OF SACRED BOOKS

550   23. Being thoroughly prepared by the knowledge of the ancient languages and by the aids afforded by the art of criticism, let the Catholic exegete undertake the task, of all those imposed on him the greatest, that namely of discovering and expounding the genuine meaning of the Sacred Books. In the performance of this task let the interpreters bear in mind that their foremost and greatest en-

[25] *Ib.,* t. X, p. 471; cf. t. V, pp. 29, 59, 65; t. X, p. 446 sq.

deavor should be to discern and define clearly that sense of the biblical words which is called literal. Aided by the context and by comparison with similar passages, let them therefore by means of their knowledge of languages search out with all diligence the literal meaning of the words; all these helps indeed are wont to be pressed into service in the explanation also of profane writers, so that the mind of the author may be made abundantly clear.

24. The commentators of the Sacred Letters, mindful of the fact **551** that here there is question of a divinely inspired text, the care and interpretation of which have been confided to the Church by God Himself, should no less diligently take into account the explanations and declarations of the teaching authority of the Church, as likewise the interpretation given by the Holy Fathers, and even "the analogy of faith" as Leo XIII most wisely observed in the Encyclical Letter *Providentissimus Deus*.[26] With special zeal should they apply themselves, not only to expounding exclusively these matters which belong to the historical, archeological, philological and other auxiliary sciences—as, to Our regret, is done in certain commentaries,— but, having duly referred to these, in so far as they may aid the exegesis, they should set forth in particular the theological doctrine in faith and morals of the individual books or texts so that their exposition may not only aid the professors of theology in their explanations and proofs of the dogmas of faith, but may also be of assistance to priests in their presentation of Christian doctrine to the people, and in fine may help all the faithful to lead a life that is holy and worthy of a Christian.

Right use of spiritual sense

25. By making such an exposition, which is above all, as We have **552** said, theological, they will efficaciously reduce to silence those who, affirming that they scarcely ever find anything in biblical commentaries to raise their hearts to God, to nourish their souls or promote their interior life, repeatedly urge that we should have recourse to a certain spiritual and, as they say, mystical interpretation. With what little reason they thus speak is shown by the experience of many, who, assiduously considering and meditating the word of God, advanced in perfection and were moved to an intense love of God; and this same truth is clearly proved by the constant tradition of the Church and the precepts of the greatest Doctors. Doubtless all spiritual sense is not excluded from the Sacred Scripture.

26. For what was said and done in the Old Testament was ordained and disposed by God with such consummate wisdom, that things past pre-figured in a spiritual way those that were to come

[26] Leonis XIII *Acta* XIII, pp. 345-346; *Ench. Bibl.* n. 109-111.

under the new dispensation of grace. Wherefore the exegete, just as he must search out and expound the literal meaning of the words, intended and expressed by the sacred writer, so also must he do likewise for the spiritual sense, provided it is clearly intended by God. For God alone could have known this spiritual meaning and have revealed it to us. Now Our Divine Saviour Himself points out to us and teaches us this same sense in the Holy Gospel; the Apostles also, following the example of the Master, profess it in their spoken and written words; the unchanging tradition of the Church approves it; finally the most ancient usage of the liturgy proclaims it, wherever may be rightly applied the well-known principle: "The rule of prayer is the rule of faith."

553 27. Let Catholic exegetes then disclose and expound this spiritual significance, intended and ordained by God, with that care which the dignity of the divine word demands; but let them scrupulously refrain from proposing as the genuine meaning of Sacred Scripture other figurative senses. It may indeed be useful, especially in preaching, to illustrate and present the matters of faith and morals by a broader use of the Sacred Text in the figurative sense, provided this be done with moderation and restraint; it should, however, never be forgotten that this use of the Sacred Scripture is, as it were, extrinsic to it and accidental, and that, especially in these days, it is not free from danger, since the faithful, in particular those who are well-informed in the sciences sacred and profane, wish to know what God has told us in the Sacred Letters rather than what an ingenious orator or writer may suggest by a clever use of the words of Scripture. Nor does "the word of God, living and effectual and more piercing than any two-edged sword and reaching unto the division of the soul and the spirit, of the joints also and the marrow, and a discerner of the thoughts and intents of the heart"[27] need artificial devices and human adaptation to move and impress souls; for the Sacred Pages, written under the inspiration of the Spirit of God, are of themselves rich in original meaning; endowed with a divine power, they have their own value; adorned with heavenly beauty, they radiate of themselves light and splendor, provided they are so fully and accurately explained by the interpreter, that all the treasures of wisdom and prudence, therein contained, are brought to light.

Study of Holy Fathers

554 28. In the accomplishment of this task the Catholic exegete will find invaluable help in an assiduous study of those works, in which the Holy Fathers, the Doctors of the Church and the renowned in-

[27] *Hebr.* IV, 12.

terpreters of past ages have explained the Sacred Books. For, although sometimes less instructed in profane learning and in the knowledge of languages than the scripture scholars of our time, nevertheless by reason of the office assigned to them by God in the Church, they are distinguished by a certain subtle insight into heavenly things and by a marvellous keenness of intellect, which enables them to penetrate to the very innermost meaning of the divine word and bring to light all that can help to elucidate the teaching of Christ and promote holiness of life.

29. It is indeed regrettable that such precious treasures of Christian antiquity are almost unknown to many writers of the present day, and that students of the history of exegesis have not yet accomplished all that seems necessary for the due investigation and appreciation of so momentous a subject. Would that many, by seeking out the authors of the Catholic interpretation of Scripture and diligently studying their works and drawing thence the almost inexhaustible riches therein stored up, might contribute largely to this end, so that it might be daily more apparent to what extent those authors understood and made known the divine teaching of the Sacred Books, and that the interpreters of today might thence take example and seek suitable arguments.

30. For thus at long last will be brought about the happy and fruitful union between the doctrine and spiritual sweetness of expression of the ancient authors and the greater erudition and maturer knowledge of the modern, having as its result new progress in the never fully explored and inexhaustible field of the Divine Letters.

§ 3—SPECIAL TASKS OF INTERPRETERS

31. Moreover we may rightly and deservedly hope that our times 555 also can contribute something towards the deeper and more accurate interpretation of Sacred Scripture. For not a few things, especially in matters pertaining to history, were scarcely at all or not fully explained by the commentators of past ages, since they lacked almost all the information, which was needed for their clearer exposition. How difficult for the Fathers themselves, and indeed well nigh unintelligible, were certain passages is shown, among other things, by the oft-repeated efforts of many of them to explain the first chapters of Genesis; likewise by the reiterated attempts of St. Jerome so to translate the Psalms that the literal sense, that, namely, which is expressed by the words themselves, might be clearly revealed.

32. There are, in fine, other books or texts, which contain difficulties brought to light only in quite recent times, since a more profound knowledge of antiquity has given rise to new questions, on the basis of which the point at issue may be more appropriately

examined. Quite wrongly therefore do some pretend, not rightly understanding the conditions of biblical study, that nothing remains to be added by the Catholic exegete of our time to what Christian antiquity has produced; since, on the contrary, these our times have brought to light so many things, which call for a fresh investigation and a new examination, and which stimulate not a little the practical zeal of the present-day interpreter.

Character of sacred writer

556   33. As in our age indeed new questions and new difficulties are multiplied, so, by God's favor, new means and aids to exegesis are also provided. Among these it is worthy of special mention that Catholic theologians, following the teaching of the Holy Fathers and especially of the Angelic and Common Doctor, have examined and explained the nature and effects of biblical inspiration more exactly and more fully than was wont to be done in previous ages. For having begun by expounding minutely the principle that the inspired writer, in composing the sacred book, is the living and reasonable instrument of the Holy Spirit, they rightly observe that, impelled by the divine motion, he so uses his faculties and powers, that from the book composed by him all may easily infer "the special character

557 of each one and, as it were, his personal traits." [28]   Let the interpreter then, with all care and without neglecting any light derived from recent research, endeavor to determine the peculiar character and circumstances of the sacred writer, the age in which he lived, the sources written or oral to which he had recourse and the forms of expression he employed.

34. Thus can he the better understand who was the inspired author, and what he wishes to express by his writings. There is no one indeed but knows that the supreme rule of interpretation is to discover and define what the writer intended to express, as St. Athanasius excellently observes: "Here, as indeed is expedient in all other passages of Sacred Scripture, it should be noted, on what occasion the Apostle spoke; we should carefully and faithfully observe to whom and why he wrote, lest, being ignorant of these points, or confounding one with another, we miss the real meaning of the author " [29]

Importance of mode of writing

558   35. What is the literal sense of a passage is not always as obvious in the speeches and writings of the ancient authors of the East, as it

[28] Cf. BENEDICT XV, Encyclical *Spiritus Paraclitus; Acta Ap. Sedis* XII (1920), p. 390; *Ench. Bibl.* n. 448.

[29] *Contra Arianos* I, 54; *PG.* XXVI, col. 123.

is in the works of the writers of our own time. For what they wished
to express is not to be determined by the rules of grammar and
philology alone, nor solely by the context; the interpreter must, as
it were, go back wholly in spirit to those remote centuries of the
East and with the aid of history, archaeology, ethnology and other
sciences, accurately determine what modes of writing, so to speak,
the authors of that ancient period would be likely to use, and in fact
did use.

36. For the ancient peoples of the East, in order to express their
ideas, did not always employ those forms or kinds of speech, which
we use today; but rather those used by the men of their times and
countries. What those exactly were the commentator cannot determine as it were in advance, but only after a careful examination of
the ancient literature of the East. The investigation, carried out,
on this point, during the past forty or fifty years with greater care
and diligence than ever before, has more clearly shown what forms
of expression were used in those far off times, whether in poetic
description or in the formulation of laws and rules of life or in
recording the facts and events of history. The same inquiry has also
clearly shown the special preeminence of the people of Israel among
all the other ancient nations of the East in their mode of compiling
history, both by reason of its antiquity and by reason of the faithful   **559**
record of the events; qualities which may well be attributed to the
gift of divine inspiration and to the peculiar religious purpose of
biblical history.

37. Nevertheless no one, who has a correct idea of biblical inspiration, will be surprised to find, even in the Sacred Writers, as in other
ancient authors, certain fixed ways of expounding and narrating, certain definite idioms, especially of a kind peculiar to the Semitic
tongues, so-called approximations, and certain hyperbolical modes of
expression, nay, at times, even paradoxical, which help to impress
the ideas more deeply on the mind. For of the modes of expression
which, among ancient peoples, and especially those of the East,
human language used to express its thought, none is excluded from
the Sacred Books, provided the way of speaking adopted in no wise
contradicts the holiness and truth of God, as, with his customary
wisdom, the Angelic Doctor already observed in these words: "In
Scripture divine things are presented to us in the manner which is
in common use amongst men." [30] For as the substantial Word of
God became like to men in all things, "except sin," [31] so the words of
God, expressed in human languages, are made like to human speech
in every respect, except error. In this consists that "condescension"

[30] *Comment ad Hebr.* cap. I, lectio 4.
[31] *Hebr.* IV, 15.

of the God of providence, which St. John Chrysostom extolled with the highest praise and repeatedly declared to be found in the Sacred Books.[32]

560   38. Hence the Catholic commentator, in order to comply with the present needs of biblical studies, in explaining the Sacred Scripture and in demonstrating and proving its immunity from all error, should also make a prudent use of this means, determine, that is, to what extent the manner of expression or the literary mode adopted by the sacred writer may lead to a correct and genuine interpretation; and let him be convinced that this part of his office cannot be neglected without serious detriment to Catholic exegesis. Not infrequently—to mention only one instance—when some persons reproachfully charge the Sacred Writers with some historical error or inaccuracy in the recording of facts, on closer examination it turns out to be nothing else than those customary modes of expression and narration peculiar to the ancients, which used to be employed in the mutual dealings of social life and which in fact were sanctioned by common usage.

39. When then such modes of expression are met with in the sacred text, which, being meant for men, is couched in human language, justice demands that they be no more taxed with error than when they occur in the ordinary intercourse of daily life. By this knowledge and exact appreciation of the modes of speaking and writing in use among the ancients can be solved many difficulties, which are raised against the veracity and historical value of the Divine Scriptures, and no less efficaciously does this study contribute to a fuller nd more luminous understanding of the mind of the Sacred Writer.

Studies of biblical antiquities

561   40. Let those who cultivate Biblical studies turn their attention with all due diligence towards this point and let them neglect none of those discoveries, whether in the domain of archaeology or in ancient history or literature, which serve to make better known the mentality of the ancient writers, as well as their manner and art of reasoning, narrating and writing. In this connection Catholic laymen also should consider that they will not only further profane science, but moreover will render a conspicuous service to the Christian cause if they devote themselves with all due diligence and application to the exploration and investigation of the monuments of antiquity and contribute, according to their abilities, to the solution of questions hitherto obscure.

[32] Cf. v. gr. *In Gen.* I, 4 (*PG.* LIII, col. 34-35); *In Gen.* II, 21 (*ib.* col. 121); *In Gen.* III, 8 (*ib.* col. 135); *Hom.* 15 *in Joan.*, ad. I, 18 (*PG.* LIX, col. 97 sq.).

41. For all human knowledge, even the non-sacred, has indeed its own proper dignity and excellence, being a finite participation of the infinite knowledge of God, but it acquires a new and higher dignity and, as it were, a consecration, when it is employed to cast a brighter light upon the things of God.

§ 4—Way of Treating More Difficult Questions

42. The progressive exploration of the antiquities of the East, **562** mentioned above, the more accurate examination of the original text itself, the more extensive and exact knowledge of languages both biblical and oriental, have with the help of God, happily provided the solution of not a few of those questions, which, in the time of Our Predecessor Leo XIII of immortal memory, were raised by critics outside or hostile to the Church against the authenticity, antiquity, integrity and historical value of the Sacred Books. For Catholic exegetes, by a right use of those same scientific arms, not infrequently abused by the adversaries, proposed such interpretations, which are in harmony with Catholic doctrine and the genuine current of tradition, and at the same time are seen to have proved equal to the difficulties, either raised by new explorations and discoveries, or bequeathed by antiquity for solution in our time.

43. Thus has it come about that confidence in the authority and historical value of the Bible, somewhat shaken in the case of some by so many attacks, today among Catholics is completely restored; moreover there are not wanting even non-Catholic writers, who by serious and calm inquiry have been led to abandon modern opinion and to return, at least in some points, to the more ancient ideas. This change is due in great part to the untiring labor, by which Catholic commentators of the Sacred Letters, in no way deterred by difficulties and obstacles of all kinds, strove with all their strength to make suitable use of what learned men of the present day, by their investigations in the domain of archaeology or history or philology, have made available for the solution of new questions.

Difficulties not yet solved

44. Nevertheless no one will be surprised, if all difficulties are not **563** yet solved and overcome; but that even today serious problems greatly exercise the minds of Catholic exegetes. We should not lose courage on this account; nor should we forget that in the human sciences the same happens as in the natural world; that is to say, new beginnings grow little by little and fruits are gathered only after many labors. Thus it has happened that certain disputed points, which in the past remained unsolved and in suspense, in our days,

with the progress of studies, have found a satisfactory solution. Hence there are grounds for hope that those also will by constant effort be at last made clear, which now seem most complicated and difficult.

45. And if the wished-for solution be slow in coming or does not satisfy us, since perhaps a successful conclusion may be reserved to posterity, let us not wax impatient thereat, seeing that in us also is rightly verfied what the Fathers, and especially Augustine,[33] observed in their time viz: God wished difficulties to be scattered through the Sacred Books inspired by Him, in order that we might be urged to read and scrutinize them more intently, and, experiencing in a salutary manner our own limitations, we might be exercised in due submission of mind. No wonder if of one or other question no solution wholly satisfactory will ever be found, since sometimes we have to do with matters obscure in themselves and too remote from our times and our experience; and since exegesis also, like all other most important sciences, has its secrets, which, impenetrable to our minds, by no efforts whatsoever can be unravelled.

Definite solutions sought

564   46. But this state of things is no reason why the Catholic commentator, inspired by an active and ardent love of his subject and sincerely devoted to Holy Mother Church, should in any way be deterred from grappling again and again with these difficult problems, hitherto unsolved, not only that he may refute the objections of the adversaries, but also may attempt to find a satisfactory solution, which will be in full accord with the doctrine of the Church, in particular with the traditional teaching regarding the inerrancy of Sacred Scripture, and which will at the same time satisfy the indubitable conclusions of profane sciences.

47. Let all the other sons of the Church bear in mind that the efforts of these resolute laborers in the vineyard of the Lord should be judged not only with equity and justice, but also with the greatest charity; all moreover should abhor that intemperate zeal which imagines that whatever is new should for that very reason be op-
565 posed or suspected. Let them bear in mind above all that in the rules and laws promulgated by the Church there is question of doctrine regarding faith and morals; and that in the immense matter contained in the Sacred Books—legislative, historical, sapiential and prophetical—there are but few texts whose sense has been defined

---

[33] Cf. St. Augustine, *Epist.* 149 ad Paulinum, n. 34 (*PL.* XXXIII, col. 644); *De diversis quaestionibus*, q. 53, n. 2 (*ib.* XL, col. 36); *Enarr. in Ps.* 146, n. 12 (*ib.* XXXVII, col. 1907).

by the authority of the Church, nor are those more numerous about which the teaching of the Holy Fathers is unanimous. There remain therefore many things, and of the greatest importance, in the discussion and exposition of which the skill and genius of Catholic commentators may and ought to be freely exercised, so that each may contribute his part to the advantage of all, to the continued progress of the sacred doctrine and to the defense and honor of the Church.

48. This true liberty of the children of God, which adheres faithfully to the teaching of the Church and accepts and uses gratefully the contributions of profane science, this liberty, upheld and sustained in every way by the confidence of all, is the condition and source of all lasting fruit and of all solid progress in Catholic doctrine, as Our Predecessor of happy memory Leo XIII rightly observes, when he says: "Unless harmony of mind be maintained and principles safeguarded, no progress can be expected in this matter from the varied studies of many." [34]

§ 5—USE OF SCRIPTURE IN INSTRUCTION OF FAITHFUL

49. Whosoever considers the immense labors undertaken by Catholic exegetes during well nigh two thousand years, so that the word of God, imparted to men through the Sacred Letters, might daily be more deeply and fully understood and more intensely loved, will easily be convinced that it is the serious duty of the faithful, and especially of priests, to make free and holy use of this treasure, accumulated throughout so many centuries by the greatest intellects. For the Sacred Books were not given by God to men to satisfy their curiosity or to provide them with material for study and research, but, as the Apostle observes, in order that these Divine Oracles might "instruct us to salvation, by the faith which is in Christ Jesus" and "that the man of God may be perfect, furnished to every good work." [35] **566**

50. Let priests therefore, who are bound by their office to procure the eternal salvation of the faithful, after they have themselves by diligent study perused the sacred pages and made them their own by prayer and meditations assiduously distribute the heavenly treasures of the divine word by sermons, homilies and exhortations; let them confirm the Christian doctrine by sentences from the Sacred Books and illustrate it by outstanding examples from sacred history and in particular from the Gospel of Christ Our Lord; and—avoiding with the greatest care those purely arbitrary and far-fetched adaptations, which are not a use, but rather an abuse of the divine

---

[34] Apostolic Letter *Vigilantiae;* LEONIS XIII *Acta* XIII, p. 237; *Ench. Bibl.* n. 143.
[35] Cf. II *Tim.* III, 15, 17.

word—let them set forth all this with such eloquence, lucidity and clearness that the faithful may not only be moved and inflamed to reform their lives, but may also conceive in their hearts the greatest veneration for the Sacred Scripture.

51. The same veneration the Bishops should endeavor daily to increase and perfect among the faithful committed to their care, encouraging all those initiatives by which men, filled with apostolic zeal, laudably strive to excite and foster among Catholics a greater knowledge of and love for the Sacred Books. Let them favor therefore and lend help to those pious associations whose aim it is to spread copies of the Sacred Letters, especially of the Gospels, among the faithful, and to procure by every means that in Christian families the same be read daily with piety and devotion; let them efficaciously recommend by word and example, whenever the liturgical laws permit, the Sacred Scriptures translated, with the approval of the Ecclesiastical authority, into modern languages; let them themselves give public conferences or dissertations on biblical subjects, or see that they are given by other public orators well versed in the matter.

52. Let the ministers of the Sanctuary support in every way possible and diffuse in fitting manner among all classes of the faithful the periodicals which so laudably and with such heartening results are published from time to time in various parts of the world, whether to treat and expose in a scientific manner biblical questions, or to adapt the fruits of these investigations to the sacred ministry, or to benefit the faithful. Let the ministers of the Sanctuary be convinced that all this, and whatsoever else an apostolic zeal and a sincere love of the divine word may find suitable to this high purpose, will be an efficacious help to the cure of souls.

Curriculum in Seminaries

567   53. But it is plain to everyone that priests cannot duly fulfill all this, unless in their Seminary days they have imbibed a practical and enduring love for the Sacred Scriptures. Wherefore let the Bishops, on whom devolves the paternal care of their Seminaries, with all diligence see to it that nothing be omitted in this matter which may help towards the desired end. Let the professors of Sacred Scripture in the Seminaries give the whole course of biblical studies in such a way, that they may instruct the young aspirants to the Priesthood and to the ministry of the divine word with that knowledge of the Sacred Letters and imbue them with that love for the same, without which it is vain to hope for copious fruits of the apostolate.

54. Hence their exegetical explanation should aim especially at the theological doctrine, avoiding useless disputations and omitting all that is calculated rather to gratify curiosity than to promote true learning and solid piety. The literal sense and especially the theological let them propose with such definiteness, explain with such skill and inculcate with such ardor that in their students may be in a sense verified what happened to the disciples on the way to Emmaus, when, having heard the words of the Master, they exclaimed: "Was not our heart burning within us, whilst He opened to us the Scriptures?" [36]

55. Thus the Divine Letters will become for the future priests of the Church a pure and never-failing source for their own spiritual life, as well as food and strength for the sacred office of preaching which they are about to undertake. If the professors of this most important matter in the Seminaries accomplish all this, then let them rest joyfully assured that they have most efficaciously contributed to the salvation of souls, to the progress of the Catholic faith, to the honor and glory of God, and that they have performed a work most closely connected with the apostolic office.

Value of divine word

56. If these things which We have said, Venerable Brethren and **568** beloved sons, are necessary in every age, much more urgently are they needed in our sorrowful times, when almost all peoples and nations are plunged in a sea of calamities, when a cruel war heaps ruins upon ruins and slaughter upon slaughter, when, owing to the most bitter hatred stirred up among the nations, We perceive with greatest sorrow that in not a few has been extinguished the sense not only of Christian moderation and charity, but also of humanity itself. Who can heal these mortal wounds of the human family if not He, to Whom the Prince of the Apostles, full of confidence and love, addresses these words: "Lord, to whom shall we go? Thou hast the words of eternal life." [37]

57. To this Our most merciful Redeemer we must therefore bring all back by every means in our power: for He is the divine consoler of the afflicted; He it is Who teaches all, whether they be invested with public authority or are bound in duty to obey and submit, true honesty, absolute justice and generous charity; it is He in fine, and He alone, Who can be the firm foundation and support of peace and tranquillity: "For other foundation no man can lay, but that

[36] LUKE XXIV, 32.
[37] JOHN VI, 69.

which is laid: which is Christ Jesus." [38]   This the author of salvation, Christ, will men more fully know, more ardently love and more faithfully imitate in proportion as they are more assiduously urged to know and meditate the Sacred Letters, especially the New Testament, for, as St. Jerome the Doctor of Stridon says: "To ignore the Scripture is to ignore Christ;" [39] and again: "If there is anything in this life which sustains a wise man and induces him to maintain his serenity amidst the tribulations and adversities of the world, it is in the first place, I consider, the meditation and knowledge of the Scriptures." [40]

58. There those who are wearied and oppressed by adversities and afflictions will find true consolation and divine strength to suffer and bear with patience; there—that is in the Holy Gospels—Christ, the highest and greatest example of justice, charity and mercy, is present to all; and to the lacerated and trembling human race are laid open the fountains of that divine grace without which both peoples and their rulers can never arrive at, never establish, peace in the state and unity of heart; there in fine will all learn Christ, "Who is the head of all principality and power" [41] and "Who of God is made unto us wisdom and justice and sanctification and redemption." [42]

CONCLUSION

Exhortation to all those who cultivate biblical studies

569   59. Having expounded and recommended those things which are required for the adaptation of Scripture studies to the necessities of the day, it remains, Venerable Brethren and beloved sons, that to biblical scholars who are devoted sons of the Church and follow faithfully her teaching and direction, We address with paternal affection, not only Our congratulations that they have been chosen and called to so sublime an office, but also Our encouragement to continue with ever renewed vigor, with all zeal and care, the work so happily begun. Sublime office, We say; for what is more sublime than to scrutinize, explain, propose to the faithful and defend from unbelievers the very word of God, communicated to men under the inspiration of the Holy Ghost?

60. With this spiritual food the mind of the interpreter is fed and nourished "to the commemoration of faith, the consolation of hope,

[38] I *Cor.* III, 11.
[39] St. JEROME, *In Isaiam, prologus; PL.* XXIV, col. 17.
[40] Id., *In Ephesios, prologus; PL.* XXVI, col. 439.
[41] *Col.* II, 10.
[42] I *Cor.* I, 30.

the exhortation of charity." [43] "To live amidst these things, to meditate these things, to know nothing else, to seek nothing else, does it not seem to you already here below a foretaste of the heavenly kingdom?" [44] Let also the minds of the faithful be nourished with this same food, that they may draw from thence the knowledge and love of God and the progress in perfection and the happiness of their own individual souls. Let, then, the interpreters of the Divine Oracles devote themselves to this holy practice with all their heart. "Let them pray, that they may understand;" [45] let them labor to penetrate ever more deeply into the secrets of the Sacred Pages; let them teach and preach, in order to open to others also the treasures of the word of God.

61. Let the present-day commentators of the Sacred Scripture emulate, according to their capacity, what those illustrious interpreters of past ages accomplished with such great fruit; so that, as in the past, so also in these days, the Church may have at her disposal learned doctors for the expounding of the Divine Letters; and, through their assiduous labors, the faithful may comprehend all the splendor, stimulating language, and joy contained in the Holy Scriptures. And in this very arduous and important office let them have "for their comfort the Holy Books," [46] and be mindful of the promised reward: since "they that are learned shall shine as the brightness of the firmament, and they that instruct many unto justice, as stars for all eternity." [47]

62. And now, while ardently desiring for all sons of the Church, and especially for the professors in biblical science, for the young clergy and for preachers, that, continually meditating on the divine word, they may taste how good and sweet is the spirit of the Lord; [48] as a presage of heavenly gifts and a token of Our paternal good-will, We impart to you one and all, Venerable Brethren and beloved sons, most lovingly in the Lord, the Apostolic Benediction.

63. Given at Rome, at St. Peter's, on the 30th of September, the feast of St. Jerome, the greatest Doctor in the exposition of the Sacred Scriptures, in the year 1943, the fifth of Our Pontificate.

POPE PIUS XII

[43] Cf. St. AUGUSTINE, *Contra Faustum* XIII, 18; *PL.* XLII, col. 294; *CSEL.* XXV, p. 400.
[44] St. JEROME, *Ep.* 53, 10; *PL.* XXII, col. 549; *CSEL.* LIV, p. 463.
[45] St. AUGUSTINE, *de doctr. christ.* III, 56; *PL.* XXXIV, col. 89.
[46] I *Mach.* XII, 9.
[47] DAN. XII, 3.
[48] Cf. *Wisd.* XII, 1.

Bibliography: Ahern, B., "Textual Directives of the Encyclical *Divino Afflante Spiritu,*" in C.B.Q., VII (1945), 340-347.

(8) Letter of the Pontifical Biblical Commission to Cardinal E. C. Suhard on the Pentateuch

Your Eminence:

577   The Holy Father has been pleased to entrust to the examination of the Pontifical Commission for Biblical Studies two questions which have been recently submitted to His Holiness concerning the sources of the Pentateuch and the historicity of the first eleven chapters of Genesis. These two questions, with their considerations and propositions, have been the object of the most careful study on the part of the Right Reverend Consultors and the Most Eminent Cardinals, Members of the above-mentioned Commission. As a result of their deliberations, His Holiness has deigned to approve the following reply in the Audience granted to the undersigned on January 16, 1948.

578   The Pontifical Biblical Commission is pleased to pay homage to the sense of filial confidence that has inspired this step, and wishes to correspond by a sincere effort to promote Biblical studies, while safeguarding for them the greatest freedom within the limits of the traditional teaching of the Church. This freedom has been explicitly affirmed by the Encyclical of the Sovereign Pontiff gloriously reigning, *Divino afflante Spiritu*, in the following terms: "The Catholic commentator, inspired by an active and ardent love of his subject and sincerely devoted to Holy Mother Church, should in no way be deterred from grappling again and again with these difficult problems, hitherto unsolved, not only that he may refute the objections of the adversaries, but may also attempt to find a satisfactory solution, which will be in full accord with the doctrine of the Church (in particular with the traditional teaching regarding the inerrancy of Sacred Scripture), and which will at the same time satisfy the indubitable conclusions of profane sciences. Let all the other sons of the Church bear in mind that the efforts of these resolute laborers in the vineyard of the Lord should be judged, not only with equity and justice, but also with the greatest charity; all moreover should abhor that intemperate zeal which imagines that whatever is new should for that reason be opposed or suspected" (*Acta Apost. Sedis*, 1943, page 319; English Edition, Vatican Press, page 22).

579   If one would rightly understand and interpret in the light of this recommendation of the Sovereign Pontiff the three official answers

Ench. Bibl. 154 (3rd ed., 161), 174-177 (181-184), 332-339 (336-343).

previously given by the Biblical Commission regarding the above-named questions—namely, that of June 23, 1905, on the narratives in the historical books of Holy Scripture which have only the appearance of being historical (*Ench. Bibl.*, 154), that of June 27, 1906, on the Mosaic authenticity of the Pentateuch (*Ench. Bibl.*, 174-177), and that of June 30, 1909, on the historical character of the first three chapters of Genesis (*Ench. Bibl.*, 332-339)—one will readily grant that these answers are in no way opposed to further and truly scientific examination of these problems in accordance with the results obtained during these last forty years. Consequently, the Biblical Commission believes that there is no need, at least for the moment, to promulgate any new decrees regarding these questions.

I. In what concerns the composition of the Pentateuch, in the above-named decree of June 27, 1906, the Biblical Commission already recognized that it may be affirmed that Moses, "in order to compose his work, made use of written documents or oral traditions," and also that modifications and additions have been made after the time of Moses (*Ench. Bibl.*, 176-177). There is no one to-day who doubts the existence of these sources or refuses to admit a progressive development of the Mosaic laws due to social and religious conditions of later times, a development which is also manifest in the historical narratives. Even, however, within the field of non-Catholic commentators very divergent opinions are professed concerning the nature and number of these documents, their denomination and date. There are indeed no few authors in different countries who, for purely critical and historical reasons and with no apologetic intention, resolutely set aside the theories most in vogue until now, and who look for the elucidation of certain redactional peculiarities of the Pentateuch not so much in the diversity of the supposed documents as in the special psychology—the peculiar processes of thought and expression, better known to-day—of the early Oriental peoples, or again in the different literary style demanded by the diversity of subject-matter. Therefore, we invite Catholic scholars to study these problems without prepossession in the light of sound criticism and of the findings of other sciences connected with this subject-matter. Such study will doubtless establish the great part and deep influence exercised by Moses both as author and lawgiver.

II. The question of the literary forms of the first eleven chapters of Genesis is far more obscure and complex. The literary forms correspond to none of our classical categories, and cannot be judged in the light of Græco-Latin or modern literary styles. One can therefore neither deny nor affirm their historicity, taken as a whole, without unduly attributing to them the canons of a literary style within which it is impossible to classify them. If one agrees not to recognize in these chapters history in the classical and modern sense, one must, however, admit that the actual scientific data do not allow of giving all the problems they set a *positive solution*. The first duty here incumbent upon scientific exegesis consists before all in the attentive study of all the literary, scientific, historical, cultural and religious problems connected with these chapters; one should then examine closely the literary processes of the early Oriental peoples, their psychology, their way of expressing themselves and their very notion of historical truth; in a word, one should collate without prejudice all the subject-matter of the historical and paleontological, epigraphic and literary sciences. Only thus can we hope to look more clearly into the true nature of certain narratives in the first chapters of Genesis. To declare *a priori* that their narratives contain no history in the modern sense of the term would easily convey the idea that they contain no history whatever, whereas they relate in simple and figurative language, adapted to the understanding of a less developed people, the fundamental truths presupposed for the economy of salvation, as well as the popular description of the origins of the human race and of the Chosen People. Meanwhile we must practise that patience which is living prudence and wisdom. This is what the Holy Father likewise inculcates in the Encyclical already quoted. "No one," he says, "will be surprised if all difficulties are not yet solved and overcome. . . . We should not lose courage on this account; nor should we forget that in human sciences the same happens as in the natural world; that is to say, new beginnings grow little by little and fruits are gathered only after many labors. . . . Hence, there are grounds for hope that those (difficulties) also will by constant effort be at last made clear, which now seem most complicated and difficult."

Kissing the Sacred Purple with sentiments of the deepest veneration, I acknowledge myself to be

Your Most Reverend Eminence's Most humble servant,
JAMES-M. VOSTÉ, O.P.
Secretary of the Pontifical Biblical Commission
Rome, January 16, 1948

ES

m him as
number
opinion
and the
with re-
tted by
n to all

in the
ts and
ust be
ks of
efend
ago
lical
ven
to
by
n a
by
nd
le
or
e

w to speak about those questions which, al- 615
the positive sciences, are nevertheless more or
e truths of the Christian faith. In fact, not a
d that the Catholic religion take these sciences
h as possible. This certainly would be praise-
of clearly proved facts; but caution must be
ather question of hypotheses, having some sort of
a, in which the doctrine contained in Sacred Scrip-
on is involved. If such conjectural opinions are
tly opposed to the doctrine revealed by God, then
they be recognized can in no way be admitted.
ons the Teaching Authority of the Church does not 616
conformity with the present state of human sciences
ology, research and discussions, on the part of men ex-
oth fields, take place with regard to the doctrine of
as far as it inquires into the origin of the human body
m pre-existent and living matter—for the Catholic faith
hold that souls are immediately created by God. How-
ust be done in such a way that the reasons for both opin-
s, those favorable and those unfavorable to evolution, be
nd judged with the necessary seriousness, moderation and
and provided that all are prepared to submit to the judg-
the Church, to whom Christ has given the mission of inter-
authentically the Sacred Scriptures and of defending
s of faith.[11] Some, however, rashly transgress this liberty of
sion, when they act as if the origin of the human body from
xisting and living matter were already completely certain and
ed by the facts which have been discovered up to now and by
soning on those facts, and as if there were nothing in the sources
divine revelation which demands the greatest moderation and
ution in this question.

When, however, there is question of another conjectural opinion, 617
namely polygenism, the children of the Church by no means enjoy
such liberty. For the faithful cannot embrace that opinion which
maintains either that after Adam there existed on this earth true men

[11] Cf. Allocut. Pont. to the members of the Academy of Science, November 30, 1941: A.A.S., vol. XXXIII, p. 506.

who did not take their origin through natural generation fr
from the first parent of all, or that Adam represents a certai
of first parents. Now it is in no way apparent how such a
can be reconciled with that which the sources of revealed trut
documents of the Teaching Authority of the Church proposed
gard to original sin, which proceeds from a sin actually comm
an individual Adam and which through generation is passed o
and is in everyone as his own.[12]

618   Just as in the biological and anthropological sciences, so also
historical sciences there are those who boldly transgress the lim
safeguards established by the Church. In a particular way m
deplored a certain too free interpretation of the historical bo
the Old Testament. Those who favor this system, in order to d
their cause, wrongly refer to the Letter which was sent not lon
to the Archbishop of Paris by the Pontifical Commission on Bi
Studies.[13] This Letter, in fact, clearly points out that the first el
chapters of Genesis, although properly speaking not conformin
the historical method used by the best Greek and Latin writers o
competent authors of our time, do nevertheless pertain to history
true sense, which however must be further studied and determined
exegetes; the same chapters (the Letter points out), in simple a
metaphorical language adapted to the mentality of a people but lit
cultured, both state the principal truths which are fundamental f
our salvation, and also give a popular description of the origin of t
human race and the chosen people. If, however, the ancient sacre
writers have taken anything from popular narrations (and this ma
be conceded), it must never be forgotten that they did so with th
help of divine inspiration, through which they were rendered immune
from any error in selecting and evaluating those documents.

Therefore, whatever of the popular narrations have been inserted
into the Sacred Scriptures must in no way be considered on a par
with myths or other such things, which are more the product of an
extravagant imagination than of that striving for truth and simplicity which in the Sacred Books, also of the Old Testament, is so
apparent that our ancient sacred writers must be admitted to be
clearly superior to the ancient profane writers.

619   Truly, we are aware that the majority of Catholic doctors, the
fruit of whose studies is being gathered in universities, in seminaries
and in the colleges of religious, are far removed from those errors
which today, whether through a desire of novelty or through a certain immoderate zeal for the apostolate, are being spread either

[12] Cf. *Rom.*, V, 12-19; Conc. Trid., sess. V, can. 1-4.
[13] January 16, 1948: *A.A.S.*, vol. XL, pp. 45-48.

openly or covertly. But we know also that such new opinions can entice the incautious; and therefore we prefer to withstand the very beginnings rather than to administer the medicine after the disease has grown inveterate.

For this reason, after mature reflection and consideration before God, that We may not be wanting in Our sacred duty, We charge the Bishops and the Superiors General of Religious Orders, binding them most seriously in conscience, to take most diligent care that such opinions be not advanced in schools, in conferences or in writings of any kind, and that they be not taught in any manner whatsoever to the clergy or the faithful.

Let the teachers in ecclesiastical institutions be aware that they cannot with tranquil conscience exercise the office of teaching entrusted to them, unless in the instruction of their students they religiously accept and exactly observe the norms which We have ordained. That due reverence and submission which in their unceasing labor they must profess towards the Teaching Authority of the Church, let them instill also into the minds and hearts of their students.

Let them strive with every force and effort to further the progress of the sciences which they teach; but let them also be careful not to transgress the limits which We have established for the protection of the truth of Catholic faith and doctrine. With regard to new questions, which modern culture and progress have brought to the foreground, let them engage in most careful research, but with the necessary prudence and caution; finally, let them not think, indulging in a false "eirenism," that the dissident and erring can happily be brought back to the bosom of the Church, if the whole truth found in the Church is not sincerely taught to all without corruption or diminution.

Relying on this hope, which will be increased by your pastoral care, as a pledge of celestial gifts and a sign of Our paternal benevolence, We impart with all Our heart to each and all of you, Venerable Brethren, and to your clergy and people the Apostolic Benediction.

Given at Rome, at St. Peter's, August 12, 1950, the twelfth year of Our Pontificate.

Pius PP. XII.

(10) 1961 Monitum of the Holy Office

Through praiseworthy enthusiasm for Biblical studies, assertions and opinions are being spread in many quarters, bringing into doubt the genuine historical and objective truth of the Sacred Scriptures, not only of the Old Testament (as Pope Pius XII had already deplored in his encyclical letter *Humani Generis,* cf. *Acta Apostolicae Sedis* XLII, 576), but even of the New, even to the sayings and deeds of Christ Jesus.

Since assertions and opinions of this kind are causing anxiety among both pastors and faithful, the eminent cardinals who are charged with preservation of the doctrine of faith and morals recommended that all of those who deal with the Sacred Scriptures, either in writing or orally, should be warned always to treat such subject-matter with due discretion and reverence and always to have before their eyes the doctrine of the Fathers of the Church and the mind and teaching authority of the Church, lest the consciences of the faithful be disturbed or the truths of the Faith be injured.

N.B. This admonition is published with the approval of the eminent cardinals of the Pontifical Biblical Commission.

Given at Rome by the Sacred Congregation of the Holy Office, June 20, 1961.

MSGR. SEBASTIANO MASALA, *Notary*

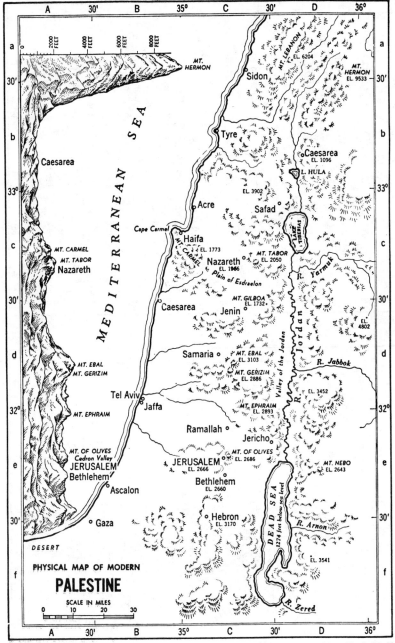

	A	30'	B	35°	C	30'	D	36°	

a

2000 FEET 4000 FEET 6000 FEET 8000 FEET

MT. HERMON

MT. LEBANON EL. 6204

Sidon

MT. HERMON EL. 9533

30'

M E D I T E R R A N E A N   S E A

Tyre

Caesarea

Caesarea EL. 1096

L. HULA

b

33°

EL. 3902

Acre

Safad

LAKE TIBERIAS

c

Cape Carmel

Haifa EL. 1773

MT. CARMEL

MT. CARMEL MT. TABOR Nazareth

Nazareth EL. 1966

MT. TABOR EL. 2050

Plain of Esdraelon

R. Yarmuk

30'

Caesarea

Jenin

MT. GILBOA EL. 1732

EL. 4802

d

Samaria

MT. EBAL EL. 3103

MT. EBAL MT. GERIZIM

MT. GERIZIM EL. 2886

R. Jabbok

Tel Aviv

Jaffa

Valley of the Jordan

R. Jordan

EL. 3452

32°

MT. EPHRAIM

MT. EPHRAIM EL. 2893

Ramallah

Jericho

e

MT. OF OLIVES Cedron Valley

JERUSALEM

Bethlehem

JERUSALEM EL. 2666

MT. OF OLIVES EL. 2686

MT. NEBO EL. 2643

Ascalon

Bethlehem EL. 2660

30'

Gaza

Hebron EL. 3170

D E A D   S E A 1274 feet below sea level

R. Arnon

DESERT

EL. 3541

PHYSICAL MAP OF MODERN

PALESTINE

SCALE IN MILES

0   10   20   30

R. Zered

f

	A	30'	B	35°	C	30'	D	36°	

Courtesy of The Catholic Book Company, New York, N. Y.

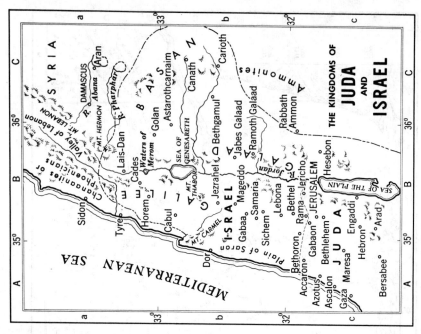

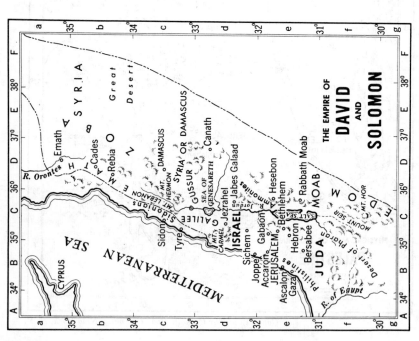

THE EMPIRE OF DAVID AND SOLOMON

THE KINGDOMS OF JUDA AND ISRAEL

Courtesy of The Catholic Book Company, New York, N. Y.

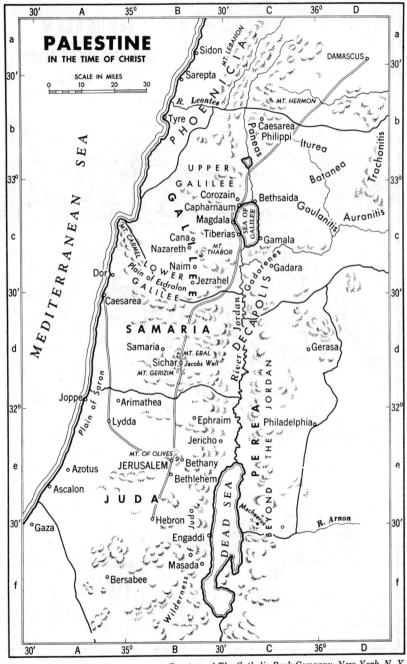

PALESTINE
IN THE TIME OF CHRIST

SCALE IN MILES
0   10   20   30

MEDITERRANEAN SEA

PHOENICIA
MT. LEBANON
Sidon
Sarepta
R. Leontes
Tyre
DAMASCUS
MT. HERMON
Caesarea Philippi
Paneas
Iturea
Batanea
Trachonitis

UPPER GALILEE
GALILEE
Corozain
Bethsaida
Gaulanitis
Auranitis
Capharnaum
Magdala
SEA OF GALILEE
Tiberias
Cana
Gamala
Nazareth
MT. THABOR
LOWER GALILEE
Naim
Gadarenes
Gadara
Dor
Plain of Esdralon
Jezrahel
DECAPOLIS
MT. CARMEL
Caesarea

SAMARIA
Samaria
River Jordan
Gerasa
Sichar
MT. EBAL
Jacobs Well
MT. GERIZIM

Plain of Saron
Joppe
Arimathea
PEREA
BEYOND THE JORDAN
Lydda
Ephraim
Philadelphia
Jericho
MT. OF OLIVES
JERUSALEM
Bethany
Azotus
Bethlehem
Ascalon
JUDA
Gaza
Hebron
DEAD SEA
Machaerus
R. Arnon
Engaddi
Wilderness of Juda
Masada
Bersabee

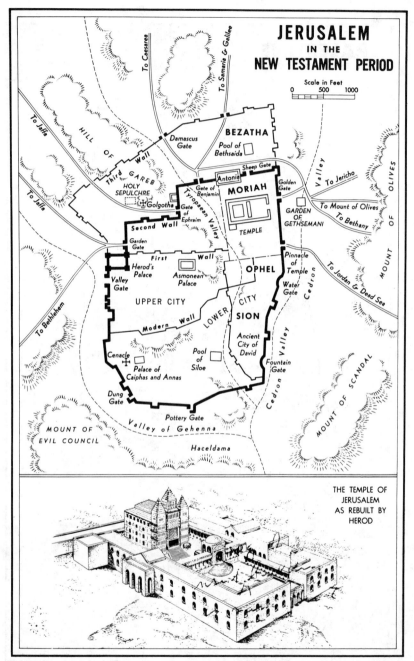

JERUSALEM
IN THE
NEW TESTAMENT PERIOD

Scale in Feet
0   500   1000

To Caesarea

To Samaria & Galilee

To Jaffa

HILL OF GAREB

Third Wall

Damascus Gate

BEZATHA

Pool of Bethsaida

Sheep Gate

Antonia

MORIAH

Golden Gate

Valley

To Jericho

HOLY SEPULCHRE

Gate of Benjamin

To Jaffa

Golgotha

Gate of Ephraim

Tyropoeen Valley

TEMPLE

GARDEN OF GETHSEMANI

To Mount of Olives

To Bethany

MOUNT OF OLIVES

Second Wall

Garden Gate

First Wall

Herod's Palace

Asmonean Palace

OPHEL

Pinnacle of Temple

Water Gate

To Jordan & Dead Sea

Cedron

Valley Gate

UPPER CITY

LOWER CITY SION

Modern Wall

Ancient City of David

Cedron Valley

To Bethlehem

Cenacle

Palace of Caiphas and Annas

Pool of Siloe

Fountain Gate

MOUNT OF SCANDAL

Dung Gate

Pottery Gate

Valley of Gehenna

MOUNT OF EVIL COUNCIL

Haceldama

THE TEMPLE OF JERUSALEM AS REBUILT BY HEROD

Courtesy of The Catholic Book Company, New York, N. Y.

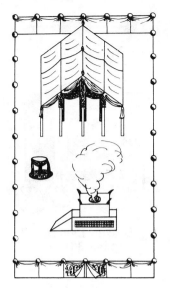

Tabernacle and Court
(page 345)

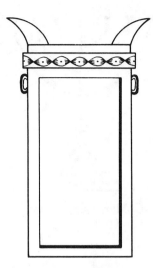

Incense Altar
(page 349)

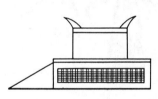

Altar of Holocausts
(page 346)

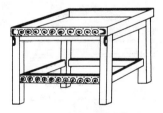

Showbread Table
(page 350)

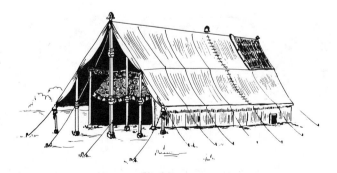

Tabernacle
(page 347)

Golden Lampstand
(page 351)

Brazen Lavers
(page 361)

Ark of the Covenant
(page 351)

Priest and High Priest
(pages 376,379)

Brazen Sea of Solomon's Temple
(page 360)

INDEX

Abelard, Peter: pre-scholastic exegete, 332
Accaron: fortified town in Philistia, 464
Acre: seaport, 464
Acta Martyrum Scillitanorum: indicates early Latin version of Pauline Epistles, 200
Acts, Apocryphal: Acts of Andrew, 148; of John, 145 f; of Paul, 146; of Peter, 147; of Thomas, 148
Acts of the Apostles: various families of Greek MSS., 179
Adrian the Monk: last writer of Antiochean school, 322
Ægidius Columna: scholastic exegete, 333
African Family: of Old Latin version, 201
Albert the Great, St.: commentaries of, 333
Albertus Patavinus: scholastic exegete, 333
*Albright, W. F.: outstanding American archaeologist, 441
Alcuin: revised Vulgate, 211; exegetical works, 328
Alcuin Family: of Vulgate texts, 211
Aldine Edition: of Septuagint, 195
Alexandria: Jewish school of interpretation, 312; first Christian catechetical school, 315 ff
Alexandrian Canon: see Canon
Alexandrian Family: of N.T. MSS., 177 ff
Allegory: use in Bible, 260
Allen, William: member of Vulgate Commission, 245 f
Alphabet: origin of, 156; principal alphabetic inscriptions, 157
Altar of Holocausts: in the Tabernacle, 346; in Temple of Solomon, 362; in Temple of Herod, 367

Altar of Incense: in the Tabernacle, 349 f; in Temple of Solomon, 362; in Temple of Herod, 367
Ambrose, St.: on N.T. Canon, 113; exegetical methods, 323
Ambrosiaster: on N.T. Canon, 113 f; exegetical works, 324
American School of Oriental Research: noteworthy in Palestinian excavations, 431
Amorites: early inhabitants of Palestine, 423
Amphilochius, St.: on N.T. Canon, 111
Analogy of Faith, application of, 302 f
Andrew of Caesarea: composed commentary on Apocalypse, 327
Anglicanism: insufficient criterion of inspiration, 54
Anglo-Saxon Versions: first translators, 236 f; see also Versions.
Animals: clean and unclean, 404 ff
Anne, St.: first mentioned in Protoevangelium of James, 144
Anselm of Laon: pre-scholastic exegete, 332
Antioch: exegetical school of, 318 ff; its principles still the basis of hermeneutical studies, 322
Antiochian Church: and N.T. Canon, 111
Antiochus IV Epiphanes: plundered the temple of Zorobabel, 364
Antiquities, Sacred: 344 ff
Antitype: use in Scripture, 262
Aphraates: on O.T. Canon, 94; on N.T. Canon, 112
Apocalypses, Apocryphal: of Paul, 151; of Peter, 150; of the Virgin, 152

593

of, 121 ff
Decapolis: location, 484
Dedication of the Temple: purpose of feast, 420
Defilement: different degrees of, 402
*Deissmann, A.: analyzes Epistles, letters, 293
Deists: on inspiration, 15
De Rossi, John Bernard: wrote on textual criticism, 338
Deutero-Canonical Books: list of the O.T. books, 77 ff; list of N.T., 103 f; mentioned by Fathers, 89 ff; see also Canon.
Diatessaron: by Tatian, 112; has western readings or text, 180
Dibon: town in Moab region, 469
Dictation: mechanical dictation of Bible, 30 f
Didache: and deutero-canonical books, 85 f, 104
Didactic Literature: found in N.T., 293
Didymus the Blind: followed Origen's principles, 318
Dies Irae: first lines quoted from Apocryphal Sibyls, 134
Diodorus of Tarsus: important exegete of Antiochian School, 320
Dionysius of Alexandria: on N.T. Canon, 109
Divino afflante Spiritu: extent of inspiration, 28; Biblical inerrancy, 36; encourages study of literary forms, 285; explains literal meaning, 258; typical meaning, 261
Douay-Rheims Version: origin, 245 f; revisions, 247 f; Challoner's revision, 247; Hay's, 248; MacMahon's, 248; Troy's, 248 f; Murray's, 248 f; Denvir's, 249; Syer's, 249; Haydock's, 249; Gibson's, 249; Poynter's, 250; Bramston's, 250
Duns Scotus: scholastic exegete, 333

Ebedjesu: and O.T. Canon, 95
Ebionites, Gospel of: see Gospels, Apocryphal
Ecclesiasticus: see Sirach
Edom: description of region, 470

Edrai: capital of Basan, 468
Egyptian dialects: 232
Egyptians, Gospel according to: see Gospels, Apocryphal
*Eichorn, J. G.: applied rationalism to O.T., 339
Elath: Edomite town, 470
Elephantine: Jewish military colony on, 368 f
Elephantine Papyri: early Aramaic MSS., 158
El-Ghor: the lower Jordan valley, 461 f
Ellipsis: use in Bible, 260
Emmaus: location of town, 481
Emphasis: use in Bible, 260
Endor: location of town, 465
English Version of Bible: see Versions of Bible
Ephraem, St.: O. T. Canon, 94; N.T. Canon, 112; comments upon Diatessaron, 229; exegetical principles, 325 f
Ephraim, Mountains of: 465
Epic: in Bible, 48 f
Epiphanius, St.: Palestinian Canon, 92; defended literal interpretation, 318, 325
Epistles of Barnabas: on O.T. Canon, 89 f; on N.T. Canon, 104
Epistle to the Laodiceans: apocryphal work, 149 f
Epistles, Catholic: various families of Greek MSS., 180
Epistles, Pauline: various families of Greek MSS., 179
Erasmus: edited Greek text, 181; edited the N.T., 335; inaccuracies of his Latin translation criticized by Sirleto, 218
Eschatology: part of salvation history, 287
Esdraelon, Plain of: remarkable for fertility, 465
Esdras: and formation of Canon, 82; apocryphal 4 Esd. and determination of O.T. Canon, 65, 70, 86; 4 Esd. apocryphal, 132; 3 Esd. apocryphal, 135 f
Essenes: and O.T. Canon, 69; name, origin, history, settlement at Qumran, literature, etc., 389 ff
Esther: deutero-canonical parts, 79
Estius, William: wrote commen-

alism to N.T., 339
*Renan, E.: applied rationalism to N.T., 339
Reptiles: all considered unclean by Jews, 405 f
Revelation: an inspiration, 22 f
Revised Standard Version: English Protestant Bible, 245
Reynolds, John: assisted in production of Douay-Rheims version, 246
Rhabanus Maurus: exegetical works, 328
Riddle: use in Bible, 260
Ritual of Jews: sacrifices, 394 ff
*Rogers, John: published whole Bible in English, 239
Romance, Historical: in Bible, 49
Rufinus: on Palestinian Canon, 92; on N.T. Canon, 114
Rule of War: among Dead Sea Scrolls, 129
Rupert of Deutz: pre-scholastic exegete, 332
Rylands Papyri: evidence on N.T. Canon, 109

*Saadias al Fayyumi: founder of philology and rational exegesis, 329
*Saadias Gaon: made best Hebrew-Arabic translation, 234
Sabbath: and Sabbath feasts, 409 ff; most important of feast days, 409
Sabbatical Year: dedicated to rest, 411
Sacred Writers: see Hagiographers.
Sacrifices of Jews: sacrifices in general, 394 f; division of sacrifices in the O.T., 395 ff; human sacrifice forbidden by the Law, 396; bloody sacrifices, 396 ff; holocausts or burnt offerings, 397; sin and guilt offerings, 398; peace offerings, 399; unbloody sacrifices, 400
"Sacrosancta" Decree: formally proclaims O.T. Canon, 91; N.T. Canon, 117; formally canonizes books of Bible, 213; text of Decree, 489
Sadducees: and O.T. Canon, 69; meaning of name, 388; doctrines, 388 f

Sadokite Document: apocryphal work, 128 f; an Essene book, 128
Sahidic: Egyptian dialect, 232
Samaria: location of town, 482; province of Palestine, 481 f
Samaritans: relations with Jews, 64
Samaritan Pentateuch: see Canon of the Jews.
Samaritan Temple: construction of, 368
Santes Pagnini: exegete, 335
Sanhedrin: meaning of the name, 384; history, 384; jurisdiction, 384 f; membership, 385; end, 385
Saron, Plain of: extolled in Bible, 464
Sayings of Jesus: His words in Gospel, 34
Scapegoat: turned loose on Day of Atonement, 418
Scholastics: doctrine on inspiration, 12 f; Thomistic school on inspiration, 20
Scholia: definition of term, 305
Scholz, J. M.: on classification of Greek N.T. MSS., 177; edited Greek text, 181
Science: and the Bible, 40 f; difficulties from natural sciences, 40; strictly scientific questions outside jurisdiction of Church, 297 f
Script, Square: its evolution, 161
Scripts, Biblical: Phoenician script used for first O.T. Books, 161; Aramaic script used during and after Babylonian exile, 161 f; Aramaic text was scriptio continua, 162; lacked final consonants, 162; lacked separation of sentences, 162; had many abbreviations, 162; may have used figures for numbers, 162 f
Sea of Galilee: description, 461
Seasons, Sacred: 407 ff
Secrets of Henoch: see Henoch, Slavic Book of.
*Semmler, J. S.: classified MSS. of Greek N.T. into families, 177; applied rationalism to hermeneutics, 339
Sense: various senses of Scrip-

1935, 250; Archbishop F. P. Kenrick revised the entire Bible, 251 f; Spencer's original translation from the Greek, 252; Confraternity Bible, 252
Victor of Capua: revises Vulgate, 209
Vincent, L. H.: foremost authority in archaeology, 433
Victorinus, St.: author of many commentaries, 323
Vogels, H. L.: edited Greek text of N.T., 182
*Von Soden: designation of MSS. of Greek N.T. too cumbersome, 173 f; classified MSS. of Greek N.T. into families, 177
Von Hummelauer: on biblical history, 44; on literary forms in Bible, 48 ff
Vulgate: history of, 203 ff; Jerome's revision of four Gospels, 204; revision of Roman Psalter, 205; his Gallican Psalter, 205; books translated from the Hebrew, 206; contents of version, 206 f; qualities of, 207 f; origin of our present text, 208; how Vulgate got its name, 208; history of version to Council of Trent, 209 ff; revisions of text, 209 f; critical editions of, 213; corrections of, 213; history from Trent till today, 213 ff; minor errors not excluded from Vulgate, 216; declared authentic by Council of Trent, 216 f; revision by Holy See urged by Council of Trent, 217; revision of text by first commission, 218; by second commission,

219 f; by third commission, 219; revision by Sixtus V, 219 f; by fourth commission, 220; revision by Clement VIII, 221; text of the Clementine Vulgate, 221; Ungarelli published much material on variant readings, 222; *"Praefatio ad Lectorem"* incriminates St. Bellarmine, 221 f; modern Benedictine revision of Vulgate, 222 f

*Westcott and Hort: classified MSS. of Greek N.T., 177; edited Greek text, 182
Western Family: of N.T. MSS., 177 ff
Westminster Version of N.T.: completed in 1935, 250
Weights: in Bible, 424 f
*Weiss, B.: edited Greek text, 182
*Wellhausen, J.: rationalistic approach to O.T., 340
*Wetstein, J. J.: edited Greek text, 181; wrote on philology, 338
Will: inspiration and hagiographer's will, 25 f
Wisdom, Book of: deutero-canonical work, 78
Wisdom Literature: found in didactic books of O.T., 292
Worthington, Dr.: assisted in production of Douay-Rheims version, 246
Writings: in ancient times, 153
Zohar: Jewish theosophical comentary on Pentateuch, 331
*Zwingli: rejects some N.T. books, 117